WITHDRAWN

D1222411

ELVIS
THE SUN YEARS

Available only through Popular Culture, Ink., P.O. Box 1839, Ann Arbor, Michigan 48106
Phone: 1-800-678-8828

Available only through Popular Culture, Ink., P.O. Box 1839, Ann Arbor, Michigan 48106
Phone: 1-800-678-8828

VILLA JULIE COLLEGE LIBRARY
STEVENSON, MD 21153

ELVIS
THE SUN YEARS
The Story of
Elvis Presley in the Fifties

by
Howard A. Dewitt

Popular Culture, Ink.
1993

ML
420
.P73
D48
1993

Copyright © 1993 by Howard A. DeWitt.
All Rights Reserved.

No part of this data may be may be reproduced, stored in a retrieval system,
or transmitted in any form or by any means, electronic, mechanical,
photocopying, recording, or otherwise, without prior written
permission of the copyright proprietor thereof.

Cover art is copyright © 1993 by
Popular Culture, Ink.
All Rights Reserved.

Book design and layout by
Tom Schultheiss.
Computer programs by
Alex Przebienda.
Cover design by
Diane Bareis.

ISBN 1-56075-020-0
LC 91-61883

Published by
Popular Culture, Ink.
P.O. Box 1839
Ann Arbor, MI 48106

PCI Collector Editions
are published especially for discerning collectors and libraries.
Each Collector Edition title is released in limited quantities
identified by edition, printing number, and number of copies.
Unlike trade editions, they are not generally available in bookstores.

10 9 8 7 6 5 4 3 2 1
(First edition, first printing: 750 copies)

Printed in the United States of America

"The best rock-and-roll books in the world!"

77590

Contents

Introduction

On September 2, 1957, I sat behind home plate in Sick's Seattle Stadium press box and watched Elvis Presley's flashy Cadillac drive through the right field fence gate. Elvis hopped from the back seat and ran up onto the temporary stage erected in center field, where he gyrated, sang, and entertained for the next hour. I was a seventeen-year-old kid who was running the press box for the Seattle Rainers, a triple-A baseball team. After serving the assembled reporters coffee, hot dogs, and the worst pastry imaginable, I watched in awe as Elvis mesmerized the crowd. In the middle of the performance, Colonel Tom Parker came to the press box and gave me two red, heart-shaped pillows with Elvis' name embroidered on them. I took them home and flung them on my bed, where they remained until my brother Dennis threw them out about a year later while I was away at college. I often wonder what they would have been worth today if I still had them.

Throughout college I continued to collect Presley records and memorabilia. Artifacts from the Sun years were always my favorites. Eventually, I acquired a Ph.D. and became a college professor. I never had any intention of writing a book about Elvis, although I continued to collect them assiduously. On an August 1977 vacation with my wife Carolyn and our one-year-old daughter Melanie, I found six new "quickie" books on Elvis in Stacey's Book Store on Hollywood Boulevard. Not wanting to carry the books around on our excursion to the San Diego Zoo and Disneyland, I piled them on a remote corner shelf with the intention of coming back for them the next day. It was August 15, the day before Elvis died. Next day, upon returning to Stacey's, we found that someone else had found and bought my entire stash of books. It was then that I decided to write a book about Presley's early years.

Elvis—The Sun Years began, then, in 1977, when Presley died. The initial manuscript was completed in 1988, and was thereafter edited by publisher Tom Schultheiss of Popular Culture, Ink. Not only did Tom polish the manuscript, he acted as a sounding board for many of my ideas. He improved the manuscript immensely. Over the years, Tom has become a good friend, starting when he helped me with another PCI publication, my book **Chuck Berry: Rock And Roll Music**. On that occasion, he took a 1200-page manuscript and reduced it to intelligent prose. (In that case as in this, any errors of fact are mine alone.) My thanks, Tom.

This work on Elvis Presley's life is not strictly a biography, but is rather an attempt to combine history, musical criticism, and ninety-five interviews with people close to Elvis. The object of the book is to reveal a great deal about the Sun Records years and a little bit about how Elvis influenced American history. As a result of eleven years of research and writing on Sun Elvis, I am indebted to more people than I can't possibly thank in these few pages. Therefore, if you are not among the following list of individuals who helped make this book possible, please accept my apologies and my heartfelt thanks.

Acknowledgements

My Sun Elvis journey began the day I called Eddie Bond in Hernando, Mississippi. Eddie put me in touch with Ronald Smith and, since that fateful day in the late seventies, Ron and I have become good friends over the decade and a half since we sat together in the Peabody Hotel in Memphis and talked about Elvis' music. Ronald Smith remains a marvelous musician, a great Elvis historian, and a walking encyclopedia of local history. He led me to many sources, made me aware of a number of previously unknown Presley concerts, and, of course, introduced me to a great many people once close to Elvis.

Unforgettable experiences punctuated my trip to Memphis:

Stan Kesler, Marcus Van Story, Paul Burlison, Eddie Bond, Kenneth Herman, and Ronald Smith all got together at Eddie Bond's club in Hernando and recreated the Sun sound for me on stage.

Marcus Van Story spent two days on the road with me in my rental car, helping me locate the small clubs where Elvis had played in and around the Mississippi-Tennessee-Arkansas area.

Doug Poindexter sat with me for two nights in his home and talked about the old days at Sun Records.

Jim and Jesse Lee Denson were excellent sources, and I grew extremely fond of Jim during our brief time together.

Marion Keisker had lunch with me twice and talked in detail about the Sun years. Nothing fancy—we lunched in a local shopping center, and the informality seemed to provide an opportunity for her to talk freely.

Malcolm Yelvington was another fountain of information. George Klein answered questions and was a marvelous help. Eddie Fadal and I talked as we stood in line to enter Graceland.

Vester Presley spent several hours with me over chicken-fried steak in a restaurant across from Elvis' home, and provided much of the material about his brother Vernon. He was surprised, after three interviews, to learn that I was a writer. Still, Vester helped beyond the call of duty.

Duck Dunn of Booker T and the MG's answered some questions about Memphis between sets at a hotel just down the street from the Peabody.

B.B. King provided some rare insights into the early Memphis years, and a telephone chat with Charlie Feathers helped clarify his role in Presley's rise to stardom.

The new owners of the various clubs that Elvis played in all cooperated, and I can only say thanks.

In Tupelo and Memphis, there are many people who helped me understand the marvelous Mississippi-Tennessee connection in Presley's life and career. Among them are John Allen Cooke, Oleta Grimes, Leona Richards, Leroy Green, L.P. McCarty, Evan "Buzzy" Forbess, Donald Dunivant, and James Ausborn.

Bob Luman, Jim Reeves, Buck Owens, Onie Wheeler, Hank Thompson and Marty Robbins all played the Wee Drop Inn in Sumas, Washington, where I worked as a bartender in the early sixties, and I took extensive notes on their views of Presley (for what purpose, at the time, I had no clear-cut idea).

Jerry Lee Lewis provided a brief interview at the Saddle Rack in San Jose, California, and Johnny Cash answered a couple of questions at the Great American Music Hall in San Francisco.

A number of fellow writers helped me with this project. My good friend Lee Cotten provided numerous anecdotes about Elvis from his vast knowledge of Presleyana, and was instumental in making Appendix 1 of this volume the most complete record or Elvis' early performances ever published. Many of the records in my record collection came from Lee's vast storage sheds. He is a great friend who has always supported my work. Dennis DeWitt, associate editor of *Blue Suede News* (who is also my pillow-pitching brother), read all parts of this manuscript and saved me from many errors. Marc Bristol, editor and publisher of *Blue Suede News*, also helped to shape the manuscript in its final form. Jerry Osborne of *DISCoveries* helped me in more ways than I can remember, lending me research materials, helping with an appendix to this book, and publishing some of my research in his magazine. Brian Bukantis, new owner of *DISCoveries*, and Peter Jancik, its editor (who provided encouragement at a late stage in this project), are also people who deserve mention for their support. Special thanks also go to Jeff Tamarkin

of *Goldmine* magazine, who, just as press time for this volume loomed, broke the story of the discovery of the second pre-Sun acetate Elvis was supposed to have recorded at Sam Phillips' Memphis Recording Service. (Just at press time, it was determined that the b-side of this acetate is truly "Without You," and not, as has long been assumed "Casual Love Affair.")

Conversations with Peter Guralnick focused my thinking on many topics. Fred Worth provided his usual in-depth comments and marvelous knowledge of Presley. Prof. B. Lee Cooper provided research leads and good ideas. Arnold Shaw, at the time Visiting Professor at the University of Nevada-Las Vegas, answered many questions on RCA and Presley.

Joan Deary was a constant source of information at Elvis fan fairs. Once she realized I was writing a book she refused to talk further, but thank you Joan for the many insights into RCA policy. At RCA, "Max" was my Deep Throat and I thank him for allowing me into the corporate files.

In Seattle, George Palmerton, Ron Peterson, Don Fulton, Little Bill Engelhardt, Rockin' Robin Roberts, Ron Holden, Andy Duvall, Paul Revere, and John Greek helped me to understand how Presley influenced the local music scene. Morten Reff in Oslo, Norway, and Willy Pauwels in Antwerp, Belgium, provided European pressings of Presley's records necessary to the completion of this project.

In the 1970s, just prior to his tragic death, Freddie Bell answered a number of questions about Elvis and Jackie Wilson during rehearsal for a Dick Clark show at the Thunderbird Hotel, Las Vegas. Larry Brazaskas, dealer extraordinaire and one of my ex-students, guided me, along with Homer Koliba, through the underbelly of Las Vegas.

Over the years, a bevy of blues musicians have helped me understand the Presley phenomenon. Among them are: Lowell Fulson, Charles Brown, Johnny Otis, Rosco Gordon, Willie Dixon, Johnny Johnson, Jimmy Beasley, Rufus Thomas, Solomon Burke, Barbara Lynn, Guitar Mac, Bob Geddins, Roy Brown, Mark Naftalin, Ron Thompson, Pee Wee Thomas, Bo Diddley, and Chuck Berry.

In New Orleans, Professor W. Kenneth Holdwitch provided anecdotes about Presley's early years in Tupelo. Jim Russell, a local record store owner, detailed his time with Elvis in Mississippi and helped me understand Elvis' relationship with June Juanico. Keith Rush was important in recalling the early days, and Jeff Hannusch provided some excellent material on Louisiana during the period 1954-55. Cosimo Matassa sat in the upstairs office of his grocery store near Bourbon Street and talked about Elvis' early days.

In Sacramento, Phil Gavant of the Sacramento Blues

Festival, a serious Presley scholar, added a great deal to this book. Thanks are also due to Delbert McClinton and his band for musical support during the final stages of this project.

In Germany, Tony Sheridan told me tales of the Beatles and Elvis, and helped me to understand the English-German rock scene of the early sixties and Presley's influence upon it. Horst Fascher was important in summarizing Hamburg's reaction to Presley, and Bruno Koschmider kindly talked with me about rock music and Presley just prior to his own death.

In England, Clive Epstein, Bob Wooler, Joe Flannery, Allan Williams, Brian Kelly, Billy J. Kramer, Mike McGear, Eddie Hoover, Sam Leach, and Ray Coleman supplied anecdotes about Presley. The Colindale Library provided periodicals from the English rock press which helped me a great deal.

Robin Rosaan was helpful in many ways, and gave me access to her extensive Presley collection. Rodney Masuoka, Hawaii's premier record collector, supplied me with a wealth of material and became a good friend. Rodney introduced me to Tommy Sands, who provided material on Colonel Parker, Sam Phillips, and Elvis. Tommy is a good friend and a marvelous person, and is even now making a major comeback as a performer.

Over the years, blues legend Jimmy McCracklin has taught me more about the blues, black culture, and the South than anyone else I know. Jimmy is one of my best friends, as well as a great blues artist. Thanks, Jimmy, for all your help.

Billy Vera and his band the Beaters put me on the pass list when I arrived in Los Angeles on interview trips. For almost fifteen years, Billy let a poor author in to see his shows for free. He is my favorite musician and a great guy. Also in Los Angeles, Elijah Perkins became like a brother and allowed me to follow Lowell Fulson around to blues festivals all over the world. Thanks Lowell and Elijah. Tina Mayfield provided support for my projects, and always listened to my ideas.

Neal Skok, Ray Meyer, Dick Schlatter, Jim Wyantt, Mark and Carol Lapidos, Steve McLaughlin, David Ray Kennedy, and Steve Marinucci provided support in many ways. Lou Holscher photocopied hundreds of articles, loaned many records, and provided a great deal of research help. Conversations with Lee Hildebrand helped to focus my thinking on Presley and the blues. Oscar Meyer and his band at Eli's Mile High Club provided me with a great deal of support during the project. Mike Lefebvre of Pepperland Records provided materials and his usual in-depth research help. David Leaf survived innumerable phone calls about rock and roll history and, while not involved in the project, gave excellent advice. Gary Hardy at Sun Records provided encouragement.

The recording session work of European super-researcher Ernst Mikeael Jorgensen and his partners, Johnny Mikkelsen and Erik Rasmussen, remains a monumental contribution to Presleyana. (Their book *Reconsider Baby: The Definitive Elvis Sessionography* is also available from Popular Culture, Ink.) A phone conversation with Jorgensen at a particularly low point in this project revived my spirits.

Although I haven't met them, the work of Colin Escott and Martin Hawkins has set a high standard of music scholarship for which to aim. Greil Marcus remains the person who introduced me to rock music criticism, and I especially value his work. He is one of the finest Elvis scholars around, and conversations with him have taught me a great deal.

Among the people close to Presley, ninety-five of them cooperated with me, although a number requested anonymity. At RCA, "Big John, the Coffee Man" and "Martha the Locksmith" helped retrieve previously unavailable sources. In terms of pure scholarship—the unearthing of new information—the help of all my Deep Throats at RCA is greatly appreciated.

At Ohlone College, my Division Chairperson, Professor Sheldon Nagel, arranged for two half-year sabbaticals to complete this work. Hans Larson placed the Learning Resources Center (formerly known as the library) at my constant disposal, and even 521 interlibrary loan requests didn't strain our friendship. I think. As always, Bob Anderson did more for my books at Ohlone than anyone. My colleagues Dr. Alan Kirshner and Professor Stacy Cole provided encouragement and a great deal of tangible support for a project they sometimes thought would never be completed. After sixteen years, it is finally done. Thanks to all of you.

My son Darin D. DeWitt, a wonderful kid, listened patiently to all his dad's ideas. My daughter Melanie did likewise, even as the CD player skipped its way through her favorite music. My wife Carolyn deserves final credit for her support of this and all my other projects. After twenty-five years of marriage, she is still a jewel.

Howard A. DeWitt
Fremont, California

CHAPTER 1

Elvis Presley:
The Final Years

The eighteen months that Elvis Presley recorded for Sam Phillips' Sun Records label in 1954-55 is a neglected aspect of Presley's career. As Elvis grew into the symbol of rock and roll superstardom, interest in his early records, concerts, and musical influences gradually diminished for all but a small band of Presley elitists. By June 1977, of course, most people were concentrating their attention upon Elvis' weight and poor physical condition. Ironically, he himself spent much of his time that fateful summer dwelling on the past. Two months later, following his death, friends would remark that he was obsessed by his early Mississippi roots and the Sun Records sessions. The disruptive pressures of rock and roll fame had long prevented Elvis Presley from leading a normal life; ultimately, they plagued him to death. Little wonder that the Sun Records era, a simpler time that allowed Presley's music to mature, should occupy his thoughts in his final months.

The contrast between Presley's career in the 1970s and the freewheeling atmosphere of the 1954-55 Sun Records era is a stark one. By examining the early years of Presley's life, it becomes easier to understand his personal decline in later decades. By 1970, Elvis was wrapped in a cocoon that generated drug dependency, personal doubt, and physical-psychological pressures that severely hampered his career. When Elvis died at forty-two, the Sun Records days were a distant if persistent memory. A study of the events of Elvis' first twenty-one years, therefore, apart from offering insights into his personal character, should serve both to break down stereotypes about his music and to illuminate his career within the context of rock and roll history. First, however, an overview of Elvis' downfall should help clarify the story of his rising star.

The End: August 16, 1977

At the time of his death—and for some time before—many critics considered Elvis as being over the hill. Yet, from January 1970 through July 1977, he charted thirty-five songs on the *Billboard* Hot 100. After fifteen years in the music business, he was still a sellout concert draw. Elvis' impact upon the first Golden Age of Rock and Roll Music remained a significant part of his mystique even in the 1970s. From 1954 onward, Presley had been a one-man gold mine for his two record companies, Sun and RCA. His long-time manager, Colonel Tom Parker, reaped extraordinary financial benefits, and the entourage that Presley acquired over the years enjoyed the trappings of a lucrative lifestyle (although many felt "underpaid" in terms of direct salary). Elvis toured constantly to maintain his way of life, his properties, and his employees. Poor management left him in a precarious financial position, however. Neither Colonel Parker nor anyone else invested Elvis' earnings, so Presley was the IRS's top citizen taxpayer. He had no tax shelters, investments, or write-offs, and ended up keeping very little of the money he earned.

On June 27, 1977, in the early morning hours, Elvis Presley returned to Memphis from an Indianapolis, Indiana, concert to ponder his future. The night before, while he rested backstage, Elvis had been presented by RCA Records executives with a plaque commemorating the pressing of two billion copies of his records.

June 1977: a bloated Elvis performing in Indianapolis, about six weeks before his death.

1

A likeness of Presley's "Moody Blue" album adorned the plaque cover. Elvis—ailing and near bankruptcy—had been nervous and uncomfortable as a CBS-TV crew followed him around to film a concert documentary.

The ensuing fifty-one days that Elvis spent at Graceland prior to his death is a mystery period. Elvis had never been off the road this long since 1969. There is no doubt that he was in ill health. His weight had increased and his blood pressure was dangerously elevated. A wide range of medications were prescribed as Elvis found it difficult to control his mood swings. He spent most of his time in the jungle room—which was unfortunately located next to the kitchen—and in his bedroom. He ate voraciously.

Elvis was worried that his health would interfere with his daughter's annual visit. Each summer, Lisa Marie arrived in Memphis to be with her father. This summer Elvis was scheduled for a brief tour following his two-week vacation with Lisa Marie. On August 2, 1977, she landed at Memphis airport. The nine-year-old was taken to Graceland, and proved to be a much needed psychological tonic for her famous father. Elvis' dramatic mood swings subsided; the sight of his daughter created a jovial frame of mind. Late on the evening of August 15, Elvis left Graceland for an eleven o'clock appointment with his dentist. He had kissed his daughter goodbye, and she was scheduled to fly home the next afternoon. Once he returned later that evening, Elvis was never to leave Graceland alive again.

Elvis was dead by the next morning. Lisa Marie Presley sat in Graceland and cried. Dan Warlick, the twenty-eight-year-old investigator for the Shelby County Medical Examiner's office, comforted Presley's daughter. She was sniffling. Warlick tried to reassure her. Lisa Marie was alone. Vernon Presley was finally in charge. He ignored his granddaughter, as did Elvis' entourage. They weren't mourning Elvis, one observer suggested, but were trying to figure out their own futures.

Ronald Smith, Elvis' first guitarist, drove over to Graceland in the late afternoon of August 16. He parked a mile away and walked to the gates. A procession of official-looking cars raced up and down Elvis Presley Boulevard. There was crisis in the air. Soon, reporters arrived to compete with the ever-growing crush of fans. Ron lit a cigarette. A tear came to his eye. He wiped it away and walked across the street from Graceland for a cup of coffee. "I thought about Elvis' triumphs," Ron remarked, "and I couldn't believe it would come to this."

A Soldier Returns

From 1956 to 1958 Elvis rose to show business star-dom with an unprecedented series of hit records. He placed ten LPs and EPs on the *Billboard* album charts—five of the albums reached number one—during his first three years with RCA-Victor. The extent of Elvis' popularity was demonstrated in 1958 when the **Elvis Golden Records** album remained on the *Billboard* charts for seventy-four weeks, an unprecedented event for the fifties. During the same period, Elvis placed thirty-four songs on the *Billboard* Pop Singles list. Almost single-handedly, then, Elvis established rock and roll as a commercial phenomenon. In 1958, when he was inducted into the army, there was speculation that his musical career was in jeopardy. Colonel Parker wasn't worried about Presley's future, however; he had every intention of maintaining his protege as a mainstream pop act and a movie star.

In March 1960, Elvis was discharged from the army and returned home. To reintroduce Elvis to the public, Colonel Parker booked him on a Frank Sinatra television special. The irony of Elvis' appearance with Sinatra was that the crooner had previously been one of Presley's nastiest critics. But the pairing of the former bobbysox idol with the King of Rock and Roll made sense. It was a show business move designed to popularize two singers with question marks looming over their futures. On March 22, 1960, Elvis left Memphis by train for Miami, Florida, where the Sinatra show was to be taped at the Fontainebleau Hotel for a May 12 broadcast. As Elvis, his guitarist Scotty Moore, piano man Floyd Cramer, and bass players Hank Garland and Bob Moore traveled to Florida, they were continually met by large, enthusiastic crowds. Southern radio stations—with help from Colonel Parker—were kept aware of Presley's travel route. "In every little town along the way the tracks were lined," Scotty Moore remarked. Hank Garland, one of America's best-known session guitarists, was frightened by the crowds. "I never saw so many people turn out," Garland mumbled. "I remember the Colonel laughing at the girls." Although the hysteria of the first Golden Age of Rock and Roll had vanished, Presley obviously still had a strong fan following.

The Timex television special was Sinatra's fourth and last show. The three previous programs had garnered poor ratings. As a result, this broadcast was titled "Frank Sinatra's Welcome Home Party for Elvis." The show would feature Sammy Davis, Jr., Joey Bishop, and Nancy Sinatra. By booking Presley, Sinatra guaranteed his final special high ratings. The $125,000 Elvis earned for ten minute's work prompted Sammy Cahn, a well-known songwriter and the show's executive producer, to comment: "You should make in a year what Frank is losing on this show." While Sinatra was unhappy with the Colonel's asking price, he paid it to capitalize on public curiosity.

Tension began to mount from the beginning, in more ways than one. During the taping of the special, a confrontation developed between Colonel Parker and executive producer Cahn. As Presley practiced for the show, Colonel Parker attempted to pack the studio audience with Elvis' fans. Sinatra's management refused to tolerate the move, so the audience ended up a relatively even mixture of Sinatra and Presley fans. During the show Elvis sang "Witchcraft," and the Sinatra tune melted the middle-aged in the audience. When Sinatra attempted Presley's "Love Me Tender," there were moments of embarrassed silence. Colonel Parker had won the battle. The audience responded with generous applause for Elvis, and the newspaper, magazine, and television reporters were deprived of a story about Presley's musical decline. The May 7-13, 1960, cover of *TV Guide* featured a drawing of Elvis with a smaller caricature of Sinatra in the background. A full-page advertisement inside *TV Guide* headlined: "Elvis Presley Returns to TV." For Elvis, the transition from rock music to mainstream pop had begun.

When the "Welcome Home Elvis" special was broadcast on May 12, it received a 41.5 Nielsen rating. Not only was this the highest rating in the time slot, but it drew twice the number of viewers that the runner-up program, NBC's "Tennessee Ernie Ford Show," earned. Still, music and television critics attacked Elvis on a personal level with a vengeance. *Billboard*'s critic, Ren Grevatt, was lukewarm in his praise. "The impression lingers...that Presley has much to learn before he can work in the same league with pros like Sinatra...." The *New York Times* was even nastier: "The recent liberation from the army of Elvis Presley may have been one of the most irritating events since the invention of itching powder," critic John Shanley commented. The negative press reaction was to have little or no impact upon Presley fans, however.

On the album front, RCA pressed 1.3 million copies of the next Presley LP, **Elvis Is Back**, which included the hit single "Fame and Fortune." The eclectic collection of songs on **Elvis Is Back** made it clear that Colonel Parker paid little attention to the music. There was no theme to the album, but it quickly went gold. Although **Elvis Is Back** only reached the number two position on the *Billboard* album charts, it was nevertheless Presley's strongest LP in the period of the sixties. The soundtrack to the movie "G.I. Blues" did reach the number one position in October 1960, and was a better indication of where Colonel Parker was focusing his—and Elvis'—energy.

Following his two-year army stint, Elvis spent most of his time making lightweight Hollywood musicals. The magnitude of the financial success of his movies has been obscured by poor reviews and a tendency to label Presley as a washed-up, first generation rock and roller. From the summer of 1960 until the summer of 1968, when he taped a spectacular television comeback show, Elvis, living in Los Angeles' Bel Air district and at Graceland, made twenty-four movies, generally low-budget productions that reaped enormous profits. In 1964, "Kissin' Cousins" was shot in seventeen days. Presley's singing stand-in, Lance LeGault, remembered that Elvis seemed distracted. The usually intense rehearsals were cut short, and Presley simply went through the motions. By 1965, the formula movies appealed to smaller and smaller audiences. Production costs remained low and the music's quality continued to deteriorate. "Clambake" was the most embarrassing movie from this period. As Elvis performed songs like "Who Needs Money" and "A House That Has Everything," he was visibly irritated by the lack of musical quality. The soundtrack for "Clambake" was recorded in Nashville, and Elvis felt he was humiliating local musicians with songs that were neither worthy of them or him.

Finally, in 1969, as a result of the response to the 1968 Singer "comeback special," Elvis returned to public performances in Las Vegas. He had not toured extensively since the mid-fifties, and there was speculation about his future. It was a calculated risk to re-emerge before live audiences. Las Vegas was a conservative and unpredictable town, and Elvis spared no expense in rehearsing for his return. The July 31, 1969, opening at the Las Vegas International Hotel was much like a coronation. Elvis was about to be crowned all over again.

Back to Live Performing (1969-70)

As Elvis prepared for his return to public performing, he was nervous about his ability to fill the cavernous 2,500-seat International Hotel showroom. Barbra Streisand had played to only small audiences the week before. Determined to do better, Elvis showed up with a large band of expensive studio musicians, experienced backup singers, and a contingent of his own musicians for two weeks of practice. The Colonel recognized Elvis' anxiety and did everything he could to relax him. To promote ticket sales, Parker's assistant, Tom Diskin, placed a harsh, high-pitched radio ad on three local stations that boomed: "ELVIS! ELVIS! ELVIS! NOW! NOW! NOW!" It rang out from the radio like a shotgun. Billboard ads covered Las Vegas and the highways leading into town.

Colonel Parker himself stood in the hotel lobby directing a gang of staplegun bearers who tacked Elvis stickers throughout the hotel. The top of the toilet seats in the men's and ladies' rooms were even covered with

Elvis posters. Wearing a straw hat, a big cigar stuck in his mouth, the Colonel bellowed to anyone who would listen that the King of Rock and Roll had returned to live performing.

The day after Elvis' opening at the International Hotel, Renee Kearns was standing outside the Mexican restaurant in the Hilton's restaurant row. Nick Naff, a public relations man for the Hilton, began talking to her and recognized her German accent.

"Where did you live in Germany?" Naff asked.

"Wiesbaden," Kearns replied.

"I can't believe it," Naff chuckled, "a decade later Elvis has one of his German fans standing outside the show. Did you come all the way from Wiesbaden?"

"No, I live in the States; to be specific, in California," Kearns stated.

"Elvis will be impressed with your loyalty."

"I wasn't sure what to think," Kearns remembered, "but I did want to meet Elvis. So I went to the party and he [Naff] bought me a screwdriver."

Shortly after she came into the party, Elvis walked up. Kearns smiled and began chatting with him. She grabbed his arm and asked him how much he weighed.

"I weigh 165 pounds," Elvis remarked. "Did you like the show tonight?"

"I loved it," Kearns gushed. She sensed that Elvis was worried about performing in front of live audiences after making movies for so many years, and that he was naturally interested in the reaction to his shows after such a long layoff. Renee Kearns assured Elvis that he was as good as ever. "In fact, I thought he was better than in the past. Not only was he a hunk but he had matured as a performer," Kearns concluded.

Renee Kearns was one of many fans who were allowed to attend the private functions Elvis held in Las Vegas and in Lake Tahoe. She reminisced for me about her years attending them, remembering how sweet and humble Elvis was at these gatherings. "He was just a regular person. Much like anyone else at the party. He was really down-to-earth." As Kearns recalled her experiences for me, she grew sad over the loss of Elvis' energy and magnetic personality.

"I was a regular at Elvis' celebrations and I couldn't believe the atmosphere. Elvis was crushed by the responsibility of meeting his fans' demands. He was a sweetie who was too good to everyone."

By the time Elvis ended his return to public performing on August 28, the election of Richard Nixon to the presidency was not very far off. The nation, now in the midst of the volatile Vietnam years, needed to reflect on old values, an atmosphere that did more than a little to re-establish Elvis' career.

In years to come, the party atmosphere of Elvis' visits to Las Vegas escalated, and he drew larger and larger crowds. In 1971, the hotel changed its name to the Las Vegas Hilton, and the profits from Elvis' three appearances in the main showroom made the hotel the most successful in Las Vegas. There was a personal magnetism to Presley's performances that brought the crowd to its feet, and this special bond with his fans spread from the performance stage to other parts of the hotel. The rooms were always reserved for his shows, the restaurants were filled, and the gaming tables reaped enormous profits. It was a partnership that made the hotel rich and created new excitement in Las Vegas.

By 1976, Elvis had performed sixteen different times in the plush Nevada setting. There was no doubt that audiences would pay big money for a chance to see the "King of Rock and Roll."

Colonel Parker had bragged in the late summer of 1970 that Elvis would take Las Vegas by storm, and Elvis did just that. "The Colonel was right," Renee Kearns remarked, "Elvis not only sold out the February and August 1970 shows, but I paid a hundred dollars to sit down front. The maitre'd told me that he had never received tips like this before."

The Hilton Hotel had run full-page newspaper ads thanking Elvis for his record-setting performances. The Colonel, for his part, had passed out promotional gimmicks in the Hilton lobby and let everyone know that Elvis was a one-of-a-kind entertainer, a bit of hucksterism that attracted promoters who hoped to organize nationwide Elvis tours. It had been a year since Elvis' first Las Vegas opening, and the decision to resume touring had been made. When Colonel Parker invited Jerry Weintraub and Tim Hulett to his office at MGM studios in Hollywood, he made it clear that they were his choice to direct Presley's tours. They were already established promoters who had handled Eric Clapton, Jimi Hendrix, and Cream, while at the same time promoting concerts for other mainstream music acts. Parker quickly agreed to a deal.

The first Elvis tour of the 1970s was set up in safe, white, middle-class towns filled with Presley fans. Phoenix, St. Louis, Detroit, Miami, Tampa Bay, and Mobile boasted sprawling suburbs teeming with Elvis' old-line supporters, all of them eager to see the King in person. When tickets went on sale they were sold out within an hour everywhere but in Detroit.

As fans streamed into the concert sites (with or without tickets), Elvis grew more and more excited about being back on the road. There was a love affair between Elvis and his fans that was almost two decades old. Unlike his early tours, Elvis was now an established act. His fans basked in the King's presence. Elvis never looked younger or healthier.

In 1968, Stanley Booth's *Esquire* article, "A Hound Dog to the Manor Born," had been one of the first serious pieces of rock journalism to grace the pages of a major magazine. In summarizing Presley's career, Booth had pointed out that "hardly a day passes in Memphis without a politician wanting to name something after him." Clearly, the national love affair with Elvis extended even to the media, and this gave Colonel Tom Parker some new merchandising ideas.

Parker loved selling old products. There were no production costs, and the finished recordings were already in the vault. Presley fans didn't seem to care that there was nothing new to buy; they supported the King regardless of the music's quality. The media's concentration upon Elvis' re-emerging talent prompted Colonel Parker to dust off the old memorabilia and sell it on the road.

It was therefore no surprise that, coincidental with Elvis' renewed public accessibility, RCA issued a catalog called *The Complete Catalog of Elvis Records and Tapes* to meet the demand for Presley's music. This thirty-pager showcased all of Elvis' currently available records. Many of the albums, though, were budget repackagings that didn't do Presley's music justice. Yet, all the albums sold well. When the Colonel mentioned that Elvis had fifty million-selling records, RCA promptly packaged them into a four-record box set—complete with a photo book—and called it: **Elvis' Worldwide 50 Golden Award Hits, Volume 1.** This album was followed by another RCA reissue containing two records: **From Memphis to Vegas/From Vegas to Memphis,** a repackaging which had been released the previous year as two separate albums. Elvis' return to live performances prompted his records to sell rapidly. There was little concern with packaging, song selection, or quality. RCA saw a means of making a quick buck, so they took advantage of the renewed interest in Presley.

Critics, too, suddenly loved Elvis. A new generation of rock and roll writers filled with honest, heartfelt appreciation was emerging. *Rolling Stone* magazine noted that **Elvis' Worldwide 50 Golden Award Hits, Volume 1** was "an absolute necessity for any rock and roll collection." The best of these critics, Greil Marcus, profiled the Elvis of the early seventies in these words: "These days...we see him singing to himself, in limousines, backstage, running, walking, standing still, as his servants fit his cape to his shoulders, as he waits for his cue." There was indeed a lonely quality to Elvis in his last decade as he waited patiently to walk on stage and entertain his fans. "Elvis has survived the contradictions of his career," Marcus suggested, and he "takes his strength from the liberating arrogance, pride, and the claim to be unique...." Long before Bruce Spring-

steen told the media time and time again that he was singing for the blue-collar worker, Elvis simply went out and did it.

An equally perceptive critic, Peter Guralnick, suggested that Elvis was "a truly revolutionary force." He was a simple kid who was "the classic American success story." Elvis never had to apologize for his talent. He enjoyed his life, celebrated the music in concert, and brought his fans a show that pleased. By giving one hundred percent of himself in the last half-dozen years of life, Elvis continued to serve his mass audience. His untimely death, as Guralnick concluded, was a "shared memory" filled with "a musical passion."

The Price of Success (1970-71)

After more than a year of concert and record successes, Elvis returned to Memphis. On December 31, 1970, he held his annual Christmas party amidst the general euphoria about his live performing revival. When Elvis walked into T.J.'s, the popular Memphis nightclub he had rented for the occasion, the crowd stood and applauded. Vernon Presley, along with his second wife of some ten years duration, the former Dee Stanley—whom Elvis disliked as Vernon's chosen replacement for Elvis' mother, Gladys—stood at his son's side, beaming.

In a few moments, all eyes returned to the stage where Ronnie Milsap, T.J.'s featured singer, was playing. Elvis' friends and employees basked in the limelight. Red West, George Klein, Billy Smith, and Jerry Schilling were all smiling at their boss. Unbeknownst to everyone, the next half-dozen years were destined to turn into a nightmare.

During the party at T.J.'s, one of Elvis' old South Side High friends remarked that Elvis was supporting too many employees. "These people are sucking you dry, friend," he remarked. Elvis explained that these people were his friends, and they depended upon him for a living. The exchange turned what had started out as a triumphant party into a bitter evening. Soon Elvis was moody and distracted. He left early and ultimately asked his dad whether or not the Memphis Mafia might not have gotten too large after all. It wasn't easy being Elvis, and the pressure showed that night.

The financial demands of Presley's entourage, the constant need for large cash reserves to maintain employees, and the continually rising costs made it necessary for Elvis to tour continuously. Elvis simply wore himself out in the 1970s—his health, his disposition, and his mental state were stretched to a precarious limit. There were whispers that his behavior had grown erratic. He fought with friends, demanded special treatment, and threw infantile tantrums. The road to self-destruction was constantly accelerated by new pressures. While there was no public indication of drug abuse, Elvis' behavior revealed that there were serious problems. Ultimately, the combination of professional pressures, prescription drugs, and a frantically-paced lifestyle would doom Elvis Presley.

Earlier that month, on Saturday, December 19, Elvis had fought with his father over money, storming from the house after Vernon chided him for spending $38,000 on guns. A few days earlier, Elvis had learned that a pending paternity suit filed by a fan, Patricia Parker, was finally going to court. The North Hollywood waitress alleged that a child, born on October 19, had been fathered by Elvis. Ultimately, after careful detective work by John O'Grady, a well-known Los Angeles private investigator, the woman's story crumbled and Elvis was cleared. By arranging blood tests, conducting polygraph exams, and searching out key witnesses, O'Grady accomplished what Presley's hillbilly entourage failed to do, but not before yet another disturbing episode—it would take a year to settle the Parker suit—had taken its toll on Elvis' peace of mind.

In the course of his relationship with Elvis, O'Grady, a former police career professional, could not avoid noticing Elvis' abnormal pulse and breathing. O'Grady surmised that Presley was taking downers, possibly barbiturates or opiates. He was alarmed, as he had developed a genuine affection for Elvis. It was to be O'Grady who prompted Elvis to meet important law enforcement officials and collect police paraphernalia, reasoning that perhaps Elvis' drug use would decline as a result. (Just the opposite occurred, however, as Presley's drug dependency steadily increased.)

In a fit of rage following his December 19 argument with Vernon, Elvis left Graceland and boarded a commercial flight to Washington, DC. He hoped to visit President Richard Nixon. While aboard his American Airlines flight, Elvis wrote a seven-page letter to the president requesting an audience. He proposed that Nixon award him a "federal agent at large" badge. Elvis scribbled to Nixon that he hoped to be instrumental in fighting the drug problem.

After he landed, Elvis took a cab to the Washington Hotel, a small, inconspicuous lodging place near the White House. Registering as Colonel Jon Burrows, Elvis began preparing for his visit with the president. Unfortunately, he had come to Washington without any of his friends. Having never flown anywhere by himself to conduct personal business, he was scared. Abruptly, Elvis flew to Los Angeles to pick up a former employee, Jerry Schilling, then working as a Hollywood film editor.

At Memphis' Catholic High School, Schilling had been a highly regarded football player. Like Elvis, he was a kid who had grown up in a tough, blue-collar neighborhood in North Memphis. He became friends with Presley in 1954 during a game of touch football. They talked after the impromptu pick-up game, and Elvis marvelled at Schilling's intelligence. Unlike most of Elvis' Humes High friends, Schilling was a bright, articulate young man who honestly expressed his feelings. Elvis, in turn, had a hypnotic effect upon Schilling. Although still in high school, Schilling soon dropped out to join the Presley entourage.

From 1964 to 1975, Schilling worked as one of Elvis's bodyguards. Once he moved into the inner circle, Schilling was an independent-minded employee. It was not easy to disagree with Elvis. Schilling had strong opinions and he left Elvis' employ a number of times as a result of disagreements. But Elvis needed Schilling. So, invariably, they patched up their differences. He was well aware that Elvis had drug problems.

On December 21, it was a skeptical Schilling who boarded a Los Angeles plane to return to Washington with Elvis, sharing a row of seats with California Senator George Murphy. Once Murphy heard Presley's request for a narcotics badge, the senator offered to bring Elvis directly to the president. Murphy, a former Hollywood actor, was a lifelong friend of Richard Nixon, and this cleared the way for Presley's visit. Elvis's request was forwarded to one of Nixon's aides, Dwight Chapin, who approached the president's chief of staff, H.R. Haldeman, with the Presley proposal.

Chapin briefed Haldeman in an inter-office transmittal: "He [Presley] says that he is not a member of the establishment and that drug culture types, the hippie elements, the SDS and the Black Panthers are among people with whom he can communicate since he is not a part of the establishment." Haldeman responded positively and said that if Nixon was busy he would arrange a meeting with Vice President Spiro Agnew. Chapin, however, was worried: "...it would be wrong to push Presley off on the vice president since it will take very little of the president's time and it can be extremely beneficial for the president to build some rapport with Presley."

At 12:30 in the afternoon on Monday, December 21, 1970, Elvis, delighted with the White House trappings and decor, was escorted into the Oval Office. Bud Krogh, one of the president's aides, kept notes of the meeting. Elvis took out his law enforcement badges from police departments in California, Colorado, and Tennessee. Nixon appeared amused, but pretended to be interested in Presley's trinkets. Elvis then made some disparaging remarks about the Beatles, and informed Nixon that the British rockers promoted anti-American

Dear Mr. President:

First, I would like to introduce myself. I am Elvis Presley and
admire you and have great respect for your office. I talked to Vice
President Agnew in Palm Springs three weeks ago and expressed
my concern for our country. The drug culture, the hippie elements,
the SDS, Black Panthers, etc. do <u>not</u> consider me as their enemy
or as they call it the establishment. I call it American and I love it.
Sir, I can and will be of any service that I can to help the country
out. I have no concerns or motives other than helping the country out.
So I wish not to be given a title or an appointed position. I can and
will do more good if I were made a Federal Agent at Large and I
will help out by doing it my way through my communications with
people of all ages. First and foremost, I am an entertainer, but all I need
is the Federal credentials. I am on this plane with Senator George
Murphy and we have been discussing the problems that our country is faced with.

Sir, I am staying at the Washington Hotel, Room 505 - 506-507. I have
two men who work with me by the name of Jerry Schilling and Sonny
West. I am registered under the name of Jon Burrows. I will be here
for as long as it takes to get the credentials of a Federal Agent. I have done
an in-depth study of drug abuse and Communist brainwashing techniques
and I am right in the middle of the whole thing where I can and will do
the most good.

I am glad to help just so long as it is kept very private. You can have
your staff or whomever call me anytime today, tonight, or tomorrow.
I was nominated this coming year one of America's Ten Most Outstanding
Young Man. That will be in January 18 in my home town of Memphis,
Tennessee. I am sending you the short autobiography about myself so
you can better understand this approach. I would love to meet you just to
say hello if you're not too busy.

Respectfully,

/s/ Elvis Presley

P.S. I believe that you, Sir, were one of the Top Ten Outstanding Men
of America Also.

I have a personal gift for you which I would like to present to you
and you can accept it or I will keep it for you until you can take it.

White House transcription of the six-page handwritten letter from Elvis to President Richard Nixon.
(Copy from the National Archives)

themes. Elvis, obsessed with the idea of restoring respect for the American flag, turned to Nixon and whispered reassuringly, "I'm on your side." Elvis told Nixon that he had been studying Communist brainwashing and the drug culture. Nixon cautioned Elvis that, in order to retain his credibility, it would be unwise for Presley to preach out against drugs. "My singing makes me accepted by young people," Elvis remarked, as he presented Nixon with a World War II Colt .45 pistol in a wooden case. Elvis thought it was the perfect gift, a symbol of the American way.

When they concluded their meeting, President Nixon suggested that Elvis record a "Get High on Life" album and appear in a new rock musical with the same theme. The president stated that if the album was recorded at the federal narcotics rehabilitation and research facility at Lexington, Kentucky, it would receive excellent publicity. Elvis left a cluster of autographed photos for the president.

When Nixon's staff drew up a two-page memorandum to serve as an official communication with Elvis, they dwelt on the recent drug deaths of Jimi Hendrix and Janis Joplin. "Their deaths are a sharp reminder of how the rock music culture has been linked to the drug sub-culture," Nixon informed Elvis.

The Nixon visit was an indication that all was not well in Presley's life. Not only had Elvis badly misjudged his impact upon American youth, but he displayed a paranoia about recent American politics that was close to Nixon's own.

As Elvis continued his live performances, his renewed celebrity grew proportionately. Unfortunately, so did the number of doctors who provided him with uppers, downers, painkillers, and diet pills. By October 1973, Elvis would be so strung out that he would need to check into Baptist Hospital for a two-week detoxification program. Following Elvis' death, Jerry Schilling would tell Memphis Police Detective Larry Hutchinson that he had tried to intercept the cache of drugs delivered by sympathetic doctors. It was virtually impossible to break the drug cycle, however, because some of those around Presley also continued to abuse prescription drugs.

There were other disturbing changes in Presley's life. As the number of death threats increased, they began to affect Elvis's mental health. He was scared to death that he was about to be assassinated. The FBI took the threats seriously enough to provide Elvis with temporary agents during his 1971 Las Vegas opening. Presley also called upon Red West, an old high school friend, and Ed Parker, a Hawaiian karate instructor, to provide extra security.

When Elvis went on stage in Las Vegas in early 1971 he carried two .45s in his waistband and a derringer in his boot. During one party in his suite, Renee Kearns patted Elvis' waist and put her arms around him. She felt something strange.

"Do you have a bad back, Elvis?" she asked.

"No, honey, those are my derringers," Elvis laughed.

Kearns was surprised by the guns, but had no idea how many death threats had been received by the Presley entourage. "Elvis didn't look or act scared," Kearns concluded.

To further compound his problems, Priscilla told Elvis that she was having an affair with her karate instructor, Mike Stone. Elvis, who had virtually raised Priscilla, was crushed by her admission of marital infidelity, although he didn't consider his own extramarital affairs indiscrete. Elvis reasoned that he never publicly flaunted his other women, but that Priscilla had broken the Southern code which governed such matters. She had violated the rules. Priscilla, for her part, would later conclude in her book *Elvis And Me*: "I couldn't believe it was over." Priscilla's immaturity—she was a young girl who had changed and now desired her freedom—indicates how little she must have been able to give to the marriage in the first place. Ultimately, Elvis was only too happy to respect her wish to be free of him, although from the point at which he first learned of her "betrayal," Presley's roller coaster ride to destruction did nothing but accelerate. He was unhappy much of the time and struggled with self doubts, feelings masked by an extravagant exterior and a boisterous attitude. Elvis' music, however, took on a sentimental, maudlin tone, and he withdrew further into his own private world. He ate too much, dieted too rapidly, and performed in too many concerts.

On February 23, 1971, Elvis returned to Memphis in a state of depression. His physical condition was poor, and he was irritable. The change in Elvis was evident in a mid-March when he began a Nashville recording session. Not only did it end up a commercial disaster, but Elvis developed a severe eye infection a few days before the session. James Burton, brought in to play lead guitar, recognized that Elvis had changed. Burton, used to a less critical Elvis, was surprised when Elvis complained about the pop sound desired by RCA. Presley particularly disparaged the cover versions of Gordon Lightfoot's "Early Morning Rain" and Roberta Flack's "The First Time Ever I Saw Your Face" that he completed during the session.

Session players who knew and respected Elvis were aware of how precise he always was in the studio. When Elvis arrived and found some of the musicians drunk and others standing outside smoking dope, he exploded.

He screamed that he had just lost his wife. Now, no one seemed to care about him or his music either. He was trying to turn out good music, but the musicians were indifferent to the process. For the first time in his life Elvis resented the party atmosphere. He complained that many of the musicians were simply there to collect their large studio fees. James Burton, Elvis' guitarist, was guaranteed $5,000 a week, and the contracts for Charlie McCoy, Norbert Putnam, and Chip Young paid an average of $2,000 a week. These types of financial costs, combined with his recent personal problems, served only to compound Elvis' depression.

The March 1971 session lasted one day. Elvis recorded only four songs—"The First Time Ever I Saw Your Face," "For Lovin' Me," "Amazing Grace," and "Early Morning Rain." None of the versions were impressive, and the session was cancelled due to Elvis' eye problem and his general frame of mind. It was another two months before Elvis went back into the recording studio. In a lengthy Nashville session from May 15 through May 21, 1971, Elvis cut thirty songs. Among these was an inspired version of Bob Dylan's "Don't Think Twice It's All Right." Elvis loved this song. It was also his way of letting RCA know that he was unhappy with the trite tunes selected for his albums. Unfortunately, RCA didn't consider the song suitable for release because it ran eight minutes. To anyone who was paying attention, this seemingly routine week of sessions could have revealed Elvis' deep concern about his music. He openly complained that he was being suffocated with poor songs and predictable musical arrangements. No one paid any attention. As far as RCA was concerned, thirty songs had been completed during this fatiguing seven-day recording stretch, and this was enough material for three albums.

The next six years were a continual downward spiral that few outsiders had any hint of because of the protective veil placed around Elvis. When he was not on tour or in Las Vegas, Elvis went to bed at eight in the morning and got up late in the afternoon. He ate breakfast as most people were coming home from work. There was plenty of time for leisure and play, but Elvis played as hard as he worked. Ever-increasing business expenses were compounded by Presley's personal spending habits. Ultimately, time off simply meant that pressures had time to build and the constant need for money to increase. No matter how much Elvis made when he did work, he spent it all and more.

There were more obvious indications of erratic personal behavior, however. Elvis bought Mercedes Benz automobiles for his friends. He had his Memphis jeweler make up expensive gifts for strangers. The Presley entourage received their full share of the diamond rings, bracelets, and TCB symbols. The number of young girls who were friends with the band suggests one reason why Presley's employees didn't complain too much about the poor pay.

Presley's vaunted entourage, for their part, had largely become Elvis clones. If he ate yogurt, they ate yogurt. If he took karate lessons, they took karate lessons. If he abused pills, they abused pills. It was unhealthy relationship demonstrated in one story after another in the devastating book *Elvis: What Happened?* Written by Red and Sonny West and Dave Hebler along with gossip column journalist, Steve Dunleavy, now a CBS-TV reporter on the show "A Current Affair," the 1977 volume recounts Elvis' drug use, sexual excesses, and his obsession with guns.

Elvis's so-called Memphis Mafia, which had begun twenty years before when Presley first invited close friends and family to surround, accompany, live with and work for him, had become largely an army of sycophants. *Elvis: What Happened?* clearly demonstrated that what Elvis had started as a cure for loneliness and the discomfort of ridicule by people whose backgrounds differed from his own was now not so much symbiosis as parasitism. The book was a double-edged sword, however. Three former bodyguards indicted themselves as well as Elvis in the book, with only the skill of professional writer Dunleavy allowing them to appear surprised by the girls and drug use.

Sonny West, for example, alleged that he had brought a young girl to Elvis' suite in the spring of 1971 while Presley was playing at the Sahara Casino in South Lake Tahoe. The girl was from Newark, California, a small blue-collar suburb south of Oakland. She had gotten on the elevator and been noticed by a member of Presley's entourage. Using a private elevator, Elvis went downstairs for a look. The girl was stunning, and, in purple prose, West retells the story of being commanded to bring the young girl to Presley. He writes as though he were a Judas goat bringing the young girl to a lamb-like slaughter. West indicated that he was surprised that she spent the night with Elvis, and was allegedly induced to drink enough Hycodan, a congestion medicine with a high narcotic base, to bring on a coma. The story was apparently intended to highlight Presley's aberrant behavior. A number of accounts of this incident in fan newsletters dispute the story—claiming that West later admitted falsely relating it—a fact less important than West's self-serving hindsight account of it. We are lead to believe that the incident actually left West shocked and angered. "Here was a girl dying...and within seconds Elvis was telling everybody it had nothing to do with him." West's rage, slow to surface, always seemed to emerge after the fact. After all, he merely kept track of these incidents for a book.

In actuality, no one got in to see Elvis Presley without Red West's approval. In 1976, after Bruce Springsteen had been on the cover of every major news magazine, he was turned away by Presley's bodyguards. "I thought for sure Elvis would see me, I had just been on the cover of *Newsweek*," Springsteen smirked. What the boss didn't realize was that Presley's hillbilly entourage didn't read. They decided who saw Elvis merely on whim.

The entire situation bothered Elvis, not only because of the expense but because he was no longer in control of his own destiny. He was surrounded by sponges who were preoccupied with things like attracting leftover girls. And from Elvis' frustration over not being able to solve the problem came an increasing reclusiveness and depression.

Despite the fact that Elvis' private life was in shambles, his professional life was in top form. His eccentric lifestyle didn't prevent him from remaining an honored entertainer. The awards continued to pile up. In February 1971, England's *New Musical Express* named Elvis as the world's top male singer. This was the twelfth time in thirteen years that the prestigious British music weekly had so honored Elvis. In the United States, the Jaycees named Elvis one of the top ten "Young Men of the Year." In 1971 he won the Bing Crosby Award for his contributions to music. In the following year, when he sold out Madison Square Garden for four shows, Elvis was to break all previous records for the venue.

Losing Control (1972-73)

On June 9, 1972, Elvis opened another tour with a series of concerts at Madison Square Garden in New York City. Earlier, at four o'clock in the afternoon, he had appeared in the Mercury Ballroom of the New York Hilton to meet the press. The anticipation of Elvis' 8:30 concert that evening was evident in the question period. At this press conference, Elvis appeared puffy and groggy. For weeks prior to the tour he had taken handfuls of diet pills to bring down his weight. No one realized the extent to which the medication was taking its toll on his body. In fact, most reporters remarked that Elvis looked physically fit. The motivation—the pressure—for Elvis, of course, was the guaranteed $70,000 (or 70 percent of the gate receipts) per show.

The New York media was also friendly for the first time, and they found Elvis in a giddy mood. The highlight came when reporters asked Elvis about his longevity.

"Elvis, why have you waited so long to come to New York?"

"Well sir, we had trouble finding a good build-ing," Elvis chuckled. "And once we found one, we had to wait our turn."

"Mr. Presley, why have you outlasted all your competition?"

"I take a lot of vitamin E," Elvis repeated with a pronounced Southern drawl. "No, actually, honey, I suppose I've just been very fortunate."

"Elvis are you satisfied with your image?"

"Well sir, it's very hard to live up to an image."

The triumph of the Madison Square Garden press conference hid the fact that Elvis was a troubled man. Surprisingly, though, these pressures didn't have an impact on his concerts. The shows at Madison Square Garden were unqualified successes. As Elvis came on stage just after nine o'clock, a flash of Instamatic cameras erupted as he walked around the stage spreading his gold-lined cape. The *New York Times* described Elvis as "...gaudy, vulgar, magnificent...." *Cashbox* wrote that Elvis deserved "...our everlasting love and envy, he has transcended the exasperating constrictions of time and place."

Nevertheless, Elvis was depressed because he was restricted from performing new songs. RCA and Colonel Parker reminded him that his popularity rested upon a time-tested formula. Colonel Parker and RCA had received numerous pleas from Elvis to include songs on his albums that he felt comfortable with in the studio. They ignored him at every turn. This pigeonholing drove Elvis to despair, a state of mind he relieved by eating himself into a stupor. After nearly twenty-five years in the music business, Elvis had become disenchanted.

RCA's complete disregard for Presley's career was evident when press releases for a live Elvis album recorded at Madison Square Garden were distributed to selected media outlets. "Elvis wasn't told," Joan Deary of RCA recalled. Beginning in 1954, Deary had been an assistant to RCA executive Steve Sholes, and had worked on various phases of Elvis' career. In 1972 she was an assistant to Jerry Jenkins, vice president of RCA, and was one of Presley's staunchest supporters. Deary, an unusually quiet person, has maintained a steadfast silence on many RCA/Elvis-related topics over the years, but even her guarded remarks suggest a personal outrage over the manner in which Presley's label handled his career. Deary retired early from RCA, apparently not without some bitterness towards the corporate monolith. This may have been the reason she dropped her guarded posture later remarks.

Eventually, Joan Deary admitted that RCA not only recorded two separate Madison Square Garden shows, but planned to release this material without consulting Presley. Elvis exploded when he heard the news. He felt betrayed. Colonel Parker and RCA were working behind his back.

Despite the fact that he hadn't been consulted about the release of the recordings, Elvis was ultimately pleased by the outcome of the New York shows. He beamed when the gross receipts for the shows were announced at $730,000. The album itself quickly sold in excess of a million copies, creating a total gross of $1.2 million dollars for six hours of work.

Whatever the successes, the pills continued and the dieting was constant as Elvis eased into a predictable work schedule during 1972. The Colonel had booked Elvis in Las Vegas in February and August, while in April, June, and November he toured in a series of one-night concerts. On the surface, Presley's schedule appeared to be relaxed. Ever the consummate perfectionist, Elvis practiced constantly for the Las Vegas shows and road tours. These pressures were punctuated by frequent medical problems, death threats, and the increasingly bizarre behavior of the Memphis Mafia. They were like little boys with new toys, basking in Elvis' limelight. Frequently they overstepped their role and often talked nastily to Elvis' face. "I couldn't believe some of the things that they said to Elvis," a California fan remarked. "In Lake Tahoe they acted like they were Elvis. They hung out in the bars looking for girls who wanted to meet Elvis. I never saw one of those girls get close to Presley," another fan remarked. "You'll get in to see Elvis through my bedroom," a bodyguard told fan Ingrid Johnson.

Mounting pressures from these and many other business and personal troubles persisted. Elvis' fascination with guns became obsessive. Since his days at Humes High, he had been a gun enthusiast. In 1972, however, it became a daily ritual for him to check his weapons. Elvis spent hours cleaning, loading, and unloading his gun collection. He diligently studied gun laws, the penal system, and police practices. He wrote to the Bureau of Alcohol, Tobacco and Firearms to inquire about a license to sell guns. This whim passed, but it indicates the serious nature of Presley's gun fetish. Indeed, surrounded by a platoon of bellicose, blustering bodyguards, many of whose members were also intrigued with weapons, there was little to discourage Elvis' fixation with firearms.

On September 4, 1972, even as Elvis continued fighting with Colonel Parker and RCA, he received word that the Colonel had negotiated an hour-long satellite television show from Hawaii. Elvis had no choice but to appear publicly delighted by the prospect of a worldwide concert. To friends, however, he described the event as depressing news. The two-hundred-word RCA memo that announced the live Elvis show from Honolulu was filled with anticipation of viewer interest and record sales. The "Aloha from Hawaii" show, to be broadcast in January from the International Convention Center, was designed to beam Elvis' music around the world.

The first formal announcement of the satellite show had come from Colonel Tom Parker's Las Vegas suite in the fall of 1972; the announcement had also triggered rumors that Elvis was looking for new management. The broadcast of "Aloha from Hawaii" a few months later temporarily quieted such talk. The spectacular picture of Elvis standing on a small stage in Honolulu as his concert was beamed around the globe intrigued the media. RCA announced a two-record album to commemorate this momentous event. The cost of the "Aloha" special had been a staggering $2.5 million, and it took the support of Rocco Laginestra, the president of RCA, to put the deal together. Although RCA covered the cost for the show, Colonel Parker received most of the credit. In reality, RCA's Laginestra was the visionary who realized that the show was an unprecedented opportunity to merchandise Presley's records.

The detailed preparation for the "Aloha from Hawaii" special indicated the precision required to complete the satellite show, which was scheduled for broadcast to the Far East on Sunday, January 14 at 12:30 in the morning. Elvis demanded extra rehearsals, and the intensity of the seven nights of rehearsal that Elvis' band ritualistically completed in Honolulu was confirmed when RCA decided to tape these sessions. While the band and backup singers worked out the music arrangements, Elvis held secret rehearsals with a select group of musicians in the Hilton Hawaiian Dome, a geodesic structure located on the Hilton's front lawn. The overall importance of these rehearsals was demonstrated when the live concert album was released.

In anticipation of the show, "Elvis Presley Day" was declared in Honolulu on January 13, 1973. The Hawaiian press lauded Elvis for making the "Aloha from Hawaii" satellite special a charity benefit for the Kui Lee Cancer Fund. Lee, one of Hawaii's best-known songwriters, died in at the age of thirty-four and Elvis promised to remember him by performing his best known song, "I'll Remember You." Elvis also contributed a check for $1,000 to the Kui Lee fund and announced that $25,000 would be raised to continue cancer research.

As Colonel Parker bustled in the background during the final preparation for the show, Elvis was filled with anxiety. For months prior to the show he had been on eating binges that had seriously affected his health. Elvis' meals usually consisted of hamburgers, assorted sweets, potato chips, and deviled eggs, and he had found it difficult to diet for the special. Upon his arrival, Hawaiian observers noted that Elvis' behavior was erratic.

The Colonel spent much of his time squelching these rumors. Everywhere Elvis went prior to the show, he complained about the possibility of something going wrong with the satellite system. The rehearsals had been lengthy and exhausting, but Elvis couldn't dismiss the thought of failure. He feared the final Friday tune-up. There were so many unanswered questions that Elvis was sorry that he had agreed to do the show.

Elvis' tensions were eased when the Friday night dress rehearsal went well. With almost six thousand fans attending the final tune-up for the worldwide television broadcast, Elvis reached into his performing bag for a little extra energy. The rehearsal show was loose and the band was tight. As Elvis' ardent Hawaiian fans cheered, RCA executives spent the last day checking the satellite and recording equipment for flaws.

The following day the concert was successfully beamed over the sophisticated Intelsat IV Communications satellite. On Sunday morning at half past twelve Honolulu time, Elvis walked on stage as a sea of cameras flashed a roar of approval. For the remainder of the show, Elvis was in top form musically, and the concert became a testimonial to his professionalism.

Elvis was as thin as a rail and as handsome as two movie stars when he taped the show. This disguised the fact that his health was in a precarious condition. His insides were giving out, and his persistent use of medication fueled a rumor that he was battling intestinal problems. There was no doubt that he was heavily medicated and addicted to a number of prescription drugs—primarily painkillers and depressants—at this point in time.

On April 4, 1973, NBC-TV rebroadcast the ninety-minute "Aloha from Hawaii" special in the United States, and this increased the worldwide audience to a billion viewers. In the American market, NBC-TV announced that the program reached an unprecedented 57 percent of the viewing audience, demolishing the ratings of the popular television show "All in the Family." While Elvis was basking in the glow of "Aloha from Hawaii," he also received a number of other honors. After more than forty albums and approximately eighty-five hit singles, Elvis won finally a Grammy for his gospel album **He Touched Me**. The recording was acclaimed as the "Best Inspirational Performance of 1972," despite its lackluster track record on the *Billboard* album charts—it reached the number 79 position during a stay of ten weeks. The award was long overdue recognition from Presley's peers, and his success as a recording artist was further demonstrated when the *Guinness Book of World Records* listed him as the artist who had sold the most phonograph records in history.

Early in 1973, MGM had begun isolated screenings of the thirty-third Presley movie, a documentary

Elvis and Glen Campbell in Las Vegas, 1973.

entitled "Elvis on Tour." When the film was released on June 6, it earned the $1.6 production costs back in three days. The reviewers were ecstatic. "At long last the first Elvis Presley movie," *Rolling Stone* wrote. The film won a Golden Globe award, and Presley basked in the critical acclaim. All of these awards made Elvis feel as though he had finally received the proper artistic recognition.

The antics of close friends continued to cause problems, however. Lawsuits grew more and more frequent, and Elvis was infuriated when bodyguards used his name for personal reasons. Young and not so young girls were constantly invited into the inner sanctum. In Las Vegas, the number of "friends of the band" was often in the hundreds. Each night young ladies even gave their room numbers to waiters in hopes of meeting Elvis. One headwaiter named Emilio directed an "entertainment" operation that kept Presley's bodyguards busy non-stop. Everyone was trying to get close to Elvis, and a hotel headwaiter seemed to have a corner on the chances for success or failure. The bodyguards were also close to many of Elvis' fans and maintained long-term friendships with many of the fan club presidents. Unfortunately, the fine line between helping the fan clubs and helping themselves to the available females was one the Memphis Mafia constantly abused.

An incident in San Francisco involving one of Elvis' entourage—Ed Parker—provoked Presley's ire. Parker, a Hawaiian-Mormon bodyguard, was one of the organizers of the California State Karate Championship. This prestigious event brought together the biggest names in karate. Since Elvis was a dedicated karate student, he decided to attend the San Francisco show. Arrangements were made for hotel rooms and a fleet of limousines. Elvis invited his personal instructor, Kang Rhee, to accompany him. When they arrived at the concert, however, the marquee read: "Elvis Presley—In Person." After Jerry Schilling pointed out the sign, Elvis paused momentarily, angrily crushed out a cigar, and ordered the limousine back to the airport.

Such abuse of Presley's name for commercial purposes was by now typical of the Presley entourage, and Elvis blamed Ed Parker, although there is no evidence that Parker was directly responsible. Parker explained to Elvis that the promoter must have taken it upon himself to add Elvis's name to the marquee. Typical of the bodyguards, however, Parker's defense took on a self-righteous tone. They all viewed themselves as larger than life characters having only the purest of motives. Everyone else outside Elvis' inner circle, the bodyguards maintained, were motivated by malevolence.

Shortly after the karate tournament incident, there was a noticeable increase in Presley's prescription drug use. Alarmed, Elvis' lawyer, Ed Hookstratten, hired Los Angeles private investigator John O'Grady to investigate and report on the extent to which prescription medicines had come to dominate Presley's life. For six weeks O'Grady made copious notes detailing the prescriptions for painkillers, depressants, and amphetamines that passed into Elvis' possession. O'Grady reported that many prescriptions were also being written for Presley's employees, many of whom were delusionally acting like *they* were the King of Rock and Roll—they not only dressed and carried themselves in a manner similar to Elvis, but took the same drugs.

In May 1973, Priscilla Presley hired a new attorney, Arthur Toll, who petitioned the Los Angeles Superior Court alleging that Elvis had practiced "intrinsic fraud" in the original property settlement, a legal means of questioning the terms of the divorce proceedings currently underway. Under California law, half of Elvis' property belonged to Priscilla, and Toll argued persuasively that the original $100,000 property settlement, $1,000-a-month alimony, and $500-a-month child support payment were paltry sums. Detailing Presley's vast wealth, Toll made an effective case for negotiating a new settlement.

The court battle was nasty. Priscilla testified that she had lived with Elvis since she was fourteen and that her life had been guided by him. In court documents, the soon-to-be-ex-Mrs. Presley described herself as a housewife with no marketable skills. The original agreement arranged by Hookstratten was labelled as an "in-house" settlement. As a result, nine months after the original divorce petition was instituted, Priscilla Presley was back in court with a new public image. She was shown in television clips as a fashionable woman who questioned Elvis' lifestyle. The argument that Priscilla's attorney used was that she had been a little girl who had been taken advantage of by an older man. Now, she was not only a mature, beautiful woman, but acting lessons made her courtroom behavior more effective. The show business education of Priscilla Presley was complete; she was now an accomplished Hollywood figure. Mike Stone, her illicit lover, had been cast aside for a more glamorous independence.

Priscilla detailed her new settlement terms. She asked for $14,900 a month for living expenses. This sum included $400 for the telephone, $2,500 for clothing, and $1,500 for incidentals. Ultimately, although she failed to secure her initial demands, Priscilla profited nicely from Elvis' willingness to meet her extravagant needs. She was awarded a $4,200-a-month alimony check and $4,000 for Lisa Marie's support and education. Priscilla also received half of the proceeds from the sale of a half-million-dollar Los Angeles house, five percent of the stock in two of Elvis' song publishing companies, and $750,000 in cash with another $720,000 paid at $6,000 a month for ten years. The $70,000 Priscilla owed her attorney was paid by Elvis.

The press wondered why Elvis had agreed to the new settlement so quickly. The simple truth is that he just gave up. The specter of a battle in open court bothered him. For decades he had maintained a very guarded private life. Generally, the Presley entourage, for all its antics, had managed to keep its innermost secrets from the eye of the media. A divorce dispute, however, was a matter of public record. It was difficult to avoid reporters and photographers, and the courtroom records were open to anyone. Elvis quickly agreed to a compromise with his ex-wife. He had always made plenty of money, and he saw no reason to contest Priscilla's demands.

Priscilla's decision to go into business just four months prior to the re-settlement had also bothered Elvis. Basically, he was troubled by Priscilla's decision to go to work, although he never publicly objected to Priscilla's business and he continued to offer her financial support. It simply made Elvis look like he wasn't supporting her. The idea of becoming an independent businesswoman had intrigued Priscilla for some time, and she had opened a designer shop located a block off Santa Monica Boulevard near Doug Weston's Troubadour Club with partner Olivia Biz. The Bis and Beaus boutique offered the latest in designer wear from an amateur who had little understanding of the fashion business. The store continued for some time as only a marginally successful curiosity "celebrity business," despite the increased support afforded by the expanded property settlement, part of which was intended to finance it.

In the end, however, it was the psychological damage of the divorce itself that had hurt Elvis most. He no longer cared about anything. The woman he loved had humiliated him. This hurt more than the money. The residue of bitterness from the divorce proceedings had a visible effect upon Presley's health. He looked drawn and haggard. Fans who saw him backstage at concerts described him as unhappy and dissatisfied. No one will ever know precisely the extent of the tension and anxiety that the divorce proceedings caused Elvis, let alone the intervening petition for resettlement. His emotional and physical health declined almost immediately after the divorce petition was filed in August 1972. His music became increasingly sentimental. When Elvis opened at the Hilton International Hotel on January 26, 1973, he performed for only forty-five minutes and the musical set had a mechanical quality. There was no longer any banter with the audience. Few people knew what was bothering Elvis, but inside observers recognized something was wrong.

Things Fall Apart (1974-75)

In early 1972, RCA had taped four dinner shows at the Hilton International for a projected live album. Tentatively entitled, **Standing Room Only**, this double LP would capture Elvis in concert at the Hilton. The album was never released, however, and RCA never offered an explanation for cancelling it. Some years later, a two-record bootleg album with the same title surfaced, but RCA itself never relented and never bothered to release a complete Las Vegas show on an Elvis LP. The reason was that a number of key RCA executives believed that Presley's appeal was limited to a narrowly-defined audience. Neither their own record sales nor the clearly outstanding concert receipts validated their thinking, but RCA continued to refuse a full-length concert album.

One close Presley observer believes that the end of Elvis' life began on New Year's Eve 1973. While hosting a traditional year-end party for thirty of his closest friends at Graceland, Elvis displayed unusually strange behavior. Rather than attending the party, he and his new girlfriend, Linda Thompson, came downstairs for only a few minutes to shake hands with the guests. The old party days were over, and Elvis was tended more and more towards reclusiveness. No longer able to maintain a friendly outward appearance, he became withdrawn and cynical.

No one knew how bitter Elvis was over his career. Colonel Parker had isolated Presley from all new musical decisions. In retaliation, Elvis threatened never to record again. RCA was aware that the King of Rock and Roll was no longer interested in recording, so they had to find a means of guaranteeing new Presley products.

Joan Deary, the executive responsible for Presley's music, came up with the idea of repackaging his old records. The result was the album **Elvis—A Legendary Performer, Volume 1**, which showcased Presley's first Sun single, "That's All Right (Mama)," as well as early RCA hits like "Heartbreak Hotel" and "Don't Be Cruel." The album also included a gospel hit, "Peace in the Valley," and Presley's best-selling movie record, "Blue Hawaii." Deary's package was a successful commercial idea that led to a series of albums. *Rolling Stone* praised RCA for finally recognizing Presley's true talent. Greil Marcus wrote that Elvis' music demonstrated "a completely innocent and mature delight in sex; a love of roots and a respect for the past; a rejection of roots and a demand for novelty...." Most newspapers, magazines, and fanzines echoed Marcus' astute comments.

Merv Griffin, Tom Jones, Elvis and comedian Norm Crosby, 1974.

Even as Elvis received critical acclaim for his music, he faced yet another series of lawsuits. During the summer of 1974, a Grass Valley, California, land developer, Edward L. Ashley, filed legal action against the Presley organization alleging that Red West, Elvis' stepbrother David Stanley, and former Palm Springs police sergeant Dick Grob had assaulted him. The facts in this case were never fully disclosed, and the lawsuit quickly faded from the public view, but Ashley's suit was characteristic of the tension swirling around Presley.

When Elvis opened at the Las Vegas Hilton on August 19, 1974, Barbra Streisand and her film producer boyfriend, Jon Peters, approached him with an offer to remake "A Star Is Born." Colonel Tom Parker wouldn't consider the proposal because Elvis was to receive neither top billing nor was he to be salaried. Sadly, accepting the part in the movie could have meant an immense change in the direction of Presley's career, finally providing long overdue recognition for his acting talents. Thanks to Colonel Parker, it just wasn't to be.

Vernon Presley, meanwhile, had separated from, Dee, his wife of seventeen years. "I started writing songs," Dee Presley remarked, "I wanted a life of my own." Now constantly at Elvis' side, Vernon's presence merely added more family responsibilities to an already burdened Elvis, who was suddenly a father to his own father. Elvis had never forgiven Vernon for marrying Dee and bringing her three spoiled children into the house. She was a Southern belle with neither the subtle beauty nor the bearing to command the attention and respect of Elvis Presley. "She was a social climber, a princess who looked for big money," one observer remarked to this writer.

Although Elvis earned more than seven million dollars in 1974, his expenses exceeded four million dollars. After Elvis paid his taxes and Colonel Parker took his share, Presley's accounting firm in Memphis, Rhea and Ivey, informed him that he had lost money. The expense sheet provided by Rhea and Ivey indicated that Elvis spent three million dollars while clearing only a million and a half. The inescapable conclusion is that no one was in charge. The lavish spending encouraged by the entourage and the lack of monetary controls had driven Elvis to the brink of bankruptcy.

In addition to his money problems, Elvis' romance with the press had ended. Elvis' concerts were no longer well-planned spectacular affairs. Fans often walked out mumbling. There were continual money problems. He was suddenly the target of ridicule. The typical headline focused on the fact that he was fat and forty. The *National Enquirer* led the onslaught with grotesque pictures of Presley in concert. A typical *Enquirer* headline read: "ELVIS AT 40—PAUNCHY, DEPRESSED AND LIVING IN FEAR." The *Enquirer* went out of its way to interview waitresses, cocktail lounge employees, and bus boys in Las Vegas and Lake Tahoe in an effort to uncover scandal. Service employees often witnessed Elvis' excesses, and they provided titillating, if unsubstantiated, bits of gossip.

One of the most crushing reviews of a Presley con-

Backstage with members of an Italian fan club, 1974.

cert came from a *Los Angeles Times* critic, Robert Hilburn. A well-known reviewer whom Elvis respected, Hilburn suggested that Elvis retire. "At forty his records are increasingly uneven, his choice of material sometimes ludicrous, and his concert performances often sloppy." Hilburn was a fan but an honest critic.

The January 13 issue of *People* magazine had a cover story on Elvis entitled "Elvis the Pelvis Turns 40, but He Isn't All Shook Up," a shallow attack upon Presley that urged him, like the Hilburn piece, to retire. Elvis had grown into a caricature of himself. His talent was no longer visible to those who had followed his career since the 1950s. Deeply depressed, he broke down crying a number of times and became even more reclusive.

As the critics deserted Elvis, so his health continued to decline. Elvis' weight ballooned to over two hundred and twenty pounds, and Bill Belew, Elvis' costume designer, simply quit measuring him for new outfits. An enlarged colon and sporadic attempts at drug detoxification sent Elvis to the hospital. He developed glaucoma. Elvis' eyes hurt day and night, and he was frightened that he would lose his sight. Upon his death, a liver biopsy revealed serious damage from years of prescription medicine. Elvis' eating habits aggravated these problems. After forty years of fried foods, sugar-rich products, and crash dieting, he was a walking time bomb.

On January 8, 1975, Elvis quietly celebrated his

fortieth birthday at Graceland. At a private dinner party with Linda Thompson, Elvis reflected on his inability to maintain intimate relationships. He was emotionally and psychologically distraught. Due to his nightmarish personal life, Elvis cancelled his January 26 to February 9 appearance at the Las Vegas Hilton. When the press speculated that Elvis was cancelling in order to diet, a Hilton spokesman countered with a press release announcing that Elvis had merely delayed his arrival until the opening of a twenty-million-dollar Hilton addition, scheduled for an April 1 unveiling. In actuality, the cancellation was necessary so that Elvis could try to recover from his personal and medical problems.

In an attempt to escape from reality, Elvis went on a buying spree. He purchased eleven Cadillacs for his friends and he bought a $1.5-million Boeing 707 jet complete with a sauna, gym, and discotheque. Later in January, Elvis entered Baptist Memorial Hospital for treatment of an alleged liver problem, actually another attempt to detoxify him. Ironically, a week later, on February 5, after suffering a massive heart attack, Elvis' father was rushed to the same hospital.

Elvis renewed his fighting with Colonel Parker over his career direction. The increased dissatisfaction with Parker resulted from the fact that the Colonel had declined two concert offers from English promoters. A British boxing entrepreneur, Jack Solomons, offered Elvis a million pounds to perform at London's Earl Court. Another English promoter, Arthur Howes, hoped to book Elvis into London's Wembley Stadium. These offers were rejected because Parker—who would naturally be expected to accompany Elvis or to explain his reluctance to do so—feared that his status as an illegal alien would be discovered. As a very young man, Parker had entered the United States from Holland without benefit of the proper immigration papers.

After a twenty-year business relationship, the strain of Presley's health and financial problems brought heated arguments. Elvis was incensed with the selection of songs included in his albums. RCA and Colonel Parker refused to spend the money for experienced songwriters. Elvis was infuriated when the Colonel authorized the release of **Having Fun with Elvis on Stage (A Talking Album Only)**, which the Colonel issued on his own Boxcar label and then allowed RCA to produce. It was a humiliating collection of bad jokes, belches, and off-color remarks.

The split between Elvis and the Colonel wasn't limited to business matters. Presley almost quit the Hilton showroom because his favorite chef had been fired. Colonel Parker scolded Elvis for telling the Hilton how to handle its employees. The argument became so heated that Elvis demanded to be released from his contract. The Colonel said fine, that he would see Elvis the next

morning with an expense sheet detailing what Elvis owed to him. No one has ever seen the bill that Parker presented to Elvis, but suffice it to say that they continued their business relationship. The Colonel had backed Elvis into a corner, and once again retained his right to manipulate Presley's career.

Because of his ill health, Elvis hadn't worked for five months prior to opening in Las Vegas on March 18, 1975. A celebration to commemorate the $20-million, 600-room Hilton Tower was planned around Elvis' opening. The Hilton hotel had capitalized on Elvis' unplanned hiatus from performing by raising the show price to twenty dollars and cancelling the dinner show. This created twenty percent more seating. The show sold out and the Hilton management loved it.

It was the twelfth time that Elvis had played the Hilton, and this particular Las Vegas opening had some new twists to it. The changes were designed to rest Elvis' battered body. Kathy Westmoreland and J.D. Sumner, Elvis' backup singers, were allowed to sing their own songs. Grossly overweight, Elvis seemed bored. He mocked his fifties image by complaining about singing songs like "Hound Dog." The Hilton, however, never once complained about Elvis' antics. Their profits were enormous.

One of Elvis' favorite pastimes during his March 1975 Las Vegas engagement was to sneak out with two bodyguards and walk into the Denny's restaurant on the strip for a strawberry shake, a cheeseburger, and french fries. Sitting in the back of Denny's, dressed in a trench coat and looking for all the world like a gangster, Elvis apparently drew some sort of solace from such moments of privacy.

By July 1975, Elvis Presley was once again erratically spending money. He gave each of the Sweet Inspirations, his backup singing group, a $5,000 diamond ring. On July 27, 1975, Elvis beat his personal record for spending by purchasing fourteen Cadillacs from Madison Cadillac in Memphis. Howard Massey, the salesman who had waited on Elvis for years, remembered that Elvis even bought a Cadillac—an $11,500 gold-and-white El Dorado—for a total stranger who had simply admired the Cadillacs as she walked by the showroom.

The spending sprees weren't the only sign of erratic behavior. Elvis was drowsy, crabby, and sweated profusely. Melissa Blackwood, a Memphis beauty queen, was one of Elvis' companions who complained that Presley was dying. Elvis bought Melissa a white Pontiac Grand Prix the day they met, but she was one of the few who cared about Elvis.

Although he dated Cybill Shepherd, showgirl Sandra Zancan, and beauty queen Jo Cathy Brownlee, Elvis was comforted most by live-in companion Linda Thompson. She was a Southern girl with a strong will and a well-developed intellect. Unlike many of Presley's companions, Linda was silent about their relationship. With a view to maintaining her position with Elvis, she was prescient enough to simply ignore Elvis' lifestyle.

The Beginning of The End (1976-77)

By 1976, Elvis was in poor physical and mental shape. RCA couldn't coax Elvis to the recording studio, so they moved $200,000 worth of recording equipment into Graceland. Presley's RCA contract called for three albums a year. The only way this contractual obligation had been met in the past was through the repackaging of old tunes. From February 2 through February 8, 1976, using his touring band, Elvis recorded his first sessions at Graceland. RCA considered the songs unsuitable for release and overdubbed most of the tunes. Elvis was still clearly troubled by his divorce from Priscilla, and it showed in the choice of songs.

In May 1976, the album **From Elvis Presley Boulevard, Memphis, Tennessee** was released with material from this session. Elvis acted as the executive producer for the album. The tunes were a strange mixture of contemporary songs that included Neil Sedaka's "Solitaire," Willie Nelson's "Blue Eyes Crying in the Rain," and Larry Gatlin's "Bitter They Are, Harder They Fall." Despite adverse recording conditions, the album indicated that Elvis was still in top musical form. The picture of Elvis on the album cover shows a slightly overweight performer. The first song on the album, "Hurt," was a million-seller, reaching number 20 on the *Billboard* Hot 100 and number 6 on the country chart. (In 1954, Roy Hamilton, a close friend of Elvis, recorded the song, and it had been a hit for Timi Yuro in 1961.) For a year prior to recording it, Elvis performed "Hurt" in concert. The album also included "Danny Boy," "I'll Never Fall in Love Again," and Roger Whittaker's, "The Last Farewell." Elvis' vocals were strong, and it remains a mystery why RCA overdubbed the album, which remains a legacy to his rich and powerful vocal talents. It also indicates that Elvis' music was moving further into a pop mold.

As Elvis' audience diversified, it grew less predictable. Newer Elvis fans didn't respect the privacy that Presley demanded. For the first time, the Presley organization began to have serious security problems. Presley was plagued by an ever-mounting barrage of death threats, paternity suits, and simple acts of violence.

The solution to Elvis' woes was provided by tough and respected Los Angeles private detective John O'Grady, mentioned briefly above. In 1970, O'Grady had been hired by Elvis to investigate potential security problems. His range of investigations was broad, and O'Grady warned Elvis of many impending conflicts. A former Los Angeles narcotics detective, O'Grady's powerful appearance and obvious integrity made him a Presley favorite. He checked out many of the girls Elvis dated. It was O'Grady who urged that Presley fire Red and Sonny West and Dave Hebler. He saw them as useless appendages to the Presley organization who did very little for their money. When the West's were finally fired, they complained bitterly about the low pay and the lack of status.

In May 1976, O'Grady and his son visited Elvis in Lake Tahoe. O'Grady was horrified by Elvis' appearance. After years of narcotics work, O'Grady knew that there was something seriously wrong. Elvis looked strung out. O'Grady devised a plan for Elvis to enter the Scripps Clinic in San Diego, but neither Elvis nor the Colonel would listen to such an idea.

There were other people who wondered about Presley's future. Ron Freitas, a California businessman, met Elvis in March 1976 while on an automobile purchasing trip. Freitas eventually bought a 1969 six-door Mercedes-Benz 600 from Presley. While buying cars in Memphis for his California dealership, Freitas was taken to Graceland, introduced to Elvis, and, subsequently, decided to buy Presley's private limousine. The dark blue limo had blue velvet and rosewood lining in the back, set with a high bar and refrigerator. "You could see the style and grace that was Presley's trademark," Freitas remarked.

"When I met Elvis," Freitas continued, "he asked me if I'd like to have a Coke. I was impressed with his manners." Freitas was Presley's guest during a May 1976 show at Lake Tahoe. "We went up to a small party in Elvis' suite, he was very cordial and friendly. The security was massive; I felt that Elvis was trapped in his suite." Freitas remembered that Presley's physical appearance had deteriorated in just a few months, and the show was a poor one. Elvis forgot his song lines, found it difficult to complete a tune, and harangued the audience with, of all things, an anti-drug speech. Freitas knew the end was near for Presley. "He must have weighed 250 pounds," Freitas lamented. "I really felt sorry for the guy. He struck me as a person who could have done anything, in any profession. Here he was trapped in Tahoe." Freitas has the gold plaque from the limo—"Built for Elvis Presley"—mounted in his elegantly furnished California home. "This man brought a lot of happiness to a lot of people; I look at the plaque and wonder what the music business did for Elvis."

Although his health was in a precarious state, Elvis

continued to tour. The sold-out auditoriums and the large gate receipts were necessary to support Presley's lavish lifestyle. Then, in the fall of 1976, Linda Thompson, Elvis' live-in girlfriend since 1972, wrote him a "Dear John" letter. The former beauty queen had grown into a mature woman and wanted her own life. She told Elvis that she still loved him, but that it was now time for her to grow beyond the confines of their life together. She returned Elvis' MasterCard after running up a $30,000 bill. Elvis smiled. Linda Thompson had earned her farewell gift.

Once Linda Thompson left Elvis, the search began for a replacement. She had to be lithe, raven-haired, and quiet, a stereotypical picture of the perfect Southern woman that Elvis had formed in his mind. A local beauty, Ginger Alden, fit the profile. Of all of Elvis' girls, Ginger Alden had the least to offer. She was pretty, but young and immature. In public she had trouble talking and fidgeted constantly. She looked like she belonged in a disco. Alden was overwhelmed by Elvis' lifestyle. She had no intellectual interests and was even bored with Presley's music. It was purely a physical attraction. Although Ginger apparently made Elvis happy during the last six months of his life, she was a clinging, lifeless figure. Yet, there was genuine affection between them and it was rumored that Elvis would marry her.

By the summer of 1977, Elvis was distraught and angry about the pending publication of the "bodyguard's book"—*Elvis: What Happened?* —penned by three disgruntled ex-employees. The West brothers—Red and Sonny—and Dave Hebler had signed the contract to do the book shortly after Vernon Presley fired them for allegedly using too much force in dealing with zealous fans. The book was published at a time when Elvis' career was flourishing in the record, concert, and television markets. On June 1, 1977, CBS television signed Elvis for a special anniversary show. Colonel Parker announced the release of an album to coincide with the television extravaganza. On June 19, while Elvis performed at the Civic Auditorium in Omaha, Nebraska, CBS-TV and RCA recording crews filmed the show. The remainder of the "Elvis: In Concert" show was filmed two days later at the Rushmore Plaza Civic Center in Rapid City, South Dakota. When the "Elvis: In Concert" special was aired in October 1977, it featured a grossly overweight and physically decimated Presley.

Despite the continuing success of his career, Elvis couldn't escape the stigma of the "bodyguard's book" in the final weeks before he died. The specter of his long-time friends, Red and Sonny West, describing Elvis as a deranged, drug-plagued maniac, prone to fits of despair, hurt Presley deeply. When *Elvis: What Hap-*

pened? was shown to Elvis, he turned to the section on Mike Stone and was shocked to see verbatim conversations in which he allegedly screamed: "Mike Stone has to die. You will do it for me. Kill the sonovabitch!" There was no way that Elvis could effectively deny such stories. He had to sit back and take the public humiliation.

After almost a quarter of a century as a rock and roll pioneer, Elvis was now at the edge of an abyss. During the last few weeks of Presley's life, the book would explode the carefully constructed myths surrounding his life. Never fully recovered from his divorce from Priscilla, Elvis longed for stability. In July 1977, when *Elvis: What Happened?* appeared in drugstores, supermarkets, and major bookstores, it fed public rumors that Elvis was physically and mentally sick. The book was an exposé that not only alleged that Elvis abused drugs, guns, and women, but also claimed that he was obsessed with religious and psychic phenomena.

It was painful for Elvis to read these sordid stories. What once seemed like simple good fun—when the Memphis Mafia partied—came across as vile and perverted. Sonny West reinforced this image of Elvis in promotional interviews on national television. A menacing figure with dark sunglasses, a beer belly hanging over his belt, West's lurid tales of drugs, sex, and violence awed the American public. Eager for scandal, many Americans purchased *Elvis: What Happened?* and it became a best seller. The measure of the success of the book was demonstrated when K-Mart ordered two million copies. Not only was this the largest book order in history, but the book forced Elvis to retreat to the safety of his bedroom as the media searched for even more scandal.

The subsequent controversy surrounding the "bodyguards book" angered Presley's fans. They labelled the tome a pack of "vicious lies." Indeed, *Elvis: What Happened?* is filled with inaccuracies; "journalist" Steve Dunleavy, a gifted writer who specializes in sensational prose, piled one sordid anecdote after another upon Presley, apparently failing to corroborate through independent research many of the tales related to him. A grossly distorted picture of Elvis as a fat, drugged-out rock star was appealing to many; sales rose to almost three million copies. By 1991, the public fascination with Elvis had kept the book in print for almost a decade and a half.

The last month of Elvis' life was a difficult time. He worried that Lisa Marie would be affected by the "bodyguards book." Each summer she would come to Memphis for a special visit, and Elvis would devote two or three weeks to entertaining her. On August 8, 1977, Elvis took Lisa Marie to the Old Fairgrounds amusement park, which had recently been remodeled and was renamed Libertyland. Elvis watched Lisa Marie ride the bumper cars and the merry-go-round, while the Memphis Mafia rode the roller coaster. Despite his personal problems, Elvis remained a strong father figure. Priscilla Presley has suggested in her book and on television talk shows that Elvis spoiled his daughter, a rather pointless criticism of the normal doting behavior exhibited by any proud father.

Despite his ill health and a strained voice, Elvis had planned yet another concert tour, beginning in about a week with a short tour in Maine. His weight was nearly 250 pounds. His attempts to diet had been futile, and a week before the tour Elvis was still eating only fruit and vegetables. He complained to the Graceland cook that he was in great pain. Scared and lonely, he had persuaded Vernon to go along on the tour. Ginger Alden, however, apparently refused to go, serving to quash rumors that Elvis would soon announce his marriage to her—rumors that few people took seriously anyway.

As Elvis became more and more of a hermit, there were numerous tales about his erratic behavior. Many of those around him complained that Elvis was caught up in his books and had no time for his friends. Indeed, he hid out in his room and read voraciously. The week before he died, Elvis was reading the Bible, books on psychic phenomena, and two Tom Robbins' books, *Even Cowgirls Get the Blues,* a chronicling of the changes in American popular culture, and *Another Roadside Attraction.* When the former work appeared as a mass market book in 1976, it became an instant counterculture classic. Elvis' favorite was *Another Roadside Attraction,* a strange tale about Christ's return to America in a traveling circus. The night that he died, Elvis had *Another Roadside Attraction* in his Graceland bathroom. An irreverent writer who made fun of pompous intellectuals, Robbins remarked: "that nothing upsets an intellectual as much as discovering that a plumber is enjoying the same book he is." Although the books caught Elvis' fancy, they were a mystery to his friends.

In the weeks before he died, Elvis concentrated upon the Robbins works because they made him feel spiritually uplifted and helped him to forget his constant illness. He also found that they were helpful in understanding the 1960s counterculture (when Robbins emerged as a major literary figure, *Rolling Stone* praised his work for reflecting the values and tensions of the sixties). What appealed to Elvis was that Robbins' fiction often made fun of religion while making a serious point. What if Jesus Christ wasn't divine? Robbins speculated about the importance of Christ's life and its influence upon Western civilization. Elvis' iconoclastic sense of humor was peaked by Robbins' sacrilegious thinking.

Elvis had apparently found a new and intriguing voice in Tom Robbins' books. The people around Elvis were worried; to them, he was reading and thinking too much, a side of his personality that most of the people around him didn't recognize.

"The King is Dead"

On August 15, 1977, Elvis experienced dental problems. He called Dr. Lester Hoffman and made an appointment for eleven o'clock that evening. Elvis arrived at Hoffman's office in his Stutz Bearcat with Ginger Alden, Billy Smith, and Charlie Hodge. With his usual good manners, Elvis introduced Dr. Hoffman to Ginger and, after some small talk, the doctor quickly filled an upper tooth. At 2:00 a.m. on August 16, Elvis returned to Graceland. After restructuring his song selection for the upcoming tour, he changed into a warm-up suit for a racquetball game.

The strenuous workout, coupled with time on an exercise bicycle, brought Elvis to a state of exhaustion. He retired with Ginger to his bedroom. There is a great deal of disagreement about the events that transpired on Elvis' last night. Ginger claims they discussed marriage. There were reports that she fought with Elvis about her decision not to go on the tour with him. Some time between eight and nine o'clock on the morning, Aunt Delta Mae Biggs knocked on Elvis' bedroom door. She had brought the Memphis morning newspaper and a glass of ice water. Elvis responded that he was going to sleep until seven that evening, only an hour before he was scheduled to fly to his concert in Portland, Maine. At nine o'clock, Ginger Alden awoke and found Elvis reading. Glancing at Ginger, Elvis walked into the bathroom—where he would later be found dead—to find some sleeping pills.

The confusion over the exact circumstances surrounding Elvis' death is due to the lack of precise information regarding the intervening period from his entry into the bathroom and his body's arrival at Baptist Hospital's emergency room at 2:56 p.m., a period of more than five hours. When the ambulance arrived at Graceland shortly after 2:30, Elvis had clearly been dead for many hours. The speculation is that, for some unknown reason, people working for Elvis delayed calling for medical help. The delay was explained in different ways by Presley's chief of security, Al Strada, his stepson David Stanley, his girlfriend Ginger Alden, and his long-time aide, Joe Esposito. When the press published their contradictory tales, there were rumors of a cover-up.

In 1991, Charles C. Thompson II and James P. Cole, a pair of investigative reporters with Memphis roots, co-authored the book *The Death of Elvis: What Really Happened?* This well-researched volume ended speculation that Elvis died of heart trouble, committed suicide, or had bone cancer. After securing a copy of the autopsy, interviewing medical people, police officials and newspaper reporters, Thompson and Cole concluded that Elvis died from polypharmacy, an accidental overdose of multiple prescription drugs. No one knew this definitely in 1977, of course, as those close to Elvis would not own up to circumstances which involved the abuse of prescription drugs.

Vernon Presley further complicated the controversy by wondering publicly how long his son had actually been lying on the bathroom floor. Both Ginger Alden and Joe Esposito, Presley's Brooklyn-bred road manager, claimed to have found the body. In the *National Enquirer*, Alden graphically described Elvis in death: "His eyes were closed...his face was a purplish color...." She stated that she had called Al Strada, the bodyguard on duty, who telephoned for an ambulance. Charlie Crosby, the ambulance driver, said that Dr. George Nichopoulos was at Graceland administering CPR to Elvis when he arrived, although the results of the preliminary autopsy indicated that Elvis had died long before the ambulance got there. Yet, both the official death certificate and the a pronouncement by Dr. George Nichopoulos indicated 3:30 p.m. as the time of Elvis' death.

During the autopsy of Elvis' body at Baptist Hospital, Shelby County Medical Office investigator Dan Warlick stayed around in his white lab coat and latex gloves to watch the proceedings. His boss, Dr. Jerry Francisco, didn't participate. Warlick watched Dr. E. Eric Muirhead, the chief of pathology for Baptist Hospital, precisely conduct the autopsy. After a good number of medical experts had examined and tested Presley, they found no evidence of a stroke, a heart attack, or cancer. (During the last year of Elvis' life, there were frequent rumors that he had cancer. Kathy Westmoreland, a backup singer for Elvis, remarked, "Not long after I met Elvis, he told me in confidence that he had a cancer-like condition." This was a common belief among Presley's inner circle. Where did this story originate? The answer is simple: Dr. George C. Nichopoulos. In an attempt to get back into Vernon Presley's good graces, Dr. Nichopoulos made up this bizarre story to explain Elvis' appearance. It soon had a life of its own. Elvis and Vernon, for their part, were embarrassed to discuss the fact that anyone in the family could have cancer.)

There were nine Baptist Hospital pathologists talking with Jerry Francisco as investigator Dan Warlick walked into the cool second floor hospital lounge. Warlick noticed three uniformed policemen and two hospital security guards standing ominously nearby. For a moment Warlick was intimidated, but he relaxed when

Francisco greeted him. As the sole investigator for the Shelby County Medical Office, Warlick took his duties seriously. He opened his notebook and took Polaroid pictures out of his pocket as he prepared to brief Francisco. As the briefing progressed, a perturbed expression came over Francisco's face as he furtively smoked a cigarette.

As Warlick eagerly talked about his research into Presley's death, Francisco appeared bored and disinterested. When Warlick talked about finding two syringes and an empty doctor's bag, Francisco failed to make direct eye contact. Warlick's conclusion that he suspected drug involvement in Presley's death was met with a thank you from Francisco that ended the conversation. Warlick couldn't believe his boss had stonewalled him.

Dr. Francisco walked into the hospital's press conference room and clumsily sat down before a line of microphones. He ruled Presley's death as due to "cardiac arrhythmia." In layman's terms, Elvis' heart simply stopped beating. Francisco had on his white lab coat and looked every bit the professional medical man. Prior to turning the microphone over to Dr. Nichopoulos, Francisco reported that the rumor that Elvis was ill with lupus was false. When Nichopoulos appeared, he looked relieved. Drugs were not the cause of death, according to Francisco, and Nichopoulos slobbered all over himself praising the ruling.

Dr. Jerry Francisco, the county medical examiner, had announced that Elvis' death was caused by a "severely irregular heartbeat," although the evidence was overwhelming that other factors were more than likely responsible. Elvis's bloated condition suggested the hereditary health problems of the Presley family, his slurred speech indicated medication abuse, and his enlarged colon and glaucoma were warnings that no one could ignore. Dr. Francisco, however, ruled that Presley's death was natural. "He had a history of mild hypertension," Francisco stated, "and some coronary artery disease."

Thus began one of the most elaborate drug cover-ups in history, a cover-up further obscured by wild rumors. Dick Grob, Elvis' security chief and former California police sergeant, tried to peddle the book *The Elvis Conspiracy*. Grob's self-serving thesis was that Elvis had been dying of bone cancer. The autopsy revealed that there was no basis for this wild conclusion. In later years, Ricky Stanley, who picked up Presley's last prescription, told a tall tale about Presley committing suicide. Eventually, Stanley teamed up with defrocked college professor and full-time rock-biography hatchet man Albert Goldman, and the duo turned out a book on Presley's alleged suicide. Long after his death, the entourage was still feasting off Presley's remains. The specter of Dr. Francisco hangs over the autopsy and all the suspect machinations that emerged during the years after Presley's death.

Few people really accepted Dr. Francisco's unconvincing conclusion. Elvis was only forty-two and there had been no previous heart trouble. The vials of prescription drugs were the real killers. The cause of death remained a controversial subject, because the medical examiner admitted that large amounts of prescription drugs including an opium derivative, two strong sedatives, codeine, and barbiturates were present in Elvis' body. The presence of two well-known painkillers, Demerol and Meperidine, suggests that Elvis was seriously ill.

Whatever the cause of his death, Elvis died in his bathroom with a book on his lap. It was a tragic way for the King of Rock and Roll to pass away. Even more pathetic was the race to cash in on Elvis' demise. Colonel Tom Parker met the press and in a monumental lapse of bad taste suggested that Elvis—by dying—had just made his greatest career move.

Elvis' fans were heartbroken, and the nation responded with an unprecedented outpouring of grief. The scene was like one reserved for a president. The entire country paused on the third weekend of August as people pondered Elvis Presley's contribution to American popular culture.

On Wednesday, August 17, 1977, the lines in front of Graceland on Elvis Presley Boulevard grew to mammoth proportions. The 13.7-acre Graceland estate had been a major tourist attraction, but Elvis' death turned it into an instant shrine. The police were called out to monitor the growing crowds. Elvis' grandmother, Minnie Mae Presley, and his aunt, Delta Mae Biggs, still lived in the house.

When Elvis' body returned to Graceland at three o'clock, almost a hundred thousand fans attempted to view it. For the next three-and-a-half hours, about twenty thousand people walked by the coffin. The public viewing of Elvis' body served only to intensify the mystery surrounding his death. Although the medical cover-up was in place, the feeling persisted that something was wrong.

Media Frenzy

Within hours of Presley's death, his life and the circumstances surrounding his death became one of the best subjects for investigative pieces in American journalism. From the earliest moments following Elvis' announced death there was a flood of media coverage. In Memphis, Dan Sears of WMPS broke the story on the three o'clock news. At 2:55, Sears had found out that

an ambulance had been dispatched to Graceland. It took him only a few minutes to discover the rest. When Sears ended his broadcast he was surprised to find skeptics at his own station.

Once Elvis' death was made public, WHBQ-TV, Channel 13, the Memphis ABC affiliate, put together a quick story. Gordon Wilson, the station's executive news producer, learned from a police dispatcher of Elvis' death. Kathy Wolfe, the news assignments editor for Channel 13, sent a photographer to Baptist Hospital. At 3:32 p.m., Gordon Wilson appeared on Channel 13 to announce Elvis Presley's death. Kathy Wolfe had held back the live television coverage until official word reached the public.

Colonel Tom Parker was in Portland, Maine, preparing for the opening show. There were stacks of souvenirs and business was as good as ever. The sound crew, musicians, and roadies were setting up the stage. In Los Angeles, Las Vegas, and Nashville, members of Elvis' band were waiting for his airplane, the Lisa Marie, to pick them up. Elvis himself was to fly in just before the thirteen-city, sellout tour began. Due to his ballooning weight, Elvis had packed only a few of his jumpsuits, but was bringing along almost five hundred scarves for the fans.

When Elvis' musicians heard of his death, there was disbelief. Kathy Westmoreland, a backup singer who had been Elvis' mistress for a short time, was stunned. During the weeks before his death, Elvis had confessed to Westmoreland his "mixed feelings" about his physical condition. During one of the last tours, Elvis had remarked to her, "I'm gonna look fat in that faggy little blue suit," a reference to one of his costumes. Then, smiling, Elvis continued, "But I'll look good in my coffin." An eerie chill ran through Westmoreland. She—unlike many Presley insiders—refused most requests for interviews and didn't cooperate with the media, although she would later publish her own book about her relationship with Presley.

The journalistic battle was on to find out who could dig up the most sensational Elvis Presley reports. One of the earliest efforts was a quick look at Presley's life by ABC's Geraldo Rivera, who anchored a "tribute" to Presley that reeked of yellow journalism. This program was planned, written, and produced only hours after Presley's death, and demonstrated that neither ABC nor Rivera knew very much about Elvis. Rivera, then a hip, long-haired, thirty-four-year-old newscaster, practiced a form of personal journalism, an unsuccessful copy of Hunter Thompson's 1960s gonzo style. Rivera, however, had neither the wit nor the personality to carry it off.

Presley's unexpected death forced Rivera to build the story on the spot. "When we went on the air," he remembered, "we had five minutes of the script written." The program reflected this lack of planning.

Chuck Berry was interviewed, and he talked about the time that Elvis and Sammy Davis, Jr. had danced down the aisles during one of his shows at the Las Vegas Hilton hotel lounge. ABC never bothered to verify Berry's story, which was inaccurate; Presley and Davis had danced across the back of the stage while Berry performed.

Bing Crosby eulogized Elvis, stretching the limits of disbelief among the fans and knowledgeable music critics.

Dick Clark, who had never spent more than five minutes with Elvis, was interviewed. Not only had Elvis never appeared on Clark's "American Bandstand," but he was contemptuous of the slick music promoter. Clark remarked that Elvis had lived like a "caged animal."

Rona Barrett, her blonde hair glistening like it had been baked in 7-Up, delivered a few personal tales from Presley's life, focusing upon her close relationship with him. She also had no idea why he was important to the music business.

Rivera himself had trouble explaining Presley's significance to American popular culture. When ABC broadcast a three-minute film clip showing highlights from Presley's career, Rivera's commentary was inane. Rivera concluded his program with personal anecdotes about Elvis on the "Ed Sullivan Show." It wasn't just the poor taste reflected in Rivera's comments; his general lack of knowledge of rock and roll was offensive, and his attempt to identify with Elvis further outraged fans.

Any Elvis-related story was fair game for the profit-hungry media. In Memphis, fans gathered outside the Graceland gates had dwindled to about three hundred in the early morning hours of August 18. Tragedy struck at 3:30 a.m., when a speeding automobile hit a young woman, killing her instantly. The driver, Treatsie Wheeler, III, was arrested on a charge of public drunkenness after leaving the scene of the accident. The *National Enquirer* made it a headline story, linking Elvis' death to the fanaticism and cult-like following of Presley fans. It sold a lot of newspapers in the supermarkets and played to the myth that there was something abnormal about Presley's followers.

The major television networks often mingled reasoned Elvis tributes with statements from people like Steve Dunleavy, who ranted about Presley's "white trash" or "hillbilly" background. Following Dunleavy's remarks, NBC's New York office received fifty telephone calls complaining that the co-author of *Elvis: What Happened?* was doing little more than promoting his book. On NBC's "Nightly News," veteran newsman David Brinkley, in a momentary lapse into bad taste, also repeated a few of the "hillbilly" myths and a number of questionable tales surrounding Presley's personal life. Brinkley—who had worked extensively in the South and should have been more aware of the facts—ended his report by summarizing Elvis' importance to the growth of rock and roll music and the impact he had made upon the entertainment business—Elvis, he concluded, had "changed things."

In Tupelo, Mississippi, State Senator Harold Montgomery watched WTWV and was incensed at Dunleavy's remarks and Brinkley's carelessness. He also resented the media's attempt to denigrate Elvis' poor Southern roots. Montgomery himself had risen from a poverty background much like Elvis' to state political prominence. Subsidized housing of the type Elvis' family had lived in at Lauderdale Court in Memphis was typical of the times, and Montgomery was furious over the media's literary license in describing lodgers as either white trash or hillbillies. Montgomery sent a thoughtful, reasoned telegram to David Brinkley pointing out the errors in his report. Brinkley recognized his mistake and returned a letter of apology to Montgomery, admitting that he had gone on the air without fully analyzing the facts of Elvis' life or impact of his death. He apologized to Senator Montgomery for any negative comments about Presley or the South.

Scandal-mongering newspapers like the *National Enquirer,* which might have actually downplayed Elvis' end had it not been for the drug rumors, cashed in on Presley's death. The "bodyguard book" had just been published, however, and the authors turned up on talk shows and in interviews with lurid tales, setting the *Enquirer* staff of experienced researchers and skilled writers hard at work. During the last week of August 1977, the *Enquirer* printed a grotesque picture of Elvis in his coffin. This "last photo" was provided by an unnamed Elvis insider, and the *Enquirer* reportedly paid $75,000 for it. Vernon Presley alleged that one of "Elvis' own cousins" took the picture. In an article in *Good Housekeeping* magazine, Vernon suggested that friends and relatives sold numerous such pictures of his son. The *Enquirer* purchased an exclusive report from the Baptist Hospital ambulance driver, and from Elvis' last girlfriend, Ginger Alden. This particular *Enquirer* issue topped six million in sales, encouraging other scandal sheets to follow suit. *The Star*, the *Enquirer*'s sub-intellectual rival, serialized *Elvis: What Happened?* with lurid headlines and titillating captions. The *Midnight Globe*, a budget version of the *Enquirer*, headlined "Elvis' Last Words," an example of preposterous journalism suggesting that Elvis had told Priscilla Presley about his death two days before it took place.

The newspaper business found that Elvis was a shot in the arm to their circulation. The *Seattle Post Intelligencer* and the *Dallas Morning News* sold ten thousand extra copies on the day Elvis died. The Jacksonville *Florida Times-Union* exceeded its previous circulation record by more than five thousand. Major American newspapers reported that their Elvis issues outsold the John F. Kennedy assassination issue. In Memphis, demand was so great that the two hometown papers—the *Memphis Press-Scimitar* and the *Commercial Appeal*—printed special Elvis editions filled with news stories about Elvis' death and life.

The major news magazines, *Time* and *Newsweek*, didn't provide cover stories on Presley's death, but they did devote lengthy pieces to the event. The *Time* article was headlined "Last Stop on the Mystery Train," and emphasized the importance of the Sun recordings to Presley's career. *Newsweek* editor Jack Kroll labelled Elvis "The Heartbreak Kid," and provided a commentary that focused upon Presley's first appearance on the "Ed Sullivan Show." All of the major accounts of Elvis' death mentioned the musical revolution of the Sun Records years and the role of Sam Phillips in crafting Elvis' sound.

Sam Phillips himself was not a safe interview, however. He confused the media by blaming Colonel Parker, RCA, and slick promoters for Elvis' problems. Because of his cranky comments the mass media generally ignored him. The perspective that Phillips provided about Presley's death was not a pleasant one. He believed that RCA hadn't properly recorded Presley's music. He also charged that the New York media had crucified Elvis for years without cause. Phillips was written off as a crazy, rather than as an astute observer of the musical scene. The media treated him like a relic from the Dark Ages of Presley's career, rather than the man who helped Elvis down the road to fame and fortune. The remainder of this book will seek to demonstrate just how important Phillips actually was to Elvis Presley and the rise of rock and roll.

For all the damage done to Elvis by the media through carelessness and profit-driven sensationalism, there were a number of reporters who were rock and roll fans as well as seasoned journalistic professionals. One of these reporters was Bob Greene, a syndicated columnist for the *Chicago Sun Times*. It was Greene who broke the story of Presley's drug problems during the last few weeks of Elvis' life. When Greene discovered that there was an exposé book on Presley, he called Ballantine's public relations office to request an author interview. Ballantine quickly agreed, and Greene interviewed Sonny West only a few hours before Elvis died. West not only made incriminating remarks about Presley's drug use, but Elvis' former bodyguard stated that RCA either didn't know or didn't care about Elvis' problems. Greene checked with RCA for a rebuttal.

True to form, RCA not only didn't have a rebuttal, they had no idea that there was an impending controversy. The *Chicago Sun Times* prepared a front-page story under the headline: "Elvis: He's In Danger of Losing His Life." Before the article was published, Presley died. The piece appeared after all the references in the story were changed to the past tense. Greene admired Elvis and was shocked by his untimely death. Visibly shaken, Greene confided to me in an interview: "Elvis was the greatest single influence of my life." Greene's syndicated column received prominent attention in other newspapers. The *Washington Star,* featuring the story in its early edition, changed the headline to read: "Elvis Presley—A Life Plagued by Drugs, Fears and Loneliness." This sensational headline provoked a storm of criticism and letters to the editor accusing the *Washington Star* of poor taste. Presley's fans complained that even in death Elvis was being castigated by the media.

Lester Bangs was the critic who came closest to understanding the importance of Elvis Presley's death. In a thoughtful piece in the August 29, 1977, issue of the *Village Voice*, Bangs asked: "Where were you when Elvis died?" He went on to suggest that Presley's death ranked alongside the bombing of Pearl Harbor and John F. Kennedy's assassination. Bangs was famous for overstating his ideas, but in this case he left no doubt in anyone's mind that Elvis was the King of Rock and Roll. "Elvis Presley was the man who brought overt blatant vulgar sexual frenzy to the popular arts in America," Bangs wrote. In the process, Elvis established a mainstream musical art form. As Bangs suggested, fans would take anything from Elvis, even disastrous repackaged albums and lackluster concerts. Since he was the undisputed ruler of rock music, there was no need to question his sincerity or his actions. Bangs perfectly captured the feelings of Elvis fans.

Hard upon the news of his death, fans expressed their public grief by purchasing every Presley record available. In New York, the Sam Goody record store chain announced that they were sold out of all of Elvis Presley's records. This seemed impossible; Sam Goody's had never exhausted its supply of any artist's records. At Rasputin's record store on Telegraph Avenue in Berkeley, California, a young man with a pin through his nose bought the last Elvis Presley album. Around the corner at Leopold's Records, a nineteen-year-old UofC-Berkeley student rushed over from her sorority building to purchase the last copy of a Presley LP. The Los Angeles, San Francisco, and Sacramento Tower Record stores posted signs requesting Presley buyers to be patient. In Cleveland, Tommy Edwards, the master of ceremonies at Elvis' show with Roy Acuff in 1955, announced that his store, the Record Haven, had stocked fifty-six different Elvis titles totalling more than 300 records. He had only two Christmas albums left at the end of the day Elvis died. The *Dallas Morning News*, the *Des Moines Register*, the *Seattle Post-Intelligencer*, the *Portland Oregonian*, the *Los Angeles Times*, and the Portland, Maine, *Press-Herald* reported that Presley's records were no longer available in any of the local record stores.

RCA was soon hit with an unprecedented demand for information about Presley's music. The media deluged Presley's record company with requests for record sales figures, biographical data, and statistics on gold and platinum records. The press was shocked to learn that RCA had never disclosed Presley's official record sales. Colonel Parker believed that this information should not be a matter of public record. Lewis Couttolenc, president of RCA Records, was pressured into delivering a statement on Presley. He responded with a press release: "Elvis Presley was the greatest legend of the modern entertainment world. He ushered in the rock music era, forever changing the tastes of the music-loving public. The legend is lost to us."

The only good-taste gesture from RCA during the period following Presley's death came from Joan Deary. Now a top level RCA executive, she believed that RCA should suspend the corporate hype for a simple acknowledgment of respect. This led to a stark full-page ad in *Billboard* that read: "Elvis/1935-1977." The page was entirely black with white letters, with only the RCA logo in a lower corner, a simple and dignified expression of Deary's long-time commitment to Presley's records.

In the aftermath of Presley's death, one veteran newsman, David Brinkley, recognized the broader implications of his musical accomplishments. To atone for his earlier impressionistic report, Brinkley and NBC prepared an 11:30 p.m. Presley special with precision and research skill. As a young man growing up in Wilmington, North Carolina, Brinkley was aware of the Yankee tendency to denigrate the South. While working in Nashville and other Southern cities in his pre-television days, Brinkley developed a feeling for the region. He had read the important Southern writers, visited the key cities, and understood the region's strengths and weaknesses. Brinkley was still smarting over the letter from Mississippi State Senator Harold Montgomery, and he hoped to demonstrate that he understood Presley's career.

When Brinkley went on the air, he placed Elvis' career in an intelligent historical perspective, pointing out how teenage America thought about and reacted to Presley's music. As part of the report, Jackson Bain, an NBC correspondent who had been flown from Atlanta to Memphis, stood at the Graceland gates and analyzed the meaning of the grief-stricken crowd. NBC then switched to a panel of disc jockeys and writers who talked about Elvis' contribution to popular culture. It was a group that included Norm Nite of WNBC radio, Murray the K, a New York disc jockey dubbed the fifth Beatle, Dave Marsh of *Rolling Stone* magazine, and writer Steve Dunleavy. Dave Marsh, the most visible rock music writer in America, and Norm Nite, a disc jockey and author of two rock music encyclopedias, pointed out why Elvis was the King of rock music. After some general comments on the music business and rock and roll music, the panel turned its attention to the "bodyguards book."

The guests discussed *Elvis: What Happened?* while Steve Dunleavy smoked a cigar and pontificated about Elvis' "drug use." Dunleavy's arrogance and continual reference to Presley's "white trash" background created tension. Dave Marsh appeared pained and uncomfortable, and the other panelists shifted nervously in their seats. Even David Brinkley returned to the air with a strained look. Rock journalists were still a new phenomenon on American television.

When the broadcast shifted back to Jackson Bain in Memphis, the young reporter eloquently described the Memphis sound and eulogized Presley's music. David Brinkley closed the show with a tribute to Presley's music that mentioned how he had outlasted Benny Goodman, jazz, Chuck Berry, and the Beatles. "Until the day he died," Brinkley remarked, "Elvis could still fill an auditorium or a ball park any time he wanted." Where Geraldo Rivera had sensationalized Presley's death, David Brinkley's comments reflected a compassionate and well-rounded sense of Presley's accomplishments from a perspective that appropriately capsuled Presley's career.

Despite the wide disparity in program quality, both NBC and ABC fared well in the ratings. Geraldo Rivera's half-baked hipness didn't prevent ABC from cashing in with viewers, and NBC ultimately used David Brinkley's seasoned and articulate image to lend credence to its eulogy to Elvis. "CBS News," for its part, ended up regretting its decision not to give the Presley story extra coverage. No one at CBS recognized the irony of their position. Elvis had received his first national television exposure on the CBS "Dorsey Brothers Stage Show." (In January 1956, Elvis made the first of six appearances on the Dorsey stage show, thereby enabling him to promote his RCA recordings. While these shows weren't ratings blockbusters, nonetheless, they provided some of Presley's most interesting early television moments. A hard-rocking, casually-dressed Elvis Presley launched furiously into his songs with Scotty

Moore on lead guitar, Bill Black on bass, and D.J. Fontana on drums.)

In the end, CBS decided that it would produce a belated Elvis tribute and make it a quality program. Charles Kuralt was brought in to anchor the CBS Elvis special. Having grown up in North Carolina, Kuralt appreciated the diverse Southern culture, and he sensed the revolutionary tone to Presley's music and stage act. In his "On The Road" segments of "CBS News," Kuralt had long been capturing and reporting on the spirit of American individualism. Unlike Geraldo Rivera, who dwelt on the sex and drug allegations surrounding Elvis' last days, Kuralt quietly lectured America on how Elvis had changed manners, morals, and popular culture. Kuralt began the program by recalling Elvis' impact in 1956. He gently pointed out that everyone and everything else from that time had faded into obscurity, while Elvis continued to fill stadiums and sell records. When he closed his moving tribute, Kuralt reminded his audience: "You never heard anybody ask, 'Elvis who?'" Few Americans are recognized solely by their first name, and Kuralt wisely reasoned that justifiable fame had made Elvis instantly recognizable. The ratings for the CBS Elvis special indicated that the network had garnered a 41 percent share of the audience—double that of the vaunted "Tonight Show." Kuralt's tribute also ended up being the highest rated CBS show for 1977.

This book, *Elvis: The Sun Years,* is an examination of the early years of Presley's life. It will lay to rest many of the myths surrounding the "Hillbilly Cat," the most persistent of which is his characterization as "white trash." As a result of interviews with more than a hundred people close to Elvis during the first twenty-one years of his life, it will be clear that Elvis was typical of young men coming of age in the South in the 1950s. He was also better educated and more articulate than biographers and media specialists have suggested. Many of Elvis' early accomplishments in school were hidden from the general public by Colonel Tom Parker, who feared that an awareness of his normal, average childhood and teenage years would serve only to jeopardize Presley's rebellious image and his popularity with record buyers.

With this in mind, let us now set aside our perceptions and prejudices of Elvis the star, and travel back to an earlier time, a time before success took its toll on a young man from Mississippi and Tennessee. There is another side to Presley's life than the one profiled above. While Elvis didn't invent rock and roll music, the ascendancy of rock music coincided with his appearance on the music scene. *Elvis: The Sun Years* is an exploration of how young Elvis Presley helped to establish rock and roll as a legitimate commercial phenomenon in the mid-1950s, and an appreciation of his role in the development of a new form of American popular culture.

CHAPTER 2
Elvis' Roots to 1941

The following chapter is predicated on the idea that a knowledge of the facts of Elvis Presley's family background can provide important insights into his character and his complex personality. Elvis' parents, Gladys Love Smith and Vernon Presley, came from families with a genealogy predating the American Revolution. The heritage of both parents was that of common, undistinguished immigrants with a strong attachment to the soil, typical of a class of Americans migrating westward during the period of Jacksonian Democracy. Their agrarian background emphasized equality, hard work, and a commitment to the American dream. Although the Presleys and the Smiths made different historical journeys before reaching Mississippi, both families could point to roots entangled in important aspects of early American history.

Gladys Love Smith's origins are particularly important in analyzing Elvis's life. As Elaine Dundy suggested in her book *Elvis and Gladys*, most biographers have ignored the maternal side of Elvis' family. Close friends would often remark that Elvis looked neither like Gladys nor Vernon. Rather, with his high cheek bones and stoic personality, Elvis—whose physical appearance seemed to have skipped a generation or two in the hereditary pattern—bore a remarkable physical resemblance to his great-great-great grandmother, Morning Dove White.

While there is little doubt that Elvis inherited his striking good looks from Gladys Love Smith's family, there are also many other qualities evident in his maternal lineage that speak to the unique character and physical stamina that typified his life. Gladys's precedents, after all, were a strong, ambitious lot who battled the rigors of the American frontier. Once the various family members achieved success, which they did with relative ease, there was a continuing emphasis upon schooling. A number of Gladys Love Smith's relatives were well-educated physicians, land barons, and businessmen. Her ancestors are prominent in local Alabama history books. It is precisely this compulsive drive for achievement which is so evident in Elvis' personality.

The Mansell Family

Gladys Love Smith's earliest influential relatives were Morning Dove White and her husband William Mansell. Morning Dove was a full-blooded Cherokee Indian, born at the turn of the nineteenth century, who married Mansell following his many years of fighting Indians. They met in western Tennessee, the home of the Cherokee nation, and wed after a whirlwind courtship. A tall, lean, striking woman, she died unexpectedly at age thirty-five during childbirth. Morning Dove White's physical beauty and calm personality were noted by many of her contemporaries. A quiet, reflective woman living between two cultures, she demanded that her children attend school and prepare for a profession. Indeed, by mid-nineteenth century standards, the family was well-educated. In her brief life, Morning Dove White demonstrated strength of character and ingenuity in raising her offspring. A strong Christian woman, she was also ballast for her wanderlust-afflicted husband.

Elvis' great-great-great grandfather, William Mansell, son of Richard Mansell, a South Carolina farmer, moved to western Tennessee in his youth to make his fortune. The Mansells were Frenchmen who immigrated to England, Scotland, and Ireland before arriving in America. This combined French, English, and Scotch-Irish heritage produced stern, hard-working, responsible personalities. William fought under Andrew Jackson during the later stages of the War of 1812, and he served another stint during Jackson's campaigns against the Florida Seminole Indians. On March 27, 1814, Mansell again served in Alabama under Andrew Jackson at the Battle of Horseshoe Bend, a victory that reduced the Creek nation's hold on land from the Tennessee border to Mobile, eventually resulting in an influx of new settlers. In 1815, the twenty-year-old Mansell left the army and drifted through the American West.

By the spring of 1818, Mansell was back in Tennessee. It had been a century since his ancestors had immigrated to America and established their homes in South Carolina. They married local Indian women, with whom lower class immigrants of the time intermarried freely. In the Mansells' case, these marriages were successful ones that provided hard-working partners who helped their husbands accumulate wealth. It was often the Indian spouse, moreover, who suggested that greater opportunity existed in the American West.

Like his ancestors, William Mansell met and married an Indian woman, Morning Dove White. Following his marriage to Morning Dove, Mansell introduced one of his friends, Moses Purser, to her sister, Mapy, and the couple was married in a brief ceremony. In November 1820, the Mansells and the Pursers, all young

27

and filled with a wondering spirit, crossed the frozen Tennessee River to settle in Marion County in northeast Alabama. The oxcart that brought the Mansells was filled with tools, seeds, and a small amount of furniture. A rich farming area close to the Mississippi border, the county was noted for its agricultural productivity. Andrew Jackson, under orders from President James Monroe, had earlier guaranteed the availability of cheap land there by taking it all away from the resident Indians.

During the War of 1812, large numbers of Scotch-Irish settlers had moved into the area, a locale which had favorably impressed Andrew Jackson's troops as they marched through. The rich alluvial soil and clean creeks made agricultural success quite easy. Over the next fifteen years following their arrival, the Mansells created an extraordinarily bountiful life. A shrewd judge of property, Mansell staked a claim to one of the most prestigious lots in Pikeville, Alabama. When the Mansell home was built on this showcase plot, located about three miles from Hamilton on a small bluff overlooking lush agricultural fields, it became one of the local attractions.

The unusually strong marriage between William Mansell and Morning Dove White was complicated only by Morning Dove's frequent pregnancy problems and miscarriages. Finally, after eight years of marriage, John Mansell was born, followed by Morning Dizenie Mansell in 1832, and by James J. Mansell in 1835. William Mansell never remarried after his wife died giving birth to James. He raised his children in a strict Christian household, taught them the importance of an education, and constantly instructed them on how to make their own fortunes. By the time they were adults, Marion County was heavily settled and the earlier economic opportunities in farming were no longer available. As a result, the Mansell children considered other options. The next step in the westward movement of the Mansells was to be the fertile farm lands of Mississippi. Offering an unlimited agricultural frontier, it was only natural for Mansell's children to seek their opportunities in this area.

Not all the Mansell children left Alabama, however. Their daughter, Morning Dizenie, remained and married Dr. Russell Palmer, a distinguished physician. During the course of a long and happy marriage they had twelve children. A number of the Palmer children attained professional success. In addition to two who themselves became doctors, there was also a merchant, a minister, and three farmers. One son, Dr. Benjamin Palmer, had a town named after him, and another son, Dr. Alexander Sherman Palmer, was an important Alabama historical figure noted for his scientific skill and philanthropic nature. Morning Dizenie's sons were courtly

gentlemen with a gracious manner and serious, scholarly personalities. Three sons who became farmers —George, Lafayette, and Grant—were respected local businessmen. They provided loans to sharecroppers, small merchants, and helped the local economy. The rise of a Saturday market was due to the brothers' entrepreneurial skills. They all had a will to succeed and a desire to make money.

One of Morning Dizenie's relatives described her as a somber, hard-talking woman who demanded and got respect. Her children were raised with an iron hand, but she retained many of the old Indian customs she had learned from her mother. When Morning Dizenie died, she was buried in the Cherokee manner with large smooth stones carefully arranged in an Indian mound around her grave, an indication of how she, like her mother, was able to combine the Cherokee and the white man's way in her life.

Morning Dove White's eldest son, John Mansell, is the seminal figure in Elvis' historical roots. He was Elvis Presley's great-great grandfather. Unlike the rest of his family, John Mansell was a hard-drinking, hell-raising frontiersman. He apparently had few thoughts about the future and lived only for a good time. A number of his contemporaries suggested that he lacked the brains and personality necessary for success. As the oldest son, he was destined to inherit the Mansell farm. Believing that his road to economic and social respectability was thus guaranteed, he had little desire to make his own living. As a result, it was not long before he ended up a total failure.

Not only did John Mansell have an unquenchable appetite for women, but he was also a notorious con man. One neighbor described him as "half Indian," and another commented that he had trouble settling down. While still living in northeast Alabama, he married Elizabeth "Betsy" Gilmore, and by the time John was in his early twenties they had nine children. As rampant rumors of illegitimate children were verified, John Mansell experienced pressures that prompted him to search for a new home. Never one to worry about convention, it turned out that John Mansell had been married to two different women at the same time and had carried on two households.

After some wandering, he settled in northeast Mississippi, hoping to make his living as a farmer near the town of Saltillo. His move to Saltillo, however, exposed the existence of his two marriages. Evangelical morality and strict Christian concepts of marriage made it difficult for Mansell to live in the town, problems compounded by the fact that both of his wives, Betsy and Rebecca, followed him there. There was strong opposition to bigamy in Mississippi, and threats from local law enforcement officials made John Mansell increasingly uncomfortable.

It was also difficult for him to make a living because most of the soil around Saltillo was harsh and unpredictable. This made the prospects for wealth and fortune dismal ones. The best land was already claimed by the large farmers, who turned small plots into sharecropping ventures. As a result of all this, there was a great deal of turnover among the smaller farmers. John Mansell, frustrated by the local agricultural climate, searched for a way out of his confining surroundings.

By 1880, John Mansell was still a fifty-two-year-old failure lusting after young girls. A woman named Mandy Bennett soon caught the attention of his wandering eye, and they married and moved to Oxford, Mississippi. No one was unhappy when John Mansell finally left Saltillo. Before leaving, he arranged to have the young children from his two previous marriages stay with his third eldest son, White Mansell. Then, in a surprising turnaround, John Mansell quickly became a successful businessman in Oxford. He purchased a large house and assumed the name Colonel Lee Mansell. Due to an articulate manner and cunning personality, it was not long before Colonel Mansell was a well-known and highly respected citizen in this picturesque Mississippi town. Whether or not there was a tradition of sexual promiscuity in the Mansell family as a whole, as some biographers have suggested, is debatable, but the family offers some interesting contrasts. The men tended to be either highly successful professionals with commensurate economic rewards, or sexually active, irresponsible con men whose brains were in their loins.

Back in Saltillo, John's son, White, had become the titular head of the Mansell family. Not only did he take over the job of raising his father's children, but he continued to provide a fine home for his own family. He married a local girl, Martha Tackett, and they had four children. The White Mansell household also included seven other relatives who lived with them after White's father left for Mississippi. This established a pattern in the Mansell family, and it was an expected duty to take in relatives.

When White Mansell became the head of the household, he provided a stability that had not previously existed. An extremely hard-working individual, White had been married ten years by the time his dad left Saltillo. After White and Martha married on January 22, 1870, there was little contact with her family. Her father, Abner Tackett, divorced Nancy J. Burdine Tackett and married at least two more times. This lack of family stability on both sides actually had a positive effect upon White and his young bride, for they established a model marriage and produced a loving family.

The Smith Family

Gladys Love Smith's mother, Octavia Luvenia "Doll" Mansell, was one of White Mansell's four daughters. Not only was she White's favorite, but the nickname "Doll" suggests a special place within the family. There is a great deal in Doll Mansell's background that influenced her daughter Gladys. Not only was Doll a beautiful, somewhat fragile, girl who was still unmarried at twenty-six, but she was constantly in ill health with tuberculosis. As a result of her persistent illness, a strange fantasy world was constructed around Doll by her father. Not only was she treated like a princess, but there were special privileges commensurate with her status. The way the family responded to Doll's demands was similar to the manner in which Gladys treated Elvis. There was love and compassion, but there was also a sense that Doll was something special. She somehow had the personality to demand special treatment without incurring the wrath of her friends and relatives. Doll manipulated people and was extremely adroit at having her every wish gratified. There were many other things, however, that Doll could not control.

In addition to her health problems, Doll experienced the social rigors of frontier life. The closed male-oriented Mississippi society made it difficult for her to grow as a person. Bright and articulate, Doll ended up preferring to be alone with her thoughts. The large number of people living in the Mansell household made privacy difficult, but Doll was able to sneak off for long hours each day. She thrived on this solitude. Her private fantasy world revolved around toys, dolls, and pretty, shiny objects. Her family constantly reminded Doll that she was an old maid and desperately needed to find a husband.

It was difficult to find a suitable mate in the remote Saltillo settlement, and it may have been just these persistent demands from her family that influenced her next course of action. As the years passed and the pressure to marry increased, she made an interesting marital choice. Rapidly approaching thirty, with prospects of remaining an old maid forever, she announced her decision to marry. Finally, in the spring of 1903, Doll Mansell married Robert Lee Smith. They were first cousins. There was nothing unusual in this, as due to the physical and social isolation of the area, many first cousins and close relatives married. Doll had known Robert Lee all her life, but she waited for three years after Obe Smith died before marrying his son. In Doll's mind, this was a sign of respect for Obe and Bob's mother Ann. Bob, the Smith's third son, was a quiet, reflective young man who had never traveled out of the Saltillo area. Few people knew Bob Smith, because, like Doll, he was a loner. Doll Mansell and Bob Smith seemed destined to meet.

When Smith's father, Obe, married Ann Mansell in 1874, they began raising a family of seven children. As a result of this marriage, the Smith-Mansell families spent a great deal of time together. Obe Smith, an itinerant wanderer, was never able to find a permanent job. In 1880, after six years of marriage, Obe and Ann were living with the Thomas Winter family. Moving from one relative's house to another, Obe's declining fortunes were evident when he was finally forced to move in with friends instead. This lack of stability in the Smith family was due to Obe's wild drinking sprees and irresponsible attitudes. After twenty-five years of marriage and seven children, Ann finally divorced him. In the 1900 census, Ann listed herself as a widow. This was hardly the stable marital situation that the Mansell's desired for their daughters and their in-laws.

Before Doll married Robert Lee, she spent many hours talking to Ann Smith. After months of close discussion, Ann remarked to Doll that the reason for her divorce was not solely due to Obe's problems with making a living, providing a home, or handling family responsibility. After twenty-five years, Ann concluded, her husband had little, if any, feeling for his family. She commented that Obe seemed oblivious to the divorce. Obe, for his part, told a different version of the story. As he continued to live with family and friends, Obe often remarked that he was mystified by the divorce. As in the case of White Mansell and Martha Tackett, however, the marital problems between Obe and Ann Smith had a positive effect upon Doll and Robert Lee's marriage. They talked for a long time about making their union a happy one. Surprisingly, despite the reclusive nature of each of them, they worked out their differences and embarked on what turned out to be a stable marriage.

The night before they married, Doll talked at length about her hopes for the future. She wanted to have a normal family and a home of her own. On September 20, 1903, Bob Smith and Doll Mansell were wed in the presence of Reverend Martin, pastor of the Union Grove Church of God. Rev. Martin had come to know Doll very well. She attended church three times a week and was very close to the congregation. The wedding day had some unusual highlights. Doll lectured Bob on the need for special clothing. As a result, both bride and groom were attired in white. For some reason, Bob wore a pin that read GRIT. It turned out the pin was given away by a local newspaper, and he put it on his jacket for good luck. There was no doubt among relatives and friends that Doll's Christian nature sobered Bob Smith, because he remarked to a number of close friends that the marriage would succeed. It was Doll's dream of a happy relationship that ultimately kept the marriage, despite its many hardships, intact.

Gladys Love Smith

Even as Doll Mansell and Bob Smith exchanged their wedding vows, the South was undergoing the first stages of an industrial and technological revolution. Lee and its neighboring counties were fertile areas producing fruit, vegetables, and cotton. Textile manufacturing, the growth of local markets, and the construction of new railroad lines promised Mississippians, including Bob Smith's children, a prosperous future.

Political change was also evident. The northern carpetbaggers who had controlled Mississippi during the Reconstruction era after the Civil War were no longer visible. A solid Democratic party political machine tried to help poor whites fit into Mississippi's twentieth-century society. There was a natural optimism about the future. In the quarter of a century since Reconstruction had ended, Tupelo, Richmond, Saltillo, and other small towns had sprung to life. The average income of the small tenant farmer had doubled, and there were new opportunities in the towns.

Not everyone shared this belief in the future or in the probable success of the Bob Smith's marriage, however. Years later, Robert's own mother, Ann, before leaving for Richmond, a nearby community where her brother White Mansell lived, would deliver a tirade that frightened both families. She chastised Doll for having married her own first cousin, who, like Ann's ex-husband Obe, she felt had no future. Worn out from raising a large family with no help from their father, Ann Smith was bitter. Having vented her frustrations, she settled into a quiet, rural existence to live out her final years.

There was also a dark side to the Smith family, to be sure. The boys lacked ambition and displayed erratic mental behavior. There was never any emphasis upon education or professional achievement. Lazy is the word many old timers used to characterize the Smiths. Sharecropping was all they knew, but most of the family avoided even this backbreaking, low-paying profession if they could. The Smiths were generally just happy to get by. There was also a pronounced tendency toward alcoholism, excessive sexual activity, and a slovenly appearance.

Robert Lee Smith was an exception to this general heritage. He was a tall, lean, and handsome man who could turn a smooth phrase with the best country preachers. Bob was described by contemporaries as a hard worker and an honest man. Few people in Lee County remember Bob Smith playing cards or staying away from home. Albert Goldman describes Bob Smith as "a merry man, and his daughter, Gladys, resembled in youth her frolicsome father." Not only is this description flawed, but it fails to accurately reflect the historical evidence. Although he was a gentle, easy-going man, Bob Smith had a serious side. This was typical of a man who accommodated everyone with his gracious manner and personality. He spent his adult life coping with a mentally unstable, sickly wife. His daughters were helpful, but he was forced to be both a mother and father to the children. To please his wife, Bob attended the Church of God services in Union Grove, and throughout his life he taught his family Christian values and a strong sense of responsibility. Mature and family-oriented, with a stoic quality to his personality, he believed that the future rewarded hard workers. It was this perpetual youthful optimism that kept Smith pursuing the American dream.

Because Bob Smith had not yet financially established himself, the young married couple moved in with his mother Ann. After their first child died, the Smiths had two daughters, Lillian born in 1906 and Lavalle born in 1908. When White Mansell moved to Pontotoc County, which was next to Lee County, Doll wanted to settle in the same area. She convinced her husband to move. Initially, Bob announced that he was going to find his own place. This was simply an idle boast. They moved in with White Mansell. In 1910, another daughter, Rhetha, was born, and two years later on April 25, 1912, Gladys Love Smith, Elvis' future mother, gave Doll the distinction of having given birth to four girls. Doll, perpetually sick, showed signs of being unable to cope with her increasing responsibilities as a mother, however. In addition, Pontotoc County had turned out to be a flat, uninspiring, dreary place, a place she had grown to dislike. Unlike Lee County where Doll grew up, Pontotoc was filled with long pastures and dusty roads. Doll was homesick. She wanted to return to Lee County. After giving birth to two more children—sons, Travis in 1915 and Tracy in 1917—Doll and Bob Smith searched feverishly for a way to provide for their six children.

Bob, determined to make his own way as a sharecropper, had no success. Because he possessed little knowledge of agricultural practices, his hard work failed to produce any crops. It was not long before his health deteriorated and the simple act of plowing a field was too much for him. Yet, he continued to try to make his way in the local fields. As World War I raged, there was an increased demand for cotton and other agricultural goods.

Then, following a trip north to Memphis, Bob suddenly found himself economically prosperous. His family had food, clothing, and some of life's necessities. No one could figure out the Smiths' overnight economic success. It seemed strange to people that the worst farmer in the area was suddenly able to make a living. Rumors filled the air. Eventually, local law enforcement asked Bob Smith to leave Pontotoc County because he was engaged in the moonshining business. People laughed at the story, but it was true.

In 1917, the family returned by wagon to Lee County and settled in the Richmond area in the small town of Gilvo. This picturesque community, located just four miles from Tupelo, was Doll's favorite spot, and her health seemed to improve after they rented the Whitehead house on the Wilburn farm. It was a dirty, depressing little shack, but it was their own.

Upon their return to Lee County, Bob Smith made a deal with the local sheriff. A deputy would collect a small tax for each bottle of Bob's moonshine. With the authorities smiling and looking the other way, it seemed like Bob Smith would be able to make a nice living for the rest of his life. He proved to be an enterprising man who had finally found his niche. A sophisticated set of copper coils and a carefully hidden still made him a respected member of the local community. Folks couldn't say enough nice things about him. Unlike many moonshiners, Bob Smith used ingredients that made his moonshine taste like bourbon whiskey or a smooth brandy. He was a consummate artist in a craft that Southerners revered. Ironically, he himself was not a heavy drinker.

Despite his newfound notoriety and economic success, after a time Bob Smith began to have some problems. He was asked to leave the Wilburn farm, and this destroyed the base for his moonshining enterprise, resulting in a decade of itinerant wandering. Gladys, only nine years old when the family vacated Wilburn farm, gradually blossomed into a young woman during a decade that found the Smiths moving from one sharecropping house to another. The homes were squalid and lacked permanence. Rather than crying or throwing a tantrum, however, Gladys was stoic and understanding. She was determined to find a better life for herself. The other children, however, lacking Gladys' inner strength, suffered more dramatically from such circumstances. It was a time of misery, sorrow, and adjustment to the gloomiest of conditions. In later years, one of the primary reasons that Gladys was able to keep her marriage to Vernon Presley together was because of the stark memories of her youth, sad memories that nevertheless provided a solid foundation for the future.

In the 1920s, the Smiths moved constantly but never within more than a ten-mile radius. They settled in places with quaint names like Parkertown, Eggville, Mooreville, Nettleton, and Spring Hill. Food was often scarce. The family was no longer able to depend upon Bob's bootlegging activity. In this environment, education was not encouraged. The family was schooled for failure, and the children became hardened at an early age. The Smiths were well known in Lee County as they settled in these small quaint places and attempted to eke out a living. It was the sharecropper's way of life, a nomadic existence that had no apparent future.

The list of new homes was endless. The family moved to Marion Parker's dairy farm, but were forced to leave because none of them had had experience with animals. Then they moved in with Bob's sister Belle, but her husband, Isom Parker, objected to Bob's moonshining. After residing temporarily with six other families, the Smith's had worn out their welcome in the ten-mile circle from Parkertown to Spring Hill. Despite their housing difficulties, Smith did everything in his power to support his family. For a week, Bob was employed to dig a ditch for Will Herrin, and he had to walk seven miles to do the job. The Presbyterian church in Spring Hill hired him to weed its cemetery. There wasn't a job that he would not take to feed his family.

Doll Smith was a fragile woman who was unable to handle the responsibility of a family—now totalling eight children. She was continually sick and displayed signs of erratic behavior. Not only did Doll spend all the family's extra money on ribbons and satin dress material, but she also collected bone comb hair ornaments. In addition to her medicine, Doll often sent one of the girls to buy large quantities of candy. A balanced diet was not part of Doll's life. Although afflicted with tuberculosis, she seemed to have an almost pathological enjoyment of her disease. It was as if she viewed TB as her job. As a result, the children were forced to take on many of the household responsibilities.

With such a large family to deal with, Gladys became an adult long before her time. Her mother's illness and erratic personal behavior prompted Gladys to become a surrogate mother. Hard work, tough times, and responsibility were thrust upon her at an early age. She never shirked these duties. In fact, Gladys appears to have thrived on the role. It brought her a sense of responsibility, recognition, and power within the family circle.

The course taken by Gladys in her personal development seems to have been due in large part to her paternal aunt, Belle Smith. Belle, the daughter of Ann Mansell Smith, was a tall, good-looking woman with a streak of independence. She took a liking to Gladys and taught her a great deal about life. On a more practical side, while living with Belle, Gladys learned to bake and cook. She also became an accomplished seamstress. Belle was a well-adjusted and loving woman who not only helped Gladys develop her domestic skills but taught her values. She also introduced Gladys to books and briefly ignited an intellectual spark in the young girl.

In the 1920s, Lillian Smith, Gladys' older sister, clashed openly with her younger sister over who would assume Doll's responsibilities. It was a job that Lillian found difficult to handle. As a result, she depended increasingly upon Gladys for help and psychological support. This tense situation was complicated by Doll's continual strange behavior. There was no doubt that Doll had serious mental problems. She retreated into a make-believe world of fantasy and spent her days talking about her poor health. As Gladys entered her teens, she was given more and more family responsibilities. A neighbor, Mertice Finley, recalls that Gladys was unusually polite and well mannered. But there was also a headstrong aspect to Gladys' personality, and this developed an independent nature. Forced to mature earlier than most young people, Gladys was a perceptive young woman who, despite the dysfunctional family unit of which she was a part, hoped one day to have a family of her own.

There was still time to think about the future, and in 1925 Gladys' thoughts were concentrated upon school and athletics. She was an unusually skilled basketball player and, in the few months that she attended school, she was also an excellent student. Her basketball coach, Mary Marville, recognized Gladys' abilities, but she couldn't persuade the Smiths to leave their daughter in school. Generally, Gladys attended classes for about four months before she was forced to re-enter the unskilled job market.

By the time she was sixteen, Gladys had lost her baby fat and was a tall, lean beauty. The family's living conditions were still primitive. The Smiths temporarily lived in a diminutive log cabin on Luther Lummus' farm. Grace Reed, who also lived on the Lummus property with her husband and five children, hired Gladys to help with the laundry and household chores. This experience temporarily soured Gladys on marriage.

In 1929, as the Great Depression began, Gladys was a seventeen-year-old beauty who looked to the future. The years of chopping cotton, cutting corn, and cleaning the house had developed her large, but firm, physique. Although she attended school only four months a year, Gladys continued to participate in the social activities at school that were important. Later on, it would be largely due to the academic frustrations of her own school years that Gladys demanded of Elvis that he demonstrate an interest in solid subjects. There is no doubt that Gladys was frustrated by her inability to attend school full-time. When she became a mother and had her own family, Gladys explained to Mertice Finley, she would make sure her children received a good education.

There was also a musical side to young Gladys Love Smith. While in her teens, Gladys was infatuated with

Jimmie Rodgers' music. A native Mississippian, Rodgers died of tuberculosis in May 1933. Rodgers' popularity in the 1920s and 1930s was similar to Elvis' in the 1950s. Not only was Jimmie Rodgers a unique singing talent, but his personality inspired loyalty and devotion from his fans. Gladys was one of his staunchest admirers.

It is ironic that Rodgers' music was ignored by record companies until 1956 when RCA Victor re-released some of his old recordings. At the height of Elvis' popularity in 1956, Jimmie Rodgers' early songs were suddenly selling once again. In the 1930s, Rodgers' songs were ones that Gladys Love Smith could sing by heart. The main themes in Rodgers' songs were love, emotion, and betrayal. Among Gladys' favorite tunes were "Mean Mama Blues" and "Any Old Time." She played these songs for hours on a neighbor's Victrola. There is no doubt that music was an important part of Gladys' early life. She often sang around her house, but she was still too shy to sing in public.

There was certainly no hint of apparent shyness in Gladys' relationships with men. After going out with a number of young men and turning down Rex Stamford's marriage proposal, Gladys even dated a married farmer. Gladys' tempestuous affair with Stamford, a casual laborer who worked with Gladys on a local farm, gave rise to a great deal of gossip about Gladys in and around Lee County. In short, there was no shortage of men in Gladys' life, but she was unable to find one that she wanted to marry.

Here, at the jumping off point for story of Gladys' influence upon her future son, we see that the marriage of Doll Mansell and Bob Smith had brought together two unique heritages. The French-Norman bloodline combined with Scots-Irish and Indian inheritance, the characteristic stubbornness of the Mansells combined with the strong silent nature of the Smiths—all worked together to produce exceedingly headstrong individuals. Strict adherence to fundamental Christian religious values was another common trait, one that promoted a parsimonious lifestyle. Many of these very traits would show up in Elvis' personality.

As she grew into a mature woman, Gladys Love Smith was nothing if not an independent spirit with her own ideas. She had a positive sense of the future and a longing for a better life. Franklin Delano Roosevelt's New Deal inspired her. Eleanor Roosevelt was Gladys' hero. She watched the Movietone newsreels at the local theater and marveled at the president's wife. A woman with her own life, her own mind, and her own direction, Eleanor Roosevelt provided Gladys with a role model. Although she wanted desperately to marry, she was extremely fussy concerning men. The long history of failed marriages and instability in the Smith family frightened her, and she was not about to settle for just anyone.

Like her mother before her, Gladys was in no hurry to get married. Marriage seemed like a life of slavery and drudgery to young Gladys. She was too bright and too cautious to make the mistakes that had robbed her mother of her independence. Family life was a drain upon her. No one could take care of themselves, and there was a communal attitude amongst the adults in which one person's treasured belonging was everyone's property.

By 1931, Gladys' father was nearly blind and in declining health. The following year, Robert Lee Smith died of pneumonia. In the last week of his life, the doctor realized that Bob had been sick for some time. He was a quiet man who never complained about his lot in life. When Bob Smith died there was universal praise for his tenacious attempts to feed and clothe his family. In the tight-knit Southern community, a man's life was judged by his hopes and dreams and not by his material possessions. The local undertaker donated a casket and Bob Smith was buried in an unmarked grave at the Spring Hill Cemetery.

After Bob Smith's death, Doll was afflicted with periodic attacks of TB and remained reclusive. In her last few years, she lived in a shallow dream world and seldom went out in public. Gladys was her mother's favorite child, and it was a tremendous strain upon the young girl to console her mother during this period. It is ironic that Doll Smith, ill most of her life, outlived her husband, lasting another five years. She would be buried beside him in the cemetery next to the Presbyterian church in Spring Hill, Mississippi.

To cope with the economic crisis caused by their father's death, the Smiths moved into a house in East Tupelo. Once they settled into the new residence, the unmarried girls went to work at the Tupelo Garment Company. The factory was a sweatshop enterprise that paid thirteen dollars a week for sixty hours of work. There was a dull monotony to sitting there all day with a group of young, silly girls. Despite the long hours and difficult working conditions, though, Gladys retained a refreshingly optimistic outlook. To counter her depression, she often sang country songs, using her musical talent to lighten the mood in the factory. This won her many new friends. At night, she would walk home across the railroad tracks and re-enter her private world of poverty and deprivation—her white, decrepit East Tupelo home. But home it was, and she loved it.

There was also a strong, fundamentalist Christian base to Gladys Love Smith's early life. After her father died, she had turned to the church for solace. The First Assembly of God church was a charismatic, fundamentalist sect that had unbending rules against dancing, however. This attitude conflicted with Gladys' notion that dancing was harmless. Gladys, who loved to dance, just couldn't conform to the strict church rules. Although she continued to date—and to dance—she suffered the pangs of Southern evangelical guilt.

The First Assembly of God church had some positive influences upon young Gladys, however. In the early 1930s, the church taught that there was a utopian future, and the pastor urged his worshippers to live in the world without being a part of it. Church doctrine concentrated upon the importance of love and the manner in which it provided salvation. The services were emotional, replete with wailing and moaning. It was the best show in Lee County, and the congregation was urged to share its joy with the local townspeople. Utopian preachers had a pie in the sky mentality that was convincing amidst the Great Depression's poverty, and the First Assembly of God church was prominent in offering hope to the locals. There was little else to inspire anyone. All of this was an important psychological release for Gladys, because she could imagine that she was a success.

Whatever the momentary escape from hardship and poverty provided by the church's guarantee of future bliss, Gladys' family's erratic mental and personal history continued to be bothersome. Bob and Doll Smith's children had severe emotional problems. Travis and Johnny Smith were heavy drinkers with a reputation for violence. There were numerous business dealings during their lives that resulted in controversy. Few people in and around Tupelo trusted the Smiths because of their reputation for dishonesty and manipulation. Neither Travis nor Johnny were able to make a living, and they reacted to criticism with unbridled violence.

Travis and his sister Lavelle each had two boys who died youthful, violent deaths. As Albert Goldman's biography, *Elvis*, states, Travis' son Junior "died of a convulsion before he was thirty, after a life darkened by homicidal madness." Another of Travis Smith's sons, Bobby, allegedly commited suicide (in the form of arsenic poisoning). He was only twenty-six. In a strangely portentous coincidence, the Shelby County coroner ruled—as later happened with Elvis—that Bobby Smith had died from a heart attack. Albert Goldman concludes that: "Elvis...we see now as possibly the victim of a fatal hereditary disposition." This conclusion is debatable, but the fact remains that the Smith family had disturbing behavioral patterns.

Consider, for example, the fate of Gladys' three brothers. They consistently demonstrated abnormal social and psychological behavior. John Smith, like Gladys, died at age forty-six after a life plagued by problems with guns, knives, and alcohol. Tracy Smith was deaf and consequently shy and withdrawn. He was psychologically distraught and few people understood his problems. Like many of the Smiths, Travis found it difficult to hold down a full-time job. In fact, he didn't secure permanent employment until Elvis became famous. Then, Travis worked as a Graceland guard and sporadically managed Elvis' Circle G Ranch. Left to his own devices, Travis was a complete failure. In general, the Smith children displayed a personal behavior that shortened all their lives.

The Presley Family

In the early 1930s, East Tupelo was sprinkled with forsaken little white frame bungalows. The town was often described by visitors as a depressing row of homes set in a dingy backwater area. The unpaved dirt streets were filled with potholes. The unassuming homes built on muddy lots had a cracker box appearance. The majority of these dwellings were on Old Saltillo Road, which leads north off the highway from Birmingham to Tupelo. There were three little side streets running off Old Saltillo Road. Both the Smiths and the Presleys lived in this rustic setting, and all seemed unaware of their poverty.

Presley was one of the common names in East Tupelo. The original double "s" spelling—Pressley—was of Scotch-Irish origin. With twenty-six Presley families in the Tupelo schools, it was the most common name in town. Before they arrived in Tupelo, the Presleys had a long and rich historical lineage.

The Presley family roots are interesting. The first Presley to immigrate to America was Andrew Pressley, an Anglo-Scottish settler, who arrived in 1745. The American colonies were then a widely diverse group of ethnically-oriented settlements. It was therefore natural that, like many Scottish settlers before him, Andrew migrated to an area filled with his countrymen. He settled in Anson County, North Carolina. In 1754, his son, Andrew, Jr., arrived. He grew up to become a blacksmith like his father, and for a time they both lived in New Bern, in central North Carolina, another area heavily populated by Scottish immigrants. A century would pass before the Pressleys changed the spelling of their family name to Presley.

The turmoil surrounding the American Revolution had a dramatic impact upon the Pressleys. Andrew Pressley, Jr., moved to Lancaster County, South Carolina, to work as the town's blacksmith. Land sales were booming, and he purchased 150 acres of prime Lancaster County property for himself. A loyal and patriotic American, he hoped to make his fortune there; indeed, it was Andrew's success in business that fed his strong sense of American nationalism. By July 1776, although he was just a simple farmer and blacksmith, he could not ignore the imminent threat of war.

When the American Revolution broke out, Andrew Jr. fought during two extended army enlistments. "I knew George Washington and General Henry 'Light Horse' Lee," Andrew Jr. wrote in an affidavit attached to his pension records. He earned a distinguished war record fighting at the Battle of Eutah Springs, South Carolina, one of 150 Carolina soldiers who courageously fought the British, taking 500 prisoners, during one of the Revolutionary War's last important battles.

After the war, being an ambitious and hard-working American who was constantly searching out new investment opportunities, he applied, through his status as a veteran, to the United States War Pension Board for a bonus land grant. Not only was the land granted, but Andrew Jr. was able to make a respectable living from it. In the last decade of his life, he talked at length about migrating even further into the American West. It was this hope for a new life that prompted him to focus his ambitions upon the alluvial soil and perfect climate of Tennessee. At the age of 101, at the time living on a $20-a-year government pension, he received approval for another land claim in Hawkins County, Tennessee. Before he could claim his new land, though, he died, never able to fulfill his dreams of a western land settlement.

Not surprisingly, Andrew Jr.'s son, Dunnan Pressley, Sr. (1780-1850), was also filled with the spirit of western exploration. Born in Lancaster, South Carolina, the ambitious aspirations of his father developed into something of an obsession for young Dunnan, one that left him without roots, destined for a wandering life.

In his youth, he lived in a dozen different homes within a 120-mile radius inside North Carolina. At the age of twenty, he moved to Buncombe County, and spent the next few decades moving about in the American West as a poor, itinerant sharecropping farmer. With an enormous capacity for moonshine whiskey, unable to read or write, he was never able to make a decent living. By the time he was forty years old, Dunnan had married twice and had fathered two boys and two girls. In 1826, following the death of his first wife, he soon married again, a young woman in her twenties. They moved to Madisonville, Tennessee, where he worked for another decade as a sharecropper. Now approaching fifty, he talked wistfully about owning a family farm of his own. The old pattern of sharecropping and odd jobs continued, however. Finally, in 1836, the promise of cheap acreage in Georgia prompted him to stake a claim on Cherokee Indian land. Ultimately, it was impossible for him to make a go of things in Georgia, and he returned again to Tennessee.

The Pressley's were actually quite typical of frontiersmen of the time. As they slowly began their jour-ney westward, they faced commonly shared frontier hardships. The best land was no longer available because squatters, banks, and Eastern businessmen had purchased it. Yet, the Pressleys, like many frontier adventurers, were oblivious to such difficulties. It was, after all, the Age of the Common Man. Ever since Andrew Jackson had been elected to the presidency in 1828, there was an eternal optimism in the South, part of the Jacksonian ethos—the notion that any man could make his fortune in the American West.

Such was the spirit of reasoning evident in the life of Dunnan Pressley, Jr. In 1846, at the age of nineteen, Dunnan Jr. enlisted in the United States Army and fought in the Mexican War with Company C, 5th Tennessee Infantry. Two years later he was honorably discharged with a two-dollar clothing allowance and a 160-acre land grant. For the next twelve years, he wandered around the Tennessee frontier, never able to plant firm roots. Jobs were temporary, and opportunity was always just around the corner. Dunnan Jr. loved to play cards, drink, and talk. He was not considered a good marriage prospect by any of the local ladies. Few people knew that, in fact, he was already married and had left his wife, preferring to act and live the life of a single man. Rather than divorce her, he had simply packed his bags and left home, deciding that the best way to avoid responsibility was to simply move to a new area.

When he turned thirty-four in 1861, Dunnan Jr. married once again. This time his bride was Martha Jane Wesson of Fulton, Mississippi. Fulton, a small town, the Itawamba County seat, was a forlorn place, and no one could figure out why Dunnan, who was not a farmer, had migrated there. In all probability, it was the lure of inexpensive land that brought him to this part of Mississippi (his quick remarriage dictated by the fact that he needed a family to settle a new land grant). Fulton had recently opened formerly restricted areas to land settlement. A treaty with the Chickasaw Indians provided a bargain price of twenty-five cents for an acre of land, strong incentive for farmers to move into the area, and for those who had the nerve to speculate about the future of the land. Another reason for moving to this remote, sparsely-populated area, of course, was to escape his first wife, who was searching frantically for him in Tennessee.

After his marriage to Martha Jane Wesson, she gave birth to two daughters, Rosalinda and Rosella. For a period of time, Dunnan Jr. was content to make a living from his farmland. This stability was atypical, however, and it was not long before he eagerly sought out a new adventure. Enlisting in Ham's Regiment of the Mississippi Cavalry, he left to fight for the Confederacy in the American Civil War.

At least the thought of going off to war was an exciting prospect for Dunnan Jr. He had romanticized his previous service in the American army during the Mexican War, bragging to his family and friends about his service with Company C of the 5th Tennessee Infantry. In reality, though, it is perhaps not strange that he waited until 1863 when the Civil War was already two years old—he was already thirty-six years old and eager to get away from his new wife—before he enlisted. In excellent physical condition, he had done everything he could in the early years of the war to escape the infantry; finally, however—and probably with the thought of collecting lucrative wartime bonuses uppermost in his mind—he joined the Confederate cause.

In order to qualify for the special incentives, Dunnan Jr. enlisted two different times in the Confederate army. On May 11, 1863, he was granted the rank of corporal during his first enlistment, collecting a $300 bounty for his horse. Shortly after he joined Company E of Ham's Regiment, however, he deserted. Members of his old unit quickly found him, giving him the choice of a public beating or rejoining another Confederate unit. The smooth-talking Dunnan convinced Ham's Regiment that he was in fact a good old boy, and they released him. Eight weeks after the controversy with Ham's Regiment, he enlisted in Company A of Davenport's Battalion of the Mississippi Cavalry. Once again he collected a $300 bonus and just as quickly deserted his unit. Leaving his wife and infant daughters behind, he took to the open road in search of yet another new life. Always eager to pass himself off as a patriot, he bragged for years about his lengthy military record.

The remainder of Dunnan Jr.'s life is inconsequential. A chronic drifter, he married four more times and demonstrated no signs of personal or family responsibility. Although he deserted the Confederate army twice during the Civil War, Dunnan had the audacity to apply for a wartime disability pension. In 1888, when he appeared before the United States Army pension board, Dunnan testified that he suffered from acute diarrhea. In a government form, he listed the source of this chronic affliction as the Mexican War. It had been forty years since he had served in the army. Not only was he granted the pension, but six years later he requested an increase. In his later years, Dunnan traveled west through Arkansas to Missouri, where he finally died in 1900. At the time of his death, the Barry County, Missouri, County Court placed Dunnan Pressley Jr.'s personal wealth at twenty-three dollars. It was an ignominious ending to an insignificant life.

From 1827 to his death in 1900, Dunnan Jr. had lived out the legacy of his Jacksonian heritage. Like his father, he had eagerly sought out fertile western land, but instead of farming it he purchased and resold it constantly, seeking to turn quick profits. As a land speculator, though, Dunnan was as unsuccessful as he was in everything else. He played the role of a small-time land baron with little success. A braggart who would stoop to any lengths to satisfy his lust for wealth, he was not considered an honest man. Dressed in expensive suits replete with a gold-handled walking stick, a diamond stickpin in his tie, and sporting glossy leather shoes, he was a dandy with an inflated opinion of his self-worth. He often talked about finding a small grassy knoll to build a home, although his stated goal merely served as an excuse for continual migration. Throughout his life, Dunnan Jr. had no concept of personal or family responsibility. He lived for the moment and liked to tell people that tomorrow would be a better day. Much like John Mansell, Dunnan Pressley Jr. was a practicing celebrant of the excesses of Andrew Jackson's democracy.

As we can see, the legacy of Jacksonian Democracy was an important one for the Pressley family. The males of the Pressley clan came to manhood at a time when the franchise was extended in western states, and this created a kinship with government and politicians. The new state constitutions fostered a zealous patriotism, leading to a strong belief in democracy and progress, and creating a spirit of optimism and a sense of mission. As the Pressleys moved westward in the midst of this euphoric setting, they epitomized the rough, energetic frontier strain that was such an integral part of American life at this time. If a person failed to make a living in one place, he simply migrated to a new locale. There seemed to be endless opportunities in Tennessee, Missouri, and Mississippi, and the Pressleys were determined to find their fortune.

Dunnan Pressley Jr.'s daughter, Rosella (1862-1924), was Elvis' great grandmother. When Dunnan Jr. left his wife Martha Jane Wesson, Rosella had been crushed. It was a traumatic event and she never recovered from it. One of Rosella's daughters, Mrs. Robbie Stacy, remarked: "My mother told me that when she and her sister were just little babies, their grandparents had taken them to church on Sunday and when they came back their grandfather Dunnan was gone." In 1980, another of Rosella's daughters, Mrs. Doshia Steele, remarked that it was not wise to ask about their father.

Rosella's life was one of continual pain and mental instability. She was a disturbed woman who bore nine children out of wedlock. After giving birth to her first child at nineteen, Rosella had eight other illegitimate children over the next twenty-eight years, refusing to identify the fathers of any of her offspring. Yet another of Rosella's daughters remembers that her mother spent most of her time alone. Refusing even simple discussion, she was suspicious of strangers.

Yet, amazingly, although no more than a wandering farmhand when it came to making a livelihood, Rosella was an excellent mother. Her youngest son, Joseph Presley, recounted his mother's poverty: "She was a sharecropper who gave half of the crops she raised to the landlord in exchange for a rough old cabin to live in." Despite these hardships, the children were virtually unanimous in praising their mother.

Elvis's Grandparents

Rosella was an iron-fisted mother with a special feeling for her children. Love, compassion, and Christian training were traits that she believed were important to instill in them. When she died at the age of sixty-two, Rosella had taught her children to be God-fearing, flag-loving Americans. They were all extremely patriotic and religious. It was Rosella's way of making up for the lack of a father figure. Yet, her attempts to raise a well-adjusted family failed with some of the children. The biggest disappointment was Jessie D. (J.D.) Presley, Elvis' grandfather. Born in 1896 in Itawamba County, Mississippi, Jessie Presley was already known as a hard-drinking, hell-raising ladies man by the age of seventeen. Continually in barroom brawls, J.D.'s behavior was the opposite of that which the Presley family praised in his brother Noah, perhaps going a long way towards explaining J.D.'s behavior. Whereas J.D. was considered a no good, shiftless drifter, his brother was viewed as a model citizen.

Noah Presley was the Presley clan's success. As a young man, he moved to East Tupelo where he opened a highly profitable grocery store. Realizing that community service and business success went hand in hand, Noah became active in local affairs. He volunteered to help out in the local school system and he even drove a school bus for a brief period. As a community-spirited merchant, Noah Presley was well liked and became prosperous at an early age. In 1936, he was elected mayor of East Tupelo. The booster spirit that prompted Noah to join local service clubs also served him well as a businessman. He had a reputation for honesty and good business sense.

It was Noah Presley's sense of family responsibility that prompted him to be financially generous. Elvis' first trips to the Memphis zoo were due to Noah. Elvis' earliest excursions out to dinner in a restaurant were with Noah. But for all their praise of him, Noah made most of the Presleys nervous. He was *too* responsible and *too* businesslike. When the rest of the family talked eagerly about President Roosevelt's New Deal programs, Noah urged them to make their own way in the world. His personality was calm and his ideas were usually understated. Not only was he a deacon in the Church of God, but he lived a clean, abstinent life.

As is often the case with brothers, Jessie was Noah's complete opposite, lacking all such business, religious, and social skills. After dropping out of school at eleven, he had never learned a trade. He tried to make up for all these handicaps with his good looks. Most Tupelo citizens remember that in his youth Jessie was much better looking than Elvis, and had the glib tongue of a gifted orator. Gay McCrae, who lived close to Jessie in East Tupelo, told Elaine Dundy: "Mr. Presley was the handsomest man I've ever seen in my life." Tupelo residents unanimously remember Jessie as tall, lean, and handsome. His wavy black hair and carefully chiseled facial features impressed the young girls. A number of people who didn't know Jessie's name called him the "tall, elegant man who had a way with the ladies." Jessie was the local widows' delight.

During his early life, Jessie worked as a farmer, a lumberjack, and a salesman. He also made a part-time living running bootleg whiskey in and around Tupelo, and his easy manner and articulate nature helped draw customers to his bootlegging enterprise. Once his illegal activities got to be too large and notorious, however, Jessie was threatened by local law enforcement officials and he quickly moved out of the area. At the tender age of seventeen, Jessie Presley vanished from Lee County.

Jessie migrated back to Fulton County, Mississippi, where he met and married Minnie Mae Hood, Elvis's paternal grandmother. He had returned to his place of birth to find a wife. Although he was still a young man, Jessie had been on his own for five years. Yet, at seventeen, he was hardly prepared to raise a family. Initially, Minnie Mae was not interested in marrying him, but he somehow convinced her that he was prepared for family life. Few people in Fulton County understood the reasons for the marriage. J.D. was a dandy with a smooth tongue, and Minnie Mae was a homely young woman devoid of personality. Nevertheless, the young couple immediately had two boys, Vester and Vernon. The marriage proved to be a rocky one. It was difficult for Jessie to make a living, and his close friends described him as "mean of hell." Jessie locked up his whiskey and ordered his wife never to drink it. When friends called, Jessie stood in the kitchen and told his wife how many pieces of cheese and baked goods to place on the table.

In addition to the couple's two boys, there were three other children—sisters, Delta Mae, Gladys Earlene, and Nashville Lorene. Despite this large brood, Jessie remained a rebellious man who loved his liquor, one who perpetually failed to mature and found it difficult to hold a full-time job. Yet, he continually bragged to his children that he was a hard worker. Years later, Vester Presley, in his book *A Presley Speaks*, reflected on his father: "Jessie is a good worker who loved his family and takes care of them...." The truth is that the local bars and a bottle of whiskey were Jessie's main forms of entertainment. Another of Jessie Presley's brothers, Calhoun, has remarked that Jessie "spent many a night sobering up in jail." He also recalled that Jessie often spent his money on fine clothes while the family went without food. Throughout his life, Jessie took off and wandered away to pursue his interests, always able to explain his absences in the most altruistic terms. A selfish, small-minded man, he had neither a concept of parental responsibility nor the sophistication to raise a family. This behavior made it difficult for Jessie to establish long-term relationships and close friends.

Jessie was basically a drifter who lacked responsibility. He loved to wear a fine suit—his pride and joy, a tailor-made, three-piece $24 brown suit with pearl buttons—smoke a fat cigar, and hang out in the local saloons. Otherwise, he was just a dreamer. When he dressed up in his fancy clothes, he called himself "the lawyer." He was a man with a penchant for affectations. A good example of this behavior was demonstrated by Jessie's use of a walking stick. When he drank in the local bars, he carried an elaborately polished stick with a gold-edged handle. It was the proper image for the would-be gentleman. He paraded around town "like a peacock," a local resident remarked after Elvis' death. "Though his family was poor, he splurged on clothes for himself."

As a result of Jessie's behavior, his marriage to Minnie Mae was doomed from the beginning. They were simply an incompatible couple. Minnie Mae was a conservative, Bible-thumping shrew who was unhappy with herself and her life. Friends described her as a tall, homely, cantankerous, poorly-dressed woman who constantly nagged Jessie. His behavior eventually brought about a marked personality change in Minnie Mae, and she developed into a harsh, nasty woman. It was not a healthy atmosphere for the Presley children.

Strangely enough, Vester Presley remembers the Tupelo days fondly. Neither of the Presley brothers took their chores seriously. "Our chores were a combination of work, fun, and a little pain...," Vester remarked. He laughs about the time Vernon almost cut off his foot chopping wood. Because of this attitude, Vester Presley developed few employable skills. The tragedy of Vester Presley's life is that he never thought beyond the present. He had no ambition, a disdain for education, and a philosophy that encouraged him to follow in his dad's footsteps. There would always be someone to take care of him, Vester reasoned.

Unfortunately, Vernon embraced a similar philoso-

phy. Young Vernon Presley watched in admiration as his dad lived in a dream world that bore little resemblance to reality, and he fantasized that his life would be like his dad's. He would be well dressed and charm the local girls. Because he lacked the ability to analyze people, Vernon failed to realize that his parents had marital difficulties. Although Jessie and Minnie Mae were married for thirty years, it was strictly a union of convenience.

When Jessie and Minnie Mae Presley finally divorced in 1947, it was a nasty and bitter court battle. It was Jessie who filed for the divorce, alleging that Minnie Mae had deserted him. In a letter to Jessie's attorney, Edwin Mengel, Minnie Mae indignantly remarked: "I didn't desert my husband. As a matter of fact, he deserted me and has been living with another woman and he hasn't sent me any money in over a year...." This letter highlighted the three decades of misery that Minnie Mae endured during her marriage.

When the Presley divorce case reached Circuit Judge Lawrence Speckman, the court's decision was a curious one. The divorce was granted and Minnie Mae Presley was awarded neither alimony nor spousal support. She was untrained for the job market, and there were few opportunities for an older woman. Eventually, Minnie Mae, whom Elvis affectionately came to call "Dodger," moved into Graceland. When she died on May 8, 1980, Minnie Mae had outlived her husband by seven years, her son Vernon by one year, and her grandson Elvis by nearly three years. There is no written record of her relationship with Elvis, but she appears to have become a substitute mother after Gladys Presley's death.

Before Jessie Presley died in 1973, he married a Louisville, Kentucky, elementary school teacher, Vera Pruitt, and was employed as a night watchman in a local Pepsi-Cola plant. Still the consummate hustler, Jessie tried to cash in on Elvis' fame by recording two songs for the Louisville-based Legacy Record label. The tunes—"The Billy Goat Song" and "Swinging in the Orchard"—were amateurish. Not only did they fail to sell, but Elvis was infuriated with Jessie's attempt to use his name for profit. In 1956, Elvis had driven to Louisville to present his grandfather with a television set, a new car, and a one-hundred-dollar bill. Jessie's brother, Joseph, remembers how proud Jessie was of Elvis, but Minnie Mae Presley made it very clear that Elvis was not to visit his grandfather again. In fact, Minnie Mae continually lectured Elvis about the shortcomings of his own father. Vernon, who, in Minnie Mae's view, was cursed with the Presley affliction, simply would not work. At age thirty-nine, Vernon convinced Elvis that he was disabled and had to retire. His alleged bad back did not prevent him from leading a full life, however. Minnie Mae urged Elvis to watch out for Vernon's "bad habits." He was an excessive man who could not control his drinking or his womanizing. At first, Elvis, who had trouble seeing anything wrong with his father, was perplexed by this talk. For a short time he passed off Minnie Mae's remarks as the frustrations of a jilted old lady, but soon realized that this truly was Vernon's style.

In fact, many of Vernon's traits would later be evident in Elvis' personality. The Presley's desire for fine clothes, elegant surroundings, and leisure were bred into Vernon at an early age. Because Vernon was an extremely good-looking man with a penchant for overstatement, he was a favorite with the local ladies. Yet, there was something missing in Vernon's personality. As Albert Goldman suggested: "Vernon was always uptight and distrustful." He was neither ambitious nor particularly bright.

In contrast, Gladys Love Smith, as we have seen earlier, was an articulate and responsible woman who was able to earn a living. She was also four years older than Vernon Presley. When Vernon and Gladys met, it was during the midst of the worst depression in American history. Yet, Gladys' optimism led her to remark that President Franklin D. Roosevelt made the Great Depression seem like a perpetual holiday.

The stability in Gladys' life came from the First Assembly of God church. Her uncle, Gains Mansell, was one of the preachers at the church. Not only was Reverend Mansell a moral influence, but he urged Gladys to wait for the right man. With Gladys' three sisters married and raising families, she was the head of the household. With the help of Reverend Mansell, Gladys found a small house on Kelly Street and moved her ailing mother and sister Clettes into the home. Doll Smith was in poor health and needed constant medical attention. The pressures upon young Gladys were enormous, but she was a strong young woman. As the early 1930s dawned in Tupelo, Gladys Love Smith and Vernon Presley were destined to meet, fall in love, and marry. This courtship and marriage would produce one son, Elvis Presley, and the influence of the Great Depression would go a long way to form young Elvis' character.

CHAPTER 3

Gladys and Vernon, 1932-1941

Gladys Love Smith was a dark-haired, medium built, attractive young lady in the early 1930s. Even as New Deal programs proliferated and President Franklin Delano Roosevelt's political rhetoric rang over the land, Gladys developed into an independent woman. Like many of her Tupelo counterparts, she became a "factory girl," a common phenomenon during the Great Depression. A factory girl was a young lady who delayed marriage while working to help out her family. She worked hard and brought money home to her parents and brothers and sisters. Gladys was typical of the factory girls who became self-reliant at an early age, and this explains why she had such a dominant personality. She didn't yearn for immediate marriage, a family, and the responsibility of full-time motherhood, and hoped instead to retain her freedom long enough to meet the right man at the right time.

A great deal about the personalities of Gladys Love Smith and Vernon Presley can be explained by examining the early history of Tupelo and Lee County. As the Mississippi countryside changed, new opportunities developed for its citizens. The structure of the Southern family also underwent enormous change, and the old roles were altered in many ways.

Tupelo

Tupelo was a typical Southern community. When it was first settled, the Gum Pond, a huge mosquito-infested quagmire, was the center of town. The harsh brown-colored soil seemed to offer little hope for flourishing agriculture, although the Chickasaw Indians had settled the area around Tupelo not only because of its mild climate but also due to the land. Eventually, the area developed into a rich agricultural locale. At first, though, mud creeks surrounding Tupelo gave it the appearance of a temporary city. All this changed in 1858 when the Gulf Mobile and Ohio Railroad built its track through the town. The railroad not only made Tupelo a permanent settlement, but it encouraged business investment and provided the impetus for Tupelo to become the seat of Lee County.

The changes in Tupelo were first evident when the train depot, two churches, a schoolhouse, and a few small homes were hastily constructed on two streets. Early visitors joked about Tupelo's "unsightly" or "temporary" appearance. In the 1860s, a group of ambitious businessmen announced that they would build a col-

lege, a courthouse, and a number of other new churches. These were only the plans of visionaries, however, typical of unfulfilled promises made by local businessmen and politicians for the next seventy-five years. Basically, Tupelo was long on dreams and short on accomplishments until the Great Depression. Always, though, there was a strong community spirit and a sense of Tupelo's future that inspired its citizens.

In 1870, Tupelo was incorporated as a city, and the town developed into a rough, bar-infested hangout for farmers and itinerant wanderers. There was a "macho" quality to Tupelo on the weekends. The local newspaper, the *Tupelo Standard Journal*, editorialized that the town's poor reputation was due to the wide open frontier atmosphere. Local citizens responded by simply not buying the newspaper, a defense of the town just as it was. In the 1880s, the St. Louis-San Francisco railroad was completed and Judge C.P. Long remarked that the new transportation system made Tupelo a "growing and expanding" city.

When World War I ended, Tupelo's Main Street was under further construction. Small businesses abounded, and a burst of high-powered electric lights brought an eerie white glow to the drab downtown buildings. A Tupelo Chamber of Commerce pamphlet of the time proclaimed: "Tupelo: Premier City of Northeast Mississippi." With a population of six thousand, Tupelo was an idyllic spot to live in the 1920s. "We had more bicycles than cars," one resident remembered, "it was a civilized place." The ice factory, the creamery, the lumberyard, and the Coca-Cola bottling plant were described by local citizens as signs of Tupelo's booming economy. There was a civic pride that Tupelo citizens suggested came from the growth of local business activity. On the agricultural front, the Memphis *Commercial-Appeal* proclaimed: "Lee County soil will grow just about everything."

Although strong trade ties between Tupelo and Memphis caused many Lee County residents to move north to the Tennessee city, there was an attempt to erase the "hillbilly stigma" that Lee County residents felt emanating from their northern neighbor. Quality of life was an important topic among local citizens. The Tupelo hospital was a model health facility, and Lee County posted signs a mile apart on the main roads which directed people to health care centers. Politicians loved to tell local citizens that Tupelo was something special, and preachers reminded citizens of their duty to God, country, and the Southern way of life.

Gladys Love Smith was also caught up in the promise of a renewed American life. She listened intently as local politicians sketched the plans for Tupelo's Federal Fish Hatchery. Gladys realized that the times were changing on a grand scale, right down to the kind of gossip people engaged in at the local beauty parlor. There was a sense of personal liberty that Gladys' parents had never experienced, and she was determined to live her life free of the social constraints that condemned the uneducated worker to the other side of the tracks.

There were strong and defined social class lines in Tupelo, a fact that troubled Gladys. The poorest local residents lived outside the city limits, in East Tupelo. Most of Gladys Love Smith's friends lived, as did she. It was a brief mile down a dusty road and up a small hill, and Gladys loved to walk home from work to the dilapidated, run-down shacks, the barking dogs, and the smell of fried meat and potatoes. The streets were filled with small, wood-frame homes where the neighbors sat out on the porches and talked to passersby. There was little diversity and few signs of change in East Tupelo, but deep down Gladys loved things constant. She was internally rebellious but longed for stability outside herself. Although it was "the other side of the tracks," it was Gladys' home. The five streets that made up East Tupelo had a homey atmosphere and gave her a feeling of security.

Along with the changes coming over America, Gladys herself was brimming with youthful optimism. She often spent hours after work wandering downtown looking in the store windows and dreaming of a better life. There seemed to be too many possibilities for future success for Gladys to think in terms of marriage just yet, an opinion encouraged by most of the Tupelo residents who knew her.

The New Deal had made strange bedfellows, and President Franklin D. Roosevelt was a hero to politicians, businessmen, and preachers alike. Brother Edward Parks, the First Assembly of God pastor, suggested that the Democratic party was working for God. It was not surprising, considering Roosevelt's faith in local Democratic votes, that he pushed through federal funds to improve Tupelo. The arguments that Roosevelt made in the 1932 presidential campaign influenced many local residents. President Roosevelt's America presented opportunities that Gladys' parents could never experience. As a result, she was caught up in the freewheeling egalitarianism of the New Deal. Listening to President Roosevelt's "Fireside Chats" on the family's antique radio, a better life appeared just around the corner.

There was a freethinking aspect to Gladys Love

Smith's personality. From her earliest days she would not submit to her parents' attempts to put her in a mold. The first sign of Gladys' independence was evident when she had convinced the family to relocate to East Tupelo. There she had the best of both worlds; although she was close to downtown, the small shotgun shacks in East Tupelo offered refuge from the complicated world. Many of Gladys' friends believed that she needed quiet, privacy, and an unhurried place where she could enjoy a sense of her own being. East Tupelo provided a familiar and comfortable setting.

Each morning she arose and walked into town. Climbing the rickety stairs to the second floor of the Tupelo Garment Factory, she went to work feeding ready-cut patterns into a buzzing sewing machine. Like hundreds of factory girls, she looked forward to the end of the day. Her meager salary brought an independence that her mother's generation had not known, and since the family depended upon her money, she had a status at home that her brothers and sisters lacked. This not only brought Gladys recognition, but respect and dignity. Earning an independent paycheck during the Great Depression was difficult for anyone, and Gladys developed a strong sense of personal worth. She was a stable member of the working class, and enjoyed a position that her future husband, Vernon Presley, could only dream about during the early days of the Great Depression.

It was while working at the Tupelo Garment Factory that Gladys developed socially. She worked with many other girls her own age, and it was common for them to go out at night after work. Many of the factory girls lived in East Tupelo, and when they crossed the Gulf Mobile and Ohio and St. Louis-San Francisco (Frisco) railroad tracks, they were home. The railroad tracks became an obsession with them and they spoke of the iron rods as the source of their "evening liberation." As a result, there was a natural camaraderie. For the first time, Gladys belonged to a group that readily accepted her. She was one of the fastest workers and one of the most popular nighttime revelers. The girls got together to secretly drink beer and complain about the bosses. They flirted with the men in downtown Tupelo and delighted in being young. Gladys loved to sing and dance, and she was generally the life of any party.

One of Gladys' greatest pleasures was shopping at Reed's department store. Not only did she love to pick through the dresses on the sale rack, but Gladys spent hours talking to her friends. After shopping, she often walked over to Roy Martin's grocery store on Lake Street to buy some food for the family. Her last stop at Miller's candy store provided a surprise for her mother.

Gladys often mentioned that East Tupelo was across

the tracks, on the "wrong side of town," a fact that appealed to her. It fed her romantic illusion of defiance and rebellion. Much like the famous son she was destined to bear, Gladys was unconventional in thought and deed. In appearance, however, she remained totally conventional, an interesting contradiction in her character. She was a good churchgoing young lady who raised hell when not in church, and it was the private moments that Gladys loved the most. With a good job, she had the same privileges that men enjoyed. One of these powers was to help select the homes that the Smith family rented.

When Gladys found a small house to rent on Kelly Street, she was overjoyed with the prospect of moving her mother into a new home. The building was tree-shaded, and the dirt road had a fresh smell to it. Orville S. Bean's dairy farm was nearby, and Gladys' brothers and sisters could work for him. Her sister Clettes was still too young to work, but she could look after their mother Doll. Gladys, now the head of the household, took the reins firmly and encouraged the rest of the family to pull their own weight. A strong-willed and independent woman, she had the brains and the practical skills to run the household. She made schedules like those at the Tupelo Garment Factory for family members, who actually showed signs of enjoying the regimentation.

From time to time, Uncle Gains Mansell and Pastor Edward Parks came by to inquire about Doll's health. The First Assembly of God church was then just a tent on a barren piece of land, but the congregation was friendly and close to one another, and Gladys continued to derive a great deal of pleasure from being a member. What Gladys loved about the First Assembly of God church was its positive view of religion. The pastors taught that God loves you, and they were actively involved in attempting to make people happy. There was little interference in daily life. The church simply hoped to solve the crises that caused families to disintegrate amidst the pressures of modern life.

Despite her independence, then, she remained true to Southern Christian values. Not only did she attend church regularly, but her youthful enthusiasm prompted her to become an integral part of a number of other local congregations. Many Tupelo residents remember her turning up at other churches. For Gladys, there was a social, as well as religious, value to church. In addition to the searching spiritual questions she posed to the pastors, she had the opportunity to meet a number of young men. Revival meetings that came through town were a special source of inspiration to young Gladys. She loved the music, the fervent preaching, and the colorful crowds. Like her son Elvis, Gladys searched longingly for spiritual truth. But, again, she confessed

that the social side of the revival meetings helped her to meet new people. She frequently confided to her Uncle Gains, who was one of the elders of the church, that although she was in no hurry to marry, the truth is that she was looking for the right man. When she found that man, they would not only marry but have a family.

Mr. and Mrs. Vernon Presley

It was just about the time Gladys turned twenty-one that she first saw Vernon Presley. She spotted him during one of her trips to Roy Martin's grocery store on Lake Street. He was four years younger than she—they would later laugh about the fact that they met just a week after he turned seventeen—but he was a handsome young man who always stood out at local dances. The Presley name was well known in Lee County, and Gladys knew a great deal about the family. Vernon's curly brown hair, blue eyes, and distinguished air made a marvelous first impression. The next day, Gladys asked a girlfriend to point out the Presley house, and she discovered that Vernon lived with his mother and father on Old Saltillo Road. Jessie Presley liked to call his home "the big house," because it had four rooms, whereas most of the East Tupelo shacks were shotgun arrangements with one big room divided up for sleeping and eating.

Once Gladys and Vernon met, friends called it a "whirlwind courtship." The physical attraction between them was immediate, and both shared an abiding disdain for conventional morality. While they were both considered fine upstanding people, there was some concern that Vernon was only seventeen and Gladys already twenty-one years old. Pressure from each family over the age difference, coupled with their own shared sense of rebellion against convention, contributed to their decision to marry quickly.

Gladys was simply swept off her feet. Not only did Vernon, a well-dressed young dandy who had wooed many young girls, talk about becoming a union electrician (a role he would later attempt to foist upon Elvis), but he had grand plans for their future family life. Star struck, Gladys was too overwhelmed to check or challenge any of Vernon's tales. When Gladys's young sister Clettes asked about Vernon, Gladys responded by introducing her to Vernon's brother, Vester, whom Clettes eventually ended up marrying. As for Gladys and Vernon, it took less than eight weeks for them to elope.

During those weeks, as Gladys Love Smith settled into the idea that she had found her man, there was still time for dating at the local roller-skating rink. It cost a nickel to roller-skate all night. Afterwards they would walk home holding hands. The roller-skating rink was located at the end of Main Street, and the long walk home gave them time to talk. It was an idyllic period as they spooned in the moonlight and planned their future. They were from the same socio-economic class, and it was obvious that they had a lot in common.

When they decided to marry, Vernon borrowed three dollars from Marshall Brown, and they took a Saturday ride to Pontotoc County. In the small hamlet of Verona on June 17, 1933, Vernon Presley made out an application for a marriage license. Since Gladys was born in Pontotoc County, she had no trouble convincing the clerk of the circuit court, J. M. Gates, that everything was fine. The marriage license was granted and the ceremony took place that very afternoon. Not only did Marshall Brown's three dollars pay for the wedding license, but Marshall and Vona Mae Brown, who came along for the nuptials, also took the Presleys out for a post-wedding dinner.

The first problem for the newlyweds was to find a permanent home. When Vona Mae Presley married Marshall Brown, there was an understanding about "family"—it was a foregone conclusion that Vernon and Gladys would be invited to stay. Although a temporary arrangement, it still placed a heavy strain on the Brown family. It was during this period that Gladys learned that Vernon had not told his parents he was married. He feared Jessie's reaction. Vernon's dad continually berated his son for being shiftless. When he was fifteen, Vernon was kicked out of the house, and he boarded with friends for portions of the next two years. Jessie Presley not only hated Vernon, but Jessie blamed him for his own unhappy marriage, continually belittling his son and suggesting that he leave the area. With Vernon's parents living on Berry Street, it was nice to have a room at 510 1/2 Maple Street in South Tupelo. Fearing his daddy's wrath, Vernon was thus able to keep his marriage to Gladys a secret.

Gladys Presley was a realistic woman. She realized from the start that Vernon was a dreamer. He had no real employment skills and no down-to-earth plans for the future. "He was like a beautiful baby and Gladys was his mother," Elvis' Memphis school chum Jim Denson recalled. Neighbors remember the Presleys as happy, but they described Vernon as childlike. His handsome face, glad-handing personality, and sense of romance seemed enough to satisfy Gladys, however.

Few realized how hard it was for Vernon. He put up a false front for most people. The smooth speech, spectacular good looks, and calm personality belied Vernon's inner emotions. He was constantly questioning his own manhood. His father was so harsh that Vernon developed a massive inferiority complex. On the outside, Vernon was boisterous, confident, and full of big talk, a bluff to hide a highly insecure and erratic

personality. Elvis would later exhibit many of the same character traits. In his early years, Elvis watched his father handle pressure and in turn formed his own responses in later life as a celebrity. It was his grandmother Minnie Mae who impressed Elvis the most, however.

A strong woman who defended her rights, Minnie Mae Presley often challenged Jessie's authority. She hollered at him publicly for disgracing her son, something which developed a special bond between Minnie Mae and Elvis that lasted a lifetime. According to many Tupelo residents, there were frequent encounters between Jessie and Minnie Mae, a great many of them witnessed by Elvis. A good example of these altercations occurred one Sunday in front of the Assembly of God church on the sixth anniversary of Vernon and Gladys marriage. Minnie Mae gave Jessie a severe tongue-lashing: "Look at him," Minnie screamed. "He thinks he's better than us. The 'lawyer' is what he calls himself," Minnie continued. "Tells his boy he's no good. Just an awful man," Minnie concluded. Vernon looked embarrassed and Jessie shook his fist. There was an awkward silence in front of the church. The Presleys quietly walked to their car, Jessie with fire in his eyes.

What was the reason for Jessie Presley's hostility? The answer is that, once he found out about it, he considered Vernon too young to be married. Wasn't Vernon only seventeen years old, Jessie would scream, when he and Gladys were married? For years Jessie had demonstrated a hatred for his own wife, an attitude that was easily re-directed towards Gladys. Often violent, Jessie thought nothing of throwing things around the house. His tirades bothered Minnie Mae, and she asked Jessie to leave her son alone. Vernon was doing the best that he could. Minnie Mae risked her personal safety defending her son, and Vernon never forgot his mother's kindness.

It was difficult for Vernon to talk to his dad. One day, however, as Vernon walked to the corner of Berry and Adams Streets, he encountered his father. They talked for a few minutes and settled their differences. Jessie even invited his son to stay at the Presley house. The astonishing turnabout in their relationship didn't surprise close friends. The mercurial Presley personality vacillated between friendship and hatred, a characteristic of the father-son relationship that had simply resurfaced because of Gladys' forceful personality. Jessie had ended up liking her, for he believed that she could straighten out his son.

Jessie suggested that Vernon purchase a lot next door to his own house. Orville Bean owned a small piece of property that sold for $180. It was ideally suited to build a small structure. Bean lent Vernon the money for the house and charged him rent until he paid off

The Presley's East Tupelo "shotgun" house.

Part of the living quarters side of the house.

the loan. The small building Vernon constructed with help from his father and brother Vester was a classic shotgun shack, a two-room house typical of the times. Stone piles were used for a foundation, and wood, paint, and wallpaper completed the task. Once it was finished, though, Vernon never remodeled the home or painted it again. It was a woefully inadequate, small house; nevertheless, it was the Presley's first real home.

Jesse Garon and Elvis Aron

When the Tennessee Valley Authority opened in November 1934, President Franklin D. Roosevelt visited Tupelo. There was a great deal of celebrating. The TVA brought electricity to East Tupelo, and residents were the only ones in the city to have electrical lines built in their neighborhood (the more affluent residents of Tupelo proper didn't yet have such access). Although the politics of the New South presented opportunities for the average person to reap new comforts of this type, for the most part the Presley household didn't seek any direct benefits from such changes. For example, they continued to use oil lamps, and never connected their home to the TVA electricity. There were just some advances that Vernon couldn't accept or afford. At the time, the Presleys adhered to an established routine and lived a life that had few surprises.

Gladys continued to walk downtown to the Tupelo Garment Factory, where she spent ten hours a day cutting patterns. Drudgery wasn't drudgery because she was happy. It seemed that everyone at work was married, and the Presley's circle of friends expanded to include co-workers Faye Harris and Annie Presley. They were "factory girls" who, like Gladys, had recently mar-

ried, and their friendships created a sense of camaraderie both at work and afterward. On weekends the couples often went roller skating, and took turns having potluck dinners. Sales Presley, Noah's son, often came by with his wife, Annie, to eat dinner. It was an idyllic time for Vernon and Gladys as they enjoyed the honeymoon phase of their marriage.

Annie Presley became one of Gladys' closest friends. They talked at length about children, family, and the future. In long talks, Gladys praised Annie's husband, Sales, and his father Noah, both of whom had developed into responsible husbands and had learned to appreciate having a family. Gladys, as she reminded Annie, wished for the same in Vernon when they finally did have a child. But they were still young people and had other things on their minds.

Over that first spring, summer, and early autumn, the Presleys and their friends talked endlessly about their future plans. They would also sing spirituals and country music tunes together on the front porches of their homes. Vester Presley was a frequent guest, and he brought along his guitar. In addition to traditional spirituals, Gladys suggested that they sing Jimmie Rodgers' "Corinna, Corinna." It had been a favorite of hers for years, and Gladys loved to show off her vocal talents. It was a festive time and the Presleys celebrated their innocent youth. Finally, a welcome surprise changed the household forever.

A year after their marriage, Gladys informed Vernon that she was pregnant. Vernon was overjoyed. In her fifth month, however, Gladys became uncomfortable. With no previous pregnancy experience, she had no idea what to expect. She wondered why she felt so poorly. It was not long before Dr. William Robert Hunt informed Gladys that she was going to have twins. The Presleys planned carefully for their new family. They would sometimes go to dinner at Clyde Reese's cafe, sitting in a corner for hours, laughing and talking. Everyone agreed that Gladys and Vernon grew closer than ever due to the anticipated arrival of the twins.

Gladys was excited about having a family. She had a feeling that they would be boys, and picked out names for them early on. (The myth has grown that Gladys and Vernon didn't know they were going to have twins. Nothing could be farther from the truth. Tupelo residents remember the anticipation and expectation that Gladys would have twins, as it was a hereditary family trait.) She chose the names Jesse, a tribute to Vernon's dad, and Elvis, Vernon's middle name. A bright young woman, Gladys realized that grandchildren would help cement her shaky personal relationship with Jessie and Minnie Mae Presley.

On Tuesday, January 8, 1935, at about 4:00 a.m., Gladys gave birth to two boys at 306 Old Saltillo Road. Not only was it a bitterly cold night, but the northeastern corner of Mississippi was covered with a sheet of freezing sleet. The first born, Jesse Garon, was dead at birth, but thirty-five minutes later Dr. Hunt delivered a healthy infant. The small baby, Elvis Aron Presley, was handled delicately by the midwife, Edna Robinson. Like many superstitious country folks, the Presleys believed that both a doctor and midwife should be present at birth, a wise precaution that required good timing, as Dr. Hunt was on call by hundreds of people.

It was a lengthy birth, but Dr. Hunt, an experienced physician, eased the problems of a difficult pregnancy. Not only was Hunt a well-trained medical man, but he had a mania for keeping accurate records. Of the 1,854 babies he delivered before he retired, Dr. Hunt had only six cases as difficult as Gladys Presley's. He also noted in his records that the Presleys could not pay the fifteen dollar fee. Instead, Hunt billed the local welfare agency. After the birth, Dr. Hunt sent Gladys and Elvis to the Tupelo hospital. She was exhausted and appeared anemic, and he wanted to guarantee Elvis' good health. After all, Dr. Hunt reasoned, welfare would pick up the bill.

When Gladys returned from the hospital, she was a different woman. She was irritable, often irrational, and the fact that she never had any more children suggests the seriousness of the birth process. The trauma of childbirth was an event she discussed regularly for the rest of her life. There were visions and images of death that she could never shake from her memory. The day after the birth of the dead infant, Jesse Garon, he was placed in a small coffin in the Presley's living room. It was common for Southern families to hold elaborate funerals at home for dead infants, a method of

grieving designed to show respect for the deceased. Since poor Southern parents couldn't afford cemetery markers, they used the funeral as an elaborate means of showing family responsibility. The wailing, weeping, and crying was not only a sign of respect that Mississippi folks liked to accord dead infants, but it made them feel that they had gone to the furthest limits for their children.

Jesse Garon Presley was buried in an unmarked grave in Priceville Cemetery, just three miles northeast of Tupelo on Feemster Lake Road. For the rest of his life, Elvis wondered about Jesse Garon's death. Gladys spent much of her life telling Elvis that his dead brother was identical to him in every way. As a young man Elvis was told that the bad side of his personality made him take the wrong path. When Elvis decided the right way, it was due to his brother's spirit. Evidence that Elvis believed his mother's ludicrous stories is strong. Vernon and Gladys believed that Elvis was a "special creation" sent by the Lord, and they speculated that he had a special destiny. From the moment he could understand, Elvis was told that he was special. The Presleys treated their little prince in a deferential manner; he was often given presents that were not in keeping with the family's financial position. The bicycles, clothes, cars, and continual gift-giving may have had more to do with Vernon and Gladys' guilt over Jesse Garon's death than with their desire to please Elvis, however. There wasn't anything that Vernon and Gladys wouldn't do to keep Elvis happy.

When Elvis became a musical superstar, he was often asked offensive questions about his dead twin brother. Not only were these questions in poor taste, but they often humiliated him. Much to his credit, Elvis never lost his temper, and his perspective on Jesse Garon's death was always a healthy one. He remembered Gladys' explanation of his twin brother's demise: the good Lord had allowed Elvis to live so that he could fulfill Jesse Garon's destiny. Still, it was a tough burden for Elvis. His brother was forever an enigmatic shadow, a weight on his shoulders that he could never escape. There is no doubt that Elvis felt guilt about his brother's death. A superstitious couple, the Presleys dwelled upon what Jesse Garon might have accomplished during his lifetime. Until her death in 1958, Gladys Presley would describe Elvis' twin brother in detail to friends.

Elvis' birthdate meant he was a Capricorn. The traits for this sign are a great deal of ambition, a persevering personality, an ability to be diplomatic with people, and the patience of a priest. Not only have biographers gone way beyond good taste in speculating about the circumstances surrounding Elvis' birth, they have tied his personality to that of his dead brother through intricately created absurdities that defy reason. A good example of such nonsense was the ridiculous story that Elvis' stillborn brother's spirit had been transferred to Elvis. Albert Goldman's biography, *Elvis*, has analyzed the twin theory at great length. Goldman claims that Gladys taught Elvis that Jesse Garon was alive in Elvis' soul. Gossip-mongering newspapers like the *National Enquirer* have persisted in reporting this tale as fact. Goldman concludes that Elvis believed that he bore the sign of an identical twin. Indeed, during his lifetime, Elvis allegedly pointed to an odd web of skin stretched between the second and third toes of his right foot as evidence that he was an identical twin. Elvis' beliefs were reinforced by Gladys' persistent story that the twins were identical, as well as Southern superstitions concerning twins which dominated Gladys' thinking.

Vernon Presley was another mythmaker. As a means of proving that Elvis was special, Vernon told about the night of Elvis' birth. It seems a blue light appeared in the sky. This was a sign of God's will to keep Elvis alive, Vernon maintained, and Gladys agreed with him. As late as 1970, Vernon recounted this story for Kathy Westmoreland, one of Elvis' backup singers, just before a concert in Portland, Oregon. He also told *Good Housekeeping* magazine that his father, Jessie, placed his hand upon Gladys' stomach after Jesse Garon was born dead and announced there was another baby in the womb. This preposterous story tells more about Vernon's mental balance, or lack of it, than it does about the birth. One of the persistent problems during Elvis Presley's life, the realities of which were often obscured as a result, was the necessity to correct Vernon's tall tales. The supposed "truth" about the Presleys' marriage, the birth of Elvis, and the poverty of the Tupelo and early Memphis years have received an inordinate amount of unfounded publicity. Most of the media reports are highly speculative and have no factual basis.

From 1935 through 1937, the Presleys struggled. A child added new pressures. Gladys had difficulty adjusting to her new life. The birth not only caused her serious health problems, but family finances suffered. After she returned from the hospital, Gladys was not her old self. She worried constantly about her young son. When she went out to the store, Dot Rutledge came over to watch Elvis. She was amazed by Gladys' love and devotion, but noticed a marked change in Gladys' personality. No longer a happy-go-lucky person, Gladys was now somber and quiet, characteristics not evident in her earlier years.

The reason for Gladys' changing personality was the death of her mother. Doll Smith's death was not unexpected, but it was still a crushing blow to her daugh-

The Presley family in the late 1930s.

ter. When Doll was buried at Spring Hill Cemetery next to her husband Bob, Gladys lost a part of her family history. Gladys' friends remarked that she was unnerved by the death, and that the future just didn't seem as bright anymore. Shortly after Doll's death, Ann Mansell Smith passed away, and was buried next to her husband Obe. Although the Presleys were not close to Granny Smith, the successive deaths exerted enormous psychological and emotional stress upon Gladys. Her security was threatened by the loss of her family.

Gladys, always the solid surrogate mother to her own mother and siblings, was frightened by the responsibility of being thrust into the role of a real mother so quickly. Vernon was no help. He was either out with his brother Vester, or selling moonshine around Lee County or in Memphis. Much like his father, Vernon concocted outlandish schemes in pursuit of quick wealth. None of his plans ever bore fruit. Real jobs were scarce in the midst of the Great Depression, and Vernon had trouble finding employment much less holding a job. In any case, the idea of steady employment and punching a time clock was foreign to Vernon Presley. He lacked the personal discipline and responsibility to report to work each day, so that whenever he filled out a job application his record was spotty and imprecise. It was not that Vernon lacked a responsible attitude. He had simply never been trained to realize that not reporting to work might cost him his job. On days that he overslept, Vernon reasoned that if he awoke after work had already started, it was simply better just to go back to bed.

Even as she grieved over her mother's death, Gladys faced another potential disaster. On April 5, 1936, at 9:04 on a Sunday evening, a tornado roared through Tupelo. Despite widespread and heavy damage, the Presley house was not hit. (To Gladys, it was a miracle that the Presley home was not struck, a happenstance that reinforced her notion that Elvis had a special destiny.) The tornado killed more than two hundred people in the area around Tupelo and injured almost five hundred others. It was impossible to assess the full extent of the damage, but federal officials listed the destruction in the millions of dollars.

One local resident recalled how, at 9:09 p.m., the Mississippi countryside stood eerily hushed, and misty-eyed citizens began emerging to view the aftermath of the storm that had leveled forty-eight blocks of Tupelo streets. Not only was a four-mile swath sliced through the town, but in the black section near Park Lane, Shakerag, which was hit hardest, dead bodies littered the streets. Local churches were turned into temporary hospitals, and clergymen spoke quietly of God's wrath. At the city hall, the Red Cross set up an emergency shelter to feed and administer to the medical needs of local citizens. There was a crisis atmosphere and a sense of urgency. The five-minute tornado had caused record damage, but large amounts of federal aid quickly rebuilt Tupelo. Nevertheless, the feeling of doom and disaster that the catastrophe wrought was not easily forgotten, and Tupelo residents were nervous and jittery for the next year.

Gladys Presley attributed the storm to God's wrath. When the tornado struck, she was attending a local Baptist church. Vernon's father, Jessie, came to the church and persuaded the family to come to his home. There was an overwhelming feeling of family as they huddled together amid the fury of the storm. Miraculously, no one was hurt. Gladys attributed this good fortune to religious protection. Gains Mansell delivered a special sermon at the First Assembly of God church emphasizing how God had blessed Tupelo, saving its most devout Christians from the storm's path.

Although her own congregation was secure, Gladys was horrified to discover that St. Mark's Methodist Church had burned to the ground. For Gladys, this was an ominous sign. She needed counseling, and went to the Reverend Mansell for comfort. He calmed her, suggesting that all churches couldn't avoid being affected by natural disasters.

As a result of the tornado, many other people received spiritual help from Reverend Mansell, and his standing in the local community grew stronger. By 1937,

it was evident that Reverend Mansell's fortunes were improving. He had personally built a new church, so that the First Assembly of God worshippers were no longer forced to meet in a tent. The new two-room wooden church on Adams Street had a crudely-painted "Welcome" sign over the doorway. For her part, Gladys Presley found renewed faith following the tornado, and over time she recovered from the difficult birth of her son and the deaths of her mother and grandmother.

Parchman

Just as Gladys regained her health, tragedy struck once again. Vernon Presley, Travis Smith, and Lether Gable were arrested on forgery charges. On November 17, 1937, the *Tupelo Daily Journal*, in a front-page story, reported that the three men—Vernon's name was spelled "Pressley"—had been indicted for forgery and required to submit $500 bail bonds, although the exact reasons for the charge remained murky. As the story later came out, it was alleged that Vernon's duplicity had developed following the sale of a hog to Orville Bean for four dollars. Unhappy with himself over accepting such a small sum, Vernon altered Bean's check to reflect a forty-dollar sum, an amount which Vernon, upon reflection, thought was the sow's true worth. Following strong pressure from his cohorts—with special encouragement from the dull-witted Travis Smith—combined with the influence of a great deal of moonshine, Vernon not only altered the check but quickly cashed it. Basically, he saw no harm in what he was doing. The Presleys needed money for food and he succumbed to a desperate plan. It was Vernon's ability to rationalize just this type of behavior that helped keep him from steady employment. Vernon, although not known as a rational or deep thinker, could usually explain away any action. No one in Tupelo was surprised.

The sheriff and local officials kept no detailed record of the specific charges or the arrest. Had it not been for the front-page story in the *Tupelo Daily Journal*, the incident might have faded into obscurity. There is no doubt the sheriff and Orville Bean were good old boys who controlled local politics, and so there was no need for a careful investigation. It was typical class-based Southern justice, and Vernon, his attention already focused beyond his own wrongdoing, was infuriated about the sheriff's casual attitude and incensed over the apparent disregard for his rights.

On January 4, 1938, two bonds were filed in the local court. Vernon's dad, Jessie, bailed out Travis Smith. Lether Gable's bond was put up by two friends. Vernon was left in jail, where he remained for the next six months. It was a crushing blow, and his own father had delivered the ultimate insult. To Vernon, Jessie had made him look like a criminal.

Before long, Vernon, in an arrogant and boisterous manner, announced that he would plead not guilty. Noah Presley, the mayor of East Tupelo, came to Vernon's aid and pressured Orville Bean to reconsider prosecuting the three offenders. They were simply young men who had made a mistake. As a result of Noah Presley's intervention, Bean reconsidered whether or not to prosecute, but Vernon languished in jail six months while Bean decided. Apparently, someone in the sheriff's office finally convinced Bean to take the case to court. Vernon Presley had made a number of enemies in the police department because of his bootlegging activity, and local police finally had a way to get even with him.

Gladys Presley was one of many people who believed in Vernon. She regularly came to visit him three days a week, bringing food and encouragement. It cemented the marriage. The Reverend Gains Mansell was another of Vernon's staunch defenders. He chastised Orville Bean for his lack of Christian charity. Noah Presley, the mayor of East Tupelo, continued to press for mercy.

It was all to no avail. Orville Bean could not be persuaded to drop the charges. Bean argued that Vernon was worthless and no good. When Bean hired him for odd jobs, Vernon seldom completed the work. Vernon was lazy, arrogant, and dishonest, Bean maintained, and this was not the first time that Presley had hoodwinked him. The intensity of Bean's feeling against Vernon suggests that there was bad blood between the two men that went back many years. When Bean used the term "long hungry" to describe Vernon, it was the worst form of insult, a label that called a person worthless in the local colloquial slang. The long period of personal animosity between Vernon and Orville Bean didn't help the prospects for a fair trial.

Finally, on May 24, 1938, Vernon Presley, Lether Gable, and Travis Smith were tried before Judge Thomas J. Johnston, who was known as a hanging judge. The long period in jail prompted Vernon to plead guilty. Gable and Smith also pleaded guilty. Judge Johnston then ordered each defendant to serve a term of three years in the state penitentiary.

This meant only one thing—Parchman Farm. It was the meanest, nastiest prison in Mississippi's Delta. Not only was it racially mixed, but Parchman was a back-breaking work camp. For six days each week the men toiled for ten to twelve hours under the hot Delta sun. They wore blue-and-white-striped pajamas, and guards stood by with menacing shotguns. A man's dignity was constantly at stake, and living conditions were primitive. The guards kept "Black Annie," an eight-foot leather belt, close at hand, and Vernon had to constantly watch his back. Inmates sometimes worked on private farms,

so Vernon was often faced with plantation owners who reminded him of his nemesis, Orville Bean. The debasing and dehumanizing atmosphere at Parchman Farm ultimately made Vernon vow to change his ways.

The summer of 1938 was a difficult time for Gladys Presley. She went to all the revival meetings that came through town. The First Assembly of God church continued to be a strong support. Elvis attended church with his mother, and he had a pleasant, well-groomed look. Much of Gladys' security was tied to her son.

Every other Sunday, Gladys and Elvis would make the long trip across Mississippi to Parchman Farm. To keep Vernon's spirits up, Gladys visited him dutifully. The prison allowed conjugal visits, and Gladys and Vernon found renewed strength in their marriage. Vernon's brother, Vester, often volunteered to make the five-hour drive, and F. L. Bobo, manager of the local hardware store, often drove them, too, marvelling at Gladys's courage.

Although Vernon was not released until February 6, 1939, he had little trouble at Parchman Farm. He reported to work, and obeyed the sergeant in charge.

Current facade of the Tupelo hardware store formerly operated by F. L. Bobo.

Vernon got along well with his fellow inmates, who were roughly eighty percent black; from his days living across from the Shakerag district, Vernon had always gotten on well with blacks. While Vernon was in Parchman Farm, Bukka White's music was recorded by Alan Lomax, and there was constantly blues music in the air.

After he was sent away, most people just tended to forget about Vernon Presley; he was ignored as the black sheep son of a poor local family. Since Gladys continued to believe in her husband, however, she single-handedly persuaded more than one hundred Tupelo citizens to write letters to the Mississippi prison system on Vernon's behalf.

With Vernon in Parchman Farm, Gladys was faced with money and housing problems. For a brief period, she moved in with her first cousin, Frank Richards, who lived at 510 1/2 Maple Street in South Tupelo. The living situation was a strain because Frank's wife, Leona, worked in the nearby Mid-South Laundry, and Gladys was used as a baby sitter. It was not long before Gladys complained that she couldn't hold down her own job, raise her cousin's children, and watch Elvis, too. Even though Gladys, like Leona, went to work each day, it was Gladys that Frank Richards expected to come home and take charge of the house. It was just too much of a strain, even though one of Gladys' sisters, Lillian, came to Tupelo and helped out during this period. Most of the Smiths, Lillian included, lived in the country a few miles from town. While this helped Elvis develop a strong sense of family, it didn't protect him from everything.

It was during Vernon's imprisonment that Elvis began sleepwalking, an affliction that followed him throughout his life. In the last six months of 1938, it was a major problem for the three-year-old boy. Since Gladys worked hard all day, she often slept through Elvis' sleepwalking episodes. Some members of the family reported that Vernon and Gladys themselves had sleepwalking experiences, indicating a hereditary condition. In all probability, Elvis was simply distraught over the absence of his daddy. Like any small boy, he didn't understand the reason for Vernon's disappearance. He often wandered downtown Tupelo and looked in the shop windows. Many people remember the little, blonde kid talking in a squeaky voice about his daddy coming home.

While Gladys and Elvis lived with the Richards, they began planning for Vernon's return home. During her visits to Parchman, Gladys noticed many changes in her husband. She believed that he was maturing and there were strong signs of repentance for his wayward past. It was a time in which Gladys and Vernon made plans for their future. Most Tupelo residents were surprised by Gladys' declaration that prison had helped Vernon. Yet, she was right.

Prison was a positive experience for Vernon. Not only did he develop decent work habits, but he pondered his future. The Mississippi Prison System archives are sparse in this period, but they offer some insights into Parchman Farm. The prison maintained a rigorous six-day work schedule and tight discipline. White prisoners were given special privileges and Vernon Presley was able to adjust to the orders of the camp sergeant. Eventually, he was able to lead a group of men in a foreman-type position. There was a work incentive program at Parchman, and Vernon's group was highly productive. He received high marks from his peers for his leadership qualities.

The fine record that Vernon established at Parchman led to an early release. There was no parole system in Mississippi, and the general attitude toward prison was not as severe as it would become in later years. Many people like Vernon made a small mistake and spent more time in jail for it than hardened criminals. On February 6, 1939, when Vernon was released from Parchman, he had learned a valuable lesson about rules, the work ethic, and the law. Although he had served nine months, he left prison a muscular, well-conditioned young man. Friends marveled that he looked better than when he entered.

When Vernon returned to Tupelo he found that people were not as friendly. His father Jessie was critical of everything Vernon did and continually berated him. Much to his credit, Vernon refused to take any more abuse. He had a showdown with his dad. They stood out on Jessie's porch hollering and shaking their fists. Then Vernon left, informing his parents that he was going to establish his total independence.

The first fruits of self-reliance were slow in coming, however, as the Presleys continued to live with Frank and Leona Richards. Not only was it an uncomfortable situation, but it was frustratingly difficult for Vernon to secure full-time employment. Apparently, there was a great deal of suspicion and hostility directed at him because of his prison term and he was forced to seek work out of town. There were government handbills, advertisements at city hall, and ads in the newspapers for WPA jobs, so he applied to the Works Progress Administration. The WPA was part of President Franklin D. Roosevelt's New Deal, and the jobs were often good ones. Vernon saw these opportunities as the only ones he could pursue.

With war raging in Europe, there was a chance for employment in the shipyard industry. Eventually, Vernon accepted a job in another part of Mississippi. Leaving Tupelo was not easy for Vernon and Gladys, but they had no other choice. No one was willing to hire Vernon. The Presleys moved to Pascagoula, an area that serviced ships brought in from New Orleans. Located in the Southeastern corner of Mississippi, Pascagoula was a depressing industrial town. It had the appearance of an instant city. The streets were lined with tin shacks hastily thrown up to house the new shipyard workers.

When they drove to Pascagoula in the spring of 1939, the Presleys were joined by their cousin Sales Presley. Sales' wife, Annie, thought the move would be fun. They would live away from Jessie and Minnie Mae and have some privacy. This dream turned out to be a nightmare, however. Housing near the Pascagoula shipyards was primitive. The small, shotgun shacks were cold in the winter and hot in the summer. The influx of unskilled labor created weekend problems due to excessive moonshine consumption and the fact that the rural Mississippi workers were angry over the way that the bosses treated them. While the money was good, the quality of life left a great deal to be desired.

The sojourn at the Pascagoula shipyard lasted for eight months. From April 15 to December 15, 1939, Vernon and Gladys Presley lived in a small, one-room cabin made mostly of screen, surviving through a hot Mississippi summer and into what was shaping up as an impossibly cold winter. Gladys refused to stay for Christmas. It was not a job, she told Vernon, it was mule work.

As a result of the Pascagoula experience, Gladys once again developed religious zeal. She prayed that Vernon would develop a sense of responsibility, and lectured Elvis about acquiring one of his own. To everyone around Gladys, it was obvious that the strain was too much. Elvis, who was about to turn five, didn't understand the household tensions. The real reason for the developing family problems was the fact that Gladys was left alone with too much time to think; she didn't work in Pascagoula, found the town depressing, and felt trapped in a set of circumstances beyond her control.

While Vernon was in prison, Gladys had begun attending religious revivals again. When a revival came through Pascagoula, she enthusiastically welcomed it. She also attended a number of local churches. Gladys told Annie Presley that she was comforted by the elaborate church buildings. The First Assembly of God church in Tupelo was still her ballast, but Gladys needed a great deal of religious support. It gave her hope. Perhaps Vernon was really the changed man that he confessed he was after leaving Parchman Farm.

Following the experience in Pascagoula, the Presleys returned to Tupelo only to find that Vernon's dad, Jessie, had sold their Old Saltillo Road home. There is no record of the sale, but it appears that Jessie took over the home's payments when Vernon went to prison. Not only was Vernon exasperated with his dad, but he realized again how little regard Jessie had for him. The Presleys moved into Vester's Reese Street house. Vester's wife Clettes complained about overcrowding, and the Presleys soon found a rental on Kelly Street. There was a great deal of concern about a war, and Vernon wondered what impact it would have upon his future.

On December 7, 1941, the Japanese bombed Pearl Harbor, and direct American involvement in World War II began. Vernon Presley was now the sole support of his family, so he was deferred from active military duty. Once the war broke out, the Tupelo economy continued to improve, and local businessmen began hiring. Unfortunately, Vernon was still not a worker that most Tupelo employers wanted. During part of World War II, therefore, he worked in Memphis. This was the reason that the Presleys moved north after the war.

The Great Depression and the first month of American participation in World War II were important watersheds for the Presley family. The Parchman Farm experience brought Gladys and Vernon closer, and the maturing young Elvis became an integral part of the household. Economic opportunities during World War II allowed Vernon to make a living for the first time in his life. Elvis attended one of the more progressive schools in Mississippi, and people increasingly forgot Vernon's errant youthful past. The next seven years were to be happy and fruitful ones for the Presleys.

CHAPTER 4

Elvis In Tupelo:
The Adolescent Years, 1941-1948

From 1941 to 1948, Elvis Presley grew to adolescent maturity in Tupelo, now a small Mississippi town with an economy evolving around the railroad, local farming, and the steady growth of small industry. The best families lived west of the railroad tracks, while to the east itinerant workers, recent migrants, and the unemployed still occupied small shacks. The railroad tracks were a common social and economic dividing line in Southern towns. It was a convenient way of defining community power, and it created class lines that everyone understood. Tupelo, the Lee County seat, was the center of local government. Situated in the northeastern corner of Mississippi, halfway between Memphis and Birmingham, Tupelo's farmland was a mixture of alluvial soil and harsh brick-colored clay. Some farmers were prosperous while others barely eked out a marginal living. "The rich folks farm the good soil, and the poor folks farm the poor soil owned by the rich folks," Vernon Presley once remarked.

The New Tupelo

The small-town merchant like L.P. McCarty and the prosperous rancher like Orville Bean were the symbols of power, prestige, and wealth in Tupelo. It was a closed society with a definite caste system. But Tupelo, like many Southern farming communities, underwent cataclysmic changes during the 1930s. Roosevelt's New Deal brought important economic advancement to the Tupelo economy, and both the New Deal and World War II ended the old Southern way of life.

During the New Deal, a fish hatchery, a cotton mill, and a fertilizer plant developed Tupelo's industrial base. The old days of bleak civic poverty were replaced by a new middle-class prosperity. In 1936, Tupelo was the first city to acquire electrical power from the Tennessee Valley Authority. The city's library bookmobile was also the first to serve Mississippi's urban and rural poor. Miss Frankie Erck, the children's librarian, made the bookmobile a special project. She allowed the children to display their art around the traveling library branch. The objective was to inspire an interest in reading.

The growth of the local economy created a reinvigorated downtown business section. As new shops, large and small, opened, local citizens had a choice of goods. Reed's department store was the first in America to hold a twenty-four-hour sale. Local citizens were proud of their progressive economic traditions. There was a feeling of community pride and a firm commitment to a more prosperous way of life.

The shacks or slum housing and abject poverty depicted in many Elvis biographies existed primarily in the black section of town, Shakerag. Like East Tupelo, it was located just over the Mobile and Ohio and the St. Louis and San Francisco (Frisco) railroad tracks. Shakerag's nondescript shacks were alive with music day and night, a sharp contrast to the dreary, monotonous routines of work-a-day life. The rough blues tunes coming out of the black section were a release for the hard-working population. As the maids, cooks, house servants, and field hands trudged back to Shakerag each evening, they were greeted by the pungent smell of home-cooked food. Many whites hung out in Shakerag, where they bought the best moonshine in town while gambling and listening to the music.

The East Tupelo area where Elvis had been born was a quarter of a mile past Shakerag on a hill on the other side of Mud and Oldtown Creeks. While Elvis often commented that he grew up living next to the black section of Tupelo, what he failed to point out was that a large body of water between the two districts made the black section quite separate and distinct from East Tupelo. Actually, Elvis identified with Shakerag largely because of the music. Also, his religious experiences were similar to those of his black neighbors. He attended the First Assembly of God church, and was weaned on a fervent evangelical Protestant faith.

In the end, there were very few similarities between white and black Tupelo once the musical comparisons were exhausted. To begin with, white Tupelo residents secured jobs, adequate housing, and an acceptable lifestyle. Consequently, World War II's temporary economic prosperity made it easier for Vernon and Gladys Presley to earn a living. Oblivious to the wartime emergency, young Elvis attended the East Tupelo Consolidated School on Lake Street, a five-minute walk for Elvis and Gladys. This school was part of a model system, with activities spanning two buildings. One was for the elementary school and the other the high school; generous taxes from large farmers and businessmen made the school progressive. There was pride in the increased literacy in Lee County, and with a classroom size of only thirty students the school district received statewide recognition. East Tupelo Consolidated School superintendent Ross Lawhon was instrumental in creating this system. He demanded discipline, respect, and community pride. The term "Tupeloan" was used to describe local boosters. There was a sense of destiny and security in Lee County.

Education

In this environment, Elvis Presley received an education that served him well for the rest of his life. The strict emphasis upon reading, writing, and public speaking was a valuable asset to Elvis in his later career, although the only hint of Elvis' future predilection for show business at the time was his strong interest in music and a willingness to perform. As a student, Elvis was generally well liked, and he participated in student government. His class pictures at Lawhon Elementary School show a young man in a clean white shirt wearing a freshly starched pair of shiny overalls.

An important part of Elvis' early development was Gladys Presley's insistence that he learn to read, write, and speak properly. Throughout his life Elvis expressed himself in an articulate manner and charmed the critics with his erudite manner. Elvis was fortunate to attend a progressive and academically sound Southern school.

In Tupelo, there was not only a sense of popular democracy but pride in community accomplishment. As early as the 1920s, East Tupelo citizens had lobbied for a modern school system. The issue of quality education was one that everyone, despite birth or economic status, took seriously. The bankers, the moonshiners, the shopkeepers, the farmers, and the casual laborers worked together to achieve this middle-class American educational dream. When the East Tupelo Consolidated School was constructed in 1926, many citizens hoped this would end references to "the wrong side of the tracks." Unfortunately, the snide comments from downtown Tupelo residents continued.

The first Tupelo high school class graduated in 1934. By 1936, East Tupelo could point with pride to a modern business department in the local school system. Within a year, vocational, agricultural, and home economics programs were an integral part of the educational curriculum. Aggressive political pressure from local citizens created a WPA lunch program, new street construction, expanded parks, and modern school playgrounds. By the mid-1940s more than seven hundred students and twenty-six teachers worked harmoniously together. The entire South was undergoing rapid educational change, and the East Tupelo Consolidated School District was an example of the area's commitment to excellence. The changes in Southern education were important. They improved the quality of life, and encouraged families to pursue a middle-class lifestyle. In the Tupelo schools, there was strong emphasis upon

developing writing skills, and Elvis took advantage of special courses in writing and grammar. Contrary to the stereotypes surrounding Elvis' background, East Tupelo wasn't a haven for poor white trash; rather, it was a thriving, progressive community.

East Tupelo's strong educational emphasis prompted parents from the nearby areas of Priceville, Briar Ridge, Oak Hill, Bissell, Beach Springs, Moore's Crossroads, Mooreville, and Auburn to send their sons and daughters to school there. School superintendent Lawhon, a no-nonsense disciplinarian with a penchant for community relations, believed that football, the school band, journalism, public speaking and writing contests created excellent community spirit. Local citizens applauded Lawhon's leadership.

The East Tupelo school system emphasized a strong academic curriculum. There was a yearly campaign to win the Lee County Literary Association's annual writing award. The writing contest, which became a popular local event in the 1920s, attests to important changes in Tupelo. For three straight years, an East Tupelo student was judged the best Lee County writer. By the time Elvis entered school, the local education system was rated one of Mississippi's best. Reading, writing, and math were the ingredients of a fine educational system, one that stressed the Three R's and also promoted patriotic, Christian education. To top things off, East Tupelo's band was the pride of the school system. Each year the East Tupelo band played at the Memphis Cotton Carnival.

In September 1941, Elvis enrolled in the East Tupelo Consolidated School District. The nation was jittery over the prospect of war, but the turmoil had little direct impact upon the Presleys owing to Vernon's deferment. Elvis attended Lawhon school on Briar Street. The principal, Aaron Morgan, spoke proudly of the elementary school, named for the legendary school superintendent, and students were expected to excel in all academic areas. As a result of the school's zealous attitude, Elvis' first school year was one of constant adjustment. Since Vernon was away from home for long periods of time, Elvis had trouble dealing with the disparity between his own home life and his classmates' stories about their comfortable family lives. Elvis' teachers reasoned that he was unable to come to grips with the painful realities of a weak father figure, and he complained continually about his daddy. Vernon Presley summarized these years succinctly: "Though we had friends and relatives, including my parents, the three of us formed our private world." It was a private world from which he was often absent, however.

Like many young mothers, Gladys Presley walked her son to school. He was a sheltered, shy child thrust into a school containing all twelve grades. It was an alien atmosphere. But Elvis profited from this experience. He received a quality education, and his early musical interests were awakened.

There were light and humorous moments during Elvis' grade school years. His first-grade friends chuckled when he persisted in using the word "duckling" to describe water. He also called milk "Butch," the name of his best friend. Although Elvis was well liked, he spent most of his time alone. This pattern persisted from the first through the third grades. Laverne Farrar Clayton, a cafeteria worker at the Lawhon Elementary School, recalls that Elvis "didn't have many friends; he didn't make friends easily. I don't ever remember him getting out of his yard. He was so lonesome, he would do anything to have somebody play with him." A reflective child with a penchant for solitude, Elvis was to grow into an adolescent who spent a great deal of time dreaming about his future. These youthful dreams were important ones in combatting his loneliness. Elvis' solitary nature seems to have been a direct result of Vernon Presley's frequent absences from home. Elvis yearned for close ties to his dad. Just as they were developing a more balanced father-son relationship, however, Vernon took a job in Memphis. While school kept Elvis busy, he nevertheless longed for a full-time father.

For a long time, Vernon Presley provided neither the economic security nor the emotional stability necessary to a young family. There were many family crises, prompting Vernon to promise Gladys time and again that he would change his errant ways. On one occasion, he came home late at night and declared that he had found Jesus, a ruse to explain why he had lost yet another job. Elvis' dad was a proud man who found it difficult to survive in the fluctuating economic conditions in Tupelo, and because he wasn't able to make a steady living, Vernon was often distant with Elvis.

On many occasions, however, Vernon displayed strong feelings for his son. A good example occurred during one of Elvis' childhood illnesses. After watching Elvis squirm in agony during a tonsillitis attack, Vernon blurted out that he was going to become a religious man. He confessed that he needed a fundamentally sound Christian faith to succeed. "That night I prayed to God that he would miraculously heal our child," Vernon recalled. Yet, signs of responsible behavior on the part of Vernon Presley persistently occurred only during family crises. Afterward, his fervent resolutions quickly dissipated, and the old deadbeat personality instantly returned. The result was that Gladys' determination to make her son successful grew. Vernon's maverick attitudes prompted her to continually push Elvis to improve himself. She was insistent that her son would not be like her husband.

There was a great deal of conflict within the Presley family over Elvis' education. Vernon frequently acted as if he was jealous of Gladys's educational goals for Elvis. To show his anger, for example, he might remark that his car needed a new window, and that if Elvis went to work the family could afford to repair the car. This was typical of Vernon's infantile attitude; it was also a means of establishing his authority. Years later, in February 1948, Gladys and Elvis went to the Lee County Library on Madison Street to fill out an application for a library card. Gladys had received a postcard from the librarian, Mary Moore Mitchell, extolling the virtues of reading. In response to the situation, Gladys tried to set up some family reading time during which Elvis and his parents would share some books. Vernon's response, as he vanished to talk with his friends at one of the local beer bars, was laughter. Behavior of this type on Vernon's part always bothered Elvis, further encouraging him to gravitate toward his mother. "Gladys was foolish about Elvis...just foolish," a Tupelo resident recalled. Undoubtedly, her influence reached deep into Elvis' character, and he did everything possible to please her. There was an intensity in Elvis' and Gladys' relationship that created a special bond.

During 1942, there were positive and dramatic changes in the Presleys' lives, improvements that stemmed from the disproportionately high wartime wages paid out in certain sectors of the economy during World War II, coupled with the general lack of consumer goods on which to spend such wages. Wartime rationing prompted the Presleys to save more than five hundred dollars. A large stocking stuffed with small change and dollar bills was kept under their bed. The money began accumulating when Vernon left Tupelo to work in a draft-deferred job in Memphis, and not only provided stability for the Presleys, but gave Elvis a feeling of security. With Vernon working in Memphis during the war, there was enough money for the Presley family to enjoy themselves.

During the week, Vernon stayed in a small rented room in Memphis. On Friday nights he drove home to Tupelo. It was a difficult time for the twenty-six-year-old; he was lonely and empty without his family. Still, he remarked to a close friend that the Memphis job had strengthened his marriage and his paternal feelings toward Elvis. His family, Vernon confided to another friend, was the most important part of his life. Despite Vernon's inner turmoil, it was a pleasant time for Elvis and his mother. A neighbor noted that Gladys' pride in her son was evident to even a casual observer. "Elvis was the cleanest child I ever saw," remarked the Lawhon school cook, a comment echoed by many Tupelo residents.

On top of the good wages and the diminished temptations on which to spend it, few people in East Tupelo realized that there was another reason behind Vernon's outgoing and happy appearance. The answer was a simple one. He made extra money by running moonshine from Tupelo to Memphis, where he had discovered that there was a demand for good, country-made whiskey. Each Monday morning, Vernon sped up Highway 78 to Memphis with a carload of Shakerag's best shine, sold his product and stuffed the money in a flour sack in the automobile's trunk. It was common for the Presleys to drive to Shakerag on weekends so that Vernon could stock up on moonshine. Elvis loved to go with his father so that he could listen to the Sanctified Church's choir practice. This black church used a guitar, tambourine, and piano to augment its choral group. The result was a big band sound, and Elvis never forgot how so few musicians were able to make so much music. In later years, Scotty Moore and Bill Black, Elvis' backup musicians, would be enlisted to re-create the full and forceful sound of the Sanctified Church choir.

There were other examples of Vernon's entrepreneurial activity. Although Elvis' father would not knowingly cheat anyone, he was a hustler who always looked for a quick buck. Since the late 1930s, Vernon had sold bootleg whiskey, so it was only natural to continue this business while working in Memphis. Another opportunity developed when Vernon discovered that there was a black market sugar ring in Tupelo, and he was able to make some nice profits from that rationed commodity.

Eventually, a warning from a local deputy sheriff ended this particular lucrative sideline, but Vernon continued to run whiskey even after the end of World War II until a local bootlegging ring told him to get out of the moonshine business, too. When the Presleys quickly moved to Memphis in 1948, it was due to threats from these same local bootleggers. During the period when he operated freely, however, the illicit whiskey business was Vernon's most successful entrepreneurial activity, and he bragged continually to Elvis about his newfound wealth.

Vernon's erratic behavior, coupled with his mother's influence over him, led Elvis to tell close friends that he experienced special religious feelings. One Lawhon classmate recalls Elvis speaking in tongues after a Saturday afternoon football game. Another remembers him grabbing a cat's leg after it was hit by a car and trying to shake the evil out of the small, frightened animal. These experiences resulted from the religious education that Elvis received at the First Assembly of God church, the church that kept Vernon and Gladys in touch with old-fashioned Southern values. Gladys believed that by encouraging Elvis' participation in church activities, she was molding his character.

Religion

The Tupelo First Assembly of God church at 206 Adams Street, located a block and a half from the Presley's house, was Elvis' second home. Not only was it a hub of social and religious activity, but the church offered solace and solutions to Elvis' problems. He spent many hours there thinking about his life. He envisioned the church as a sanctuary from the world's pressures. Elvis loved to watch the sunlight come through the majestic church windows, and he confided to Leroy Green that he felt calm when he was inside.

The Presleys, like most other people who attended the First Assembly of God church, were an average family who didn't stand out in the congregation. The Reverend Frank W. Smith recalled that the Presleys were like anyone else trying to make ends meet and survive during the war. Vernon and Gladys didn't sing in the church choir, nor were they particularly active in church affairs. Yet, the various First Assembly of God pastors who ministered to the Presleys' needs, Edward D. Parks, James F. Ballard, and Frank Smith, had great respect for Gladys' Christian attitudes. The pastors remarked that Gladys was the force that kept the Presley family intact.

Reverend Ballard influenced Elvis with lectures on the necessity of hard work. Brother Frank Smith, a young, energetic pastor, was another strong influence upon Elvis. The Reverend Smith, a naturalist, impressed upon Elvis the importance of nature's balance. One Saturday afternoon while hiking in the woods with Reverend Smith, Elvis spotted a dead lizard. The young preacher used the lizard to weave an allegorical tale regarding the importance of life. After an extended personal sermon, Reverend Smith dramatically buried the lizard in a small, tree-shaded area. This lesson in nature's gifts was a lasting one, and during his years as a rock music superstar Elvis frequently acknowledged Reverend Smith's teachings.

The preacher also had a strong musical influence upon Elvis. During services at the First Assembly of God church, a hard-driving, blues-oriented piano was used during key musical numbers. The piano sound combined with Reverend Smith's guitar to help stimulate Elvis' interest in music. An unusually talented performer, Reverend Smith brought the church to its feet with his inspired playing, something which later encouraged Elvis to practice his guitar regularly. Elvis' uncles, John Smith and Vester Presley, were also guitar players, although they lacked Reverend Smith's discipline and musical dexterity. Thus, it was to be Reverend Frank Smith who explained the complexities of chord progression and guitar riffs to the budding King of Rock Music.

As a result of his desire to listen to the music that praised the Lord, Elvis also attended other churches. At the nearby Free Will Baptist Church, Elvis and Vernon joined Marie Lummus Kate to perform a rousing version of a new hymn, "If We Never Meet Again This Side of Heaven." Elvis regularly sang in churches around Tupelo. During these sessions, he acquired some skill both on guitar and piano. The piano was actually Elvis' strongest instrument, but Colonel Tom Parker later created the myth that Elvis was really only minimally talented as a guitar-piano stylist. In fact, some of Elvis' best music resulted from sessions in which he played piano.

As Elvis matured, religion was the guiding light in his life. He seldom made important decisions without considering the religious implications. During school and at services held at the First Assembly of God church, Elvis was mesmerized by music with a religious-patriotic mix. The gospel choir at church and the country music at home shaped Elvis' basic musical interests. "We used to go to these religious singing's all the time," Elvis recalled, "and this music was my favorite. I knew all them songs." It was while he watched choir practices from the back of the church that Elvis noticed the intricate musical arrangements, the integration of guitar and piano solos in the church's music, encouraging him to daydream about a career in music.

The musical influences in the First Assembly of God church prompted Elvis to listen to religious music on the radio. During his adolescence, Elvis also heard a great deal of country music. He heard it on Tupelo's street corners, over the radio, and on the front porches of local homes. On one occasion Elvis remarked: "I'll never forget the cowboys on the street corners, their songs were a slice of real life." At an early age, Elvis acquired a musical education that provided the foundation for his later successes. It was not long before Elvis was looking at guitars in the window of F.L. Bobo's music store, although he was still too unsure of himself to confess that he really wanted a guitar of his own. Elvis simply listened and watched.

When World War II broke out, President Roosevelt issued Executive Order 9066 establishing relocation camps to intern Japanese-Americans alleged to be a security risk. Like most Americans, Vernon Presley was a superpatriot who condemned the Japanese, but he also informed the local draft board that he was ineligible for active duty. As the sole support of his family, and with an alleged chronic bad back, Vernon was deferred from active duty.

When the news leaked out that a relocation camp was being built in Como, Mississippi, Vernon drove the one hundred and seventy-three miles to this desolate rural town to apply for a job. He discovered the camp was being built to house captured German POWs, and he was hired as a day laborer. The WPA project paid a small wage, and Vernon was one of the first hired. It turned out that Vernon, as a result of his bootlegging activity, knew one of the Democratic party politicians who handled the project.

During the winter of 1942-43, Gladys got pregnant again, but she had trouble carrying the baby. That spring, a distraught Gladys showed up at the Tupelo General Hospital on the verge of a miscarriage. She suffered a placenta previa, which caused the baby to abort. It was a long and traumatic experience for her, one that Elvis shared with his mother. Leona Miller, a nurse at the Tupelo hospital, alerted Noah Presley, who came and took Elvis home with him during the ordeal.

Much to his surprise, Vernon was abruptly fired from his construction job at the relocation camp in Como. One of Vernon's friends, Bill Parham, who remained on the job, was also mystified by the firing. To those who knew, the reasons for the dismissal were clear. Vernon would not do a full day's work. He spent too many nights in the local beer joints and openly sold bootleg liquor.

It was now May 1943, and Vernon had no choice but to drive to Memphis to look for work. A number of the Presley's Tupelo friends believed that Vernon dismissal was a stroke of luck, eventually enabling him to find employment in the bustling Memphis wartime economy. There was no doubt that Vernon's bootleg whiskey sold much better in Memphis. He also preferred the night life and beer bars of the big city to those of Como.

When Vernon came home on weekends, he often went fishing with Leston Marcy. In quiet moments, Vernon vented his frustrations. He wondered if he would ever find a decent-paying job. He often talked of becoming a salesman. Somehow, though, he could never quite find the right job. Yet, Vernon, whether he had a job or not, was always ready for a good time. "The eagle flies," Vernon would remark. One neighbor called Vernon the "weekend dandy" because he dressed up in a fine suit and acted like he was a salesman, behavior very similar to Jessie Presley in his dandified "lawyer" days. Always decked out in his nice clothes on card-playing Friday nights, Vernon's posturing was a simple psychological release from the tension and frustration of a failed life.

Because work kept Vernon away from home during the week, Elvis grew closer to his mother than he had ever been in his life. She was a source of security and Elvis' best friend. The relationship between Elvis and Gladys prompted Mrs. William Farrar to comment that Gladys "would go to school with Elvis—rain or shine."

Mrs. Farrar shared a belief common among Tupelo residents that Gladys was both mother and father to Elvis. One church member recalled that Elvis regularly prayed for his dad. As Gladys' family responsibilities increased, a close friend noted that Elvis "always went to her for guidance, right up until she died." Gladys and Elvis regularly attended the First Assembly of God church. The weekly prayer sessions and a special bible study group occupied much of their spare time. "We used to go to the singings all the time," Elvis recalled, "there were these singers, perfectly fine singers but nobody responded to them. Then there was the preachers and they cut-up all over the place, jumpin' on the piano, movin' ever' which way. I guess I learned a lot from them." The church, the training ground for Elvis' rock and roll style, was also important in maintaining his personal, as well as spiritual, equilibrium.

Despite the close relationship with his mother, Elvis was a typical eight-year-old with a third-grader's curiosity. His classmates that year remember Elvis as a "bundle of dynamite," interested in all sorts of things. When Elvis' teacher, Mrs. Bell, asked the students to describe their favorite story, Elvis selected *The Wizard of Oz*. Since 1939, when the film began its yearly tour through the movie theaters, children were fascinated by Dorothy's adventure along the Yellow Brick Road. It was a story that intrigued Elvis, because the Tin Man, the Cowardly Lion, and the Scarecrow all found inner strength despite their spineless personalities. There was a psychological transference in Elvis' mind, and he wished that his dad could find some of the strength of character inherent in *The Wizard of Oz* characters. Elvis was satisfied that he could succeed in meeting his mother's expectations, but he worried about his relationship with his dad.

Elvis continually tried to make his mother happy. Harold Lloyd, Elvis' cousin, remarked: "I have never in my life seen a parent and child that close." Uncle Vester Presley remembered that Gladys watched Elvis "close as hell. He was a quiet, obedient boy who lived to please his mother." It was Elvis who accurately summed up his relationship with his mother: "I was an only child...a protected only child and I never did anything that my parents didn't tell me. See...I would get up in the morning and my mother would tell me what to wear, what to do, what to eat and when to do it...."

Despite these constraints, Elvis showed signs of independence. A good example of this attempt to break away occurred in 1945 when he set out to find a job. He was only ten years old, but he went around Tupelo inquiring about delivering groceries. A number of downtown businessmen joked that Elvis was more responsible than his father. He also began to enjoy the company of two new friends, Odell Johnson and Guy Har-

ris. The three boys were frequently seen cooling off with a nickel ice cream cone at Martin's store.

Although Gladys Presley's dominance shaped his early life, Elvis and Vernon shared the brief moments that are common to fathers and sons. In the summer of 1944, for example, Vernon let nine-year-old Elvis drive the Presley's 1934 Ford. It was a comical sight, one neighbor observed, to see blond-haired Elvis bobbing in the front seat of the old Ford driving down East Tupelo's dusty streets. It was a rare moment of togetherness between Elvis and his father.

Music

For Elvis' ninth birthday, his parents secretly bought him a small guitar. On Saturday, January 8, 1944, at Elvis' party, the $7.75 guitar was given as one of his gifts. Legend has it that Elvis wanted a bicycle, but that it was Vernon who encouraged his son to settle for a guitar instead. This is a myth. Elvis himself had spent months talking about a guitar, steadily gaining support from his mother. For six months, Elvis stared longingly at the guitar showcase in F.L. Bobo's front window at the Tupelo Hardware Company. Eventually, Vernon purchased one of the less expensive models. (In our taped interview, Bobo recalled that it was he who sold Elvis' first guitar to him, accompanied by Gladys. "I showed him a rifle first," Bobo remarked, "he couldn't decide whether to get a guitar or a rifle. When I told him he

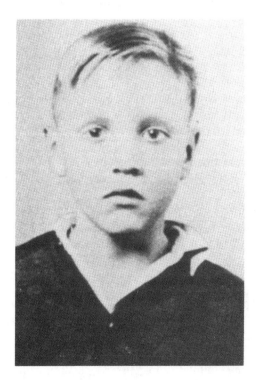

Elvis in 1944.

might kill one of his friends, he bought the guitar," Bobo concluded. It is more likely that Elvis' parents purchased his first guitar as a gift, not Elvis himself. Perhaps Bobo's statement refers to a later purchase, or is a recollection influenced by one of Colonel Parker's press releases about how Presley came to play guitar.)

Although his dad was critical of Elvis' plans for a career in music, his son was so compulsive in his pursuit of singing that Vernon remarked: "You can practice with Gladys' brother." Elvis persuaded his uncles to teach him a number of popular country songs, and it wasn't long before Elvis was moderately proficient with his guitar. Elvis often wandered downtown and played in front of the Tupelo radio station—WELO. "The Smith family has musical talent; my brothers are teaching Elvis to play the guitar," Vernon later bragged to F.L. Bobo. Mrs. J.R. (Janelle) McComb, one of the Presley's closest Tupelo friends, observed of Elvis: "He always saw the talent of other people before his own." In 1954-55, Elvis was to sing many of these same country tunes in the Sun studio, songs that he had spent a decade practicing. Traditional country ballads like "Old Shep" were interspersed with the music of Roy Acuff, Bill Monroe, Paul Womack, Paul Howard, and Ernest Tubb. Elvis' musical exposure was broad and included gospel, hillbilly, and blues tunes. (Elvis heard "Old Shep" for the first time when his Uncle Vester played it on the Presleys' porch. Young Elvis loved the tune. It was the main reason that he wanted his own guitar. When Red Foley released "Old Shep" in 1940, it immortalized his dog and later caught on with a war-weary nation. Many Tupelo residents remember how Elvis was preoccupied with "Old Shep." The Reverend Frank Smith recalls Elvis sitting on the porch of a half-dozen houses that the Presley's lived in, playing the guitar and singing the song.) By all accounts, young Presley's interest in country music was already extensive. Whenever country singers came through town, Elvis was waiting to hear them.

Unfortunately, Elvis biographers have tended to ignore the Tupelo years. The zeal to explain Elvis' life in terms of the "Hillbilly Cat" stereotype has led biographers like Albert Goldman to ignore Elvis' normal social adjustment and strong report card. From his earliest school years, Elvis had an intense interest in art, music, history, and literature. A quick wit and sharp mind was an integral part of Elvis' personality. Yet, Goldman alleges that Elvis' schooling can be reduced to a fondness for shop and manual training courses. An examination of yearbooks, interviews with friends, and a survey of Elvis' report cards indicates that he was not only academically sound but active in many school clubs and organizations.

Elvis' biographers also ignore the socio-economic changes in the South during the 1940s and early 1950s. The terms "hillbilly" and "poor white trash" no longer applied in Tupelo. The birth of new industry and better-paying jobs created a precarious but clearly defined lower middle-class status that included the Presleys. Significant changes in Elvis' character resulted from the transformation of values in Southern life, a transformation that brought a new cultural sophistication to the South as a whole. Suddenly the traditional Mississippi social structure was modified, and a newly enfranchised lower middle-class emerged to challenge the values of the old South.

Vernon and Gladys Presley were part of the formerly rural poor who moved into the lower middle-class stratum. They had consumer dollars that previous generations lacked, and this increased their status. Although the Presley family was poor, in contrast to past generations, they had the means to escape the South's rural poverty. The goods that languished in Tupelo stores in the 1920s and 1930s were purchased by workers like Vernon and Gladys. While opportunity was still determined largely by race and class, the prospects of a more prosperous life loomed large.

Some aspects of Southern life remained intact, however. Young people from the Presley's social class were encouraged to date at an early age. It was not uncommon for marriage to occur from thirteen to fifteen years of age. Consequently, when Elvis began casual dating he was only ten years old. Elvis' first social contacts came when he attended movies at the Strand Theater in Main Town. The myth persists, largely due to Elvis' early interviews, that he didn't attend the movies in Tupelo. Nothing is farther from the truth. Elvis was a regular at the local movie theater. He attended the special kid's shows in East Tupelo, and frequently walked downtown for a movie. Charles Farrar went to these shows with Elvis and remembers that Presley was a typical kid. Unlike the biographers who suggest that Elvis was tied to his mother's apron strings, most of his Tupelo friends, like Leroy Green, assert that he was just "another boy trying to grow up."

Like most of his Tupelo friends, Elvis talked about dating girls. This was simply a part of adolescence. When World War II ended, ten-year-old Elvis was dating Caroline Ballard. Elvis met the daughter of Reverend James Ballard during a First Assembly of God youth group service. As a preacher's daughter, Caroline was raised to excel. There were many qualities about Caroline that Elvis admired, but her speaking skills especially inspired him. Elvis remarked to his dad that he envied Caroline's confidence and poise. Caroline, out of the sight of her parents, was a typical young girl. She met Elvis at the Strand Theater, and they spent many nights in the theater's last two rows holding hands and smooching. Because of her family background, Caroline was imbued with religious fervor. This rubbed off on Elvis, and his commitment to Christian values increased. Because of his strong feelings for Caroline, Elvis even considered becoming a minister.

Typical of most boys his age, both Elvis' romantic attachments and his career aspirations were constantly in a state of flux, however. By 1946, for example, he was walking Becky Martin to school, often stopping at the end of the day for an ice cream cone at her father's store. Around the same time, dreams of a musical future aside, Elvis would talk to his friends about possibly becoming a policeman. "One day I'll be a real deputy," he bragged to Becky Martin. Because of this interest, Elvis would sometimes follow police officers around Tupelo, an activity which made Vernon somewhat nervous. Law enforcement was a respectable dream for Elvis, but Vernon's shady dealings quickly put an end to that dream.

Mississippi Slim

There were overpowering musical interests that deterred Elvis from the pulpit, however. In 1944, a local musician, Mississippi Slim, became Elvis' first entertainment role model. In the process, Mississippi Slim changed the course of Elvis' life. Carvel Lee Ausborn, an East Tupelo native, performed under the stage name Mississippi Slim. Slim's gaunt appearance and fancy cowboy clothes made a lasting impression upon Elvis. Because of his unique guitar and harmonica sound, Mississippi Slim performed in a wide variety of clubs and halls. On weekends he would play the local hillbilly bars, juke joints, black clubs, or American Legion or Rotary Club halls. To survive, Slim played everything from straight country to blues to up-tempo hillbilly/ rockabilly music. There were a number of Mississippi Slim songs that appealed to the locals—"Play Her Little Game," "Married Man," and "Unpaid Bills"—autobiographical tunes that Slim wrote and performed for people with the same problems. A hometown singer-songwriter, Slim's music reflected the blend of hard and good times well known to his local audience. In his performances around Tupelo, Mississippi Slim was accompanied by Little Nellie Lubin, a country singer who looked like Brenda Lee and sounded like Dolly Parton. Like Slim himself, Little Nellie combined a blues-country voice with a rockabilly sound.

Early on, so few of the town's residents paid enough attention to Mississippi Slim's music that he was forced to look—without success—for greener musical pastures in Memphis and Nashville. Although he wrote original songs and had a gregarious personality, Slim was destined to make his name back in Tupelo. For two decades, he appeared on Tupelo's WELO radio station. His initial show was a fifteen-minute Saturday morning broadcast, "Singin' and Pickin' Hillbilly." As the popularity of Slim's music grew, it led to a thirty-minute program, which expanded into an hour a day, five days a week.

The bluesy quality of Mississippi Slim's recordings were greatly influenced by a number of piano players. In the early and mid-1940s, Slim worked with piano players like Adelaide Hazelwood, a country piano artist who also recorded for the Tennessee label. One of Slim's primary influences, she played a barrelhouse-style piano reminiscent of the Memphis and New Orleans whorehouse pianists. During the same period, Del Wood came through Tupelo with a traveling show. She met Slim, changing his style into a neo-rockabilly one. Wood later secured a recording contract and, in 1951, had a minor hit on the Tennessee label, "Down Yonder." She was the one who urged the label to consider recording Mississippi Slim. Her ability to combine blues and country piano styles intrigued him. She taught Mississippi Slim a great deal about integrating the piano with the guitar and harmonica. As a fledgling rockabilly piano player, Del Wood also influenced the future careers of Jerry Lee Lewis and Elvis Presley. Their music was the direct result of the freewheeling piano style that she infused into traditional country music. At the urging of Mississippi Slim, Elvis listened to Del Wood's early recordings. Because Mississippi Slim talked so much about the piano, Elvis took up a greater interest in the instrument. Although he was only nine years old, Elvis hung around Mississippi Slim and asked him many questions. "Mississippi Slim loved Elvis like a son," James Ausborn remembered, "he taught that little boy a lot and let him perform on his radio show."

On May 15, 1944, Elvis made his first public appearance on WELO's "Black and White Jamboree." Mississippi Slim urged the station manager, Charles Boren, to bring Elvis onto the show. The local sponsor, the Black and White store, thought that it was a good idea; he was a cute little boy who would help sell goods. On Slim's show, Elvis, not surprisingly, nervously sang Red Foley's classic, "Old Shep." He was given a small ribbon. It was a happy time for young Elvis as he ran through the Tupelo streets showing off the prize.

This appearance with Mississippi Slim began a lifelong friendship. Elvis not only learned a great deal about music and life from the wandering troubadour, but he found a valued friend. Slim's ramshackle East Tupelo house was one of Elvis' favorite haunts. In addition to country and blues tunes, Mississippi Slim was versed in old standards like "Blueberry Hill." He had a large music collection and willingly shared his knowledge with Elvis. After years of playing in honky-tonks,

Mississippi Slim.

Mississippi Slim was able to impart a great deal of musical history. Elvis never forgot the lessons.

Sam Phillips "discovered" Mississippi Slim in 1952, recording fifteen of his songs for Sun Records. The tunes were not considered suitable for commercial release, however; Phillips believed that they were too raw. Nevertheless, there was a persistence to Mississippi Slim that compelled him to continue to strive for stardom. Slim eventually recorded for the Tennessee label, his songs there included "Honky Tonk Woman," "Tired of Your Eyes," and "I'm Through Crying Over You." None was a hit and by the early 1960s his dream had faded. After three marriages and more than forty years of attempting to find a hit song, he would ultimately pass away in Tupelo, the luster to his epitaph being his little known influence on a local youth named Elvis Presley. Although he lived and died a "local artist," Mississippi Slim's work did finally receive historical recognition. In the Nashville Country Music Hall of Fame, four Mississippi Slim tapes showcase his original talents.

Kith and Kin

By employing the term "the Hillbilly Cat," Elvis' biographers have perpetuated the enduring myth of Elvis' "backwoods" roots, conjuring up Lil' Abner-type images of barefoot bumpkins brewing corn whiskey in the holler. To the contrary, as Greil Marcus noted in *Mystery Train: Images of America in Rock and Roll Music*, "Elvis's story is so classically American (poor boy makes good in the city) that his press agents never bothered to improve upon it."

The most damaging statements about Elvis' hillbilly origins are contained in Albert Goldman's *Elvis*. From the perspective of a New York Jewish intellectual, Elvis was the product of a "race of Rip Van Winkles" who "awoke in the twentieth century...." Goldman's study makes judgments that cannot be substantiated, and he employs a pseudo-psychology that undermines the credibility of his work. His unsubstantiated generalizations not only hurt the book's credibility, but suggest a significant degree of non-scholarly bias. A good example of this tendency is Goldman's statement that Elvis was the product of a "deracinated and restless race." In order to validate his poor white trash thesis, Goldman graphically portrays Elvis' earliest recordings and tours as vulgar, tasteless affairs by a mediocre and minimally-talented performer. By constantly referring to Elvis as "The Hillbilly Cat," Goldman obscures the importance of Presley's early years.

The facts of the Tupelo period refute Goldman's arguments, however. Not only did Elvis develop excellent character traits, but he was interested in music, sports, and education. A number of Tupelo residents remember Elvis' insatiable intellectual curiosity. At school, he excelled in science, English, and history. He was also elected to student council positions by his peers. This record of achievement suggests that Elvis was a student leader in Tupelo, not the type of behavior consistent with the white trash stereotype.

Elvis was a serious student who practiced diligently for the Lee County annual writing contest. Elvis' interest in the writing award further challenges the myth that he was just poor white trash. For one of his essays, Elvis spent a great deal of time researching a paper on Mississippi's role in the Civil War. This essay was inspired by a relative who had fought for the Confederacy. In the end, because he was berated by Vernon for wasting his time, Elvis didn't submit the essay to his teacher. It remains an important example of Elvis' commitment to literacy and education. The poor, white country bumpkin approach to the Presley myth was great material for publicists, Hollywood agents, and gossip columnists, but it distorts Elvis' personality and abilities.

Many Tupeloans also remember that music was Elvis' primary outside interest. He was constantly playing his guitar, singing, or hanging out at WELO. Elvis fantasized about becoming a well-known singer. This dream was buoyed by Gladys when she played records on the family's Sears & Roebuck Victrola, an activity that further stimulated Elvis' interest in country music. Gladys instilled a sense of pride in her son and convinced him that he was talented. At times, Vernon's remarks would be too harsh, or Uncle Vester would laugh, as he frequently did, at Elvis' guitar playing, and it would be Gladys who shielded Elvis from criticism and supported his efforts.

The influence of Elvis' mother clearly forms the basis of his strong character and serves as a major factor in his later success. As one observer remarked: "Mrs. Presley treated Elvis as a mother bear cossets her only cub, spoiling him she also gave him the means of earning respect from others, feeding him something that seemed a cross between Emily Post and a rigid sort of Christianity." This comment by Elvis' most perceptive biographer, Jerry Hopkins, is the best definition of Gladys Presley's influence upon her son.

Gladys introduced the middle-class value system and Christian sense of dignity that characterized Elvis' life. To mask the family's poverty and insecurity, Gladys provided Elvis with an abundance of material goods. This isolated Elvis psychologically from the hard times—providing a strong sense of security. Elvis' recollections of the Tupelo years were positive. This impregnable lower middle-class value system made Elvis proud of his heritage and ancestry. While he lived amongst and identified with Tupelo citizens, Elvis was never the "white trash hillbilly" that Hollywood press agents and publicists portrayed. In many respects, Elvis was the first blue-collar, working-class rock and roll hero. Long before Bruce Springsteen made millions from blue-collar, bar-band tunes, Elvis was living and playing working-class rock 'n' roll. Elvis' roots and values were part of the reason that his music reached such a diverse cross section of American popular culture.

Of course, a portion of Elvis' blue-collar musical image resulted from the social relationship between the Presleys and Travis and Lorraine Smith. The Smiths, along with their sons, Billy and Bobby, continually reinforced rural Mississippi country values, and they also had some of the old redneck character traits. They baited Elvis and ridiculed his goal of a high school graduation. The Smiths were—in the truest sense—"hillbillies." They had little respect for education, almost no concern for each other, and they were a violent lot. In November 1937, Travis was instrumental in the foiled plot to alter Orville Bean's check. For the next decade, Travis led Vernon by the nose from one beer bar to another and through weekend jaunts to Shakerag. Albert Goldman describes the Smiths as "heavy drinkers and dangerously violent when drunk, given to brandishing knives and guns."

The Smiths were indeed a family of multiple contradictions and violent, bizarre behavior. Tracy was born deaf. Travis, a heavy drinker prone to violent outbursts, constantly meddled in the Presley's marriage. He died at the age of fifty-one, a troubled, psychologically diminished person. The Smith children, Bobby and Billy, were loud and uncontrolled. Gladys worried that they might have a detrimental effect upon Elvis. When the boys played together, Elvis complained to Gladys that Bobby lacked self-control and needed discipline, a portent of Bobby Smith's later violent and wasted life. (On September 13, 1968, after decades of strange behavior, he committed suicide by allegedly swallowing arsenic. Elvis felt sorry for Bobby's brother, Billy Smith, and so hired him to work at Graceland, where he lived in a trailer behind the main house until Elvis' death.)

Gladys' sister and Elvis' aunt, Lavalle Smith, had two children, Junior and Gene, who were very close to Elvis. Junior Smith's life was also tragic. A poor student in school with tendencies toward anti-social behavior, Junior was drafted into the army during the Korean war. When he returned from the service, he was still psychologically troubled. He had been given a medical discharge because he had allegedly killed a Korean family who were attempting to surrender. As Albert Goldman remarked, "Junior...looked exactly like what he was: a psychopathic killer." In later years, Elvis hired Junior as a bodyguard; other performers referred to Junior as "the hillbilly creep." He died from convulsions before he was thirty, his life testimony to a mental disorder that produced borderline madness.

As Elvis watched the lives of his relatives unfold, he had a sense of foreboding. Worried about heredity, acutely aware of Billy and Bobby Smith's peculiar mental conditions, Elvis' bloodline was a constant source of concern to him. There were relatives from the Tupelo days who were bright and well-adjusted, however. Buck Presley, the first cousin to Elvis' grandfather, dropped by to talk music with Elvis. An avid reader, Buck often quizzed Elvis on world affairs. It was a strange sight to see Buck and Elvis talking about World War II. In Buck's eyes, Elvis was the smartest kid he had ever seen. Another cousin, Arnold Smith, taught Elvis to play new country songs on the guitar. Only a few years older than Elvis, Arnold was an accomplished musician. Unfortunately, Arnold was also the first relative to destroy one of Elvis' cherished childhood beliefs. During the 1942 family Christmas celebration, he told Elvis that there was no Santa Claus. Elvis cried for days, and, in childhood terms, complained for weeks about Arnold Smith's insensitivity. It was a family trait, one that would surface again and again even in the best of them.

On Sunday, December 20, 1942, Elvis went to the

First Assembly of God church to pray for Santa's safe arrival. As Elvis tried to come to grips with the Santa Claus crisis, his plight was observed by Mrs. Faye Harris, who lived in a small house on Adams Street across from the church. Watching Elvis enter the church, she realized that he was troubled, and inquired about the boy's distress. Mrs. Harris, Gladys Presley's best friend, warned Elvis' mother about what had happened, and Gladys quickly explained the cruel remark and attempted to soothe Elvis' feelings.

Vernon, for his part, couldn't understand the problem, a response typical of Elvis' father. He, too, lacked a basic sensitivity for the feelings of others, and the incident only serves to illustrate further Vernon's inability to deal with crises in his son's life. Vernon's behavior prompted Clint Holmes, a furniture store owner, to take Elvis aside and explain that the idea of Santa Claus was really just the imagery used to express a Christian feeling, an explanation that helped Elvis to understand the symbolism and importance of Christmas.

Vester Presley was one of the more astute observers of the Tupelo years. He, along with Gladys' sister, Clettes, who married Vester, spent a great deal of time with Elvis. Clettes recalls that Elvis' sense of humor was often demonstrated in his relationship with his Uncle Vester. When Vester entered the Presley home, Elvis would scream out a warning that his uncle had come to steal peanut butter. At other times, Elvis good-naturedly accused Vester of stealing chickens from his parents. (the fact that Vernon didn't own any chickens was irrelevant). Vester suggested that Elvis' humor was simply his way of letting his uncle know that he loved him.

Home Sweet Home

Between 1943 and 1945, the Presleys were constantly on the move, relocating from one house to another in dizzying succession. This transiency was partially due to Vernon's on again, off again employment, but was also prompted by changes in Tupelo housing patterns. Rental units were scarce and their availability unpredictable. Mrs. Mildred Merchant, secretary at the East Tupelo Consolidated School, recalls that Elvis didn't seem to suffer academically from the frequent moves. Actually, due to the moves, he made a lot of new friends. When he showed up at a fifth-grade dance with Eloise Bedford, Elvis remarked that he had met her during a lengthy moving session.

Tupelo was growing rapidly in 1944 when the Presleys moved into a small house on Adams Street near the First Assembly of God church in East Tupelo. The landlord, a local doctor, maintained the house nicely, and it was only a short walk to school. Vernon bragged to his family that he was doing a good job of providing for them, a boast that was far from the truth. The old patterns of erratic employment, money problems, and shortsighted planning surfaced, and suddenly Vernon couldn't pay the rent. Vernon was a man who just couldn't plan from one day to the next.

The family's economic problems finally reached the point where the Presleys were forced to live with relatives on Old Saltillo Road. Many of Vernon's friends were moving north. The post-war migration to Memphis and Chicago reflected the area's overall economic plight. Blacks and whites alike were fleeing north for better jobs. When some of Vernon's friends returned to Tupelo, they complained about the vicious stereotypes they faced in Memphis. "They treat us worse than the Negro," Travis Smith remarked. Diehard Tupelo residents, like Vernon and Gladys, tried to hang on in the midst of a changing economy. There were some new opportunities in Tupelo, but not everyone could find good jobs.

In the midst of bad times, Vernon Presley astonished the family by purchasing a house on August 18, 1945, with a $200 down payment. The four-room white frame building was modestly constructed and many Tupelo residents thought the $2,000 price too high. Located on Berry Street, the house was Vernon Presley's dream of respectability. The surrounding run-down neighborhood went unnoticed by Vernon, who was consumed with the notion of having his own home. The dream quickly faded when Orville Bean threatened to foreclose and refused to extend the Presleys credit. As usual, Vernon had not planned carefully for the purchase.

Much of Vernon's bad luck in Tupelo was due to Orville Bean. Not only was Bean Vernon's former employer, but he was also the white landowner who sold property, arranged credit, and secured employment for Tupelo's unskilled working-class population. Bean's economic practices harkened back to the nineteenth century, a form of modern feudalism that continued into the twentieth century. On the surface, Bean was an honest man, but he repeatedly took advantage of unskilled and uneducated laborers. It was simply good business. He was "the boss," and no one crossed him. The price that Bean asked for his land was extraordinarily high. But other Tupelo dreamers also bought these parcels. On October 11, 1945, for example, Bean sold a lot on Kelly Street that was the same size as Vernon Presley's. No one was surprised that the price was more than $2,100. The tragedy of doing business with Orville Bean was that his contracts were sophisticated. The thirty-dollar monthly payments were complicated by a six percent monthly tax. It was a no win situation because the contract's language made it impossible to pay off the land or house. Somehow Vernon managed to keep up the payments, but he knew that he would have to eventually sell it.

Enrolled in the fifth grade at Lawhon School, Elvis was unaware of the family's problems. He was like any other grade school student, interested in sports, music, and his studies. For some time, the Lawhon School teachers had recognized Elvis' musical talent. Consequently, in September 1945, he sang "God Bless America" during a school program. J.D. Cole, then the Lawhon principal, suggested that Elvis' homeroom teacher, Mrs. J.C. (Oleta) Grimes, fill out an entry form for Elvis in the Mississippi-Alabama State Fair talent show. Before she married, Mrs. Grimes was none other than Oleta Bean, daughter of Orville Bean. "My daddy had strong feelings for the Presleys, and he did everything he could for the family," Mrs. Grimes recalled. "I saw his [Elvis'] talent in my classroom and tried to develop it." Oleta Grimes worked with Elvis on his diction, posture, and writing style. She was an old-fashioned teacher who believed that participation in the school talent show should be reserved for the best students. She clearly viewed Elvis as the best, and he was selected to represent the school. It was an honor to be a contestant in the talent contest, and only one student from each school was selected to participate. Elvis was proud of this accomplishment, and he practiced diligently.

On October 3, 1945, Gladys and Elvis walked to the Children's Day talent show at the Mississippi-Alabama State Fair in Tupelo. Vernon was out drinking and had failed to come home. After talking it over with his mother, Elvis elected to perform "Old Shep." He had sung the tune hundreds of times. Since the fair was only half a mile from Elvis' house, he wasn't nervous about performing. Mississippi Slim gleefully informed Elvis that WELO was going to broadcast the show. Once the contest concluded, Elvis won the five-dollar second prize as well as free admission to all the carnival rides. Shirley Jones, who also attended Lawhon School and often sang at school with Elvis, won first prize. Later in the school year, Elvis and Shirley sang Gene Austin's "My Blue Heaven" together during a school assembly. It was a pleasant time for Elvis even though Vernon Presley had trouble keeping a job and was away from home for days. Elvis' father complained that the prosperous war economy had ended, and as a result he was no longer able to secure adequate employment.

Although he was basically unaware of the Presleys' housing problems, there were other events in Tupelo that left a mark on young Elvis. As he was preparing to celebrate his eleventh birthday, Elvis was caught in the midst of a tornado. On Monday, January 7, 1946, at 5

a.m. a tornado rampaged through Lee County, and, although it was a mild twister, it scared Elvis. The family talked about the storm for the next two years.

Vernon once again experienced job problems. When Orville Bean again threatened to foreclose, Vernon sold the house to his friend, Aaron Kennedy, on April 18, 1946. The profits went directly to Orville Bean to clear up overdue mortgage payments. The escrow instructions granted Vernon ninety days to find a new living situation for the family. Finally, on July 18, the Presleys moved to a Commerce Street apartment on Tupelo's east side.

Jessie Presley was also having problems with Orville Bean. Like many Tupelo citizens, Vernon's father also owed Bean money. As a result, Jessie sold his own Berry Street home to pay off a thousand dollars in back payments. Watching his daddy lose everything to Orville Bean hurt Vernon. But, like other Tupeloans, he had no choice but to swallow his pride.

The new apartment that Vernon rented was located in an area of small shacks. The streets were treeless, and there was little relief from the sweltering heat. Fortunately, the Commerce Street apartment was only a temporary residence. After searching for a job for weeks, Vernon was finally hired by wholesale grocer L.P. McCarty for $22.50 a week. Because he had previously worked for McCarty, Vernon was able to step into the job without difficulty. As a vegetable wholesaler, McCarty serviced a large geographical area and the job required a great deal of Vernon. "I never thought he had it in him to work for that McCarty," Jessie Presley remarked, "but I guess my boy tried to prove himself from time to time."

Long work days and backbreaking conditions characterized Vernon's time with L.P. McCarty. He drove two hundred miles a day, and loaded and unloaded an average of twenty-five crates. The small stores that Vernon delivered his goods to were owned by unpleasant shopkeepers who complained continually about high prices. It was a depressing job. Much to Vernon's credit, he stuck with it. Part of the reason for his responsible attitude was due to the fact that Vernon's mother, Minnie Mae Presley, had moved in with the family. He could not expect Gladys to accept his mother unless he was making a decent living.

For a time Vernon became so responsible that L.P. McCarty allowed him to use the truck on Sunday, and the Presleys went to church in it. Elvis learned to drive behind the wheel of McCarty's delivery truck. The truck was an important status symbol for Vernon because it proved to everyone that he was employed. Never one to let a good thing go unspoiled, the truck also allowed Vernon to drive to Shakerag for bootleg whiskey. A short drive north across the Tennessee border to Millington secured a buyer for the whiskey. The Memphis Naval Air Station was filled with customers, and a bootlegger in Frayser convinced Vernon to sell him his liquor. To Vernon, it was a sweet arrangement. The Sunday trip to Memphis was like a holiday, and Vernon spent much of his profits in the beer bars in North Memphis. When the Presleys finally moved to Memphis, they settled within a few blocks of the taverns where Vernon drank beer during and after World War II.

Jim Denson remembers Vernon and Elvis walking around Memphis most weekends in 1947 and 1948, a year prior to the Presleys move to that city. Travis and Lorraine Smith were already living in Memphis and the job market was a strong one. Gladys didn't want to leave Tupelo and Vernon was incensed over her attitude. "I saw Vernon in the beer bars and he was an unhappy man," Denson recalled. "Elvis was always with his mother, she wouldn't let him out of her sight." Basically, the Presleys made frequent trips to Memphis so that Vernon could make enough money from selling illicit liquor for the family to continue to live in Tupelo.

The money from bootlegging and the promise of permanent employment next prompted the Presleys to move into a house on Mobile Alley near the Tupelo fairgrounds, one of the poorest parts of Tupelo. Vernon's unhappiness with his situation became so disruptive that it forced the Presleys to again consider moving to Memphis. "Vernon was so dandified, we wondered where he got the money to dress like an aristocrat," W. Kenneth Holdwitch remarked. It was not from working. In the end, like most of the Presley's homes, this one just didn't work out. The landlord on Mobile Alley had a number of fights with Vernon about the late rent. They stood out in front of the ramshackle house and hollered at each other. Finally, the owner evicted them when Vernon announced that he was never going to pay the rent again.

Elvis made some new friends while living on Mobile Alley, however. Wayne, Bobby, and Billy Crabb lived next door and they played with Elvis. They laughed at his overalls, because he used a nail to hold his pants up. The Crabb boys' mother, Phyllis, remembers Elvis was poorly dressed, but "was a nice boy, shy, and sensitive."

After a short period of time, the Presleys again found new housing. A giant step down from even the Commerce Street and Mobile Alley residences, the Presleys were forced to move to Mulberry Alley. As the name suggests, it was Tupelo's least desirable spot. Located next to the city dump, Mulberry Alley was the closest thing to skid row in the area. On summer nights, the smell wafting over from the dump was sickening. There was a rancid, low-life quality to Mulberry Alley.

This new living arrangement was the result of Vernon's persistent drinking. (From 1945 to 1948, periodic alcohol sprees rendered Elvis' dad unsuitable for full-time employment. When he had money, he spent it on liquor. Gladys stuck by her husband, eventually agreeing to move to Memphis so that Vernon could rehabilitate himself.)

There was, however, one benefit to living in Mulberry Alley. It was located in Tupelo proper and Elvis could attend Milam Junior High School. This large, impressive brick structure was the cornerstone of Tupelo's middle school system. Located at the corner of Gloser and Jefferson Streets, it was a modern building with an excellent educational reputation, a progressive school with a curriculum designed to foster job skills. In September 1947, Elvis walked to class for the first time, and it was not long before he was active in school politics. Not only was Elvis elected a room monitor, but he planned to run for student council. The fact that Elvis was elected by his peers to a position of responsibility suggests his stature and academic progress.

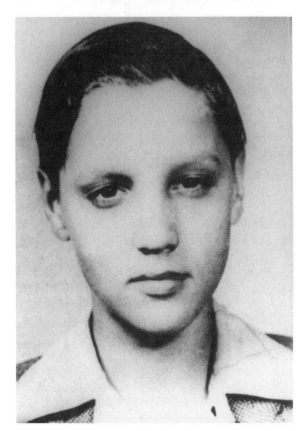

Elvis in 1947.

Vernon finally moved the Presleys into their last Tupelo home, 1010 North Green Street. Gladys complained about the move; she was tired of relocating. It was the Presley's third home in eight months, and the strain showed in Vernon and Gladys' relationship. Gladys, for her part, at times did things that didn't help the situation. She loved to help her relatives and neighbors, for example. Her impromptu generosity reached new heights when Harold Lloyd, Elvis' sixteen-year-old cousin, moved in with the Presleys. He had previously lived with them on Berry Street and now showed up to sleep on the couch in the North Green Street home. Not only did Gladys treat Harold like a member of the family, but she bought him whatever she could. Although she aimed to please everyone, Gladys' behavior often had an unsettling effect upon the Presley household.

Located in northeast Tupelo, the Green Street house was a four-room building on the edge of the Shakerag. There were black families living in the same block. Tupelo simply ignored this early form of socio-economic integration. All the poor—of whatever color—simply lived together in the worst housing. There was no color line between the Presleys and their black neighbors. They were all poor people surviving the post-World War II economic cycle of boom and bust.

Many of the Presley's old friends had ridiculed their move to North Green Street. One of Gladys' neighbors, Corene Smith, further increased the Presley's unhappiness by pointing out that their new home was again on the wrong side of the tracks. Earlier in their friendship, Gladys had heard similar disapproval from her friend. As Corene Smith stated to author Elaine Dundy, East Tupelo "was only a mile from Main Town, but it was a long mile." Now the Presleys had moved from East Tupelo into town, only to end up on North Green Street. As one citizen remarked, "it was too close to the Negroes."

Despite the turmoil created by constantly having to relocate, Elvis actually looked forward to moving from one house to another. His uncles, Vester Presley and Johnny Smith, were always around to help move, and they would spend time teaching Elvis songs by Roy Acuff, Ernest Tubb, and Bob Wills. The move to North Green Street also placed the Presleys next door to a black church. The degree to which Elvis was influenced by the Sanctified Church's music is impossible to determine, but a number of Tupelo residents suggested to me that it would have been impossible for Elvis not to have heard the choir on numerous occasions; it seems clear that the piano, guitar, and drums resonating through the church walls would not have left Elvis unmoved. Throughout his life, although Elvis never mentioned the church, he was undoubtedly influenced by its raucous brand of gospel music.

John Allen Cook lived with his family in the same area as the Presleys, at 502 North Green Street. Although Cook lived five blocks from the Presley's home,

Elvis eventually found his way to Cook's door. The grocery store in the North Green Street neighborhood was owned by a black businessman, D.L. Andrews, and John Allen Cook was hired to deliver the groceries. Elvis would follow Cook around on his delivery route. Cook recalls that Elvis was shy and loved music. "I loved to talk with that young boy," Cook remarked, "he sure knew black music." To Elvis, it was a wonderful spot. He loved the old black men who played music on the front porches, and the smell of barbecued meat was always in the air.

The Green Street house proved to be an important influence upon Elvis. He saw many sights not witnessed by too many young Southern white kids. As both blacks and whites struggled to make a living, they shared a common bond. To outsiders there appeared to be an uneasy truce between the races. The truth is that the poor whites and blacks had common problems and recognized their similar plights. D.L. Andrews extended Vernon credit and frequently threw in a little extra food; in turn, Vernon would help the black workers load the trucks, and when the sun went down they drank together in the same juke joints.

Milam Junior High

As has been noted above, one of the most important effects of the Presley family's move from East Tupelo into Main Town was the fact that Elvis could attend Milam Junior High School. He entered Mrs. Clay Camp's sixth-grade English class and found a rich academic environment. Since Elvis was from East Tupelo, however, many of the students looked at him with curiosity. The new rich in Tupelo perpetuated an atmosphere structured along class lines, so that there was still a social stigma attached to students who came from "the other side of the tracks."

During the period that Elvis attended Milam, Tupelo was undergoing a great deal of change. W. Kenneth Holdwitch, a professor of English at the University of New Orleans, was also a student at Milam Junior High. He recalls that Tupelo was full of new money. "There were class distinctions in Tupelo that had a haughty affectation," Holdwitch commented. The sense of aristocratic behavior and the snobs that resulted from it hurt people like the Presleys. "The Leakes and the Goodlets considered themselves aristocrats and weren't above letting the rest of Tupelo know it," Holdwitch remarked.

Mrs. Camp was fully aware of the social pressures that prevailed even among her grade school students, and tried to bring them together through participation in weekly classroom shows. Mrs. Camp recalled her first efforts to get Elvis to perform in just such a Friday talent show; in response to her question as to what he liked to do, Elvis was answered with conviction.

"I sing," Elvis replied.

"Bring your guitar Friday," Mrs. Camp urged.

After walking back to his seat, Elvis whispered to Leroy Green: "I's scared."

It was a wonderfully innocent moment tinged with meaning and importance for Presley's future career. That Friday, he dutifully brought his guitar to school and performed. After Elvis sang, Mrs. Camp took him down to Virginia Thomas' math class where he sang another song. After visiting yet another classroom, Mrs. Camp quietly brought Elvis back to his homeroom. "Teachers didn't have much freedom in those days," Mrs. Camp recalled. "So I had to take Elvis around quickly." Her interest and encouragement was just the type of recognition that allowed Elvis to enter easily into the mainstream of his new school's social and political life.

"His school work was very good," Mrs. Camp remembered. "He was a happy-go-lucky somebody who loved to play and sing. He flirted with the girls and one girl asked me to keep Elvis away." Mrs. Camp also held homeroom chapel programs. "Elvis was always one of the main characters in my plays," she noted, recalling how eager Elvis was to play in these classroom productions.

At Milam Junior High School, Elvis was inclined

Front facade of Milam Junior High (mid-1980s).

to perform country or traditional folk songs. "Old Shep," "Keep Them Cold Cold Icy Fingers Off Of Me," and "Barbara Allen" were favorites. "Elvis liked to sing," Leroy Green recalled, "there was nothing shy about him in front of the classroom." Another classmate, Maude Dean, told author Elaine Dundy that Elvis preferred slow ballads and traditional folk songs, but her comments implied that Elvis had a wide musical repertoire and eclectic tastes, which he did.

It was a combination of his academic and musical ability that made Elvis a popular student at Milam Junior High. Not only was he selected as a homeroom monitor, but Elvis was active in a number of clubs. The energy and enthusiasm that Elvis maintained in school was matched by his outside activities.

Apart from Mrs. Camp, the Milam school favored Elvis with other teachers who encouraged and influenced him in positive ways. Mrs. Virginia Plumb, another sixth-grade teacher, was a large lady with two children of her own. She urged Elvis to take his musical talents seriously, and to recognize his gifts in that area. Essie Paterson, another of Elvis' teachers, pointed out his academic skills to him. One of Elvis' good friends, Billy Welch, kidded him about all the attention he was getting from the teachers. When instructor Montrose Tapscott talked about history, Elvis listened with great excitement. "I think Elvis had a special talent for history," Tapscott remarked, "he sure did love to read." In short, there is no doubt that Elvis had a special quality about him and that his teachers recognized a budding talent that they couldn't fully define at such an early age.

There were some unsettling moments for Elvis at Milam Junior High School. On one occasion, one of the class bullies called Gladys a "factory worker." Elvis was incensed over the snide remarks about people who worked for the Reed's shirt factory, which, among the social elite, was not considered a proper place for young women to work. There was almost a fight, but Elvis controlled his temper and did his best to ignore the comments. There had always been bullies in Tupelo who made Elvis' life miserable at one point or another. In the past, there were those who had chided him over the fact that white people did not—as the Presley's sometimes had—eat fish from Gum Pond. Also, before enrolling in Milam, Bitsy Savery, a football player, allegedly made fun of Elvis' roots. Bitsy's father, Ikey Savery, was a local insurance agent, and the son flaunted his dad's money and social position. In Tupelo, class depended upon money, and, in relative terms, the Presleys were dirt poor. Ruminating on the Tupelo days, Leroy Green, one of Elvis' boyhood friends, recalled of him: "He was the only kid who had less than I did, we both wore overalls." Incidents like these serve to reflect Tupelo's stringent class divisions. These distinctions were so great in Tupelo that it formed an indelible part of Presley's character, and throughout his life Elvis would go to great lengths to demonstrate that he was not a social class snob.

It was Professor Holdwitch who provided me with the interesting information about Elvis Presley's fondness for sacred harp music, a form of music familiar to inhabitants of the rural South. Sacred harp music dates back to Elizabethan England, and features four-part harmony. Bands of sacred harp performers used a strange-looking oblong hymnal and performed without musical accompaniment except for a tuning fork. Groups typically sold out churches, grange halls, and tent shows throughout the South. "Elvis loved sacred harp music and identified with it," Holdwitch stated. Sacred harp singers had a definite influence on country music, and it was no surprise that the style appealed to young Presley. During the hot Tupelo summers, Elvis regularly attended the all-night gospel songfests held in the big tabernacle behind the First Baptist church, where touring gospel groups offered up sweet harmonizing music. "Elvis showed up at the gospel concerts; we all loved it," Holdwitch concluded.

There were also the gospel concerts broadcast on WELO. On many Sundays, Sister Rosetta Tharpe's booming gospel voice rang out over the airwaves, reaching out to an avid young listener bound for a glory of his own. Indeed, Tharpe's versions of "This Train Is Bound for Glory" and "Peace in the Valley" were among Elvis' favorites. When Elvis would listen to "This Train," he would jump around to its furious beat; Sister Rosetta's guitar-playing dazzled the young Presley. Entranced by Tharpe's gospel interpretations, Elvis often delayed running out to play until her program ended.

Memphis

During the summers of 1947 and 1948, Velma Dougherty allowed Elvis to ride horses on her ranch. She recalls that he was very good with animals and had a natural affinity for them. Mrs. Dougherty also remembers that Elvis loved to play in the fields for hours. The idyllic 1947-1948 summers were indeed a pleasant time in Elvis' life, but they were also his last chance to enjoy the pastoral Mississippi countryside as a carefree youngster.

The Mississippi outdoors provided Elvis with a great deal of leisure. He loved to walk to small, isolated spots on the outskirts of Tupelo. Serenity and solitude were important to him, and he took every opportunity to be alone with his thoughts and dreams. But Elvis also had friends. During the summers, Elvis went swim-

ming frequently with Odell Clarke and Guy Harris. They built a flying jenny and apple cart wagons to race in the East Tupelo streets. "We were all sort of short on cash back in those days," Odell reminisced. He also remembers Elvis's preoccupation with music of all kinds. "This one boy made a guitar out of a five-gallon can and traded it to Elvis. He banged it for a while," Clarke recalled. One day in Mrs. Jewel Webb's cafe, Guy Harris was startled when Elvis suddenly began singing some gospel songs even as bemused patrons continued to eat their home-cooked meals. To kill time, Elvis often wandered down to Tupelo's black section and listened to guitarists, washboard players, and piano artists. Although he was only twelve years old, Elvis was already heavily influenced by the musical style of local blues artists.

In September 1948, Elvis entered the eighth grade at Milam Junior High. He had grown almost four inches over the summer, and there was a noticeable change in his personality. This change was the result of his election to the Milam Student Council. The September 12, 1948, *Tupelo Daily Journal* listed Elvis as one of the students elected by his peers to represent his homeroom in the school council. Gladys was so happy that she couldn't contain herself, showing a copy of the newspaper article to everyone. Unfortunately, hard upon his election to the student council, only a a few days were to pass before the family moved again—to Memphis, Tennessee.

It was in September 1948 that Vernon Presley was once again fired by L.P. McCarty; this time there were unusually bizarre stories surrounding the family's subsequent move to Memphis, however. They ranged from a police crackdown on Vernon's bootlegging activity to a preposterous story allegedly fabricated by Vernon about a neighbor. This tale was one in which a "cab driving neighbor...beheaded his wife after a family argument," allegedly burying her in the backyard of their home. Gladys Presley, scared out of her wits, supposedly demanded that the family move the very night that the body was dug up. There is no record of such a murder or exhumation having occurred, however. Vernon apparently told this story to Jim Denson and others in Memphis to justify his quick decision to move from Tupelo.

"Dad packed all our belongin's in boxes and we put them on top and in the trunk of a 1939 Plymouth. We left Tupelo overnight. We were broke, man, broke," Elvis recalled. The Presleys' move was not entirely an unplanned one, though. Travis and Lorene Smith and their two boys, Billy and Bobby, were in Memphis, and the couple had long urged the Presleys to come north to the land of milk and honey. Vernon's split with L. P. McCarty was simply the last straw. Gladys agreed to the move, and cleaned up the North Green Street house so that her sister Lillian could move in and take over the tenancy.

So it was that the end of Elvis' idyllic Tupelo life came abruptly on that Sunday in September of 1948. For the rest of his life, Elvis had fond memories of Tupelo. He never fully understood the quick move to Memphis. The simple truth is that Vernon Presley had failed to find a permanent place for his family in Tupelo. He reasoned that Memphis could be no worse. Elvis' parents were just not able to cope with the volatile Tupelo economy, and never really got beyond the serious economic problems created by Vernon's inability to find and hold a job. Elvis, who had previously found positive aspects to all the moves made within the confines of Tupelo, was less than enthusiastic about going to an unfamiliar place where he had no friends. Finally having gained a measure of acceptance and stability at Milam school, it seemed to Elvis in his discomfort that the Presleys would never stop moving from one apartment to the next.

Elvis' classmates were sorry to see him move. Recalling Presley's days at Milam Junior High, Elvis' friend Leroy Green recalled the time when some bullies cut Elvis' guitar strings: "We chipped in and bought him some new strings." The teachers at Milam loved his music, and the class as a whole was proud of him. Leroy Green remembered that Elvis sang for twenty minutes during his last day in school. After singing one last traditional tune, "A Leaf on a Tree," Elvis left for Memphis, leaving behind many friends and fond memories.

During his lifetime, Elvis himself was responsible for creating a few myths about his Tupelo years that were important to his survival. That being said, we can conclude with great confidence that Elvis never forgot the tree-shaded streets, the good times in the open country, the short walk to the Mississippi-Alabama Fair, the sights, sounds and smells of Shakerag, the country and gospel tunes he heard on WELO, or the experiences he enjoyed—religious and musical—in Tupelo's First Assembly of God Church and the many other more humble places of worship that he frequented.

CHAPTER 5

Memphis:
The Obscure Years, 1948-1952

During the summer of 1948, Vernon and Gladys Presley had debated their future. It was difficult for Vernon to find work, and they had moved from one small house to another for more than a decade. Although Vernon made small sums of money selling moonshine whiskey, it was just not adequate—by itself—to support the family. Having had at least some success working in Memphis during World War II, Vernon ultimately came to view it as the promised land.

Transition: Tupelo to Memphis

Elvis, just entering the eighth grade, was surprised by his parents' decision to move from Tupelo to Memphis. True, they had talked about it at great length, but Vernon had seemed to have difficulty making a firm commitment to a new life in the big city. Gladys, ever-reluctant to leave Tupelo, finally urged him to think about his future; she felt that the family would be better off in a new environment, or at least said so.

Elvis, popular in school activities, had for some time been interested in student government. He talked with his close friend Leroy Green about running for an office. Green encouraged Elvis, as did a number of other friends. The first week of school, Elvis was elected to the Milam Junior High School student council. It was an honor that his peers accorded him because he had campaigned hard for the job. Not only was popularity required to achieve the position, but the homeroom teacher had to agree that the student was academically sound. Elvis met both criteria. Then, just as he had achieved a degree of acceptance and popularity, Elvis had to move.

On Sunday night, September 12, 1948, the Presleys loaded their 1939 Plymouth coupe and left Tupelo for good. Elvis, puzzled by the sudden departure, nonetheless accepted the change. To explain the move to Memphis, Vernon began telling people that a neighbor had murdered his wife. Everyone that Vernon met during his first few months in Memphis remembers the grim story of the cab driver who had cut his wife's head off during a domestic quarrel. The head, according to Vernon, was buried somewhere in the back yard of the home next to his former Tupelo residence.

The imperative behind the Presley's move to Memphis was actually made somewhat more smooth by the same factor that really caused it, however: the moonshine whiskey business. During World War II, middle

Tennessee stills had been closed down by law enforcement officials, and cooks that produced the illegal brew had moved to Tupelo. The lax attitude of Lee County law enforcement, combined with a geographical proximity to half a dozen major Southern cities, made moonshining a major Tupelo industry. "Vernon Presley wasn't a cooker," one of the old moonshiners recalled in 1986, "but Elvis' daddy bought my whiskey and acted like a big man selling it." In Memphis, Vernon not only found a ready market for moonshine, he had regular customers. The list included a number of bars on Poplar Avenue that sold the whiskey from their back rooms.

The final impetus for the move came when a competing bootlegger complained about Vernon's moonshine activity. In Tupelo, Vernon was well known as a moonshine whiskey runner, a business which had its germination in Vernon's use of L.P. McCarty's delivery truck to run the product around town. A prominent local businessman told Elaine Dundy that "bootlegging was then a way of life." What this citizen failed to mention is that Vernon had attempted to set up his own bootlegging business. It was at this point that local law enforcement began to watch him. There was a pecking order in small Southern towns, and not everyone could make and sell bootleg whiskey. It was not long before a local deputy sheriff was collecting evidence to arrest Vernon on illegal whiskey sales. With the eyes of the Tupelo police on him, Vernon finally decided it was time to move the family north. In addition to his failed "business," Vernon also had to leave Tupelo because of anger over the number of stolen horses, hogs, and chickens he had sold to unsuspecting friends. Elvis' father had simply worn out his welcome. It was time for a new start. Vernon, whose enterprising spirit blossomed whenever there was easy money to be made, and smitten by the desire to live in the big city, merely seized the opportunity.

The move to Memphis didn't surprise the Presley's closest friends. To some observers, of course, it had looked all along as though they already lived up north, visiting there almost every weekend between 1946 and 1948. In particular, from the early summer until the fall of 1948, the family made frequent trips to the city, scouting for both the jobs and housing in Tennessee that had eluded them in Mississippi. Relocating was no easy matter, however, and they spent considerable time visiting friends in and around the greater Memphis area while they looked. "I remember Elvis standing around the streets near Poplar Avenue in 1947," Jim Denson remarked. "I had just gotten out of the service and the Presleys were living in Memphis." Denson, like many others, was wrong; the family still had a home in Tupelo. Denson had originally met Elvis, Vernon, and Gladys near his father's church in Memphis. "Elvis lived in Memphis in 1947 and went to school," Denson incorrectly recalled. "I saw the Presley family around town all the time." Uncle Noah Presley had brought the family north many times, and Vernon Presley often told people he lived in Memphis, factors which added all the more to the confusion. Despite the frequent visits, though, Elvis was still going to school in Tupelo. (This explains why Elvis was absent so many days from the Tupelo public schools in 1947.)

The memories of Elvis' move north provided by a Memphis neighbor suggest that there was a great deal of turmoil within the Presley family. During the trip, Elvis and Vernon apparently didn't discuss the move at all.

As Elvis left Tupelo, his friends recall that he had mixed feelings, because it was the only home he had ever known. Throughout his formative years, the ideas Elvis developed in the sleepy Mississippi countryside had greatly influenced his character. He had memories of a happy childhood. In fact, throughout his career Elvis spoke fondly of his Tupelo years. In recalling Tupelo, Elvis pointed out the close relationship between his mother and father and the strong sense of family unity. There was definitely a romanticized attachment to the small downtown shopping area, the black Shakerag section, and the fairgrounds near the railroad tracks where the Mississippi-Alabama State Fair took place.

As the Presley's car rolled along Highway 78 toward Memphis, however, inescapable changes came into Elvis' life with every passing mile. As a member of Tupelo's First Assembly of God church, for example, Elvis was not supposed to attend dances or movies (although, it seems clear, that attending movies was one of his favorite youthful pastimes). These simple pleasures were ones that would become an integral part of his new Memphis life. Looking back on the Tupelo years, Elvis later remarked, "I don't like a church where you can't enjoy small pleasures." This innocent remark was an important comment on the personality transformation that young Elvis experienced as a teenager. He was thirteen years old, and he was changing his values. The move to Memphis offered new freedoms, a chance to make important decisions, and a means of acquiring a new lifestyle.

Memphis Blues & Rockabilly

During the year prior to the Memphis move, Elvis had come to know Memphis as an exciting city with a reputation for enlightened city government. Memphis was, in fact, one of the South's most progressive cities. It was also a natural gravitational point for white and black musicians.

In 1909, W.C. Handy settled in Memphis. Handy was lured not only by the rich heritage of Memphis blues, but found the social atmosphere an integrated one. To Handy and other blacks, Memphis was a symbol of escape from the grinding rural poverty enslaving Southern blacks. Soon Handy's "St. Louis Blues" became a national hit. Through his interpretation of the blues, W.C. Handy, a trained band musician, helped to popularize this musical form, incorporating folk blues into his ragtime songs.

It was not long before many other country bluesmen migrated from western Tennessee, north-central Mississippi, and the Delta in search of new performing venues in Memphis. Although segregation was still prevalent, when the sun went down, white and black musicians played side by side in the small clubs. Memphis' famed entertainment district, Beale Street, featured fledgling blues artists like B.B. King, Howlin' Wolf, Walter Horton, Joe Hill Louis, Little Milton, Lowell Fulson, and Rosco Gordon. Before too long, these artists made records that found their way into Elvis' life. It was therefore no accident that performers like Elvis Presley copied the frenetic vocal style of local black blues artists, characterized by rough vocals with an energetic personal flair.

There were other influences from black musicians. The guitar and piano accompaniments of many black blues acts could provide the rhythm and power of what seemed like a whole orchestra. Early commercial recordings of Memphis blues artists of the time often feature two-guitar teams. Yet, these were just two-piece backup bands, usually augmented by the singer's guitar. Long before Elvis Presley, Scotty Moore and Bill Black amazed white audiences with their "big band" sound, the black musicians of Memphis had already broken the original mold.

During the 1940s and early 1950s, Memphis country radio stations broadcast live concerts by artists like Hank Williams and the Delmore Brothers, and became the center of an original brand of hillbilly music, one which was to become an integral part of the Memphis music explosion. The blend of hillbilly, country, and early rock and roll music turned out a unique sound known as rockabilly. Performers like Jackie Lee Cochran, Roy Hall, and Johnny Carroll interpreted blues, country, and rockabilly songs in a manner very similar to the way in which Elvis did. These young performers were invariably pleasing on stage, and they were one of the reasons that so many bar bands began playing around Memphis. As the demand for rockabilly music increased, bar owners wisely booked the new bands for small sums to play for their wildly enthusiastic customers. Many such obscure rockabilly bands performed in local bars, and the city was alive with new musical sounds. It was just this blend of blues, hillbilly, and rockabilly music that made Elvis so popular, and it was precisely this type of music that dominated the city when the Presleys arrived.

On Beale Street, black musicians found a place to employ their talents. The Monarch Club, with its mirrored walls and black-cushioned seats, attracted the best crowds and the most innovative musicians. Gambling clubs with names like the Slop Crowder and Casino Henry offered card games, casino-type gambling, and a back room complete with girls, whiskey, and a comfortable lounge. The musicians usually hung out at Pee Wee's Saloon on Beale Street. The owner, an Italian immigrant, Vigello Maffei, and his son-in-law, Lorenzo Pacini, were typical of the recent immigrants who populated Beale Street in the 1940s. They offered a good meal, excellent music, and a warm atmosphere. The beat policemen kept order, and Beale Street was a safe place to roam day or night. Open prostitution, drug use, and fights were not tolerated. Gambling, illicit liquor sales, and boisterous behavior were ignored by the police. "Beale Street was a male hangout," Ronald Smith, Elvis' first guitarist, recalled, "there were very few girls in the clubs. The musicians came to compare styles and play their music."

For blacks, Beale Street was a symbol of escape from white prejudice; it was one place where musicians were judged by talent, not by color. In turn, black musicians often accepted white artists who had a real feel for the blues. It was a time of musical ferment in which black and white music was blending into a new hybrid—rock-and-roll music.

When Paul Burlison, a member of the Rock 'N' Roll Trio, was brought in through the back door of many West Memphis, Arkansas, clubs by Howlin' Wolf to play for black audiences, he learned some of the blues tunes that made the Rock 'N' Roll Trio so popular. Burlison's lead guitar work on the Rock 'N' Roll Trio songs "Honey Hush," "All By Myself," and "Drinking Wine, Spo-Dee-O-Dee" was exceptional. He played these songs with Howlin' Wolf and other black performers in the small honky-tonks around Memphis for years. Burlison's experience was typical of local white musicians.

On the other side of the coin, when radio station WDIA hired a black disc jockey, Nat D. Williams, it was a recognition of the emerging purchasing power of Memphis blacks. Not only did WDIA initially aim its programming at a predominantly black audience, but they publicized Williams as the Mid-South's first "Negro" disc jockey. What made Williams unique is that he played a strange blend of black and white music. He didn't recognize strict musical color barriers.

WDIA's sound was eagerly adopted by a white audience. Williams hosted a radio show, the "Tan Town Jamboree," showcasing blues, rhythm and blues, and jump music, and the listening audience was estimated to be at least fifty percent white. As Nat D. Williams once jokingly suggested: "The only black record the station had was 'Stompin' at the Savoy,' which became the theme song for my show—and it was by a white writer." Despite this comment, Williams did indeed play important black music. It didn't take long for Nat D. to develop a local audience with artists as diverse as Arthur "Big Boy" Crudup, Big Bill Broonzy, and Louis Jordan.

Both the experiences of Paul Burlison and Nat Williams mirror the subtle blending of black and white music that was so important to Elvis Presley's emergence as a star.

In sum, the atmosphere in Memphis was a very special one. On street corners, country bluesmen played for tips. In Handy Park, jug bands vied with informal groups that played the blues and popular songs for the crowd's attention. The theaters along Beale Street featured vaudeville blues singers such as Bessie Smith, Memphis Minnie, and Ma Rainey. Young musicians like Memphis Slim and Sunnyland Slim, who drifted in as supporting musicians, wound up as local celebrities. The Memphis blues scene soon took on a professional quality. When Elvis began frequenting Beale Street in the early 1950s, it was in the midst of a revolution.

There was one club, the Hippodrome, that catered to young white kids. "If you looked like you wouldn't make trouble, they'd let you in," Ronald Smith recalled. "We loved to go there and watch the black musicians," Elvis' friend Kenneth Herman remembered. It was at the Hippodrome that Elvis continued to develop his musical style during the period 1952-53. Performances at the club also inspired Elvis, Ron, and Ken to talk about making a record.

As the bands and singers on Beale Street began making records, it was natural for everyone to get the idea that they ought to record their own music. The growth of small local record labels provided the opportunity for many of the performers. Memphis musicians all wanted the same thing—a hit record. When there was a success, as occurred in 1951 when Ike Turner and his Kings of Rhythm hit the charts with Jackie Brenston singing lead on "Rocket 88," everyone's enthusiasm was renewed. This song, with the musical revo-

Elvis' friends Kenneth Herman (left) and Ronald Smith.
(Photo courtesy Ronald Smith)

lution on Beale Street as a backdrop, helped bring rock and roll to life. Memphis was not only the cradle of this new black music, it was the central focus of an emerging white style.

Settling In

In 1948, as the Presleys drove into Memphis, there were also indications of a social and economic renaissance. The Black and White store and the local Kress' had lunch counters open to blacks, and there were signs of progress in employment, education, and entertainment. Blacks were key consumers in Memphis, and it was just good business to appeal to their needs. The *Memphis Commercial Appeal* covered black events with dignity and grace, and there was little evidence of media discrimination.

The newly arrived Presleys were initially unaware of the full scope of Memphis' musical underpinnings—Beale Street, rockabilly, WDIA. It was natural for them to gravitate to the part of Memphis that locals called "Little Mississippi," which was filled with people who had migrated from small northern Mississippi towns. They rented a room in a boarding house on Washington Avenue, and Vernon quickly walked down to one of the seven beer bars on nearby Poplar Avenue, along with Gladys' brothers, Johnny and Travis Smith. The Smiths had also moved their families—along with Grandma Minnie Mae Presley—to Memphis, and were working at Precision Tool while looking for better hous-

ing. As Vernon and the Smith brothers left to drink beer, Gladys and Elvis quietly celebrated their arrival in Memphis by going to Loew's theater to see "Abbott and Costello Meet Frankenstein." It was not long before Elvis was a regular at the nearby Suzore #2 Saturday afternoon bargain matinees. With dreams of movie stardom filling his head, young Elvis was soon trying to dress, walk, and talk exactly like Tony Curtis. It was also not long afterward that Elvis discovered Beale Street and WDIA.

The musical changes during Memphis' postwar economic and population boom were paralleled in other areas. The city's population increased to more than 300,000, bringing new employment opportunities. Rural Southerners viewed Memphis as a chance for a new life. Black and white Southerners alike were attracted to the promise of good jobs and the lure of bright lights. Like many Southern cities, Memphis' economic boom was short-lived, however. It was not long before the supply of available workers quickly glutted the job market. The reservoir of surplus labor periodically led to poor working conditions and inadequate wages. Like everyone else, the Presley family was influenced by these boom and bust cycles. Vernon soon realized that the family had traded a workable rural lifestyle for urban deprivation.

Indeed, the Presleys' first Memphis family crisis was due to housing. A few weeks after they arrived in Memphis, they moved from Washington Street into a small, one-room apartment at 572 Poplar Avenue. The

An eerie mid-1980s photo of a boarded-up 572 Poplar Avenue.

$35-a-month rent for the small apartment in the large, multi-storied building was within Vernon's budget, and there were a number of other important reasons for renting it. The ground-floor efficiency was only a brisk walk from Beale Street, and it was close to the growing downtown business section. The once luxurious house, though, was in a sad state of disrepair, and the owner neglected to maintain it. The Presley family had to share a bathroom with other tenants. The North Green Street house they had left in Tupelo began to look like a mansion compared to this Memphis dwelling. Nevertheless, the family remained in the decrepit little hovel for a year. It was a depressing home in a neighborhood that reeked of white poverty. Elvis never forgot the toilets, the stench from the kitchen facilities, or the degrading appearance of the makeshift rooms. Gladys, for her part, never complained about the squalid living conditions. Vernon, on the other hand, was constantly depressed. The local beer bars continued to be Vernon's favorite haunts.

The first few months in Memphis were not a pleasant time for the Presleys. It was Gladys' humor and steadfast belief in God that held the family together during this ordeal. She talked openly and at great length of her faith in God, and she urged Vernon and Elvis to think positively about the future. To alleviate the pressures surrounding the sudden move to Memphis, the Presleys joined the First Assembly of God church at 1085 McLemore Street. They found people much like themselves there—a group of recently displaced, rural Southern migrants attempting to cope with the rigors of big city life.

Nat Williams and B.B. King

The lure of black music became increasingly important in Elvis' life, and he began wandering around Beale Street looking at the sights and listening to the music. Whenever possible, he listened to Memphis' radio station, WDIA. One of Elvis' early musical favorites was B.B. King, who had started out on WDIA singing commercials for Pepticon, a health tonic. It was during the 1951 Christmas season that Elvis first heard King's record "Three O'Clock Blues." The song, written by Lowell Fulson, reached number one on the *Billboard* rhythm and blues chart in 1952, remaining there for fifteen weeks.

When WDIA began broadcasting on June 7, 1947, the station had a minuscule output of 250 watts. The two white Memphis businessmen who owned the station, John R. Pepper and Bert Ferguson, were not the least bit interested in the blues. The following year, however, Ferguson shrewdly recognized that blacks were being ignored by local radio. He approached black businessmen with an idea for a black-oriented musical format, and they agreed to advertise. When Nat Williams was hired, the station began its transition into a major blues force. A 50,000 watt transmitter turned it into one of the pre-eminent radio stations in the South. After Rufus Thomas also went to work as a disc jockey, the station not only became more popular, but the black community responded with strong support.

B.B. King was the superstar on WDIA. When King walked into WDIA looking for a job, the station had just won the advertising account for Pepticon. It was a product that attempted to compete with Hadacol. Both were health tonics heavily laced with alcohol, and neither one had any redeeming medical benefits. Sonny Boy Williamson sold Hadacol on KWEM in West Memphis, Arkansas, and KDIA was looking for someone to sell Pepticon. As a result, B.B. King became the "Pepticon Boy."

His daily radio show soon established King as a commercial artist in Memphis; he also played nightly at the Sixteenth Street Grill. Standing on the small stage each night, King's guitar repertoire rapidly garnered him a sizable following, and his blues vocals set a new standard for soul. The word spread to Humes and South Side high schools about a cat playing guitar down on Beale Street. Ronald Smith was one of the first to recognize the power of B.B. King's guitar work, and he alerted Elvis to the new sound. "Elvis loved B.B. King," Smith remarked, "he couldn't get enough of his blues vocals." Many other musicians cut their teeth on B.B. King's blues, and he soon became a local celebrity.

Eventually, B.B. King took over a prestigious radio show, the "Sepia Swing Club," and played records by local musicians as well as national acts. King's show was rivaled by the musical sophistication of Nat Williams' "Tan Town Jamboree." The latter program attracted as large a white audience as a black one. The music played during the "Tan Town Jamboree" helped Elvis to select records to buy. Soon, he was acquainted with the music of Fats Waller, Ivory Joe Hunter, Roy Brown, Louis Jordan, and T-Bone Walker. Williams' show provided Elvis with a musical education as well as taking his mind off the Presley family's squalid living conditions. The crisp guitar licks and bluesy vocals on King's radio show served to inspire Elvis the musician. The two together—King and Williams, the Memphis blues and the emerging rhythm and blues sounds—came to form the core of Elvis' musical roots, and is something we'll explore further in the next chapter.

Becoming Memphians

The strain on the Presleys was doubtless eased by

the close proximity of Travis and Lorraine Smith and Grandma Minnie Mae Presley. Just a month before the Presleys moved, the Smith's had brought their sons Billy and Bobby to live in Memphis. Travis, working for Precision Tool, found a job there for Vernon. Lorraine Smith had previously written Gladys two letters extolling the virtues of Memphis life. It was, by all accounts, the "Promised Land" that the Presleys had hoped to find. The Smiths, who had also originally settled in a Washington Street rooming house, soon moved to Poplar Street to be near the Presleys.

When the Presleys arrived in Memphis, Vernon convinced Travis to loan him twenty-five dollars, and the families celebrated the next weekend with salt pork, potatoes, and greens. Vernon's hopes for a new life were not to be realized, of course, because he had no marketable job skills and had never been able to hold a job for any amount of time. His silver tongue and smoky good looks helped him to explain away his faults, but in Memphis he soon experienced the same problems that had plagued him in Tupelo. As a result of his lack of responsibility, Vernon had trouble keeping his job at the Precision Tool Company. It was not long before he was laid off. Eventually, he found part-time work driving a truck for a wholesale grocer, but it provided little financial security.

The family fortunes improved in October 1948 when Gladys found work as a seamstress with Fashion Curtains. It was tough work sewing small curtains from early in the morning till six o'clock at night. Soon the long hours began to tell, and she deteriorated physically and emotionally. Tension between Vernon and Gladys increased due to their economic plight. Gladys was drinking beer heavily and often hollered at Vernon late into the night. He responded by leaving the house and walking down to the beer bars.

Finally, in February 1949, Vernon found full-time employment at the United Paint Company. It was a tough job requiring him to handle hundreds of cases of paint each day. Vernon's job was the hardest he'd ever had, but he kept it to prove that he could work full-time. One person referred to the United Paint Company as a place for "mule work." It required an extraordinary amount of physical stamina, and the working conditions were primitive. Vernon, however, was just happy to be employed full-time, and he began to acquire a renewed sense of his self worth. As a result of Vernon's employment, Gladys quit her job as a seamstress and went to work part-time as a waitress. The Presley family now had a combined income of sixty dollars a week. This allowed Elvis some spending money and temporarily eased tensions at home.

When Elvis entered school in Memphis, he enrolled at the Christine School on Third Street. The Presleys waited nearly two months to send him to school, apparently in order to make sure they got settled first, because Memphis school system records indicate that Elvis' first day in class was November 8. Jim Denson recalls Elvis hurrying to school with Gladys following closely behind. "He was a mama's boy. I don't think he had much freedom," Denson remarked. "Vernon was in the beer joints every night and Gladys wanted to protect the boy." Denson, a Korean War veteran, was older and considerably wiser than the other boys, and he helped Elvis to ward off the neighborhood bullies. Denson recalled for me the musical influences upon Presley, and remembers how Elvis' musical education was furthered by people like his brother, Jesse Lee Denson, as well as other Memphis musicians—Ronald Smith, Kenneth Herman, Eddie Bond, Paul Burlison, Johnny Black, and Doug Poindexter. "Elvis had his own special talent," Denson concluded, "but he was taught a lot of things by my brother, Jesse Lee." As Denson suggests, Elvis had a great ability to copy other musicians; throughout his career Elvis used demo singers to help craft his sound, something that began in his relationship with early friends like these.

It was not long, however, before Elvis began to make new friends. George Klein, who eventually became the senior class president at L.C. Humes High, befriended Elvis during the ninth grade. Initially, it was not a close relationship. Klein was a slick politician interested in maintaining his popularity. As a result, he was friendly to everyone. Red West had introduced Elvis to Klein at Humes, but Elvis was initially nervous around the overly-aggressive and socially-mobile Klein. Few people remember George Klein as one of Elvis' friends during Elvis' years at Humes. Kenneth Herman, Eddie Bond, Ronald Smith, and Jim Denson all recalled that Klein was personable and nice to everyone, but that he was simply not one of Elvis' closest high school friends. Klein's lifelong friendship with Elvis did not really begin until 1956, after graduation.

A few days after Elvis met George Klein, Mrs. Elsie Marmann, Humes' music teacher, persuaded Elvis to perform for her music class. He sang "Old Shep" and "Keep Them Cold, Cold Icy Fingers Off Of Me." Elvis had sung these songs many times in Tupelo, and felt comfortable with them. Evan "Buzzy" Forbess was one of Presley's new friends who remembered how nervous Elvis was during the songfest. "He was shy," Forbess remarked, "but we loved to hear him sing." The reason that Mrs. Marmann asked Elvis to sing was because he often carried his guitar to school. Mrs. Marmann thought that this was a peculiar habit and hoped to cure him of it. Jane Lazenby, a student in the music class, recalled that Elvis often walked through the Humes high school halls, his collar turned up, plunking away at his guitar. After the short singing session, Mrs. Marmann was critical of Elvis' singing. "A person can't understand the words Elvis and you sing the song too quickly," Mrs. Marmann intoned. The incident apparently had no effect, as Elvis and his guitar remained inseparable.

Lauderdale Court

As the Presleys adapted to Memphis, the family gradually became economically secure. With both his parents working and the adjustment to the new Memphis lifestyle completed, Elvis no longer missed Tupelo. During the spring of 1949, Vernon Presley was placed on the permanent payroll at the United Paint Company, and the family petitioned the Memphis city government for a subsidized apartment. Vernon's wage was $38.50 a week, with four hours of overtime built into the workweek. In order to qualify to live in a Memphis Housing Authority unit, Vernon's boss had to report his income twice a year. Vernon was humiliated by this request, but it was necessary if the Presleys were to move into better housing. (It bothered Vernon that he had to disclose his earnings, because he feared the Memphis Housing Authority might discover that he was still selling a bit of moonshine whiskey. Not only could he supplement his income this way, but it gave him an excuse to return to Tupelo each month. Although the United Paint Company paid $38.50 a week, Vernon was able to add another $12 or $13 a week by continuing to sell small quantities of shine.)

In 1949, Memphis was governed by a model progressive city government whose image centered around its excellent public housing projects. When Vernon applied for public housing assistance, Mrs. James Richardson, a case worker for the Memphis Housing Authority, remembered that the Presleys "were just poor people. But they seemed nice and deserving." She recommended that they be allowed to move into a project called Lauderdale Court. Located at 185 Winchester Street, the project had been constructed with federal funds and was an excellent example of Democratic party patronage. Although Albert Goldman has described the Lauderdale Court as "a drab little pile of red brick...," the truth is that the complex was excellent public housing which instilled pride in its occupants. It was also the first step for many Southerners into a precarious, lower middle-class life. The appearance of the three-story brick building was actually something akin to a college dormitory. Just across the street, a predominantly black neighborhood stretched for blocks.

On Sunday, May 1, 1949, Elvis and his family moved into Apartment 328. The Lauderdale complex housed four hundred families, and to Elvis it was a magnificent

Elvis in Lauderdale Court, 1949.

new home. Each unit had a living room, two bedrooms, a kitchen, and a freshly-painted bath. Inside, the smell of disinfectant created the illusion that the apartment was cleaner than any place Elvis had lived. When Elvis mentioned the apartment's cleanliness to Gladys, she laughed at her son's newfound pride. She explained to Elvis that the Lauderdale Court also had more than a hundred rules for the tenants. Gladys pulled out the list of do's and don'ts and proceeded to lecture Elvis on what was expected of him.

The day after the Presleys moved into the Lauderdale Court, the telephone company installed a desk phone in the front room. Elvis quickly memorized the telephone number and urged everyone that he knew to call him. It was indeed an important period for the Presleys. They had finally moved into a clean, well-kept two bedroom apartment with all the amenities. The $35 monthly rent was reasonable, and Vernon's income, which now averaged $200 a month, was more than adequate to meet family expenses.

Just as things began looking up for the family financially, however, they were faced with the prospect of a new boarder. Minnie Mae Presley, Elvis' fifty-four-year-old grandmother, had recently ended her thirty-four year marriage to Jessie D. Presley. In fact, Minnie Mae had moved to Memphis ahead of Gladys and Vernon, determined to live a quiet life. After raising five children, including Vernon, Minnie Mae was ready to retire. She was a fussy, cantankerous old lady who worried about her health, and gave Gladys and Vernon more advice than they could stand. Yet, they loved her and were willing to put up with her eccentric behavior. As a result, when family pressures forced her to move from living with the Smiths, she found a place with the Presleys.

Minnie Mae was either unable or unwilling to work, and so contributed little to the household finances. Vernon began to urge Gladys to return to full-time employment, and they argued incessantly about the financial strain his mother placed on the family. The short-lived bliss that had developed after the family moved into the Lauderdale Court was replaced by constant tension. This time money was not the issue. Gladys and Vernon simply had no privacy, and they battled with one another over the direction of their lives.

Elvis, even though in high school, was willing to work, but Gladys made it very clear that her son was going to finish his education. It was a tense time for the family, but they were really no different than other poor white families struggling to make ends meet in the post-World War II recession. Despite the rapid changes in the Presley's lifestyle, they enjoyed Memphis and adjusted quickly to city life. For the next three and a half years, the Presleys lived comfortably in the Lauderdale Court. Elvis played football, made friends, and his life took on a predictable quality.

In the summer of 1949, Elvis mowed lawns for fifty cents, and he organized a business to sell spoiled fruit picked out of a refuse can at a local market. After work, Elvis often slipped quietly into the black ghetto to listen to music. He was intrigued by the language and mannerisms of the black Memphis subculture and, as there were no blacks at Humes High, Elvis made friends with them during pickup football games. In a time of personal and musical growth for Elvis, his experiences with blacks were educational ones. In fact, it was from some early black friends that Elvis and Billy Smith got the idea to build the makeshift fruit stand that became so profitable for them. They made signs advertising the discarded fruit as recently picked country produce, and few people suspected that they were actually selling the bruised items thrown away by local merchants. Elvis, Billy, and Bobby Smith used the profits to purchase movie tickets and buy snacks at a local drive-in restaurant. Every day, they walked over to the drive-in and gorged themselves on shakes and hamburgers.

Elvis' early Memphis years were happy ones. He was like any other country boy who migrated to the big city with his family after World War II. After the Presley family adjusted to the exploitative labor market, the bureaucratic maze of public housing assistance, and the trauma of helping Elvis adjust to L.C. Humes High School, they settled into a well-adjusted lifestyle. Elvis grew into adolescence as a healthy young man fighting the forces of the city.

There was a definite blue-collar, working-class side to Elvis Presley's personality. He loved to work. Elvis had been the organizer and instigator of the fruit business. Elvis often bragged to his friends that work was more important than high school. In private, however, Elvis confided to other friends that he also loved school.

In November 1950, Arthur Groom, the Loew's Theater manager, hired Elvis to work as a part-time usher. The $12.75 that Elvis made each week further supplemented the family income. For almost a year, Elvis worked five hours a night, seven days a week at Loew's. Despite a heavy load of five classes at Humes High, Elvis doggedly reported to work. After work, he would walk down to the Grit-Iron Cafe to meet Ronald Smith and Curtis Lee Alderson. The restaurant, located across the street from the Peabody Hotel, was an all-night hangout.

It was while working for Groom at Loew's Theater that Elvis began talking about his musical future. "Elvis talked about music all night when we met him. He sure did keep up with the scene," Ronald Smith concluded. The job forced Elvis to quickly complete his homework, which created guilt about neglecting his studies. His job at Loew's Theater ended when a concession girl not only flirted openly with Elvis but let him eat all the candy he wanted. Another usher told the boss that Elvis was eating free candy, a fight broke out, and Elvis punched the boy in the nose. Groom fired both boys, but Elvis soon became an usher at the Malco Theater.

While working at Loew's Theater, Elvis dated Betty McMahan. She lived in a third-floor apartment at the Lauderdale Court, and they frequently went to the Suzore #2 theater. Betty loved to dance. She continually pressured Elvis to take her to the St. Mary's dances. Elvis confessed that he couldn't dance and pleaded that the crowds made him nervous. Consequently, they spent many afternoons at the bargain matinees in the Suzore #2. Elvis liked to strum his guitar at home and play it at parties, although he demanded that the lights be turned out. His second girlfriend, Billie Wardlow, remembers that Elvis loved to sing Eddy Arnold's "Won't You Tell Me Molly Darling." When he sang this song, Elvis playfully changed the girl's name to Billie.

Eventually, after the ushering job and the girls in the Lauderdale Court had contributed to a decline in

Elvis' grades, Gladys forced the boy to focus his attention upon his school work. After Elvis was fired at Loew's Theater, Gladys went back to work as a nurse's aide at St. Joseph's Hospital. Elvis loved to watch his mother put on her aqua-green aide's uniform, and he affectionately called her "Nurse Gladys." When she came home from St. Joseph's, Gladys invariably brought cookies, cakes, and pies for the family. They were hospital leftovers, but they were special to Elvis.

Gladys' job at St. Joseph's was important in another sense. It was the first time that Gladys talked with Elvis about socio-economic differences. She pointed out that many patients were finely dressed. A man who came to visit his wife in a pink Cadillac was Gladys' favorite. She dreamed of a better life, and used the patients at St. Joseph's to fantasize about her own middle-class aspirations. Elvis laughingly promised his mother a new pink Cadillac when he became rich.

Music, Music, Music

During 1950-51, Elvis spent an great deal of time playing his guitar and singing. One of his favorite songs was Ivory Joe Hunter's "I Need You So." In April 1950, Hunter's tune was played on Southern rhythm and blues radio stations, and Elvis identified with the slow, soulful direction in Hunter's music. (Elvis recorded "I Need You So" in 1957, and it appeared on the **Just for You** EP and the LP **Loving You**.) Another 1950 song that influenced Elvis was Bob Wills and the Texas Playboys' "Faded Love." When Wills' group played in Memphis, Elvis was greatly impressed by the Texas Playboys lead vocalist Tommy Duncan. In addition to singing country or hillbilly music, Duncan performed blues and rhythm and blues songs. In 1953, Duncan covered Willie Mae Thornton's "Hound Dog" on the Intro label. Ron Smith remembers Elvis practicing the Duncan-inspired version of "Hound Dog." Bob Wills and the Texas Playboys influenced Elvis musically in yet another way. Their stage show was more like a big band dance concert than a rock-and-roll show, but Elvis was intrigued by the way they persuaded the crowd to dance.

The close friendship that Elvis had with Ronald Smith and Johnny Burnette further helped to develop Presley's music. Burnette was a country music enthusiast who loved the blues, and Smith could play blues riffs on his guitar. Lonzo Green, another Memphis musician, remembers an attentive Elvis following his chord progressions on guitar. Anyone who played a guitar became Presley's friend.

Black musicians remained a strong influence upon Presley. He prided himself as a person who could search out new songs. "Elvis loved the record stores," Ronald Smith remembered. "He loved to find obscure tunes."

The best new records were sold in small shops, at shoe-shine stands, or in small catchall shops. "We were all searching for a sound," Smith remarked. "No one knew what type of sound, so we looked for new records. When we went to Ruben Cherry's store, he was nervous about us; a younger guy let us listen to records," Smith maintained.

When Elvis finished the ninth grade in June 1950, one of his Humes High School teachers, Susan Johnson, remarked, "Elvis liked to sing songs to a few friends during lunch or at a school assembly." As Ronald Smith pointed out: "He even went to South Side High to appear in the shows. Everywhere there was music Elvis appeared; sometimes we didn't want him to play," Smith remarked with a twinkle in his eye.

"The Ink Spots were one of Elvis' favorite acts," Susan Johnson stated, "I couldn't figure out why for the life of me." Ronald Smith knew why: "Elvis loved the vocal harmonies of the Ink Spots." Due to the Ink Spots' influence, Elvis practiced a version of their hit, "My Happiness." He also listened intently to their rendition of "That's When Your Heartaches Begin." The group's vocal harmonizing intrigued Elvis, and when, in later years, he decided to use the Jordanaires in recording and concert appearances, it was as a direct result of the impact made upon him by the Ink Spots.

Gospel music was another important source of musical inspiration. While living in the Lauderdale Court, the Presleys attended church regularly for the first time since leaving Tupelo. The Memphis-based First Assembly of God church was larger than its Tupelo counterpart, and featured an extensive program of church events. Not only did the church have its own gospel choir, but it sponsored gospel songfests. A fleet of buses brought worshippers from every part of the city. The church's elaborate weekly schedule included gospel singing events that Elvis enjoyed; in fact, it was gospel music that brought Elvis actively into the First Assembly of God church.

In the Lauderdale Court, Elvis became friends with Evan "Buzzy" Forbess. In December 1950, Elvis and Buzzy talked about the Christmas presents that they had bought their parents. Elvis had saved fifteen dollars and purchased a garish picture of Jesus imported from Mexico for his mother. The portrait hung in the Presleys' bedroom until Gladys died; she called it her favorite present. Buzzy remembers that Elvis, persuaded to sing for his tenth-grade class Christmas party, purposely forgot his guitar; it was obvious that he was still self-conscious about performing.

During his sophomore year at Humes High, Elvis discovered the Odd Fellows Hall. An assortment of country and gospel artists performed there, and Elvis learned a great deal about their music. He was initially hired to clear tables at the hall, but always managed to stay for the first musical set. It was at the Odd Fellows Hall that Elvis first saw his future bass player, Bill Black, perform.

In 1951, at a Hardrock Gunter concert, Bill Black played bass with Doug Poindexter's hillbilly band. Gunter had just made his first Decca recordings, and Elvis was amazed that they covered Billy Ward and the Dominos' recent r and b hit, "60 Minute Man." The sight of a hillbilly band playing black music intrigued Elvis. After the first set, he approached the band.

Striking up a conversation with Bill Black was easy. Elvis lived in the Lauderdale Court near the Blacks, and was a good friend of Bill's younger brother, Johnny. They talked, although getting Black to listen was a little harder; Black paid very little attention to Elvis. Bill Black knew Elvis casually and listened to him talk about music, but he didn't take Elvis seriously as a performer until the day they recorded for Sam Phillips' Sun label. Elvis, on the other hand, picked up a great deal of performing knowledge from Black's extroverted stage performances at the Odd Fellows Hall.

While watching Hardrock Gunter perform, Elvis listened to the musicians talk about Walter Horton's new record, "Hardheaded Woman." Elvis never forgot this discussion, and in 1958 he recorded Horton's tune. An integral part of Elvis' approach to music, he always made it a point to search out the best new blues or rhythm and blues records and practiced them in his unique style.

Many other musicians provided me with excellent examples of Presley's musical apprenticeship during this period. Doug Poindexter's group, the Starlite Wranglers, had the best musicians in Memphis. Elvis loved their combination of big band and country music influences. Scotty Moore's lead guitar work caught Elvis' eye, and he went home and tried to duplicate Moore's riffs. It was absolutely impossible; Moore had a way of playing that Elvis just couldn't master. Three years later, both Bill Black and Scotty Moore became the Blue Moon Boys, and were instrumental in shaping Elvis' unique brand of rock and roll music. It was due to their skilled musical training and long apprenticeship with hillbilly bands that Scotty and Bill were able to step in and play behind Elvis. They easily followed Presley's blues-oriented and rhythm-and-blues inspired musical direction.

Another ingredient in Elvis' musical training was his intense interest in collecting records. A friend joked that Presley had the "vinyl disease." Many of the songs that Elvis listened to were discovered at Ruben Cherry's record store, "The Home of the Blues" on Beale Street.

Cherry's store was a second home to Elvis, who frequently wandered down to listen to the new records. A slight, kindly man, Cherry often reminded Elvis that a purchase was required, and this prompted Elvis to begin collecting rhythm and blues records. In the summer of 1951, Vernon surprised Elvis with an eight-dollar Sears-Roebuck record player. During his last two years in high school, Elvis would dance around the house as the small record player blasted away in the living room, which had become his bedroom now that his grandmother had occupied the second bedroom. To Elvis, this was a fine arrangement, and he imagined that the living room was his own little apartment. He would walk around the room impersonating Tony Curtis, and repeating dialogue from Curtis' latest movie.

Family Matters

During the 1950-51 Christmas season, the Presleys celebrated their newfound prosperity when Vernon received a ten dollar monthly raise. The joy over Vernon's salary increase soon vanished, however, when the Memphis Housing Authority discovered Gladys' income at St. Joseph's Hospital. The family's monthly earnings now exceeded the amount allowable to live in the Lauderdale Court. As the Presleys debated their problems, Vernon hurt his back and was laid off from work. Unable to pay their rent, they fell $43.74 behind in their payments to the Memphis Housing Authority. Eventually, the housing authority informed the Presleys that a dollar-a-day fine would be levied against them until the delinquent bill was paid. Only a loan from Travis Smith allowed the them to escape eviction.

Vernon was once again at the center of the Presleys' economic problems. Elvis' dad often stated that his back "was constantly in pain and rendered him useless." Vernon's close friends suggested that he was a malingerer at work. He was also a spendthrift. A good example of Vernon's inability to manage his money occurred two years later, when he told everyone that he had bought Elvis a fifty-dollar green Lincoln coupe for his eighteenth birthday. "The green Lincoln was Vernon's car," Ronald Smith commented, "but Elvis always had it and said it was his." To friends of Vernon's with any sense of their own, Vernon just lacked good sense. The Presleys were broke, but he persisted in trying to please his son and act as though he had money.

In January 1951, Elvis took and passed the written and road tests for a Tennessee driver's license. Elvis loved to sit for hours parked at a local hamburger stand in the ostentatious green Lincoln. With his collar up and his shoulder jammed against the car door, Elvis was the epitome of the angry young rebel, a pose not uncommon to many youths in the 1950s. "I helped Elvis push that green car around Memphis," Ronald Smith remarked. "Elvis loved that car." A well-known Sun Records session musician, Marcus Van Story, also remembered "Elvis sitting in the front seat looking unhappy. That damned car never ran right, but he pushed it all over Memphis."

Football and the Army ROTC program also occupied much of Elvis' attention. At six feet and 150 pounds, Elvis was too small for the football team. As a result, ROTC was a natural outlet; Elvis excelled in this pseudo-military environment. He loved the uniform and gadgetry that went along with ROTC. Unfortunately, he didn't have enough time to put into it, and quit after a year.

Elvis looked forward to the twenty-minute walk to Humes High each morning, and he was eager to absorb all he could from the 1,600-member student body. Each day, upon entering Humes High, Elvis would install himself in his perch, a small corner to the left of the main entrance. He'd stand there like a proud peacock, and from his nesting spot he'd eyed the girls. It was a means of asserting his identity.

Elvis also loved searching through the library. He spent hours reading history and literature books. For almost a year, Elvis worked at restacking the shelves in the library. His friends kidded him unmercifully about being a bookworm. Peer pressures ultimately forced Elvis to become a closet reader, hiding his intellectual interests.

Although he adapted to Humes High's progressive educational program, Elvis was more often ignored by his peers and teachers. As Thomas C. Brindley, the principal, pointed out: "We never bothered Elvis about his dress. I recognized he was different from other students. We allowed him to grow up his way." With a mammoth student body, there were rules but no rigid requirements for graduation. Humes High had few social problems. The faculty fostered a down-to-earth-basics approach to education, and the student body was directed toward immediate employment, not college. Correspondingly, Humes' educational philosophy included a liberal dose of nationalism. As a result, identification with and defense of things American became an integral part of Elvis' personality. Principal Brindley was fond of pointing out that his job was to personally see to it that each student graduated into the labor market.

Between Gladys' influence and the school's strong emphasis upon a good education, Elvis was motivated to meet all the graduation requirements. By the time Elvis graduated from Humes, he was an above average student who did very well in English and history. The myth that Elvis was a mediocre plodder is untrue. Despite his humble origins, Elvis had virtually a photographic memory, and was able to pick up his school work easily. Elvis' report card reflected a sprinkling of Bs and Cs, and he was praised by his history and English teachers. They wished that he had more time to devote to his studies. He was a competent student who read voraciously. At home, Elvis spent long hours pouring over books on the Civil War, the growth of religion, and changes in American literary themes.

There were also moments of trauma during Elvis' years at Humes High. In fact, the first day he entered Humes, Elvis ended up wandering home rather than face new classmates and an alien environment. By the 1950-51 school year, however, he was well-liked and maintained a small but close circle of friends. A myth perpetuated by Elvis' biographers is that he dressed and acted differently from other Humes students. There is little evidence to suggest that he was an iconoclast or a genuinely unrequited rebel, despite the image he projected. The truth is that Elvis was much like other teenagers. He was merely part of a highly identifiable subculture—the greaser, the type of student whose most defiant qualities generally expressed themselves in a preference for hanging out at the local hamburger stand rather than in the school lunchroom. There, they listened to music and talked about cars. Elvis' most extreme rebellious quality was probably his passion for rhythm and blues music. For Elvis, listening to Billy Ward and the Dominoes, Ike Turner's Kings of Rhythm, and Sonny Til and the Orioles was simply an aspect of his education and his maturation. The greaser sported his rebellion with a clothing, a highly-defined musical backdrop, and a casual approach to life. It was a healthy rebellion reflecting the general changes in American culture and the tensions of an urban-industrial society. It all brought a new sophistication to Elvis Presley.

The Lure of Performing

In May 1953, just before graduating, Elvis would became part of a band almost by accident. Ronald Smith was hired to play a supper club, the Hi-Hat. The owners, Tom and Mary, were former Arthur Murray dance instructors who had invested their profits in the creation of a beautiful music club. They wanted a pop music band, but most of the Memphis groups performed country or hillbilly music. Eddie Bond and his group, a country artist and band that were decidedly un-pop, were reorganized by Ronald Smith, who also urged the hiring of Elvis as a guest vocalist. Ronald and Eddie Bond, who were also performers on KWEK in West Memphis, gave away tickets to the Hi-Hat's Saturday night show.

"I asked Elvis to bring Dixie Locke out to the Hi-

Hat," Smith recalled. "Elvis was nervous but I told him the band could play anything." It was at this May 1953, club engagement that Elvis was first introduced to Eddie Bond. "We went outside and talked in my car," Bond remarked. "I was amazed by Elvis' knowledge of pop music; he knew all the songs on that 'Hit Parade' show." When Smith took over Bond's Stompers for nightclub dates, he often brought in Ace Cannon; so it happened that when Elvis performed with the band, he was backed by some of Memphis' best musicians. "Elvis loved the Hi-Hat Club and couldn't stop talking about singing there," Ronald Smith remembered. The music was pop and there was no brawling.

Months earlier, however, Elvis had begun frequenting the rough hillbilly bars on Highway 78. During the spring and summer of 1952, Presley had discovered the Eagle's Nest nightclub, a large and popular country music bar that was undergoing a musical transition. Many of the future rockabilly and rock and roll stars tried out their new songs at the club. Johnny Burnette, while still working for the Crown Electric Company, would often play guitar on weekends there, and it was Burnette who got Elvis a job cleaning up in the club. Burnette played country music, and was thinking about forming his own band. He then began experimenting with rockabilly sounds, and this drew like-minded musicians out to the Eagle's Nest. One of those musicians was a superb guitar player, Paul Burlison, who ultimately helped set the standard for rockabilly music.

In 1953, Burnette and Burlison would form the "Rock 'N' Roll Trio." The third member, Dorsey Burnette, was Johnny's brother. When the Rock 'n' Roll Trio came to prominence on the "Ted Mack Amateur Hour," the national exposure made the boys Memphis celebrities. (What is ironic is that the Rock 'N' Roll Trio were actually professional musicians who had recorded prior to their appearance on the "amateur" hour.) Eventually, in the 1960s, Johnny and Dorsey Burnette would emerge as successful solo artists. In the early 1950s, however, they played at the Eagle's Nest, providing Elvis with invaluable opportunities to nurture his talents. As Elvis watched bands like these perform, he longed to be able to sing in a group. He approached Ronald Smith with the idea of appearing in a South Side High talent show, and Smith agreed to perform with him.

On Thursday, November 15, 1952, Ronald Smith nervously prepared for the South Side amateur show. The sixty-cent admission benefited the school band. Ron and Elvis performed as a duo, with Elvis singing cover versions of Lefty Frizzell's "Till Then" and Billy Ward and the Dominos' "60 Minute Man." The Shelby Falen band were special guests on the show, but weren't allowed to compete for prizes. Falen's group was semi-professional and solidly-booked into local clubs. Paul

Ronald Smith performing at Ellis Auditorium, March 9, 1952. (Photo courtesy Ronald Smith)

Burlison played lead guitar for the group, and he was intrigued by Elvis' talent. Burlison, a close friend of Ronald Smith's, was extraordinarily gifted on guitar, and he engaged in a friendly guitar duel with Smith that night. Elvis benefited greatly from such musical battles.

Although Ronald and Elvis failed to earn enough applause for an encore, they left feeling good about the show. Ronald took Barbara Hearn home, and Elvis, after dropping off Dixie Locke, quickly drove to Mississippi Street to spend the night with his secret girl friend, Patti Philpott. She was only fifteen years old, but had the body of a mature woman. And she loved Elvis. "Elvis told me that Patti had to buy a whole lot of lipstick to keep up with him," Ronald Smith chuckled. This torrid but secret affair was important to Elvis, who wanted both the respectability of girls like Barbara Hearn and Dixie Locke while still sharing the luscious curves of Patti Philpott—a lifelong predilection for dalliance that never left him.

Each night as Elvis prepared the Eagle's Nest for its musical explosion, he talked with the musicians. Almost everyone ignored Elvis; he was simply another nice kid talking music. Doug Poindexter and the Starlite Wranglers played regularly at the Eagle's Nest. "That boy was always around the music scene," Poindexter remarked thirty years later. "I knew he had something special, and my boys were jealous of him," Poindexter commented sipping on a whiskey. "I think Elvis judged himself against the other boys." Poindexter's remarks confirmed that Elvis studied and adopted the best that local musicians had to offer.

It was as Elvis watched Poindexter's group that he concluded that he had to form a backup band for himself. So, Elvis began looking. One person he admired was Paul Burlison, lead guitarist for the Rock 'N' Roll Trio. Not only was he a musician that Elvis envied, but Burlison had a style that Elvis loved. No one could play lead guitar like Burlison; that is, until Elvis saw the musicians in Doug Poindexter's band. He realized that Scotty Moore's guitar and Bill Black's bass were the best he had ever heard. They had a sound that Elvis believed could transform his voice. As he entered his final year at Humes High, Elvis had finally acquired the confidence to pursue a musical career.

Many Elvis biographers, notably Albert Goldman, dismiss the importance of these formative years. The most contrived description of Elvis' adolescent years is contained in Goldman's book, *Elvis*. In a chapter entitled "Portrait of the Artist as a Young Punk," Goldman draws a highly inaccurate picture of Elvis' high school years. Elvis is portrayed as simply a shy student who blended in unnoticed with the 1,600 other students at Humes High. While there is some truth to this generalization, it fails to mention that Elvis was active in academic clubs, worked in the library, and dabbled in sports. Elvis was not a "prisoner in some old-fashioned penitentiary," as Goldman charges; rather, he was a simply a young man in the process of molding his character.

True, during his years at Humes High, Elvis had never fit into the football pep rally, school dance, talent show scene. He reluctantly participated in these activities—performing at school assemblies as he gradually perceived them as the start of the road to a musical career—but yearned for freedom from the necessity of having to go through them. Elvis instead took full advantage of the ice cream parlors, poolrooms, and record stores near the Lauderdale Court. He also attended concerts at Ellis Auditorium and was a regular at the St. Mary's church dances. The teen canteen, a small building in the Lauderdale Court, was another place that Elvis often played his music. In September 1952, Elvis' parents allowed him to begin to hold parties in the family's Lauderdale Court apartment. "Elvis was a central part of the neighborhood," Buzzy Forbess remembers. "Most of the parties were at his house, and in the evenings things centered around Elvis and his guitar." Elvis was so busy playing the guitar that he seldom danced. When Elvis did dance, it was to Kay Starr's "Harbor Lights."

In retrospect, Elvis was like many other high school students in the 1950s; he was bored with school, interested in music, considering his options, and was searching for his place in society. By looking forward to the special events like the May Memphis Cotton Carnival, Elvis escaped school's drudgery. He also dated a large number of girls, and developed a great deal of self-confidence.

Coming of Age

In the early 1950s, Humes High was a training ground for marriage, an eight-to-five job, and blue-collar, working-class life. Like most young men, Elvis reflected the values and contradictions of the Eisenhower years. The black pants, pink shirt, narrow purple suede belt, and wild sport coat were symbols of a newly emerging teenage subculture. Elvis didn't create this phenomena; he was simply a reflection of it. The only difference is that Elvis became the symbol for a generation. Elvis didn't reject the lifestyle and values of the mass consumption fifties American teenager; rather, he embraced and popularized these ideas. His career and personality celebrated the rejection of conformity and the rise of monetary hedonism. Rock and roll music was part of the phenomena that teenagers used to proclaim their newfound individuality.

The view that Elvis was a mediocre nonentity who accidentally burst into rock and roll fame is a myth growing out of an insufficient knowledge and awareness of what went on during his high school years. This viewpoint suggests that Elvis simply stole the essence of black music and transformed the themes inherent in rhythm and blues and blues music into the mainstream of white culture. During his years at Humes High, Elvis did talk about copying black musicians, an innocent statement that has been taken out of context to suggest that Elvis merely mimicked black artists.

During his years at Humes High, Elvis pondered his future. Vernon's unstable lifestyle was motivational, because it prompted Elvis to make important career decisions. When Sam Phillips released "That's All Right (Mama)" on Sun Records in July 1954, Elvis remarked to reporters that he was enrolled in an electrician's school. Elvis' earliest dream was to become a skilled tradesman, and this resulted in an innocent fictional story designed to impress others with his career goals. This tale offers an important insight into Elvis' character. The electrician myth that Vernon and Elvis invented reflected the dream of a lifetime job with a guaranteed income. Elvis had watched his father move from one job to the next and vowed to find a stable career.

But Elvis often wondered if hard work guaranteed success. He remarked to Buzzy Forbess that his parents were making more money than ever, but they couldn't tell anyone for fear of being evicted from the Lauderdale Court. Johnny Burnette, who graduated from Humes High in 1952, was a frequent visitor to the Presley household; Johnny and Elvis would sit around and play their guitars. They spent long hours talking about different types of music and trying out new songs. Burnette talked with Elvis' about his family's bleak economic future. One of these counseling sessions stood out in Elvis' memory. He continually talked about the time on Thanksgiving Day, 1952, when Johnny Burnette came home on leave from the U.S. Navy. Burnette came over to the Presleys' house and persuaded Elvis that better times were ahead. Like the old days during their youth, they played and sang for hours. Johnny suggested that Elvis develop the same unique rockabilly sound that they both enjoyed, and he urged Elvis to consider forming a group.

As a result of their son's show business ambitions, Vernon and Gladys continually prodded him to instead find a good profession. Their remarks made Elvis feel guilty, and he searched continually for the perfect job. The constant pressure from his dad prompted Elvis to pay homage to the idea of a respectable job even as he ached for center stage. "Elvis had pressures none of us understood," one close friend remarked. This was the consensus of the people who lived in the Lauderdale Court. Elvis had also made a number of friends at South Side High School, and they, too, recalled that Vernon pressured Elvis to find "decent" work.

For some time prior to his senior year, Elvis had been going around with Travis and Johnny Smith in search of a job. Unfortunately, they were all wild-eyed young rebels who frightened most employers. Even mule-work employers turned down the Smiths because they were "frightening to look at." One prospective employer remarked, "Travis and Johnny looked and acted like they came from the hills. They couldn't do much work. Their wild hair-dos and asinine grins made us feel strange." When they did get employment, it was due to Elvis. He was a personable and intelligent young man, and he had a way with local businessmen. Eventually, Elvis decided to lie about his age and go to work for Precision Tool. The Smiths, hired just prior to Elvis' application, helped him get the job.

Before he applied, Elvis walked over to the 1132 Kansas address to take a look at the building. He then went home and called Whitehall 8-1652 and asked if they were hiring. A day later, on June 3, 1951, Elvis filled out an employment application and was hired to work from 7:00 a.m. to 3:20 p.m. The employment application was a simple one; sixteen-year-old Elvis put down that he was eighteen. When one of his fellow workers mentioned that Elvis was going to be a junior at Humes, Elvis was promptly fired. He was told to turn in his badge, number 78; a prized possession, he instead told Precision Tool that he had lost it. Elvis later gave the badge to Ronald Smith. Although Precision

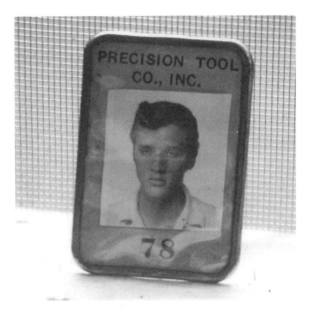

Elvis' Precision Tool badge, pictured here for the very first time. (Photo courtesy Ronald Smith)

Tool were impressed with Elvis' work, the company demanded that its employees be eighteen years old.

In September 1952, when Elvis began his senior year at Humes High, he took a part-time job at the Marl Metal Company. On the application he filled out at Marl Metal, Elvis listed his previous job at Precision Tool. When the supervisor at Marl Metal called the Precision boss, he received a glowing report about Presley's work. He was told that Elvis was let go because he was too young, but the supervisor noted that he was an aggressive and responsible worker. At Marl Metal, Elvis had a dead-end janitorial position. All he did was sweep up during the evening shift, but the dollar-an-hour pay was excellent. In less than eight weeks, though, Elvis' school work suffered dramatically. Gladys made him quit the job and again lectured him on the necessity of an education.

By January 1953, Elvis Presley was a mature, eighteen-year-old high school student. He had developed a strong sense of self worth, and no longer needed one girlfriend to feel confident. By the spring of 1953, Elvis was hanging around with a group of local truckdrivers. Their big trucks, long hair, sideburns, and free lifestyle intrigued him. Although his own sideburns had been long for some time, his hair greasy, and his collar turned up, it was in the early months of 1953 that he accentuated these affectations into a distinctive personal style. The truck driver mystique was one Elvis loved, and he imagined himself as a tough, blue-collar trucker.

Albert Goldman's biography contends that in 1953 Elvis was the "weird kid with the sideburns." This conclusion ignores the fact that Elvis was also—in many other ways—much more like any other Humes High student. Searching for the proper image to carry out his high school fantasies, the macho, tough truck driver was the perfect model for Elvis. His fantasy was a healthy one, and helped him to grow up with a strong sense of working class values; in fact, Elvis was so well adjusted that many of his friends described him as "boring."

In his chapter on Elvis' high school days, Goldman contends that Elvis suffered from severe emotional problems. To support this contention, Goldman weaves a narrative picture of a paranoid young Elvis wandering around the hallways of the Lauderdale Court at night naked except for his underwear. Goldman observes that since the Presleys were "hillbillies," they never considered consulting a doctor about Elvis' sleepwalking. What is troublesome about this line of reasoning is that Elvis' behavior was no different than any other family member. They were a strange lot, but there was no sign of mental illness. The wild paranoid delusions described by Goldman were not part of Elvis' public life. Nor is there any evidence that these patterns dominated his early years. Another problem with Goldman's biography is that he describes Elvis as crowning himself with "the world's most celebrated hair style." The greasy look was part of a larger, teen-oriented rebellion, and it reflected the beatniks' concept of "cool" mixed with the new power of the rock and roll rebellion. Most teenagers of the time used these badges to protect themselves from the adult world. In reality, Elvis was much like any other teenager surviving high school during the 1950s. He was cool, confident, and musically inclined.

The change in Elvis' personal appearance, then, was merely symbolic of an internal metamorphosis. He was struggling to assert himself and to tell the world that he wanted to become a professional singer. During his last year at Humes High, Elvis continually talked about the lure of show business. By all accounts, it was an obsession with him. A man must make a living, Vernon Presley lectured Elvis, and he pointed out that it was difficult to make it in the music business. Undaunted, Elvis continued to plod toward his musical goals.

Cypress Street

On November 28, 1952, the Memphis Housing Authority notified the Presleys that they no longer qualified for public housing. The family income exceeded the amount required to live in the Lauderdale Court. It was difficult for Vernon to find adequate housing in the ninety days allowed him, but finally, after the Christmas vacation, the family found an apartment at 398 Cypress Street. The new apartment was located in a seven-room house, which offered occupancy for four families. The Presleys paid fifty-two dollars a month for two rooms. It was a small, depressing living situation. Elvis constantly complained to his dad that his friends wouldn't visit him in the Cypress Street apartment, and he urged Vernon to get a real job. For the first time in their life, Elvis and Vernon fought with one another over money.

Despite the circumstances, Elvis tried to make the best of the apartment. After the Presleys moved, Elvis performed in the December 1952 Humes High Christmas talent show. He sang his standard repertoire— "Keep Them Cold, Cold Icy Fingers Off of Me" and "Till I Waltz Again with You." Elvis was the only act awarded an encore; he performed his good luck song, "Old Shep." Elvis' history teacher, Mildred Scrivener, remembers how nervous Elvis was performing in front of his classmates. "He was standing on the edge of the stage, half-hidden by the curtain when I told him, it's you, Elvis, go out and sing another song." Suddenly Elvis' stature and popularity hit a new high. After Christmas, as Elvis sat outside Kay's Drive Inn, his newfound confidence was demonstrated in casual banter with close friends. He was like a regal king, eating cheeseburgers and drinking double-chocolate shakes.

Frequently ensconced at Kay's Drive-In, Elvis got many invitations to perform at house parties. When he sang for friends at these dimly lit affairs, he often covered recent rhythm and blues tunes. He also indulged in the luxury of smoking cigars. "It makes me feel like a man," Elvis remarked to his cousin, Billy Smith. These gatherings gave Elvis a chance to perform the rhythm and blues hits that he spent so much time listening to and learning. Yet, as we know, this was only one form of music that interested Presley.

Throughout his years at Humes High, Elvis was intrigued by gospel music. His interest in gospel songs was a lifelong one. He found it inspirational, but also a natural release for his fundamentalist religious guilt. One of the earliest gospel concerts that Elvis attended was held in August 1951. Just before starting his junior year at school, Elvis went to an all-night gospel concert at Ellis Auditorium. He was mesmerized by the style that gospel singers employed to reach their audience; the singers used a personal plea, and he loved its impact. That night, Elvis first saw the Blackwood Brothers perform, and for the next three years he listened to records by the Blackwoods and their younger counterparts, the Songfellows. The Blackwoods were also featured in a weekly radio show broadcast from the Peabody Hotel. They frequently chatted with Sam Phillips over the radio and in the Sun studios. Elvis observed their shows intently, and began incorporating the Blackwoods' music into his practice sessions.

There were a number of gospel quartets who were as important as the Blackwood Brothers in the early 1950s. Elvis' favorite group was Hovie Lister and the Statesmen. The lead singer, Jake Hess, was an extremely influential figure in Elvis' musical development. Not only was Hess able to mesmerize the audience with his unique singing style, but he radiated a charismatic sincerity that turned these concerts into lovefests. His performance was similar to Presley's during the latter's touring heyday. In 1946, Hess participated in the first all-night gospel concert in Atlanta, and the sound he created was a unique one. By the early 1970s, rock groups like Lynyrd Skynyrd, Wet Willie, the Allman Brothers, and the Marshall Tucker band had transformed Hess' vocal style and gospel backdrop into a special brand of Southern rock and roll.

Another group that influenced Elvis was the Sunshine Boys. They frequently traveled up from Florida for concerts, and the groups' bass singer, J.D. Sumner, met Elvis in 1949 at a church songfest. It was not long before Sumner joined the Blackwood Brothers. Sumner's ability to employ the black spiritual within a pop-religious framework intrigued Elvis. The notion of using Sumner's bass voice in much the same manner the Mills Brothers used their bass sound stuck in Elvis' mind.

It was J.D. Sumner who first noticed Elvis hanging around Ellis Auditorium in 1951-52, and he spent a great deal of time answering young Elvis' questions about gospel music. "When Elvis auditioned for the Songfellows, J.D. Sumner told him to forget the music business," Ronald Smith remarked. "I was amazed when Elvis hired Sumner to work with him." As Smith suggests, Elvis had many people throw barbs at him, only to turn around later and hire them. Since Presley loved Sumner's voice, he saw no conflict in putting J.D. on the payroll.

In 1952-53, the level of Elvis' musical talent was demonstrated when a number of Memphis gospel groups considered hiring him. In the early 1950s, the Blackwood Brothers moved to Memphis, and they selected the First Assembly of God church as their base. Cecil Blackwood, a student in Elvis' Sunday school class, recognized Presley's talent. Cecil and two other members of the Blackwood Brothers attended the same church. The Stamps were another gospel quartet who attended the First Assembly of God church. The Stamps featured J.D. Sumner's bass voice, and were continually on the lookout for new talent. Since he had known Sumner for some years, Elvis was allowed to practice with the group. It was common to see Elvis at Kay's Drive-In eating with the Songfellows or the Stamps. The Stamps listened to Elvis sing and suggested that he audition for a gospel group. He talked to anyone who would listen about becoming a member of one of the local gospel quartets. It didn't work out, but this encouragement prompted Elvis to continue his quest for a singing career. Whenever Elvis watched the Blackwoods perform at local concerts, he would talk to Ronald Smith, Kenneth Herman, or Leroy Green about his gospel singing ambitions. It was common to see Elvis backstage at these gatherings. When Johnny Burnette asked Elvis why he hung around the gospel concerts, Elvis replied: "Because it's the best music in Memphis."

While he pursued his interest in white gospel music, Elvis also immersed himself in black gospel sounds. The Soul Stirrers, featuring young Sam Cooke, helped Elvis mold a soulful approach to his own music. Elvis admired the ballad artist, but his musical interests remained eclectic ones. Such ballad artists as Nat King Cole, Billy Ward, and Charles Brown were balanced by the more raucous sounds of Roy Brown, Wynonie Harris, and Ray Charles. These varied influences helped Elvis blend his music into a mainstream pop-gospel sound.

An important influence in this period was an obscure songwriter, Percy Mayfield. As a performer largely confined to the chitlin circuit, Mayfield was an unknown rhythm and blues and blues performer until he began writing hit songs for Ray Charles. Soon, Charles hired Mayfield as a full-time songwriter. In the summer of 1953, Elvis discovered some of the songs Mayfield had written for Ray Charles. It was while listening to "The Sun's Gonna Shine Again," "Losing Hand," "Mess Around," and "It Should Have Been Me" that Elvis discovered a unique blend of pop and rhythm and blues songs that fit his own style. It was therefore not surprising that when Elvis later appeared on the "Louisiana Hayride," he performed Ray Charles' classic tune "I Got a Woman." Charles' music was the perfect blend of blues, rhythm and blues, and pop music.

While listening to Charles' records during his senior year at Humes High, Elvis talked at length to Ronald Smith about his hopes for a music career. Elvis' early thoughts about show business were also articulated to the son of the First Assembly of God pastor, Jimmy Hamill. By the summer of 1953, as Elvis walked down to the First Assembly of God church at 960 S. Third Street, he considered his musical options. "Elvis wanted to be a gospel singer," Ronald Smith remarked. "He liked pop and hillbilly music, but it made him uneasy. He was a religious young man with a feeling for the church."

The period from 1948 through 1952 was a rich one for young Elvis. He blossomed as a student, expanded his musical knowledge, and began to dream of a show business career. Elvis looked forward to high school graduation and the prospects of finding his place in Dwight Eisenhower's America.

CHAPTER 6
The Making of a Performer, 1953

In June 1953, as Elvis Presley prepared to graduate from L.C. Humes High School, his future appeared bright. Not only was the Memphis economy growing rapidly, but there were unprecedented employment opportunities for high school graduates. The prospects for Elvis to earn a steady income delighted Vernon, who bragged to his friends in the local beer joints that prosperity was just around the corner. Vernon's lower-class Southern value system demanded that the prodigal son bring home a paycheck. Gladys was equally proud of her son, but for different reasons. Not only was Elvis the first Presley to graduate from high school, but he was the first family member to easily secure a job. Yet, it is surprising how little Vernon and Gladys knew about Elvis' academic potential. They were so busy making a living and adjusting to life in Memphis that they were oblivious to his present and future educational needs.

The shortsighted view that Vernon Presley had about the future provides an important insight into Elvis' character. Continually striving to please his father, Elvis never challenged Vernon's attitudes concerning education. To many of his close friends, however, Elvis expressed a desire for more schooling. College was out of the question, but he hoped to at least learn a trade. It was important for Elvis to be someone, but a good Southern boy didn't disobey his father.

Not only was Elvis a loyal son, he considered it improper to debate his father. Vernon was a manipulator who viewed his son simply as another arm of the Presley family economic machine, a role that Vernon himself had manifestly failed to fulfill much of his life. As a result, there was tension between Vernon and Elvis that remained until the day that Gladys Presley died. Vernon couldn't understand why Elvis' mother loved her son so much. He was openly jealous of Gladys' relationship with Elvis. As a result, fights between Vernon and Gladys colored both their overall views of Elvis' life.

Lost Ambitions

Vernon and Gladys either ignored or just couldn't appreciate an important aspect of Elvis' development at Humes: his interest in the math and English clubs, an indication of his intellectual curiosity, ability, and achievement that totally escaped them. As early as the fifth grade in Tupelo, Elvis had also demonstrated leadership in school politics. While he participated in a wide variety of activities during his senior year in high school; however, he ended up steering clear of student government activities. In the early 1950s, it wasn't considered "cool" to be a student officer. This is one of the reasons that Elvis admired George Klein. The years that Klein served in student government at Humes were ones in which Elvis had the same unfulfilled aspirations.

A number of Elvis' friends remember him talking about how much he enjoyed being in school. His parents, on the other hand, believed that high school was enough education for a Presley—in fact, a stellar achievement. Vernon and Gladys had assumed that Elvis worked in the school library, for example, for monetary reasons, not because he had any academic interests. Elvis' parents had no way of knowing that he was a better student than his grades indicated. Elvis often relaxed in the school library, a warm spot where he could unwind. He liked to read historical fiction and biographies, which provided an element of fantasy, escape, and a glimpse of far horizons. As a young man, Elvis' keen intellectual interests were responsible for secret reading habits that satisfied his quest for knowledge.

Elvis' favorite extracurricular school activity, the English club, provided him with an excuse to read a number of historical novels. Since his earliest days in Tupelo, Elvis had been a voracious reader. During his grade school years, Elvis and a classmate, Wayne Earnest, read comic books. Hopalong Cassidy, Batman, Superman, and Tarzan were Elvis' favorites. Eventually, he became obsessed with Captain Marvel comics. This was the quiet part of his education, and few people were aware of his reading habits. The music hid this side of Elvis' character. (Elaine Dundy's book, *Elvis and Gladys*, suggests that Elvis copied Captain Marvel's personal logo to produce his own trademark TCB lightning bolt. The lightning bolt on the front of Captain Marvel's costume intrigued Elvis, and he frequently made references to it. Whether or not Elvis copied the Captain Marvel logo is impossible to prove, but there is no doubt that Presley was a persistent and ambitious reader.)

Once he was out of school, Elvis read more than ever. Throughout the rest of his life he read constantly on a wide variety of subjects, and even brought a trunk of books on his tours. This love for books and knowledge was a trait that never left him, and one which helped sustain him for more than twenty years in the rock and roll musical jungle.

In the spring of 1953, during his last few months at Humes High, Elvis disguised his love of learning to most of his friends. Only a few of them were aware of and recognized his intellectual curiosity. As a consequence of his serious academic side, Elvis sought out South Side High School students like Ronald Smith. Not only was Smith Elvis' friend, but he provided a sounding board for Presley's ideas. It was obvious that Elvis' friends at Humes—an odd assortment of rednecks and aggressive poor kids more interested in their social life than in pushing for a better grades—would find it difficult to believe that he loved books. It was virtually impossible for Elvis to talk with dull, pedantic people like Red West or aggressive social climbers like George Klein. The students that Elvis hung around with at Humes had very little interest in school. As a result, when Elvis relaxed in Memphis with his Humes High chums, books were the last thing they would talk about.

Friends from nearby South Side High—Ron Smith, Ken Herman, Barbara Hearn—were the ones who fed Elvis' intellectual and musical appetites. The few people who saw this side of Elvis were intrigued by his persistent academic curiosity. When Ronald Smith introduced Elvis to Barbara Hearn, Elvis was impressed with her knowledge of politics. She was not only a beautiful girl, but had a strong interest in Republican Party politics.

For a time, Elvis dated Barbara, who provided him not only intellectual stimulation but a glimpse into a world of political ideas that had previously been alien to young Presley. Elvis' close friends remember that he was mesmerized by Barbara, and followed her around like a puppy dog. She possessed the class and academic savvy that Elvis desired. Bound for college, she was the most impressive person Elvis had ever met; her aura of personal power transfixed him. Elvis, on the other hand, could only dream of college; he had family responsibilities. Hearn eventually married a CIA agent, James Smith. (Her engagement ring allegedly once belonged to Francis Gary Powers, shot down over Russia during Dwight Eisenhower's presidency.)

Getting Ready to Rock

By June 1953, Humes High alumnus Elvis Presley would be ready for a full-time job. Not only was the local economy booming, but there were signs of an increasingly vibrant teenage consumer society. In the record shops, clothing stores, and drive-in hamburger spots, young people were spending money at phenomenal rates. There was a quiet revolution brewing in young people's record-buying habits. Rhythm and blues discs—the type of songs that evolved into mainstream rock and roll—sold

Ronald Smith and Barbara Hearn,
South Side High School Junior Prom, May 1954
(Photo courtesy Ronald Smith)

well in local stores. Elvis himself spent virtually every free waking hour listening to the radio or playing his records.

There was a reason for Elvis' obvious interest in records. Although he knew he was now bound for the job market that Humes High had prepared him to enter, he had made the decision to pursue a singing career. His success during the December 1952 Humes High variety show had spurred his show business ambitions. It would not be until after graduation that Elvis would finally have the time and money to pursue his avocation, however. Meanwhile, he planned to continue to haunt the local clubs and fully develop his musical talent. Elvis confided his thoughts to Ron Smith and Ken Herman, hoping that they wouldn't scoff at his chances for success. They didn't. In fact, they encouraged Elvis and listened to his youthful dreams.

As noted earlier, just before he graduated from Humes, Ronald Smith had taken Elvis to the Hi-Hat Supper Club on Third Street to meet Eddie Bond. Although he was not yet a recording artist—they did not record until 1955—Bond was a highly respected local musician. Bond's band, the Stompers, included some of the finest Memphis musicians and played in all the local clubs, combining traditional country music with pop tunes.

Bond not only encouraged Elvis, but often hired him as a pop singer so as to broaden the band's appeal. When Eddie Bond and the Stompers played at a local club, Elvis was always ready to jump up on stage for a number. It was due to these impromptu sit-in sessions that Eddie Bond decided to hire Elvis for special club dates. "Elvis could sing all the pop songs," Bond recalled. "He was like a jukebox. Elvis could sing all the songs on the *Billboard* pop chart. I hired him for the older people. The ones who liked ballads."

It was obvious to Eddie Bond that Elvis spent a great deal of time watching television. "He sounded like Snooky Lanson, that guy on the 'Hit Parade'," Bond recalled. ("Your Hit Parade" was a television show featuring Snooky Lanson's smooth ballad style.) Bond chuckled as he expounded, "He could sing almost every song on the 'Hit Parade'." As a result of watching television, Elvis often performed tunes that didn't suit his vocal range. The important part of Elvis' early training was that he was willing to experiment with any type of tune.

Eddie Bond, flanked by Ronald Smith (left) and Johhny Fine, at the Peabody Hotel, Spring 1954.
(Photo courtesy Ronald Smith)

One of the first clubs that Bond hired Elvis to play at was the VFW hall in Hernando, Mississippi. A picturesque, rural town, half an hour from Memphis, Hernando was home to a long, white VFW building with a huge parking lot, one often used by moonshine whiskey drinkers. It was located on the outskirts of town and, according to Bond, "drew a hell of a crowd." Sat-

urday night dances were a tradition, and people of all ages showed up for the music. The young men dressed up and the girls had on their finest dresses. At intermission time, the parking lot was filled with refreshment seekers. "Elvis was nervous that hot summer night in Hernando," Edyth Peeler, a local resident recalled. "He wore a pair of faded blue jeans and a plaid jacket. We had no idea who he was." Mrs. Peeler did notice that the girls sitting on the edge of the stage liked Elvis. "They surrounded him at the intermission. He sure was a good-looking boy. Now that I recall, I also liked his singing." Comments like these were repeated by a number of other Hernando residents, all of whom had fond memories of the night Elvis performed in their little white VFW hall.

Elvis' appearance with the band provided some insights into his future career. When Elvis arrived in Hernando and got out of his car, he was horrified at the dance site. "Elvis hadn't played any country honky-tonks," Eddie Bond recalled. "He was stunned by the drinking in the parking lot." Moonshine whiskey was in abundance and it was not unusual for a gun to fire followed by a rebel yell. The VFW dance was a place where the farmer, the small businessman, and local workers could let loose. Young girls, not so young women with big breasts, and the traditional-looking army couple crowded the dance floor. To Presley, it was a strange environment to sing romantic ballads. Elvis told Eddie Bond that he would convert the crowd to his kind of music. Bond had no idea what Elvis meant. When Elvis performed Guy Mitchell's 1950 classic "The Roving Kind" and Johnny Ray's 1951 hit "The Little White Cloud That Cried," it was clear that he selected songs the locals liked. "I saw those tunes on the jukebox inside the hall," Elvis laughed. "I knew those folks would like those songs," he told Bond.

During his performance, Elvis sang two sets of songs. During each set he sang "Crying in the Chapel." No one was really sure why Elvis repeated his songs, considering how many he knew. The reason was simple. He used these small shows to perfect his delivery of a particular tune. Since he favored pop ballads, no one really cared if Elvis sang a song more than once—he was able to work the girls into a frenzy with anything he sang. What it amounted to, though, was that long before Elvis became the first rock and roll superstar, he was consciously practicing the act that would take him to the pinnacle of show business success.

Elvis' musical ambitions soon took on something of an obsessive-compulsive character. He was determined to find the key to success. Ron Smith, who played lead guitar in the Stompers, remembers that Elvis would show up to sit in at many of the band's club dates. Eddie

The original lineup of Eddie Bond and the Stompers, early 1953.
(L. to r.): Ronald Smith, hot guitar; Enlo Hoskins, bass; Johnny Fine, drums;
Curtis Lee Alderson, vocals, dancer; Jody Chestine, steel guitar; Eddie Bond (kneeling), vocals.
(Photo courtesy Ronald Smith)

Bond often looked for Elvis to show up. "I liked to bring him on stage, it added something to our show," Bond recalled. Even when the band didn't mention where it was playing, Elvis would often be waiting to sit in. "Any place we played, Elvis showed up," Ronald Smith remarked. "I remember one night we played at a home for the crippled; it was a small-time charity gig, but Elvis showed up to sit in." "We wouldn't tell Elvis we were playing there," Ronald Smith recalled, "but he would show up to sit in with us." (To further their musical skills, Eddie Bond and the Stompers played the Home for the Incurables. It was a residence for the physically handicapped, and the patients loved to see live musicians. Johnny Fine was the group's bass player, and he remembers that Elvis' ballads had a soothing effect upon the patients.) Ronald Smith often had to defend Elvis, because some of the other musicians were tired of seeing him show up at the gigs.

"I used to bet Elvis would be waiting for us," Kenneth Herman remarked, "but we always let him sing something." Ken Herman continued to reminisce: "We still don't know how Elvis found out we were playing." At the country or hillbilly nightclubs, Elvis was adept at jumping on stage to fill a few intermission minutes or to appear in an amateur night spot. It was typical of Elvis to find every opportunity he could to play his music in front of an audience—any audience.

The Memphis music scene was a very competitive one, and it was a natural place for Elvis to develop his talent. In small clubs like the Silver Slipper, the Silver Stallion, the 1600 Club, the Green Owl, the Green Beetle, the Rosewood, the Officers Club Airport, the Blue Haven, the Bon Air, the Palms, the Coral, the Wayside Inn, the Gypsie Village, the Hut, the Hi-Hat Supper Club, the 5 Gables, the Cottage Inn, the Peabody Hotel, the Hotel Chesca, the Hotel Clarage, the Cotton Club, Danny's, the Wagon Wheel, the Plantation Inn, and the VFW hall in Hernando, Mississippi, Elvis learned his craft. These little, out-of-the-way clubs provided the training ground for a number of other Memphis musicians who were soon to burst into the national spotlight (more on the club scene follows below). There was also a "Teen Canteen" that offered an opportunity for fledgling musicians to find an audience. It was a unique time for Memphis musicians, because there were many places to craft their musical skills. The pay was minimal, but the chance for musical exposure was very great indeed.

One Saturday morning, Elvis was awakened by a phone call from Ronald Smith. One of Ronald's friends, Mary Scott, had suggested that her dad hire a teenage band to play at the Columbia Mutual Towers. This engagement, in May 1953, a month before Elvis' high school graduation, was part of Memphis' annual Cotton Carnival celebrations. Ronald and Elvis joined with Ray and James Damon Sexton to play in the activity room at the twelve-story Columbia Mutual Towers building. The dance was an adult affair, and the band stuck primarily to country and pop tunes. Elvis was delighted with the job.

It was also about this time, as discussed earlier, that he began showing up regularly at the Hi-Hat club to watch Eddie Bond and the Stompers. The importance of the influence of the band that Eddie Bond put together for the Hi-Hat should be further emphasized. In addition to Ronald Smith on guitar, it included drummer Mark Waters, and piano player Aubrey Meadows. Dixie Locke frequently came with Elvis to the Hi-Hat, and he loved to show her that he knew the musicians. The tight musical arrangements and energetic country songs of Eddie Bond and the Stompers impressed Elvis, and he told Ronald Smith that it was his goal to one day be as professional on stage as the Stompers.

It was also Eddie Bond who tried to persuade Elvis to play at Red's Place on Highway 61. Red's was a bucket-of-blood-type saloon that drew the worst local rednecks. Most bands were afraid to play to this crowd because of the nightly brawls. A sign at the door warned people not to urinate inside the club, and a bouncer checked patrons for weapons as they entered. The police came in every hour, looked around, and checked the bathrooms for troublemakers. People who ignored the club's signs were the least of its problems; the club was plagued by fistfights, knifings, and an occasional shooting. Paul Burlison, lead guitarist with Johnny and Dorsey Burnette's Rock 'N' Roll Trio, remembers the band having to fight its way off stage because a small coterie of roughnecks didn't like the way that they played a Bob Wills song. "They stood by the stage and hollered at us," Burlison recalled. "I was a Golden Gloves boxer and I thought to hell with them, I'd kick their ass." It was into this environment that Eddie Bond tried to coax Elvis, who refused to be coaxed. It was not only too rough, but few people listened to the music. "I can't play that place," Elvis told Ronald Smith. "They'll tear my head off." Smith laughed, but Eddie Bond persisted. Elvis instead persuaded Bond that he should sit in with the Stompers at the Hi-Hat, and he'd think about playing Red's. Frightened by the "ambiance" at Red's Place, Elvis never did.

At this stage in his life, Elvis had grown as concerned about clothing as he had his music. Not only did he spend an inordinate amount of time in front of the family mirror, but he shopped frequently at Lansky's clothing store. Located on Beale Street, and featuring the latest in hip new styles, Lansky's was one of Elvis'

Mid-1980s photo of Lansky's on Beale Street.
The sign to the right of the entrance reads:
"CLOTHIER TO THE KING."

favorite haunts.

In addition to hanging out at Lansky's clothing store, Elvis often wandered into Henry's Record Shop and Shine Parlor. Robert Henry, a Memphis businessman, had promoted every conceivable show business venture. Henry had booked musical acts like Fats Waller, Duke Ellington, and Earl "Fatha" Hines into Memphis theaters. As a result, Henry's Record Shop was a place where black musicians congregated, and therefore a focal point for Elvis. "That boy listened to our music, and took it to the bank," Jimmy McCracklin remarked. McCracklin was one of the performers booked by Robert Henry, and loved to play Memphis in 1953 because of the blues crowds. "They loved my music, and I couldn't wait to get back to Beale Street," McCracklin reminisced. Between Lanksy's and the nearby record stores and food stands, Beale Street was also Elvis' version of paradise.

During the six months after graduating from Humes High, Elvis would cultivate an extensive knowledge of urban Memphis blues. His acquaintance with rural Mississippi blues tunes was already quite strong. There was a special feeling in blues records that excited young Presley. It was the blues that inspired Elvis to alter his country and western and pop stylings, and craft his mu-

sic more towards a distinct rockabilly sound.

He began performing tunes by Memphis blues artists like Rosco Gordon, B.B. King, and Little Junior Parker, developing himself into a white blues singer with rockabilly overtones. The result would become apparent in July 1954, when Elvis entered Sam Phillips' Sun studio to record his first song. By that time, Elvis had mastered the Memphis sound, and the influence of local musicians like Eddie Bond, Marcus Van Story, Kenneth Herman, and Ronald Smith would be evident.

The Family Moves Again

During Elvis' last six months at Humes High School there were many problems. On January 7, 1953, the Presleys moved into a small flat at 698 Saffarans Street. It was a small apartment house in which—for $52-a-month rent—they secured two downstairs rooms. Elvis was miserable in these primitive living conditions, but Vernon had seven beer bars and a Pentacostal gospel mission nearby for entertainment. The Rev. Jesse James Denson ran the mission, and his sons Jimmy and Jesse Lee were among young Elvis' closest friends. Jim Denson, who claims to have first seen Elvis late in 1947—again, when the family had not yet moved to Memphis—had finally made his acquaintance while walking the few blocks to high school. Elvis was immediately attracted to Jim, the older Denson brother. He was not only a Golden Gloves boxer but a fisticuffs legend around the Lauderdale Court. Jesse Lee Denson, a talented country musician with a pop singing style, was eager to teach others his guitar licks, and Elvis was one of his earliest students. The Denson brothers re-

Site of Reverend Denson's Pentecostal mission.

Jim Denson, 1986.

to reap the benefits of the American dream. At the nearby beer bars, Vernon bragged about not having to file an earnings statement with the Memphis Housing Authority. Elvis shook his head at his father's logic and complained constantly about the living conditions at the Saffarans Street apartment. Gladys did her best to preserve a precarious peace, and she was the ballast that kept the family stable. In a psychological sense, Vernon was now in charge of the Presley family fortunes. The $52-a-month rent Vernon paid the new landlord was his first sign of fiscal independence.

There were other reasons for Elvis' unhappiness with his new surroundings. Each morning he arose and complained about the squalid sanitary conditions. The common bathroom was down the hall, and Elvis found it cold and dirty. The water was never hot and the bathtub was always filled with hair. His experiences at this apartment created an aversion to bathing, and Elvis showered only when absolutely necessary. He cultivated the habit of purchasing large bottles of Aqua Velva after-shave, and splashed the lotion all over his body. The result was a disconcerting smell, a cross between body odor and lilacs.

When Elvis' friends from the Lauderdale Court came by to talk about music, school, and girls, he appeared confident and outgoing. It was hard for Elvis to admit that he was unhappy with the new apartment, so he, too, put on a false front and bragged that his dad earned enough money to keep the Presleys out of public housing. Despite his personal hostility to the Saffarans Street apartment, however, Elvis suddenly had more money and free time, and this nurtured a more carefree attitude. He was not only evolving into a mature young man, but he had the time and money to pursue his musical interests. The exploding club scene, the guitar and singing sessions, and the influence of his high school peers made music Elvis' most important goal.

Ronald Smith

The influence of Ronald Smith upon Elvis' music is a generally ignored topic. Smith, like Elvis, came of age musically in Memphis in the early 1950s. "I first met Elvis in 1950 at a birthday party," Smith remarked. "He was singing an Eddy Arnold song, 'Please Mommy Please Stay Home with Me'." It was Pattie Philpott who introduced Ron to Elvis, and they quickly became close friends. Jesse Lee Denson was at the party, and they all played together and sang into the night. "Elvis sang some Hank Snow songs, and he really liked Lefty Frizzell's music. I was impressed," Smith remarked. "I had never seen a guy with that much knowledge."

For the next three years, they all hung out together, listened to music, and chased girls. Ronald Smith would

call Elvis as a shy boy who was often reticent to mix with the other kids, something that may have been due partially to the Presley's perpetual housing problems.

It was easy to understand why the living situation at 698 Saffarans Street depressed Elvis. In the late 1940s and early 1950s, however, many homes were divided into small apartments. The four families living in these buildings liked to reassure one another that they were a cut above the public assistance housing tenants who lived in the nearby Lauderdale Court. In theory, 698 Saffarans was a step above public housing because the rent was higher and the Presleys no longer had to go through the ritual of qualifying for low-income housing. In terms of comfort, however, the Saffarans Street apartment was disastrous. It was a small unit desperately in need of paint, new plumbing, and adequate lighting. It is ironic that by foregoing subsidized public housing, the Presley's living standard actually declined. Now they were part of the upwardly mobile lower class, who were forced to rent substandard housing because of increased income. This was an anomaly of the 1950s that Elvis could not grasp. Although Vernon Presley earned more money, there were fewer luxuries. Elvis continually expressed concern to his dad about the family fortunes. Maybe they should return to Tupelo. The Presleys were working harder then ever, but their money produced only a substandard lifestyle.

To counter Elvis' fears, Vernon constantly reminded his son that they were no longer dependent upon support from the city. The family was now a solid middle-class success, Vernon argued, and they would continue

Elvis' South Side High friend Ronald Smith, 1986.

drive his car down to pick Elvis up and they would drive toward South Side High School to pick up Ken Herman or see Eddie Bond. Elvis was one of the boys and he loved it. There was no pressure from his new friends and Elvis fit in nicely. He didn't have to prove himself as a "stud" or "macho fighter," traits admired by some of Presley's Neanderthal friends at Humes.

Smith and Presley loved the Memphis music scene. They went to the clubs to hear the new music. For a time, Ronald dated Barbara Hearn, and this is how she came to know Elvis. It was shortly before Smith graduated from school that Elvis himself began dating Barbara. Soon they were seriously involved, and Ronald Smith often came along with his own date.

In May 1953, when Ronald Smith and Elvis attended the Memphis Cotton Carnival and played for Mary Scott's dad at the Columbia Mutual Towers, Barbara Hearn came along for fun. During this appearance, Elvis talked to Barbara and Ronald about the Memphis music scene. He was aware of Sam Phillips' Sun Records label. When Phillips' second group of records was released in March 1953, Elvis went to the House of Records and found the recordings. Smith and Ken Herman were constantly amazed by Elvis' ability to come up with new musical sounds. Joe Hill Louis and Willie Nix were artists that Elvis enjoyed, but it was Rufus Tho-

mas' song "Bear Cat" that excited young Presley the most. The song, an answer tune to Big Mama Thornton's "Hound Dog" was described by Elvis as the best rhythm and blues song he had ever heard. Presley continually raved about it to Kenneth Herman. As Elvis' South Side High friends recalled, he often used his musical knowledge to win new friends. Yet, others of his contemporaries felt that Elvis tried too hard. Paradoxically, it was this intense preoccupation with music that ultimately either drew friends closer to Elvis or helped create barriers.

Some of his friends referred to Elvis as "Farley." This was a term that suggested that while Elvis was almost like the other fellows, nevertheless, he was still just a little bit different. In other words, as Ron Smith recalled, "Elvis tried so hard to be cool that he was often a little hard to take." Still, there was nothing to laugh at in his music. Even at this neophyte stage, Elvis was an exciting performer. J.D. Sexton, a marvelous fiddle player, was one of the Presley's friends who believed that there was a bright future for the unknown Humes High graduate. When Sexton played instrumental breaks during early performances, he was amazed at how Elvis worked up the crowd by dancing around the stage. There was no way to explain Elvis' moves, Sexton remarked, "he simply couldn't control himself while performing."

Borrowing from the Blues

Once he went to work, Elvis used a good portion of his earnings to frantically expand his rhythm and blues and blues record collection. He also broadened his musical knowledge by continuing to hang out in the Beale Street blues clubs, which provided an education for a neophyte performers and introduced them to new songs. Although it was in a period of decline, Beale Street was still a vibrant blues center. "I remember the white boys coming into some of the black clubs," Jimmy McCracklin recalled. It would be some time before McCracklin's hit "The Walk" established him as a major blues-rock act, but many white Memphis musicians showed up to catch McCracklin's Arkansas blues.

When Elvis wasn't trying to perform in the country and western bars, he was on Beale Street looking for new music. B.B. King remembers Elvis shyly standing in the background at the Beale Street clubs. "I saw Elvis many times," King remarked, "and he appreciated the blues." Nat D. Williams, the unofficial mayor of Beale Street, recalls that Elvis collected records by Arthur "Big Boy" Crudup and Big Bill Broonzy. "Elvis Presley when he first started on Beale Street was a favorite man," Williams remarked. "When I got to Beale Street," Paul Burlison of the Rock 'N' Roll Trio remarked, "I saw this white kid with long hair digging the blues, it was Elvis."

Nathaniel Dowd Williams' career provides some important insights into black and white relations in Memphis. Like many young blacks, Williams grew up torn between his grandmother's religious preachings and his affection for the blues. The black church considered the blues the work of the devil, and Nat Williams' conscience struggled constantly with his love for the blues. It was difficult for Williams to admit to himself that he wanted to sing "the Devil's music." Like Elvis Presley, Williams was deeply religious and concerned with moral values. Instead of following a musical career, Nat went to college and became a local high school teacher. A man caught between two lifestyles, Williams just couldn't contain his love for the blues, however. It was a schizoid heritage and Williams often gave in to his show business ambitions. During various periods, he was a well-known Memphis disc jockey, a respected musicologist, and a part-time promoter. He wore many musical hats, and it was impossible to categorize him. Many in the black community criticized him for publicly praising the blues—a man with his education was lowering himself by trumpeting the virtues of such music, his critics remarked. Supporters have pointed out that Nat Williams almost single-handedly popularized the Memphis blues. A strong promoter of black history and culture, few people recognized then that Williams was ahead of his time when he preached that the blues reflected black history.

As discussed in the previous chapter, Elvis, like many Memphis teenagers, listened to Nat D.'s show on WDIA. WDIA's audience was predominantly white; the Memphis black aristocracy complained that Williams was more of a clown than an air personality. Such criticism was unfair. Williams began each show with a brief sketch of black history. He followed his opening with a wide variety of black music. The "Tan Town Jamboree," as Williams' show was known, educated the white Memphis community about black music. It also reinforced awareness of the small elements of black history that filtered through to the local white community. Even though Memphis had a progressive school system, there was no mention of black history in classes. Elvis Presley, like many other white Memphis teenagers, unwittingly acquired an early appreciation for black culture from Williams' radio shows.

It was not long before Elvis was hanging out at WDIA. He met Nat D. and was soon friendly with a number of entertainers. Robert Henry, the owner of Henry's Record Shop and Shine Parlor, took Elvis to the Hotel Improvement Club and other nightclubs. (Henry claims that Elvis saw Charlie Burse sing and shake on stage and adopted this affectation in his own act.) They also went to the Palace Theater, where a weekly amateur talent show allowed Elvis to perform with other neophytes. (Immediately after high school graduation, Elvis entered every conceivable local amateur contest he could find.) Robert Henry told Margaret McKee and Fred Chisenhall that Elvis "had a way of singing the blues that was distinctive." While Henry didn't believe that Elvis had the "Negro feel," nevertheless, Henry remarked that blacks "were crazy about Elvis."

The Club Handy was another Beale Street club that Elvis frequented. The club was a gathering place for rhythm and blues performers, and the manager, Andrew "Sunbeam" Mitchell, brought in young and untried acts. He made a nice profit by allowing exceptionally-talented musicians to perform at the Club Handy. They played for so little that a fraternal atmosphere was necessary to survive the lack of pay. The musicians slept in small rooms adjacent to the club, so it was tantamount to a boarding school. He watched intently as vocalists and musicians interwove the blues with pungent vocal stylings.

While frequenting Beale Street, Elvis began listening late at night to Gene Nobles and John "John R" Richbourg, who broadcast out of Nashville and played rhythm and blues tunes. These disc jockeys were much like Dewey Phillips on WHBQ in Memphis; they howled, screamed, and breathed a dangerous life into the new music. (Nat Williams aside, it was generally white disc jockeys who brought black music into the bedrooms of young teenagers. It was on one of these programs that Elvis probably first heard Jackie Brenston's "Rocket 88.")

Sam Phillips also saw white and black music blending into a strange hybrid early on. Even as Phillips sold his masters to the Leonard Chess or the Bihari brothers, he began to see an opportunity for himself. When they met, it was not surprising that Elvis and Sam hit it off. They had the same vision. A music that would combine the black and white experiences, an integration of musical styles, and a market for records that would be without racial lines.

In 1953, integration and equality were creeping slowly into American life. There was a new freedom for blacks, but it was mostly a musical freedom at a time when jobs, education, and equal housing were years away on the national level. While the major changes brought about by the civil rights movement were still a decade away, blacks in Memphis were quietly moving into new jobs in 1953. They were part of the service industry, used for manual labor in the Memphis building boom, and this often led to better housing and a higher standard of living. There was economic progress in the South for everyone, and this made blacks active consumers.

In Memphis, the civil rights revolution also meant that blacks were no longer confined to Beale Street. This change in attitude allowed whites a new freedom to listen to black music. There was another side to this revolution. Blacks moved downtown. Movie theaters, department stores, and restaurants catered to the local black population. This caused Beale Street to disintegrate as the center of local black culture. In 1953, however, it was still the apex of the black music.

The rise of black rhythm and blues musicians in Los Angeles, Harlem, Chicago, and Detroit, among other urban centers, attested to a new musical vibrancy. The sounds of Glenn Miller, Jimmy and Tommy Dorsey, and the white pop crooners were antiquated to teenagers. Sex and booze were increasingly a part of the American musical consciousness. Since May 1951, when the Dominoes' "60 Minute Man" was released, there had been an excitement about rhythm and blues music. In 1953, *Billboard* reported that two and a half hours of rhythm and blues music was played each week on radio. This was a small figure, but it was a beginning.

In July 1953, Sonny Til and the Orioles' syrupy r and b tune "Crying in the Chapel" wound up in the number 11 slot on the *Billboard* Hot 100. Black vocal groups, musicians, and at times even a producer were becoming a part of the record industry.

Jerry Leiber and Mike Stoller, two young white kids from Los Angeles' Fairfax High School, were busy writing songs for Atlantic Records that changed the course of rock and roll music. These angelic-looking young kids turned out tough urban rhythm and blues, and unwittingly began a musical civil rights revolution. White writers, black producers, and black and white musicians were all combining to produce a new music, a trend that was mirrored in other parts of American life.

In 1953, the early signs of integration were apparent in Memphis clubs, dance halls, and out-of-the-way juke joints. "We didn't know what the hell was going on, but we were playing music with the blacks behind closed doors," Marcus Van Story remembered. "I think that Howlin' Wolf liked us crazy hillbillies," Kenneth Herman remarked, "he saw us as kindred spirits." It was an integration in attitude as well as in entertainment facilities. Paul Burlison, the lead guitarist with Johnny and Dorsey Burnette's Rock 'N' Roll Trio, remembers playing with Howlin' Wolf in West Memphis, Arkansas, juke joints. "We came in the back door and Wolf watched out for us."

The clubs across the river in West Memphis were a daunting sight. They were located in small, ramshackle buildings and had antiquated sound systems. The bars were creaky and ill-stocked. The crowds were abusive, violent, and hard to please. Small radio stations that broadcast the blues would urge people to come to these clubs. Howlin' Wolf used to come straight from laboring in the fields to do his show. A hulking man with a soft heart, he loved to see the white boys playing the blues, and often picked up a great deal from them himself.

Marcus Van Story

One of the more progressive Memphis musicians, Marcus Van Story was on the radio regularly in West Memphis. Van Story had a show that came on just after Howlin' Wolf's program on KWEM. For a time, Van Story worked with Texas Bill Strength on the radio and made his reputation playing with bands like Slim Scoggins and the Drifters and the Snearly Ranch Boys. A close friend of guitarist Stan Kesler, Van Story was a multi-faceted country musician with strong blues influences. He could play lead, rhythm guitar, violin, and harmonica. Deford Bailey, the black harmonica player on the "Grand Ole Opry," was an early influence upon Van Story. "It was a long time before I knew that Bailey was black," Van Story recalled. "It didn't matter to any of us, we were only interested in the music." Another important influence upon Van Story was a fiddle

Marcus Van Story, 1986.

(L. to r.): Stan Kesler, Marcus Van Story, and Ronald Smith entertain the author with an impromptu jam session.

player, Blueford Hood. He wrote the "Carroll County Blues" and combined country with blues music.

"I really learned my craft playing with the Snearly Ranch Boys," Van Story recalled. "We played all types of music from bluegrass, country and blues...." Musicians like Van Story and Stan Kesler grew up with the blues. "It was natural for us to listen to black music from childhood on up," Van Story commented. The musicians in the Snearly Ranch Boys either lived at Ma Snearly's Boarding House or hung out to jam. They included Smokey Joe Baugh on piano, Paul Burlison on guitar, Clyde Leoppard on drums, Hank Bowers on guitar-trumpet, Barbara Pittman on vocals, and Stan Kesler on bass. The Snearly Ranch Boys were one of Memphis' best bands, and they provided the studio musicians that made Sun Records successful. "Elvis had only heard about the Snearly Ranch Boys," Van Story remarked, "but he eventually came to know all of the boys who played in the band." With characteristic modesty, neither Van Story nor Kesler would pinpoint the Snearly Ranch Boys as a direct influence upon Elvis. Yet, their influence is unmistakable.

"Elvis was around watching what we were doing," Van Story remarked. "He was always so nervous," Van Story continued, "but he was learning about the music, no doubt about that." Van Story played a number of small concerts with Elvis in 1954-55. "Elvis was friendly with everyone," Van Story remembered. "Key Sheriff,

a disc jockey on WHHM, told me he played Elvis' records because he was such a nice kid. Everyone recognized that Elvis had a special way with the music," Van Story added.

"I went with Elvis to Sikeston, Missouri, on January 19, 1955, and he performed with such intensity that he came off stage and went straight into the men's room with water dripping from his head," Van Story recalled. "I asked him why he was performing so hard," Van Story continued. "It's because of Tupelo, Marcus; I can't forget Shakerag," Elvis replied. That night, they drove back to Memphis and stopped in Truman, Arkansas, for some food. "Elvis ate three cheeseburgers and then ordered three more," Van Story chuckled. "The lady asked Elvis if he planned to pay for everything."

"Yes, ma'am," Elvis replied.

"That night Elvis unburdened himself," Van Story continued. "He told me that he never forgot how poor he felt living in the Lauderdale Court. Elvis was haunted by his poverty. So, he was committed to the music," said Van Story. "He would practice in the washroom downstairs at the Lauderdale Court and try to learn from other musicians." Van Story remembered the full intensity that Elvis Presley displayed toward rock and roll music, an intensity obviously fueled not only by a love of music, but by a determination to put the poverty of places like Shakerag and Lauderdale Court behind him. In this, as we shall see when we examine the life of Colonel Tom Parker, Elvis apparently shared a psychological trait with Parker—a consuming dread of being poor—that drove him to make and adhere to alliances sometimes less beneficial than they might have been, among them his alliance with the Colonel.

One of the most obscure but significant Memphis musicians influencing Elvis was a harmonica player named James Cotton. In 1953, Cotton's band featured guitarist Pat Hare, and in December of that year Sam Phillips brought Cotton and his band into Sun Records to record two songs, "My Baby" and "Straighten Up Baby." Cotton's band had performed these tunes for some time in the Memphis area. Although Sam Phillips didn't record Cotton's songs until December 1953, Elvis had long been aware of these tunes from watching the band in local clubs.

In an interview with Helen Doob Lazar that appeared in a 1987 issue of *Living Blues*, James Cotton recalled his early Memphis days. He had a radio show six days a week for fifteen minutes on KWEM in West Memphis. "I guess Sam Phillips used to listen to the show," Cotton remarked. "He called me up one day and asked me how would I like to do a record." When "My Baby" b/w "Straighten Up Baby" (Sun 199) was released in April 1954, the record went unnoticed.

Cotton's vocals appealed to Elvis, however, and he attempted to copy them. Elvis found it difficult to emulate Cotton's style, but it suggests how far he went to develop his talent.

The Club Scene

As the summer of 1953 progressed, Elvis discovered the music at the Cotton Club in West Memphis, Arkansas. This was one of the most popular spots in the area for musicians to play after hours. Although an inconspicuous figure, Elvis learned a great deal at the Cotton Club. Johnny Burnette often accompanied Elvis, and they were greatly influenced by the blues and rockabilly sounds that local musicians employed in extemporaneous jam sessions. Paul Burlison remembers going in the back door of the Cotton Club to talk to Howlin' Wolf. "We all loved the Wolf's music, it had something special to it." Also at the Cotton Club, Elvis watched Harmonica Frank play a small harmonica. "Harmonica Frank could put that thing in his mouth and play it like a violin," Marcus Van Story noted. "No one could play blues licks better than Harmonica Frank," Ronald Smith added. "Elvis was in awe of his talent."

It was at the Hi-Hat club during the summer of 1953 that Elvis tried out some blues tunes. Dixie Locke and Ronald Smith were with Elvis at the Hi-Hat, and watched his talent develop. "Elvis loved the blues," Smith remembered. "He had a feeling for black music." Memphis Slim was another influence that summer; Ronald Smith continually talked with Elvis about the piano style of this well-known local blues artist.

Carolyn Lepley, then Sleepy-Eyed John's wife, was typical of Memphis observers who noticed Presley's emerging talent. "He was special," Lepley remembered. "There were a lot of people who saw something in Elvis," Kenneth Herman recalled. "They had no idea that he would become a recording star, but Carolyn Lepley knew crowds at the local clubs loved Presley's impromptu sets." Eventually, Carolyn Lepley, one of Presley's strongest local boosters, married the disc jockey Uncle Richard (Dick Stewart).

On weekends, Ronald Smith and Kenneth Herman would wander down to Old Red's on Third Street to play for a crowd of boisterous beer drinkers. "We would play for a couple hours and they would pass the hat," Kenneth Herman remarked. The band included Gerald Ferguson on bass, Herman on steel guitar, and Ronald Smith on lead guitar. Sometimes there was a drummer, other times the band simply played without drums. Old Red's Place was located near the Hi-Hat club, and Elvis sometimes dropped in to play with the band. In this bar, Presley sang country music tunes.

At the Hi-Hat Club, Kenneth Herman played the banjo, bass, steel, and lead guitars and often sat in on the drums. Elvis loved to listen to Herman tell tall tales about his pursuits (Ken was attending Keegan's Radio School and Elvis loved to listen to him impersonate local disc jockeys), but there was a serious side to Herman. He was an accomplished country musician who was a veritable storehouse of musical knowledge. Many of the Ernest Tubb, Bill Monroe, Hank Snow, Faron Young, and Eddy Arnold tunes that Elvis performed in small clubs resulted from conversations with Herman. At the December 4, 1956, Million Dollar Sessions in the Sun Records studio, Elvis sang Young's "Is It So Strange," Monroe's "I Hear a Sweet Voice Calling" and "Little Cabin on the Hill," and Ernest Tubb's "I'm in the Crowd, but Oh So Alone" as a result of Herman's influence. Elvis gave Herman a tape of the session by way of thanks.

This was all very typical of Elvis' musical acumen: he used other people's knowledge to build his repertoire. Another good example of this musical osmosis occurred when Elvis listened to Moon Mullican's "Whatcha Gonna Gimme" and "Jole Blon." These songs, as interpreted by Elvis, evolved into mainstream rockabilly music. During this time, Gladys Presley also encouraged her son to sing Leon Payne's "I Love You Because" and Hank Snow's "I'm Moving On," songs which Elvis easily covered.

One of the by-products of Elvis' visits to local clubs was that many owners and performers later claimed to have either auditioned or hired Elvis at one time or another. A good example of this myth is detailed in Nick Tosches' excellent book, *The Unsung Heroes of Rock 'n' Roll*. Tosches interviewed Roy Hall, a piano player who claimed to be the model for Jerry Lee Lewis. It was Hall who first recorded "Whole Lotta Shaking Goin' On" in September 1955, but a series of poor business decisions and a nasty divorce doomed Hall's career. Hall also told Tosches that, in the summer of 1954, Elvis Presley came into his Nashville club looking for work. "I was drunk that night, didn't feel like playin' piano, so I told 'im to git up there an' start doin' whatever in hell it was he did," Hall remarked. "I fired 'im after just that one night. He wern't no damn good." There is no way to verify Hall's story, but it fits the general pattern of Elvis' musical wanderings. He would play anywhere, anytime, and in front of anyone in order to further his career.

The Eagle's Nest

In March 1953, Vernon Presley bought his son the 1942 light green Lincoln Zephyr mentioned previously. This post-birthday (Elvis turned eighteen in January)/

pre-graduation present was a catalyst to Elvis' musical education, and was one of the reasons Elvis spent so much time around Beale Street. It provided the transportation as well as the image necessary in pursuing his musical dreams. The fifty-dollar car immediately became Elvis' pride and joy. Every Saturday morning, Elvis washed and waxed his prized possession, and almost every night he cruised the parts of Memphis where his friends hung out. Elvis loved to drive around the Peabody Hotel and circle the nearby Suzore Theater. It was a frivolous time for Elvis, and his confidence grew as his social popularity soared. "We pushed that car around Memphis as much as we drove it," Ronald Smith remembered. "We had a good time with that car and Elvis was just one of the fellows."

Elvis' favorite music hangout continued to be the Eagle's Nest nightclub. It was a large honky-tonk night spot out on Highway 78 that featured the best in local music. There was a swimming pool on the premises that opened each day. Clearpool, as the pool and club was referred to by locals, was a good place to meet a young lady. Good music, food, and a dance floor filled each night and made the Eagle's Nest a great bar.

The impact of the revolution in American manners and morals frightened Elvis somewhat, however. He was nervous around the girls at the Eagle's Nest, often remarking that it had gotten a little too easy to pick up girls. This moral dilemma was one that bothered Elvis much of his life. Like Jerry Lee Lewis, Elvis worried that rock and roll music was damning his soul. Kenneth Herman remembers both Jerry Lee and Elvis wringing their hands over the language, atmosphere, and morals of the early rock and roll revolution. In private they complained to Herman about the lack of "God fearing" people in the rock music business. "I saw a strong, fundamentalist Christian side to Elvis," Herman remembered, "and this caused him personal anguish. Rock and roll music simply didn't square with Elvis' religious beliefs."

Despite these conflicts, Elvis continued to immerse himself in Memphis nightlife. The clubs were packed seven nights a week, and each night a new band vied with old favorites to please the crowds. The style of music was changing, and rockabilly and blues artists dominated local musical tastes. It was a good time for Elvis to develop his singing talent. After appearing for almost a year as an amateur performer at the Eagle's Nest and other clubs, Elvis was primed to begin his own musical career. Although still in high school, Elvis spent most of his nights at the Eagle's Nest, to some degree because he simply dreaded returning to the family apartment.

There was an excitement at the Eagle's Nest that drew Elvis in like a magnet. Bands like Eddie Bond's Stompers, featuring Barbara Pittman's lead vocals, played there regularly. "We played rock 'n' roll and rockabilly," Ronald Smith remembered, "and Elvis watched our every move." Smith, a boyish-looking guitar wizard, also played with Jerry Lee Lewis and Billy Lee Riley. As one of Elvis' close friends, Smith displayed a guitar style similar to Scotty Moore's. In fact, many Memphis guitarists employed riffs like Moore's. They didn't simply copy Scotty Moore; their sound was due largely to the generalized demand for the distinctive rockabilly guitar sound that dominated Memphis.

Alabama Street

As Elvis pursued his musical dreams, the Presley family fortunes took another important turn. In April 1953, Elvis was overjoyed when Vernon and Gladys announced that the family was moving into a new apartment. The Presleys rented the bottom floor of a large house at 462 Alabama Street. This was right around the corner from the bars that Vernon initially frequented when the Presleys arrived in Memphis. Elvis liked the location because it was near Lauderdale Court. Vernon paid fifty dollars a month for the apartment, and the Presleys installed a telephone. Soon Elvis was entertaining his friends. There was more money for the family, and Elvis once again intensified his record collecting. A typical teenager, Elvis always measured the family's increased financial security by the size of his expanding record collection. He loved to show off his collection to friends, and Johnny Burnette often dropped by Elvis' house to listen to blues or rockabilly songs. Young Burnette was working days and playing music nights, and he loved to talk to Elvis about his new rockabilly sound.

For a year and a half, Elvis lived with his family in the Alabama Street apartment. It was here that Elvis plotted his earliest career moves. The two-story brick building was comfortable, and Elvis spent hours practicing his music in the living room. Minnie Mae Presley, Elvis' grandmother, would jokingly ask Elvis to quit singing because it interfered with her naps on the couch. In private moments, however, Minnie Mae encouraged Elvis, and they developed a bond that gave Elvis a great deal of security.

Vernon Presley, as usual, continued to have money problems. Since Elvis worked, though, he was helping pay the rent. In the summer of 1953, when Elvis cut "My Happiness" at his own expense in the Sun studio, Vernon had a fit. He lectured Elvis about his frivolous approach towards money, never seeing the irony in his attitude towards his son. In the long run, of course, Elvis' decisions produced more income for the family—income beyond their wildest dreams. Once he began touring in 1954, Elvis would send money home regularly to help pay the bills. In the spring and summer of 1953, though, Elvis was still far from a music career.

Graduation

The intensity of Elvis' musical desire was demonstrated the week of his high school graduation. On May 26, 1953, the First Annual Jimmie Rodgers Memorial Festival opened in Meridian, Mississippi. The celebration commemorating the singing brakeman's musical feats was not yet a highly commercial event. Although Rodgers' untimely death of tuberculosis at age thirty-six established his musical legacy, nevertheless, many of Meridian's citizens were unhappy about the celebration. As a result, there was a mixed community reaction when Rodgers' Mississippi friends organized the weekend feat. The *Meridian Star* advertised a talent contest open only to local Mississippi performers. This musical talent contest was an attempt to showcase local artists and popularize Jimmie Rodgers' music. Unwittingly, the contest promoters attracted many fledgling rockabilly singers like Elvis, performers who were young men dreaming of fame and fortune, and who, like Elvis, weren't necessarily local Mississippi performers any longer.

Elvis was only a week away from high school graduation, but the Jimmie Rodgers talent contest occupied all his thoughts. In order to convince Gladys that a trip to Tupelo was necessary, Elvis informed his mother that he wanted to go and invite some old Mississippi friends to his graduation. Gladys agreed to let Elvis go, unaware that he was actually embarking on a 240-mile trip to Meridian. It took Elvis' last few dollars for gas to make the trip, but there was no question in his mind that he had to perform in the event.

When he arrived in the sleepy Mississippi town, Elvis went immediately to the Lamar Hotel. It was in this hotel that Jimmie Rodgers was treated by his Meridian physician, Dr. Inman Cooper. To local citizens, the hotel symbolized Rodgers' tragic end. Consequently, it was selected as the site of the amateur singing contest. This magnificent old Southern hotel had a spacious ballroom, an open garden sitting area, and a sumptuous dining room. The crowd milling around the Lamar consisted largely of country music purists. Red, white, and blue bunting covering the stage of the hotel, an idea proposed by the *Meridian Star*, mirrored a patriotic theme that pleased most people. The contest rules were strict ones; each performer was to be given a maximum of four minutes to perform his song. The audience ended up being shocked by some of the entrants, which included a bunch of young kids singing uptempo rockabilly songs that, according to one observer, vio-

lated all the hallowed traditions of country music. Clearly, although the rockabilly revolution was on its way—with Elvis Presley was in the vanguard of the movement—it would be an uphill battle.

Before he performed, Elvis, like many of the contestants, wandered around Meridian. He walked to the small city park and looked curiously at a 1904 Baldwin locomotive with eight wheels. The locomotive was painted red and protected from the public by a fence. Next to the locomotive, a statue of Jimmie Rodgers occupied a conspicuous spot. A small plaque praised Rodgers' contribution to country music.

During the day's celebration, a unique event occurred when Bill Bruner, a local musician who had recorded for Okeh Records, donated a guitar that Jimmie Rodgers had given to him. During a 1929 county music show in Meridian, Rodgers was too sick to perform, and Bill Bruner took his place. After the show Rodgers showed his appreciation to Bruner by giving him the guitar. It was one of Bruner's prized possessions, and he decided to pass it on to a deserving country musician. In 1953, Bruner presented the guitar to Hank Snow's son, Jimmy Rodgers Snow. As Elvis viewed the ceremony, he had no idea that in the next two years he would be touring with Hank Snow and his manager Colonel Tom Parker.

As Elvis waited to go on stage, he nervously paced around behind the contestant's area. What song should he sing? What type of vocal presence should he cultivate? There was always one song that Elvis felt safe performing: "Old Shep." But was this song right for the Jimmie Rodgers celebration? The singing brakeman was the type of performer who appealed to Gladys Presley. Elvis had heard Rodgers' "Mean Mama Blues" and "Corinna, Corinna" on the family Victrola and knew them by heart, but for years he was too nervous to sing them. Elvis had sung "Old Shep" many times at home, and to conquer his shaky nerves he decided to perform it in Meridian. Elvis finished second in the contest and won a new guitar. The *Meridian Star* didn't publish a list of contestants nor the prizes awarded, and Elvis' performance generally escaped public notice, but the new guitar was prize enough. With summer approaching, Elvis planned to continue performing at amateur nights in local Memphis clubs, so a new guitar was a nice bonus.

When he left the Jimmie Rodgers festival, Elvis had taken his first serious step toward a professional musical career. His performing style was still largely country, but Elvis was responding to the signs of musical change. The clubs that he frequented in Memphis, northern Mississippi, and West Memphis, Arkansas, were vibrant with rockabilly sounds.

During his last week at Humes High School, Elvis was excited about the prospect of working days and playing music nights. At Humes High, Elvis' popularity had increased due to his musical talent. He was more frequently invited to parties and constantly expanded his group of friends. Since many of Elvis' friends were from South Side High School, he lived in two worlds. Not only were the South Side students from better homes, they had cars and serious musical interests that appealed to Elvis. The students at Humes High were blue-collar and often came from broken homes. The family stability that Elvis craved was buttressed by his friends from South Side High.

Since December 1952, when Elvis performed at the Humes Christmas Variety Show, he had risen in popularity, dating a number of different girls. It was Humes High's class president George Klein and football star Red West who were the big men on campus, however. While they were friendly with Elvis, they never went out of their way to be with him. In later years, Klein and West would make a career out of their high school relationship with Elvis, but many former Humes students remember that Klein and West had little intimate contact with Presley at the time.

In addition to performing at the Humes High Christmas show, Elvis also appeared at the South Side High School Annual Talent Contest in November 1953 in a band with Ronald Smith and bass player Curtis Lee Alderson. The band finished second to a Jerry Lewis comedy impersonator. "Elvis was nervous and couldn't hold his pick very well," Ronald Smith chuckled. Despite the pressures of performing, Elvis was drawing a great deal from these appearances. He was slowly developing into a well-rounded and moderately seasoned performer, and there was also a silent confidence developing in Elvis as his popularity at Humes High grew.

The newfound confidence that Elvis displayed prompted his shop teacher, Mr. Hiltpole, to remark that young Presley seemed like a different person. Not only did he get into good-natured woodchipping fights with the others, but for the first time in his life Elvis mingled easily with his fellow students. As the woodshop teacher remarked: "Elvis was in a shell until his last few months at Humes."

In *Elvis: What Happened?* Red West recalled how the annual Humes High variety show brought about a change in Elvis' personality. Not only did he win the talent contest, but he performed three songs with near professional skill. There is no doubt that Elvis had practiced his repertoire for months. The ease, grace, and skill he displayed on stage was part of an act he had perfected in amateur night contests in many Memphis clubs. It was also an indication of how much he had learned about playing the guitar from Ronald Smith. "I

don't know of anyone who tried harder to perfect his music," Smith commented about Presley.

Graduation day was a busy time for Elvis. During the afternoon he went to the Tennessee State Employment Security Office to apply for a job. Prior to the interview, Elvis spent an inordinate amount of time combing his hair and selecting his clothes. He was determined to make a good impression in the job market. He was interviewed by Mrs. Weir Harris, and she was impressed by Elvis' ability to articulate his career goals. After Mrs. Harris took one look at Elvis' clothes, however, she quickly decided against trying to place him in a sales training position. Elvis' fashion statement just hadn't gone over well with his conservative interviewer.

Owing to Elvis' strong interview, though, Mrs. Harris administered the General Aptitude Battery Test to evaluate his potential job skills. The test results revealed high scores on the manual skills sections. There were also excellent marks on the verbal reasoning and written aptitude portions of the exam. These tests suggested that Elvis not only possessed excellent manual training skills, but that he was strong in traditional academic areas. Elvis' work in English classes at Humes High was outstanding, and his mathematical scores indicated a talent for geometry. This was exceptional because, like most lower middle-class American high school students, Elvis wasn't encouraged to develop his English or math skills. Boys from a Lauderdale Court background typically entered the blue-collar work force. If they possessed academic skills, that was fine, but these areas were not the focus of a Humes High education. The test scores flustered Mrs. Harris, because Elvis' high school record indicated that he was an average student educated primarily for manual labor. The GAB results, however, indicated that he was also likely to fit into a semi-professional white-collar position.

After Mrs. Harris coded Elvis' test results, she scanned the files requesting temporary help. A flyer from the M.B. Parker Machinists' Shop, a tool company in North Memphis, caught her eye. The Parker brochure requested a manual laborer to take machinery apart prior to reconditioning it. The day after Elvis graduated from L.C. Humes, he reported to work at the Parker Company. Elvis was determined to bring money home to help his parents. Although many Humes High teachers suggested that Elvis consider continuing his education, college was not a possibility. He did perpetuate the myth that he attended night school to become an electrician, so as to pay lip service to those encouraging him; this was an implausible story, however, because electricians trained on the job. This tale did, however, satisfy well-wishers, as well as Elvis' dad, who continually lectured Elvis about the necessity of finding a skilled trade.

When Elvis graduated from Humes, he was a well-adjusted, articulate young man who easily charmed people. This was an important personality trait during the few months following high school graduation. It allowed Elvis to experiment with a number of jobs while pursuing his musical interests.

On June 3, 1953, Elvis' L.C. Humes High School commencement, a joyous moment for the Presley family finally arrived. Vernon bought a new suit and Gladys sewed a fine, new print dress. On that muggy Wednesday night, Elvis anxiously entered the spacious Ellis Auditorium for the graduation ceremony. His parents, bursting with pride, had invited everyone they knew to a post-graduation party at their home. In his subdued black tie and new white shirt, Elvis felt awkward as he walked into the hall with his classmates. As the 202 members of the Humes class of '53 marched forward to accept their diplomas, there was an uncomfortable feeling in Elvis' stomach. It was time to face the real world.

As Elvis wandered into the Ellis Auditorium, he met George Klein, the Humes High class president. They exchanged pleasant greetings and vowed to keep in touch during the next few months. Then they marched inside and faced their proud families and friends. Although they were not particularly close in high school, Klein and Elvis developed a strong friendship in the post-high school years. They were both poor boys who were highly successful overachievers. Elvis admired Klein's poise and self-assurance, and Klein was smitten with Elvis' musical talent.

Elvis' Humes High yearbook photo.

As the Humes High School commencement began, Klein welcomed the guests with a short speech. A gaunt young man with sharply chiseled features, Klein made the predominantly blue-collar, working-class crowd feel at home. The ceremony was a rapid one, to everyone's joy.

The bubbly sense of anticipation that erupts during a high school graduation was evident as each student shook principal T.C. Brindley's hand and received a diploma from the superintendent of the Memphis public schools, E.C. Ball. As Elvis left the stage, he turned to Billy Leaptrott, a classmate and photographer, and remarked: "I don got it." It was Elvis' humorous way of suggesting that, despite his rural Southern background, he was smarter than many people realized. Elvis always took care to use proper English, and his remark was a cutting reference to the strict class lines that prevailed in Memphis society.

During the ceremony, Vernon and Gladys beamed proudly from the audience. Elvis' aunt and uncle, Travis and Lorraine Smith, sat next to Jeanette and Alfred Fruchter, and they all smiled as Elvis walked across the stage. The Fruchters were the Presley's neighbors, sharing the duplex with them on Alabama Street. Consequently, they were very close to young Elvis, and encouraged his musical interests. Elvis' fondest graduation party memory was the tie clasp and cuff link set that the Fruchters gave him. The Fruchters were acutely aware of Elvis' obsessive-compulsive desire for musical stardom. Many of Elvis' biographers have perpetuated the myth that he didn't own a record player. Nothing was further from the truth, according to Jeanette Fruchter, who told Vince Staten that she never loaned a record player to Elvis. She indicated that the Presleys not only owned their own record player, but that Elvis was an avid collector of different types of music. It is obvious from the Fruchter's observations that Elvis was already well on his way to pursuing a musical career.

Afterwards, the Presleys went home for a celebration, laughing together with friends over the remarks in Elvis' high school yearbook. To reinforce the notion that Humes High prepared its students for the work force, there was an indication in the yearbook of what the student considered his or her major subject. Elvis' vocational goal—something taken seriously by uninformed biographers like Albert Goldman—was irreverently listed as "Shop," whereas Elvis' honors, including things like the History Club and English Club, clearly belied the wood shop reference. Although Gladys and Vernon loved to display the crude salad bowl that Elvis had labored over for eight months in shop class—anyone who saw the poorly carved bowl knew that Elvis' future was not as a skilled craftsman—Elvis often remarked to Ronald Smith and other friends that academic subjects were the most important to him. The talents that Elvis possessed were best displayed in dramatic history readings, were evident in the English Club and the Speech Club, all of which provided outlets for his creativity.

Starting Work

When Elvis awoke on a hot, muggy Memphis morning on June 4, 1953, it was time to enter the work force. That Thursday morning was the day that Elvis reported to work at the M.B. Parker Machinist Company. Elvis was immediately bored with his new job. There were, however, some positive aspects it. Elvis remarked to a friend that his new paycheck would not only provide record money, but funds for clothes, movies, and hamburgers. Elvis was finally an independent adult who believed that he had the freedom to make his own decisions.

There were some minor conflicts between Elvis and Vernon during the first month following high school graduation, but these spats were little more than the usual family disagreements. Elvis' parents wanted the best for him, so it was only natural for Vernon to lecture Elvis on the necessity of learning a skilled trade. Fundamentally, such talks were a reflection of Vernon's own frustrations.

Despite occasional differences between Vernon and Elvis, the Presley household was a happy one. During the summer of 1953, as Vernon's income increased at the United Paint Company, family fortunes improved. Vernon Presley's paycheck also brought him a new respectability. He was the primary breadwinner again, even though Gladys continued to work part time at St. Joseph's Hospital as a nurse's aide. Part of Elvis' check was used for household expenses, too, and this allowed the Presleys the unusual luxury of some extra spending money. To celebrate their newfound prosperity, the Presley family began going out every Thursday night for hamburgers, french fries, and milkshakes.

While family times were pleasant, Elvis grew increasingly unhappy with his job. The first sign of dissatisfaction with the Parker Company occurred when Elvis reported to David Parker, the boss' son, and complained about being assigned to an eight-man crew stripping nail kegs from equipment about to be reconditioned. The tedious work bothered Elvis, so he talked at length about his show business aspirations. It was not a form of bragging; in Elvis' own mind, he sounded as good as the major crooners like Dean Martin, Frank Sinatra, Nat King Cole, and Frankie Laine. When his co-workers taunted Elvis, he would sing like Dean Martin. At work, he once sang the soundtrack to the recent Dean Martin and Jerry Lewis movie. This behavior not only

demonstrated his encyclopedic musical knowledge, but suggests he had confidence in his singing.

There were other insights gained into Elvis' character while he was employed at Parker. His co-workers remembered that he talked for hours about joining the National Guard. Elvis spoke glowingly of the Guard's sophisticated weapons. He was intrigued by the uniforms, the guns, and the two weeks of summer training. At Humes High, remember, Elvis was briefly a member of the ROTC unit; it had a strong impact upon his character. Elvis developed a passion for guns and uniforms as well as a finely-tuned patriotism. He was a typical young Southerner, schooled to believe in his country and its goals.

A transformation in Elvis' character was also evident to his close friends. This change was noticeable as early as March 1953, when Elvis began spending more time hanging out in the Beale Street clubs. The blues that Elvis heard in these bars was transformed into a new sound. In cowboy bars like the Silver Stallion club at 1447 Union Avenue, it was possible for young Elvis to perform blues-tinged cowboy tunes with a rockabilly flair. The Silver Stallion paid off the beat cop to let underage people into the bar, and they held amateur shows each week. Elvis often wandered down and sat in at these events. He not only learned a great deal about country music, but was able to meet a wide variety of musicians.

The amateur nights at the Silver Stallion were ones that Elvis loved, because they provided some of his strangest moments as a neophyte performer. One night, the owner of this club decided to bring in some show horses to do tricks on the dance floor. Much to Elvis' horror, he was to follow the horse show with an acoustic guitar set. Not only was Elvis unsure how the crowd would react to a singer following the horses, his nose told him there had been an accident on the floor. The crowd roared as Elvis came on holding his nose. He laughed and the crowd cheered him. This incident was so well known in Memphis that there was even an oblique reference to it in the Humes High School year book. It was during incidents like this one that other musicians began noticing Elvis' singing talent.

One night during the summer of 1953, as Elvis sat in the back of a Beale Street club, a young, black piano player, Billy "The Kid" Emerson, approached him, and they spent some time talking about the local music scene. Emerson, a native of Tarpon Springs, Florida, was on leave from the U.S. Air Force. He would shortly join Ike Turner and the Kings of Rhythm. Billy The Kid went on to record five singles and influence a wide variety of musicians. His unique sound prompted white musicians like Warren Smith, Billy Lee Riley, Carl

Mann, Sonny Burgess, Paul Burlison, Marcus Van Story, and Elvis Presley to listen to and emulate Emerson's tunes. While growing up in Florida, Emerson learned to combine a soft piano touch with a jump blues vocal style. Ike Turner recognized Emerson's talent, and by 1954 he was recording for Sun Records.

During one of his visits with Elvis, Emerson played a number of Big Joe Turner songs. Afterward, as they talked, Emerson told the story of a song he had written while listening to Turner. The tune was entitled "When It Rains, It Really Pours," and it had a powerful impact upon Elvis. "That song," Emerson remarked to Colin Escott, "was nearly a monster seller. I wanted Elvis to cut it." Its blues-drenched lyrics were combined with a plaintive musical background that appealed to Elvis' musical instincts. The following year, on September 18, 1954, Emerson and Elvis met again just as Billy was about to record the song for Sam Phillips' Sun label. Ironically, in the fall of 1955, Elvis ended up recording Emerson's tune instead. The song remained unreleased in the Sun Records archives, and in 1956 its ownership was transferred to RCA. Finally, in the 1980s, RCA released Elvis' version of "When It Rains, It Really Pours," another example of how Elvis' musical apprenticeship was impacted by the blues.

Charlie Feathers

An important part of Elvis' show business education during the summer of 1953 resulted from discussions with musicians who cut their own records. The proliferation of small records labels, the rise of vanity recording studios, hobbyists operating in garages, and the hustling businessmen who promoted this product led to a boom in homemade records. Everyone thought that they could produce a hit record. No one was more confident of his ability to cut his own records than Charlie Feathers.

While he was growing up in Holly Springs, Mississippi, Feathers remembered how "the cottonpatch blues" used to inspire him. This was the music played by black field workers, and it became the most important influence upon his unique country-rockabilly style. "When you take the blues out of country or rockabilly," Feathers remarked, "you ain't got no more country music." With Stan Kesler, Feathers wrote "I Forgot to Remember to Forget," and he became a Memphis musical legend. Long before Elvis appeared in clubs or recorded at Sun, Feathers was performing a rockabilly type of music very similar to that heard on Elvis' Sun recordings. Sam Phillips discovered Feathers' talent and hired him as a studio musician, house songwriter, and musical arranger. Not only was Feathers present at Elvis' recording sessions, but Memphis musicians spoke constantly of Feathers' contribution to Elvis' music. Stan Kesler, Marcus Van Story, Ronald Smith, Paul Burlison, Kenneth Herman, and Doug Poindexter were around the Sun studio in 1953 and 1954 and remember Feathers.

In March 1955, when Charlie Feathers recorded his first Sun single, "I've Been Deceived," his music was rockabilly. There is no doubt that he influenced Elvis, because Feathers was an open, somewhat naive, man who readily shared his musical ideas. For years, the critics have scoffed at Feathers' claim that he influenced Elvis. Yet, every important musician who hung out at Sun Records or recorded with Sam Phillips speaks of Feathers' contribution. Elvis listened and watched and used the best of Charlie Feathers' material. In most of his songs, Elvis was a singer who copied other styles, and Feathers was one of Elvis' earliest influences. Since Feathers talked about cutting his own records, it was only natural for Elvis to do the same. Feathers does not appear to be an important influence upon Elvis only because his reputation has never been more than that of an obscure legend. To some, Feathers is a legend in his own mind. To others, he is a legitimate rockabilly pioneer. After interviewing a number of Memphis musicians, it is clear that Feathers is a seminal figure in the Sun Elvis story. "It's not that Elvis copied Charlie Feathers," Ronald Smith remarked, "but he sure did build on Feathers' music."

A gregarious individual who performed at the drop of a hat, Feathers believed in cutting his own records. For a few dollars, it was possible to record a demo record that might encourage one of the independent labels springing up all over the South to release it. One of the demos Feathers cut was "I Forgot to Remember to Forget." No one can remember the exact date, but the summer of 1953 is probably the time that Feathers' cut the song. "I wanted to give Charlie at least half the songwriting credit," Stan Kesler remarked, "because without his demo, Elvis never would have recorded the song."

It was Charlie Feathers' constant talk about hit records that prompted Elvis to consider going into Sam Phillips' Memphis Recording Service for a recording session. In July 1953, Elvis talked frequently about cutting a vanity record. After hanging out in the Beale Street nightclubs and in the hillbilly bars around Memphis, he was excited about making a recording. He reasoned that there were many other singers who cut a demo record, and that if Sun Records wasn't interested, perhaps one of the other record company magnates like Leonard Chess, Huey Meaux, Don Robey, or Lew Chudd would consider the song. Ronald Smith had told Elvis about the outsiders who came into Memphis with big cigars and shiny suits and bought acetate dubs. They were Phillips' competitors and their agents, and frequently urged artists to cut their own records.

A good example of how self-produced records could hit the charts is evident from the career of Jimmy McCracklin. Every song that McCracklin had on the rhythm and blues charts in the 1950s was written, arranged, and produced by him. The record company simply pressed the master and released the songs. McCracklin was typical of the artists who gravitated to Memphis, Chicago, and Los Angeles to find a record deal. Eventually, McCracklin's single "The Walk," on Checker Records, a Chess subsidiary, established his musical career. Like many fledgling songwriters and performers in 1953, McCracklin spent time on Beale Street. "You couldn't help but be influenced by those cats," McCracklin remarked about B.B. King, Bobby Blue Bland, and Johnny Ace. "I took the records I was producing and went from one company to the next; it worked," McCracklin concluded. Elvis was much like McCracklin, in that he, too, hoped to make a record that would garner a recording contract. It was every local artist's dream, and they flooded to Sam Phillips' Memphis Recording Service to make their product.

"I was always trying for that crossover sound," McCracklin noted. "Elvis got it and all our money, too!" Like many black performers, Elvis' friend Billy "The Kid" Emerson had the same idea. He lectured Elvis that a crossover sound combining rhythm and blues and blues music was the emerging sound to cultivate.

Doug Poindexter

A number of country musicians, among them Doug Poindexter, also urged Elvis to make a record. A respected local musician, Poindexter led the Starlite Wranglers to Memphis musical success. The band organized in 1953, and featured Scotty Moore's lead guitar and Bill Black's slapping bass. Poindexter, who was born on October 19, 1928, in Van Dale, Arkansas, developed his musical talent listening to Ernest Tubb. Poindexter's first and only musical group was the Starlite Wranglers, and they combined a country sound with a rockabilly spirit. Doug Poindexter remembered that he and Scotty Moore organized the Starlite Wranglers. It was natural to bring in Bill Black into the group, because he was a long-time friend of Poindexter's. "I was around clubs where Bill played, and he was the best bass player in Memphis. He was a real professional with a musical future," Poindexter remarked. As a musician, Black had few peers, and Poindexter convinced him to join the Starlite Wranglers.

"I liked to fool around with different guitar sounds," Poindexter recalled. "By experimenting with my guitar, I found a way to develop unique sounds." This innovation was not lost on Scotty Moore, and he copied a

great many of Poindexter's licks. It was this sense of a new musical direction that separated the Memphis rockabilly musicians from the traditional country pickers.

Doug Poindexter was Memphis' best-known band leader in 1953. A large, quiet, soft-spoken man, Poindexter, like Charlie Feathers, eagerly shared his musical knowledge with young Elvis. In 1953, Poindexter's band played live for Tom Rome over radio station KWEM, and Elvis often showed up at the radio station when the Starlite Wranglers played. Intrigued by their sound, Elvis also sat in with the band whenever he could. Poindexter recalls a number of interesting stories about the times that Elvis played with his band. He also vividly remembers the snide remarks directed toward Presley's unique talent. "It was awful the way some of them treated that boy," Poindexter recalled.

When Elvis appeared with the Starlite Wranglers, according to Poindexter, there was a great deal of petty bickering. The other musicians didn't seem to understand Elvis' music, and they were miffed over his popularity in the local clubs. "The other musicians were jealous of Elvis," Poindexter remarked. "It wasn't just that the girls liked Elvis; some of the musicians couldn't accept his new direction."

It was Scotty Moore, Poindexter suggested, who made Elvis' sound so strong. But it was the rockabilly sound bursting out all over Memphis that really developed Elvis' talent. Poindexter believes that rockabilly music was a catalyst to Elvis' popularity. "There were a lot of musicians who had the sound Elvis later popularized," Poindexter remarked. Even the big name musicians felt threatened by Elvis. Poindexter laughed about the number of commercially successful show business figures who predicted no success for Elvis. "I could tell that boy was a good one," Poindexter concluded. "He knew how to move a crowd."

A good example of a country superstar's nasty reaction occurred in late July 1954, when Webb Pierce made an unadvertised appearance at the Eagle's Nest. Pierce was on his way to Nashville, and he dropped into the Eagle's Nest to watch a bill featuring Doug Poindexter and the Starlite Wranglers. The special intermission act was Elvis Presley. It was only a week after the release of Elvis' first record, and Webb Pierce was extremely critical of Presley's music. "I remember that Elvis went up and was going to shake hands with Webb Pierce, and Pierce called him a son of a bitch. He told him [Elvis] that he would never appear with a singer who performed like Elvis," Poindexter continued. "I couldn't figure, it didn't make sense to me."

On May 25, 1954, Doug Poindexter and the Starlite Wranglers recorded "My Kind of Carrying On" for Sam Phillips' Sun label. Phillips hoped to release Poindexter's tune in the rockabilly market. Reminiscing about the changes in the Memphis music scene, Poindexter recalled that "after Elvis it boomed." Doug Poindexter and Malcolm Yelvington's bands broke the ground for the new popularity of rockabilly music. "When Sam got that song 'My Kind of Carryin' On,' on tape his wheels started turning," Poindexter remarked, "and when he heard Elvis he stopped there." Poindexter suggested that at this point Phillips had the new "Sun sound" fully in mind.

Out of respect for Doug Poindexter's musical knowledge, Sam Phillips quietly brought him into the studio to listen to Elvis' early Sun cuts. This was typical of Phillips' shrewd business acumen. Sam wanted to take advantage of local musical knowledge to help produce Presley's records. Poindexter stated that Sam Phillips had him play guitar on Elvis' recording of "Good Rockin' Tonight" on September 25, 1954. Poindexter employed a technique in which he ran a strip of paper through his guitar strings to come up with the unique guitar sound that characterized the recording. "Sam Phillips was broke," Poindexter said. "Sam used me on three of Elvis' sessions. I was happy to play," Poindexter remembered. "I just remember recording for a man that was flat on his back," Poindexter said of Sam Phillips. "He was a genius. Sam was a businessman, he was shrewd. I've always admired him and respected him." Since Phillips didn't want to pay union costs, he failed to list Poindexter's guitar work. "Everybody knew Sam only reported the union musicians on these early recordings."

Reminiscing about his days at Sun Records and Elvis Presley, Poindexter stated, "I played on three of Elvis' records, and I'm proud of it. It makes me a little mad that I didn't get credit for the Presley sessions." After searching his memory, Poindexter remembered that in addition to "Good Rockin' Tonight," he appeared on the next two songs that Elvis recorded. This was at the session held during December 1954, Poindexter recalled, when Elvis recorded "Milkcow Blues Boogie" and "You're a Heartbreaker." As a highly-skilled country musician, Poindexter's guitar style fit these songs; Scotty Moore's guitar would have been too rockabilly. Since Poindexter had once employed Moore and Black in his band, it was only natural for them to encourage Elvis and Phillips to bring in their former boss for the session. It was apparently Colonel Tom Parker who prevented Poindexter from receiving the credit he was due on Presley's early records. The Colonel believed that Poindexter was too country for Elvis' fans, an association he wished to play down. It was after Colonel Tom Parker came into the management picture that Poindexter noticed some important changes in Elvis' career direction. Poindexter remarked that Colonel Tom Parker got rid of everyone close to Elvis. Sam Phillips was just the opposite; steel guitarist and bass man Stan

Kesler continues to operate a part of Phillips' record business even today.

Ultimately, of course, it was Poindexter's best musicians from the Starlite Wranglers, Bill Black and Scotty Moore, who were to help make Elvis a star. Despite Elvis having hired away his two key backup men, Poindexter and Presley always remained friends. By 1954, Poindexter had left the music business to raise a family, while Scotty and Bill went on tour with Elvis.

Little Junior Parker

Another important song that Elvis listened to in 1953 was Little Junior Parker's "Mystery Train." This Sun Records product was Sam Phillips at his best. There is a great deal of Southern music in Parker's roots. Little Junior Parker was born March 27, 1932, in Coahama County, Mississippi, and he crafted his harmonica skills by listening to local field hands. This created a rural feeling in Parker's music. Yet, there was also a tinge of country influences. In 1947, while still a teenager, Parker moved to West Memphis, Arkansas, and the following year joined Howlin' Wolf's band. A wild performer with a penchant for alcohol, Parker's soulful ballads and frenetic vocals tellingly foreshadowed rock and roll music. Because of his close friendship with the hulking Howlin' Wolf, Parker was dubbed "Little Junior." By 1951, he was recognized as one of the best harmonica players around Memphis, and he was ready to record music.

The following year, Junior Parker made his first significant recordings with his backup band, the Blue Flames. This band included guitarists L.C. Dranes and Matt Murphy, pianist Bill Johnson, with Ike Turner sitting in on piano. As a talent scout for Modern Records, Turner provided a much needed piano on these sessions, and then acted as the agent selling the sessions to various record labels. These recordings demonstrate a fine blend of blues and country musical influences. Sam Phillips quickly signed Parker to his Sun label.

As one of the first bluesmen to record for Sam Phillips, Little Junior Parker was blessed with Phillips' own vision. Not only did Sam restructure and craft Parker's music, but he added Pat Hare on guitar to strengthen the sound. Little Junior Parker's first Sun record, "Feelin' Good," was a classic boogie-blues tune with a distinct rockabilly feel. By this time, Parker was strictly a vocalist, and the talking introduction to "Feelin' Good" was the reason that the record did so well in the blues market. Pat Hare's guitar licks were also a model for Scotty Moore's backup guitar work with Elvis. It was Parker's version of "Love My Baby" that contained the same guitar lines Moore used in Elvis' recording of "Mystery Train." Yet, these licks were not even original with

Pat Hare, as the Carter Family had recorded "Worried Man Blues" in 1930 employing a similar musical styling.

In 1954, Little Junior Parker moved to Houston to record for Don Robey's Duke/Peacock Record Company. The night life in Houston and Robey's flashy lifestyle swayed Parker, but he failed to reach the same musical brilliance in the seedy Duke Record environment. From 1954 through the early 1960s, Parker and Bobby Blue Bland toured as Blues Consolidated, playing before predominantly black audiences all over the country. Although Parker had a number of important hits on Duke—"Next Time You See Me" (1957), "That's All Right (Mama)" (1958), "Driving Wheel" (1961), "Annie Get Your Yo-Yo" (1962), and "Someone Somewhere" (1963)—these songs ranked only between numbers 51 and 95 on the *Billboard* Hot 100. Had Parker remained with Sam Phillips, his records might have had a stronger impact among white listeners. Little Junior Parker had the sound to cross over, but he was unable to record for a label like Sun that specialized in reaching white audiences with the blues.

Before he left Sun, Little Junior Parker recorded "Mystery Train." It was Parker's 1953 lazy and often erratic vocal styling on "Mystery Train" that Presley turned into a frenetic, rockabilly classic. A slow, bluesy direction with the smooth saxophone sound of Raymond Hill made the song initially unsuitable for Elvis, but when Sam and Elvis listened to Parker's "Love My Baby" they found the perfect instrumental backing for Presley's version of "Mystery Train." Parker's music was one of the last influences necessary in producing Elvis Presley's Sun Record sound.

Other Influences

Another band that influenced Elvis was Malcolm Yelvington's Star Rhythm Boys. They were an outstanding rockabilly and country music group that brought the crowds in the local honky-tonks to their feet. A hint of rhythm and blues and blues influences crept into the Star Rhythm Boys instrumental breaks. Their piano player, Frank Tolley, did a mesmerizing solo performance, and he was able to bring the crowds streaming onto the small dance floors.

Yelvington's signature song, "Drinkin' Wine Spodee-O-Dee," was an old rhythm and blues tune made famous by Sticks McGhee. This was one of many tunes in which Yelvington and the Star Rhythm Boys incorporated black influences into their music. Yelvington recorded his signature song after Elvis finished cutting Sun Record No. 210, "I Don't Care If the Sun Don't Shine" and "Good Rockin' Tonight." The previous year, Elvis listened to Yelvington perform "Drinkin' Wine

Spodee-O-Dee" many times in local clubs. "Elvis stood out in the crowd, but he never talked to me," Yelvington recalled. "He was a fine singer. The boy was always looking for a piano player. He liked our man and that's why he hung out around us." Yelvington also re-emphasized that he had never played with Elvis. "I understand there's a book that says that, but it's not true."

The radio was another important influence upon Elvis' musical growth. One of young Presley's favorite shows was Bob Neal's program over radio station WMPS. On his show, beginning in late 1952, Neal opened and closed by playing the Ripley Cotton Choppers record "Silver Bells." It was a typically corny country tune, but Elvis loved it. He had as much interest in traditional country music as the new rockabilly sound. Johnny and Dorsey Burnette also listened to Bob Neal, but they didn't like traditional country music. Johnny Burnette frequently came over to Elvis' house on Saturday nights to listen to the "West Memphis Jamboree." This radio show, hosted by Dick Stewart, Charlie Feathers' brother-in-law, was popular due to its wide musical mix. It was while listening to the "West Memphis Jamboree" in 1952 that Elvis heard Tennessee Ernie Ford's "Blackberry Boogie," and the following year Ford's version of "I Don't Know It" also intrigued him. These songs were country-tinged, but they had a hint of rock and roll music.

There were still others who shared Elvis' musical interests. One of the people who hung around with Elvis was Marshall Ellis. He had converted his garage into a crude recording area, and was a kind of minor league Sam Phillips. In a few years, Ellis would found Fernwood Records and, with Thomas Wayne's hit "Tragedy," hit the *Billboard* pop chart. Like Elvis, Marshall Ellis was caught up with local Memphis music, and hoped to turn out his own records. Ellis and Elvis spent a great deal of time talking about the records played on the radio.

In addition to the radio, Elvis continued to spend a great deal of time listening to new records. Over night, small record stores sprang up all over Memphis to service the growing teenage market. In a dingy back-room record shop on Beale Street in 1953, Elvis listened to Franklin McCormick's vocal on "Are You Lonesome Tonight." McCormick, a Chicago radio announcer, was the lead singer for the Blue Barron's Orchestra in the late 1940s and early 1950s, and his vocal stylings were similar to those Elvis used in his own ballads. Elvis listened to McCormick's song, and his own version of "Are You Lonesome Tonight" ended up a virtual copy.

The First Recording

Elvis was fixated on the idea of recording a $3.98

ten-inch master, but was having real problems working up the courage to take the plunge. He was too shy to tell anyone, so he decided to secretly make a personal recording. To pay for his own record session, Elvis went to his boss, M.B. Parker, Sr., and inquired about a salary advance to buy a car (actually, Elvis' parents had recently purchased him the Lincoln). In reality, the money Elvis asked for was to be used for a demonstration record to impress Sam Phillips. The many hours that Elvis had spent at Taylor's Cafe, next to Sun Records, encouraged young Presley to cut his own record. Charlie Feathers and a number of other rockabilly artists shopped crudely recorded songs among the small labels and talent scouts that frequented Memphis, and talked about how they were going to make a hit record. Eddie Bond frequently dropped in and talked about his record. Marcus Van Story was always hanging around the studio. Doug Poindexter and the Starlite Wranglers encouraged Elvis to make his own record. Other people he knew—Stan Kesler, who played on a number of vanity records, and Smoky Joe Baugh, whose piano was evident on some sessions, were doing it—so why shouldn't Elvis make a record?

On Tuesday, July 14, 1953, M.B. Parker rolled a cigar in his clenched teeth and listened to an impassioned plea from Elvis, who wanted his paycheck early. Elvis was a good employee and Parker saw no reason to deny the request. He wrote out a thirty-three dollar check and Elvis ran across the street to a liquor store to cash it. He took twenty dollars home to Gladys, and set the remainder aside for the record. During the next three days, Elvis spent a great deal of time in the bathroom practicing his vocal skills. Since Elvis hated bathing, Vernon and Gladys were more than curious about such long, sequestered spells in the privy.

Despite the practice, and having the money all set aside for the session, Elvis still couldn't work up the courage to make a recording just then. His confidence simply hadn't reached the point where he was willing to test the water. Instead, he continued to listen to songs that he might record. He listened intently to the Pied Pipers' 1948 hit "My Happiness," and when he was tired of it, he'd play the Ink Spots' "That's When Your Heartaches Begin" on the family Victrola. Vernon loved the Ink Spots and he spent hours talking about their music. (There is no evidence that Elvis listened to or was influenced by country singer Bob Lamb's version of "My Happiness.")

Elvis and his friends were so consumed with the music that they couldn't think of anything else. "Elvis wanted to cut a record real bad," Ronald Smith recalled, "and he asked us a lot of questions about music." The Presleys loved to listen to Elvis practice, and they did everything possible to encourage him. Vernon

and Gladys were so intrigued by Elvis' behavior that they insisted the family have a special weekend dinner. On Friday night, July 17, 1953, Vernon, Gladys, and Elvis spent the evening talking about the family's success. Vernon was happy that Elvis was employed full-time. Gladys talked at length about her son's singing ability, and they all laughed into the night. Elvis decided that very night to finally make a record to surprise his mother and father, quietly vowing to sing the two songs he had been practicing for so long.

The next day, July 18, 1953, Elvis cut the songs "My Happiness" and "That's When Your Heartaches Begin." The encouragement of his parents the night before must have been the last straw. Besides, it would be a way to get Sam Phillips to notice him—perhaps he could even get a Sun Records contract. A close friend from Humes High School was also instrumental in Presley's decision to cut the record. "I had been trying to persuade Elvis for quite some time to try his hand at making a record," Ed Leek told author Jerry Osborne. "After all, he was always going around singing." The record had nothing at all to do with Gladys' birthday, as some chroniclers have claimed, as that had already passed on April 25. After Elvis cut the $3.98 ten-inch acetate of "My Happiness" and "That's When Your Heartache Begin," a Sun label from the Prisonaires' "Softly and Tenderly" release was pasted on Presley's record. The Prisonaires' record was a 1953 release and, as Stan Kesler remembered, it was common to take any label and put it on one of the "amateur records." The words "Elvis Presley" were written on the label, and Elvis took it with him when he left Sam Phillips' recording service. He went immediately over to Ed Leek's house. Eventually, after spinning it for his parents, Elvis let Leek take the record home. Ed stored the disc and forgot about it over time. It was not until August 1988, when the story broke nationally, that Ed Leek sought authentication of the record. It came quickly. There were a number of people in Memphis who were aware of it. One of them was Marcus Van Story. He was sitting in a local cafe on the hot August day in 1953 that Elvis decided to record his two songs.

"I had nothing to do and was hanging around Taylor's Cafe," Van Story remarked. "In walked Elvis and we talked for a moment. He wasn't nervous," Van Story continued. Van Story walked with Leek and Presley next door to Sun Records and left to do some errands. "When Ed Leek and Elvis walked into the Memphis Recording Service, I didn't think anything of it," Van Story concluded.

As 1953 ended, Elvis spent Christmas with Vernon and Gladys, and continued to talk about his show business ambitions. The road to rock and roll fame was still a long way off, although Elvis had begun to feel comfortable and confident with his music.

But it wasn't just Presley's music. The "street-corner symphony" was taking over America, the rhythm and blues music that was essential to the future of rock and roll. When the Drifters' "Money Honey" was played on Memphis radio, Elvis sang along and talked eagerly about his r and b record collection. The gospel-tinged vocals that Clyde McPhatter laid down with the Drifters were special to Presley, who was amazed that many local radio stations continued to ban black music. In 1953, record banning was in its infancy. Despite the new freedom, the increased prosperity, and the lessening of racial tensions, not everyone believed that the new music was positive. Station WDIA eventually banned the Bees' "Toy Bell"—a song that would later become known as Chuck Berry's "My Ding-a-Ling"—one of many that Memphis censors talked disparagingly about in the changing social-cultural environment because it contained "bad words."

"We knew that something special was happening with black music," Ronald Smith recalled. "So we listened to as much of it as we could get." Elvis, according to Smith, had a mission. It was to combine his musical interests into a unique style. "I don't think Elvis knew what he was doing musically," Smith concluded, "but he sure as hell sounded good."

CHAPTER 7

The Key Influences:
Colonel Parker and Sam Phillips

The key career influences in Elvis Presley's early musical life, Colonel Tom Parker and Sam Phillips, came from very different backgrounds, and each made distinct contributions to Presley's music. It was Phillips' ability, for example, to capture Elvis' talent on record in the Sun studio that provided Parker with the opportunity to publicize Presley. This in turn attracted the interest of RCA-Victor Records and the general American public. Whether or not publicity was the seminal ingredient in launching Elvis' career is debatable, but there is no doubt that without Sun Records, Colonel Parker would not have had a product to sell.

Critics have long been divided over whether the Colonel was an overall help or hindrance to Elvis; there is so much myth associated with Parker that it is difficult to assess his impact. In most of the early Presley biographies, Parker is single-handedly credited with Elvis' national popularity, an unfortunate distortion of the historical record. It was Sam Phillips who produced Elvis' Sun Records hits and guided his early career. To this writer, Phillips was the pivotal figure in Presley's eventual stardom. Had Phillips not recorded songs for Elvis like "That's All Right (Mama)" and "Mystery Train," Presley wouldn't have had the musical success that caught the attention of Colonel Parker. By comparing and contrasting the backgrounds and influences of Colonel Tom Parker and Sam Phillips, it is possible to analyze further their respective impacts upon Elvis' career.

The Making of a Flimflam Man

For many years Colonel Thomas A. Parker was described by the press in glowing terms. The media unanimously agreed that Parker's image as a country bumpkin masked a shrewd gift for promotion. Always eager to contribute stories of his past triumphs, Parker deftly manipulated the press. A good example of his skill with the media occurred on May 16, 1960, when *Time* magazine printed a lengthy article about him. Despite its investigative reputation, *Time* accepted Parker's stories about his origins and background without questioning the Colonel in depth or verifying the accuracy of his tall tales. When Parker claimed that Huntington, West Virginia, was his birthplace, one could almost smell the collard greens and fried chicken. Colonel Parker had the unique ability to place the American dream into a corn-pone country perspective that blinded jour-

nalists. For years these stories filled newspaper pages. The earliest fabrication was Parker's confession that he was an orphan adopted by Uncle Parker of the Great Pony Circus. "Orphaned as a child," *Time* reported, Parker "had his own pony-and-monkey act in his teens." It was this training in the circus, according to *Time*, that developed Parker's promotional genius.

The stories concerning Parker's legendary feats were largely self-proclaimed ones. As a young man, to hear the Colonel tell it, Parker sold foot-long "hot dogs" consisting of small pieces of meat at each end of a bun, the middle filled only with condiments. If an unsuspecting customer complained, the Colonel pointed to a piece of meat on the ground and bellowed: "You dropped your meat, boy." The original flimflam man loved to recount these stories to Yankee reporters. Much of Parker's legendary status was due to these self-serving anecdotes.

There was a method behind Colonel Parker's seemingly innocent tales. He succeeded in creating the image of a good old boy: a down-home Southerner who was shrewd, honest, but not above a harmless prank. Like P.T. Barnum, Parker presided over a circus where the fun and good times were more important than the money.

In Parker's role as Elvis' manager, he prided himself on perpetuating the myth that they worked together on a handshake. The Colonel loved to tell people that he had never signed a contract with Elvis. His boy trusted him, the Colonel bellowed. For years the Presley family leaned on Parker for advice. Why would the Colonel take advantage of Elvis? It didn't make sense. No one knew that the Colonel's Svengali-like behavior cut Elvis out of much of the decision making. Nor was it common knowledge that the Colonel's cut of Presley's earnings was as much as fifty percent. No one questioned the Colonel about business; it was simply futile to bring up the subject. Parker let everyone know that he was the best manager in the business. It was not until after Elvis' death that the extent of his self-serving deals with Elvis became public knowledge.

To reinforce his corn-pone image and keep attention away from more substantive matters, Parker continually plied the press with colorful stories. These tales were used to reinforce the notion that Parker was a shrewd businessman. While managing Eddy Arnold, Colonel Parker remarked, he often discovered that a state fair charged a twenty-dollar tax for entertainment

Early 1950s photo of Colonel Tom Parker in his element.
(Photo courtesy Tommy Sands)

acts that didn't have a livestock exhibit. To escape this tax, Colonel Parker carried two chickens in a cage with a sign proclaiming: "Livestock Exhibit." One night, Eddy Arnold was sick and couldn't perform. Parker advertised a new attraction: "Eddy Arnold's Dancing Chickens." The Colonel sent an assistant to a nearby hardware store to purchase a two-dollar hot plate and an extension cord. The plates were plugged in at low heat beneath a straw-filled chicken cage. To the amusement and delight of startled patrons, the chickens danced to the tune of Bob Wills and the Texas Playboys' "Turkey in the Straw." It's a good story, but probably not a true one. Such tales were designed to contrast Colonel Parker's show business genius with the poor country bumpkins at local fairs who were taken to the cleaners. It was good fun and a good story. No one got hurt. It was the kind of fabrication that Yankee journalists loved, even though such stories were usually not verifiable.

The height of Colonel Parker's storytelling genius is demonstrated in his carnival promotion schemes. Parker alleges that he painted sparrows yellow and sold them as canaries to unsuspecting country yokels. He also claims to have spread cow manure over the exits of his shows so he could charge departing revelers a nickel for pony rides to the parking lot.

The New York media loved to recount how Parker took advantage of unsuspecting country rubes. For years, Parker managed country music acts and was famous for convincing the locals to part with their money. When

he arrived in town with a musical act, Parker sold photos and programs like they were a health regimen possessed of a miracle cure. After the concert, the Colonel hired young kids to pick up the discarded photos and programs left on the seats, and subsequently resold them in the next town. Tom Parker was always proud of the fact that he was a businessman who was able to make a quick buck and still have a few laughs.

Andreas Van Kujik

For years this ruse disguised the fact that Colonel Tom Parker was an illegal alien. Parker was actually born Andreas Cornelis Van Kujik on June 26, 1909, in Breda, a city in southern Holland. His father, Adam Van Kujik, a renowned horseman and a soldier, operated a livery stable in the city's old quarter. His mother, Marie Ponsie, was a woman of French descent whose family owned a carnival. She was also an unusually religious woman. Although the Van Kujiks were Catholics, there was a distinct fundamentalist religious strain in the Van Kujik household. This religious fervor was similar to that of Southern evangelicals, an influence that was later to prove an asset to young Andreas.

Another unique and helpful character trait was the young boy's obsession with things American. He watched movies and learned about the Wild West. Through early reading, he learned about country music. In the 1930s, years after he had come to the United States, Parker, smitten with Jimmie Rodgers' songs as a youth, would recall listening to Rodgers' "In the Jailhouse Now" and "I'm Lonely and Blue" in his early days. The hunger and poverty that Rodgers experienced was something that Parker identified with as a boy who grew up during the Great Depression. Young Andreas also liked city life, and read everything he could find about New York and Hollywood. Whether it was the movies or American music, he immersed himself in his new interest, so much so that his childhood friends called him "the American." It was not long before Andreas Van Kujik vanished—off on a trip to the United States. His love affair with America was an on again and off again thing, however; he would travel to New York a number of times before he finally settled in the States.

When Andreas would return to Holland, it was usually his love for the circus that brought him back. It was in Holland that the youth learned about animals, knowledge which would provide him with a familiarity which would eventually enable him to find work in America. For years the boy's father operated a livery stable—the Van Kujik's lived above the stable—and young Andreas tended the horses. Andreas not only grew to love the animals; they were his best friends. He also identified with the circus performers who showed up to train with their menagerie of exotic pets.

Because Breda was a traditional Dutch Catholic town, the youngster's mother was not only a devoutly religious woman, but one who believed strongly in a religious education. For years she preached the necessity of religion, and her son's schooling confirmed the place of God in his life. All this had a profound influence upon the adult Tom Parker, who would donate large sums of money to various churches throughout his lifetime. There were contradictions in the feelings Andreas had towards religion, however. The intensity that he demonstrated toward animals, the circus, and making money challenged his Catholic beliefs. Eventually, his interest in worldly matters caused him to have trouble retaining his mother's religious faith.

Parker's developing character was formed under influences other than these two, of course. Perhaps the most significant one was his mother's storytelling sessions. Often in ill health, there was nevertheless a light-hearted side to Parker's mother; Marie Ponsie continually spun intriguing tales about the family circus. A born storyteller who could fascinate visitors for hours with elaborate vignettes of circus lore, her ability to weave tall tales, her dramatic sense, was one which carried over into her son's career.

Andreas' early life quickly took some sour turns. In 1925 his father died, and he moved to Rotterdam to live with an uncle. For two years, Andreas Van Kujik stayed with Johannes Ponsie, an itinerant ship captain.

Captain Ponsie, a larger than life character, lived from day to day. He had no thought about the future and disdained money. It was in reaction to Uncle Ponsie's disregard for money that created a Scrooge-like financial attitude in young Andreas. It was frightening to Andreas to watch Captain Ponsie spend a month's salary in one night of revelry.

But there was also a redeeming side to Andreas' uncle. For hours he would regale Andreas with tales of the sea and of the women he had found in exotic ports. There were no stories more intriguing than those concerning the American ports. In Atlanta, Miami, and New Orleans, Captain Ponsie purportedly won the hearts of many local damsels while downing large quantities of beer. Unwittingly, Captain Ponsie prepared Andreas Van Kujik for a new life. Andreas' own storytelling was encouraged by his uncle, and he began to spin effective tales about circus life.

It was also Captain Ponsie who further excited young Andreas with tales of American music. The force of New Orleans jazz, the plaintive feel of country music, and the gutbucket blues that ran rampant in major Southern ports had an immediate impact upon the seafaring Dutchman, one which he transmitted to his nephew.

On September 2, 1927, Andreas returned to Breda for his mother's birthday. He spent the next two weeks with family and friends. To celebrate Andreas' return, a joint celebration was held on September 15 to commemorate sister Adriane's birthday, as well as the return of the prodigal son. The following day, without telling his family, he sailed quietly from Holland bound for America. Andreas had been noted for his ability to relate spellbinding tales of the American West to his unsuspecting young Dutch friends and their children, but Andreas' family had had no idea that the young boy was so intent upon becoming an American. They had also failed to recognize the degree to which his fantasies were preparing Andreas for a new life. After reading about Southern cities and the glory of the Confederate cause during the American Civil War, Andreas had come to picture himself in the role of a Southern colonel, a fantasy that sustained him through many youthful failures. Once he landed in New York, however, Andreas found it difficult to cope with the new and vast land.

After spending a few nights in New York City with a Dutch family, eighteen-year-old Andreas walked down to the New York stockyards and watched the trains come in from all over the United States. It was not long before he struck up a conversation with some hoboes, and these itinerant Americans urged him to hop a train and see the country. The temptation was too great to resist, and for a year Andreas did just that, wandering around the South. He was intrigued by Florida, West Virginia, and Tennessee, states varied in terms of people and geography. During this trip, he established his plans for a show business future; he envisioned great potential for a young man interested in the circus.

A year later, Andreas returned to Holland to once again celebrate his mother's birthday. Not only did he bring presents from New York, but he was filled with stories of the American West. To his family, the legends and folklore of this vast nation intrigued the young Dutch visitor beyond comprehension. He had grown even more fascinated by cowboys, carnivals, and clubs featuring Western music.

His brief taste of American life prompted Andreas to consider permanent residence in the United States. The level of economic opportunity in America had simply overwhelmed him. Determined to become a circus employee and eventually an independent promoter, he made his plans to return. Not only was the South his favorite region, but he found the people warm, friendly, and naive. To Andreas, it was the perfect place for a young storyteller inspired to make a fortune in show business. During the summer of 1929, Andreas left Holland for a another trip to America.

While on board the ship, Andreas concocted a plan to become a U.S. citizen. On the boat he met an American family, eventually using them as a point of reference for a new American identity. With a flair for historical facts, he invented a detailed background for himself after learning everything he could about the family. Eventually, he enlisted in the United States Army. In the midst of the worst depression in American history, the army failed to check the bogus birth information presented by the young inductee. Andreas' thereby established an American identity.

But Andreas did not totally abandon his roots. He experienced a twinge of conscience and still felt an enormous responsibility towards his mother. In January 1930, Andreas' mother was shocked when she received her first monthly check from the United States Army. Andreas had made sure that she received his allotment, a monthly stipend that relieved his guilt and made his decision to immigrate to America easier. For the next two years, twenty-six dollars a month arrived in Holland. Andreas also wrote lengthy letters to his mother detailing his successes, and sent pictures documenting his new American life.

During his service in the United States Army, Andreas was stationed at Fort Barrancas in Florida and at Schofield Barracks in Hawaii. For the remainder of his life, Florida and Hawaii were the Colonel's two favorite spots. This explains why Tom Parker moved to Tampa, Florida, after leaving the army, and why he had Elvis perform two benefits for the military (very near the Schofield Barracks) in Hawaii. Florida and Hawaii had offered Colonel Tom Parker solace—early in his life, he was happy in these two locations.

It was at the Schofield Barracks that many of Parker's most important adult attitudes were formed. He watched the local Japanese and Filipino farm laborers compete with the Hawaiians for jobs. On weekends these groups spent their money at carnivals, cockfights, and gambling dens. Parker was excited by the hustle: it whetted his appetite for carnival life. When he would leave the vast army base, he would ride the bus into Honolulu. He was intrigued by the bargaining for goods in the marketplace. Every Saturday there were two or three special commodities that sold out quickly in the open air market. This intrigued Parker and proved an early lesson in supply and demand. He haunted Hotel Street in downtown Honolulu at night, and like every enlisted man enjoyed its offerings. Hawaii left a lasting impression upon him, and he never forgot the turbulent, frontier-like atmosphere of what was then a somewhat remote American province.

Finally, with his discharge from the army on the horizon, it was time for Andreas to establish his new identity, something which proved to be a difficult task. He was a large, cordial, outgoing man, but he found it difficult to make lasting friendships. There were also inner doubts and personal turmoil in his life. He wanted desperately to become someone important. The trappings of success were fundamental to the young man. For years he brooded about his Dutch background; his tyrannical father and angelic mother had fostered many personality conflicts. Would he become a worthless storyteller like his uncle? Would he become a tyrant like his father? Would he turn into a sweet, manipulative person like his mother? The anxiety created by these questions ultimately prompted him to simply sever all his family ties. Andreas Van Kujik was buried. Suddenly, beginning in January 1932, the Van Kujik's no longer received letters from Andreas. He was now Tom Parker, and he had turned his back upon his Dutch heritage. His personality underwent a radical change: he became the Southern colonel of his fantasies. In later years, not a single soul realized that Elvis Presley's manager was actually an illegal alien who had hidden his real identity by shrewdly enlisting in the United States Army. If a boy couldn't produce his birth certificate, certainly an honorable discharge from the army was adequate proof of citizenship. Patriotism was the perfect way to enter the mainstream of American life. Tom Parker was a brilliant man with a penchant for self promotion and grandiose schemes, and his short army stint perfectly covered his illegal entry into the United States.

Tampa: Time Well Spent

The name Tom Parker was a result of Van Kujik's army service. While stationed in Hawaii, he had met a Captain Tom Parker. He took a liking to the career army officer and subsequently assumed his name. It was easy to fabricate a new identity during the turbulent 1930s.

After finishing his two-year enlistment, Parker moved to Tampa, Florida. This small Florida city, then dominated by organized crime, was a mob-infested bastion of gambling, illegal liquor, and prostitution—the perfect place for a fledgling show business personality. Since the major circus companies wintered in Tampa, Parker could easily learn more about the circus business. Tampa was also a city of opportunity for the quick-talking entrepreneur. In the 1930s, Colonel Parker ingratiated himself with local political bosses, and he was eventually given the honorary job of city dogcatcher. The job was a sinecure; one that allowed the local dogcatcher to sell all the animals he took in and split the money with city officials.

By the 1940s and 1950s, Tampa was the easiest place in the world to make a quick dollar. Vice and crime thrived on every street corner. A group of Cuban gamblers ran illegal lottery tickets, and bootleg whiskey was professionally produced with seemingly legitimate tax labels. The fraud was so rampant that the U.S. Treasury Department's elite Bureau of Alcohol, Tobacco and Firearms unit opened an office in Tampa to investigate local whiskey bootleggers. They found an operation that had the quality control and professional appearance of a legal whiskey distillery. New York gangster Frank Costello provided the money for the whiskey business. Much of the liquor was manufactured in Puerto Rico and smuggled in through customs. One can only assume that Parker watched these illegal enterprises with great interest. His honorary title of Tampa dogcatcher was a nice patronage position, the Colonel was well connected in Tampa politics, and he admired inventiveness of the type that sometimes characterized the illicit activity of local businessmen when it came to moneymaking.

One of Colonel Tom Parker's closest friends, the Hillsborough County Sheriff, "Melon-Head" Culbreath, made it clear that Parker was a trusted city official. The aura of power that Sheriff Culbreath radiated attracted Colonel Parker. Not only was he Tampa's head dogcatcher, but Parker was also able to sell animals for his own profit. The proceeds from the animals wound up in many pockets. It was the good-old-boy system; Sheriff Culbreath freely distributed favors and raked in his share of the economic rewards.

After years of abusing his power, Culbreath was investigated by the Kefauver Crime Commission. This federal commission, headed by Senator Estes Kefauver, was instrumental in publicizing criminal activity among the police. The influence of organized crime was evident at many levels in America. The Kefauver Commission forced a solution to some of these problems. As a result of the Commission investigations, Sheriff Culbreath was indicted in March 1951, but the prosecution found it difficult to prove criminal wrongdoing. The indictment was little more than a slap on the wrist. Evidence was skimpy and witnesses either refused to testify or temporarily lost their memory. Sheriff Culbreath was acquitted by a local jury, and he held a press conference proclaiming his innocence. The Spanish-speaking population laughed at Culbreath's acquittal; they referred to Tampa as "Casa de Melon"—Melon Head's house. Everyone took it for granted that open graft and corruption was and would always be a part of Hillsborough County. For the nineteen years that Sheriff Culbreath's iron hand controlled Hillsborough County, Colonel Tom Parker had an opportunity to learn a great deal about power and manipulation from the sheriff's methods.

The Colonel's most important lesson was that a bluff could carry a person a long way. Parker was also learned to reward his supporters, an axiom of business which he carried into his show business career. For almost four decades, Parker worked with the same staff. This was an unheard of type of allegiance in the music business, but this loyalty produced excellent promotional results. Each detail was worked out with skill and precision owing to Parker's experienced staff. While he rewarded his workers with bonus payments and excellent salaries, however, the Colonel still found it difficult to spend his own money on himself.

No matter how much money he made or what amount of influence he possessed, Colonel Parker was frightened about the prospects of future poverty, a frugal Dutch character trait that haunted him throughout his life. He could never take a vacation, relax, or plan a long-term project. Parker's rationale was that the suckers would eventually catch on, and he would be out in the cold. Due to this notion, the Colonel remained the consummate hustler. He saw the entertainment business as a con game, and this accounts for his management style. Thus, the political connections in Florida were an important factor in rounding out Parker's approach to show business.

It was this ability to ingratiate himself with individuals in positions of authority—like "Melon-Head" Culbreath—which helped to mold his character and career. Close ties to Florida politicians and a good-old-boy manner helped Parker persuade Louisiana Governor Jimmy "Pappy" Davis to grant him the honorary title of "Colonel." Not only did such men provide effective role models, but Parker quickly made people aware of his connections with the rich and powerful.

Beginning in the 1930s, then, Tom Parker learned a great deal from living in Tampa, not all of it related to politics. For a time, he dabbled in dog racing and circus sideshows. Neither of these ventures were prosperous ones. Suddenly, Parker developed a new interest. He began listening to the "Grand Ole Opry" and other country radio shows, casually following the careers of a number of country singers. The most influential performer, Gene Autry, provided Parker with a model for his later dealings with Elvis Presley.

From 1930 to 1934, Parker listened to Gene Autry on the Chicago-based WLS program "Barn Dance." When the show first went on the air on April 12, 1924, WLS was a Sears Roebuck station (the call letters meant World's Largest Store). Parker loved this form of commercial hucksterism. He realized that the WLS show was helping to create a broader market for country music. As Southerners migrated to the northern factories, their music followed; WLS's "Barn Dance" was one of many shows to exploit the burgeoning hillbilly audience "up north." The show was broadcast on a strong, clear transmission heard throughout the South as well. The success of the show prompted Hollywood to offer Autry a movie contract. Autry created the archetype of the perfect cowboy, and soon became the first person to sing in a money-making western movie.

By the late 1930s, acutely aware of Gene Autry's success, Parker was looking for his own singing cowboy. He had booked Gene Austin a few times in 1939, and decided in the absence of a cowboy to continue booking Austin into small towns in Florida and Louisiana until something better came along. Still honing his showman's art, Parker established the same booking procedure that he would later use with Elvis Presley. Arriving in town before his singer, the Colonel would distribute posters, hype the radio market, and grease some palms at the local newspaper, sheriff's office, and town hall. Gene Austin drew large crowds, and everyone made money.

Austin approached Parker about managing him full time and moving to Nashville, but the Colonel refused. Parker realized that there was little life left in Austin's career. He would be managing a marginal act, something that had no appeal for Parker. There was always the job with the Tampa Humane Society as a field agent to fall back on—he had a title, a desk, and a ready source of income. Gene Austin was just too uncertain an act. His one big hit record, "My Blue Heaven," had

been forgotten by all but the most ardent fans. He was through as a major show business figure, and Parker knew it.

Suddenly, on December 7, 1941, the Japanese bombed Pearl Harbor and war broke out. When the Selective Service System sent Parker a registration form in 1941—it was, after all, not "Tom Parker" who had already served two years in the army—he wrote that he was married with a child, and he listed his occupation as Gene Austin's manager. This information prompted the draft board to classify the thirty-two-year-old Parker as "3-A," exempt from military service by virtue of "extreme hardship and dependents."

During World War II, Parker took time to carefully consider his future. Although he himself had avoided further army service, Parker read curiously about the influx of musical and movie talent into the military camps. This phenomena persuaded Parker to rethink his career direction. He loved the circus, but show business people held a special allure for everyone. Although aware of the enormous possibilities for financial gain in the entertainment field, he decided at that point that he felt more comfortable pursuing his first love—the circus life.

After a period of time working odd jobs, Parker became a promoter for touring circus groups. Due to his political contacts and extensive knowledge of animals, he was again appointed to impound stray animals by the Tampa city government. As a result, he had plenty of time on his hands and spent it at the local circus headquarters. Since Tampa was the winter headquarters for professional circus performers, he was constantly reminded about the financial rewards of the performing life. But Tom Parker also had other concerns.

During the Great Depression, Parker had met his future wife, Mrs. Marie Mott. She had been married twice before, and was known as Marie Ross to many of her friends. She was a widow, and the perfect companion for Parker. Not only was Miz' Rie, as Parker fondly called her, a strong person, she was a well-dressed, business-oriented woman with a brilliant mind. Miz' Rie was the only sounding board the Colonel needed during his lifetime. They had a storybook marriage. The Colonel was consumed with money matters, but he also helped his wife raise her son by a former marriage, Bobby Ross. Afflicted with multiple sclerosis at an early age, Bobby was treated kindly and affectionately by Colonel Parker. Much to the Parker's credit, he helped Bobby set up a successful public relations business in Tampa. Until his death in 1977, Bobby Ross was one of Florida's most respected businessmen.

It was Miz' Rie and Bobby Ross who encouraged many of the Colonel's early ideas. The Colonel's business schemes were carefully thought out, and he went over the details of every move many times. In the end, a business plan always required Miz' Rie's approval. After a series of long conversations with his wife, Parker signed his first major country music artist, Eddy Arnold, to a management contract. Arnold, a young singer from Henderson, Tennessee, had made his radio debut in 1936 as a solo artist and was promptly signed by Pee Wee King's Golden West Cowboys. Known as the "Tennessee Plowboy," Arnold developed a vocal style similar to Gene Autry's and became a mainstream country music star.

Bucking the Establishment

By signing Eddy Arnold, Tom Parker made some early enemies in the country music business. The "Grand Ole Opry" booking agency, which had monopolized the booking of key country musicians, often challenged Parker's shows. Initially, the growth of the "Grand Ole Opry" made it difficult to challenge its power. The "Opry" had become very influential since the 1930s, and its booking agency was powerful in the industry. In the 1940s, Parker was one of many independent promoters who fought the establishment. Control of the country music business by the "Grand Ole Opry" was nearing its end, however, and Tom Parker was instrumental in changing the face of the country music business.

In July 1939, the "Grand Ole Opry" moved its shows to Nashville's War Memorial building, which boasted a seating capacity of 2,300. This move increased the Opry's popularity, so in 1943 the even larger Ryman Auditorium was secured as a concert site. As the fame of the "Grand Ole Opry" spread, Jim Denny, a young souvenir hawker, reorganized the Opry's booking service to take advantage of the increased demand for country musicians. The rumor was that if you played for Denny for a small fee, a "Grand Ole Opry" appearance was guaranteed. It was a legal form of payola that riled Tom Parker, and he was determined to fight it.

In November 1946, Denny left his full-time job with the National Life Insurance Company to head the Artist Service Bureau at the "Grand Ole Opry." In a few years, Denny was the most powerful promoter in Nashville, a position that he abused for years. He booked his girlfriends, new acts that he secretly managed, and anyone else he liked into local clubs. Denny ran the circuit of the clubs and demanded to be treated like a king. Although he was married, he constantly showed up at clubs with other women. Few people liked him, but everyone feared his power in the music industry. (Prior to his management agreement with Colonel Tom Parker, a young performer named Elvis Presley appeared on the "Grand Ole Opry" in 1954, only to be insulted by Jim Denny, who told Elvis that he ought to

consider going back to driving a truck for a living.) Colonel Tom Parker was one of the few promoters to stand up to Denny's bullying. Not only did Denny respect the Colonel's promotional skills, but he acknowledged his business acumen.

It was because of Jim Denny's abuse of his power that Colonel Parker was able to persuade Eddy Arnold to leave the "Grand Ole Opry" booking agency. Although it was a calculated risk, Arnold was soon making more money. Tom Parker was one of a number of maverick promoters who challenged the traditional monopoly that Denny and the "Opry" had upon country music bookings. When Elvis Presley became a major regional star in 1954 and 1955 for Sun Records, it was due in some degree to the changes in booking procedures in the country music field brought about by the likes of Tom Parker.

Prior to Denny's time, between 1934 and 1946, under the guidance of George Hay, the Opry's booking service had been the best in the country music field, and it generated excellent wages for the country music artist. Not only was the performer guaranteed an appearance on the "Opry" by booking with Hay, but local concerts were arranged to cut travel expenses. Changes had begun in the 1930s and early 1940s, however, when country and western entertainers were increasingly booked by independent promoters, and a system of competing promoters developed to challenge traditional booking practices. Many radio stations began to offer their own booking service and received a percentage from each concert for booking and producing an artist. All this effectively ended the booking monopoly of the "Grand Ole Opry."

Tom Parker was one of those who believed that there was room for the independent booking agent. As a result, he challenged the Opry's monopoly by offering cut rate concert fees to promoters and club owners. One reason that Parker felt confident about standing up to the establishment was Jim Denny's fondness for beautiful women. By 1946-1947, Parker was telling anyone who would listen that Denny was too busy with his girls to book acts. It was Parker's way of undercutting Denny and establishing his own booking agency.

Since Colonel Tom Parker was a moralist, he reasoned that Jim Denny's liaison with a local dancer, Dollie Dearman, would ultimately alienate the conservative country music community. Denny's wife, Margaret, a financially secure woman, disdained Denny's show business friends. Their marriage persisted merely as a matter of convenience. Early on, Colonel Parker recognized that he could manipulate Jim Denny to his own advantage. Many country music promoters have charged that despite Colonel Tom Parker's criticism of Denny, he often paid Denny large sums to guarantee the Colonel that "Grand Ole Opry" acts would not play in cities in and around Eddy Arnold's concerts. While there is no direct proof that Denny protected Arnold in this way, there is evidence that the Colonel received preferential treatment from the Opry's booking agency. "Denny would make sure that no 'Opry' act went into a town within two weeks of Arnold," one country music promoter recalled. It was a convenient arrangement, one that made Arnold a great deal of money and still allowed Denny to take his small bribes. Denny retained his illusion of power and the Colonel filled large dance halls. "I wouldn't say that the Colonel blackmailed Jim Denny," country music star Jim Reeves remarked, "but he sure did get preferential treatment from Denny."

There is no doubt that Colonel Parker was a well-known and respected figure in Nashville. But what are the reasons for Parker's influence? Most observers failed to recognize that Parker usually had friends in high places. Or that, more often, he consorted with show business legends to get his way. When he arrived in Nashville, Parker struck up a strong friendship with Roy Acuff. In Florida, Parker had helped Acuff with some business deals. "I suggested he come to Nashville, meet the boys," Acuff remembered. Just a few days after settling in Nashville, Parker proposed a management deal to Acuff. After thinking about it, Acuff told Parker that, yes, he was interested in a business arrangement. Much to Acuff's astonishment, and in a move which anticipated Parker's future managerial style, the Colonel then suddenly withdrew his offer! The "Grand Ole Opry" and Jim Denny had contractual arrangements with Acuff, and Parker viewed these agreements as negative ones. He wanted total control over Acuff's career. Parker also believed that the "Grand Ole Opry" was moving out of the mainstream of country music. The Colonel astounded the Nashville musical establishment with his bold remarks. "He wouldn't take anyone who just wanted to stay with the "Grand Ole Opry," Acuff recalled. There is no doubt that many of Parker's later promotional schemes with Elvis Presley were nurtured during these early days as a fledgling country music manager. The Colonel had extravagant promotional ideas that were more grandiose than performers like Gene Austin and Eddy Arnold could comprehend.

Eddy Arnold

It was while managing Eddy Arnold that Parker developed into an effective country music promoter. Before he hooked up with the Colonel, Arnold had already enjoyed enormous popularity with Pee Wee King and his Golden West Cowboys. In 1940, Arnold increased King's popularity, and went on to work with the diminutive bandleader until 1943. King's group played on WSM radio in Nashville, a 50,000-watt station, and the band was well received in country western circles. Despite the notoriety, Arnold felt he wasn't receiving a livable wage, and so decided to leave King's band. Hired directly by radio station WSM, Arnold continued to develop his songwriting and singing talents. "I kept on working clubs, schools and other events, and pretty soon I was earning as much as one hundred dollars a week." In 1943, RCA-Victor auditioned Arnold and signed him to a contract—something it had taken him eight years to achieve.

In 1944, when Tom Parker persuaded Arnold to sign a management contract, he became an integral part of Arnold's life. "Tom was booking acts in small towns at that time," Arnold remembers, "and he decided that he wanted to be my manager; and I decided I wanted him to be my manager...." Under Parker's management, Arnold's career blossomed, and he graduated from tent shows to theaters. During these years, Parker also cultivated a friendship with RCA's most productive country music producer, Steve Sholes. In 1944, Sholes' friendship with Parker was enough to persuade Sholes to produce Eddy Arnold.

As the best country music producer at RCA, with a knack for finding a hit song, Arnold was fortunate to work with Steve Sholes. It was Sholes' ability to adapt to his artist's talent that made him so successful. (In 1956, when Sholes produced Elvis Presley's first RCA record, he demonstrated the same musical genius.) By 1946, Colonel Parker and Steve Sholes were mapping out Eddy Arnold's career with RCA. They talked about a series of mellow, middle of the road country hits that were neither too energetic nor too ballad-oriented. Sholes, like Parker, realized the importance of a "pop country" sound.

To pay for Eddy Arnold's music, Colonel Parker convinced the Ralston Purina Company to sponsor a radio program on the Mutual Broadcasting network. The program, "Checkerboard Square," was broadcast at noon for fifteen minutes each day all over the United States. As Arnold hosted popular guests like Hank Williams and Tennessee Ernie Ford, his own music became more popular. "Tom Parker kept on pluggin," Arnold remarked. "He started getting me guest spots on national programs, and he finally convinced me that the royalty checks were real...." To Arnold's recollections, there was no hint of bitterness or dissatisfaction on his part with Colonel Parker's management style up to that point.

As Arnold's hit records began to top the million mark, Parker worked with the William Morris Talent Agency to secure a movie contract. Arnold, however, did become unhappy with Parker when he found out that Parker had signed him to make two movies in three months. Worried about the quality of the movies and the impact upon his career, he began to question his manager's judgement. In his autobiography, *It's a Long Way from Chester County*, he recalled a conversation with Parker about the movie deal.

"Well, they'll be a little lean on quality and budget, but they'll be acceptable pictures," Parker remarked.

"I'll be terrible in all of them," Arnold suggested, "but if Hollywood will gamble on me, I'll gamble on Hollywood."

"Just sing and play your guitar," Parker concluded. The two movies, "Feudin' Rhythm" and "Hoedown" were designed to showcase country music talent. When they were released in 1950, they made Arnold uncomfortable; he felt out of place in this new industry.

Eddy Arnold's career is a microcosmic reflection of Parker's future management style. It was during his years managing Arnold that Parker developed the tactics that he would employ so successfully with Elvis Presley. There were three aspects of Parker's management style that carried over into the Presley era. First, Parker overexposed his act when they were popular. In 1950, at the height of his popularity, Arnold was signed to the movie deal. (His earlier hit records, "That's How Much I Love You" and "Don't Rob Another Man's Castle," had already made him a major star.) Second, once Arnold reached this peak level of stardom, Parker booked him on every major radio show. A half-page ad was purchased in *Billboard* announcing Arnold's appearances on prestigious radio shows such as the "Spike Jones Show," "Hayloft Hoedown," the "Breakfast Club," the "Paul Whiteman Club," and the "Western Theater." Third, Parker arranged a backbreaking concert tour to cash in on the publicity. Arnold was performing ten shows a week and he was exhausted from the frenetic schedule.

From 1944 through 1954, Parker successfully guided Arnold's career. In Arnold's autobiography, although bothered by Parker's obsessive management style—when Arnold suggested that Parker take up a hobby, the Colonel replied: "You're my hobby"—he characterizes Parker as a wonderful manager and a good friend. A persistent booking agent, Parker sometimes promoted tours that included bookings in different cities *for the same night*. It was not uncommon for a show to begin at 6:00 p.m. in one town and, after a forty-minute session on stage, see the first act drive a hundred miles to open an 8:30 p.m. show in another city. Hard on the concert artists, but it did maximize concert profits.

On a financial level, Eddy Arnold profited handsomely from his management deal with Parker. In 1947, Arnold's "Bouquet of Roses" sold a million copies. It

was not long before Arnold eclipsed Roy Acuff in popularity. The only real challenge to Eddy Arnold was Hank Williams. (On February 25, 1949, MGM Records released Williams' "Lovesick Blues," and this song made the erratic singer-songwriter a major country music star. During one "Grand Ole Opry" show, Williams was called back for six encores. Jim Denny was amazed at his popularity.) Eddy Arnold continued to occupy the top spot in country music sales and polls, although Hank Williams and Eddy Arnold took turns topping the various country music charts. It was Arnold's smash hit, "Don't Rob Another Man's Castle," which prevented Williams from placing his first five records on the top of the country charts. Among Williams' songs in late 1949, "Lovesick Blues" and "Wedding Bell" were numbers 1 and 3 on the country charts, and only Arnold's "The Echo of Your Footsteps" prevented Williams from having the top 3 songs on the Best Selling Retail Folk (country & western) Records popularity chart. It was Hank Williams' enormous popularity that made Parker even more assiduous in pursuit of Eddy Arnold's success; he worked diligently with disc jockeys, jukebox operators, one-stop distributors, and booking agents to continue Arnold's record sales.

Parker very shrewdly directed Arnold's career, but Arnold's popularity was such that it consumed his private life. The Colonel successfully negotiated for national radio shows, appearances at the thriving Las Vegas casinos, and a financially lucrative contract for two Hollywood films. Parker insisted that Eddy tour constantly, and he never gave his star time to be with his family. Parker often negotiated business deals without even fully informing Arnold. This infuriated Arnold because it often took him away from home for months. The Colonel, however, expected Arnold to concentrate all his energies upon his career. Soon Parker and Arnold were fighting over management style and career direction. Arnold was embarrassed by the Colonel's methods. Not only was Arnold expected to constantly sign memorabilia, but the Colonel demanded that his artist continually hold radio press conferences.

The most humiliating example of Parker's corn-pone promoting style occurred during Eddy Arnold's first appearance in Las Vegas. The show was booked by the William Morris Agency. Not only was the William Morris Agency the largest booking agent in America, but they were also the key to crossing over from the country into the pop market. To the astonishment of everyone in the music business, Colonel Parker demanded that the William Morris Agency pay for Arnold's two-week appearance in advance. The Colonel always liked to get his money up front, and he didn't care if someone was alienated in the process. Many of Colonel Parker's critics have suggested that he was a hick for collecting up front from the William Morris Agency; they claim that the Colonel really believed that the Las Vegas casinos might go out of business in two weeks. A more plausible explanation is that the Colonel was simply flexing his muscles and letting the William Morris Agency know that he was a powerful management figure. Parker's assistant, Oscar Davis, tried to explain to Parker that alienating the William Morris Agency was a mistake. The Colonel laughed. He had learned his lessons well in Tampa. Never let the big promoters push you around.

The best insights into Parker's career are offered by Gabe Tucker. As a fledgling entertainer and country music promoter, Tucker was friendly with Parker during World War II. Tucker worked as a publicist at the Ernest Tubb Record Shop in Nashville, where he first met Parker. Gabe was an aspiring musician and a would-be promoter. A guitar, trumpet, and bass player of limited talent, Tucker loved show business and hung around the "Grand Ole Opry." A wildly dressed character with a penchant for self-promotion, Tucker eventually went to work for Colonel Parker and became one of the Colonel's close friends. Still, Parker is also portrayed in Tucker's book, *Up and Down with Elvis Presley*, written with Marge Crumbaker, as a freeloader, a man always looking for a quick buck, behavior very characteristic of Parker's early years.

At one moment, says Tucker, Parker was a highly sophisticated promoter, at another time he would act like a hillbilly. A good example of this type of behavior took place in Tampa. Although Parker made plenty of money managing Arnold, nevertheless, he never passed up a chance for an easy dollar. During his early management days with Arnold in the 1940s, the Colonel continued to operate a small business in Tampa. He met a young man, Bevo Bevis, who helped Parker set up a pet cemetery. It was not long before Parker was burying pets for outrageous sums. There were also rumors that horses, ponies, cows, and other forms of livestock showed up at the pet cemetery. This lucrative sideline offers an important insight into Parker's character. Although he was managing a major country music act, Parker was deathly afraid of poverty.

The Colonel used every available device to make money, and he spent very little of his fortune. In 1944, reports Tucker, he and the Colonel traveled together with Eddy Arnold in a tent show. Gabe was playing bass fiddle and learning to publicize country music shows. The Colonel was in charge of the show's promotion and traveled a day ahead of the entourage. Prior to managing Eddy Arnold, Colonel Parker had always dressed frugally in military boots, a worn shirt, old trousers, and a wrinkled windbreaker. Only when Parker went on the road with Arnold did he hire his old friend, Jack

Garns, now a Beverly Hills, California, tailor, to sew up some fancy new clothes.

Another interesting personality quirk that Colonel Parker demonstrated was his love for uniforms. Gabe Tucker remembers the Colonel traveling hundreds of miles to get a free uniform from a service station attendant, a hotel porter, a sailor, or a theater usher. (He often told people that Eddy Arnold would enjoy having a certain uniform, but kept them for himself.)

When the Colonel lectured Bevo Bevis about pet cemetery decorum, he often stated: "Now Bevo, if you are to look your best, you must have a uniform." Tucker always laughed at the Colonel's comments. Soon the Colonel himself was wearing a well-pressed, hospital-type smock to catch pets in his role as dogcatcher. Not only did Parker consider this a professional look, but he used the uniform to convince people to bury their pets in his cemetery.

By the early 1950s, Parker's style was so firmly developed that his relationship with Eddy Arnold was strained beyond repair. They fought over bookings, management tactics, and the Colonel's propensity to over-promote Arnold's shows. By 1953, Parker had brought Arnold into Las Vegas' lucrative casino showrooms, but believed that Eddy would not fit into the new musical mold, and felt that he had pushed Arnold's career to its artistic and financial limits.

The Colonel and his wife had moved to Nashville and purchased a large four-bedroom home in Madison, Tennessee. Located just outside Nashville, the Madison residence was the center of Parker's burgeoning management fiefdom. To merchandise Arnold's music, the Colonel negotiated a music publishing contract with the most influential Nashville house—Hill and Range. Not only was Hill and Range the best-known country music publisher, but they were expanding into the pop music. They were perfect for Colonel Parker's plan to move Eddy Arnold into the Northern and Western pop music markets. Parker's intention was to make Arnold a multi-market star. He failed, but the idea persisted until the Colonel found Elvis Presley.

Because of Parker's obsessive-compulsive need to promote his singer's career, he spent every waking hour at Arnold's house. Eddy's wife, Sally, constantly complained about Parker's lack of social grace. The Colonel showed up at the Arnold house any hour of the day or night, taking complete control of the household. Parker, his wife Miz' Rie, and Gabe Tucker often stayed with the Arnolds for days while working out business deals. It was more than Eddy Arnold's family could stand, and they couldn't understand the Colonel's single-minded devotion to Arnold's career. Gabe Tucker suggests that Sally Arnold liked Colonel Parker, but she finally demanded that something be done to keep him out of the family kitchen.

While performing in Las Vegas in 1954, the tensions between Eddy Arnold and Colonel Parker finally exploded over business matters. In reality, there had been a decade of differences, and the problems simply surfaced in Las Vegas. The rift came when Arnold made an unannounced visit to Parker's Las Vegas suite, and the Colonel quickly stuffed a huge batch of papers into a drawer. When Arnold demanded to see the papers, Parker refused. Angrily Arnold yanked the papers from the drawer. They revealed an ambitious merchandising campaign for Arnold's next RCA release. Colonel Parker explained that he was preparing a surprise advertisement to aid his client's career. Eddy Arnold, according to Oscar Davis, one of the Colonel's trusted employees, was convinced that the Colonel was keeping something from him. The pair exchanged angry words and a fistfight was narrowly averted. That evening Arnold and Colonel Parker separated as business partners. Strangely enough, they remained close personal friends, but the strain of togetherness on the road for a decade had taken its toll. Arnold simply could not understand why the Colonel had to spend so much time and money promoting his career. He was already an established country act, and Arnold's RCA recording contract was one of the most solid in the business. His fans had remained true to his music for a decade. The Colonel had always argued that money was needed to prepare an advertising campaign to generate more sales for Arnold's records. "You never can tell when they'll catch onto us," Parker told Arnold.

By 1954, Arnold began to consider retirement. He was successful, had invested his money wisely, and had a happy marriage. For his part, the split with Arnold had prompted Colonel Parker to search for another performer to manage. It was the first significant crisis in Parker's management career, and he come through it without rancor. He went home to Madison, Tennessee, and prepared to find his next act. This was exactly the moment that Elvis Presley's Sun recordings were causing a sensation in the Southern market. In his book, Gabe Tucker takes credit for convincing Colonel Parker to sign Elvis. There is little validity to this claim, but Tucker's book otherwise offers a valuable inside view of Colonel Parker's business life.

Tom Parker was himself acutely aware of important changes in the music business, and was perfectly capable of prospering without Tucker's insight. When Hank Penny's 1950 King recording, "Hillbilly Be Bop" and Moon Mullican's 1951 record, "Cherokee Boogie," hit the charts, Colonel Parker recognized the blues direction in country music. When black artists began recording country songs, Parker carefully monitored the sales. Ivory Joe Hunter's 1949 record "Jealous Heart" and Wynonie Harris's 1951 hit "Bloodshot Eyes" were solid records demonstrating that a black cover record of a Western swing song could sell. It was then that Parker began looking for a white singer who could cover black songs. Like Sam Phillips, Parker was an astute judge of changing musical tastes. The new style in Hank Williams' hit records, and the popularity of Little Jimmy Dickens' "Hillbilly Fever," Hank Snow's "I'm Moving On," and Lefty Frizzell's "If You've Got the Money, I've Got the Time," focused Parker's attention on the fact that electrical background, blues instrumental and vocal influences, and the rise of realistic lyrics were profoundly changing country music. Inasmuch as both black and white artists were recording country songs, the affinity between rockabilly and black music in the early 1950s was clearly broadening the base of the country music market.

"Grand Ole Opry"

Because of business problems, Parker didn't finish his dealings with Eddy Arnold until the late summer of 1954. Ironically, the week he concluded his arrangement with Arnold, he first heard industry gossip about a new hillbilly singer named Elvis Presley. Parker didn't pay too much attention to the rumors, although he filed away the information for future reference. Opportunities presented by the "Grand Ole Opry" continued as Parker's main preoccupation.

It was only natural for the Colonel to look toward Nashville's premier musical hall for another performer. WSM broadcast the "Grand Ole Opry" radio show on one of the strongest signals in the South. Hadn't every major country star emerged from the Opry's stage?

When Parker returned to Nashville, he walked the one block from Ryman Auditorium to the Ernest Tubb Record Shop. Much to Parker's surprise, Tubb was himself waiting on customers. They talked for a long time about the emerging rockabilly sound. They both liked Hardrock Gunter's music. It was while in Tubb's store that Parker listened to Gunter's 1951 recording "Boogie Woogie on a Saturday Night." After listening to it, Parker thought again about young Elvis Presley, whom he would first see perform in Boston, Texas, later that year. Tubb had Presley's first single in the shop, and they listened to "That's All Right (Mama)." The visit to Ernest Tubb's store had revived the Colonel's interest in Presley.

Tom Parker was anxious to disprove Eddy Arnold's notion that business and family matters had to be separate. The Colonel hoped to find an artist whose passion was so great for stardom that he would devote every minute to show business. In many respects, Elvis' compulsive nature was an important aspect of Parker's interest in him. The Colonel was not committed to managing Elvis in late 1954 and early 1955, but he started watching the kid.

During Colonel Parker's search for another client, he spent hours looking at talent. Bill Williams, *Billboard*'s Nashville representative, remembers Parker hanging around Ryman Auditorium, constantly chewing a cigar and boisterously talking with other independent booking agents. Jim Denny was still running the Artists Service Bureau from the Opry's main office as small-time promoters hung around in the hall looking for acts to book. At nine each morning, WSM's lobby quickly filled with colorful characters who badgered one artist after another. The rise of small clubs, the increased number of releases by independent record labels, and a new prosperity in the Southern economy led to an explosion in regional record sales. With the right acts and extensive knowledge of where and when to book talent, fledgling independent booking agents could survive and even prosper. Colonel Tom Parker was not alone in entering the golden age of the independent booking agent.

Ever since he was appointed head of the Artists Services Bureau in 1951, Jim Denny had instituted a number of reforms designed to thwart the hustling, small-time promoters. Over the years, however, the booking agents and managers who roamed the Opry's halls had gotten an annoying foothold, regulars whose daily visits were grudgingly acknowledged and accepted by the Opry's management. By 1954-55, though, Jim Denny had begun to question the legitimacy of the presence of these show business promoters. It was not long before he raised a storm over their actions. In the main lobby, for example, agents could use the telephone free of charge. Eventually, "Opry" management discovered that their phone was being used to book acts other than those promoted by the Opry's booking agency. When Denny found out that the free telephone was being thus abused by the booking agents, he cut off the privilege.

Actually, Jim Denny was basically just furious over the agents' behavior in general. He issued a series of memos which brought a corporate structure to the "Grand Ole Opry," reforms which ended the "good ole boy" country entertainer atmosphere. There were suddenly restrictions on the use of the phone, the lobby was monitored for unauthorized personnel, and a system of checks and balances upon "Opry" management was instituted by a group of newly-hired accountants. Denny was certainly not acting in the spirit of country music. As an honorary Louisiana Colonel, Tom Parker blustered about the lack of protocol, and he urged Denny to restore the old system. With a twinkle in his eye, the Colonel suggested that Denny could one day book one

of Parker's more obscure acts to rectify his hurt feelings. Denny laughed and agreed.

Predictably, the changes in "Opry" policy had no immediate impact upon Tom Parker. He simply became friendly with the disc jockeys and low-level management types who operated the lobby. It was not long before he was using the free phone in the station announcer's booth. The Colonel also recognized that the perception of his status at the "Grand Ole Opry" was not that of a well-known promoter. He concluded that Southerners were not only impressed by titles, but were exceptionally deferential to those individuals with special monikers. In 1953, Governor Frank C. Clement of Tennessee was persuaded, owing to a sizeable campaign contribution, to grant Parker the title of Tennessee Colonel, his second anointment, as it were. It was an important step in Parker's management strategy, because it again made him appear close to important politicians. In the South, his was a credential that businessmen could not overlook. The action also guaranteed that the Colonel would be taken seriously in Nashville music circles.

In order to facilitate a career in the Tennessee music industry, as mentioned earlier, Parker had relocated his management company, Jamboree Attractions, to an eleven-room flagstone house on Gallatin Road in Madison, Tennessee. Located just a few miles from Nashville, Parker's new home was perfectly suited for his constant business dealings. Initially, Jamboree Productions was located across the street from Eddy Arnold's home, a situation which allowed the Colonel to spend as much time as he desired directing Arnold's career. When Parker and Arnold went their separate ways, the Colonel still found his home an ideal location to conduct his business affairs.

The intensity that Parker felt about his business was demonstrated in the converted garage that became Jamboree Attractions' office. Not only was no expense spared on telephones and equipment, but the walls were plastered with photographs, souvenirs, publicity shots, and honors the Colonel had wrangled over the years. To visitors, Jamboree Attractions was a shrine dedicated to Colonel Parker's single-minded devotion to his clients.

There was another important element in Colonel Parker's success; namely, his assistant Tom Diskin. Diskin, Parker's brother-in-law, was a loyal employee with a devotion to show business second only to the Colonel's. When Parker married, he had promised his wife that her family would share in his business success. No one was better suited to be the Colonel's alter ego than his brother-in-law Tom. A quiet, physically slight man who never directly challenged the Colonel, Diskin's background was an important asset. Tom Diskin grew up in

Chicago, and early in his life developed a shrewd business mind. It wasn't just Diskin's management skills that Parker admired; his loyalty was unquestioned and greatly appreciated.

Much of Jamboree Attractions' success was due to Diskin's penchant for detail. He was an organization man who spent eighty hours a week planning where, when, and how Jamboree Attractions would present its acts. Much of the double-booking activity that Colonel Parker engaged in was due to Diskin's skill at logistics. He could book one of Parker's attractions for two shows within a one-hundred-mile area, and make both concerts run smoothly. In fact, by 1954 Diskin had organized the Madison, Tennessee, office so efficiently that Colonel Parker dispatched his brother-in-law to open a Jamboree Attractions office in Chicago.

Hank Snow

In September 1954, Colonel Tom Parker was back in the management business with Hank Snow. (Ironically, it was in August 1954 that Scotty Moore first approached Tom Diskin about booking Elvis Presley.) A Canadian, born in 1914 in Liverpool, Nova Scotia, Snow had appeared at the "Grand Ole Opry" for five years when he agreed to a management contract with Parker. The forty-year-old Snow was at the peak of his performing powers, and had recorded for RCA-Victor Records. Parker still had excellent relations with RCA because of Eddy Arnold's old contract, so it was relatively easy to convince Snow that the Colonel could do big things for his career. Snow, for all his experience, was still having difficulty adjusting to American life. The Colonel argued that Jamboree Attractions was the answer to his problems.

To demonstrate his faith in Snow's future, the Colonel offered him a partnership in Jamboree Attractions. It was not a good-will gesture, however. Parker was keen to forge a business relationship with a major country star. Hank Snow was a top act, and the Colonel knew he could make a lucrative income from Snow. Under the arrangement, Parker was allowed to work independently with other acts, and Jamboree Attractions quickly evolved into one of the most important independent booking agencies in the South. But it was Hank Snow who paid the bills.

In 1954, the Colonel assembled an impressive traveling unit known as "Hank Snow's Jamboree Attractions." The lineup of supporting acts read like a who's who of country music. Among others, Mother Maybelle and the Carter Family, Slim Whitman, Martha Carson, Ferlin Huskey, the Wilburn Brothers, Faron Young, Webb Pierce, Onie Wheeler, Minnie Pearl, and Jimmy Rodgers Snow traveled with Hank Snow. A good businessman in his own right, Snow was cautious about money, and found it difficult to easily trust in the prospects of a partnership with Colonel Parker. On his own since age fourteen, Snow was careful in his business dealings and took great pride in his reputation. For years he had developed a God-fearing, flag-loving reputation, and this bore a great deal of fruit at the box office. There is no doubt that in 1954, Colonel Parker and Hank Snow were both well aware of Elvis Presley's reputation. The Colonel had followed Elvis' development for a long period of time. Hank Snow, while not a fan of Elvis' music, was certainly aware of his commercial appeal. It was not until Colonel Parker booked Elvis with "Hank Snow's Jamboree Attractions" that he realized Elvis' full potential. Unfortunately, confirming his misgivings about the Colonel, Tom Parker ultimately finessed Snow out of any share in Elvis Presley's future earnings. However, this should not obscure the fact that Snow was a shrewd businessman and consummate showman. When the Colonel and Snow first worked together, Elvis was viewed merely as a talent to watch; Snow simply didn't have the good fortune to buy into Presley's future.

Taking full advantage of his right to make separate management deals, the Colonel listened intently as fellow performers lauded Presley. The praise that singers Tommy Sands, Johnny Tillotson, Bob Luman and others accorded Elvis was important in Parker's final evaluation. Sands, Tillotson, and Luman were beginning their careers in the music business when they talked to Colonel Parker, but they were extremely astute observers of the new music. The Colonel always believed that the little guy or the amateur was the best judge of talent. So, he eagerly sought out opinions from unknowns. These evaluations of Presley's talent were an important influence on Colonel Parker's eventual decision to manage the Memphis singer.

Before he signed Elvis to a management contract, the Colonel talked at great length with aspiring rockabilly singer Tommy Sands. Sands not only believed that Elvis was the forerunner of a new musical style, but he urged the Colonel to quickly sign Presley to a management contract. When Sands appeared in Houston and Dallas as a country singer, he also performed pop songs. Later on, after Tom Parker became involved in Elvis' career, Scotty Moore and Bill Black, recognizing that Sands had a talent much like Elvis, hired Sands to appear with them. "There were obvious strains between Scotty Moore, Bill Black and Elvis," Sands remarked. "I went on the road with the Blue Moon Boys for one night. It just didn't feel right, so I never performed in the Elvis vein again." After the one concert in Texarkana, Texas, Sands informed Scotty and Bill that he couldn't take Elvis' place. "Not only did we call Elvis

(L. to r.): A 1953 shot of Tommy Sands, Colonel Parker (holding a coin), and two unidentified men (who look to be father and son). Which way is the coin passing? Well, who has the biggest grin?
(Photo courtesy Tommy Sands)

'the Cat" because of his good looks, it was also a compliment on his singing style. No one could replace him," Sands concluded.

The night that Sands appeared as the lead singer in the "Blue Moon Boys," there was a great deal of discussion about their future with Elvis. Bill Black wanted to front his own band. Scotty Moore had just completed a solo recording session for Sam Phillips' Sun label, and he was anxious to have his own record released. In December 1954, Scotty recorded "Blues Stay Away from Me" and "How Do You Think I Feel." The record was not released, because Sam Phillips was too busy promoting Elvis. This further strained relations between Presley and his backup musicians. They resented the attention he received, and pointed out that his sound wouldn't be the same without their skilled musical accompaniment. By going on the road with Tommy Sands, Scotty and Bill were trying to replace Elvis. The Colonel was furious when he found out about the Texarkana concert. It was a signal to Parker to replace Scotty and Bill. By late 1955, he would begin isolating them from Elvis. The Colonel would not tolerate competition, and he knew that internal friction could hamper Elvis' performance. There were many calls from the Colonel's number in Madison, Tennessee, to other musicians, and

Parker carefully laid advance plans to break off contacts with all of Elvis' Sun Records associates.

By the time the Colonel signed Elvis to a management contract, then, he had spent years in country music. His experiences with Gene Austin, Eddy Arnold, and Hank Snow gave Parker a deep understanding of the record business. He was already a proven concert promoter, and was recognized widely for his business skill. Elvis Presley was the act destined to provide Parker the strength on stage, the looks off stage, and the mystique in the press that created a million-dollar superstar.

Sam Phillips

Sam Phillips' career was one of stark contrast to that of Colonel Tom Parker. Phillips was born in Florence, Alabama, on January 5, 1923, the youngest of eight children from a tenant farming family. Phillips was raised on a 300-acre farm located on the Tennessee River on the outskirts of Florence. When Sam was six years old, the Great Depression ruined the family farm business. As Phillips watched his father struggle for a living, he developed the determination to be his own man. When his father died just after the Japanese attack on Pearl Harbor, Sam dropped out of high school. He quickly found a job to help support his aunt and recently widowed mother.

For a time Sam worked in a grocery store and then found employment in a funeral home. Neither job was to his liking. Phillips looked around Florence for a career model. He found a local lawyer that he admired, and announced his new career direction. Lack of money and local educational opportunities were to turn Phillips' attention away from the law, however. His interests gravitated towards radio, and he studied audio engineering, production, and announcing at the Alabama Polytechnical Institute.

As a young man growing up in the heart of the Bible Belt, Phillips developed an understated personality and a gracious manner. He had a sincerity that appealed to people, and his voice was described as "honey-toned." A well-dressed dandy with a penchant for sweet talk, Phillips had a natural facility for language, and described himself as a "frustrated criminal defense lawyer." He was also a frustrated musician, and he loved black music. Clearly, Sam Phillips was the new breed of Southerner. A student of music, he was aware of the musical history surrounding Florence. W.C. Handy had grown up in the small Alabama town, and there was otherwise a historically strong musical heritage connected with it. The streets were filled with country and blues musicians on weekends, and the black field hands could be heard playing and singing in the local juke joints.

In the mid-1930s, a fifteen-year-old Sam Phillips walked the streets of Florence pondering his future. In addition to pursuing his studies in radio, young Sam's course in life was strongly influenced by the cultural direction of the new South; his appreciation for the mix of musical styles in Florence would inspire him to enter the field of show business. The only natural course was to become a disc jockey. Beginning in his youth, Sam worked as a radio station engineer, a small-time concert promoter, and a disc jockey, although when and where he gained this experience is still shrouded in mystery.

Like many young Southern boys, Phillips was influenced by a particular black musician. In Sam's case, it was Uncle Silas Payne, a black field hand who played blues tunes on a guitar and harmonica, and thus helped bring the blues into Phillips' life. Payne also helped Phillips develop a commitment to black civil rights. Sam believed that blacks were not able to properly record their music. When Charlie Christian played his guitar with Benny Goodman in 1940 and 1941, Phillips was enthralled with the sound of this legendary guitarist. Christian's guitar solos on such songs as "Flying Home," "Honeysuckle Rose," and "Seven Come Eleven" opened up new possibilities for the guitar. Christian's musical innovation was not lost on Phillips; he believed that the black guitarists were the best in the South. Phillips recognized that Beale Street in Memphis held a special allure for these performers, and resolved to move there. In 1942, before leaving for Florence, Sam married his sweetheart, Rebecca Burns.

Prior to moving to Memphis, however, Sam also spent three years at WMSL in Decatur, Georgia, learning more about the radio business. He haunted beat clubs featuring black music, and was also seen at the hillbilly dances. By 1945, as World War II ended, Phillips was in Nashville working for WLAC. The next stop was Memphis, where he would pursue the recording studio dream that he had nurtured since his youth.

As a young man, music was Phillips' first love. He had learned to play the sousaphone and the drums, but was not an outstanding musician. "I played music from the sixth through the eleventh grade," Phillips told Colin Escott. "I was never a very good musician. I could always see the people that did have the talent." Phillips had a large record collection, and often complained to friends about the recording quality of these discs. The records featuring black artists were of especially uneven quality. Their sound was not well recorded, and Phillips often liked to point out that artists like Charlie Christian were musically too sophisticated for Benny Goodman. "The Negroes had no place to record in the South. They had to go up to Chicago or New York to get on record and even the most successful of the local entertainers had a hard time doing it," Phillips stated.

Because of his desire to record black artists, Phillips moved into the radio business with a new zeal. From June 1945 to 1949, Sam broadcast over WREC in Memphis. He was also caught up in Memphis' extensive nightlife. The blues were alive on Beale Street, the Peabody Hotel had dance band concerts, and local beer bars featured hillbilly music. On the weekends, Memphis was filled with would-be singers and musicians. Phillips' brother, Judd, also worked at WREC, singing with the Jollyboys Quartet. Judd not only educated Sam about the locals, but he opened a number of doors for his brother.

At four o'clock each afternoon, Sam hosted "Songs of the West." He signed on using the name "Pardner," and then proceeded to wow the locals with country music. But the show bored Sam, and he looked for another creative outlet. He found it by working with Milton Brame, who was the show's transcription manager. In an era when shows were not taped, the transcription manager instead produced sixteen-inch acetate discs. This meant that a radio engineer like Brame could teach Phillips the hands-on skills of a recording engineer, which Sam quickly acquired, learning many of the subtle

Sam Phillips.

125

nuances of craft necessary to his later career.

While at WREC, Sam also searched out on-air sound effects for the station, and helped to build up the disc jockey library. "One of my first jobs," Phillips remarked to Colin Escott, "was to go to the 'Home of the Blues' record store and buy up any records that WREC wasn't getting shipped to them." This was an ideal way to learn what made a record popular.

Prior to his decision to give up his full-time jobs, then, Memphis accorded Sam a valuable musical education. He loved the blend of musical styles in the city. The blues and country music bands were his favorites. "It seemed to be that the Negroes were the only ones who had any freshness in their music," Phillips remarked. Phillips was also one of the earliest Memphis music figures to recognize the popularity of the new dance bands. As an engineer at WREC, he was responsible for the CBS network broadcasts from the Skyway Room atop the Peabody Hotel. There were long lines to see the bands, but the musicians complained that they had trouble obtaining bookings. It was not long before Sam Phillips was making a good living booking bands into the Peabody. He had a knack for selecting the right groups to perform in the large ballroom, and this resulted in excellent musical connections.

Because of his extensive knowledge, Phillips soon hosted the WREC "Saturday Afternoon Tea Dance." This program was not only popular with local listeners, but it attracted the attention of bands. Sam was flooded with requests to play jazz, blues, and pop records. The leaders of local bands hung out with Sam, drank with him, and talked to him about their dreams. Sam Phillips had his own vision, too.

Memphis Recording Service

Sam Phillips' early years were tough ones. "I had obligations all my life," Phillips lamented to Colin Escott. "I was the youngest of eight kids, lost my father early on, I had a deaf mute aunt...." But Sam was driven to succeed in the music business. His wife Becky encouraged him, and he concentrated his efforts on music. The decision to give up his full-time employment was not an easy one. "I went home one night and told my wife Becky, I can't stand it." With this declaration Phillips vowed to make a living his own way. "I had no income except what I could hustle up," Phillips concluded.

Phillips leased the building at 706 Union Avenue in October 1949 and, in January 1950, quit his job at WREC and opened the Memphis Recording Service. The times were not good ones for a small record company. He told everyone it was basically just a hobby, and that he didn't expect to make money from it. Phillips had a realistic attitude, so he sought out part-time work to guarantee his family a livable income. Deep down, however, Phillips was serious about producing the best black music in America. When he explained why he started the company, Sam pointed to the likes of Uncle Silas Payne as his first choice for special studio treatment. "I set up a studio in 1950 just to make records of those great Negro artists," Phillips remarked. Much like a feudal baron who hoped to create a new society, Phillips was determined to bring the black music that he loved to a wider audience. A quarter of a century after opening the Memphis Recording Service, Sam Phillips spoke at length with Martin Hawkins. Phillips confessed that he began his business to record music "that people should be able to hear." The blues was the music Phillips had in mind. "My main aim was to try to record the blues," Phillips continued. Black artists flocked to Phillips, because he didn't charge a studio fee. "You see, until then," Phillips remarked to Hawkins, "the artists did not feel that anybody was really going to help them." Not only did Phillips record some excellent blues tunes, but bluesmen recognized that he appreciated and understood their music. Sam Phillips vowed to provide the black artist with the proper recording atmosphere, and, much to his credit, he did it. The immediate goal of Phillips' new business, however, was to make enough money recording bar mitzvahs, weddings, and local talent to help finance a new record label. Initially, Sam Phillips viewed the Memphis Recording Service as a springboard to a large record company. It took him two years to launch Sun Records.

The original site for what became Sun Records was a narrow one-story building that created the illusion of being squashed into Union Avenue. Once inside, however, the recording studio was a comfortable thirty-by-eighteen-foot room lined with white acoustic tile. There was a make-shift control booth that allowed Phillips to direct the recording sessions. Eight mikes were visible in various positions, but they weren't placed in a particularly scientific manner. Jack Clement, Sam's chief engineer, worked with Phillips setting up the studio, and, over the next few years, Stan Kesler, Marcus Van Story, and Charlie Feathers worked on arranging the mikes. (The famous "Sun sound" was actually produced by one mike bleeding into the next.)

Creating the studio had been a tremendous remodeling job. On the plus side, the presence of carpenters, plumbers, and moving vans had attracted attention. Country performers, street musicians, blues artists, and big band members watched Sam Phillips develop his new company. When Phillips formally opened the Memphis Recording Service, large numbers of local blues musicians walked through the company front door. In order to understand Phillips' success, it is necessary to examine his relationship with Memphis musicians and key figures in the music business.

At the time, the record business was dominated by corporate giants. The major record labels—Decca, RCA, Columbia, and Capitol—soon found that they were challenged by three new labels: MGM, Mercury, and London. To Phillips' surprise, none of these companies paid any attention to the blues. Several small labels—Chess, Atlantic, Imperial, and others—were competing for the artists at the center of Sam Phillips' attention, however. At first, Memphis Recording Service simply recorded master tapes for these other small labels to release. Leonard Chess or one of the Bihari brothers would order a tape, and Sam Phillips would record the artist. While there was no money in making these recordings for others, Phillips found it excellent training for future success with his own label. "I had great, great artists that I was working with like B.B. King, Rosco Gordon, and the Howlin' Wolf...," Phillips reminisced.

Initially, Phillips' plan was to sign and record some of the best local artists, and sell the master tapes to the growing army of independent record labels. "I opened the business," Phillips stated, "with the intention of recording singers and musicians from Memphis...I'm talking about blues...I always felt that the people who played this type of music had not been given an opportunity to reach an audience." He began asking around about music groups that he could record. If a band could be recorded effectively, Phillips reasoned, the master could be sold to a name record label by his recording company.

Bill McCall of 4-Star and Gilt-Edge Records became one of Phillips earliest customers. 4-Star, a Los Angeles-based company, had discovered Cecil Gant, a black crossover piano player with a boogie-woogie sound. McCall also bought songs from an Oakland-based songwriter, Bob Geddins. Geddins was one of many black songwriters who convinced McCall that black artists could record in a white vein. The ties that Phillips established with McCall not only helped educate Sam about the record business, but McCall provided an example of a slick record promoter whose astuteness interested him in even more in the commercial possibilities for black music.

When Bill McCall asked Phillips to cut some demos for 4-Star, Sam jumped at the chance. In May and June 1951, Phillips recorded two blues artists, a piano player, Lost John Hunter, and a blues guitarist, Charlie Burse, as well as two country musicians, Slim Rhodes and Buck Turner. One song from this session "Cool Down Mama" (4-Star, 1942) by Lost John Hunter and the Blind Bats was registered with BMI in September 1951 and released to immediate obscurity. However, it is an important song, because this was Phillips' first blues release. When Sam saw the 78 that 4-Star released, he

was determined to produce more blues tunes. McCall failed to pay Phillips a fair price for these early tapes, however, and their business arrangement fell apart.

Sam Phillips also entered into an agreement with Modern Records magnates Jules and Saul Bihari to produce tapes for their new RPM label. After recording Joe Hill Louis, Phineas Newborn, and the Gospel Travelers, Phillips once again was struck with the notion of turning out his own records. The Joe Hill Louis tapes intrigued Phillips because he realized that Louis' versatile musical talents could be used in the studio to back other artists. One of the strengths of Sun Records was that the backup musicians provided excellent musical accompaniment. The fact that Phillips recorded original songs, written by the artist, prompted a large number of singer-songwriters to approach him. This was fifteen years before the singer-songwriter became a commercial phenomenon. The large number of musicians who approached Phillips caused the Bihari brothers to complain that Phillips was encroaching upon their territory.

The Biharis recognized Memphis' unique musical talent. In the summer of 1949, B.B. King signed a contract with the RPM label and recorded songs that became Memphis hits. B.B. King's "Woke Up This Morning," "B.B.'s Blues," and "B.B.'s Boogie" were songs that Sam Phillips loved, and they influenced his decision to open his own record business. RPM had not only released B.B. King's records, but regularly scouted local Memphis clubs for new acts. When some of the artists that Phillips recorded for the Biharis opted for other labels, there were harsh words. By late 1951, the tensions between Phillips and the Bihari brothers were obvious to most musicians hanging around the Memphis Recording Service; Phillips, everyone also noticed, talked incessantly about turning out his own records. Once Phillips began recording local artists, the Biharis became increasingly aggressive and hostile. Sam was incensed with the Bihari's arrogant attitude and there were strong words exchanged one night in a Memphis bar.

Phillips' reputation as an innovative producer was largely due to his recording of "Rocket 88." The tune featured the lead vocal of Ike Turner's saxophonist, Jackie Brenston. When Ike Turner and the Kings of Rhythm traveled from Clarksdale, Mississippi, to Memphis, they specifically sought out Phillips to record their music. In his role as producer, Phillips took a jump blues song and turned it into one of the first rock and roll records.

While the record was being produced, Phillips had realized that Turner was ruining the song. He made "Rocket 88" a success by placing Turner, the would-be producer, in the background, and by controlling the raw,

Jackie Brenston of "Rocket 88" fame.

rough edge of Turner's band. Not only did Sam cut the tune, but he leased it to Chess Records. It had taken all of Sam Phillips' persuasive powers to convince Ike Turner to allow Jackie Brenston to sing the lead. Turner was an excellent talent scout as well as a superb musician, but he was also a shortsighted egomaniac. He fought with his best lead vocalists and placed those with hits in the background. Often, young girls with strengths other than their vocal talent fronted Turner's band. At this stage in his career, however, Ike Turner couldn't afford to ignore Phillips.

When Sam Phillips approached Leonard Chess with "Rocket 88," Chess raved to Phillips about its commercial potential. "I'll show you how to merchandise a record," Chess growled to Phillips. Because of contractual problems with Ike Turner and the volatile situation in the band, Chess released "Rocket 88" under the lead singer's name, Jackie Brenston and His Delta Cats. In April 1951, "Rocket 88" was released on Chess Records, and the following month, as Leonard Chess had predicted, it was number 1 on the *Billboard* rhythm and blues chart. In "Rocket 88," Phillips had recorded archetypal rock song lyrics. The imagery of the new rocket-tailed Oldsmobile 88 foreshadowed the automobile themes that would dominate early rock and roll music. Chuck Berry was similarly influenced by "Rocket 88," and used it to craft a crude early version of "May-

bellene." Sam Phillips was unhappy about selling this recording to Chess, and the incident went a long way to ending Phillips' practice of making acetate demonstration recordings and selling them to other companies. Now he wanted to produce his own records. As the golden age of rhythm and blues music burst upon the American music scene, Phillips was ready to find the best new talent and record it. The first two years that Sam Phillips was in the record business was a training period.

Ike Turner and Jackie Brenston soon fought over the rights to "Rocket 88." The feud grew so bitter that Turner would not allow Brenston to perform the song in concert. Sam Phillips stepped into the fray and signed Brenston to a personal management contract. Quickly recruiting a band, the Delta Cats, Brenston toured to capitalize on his hit. A heavy drinker and an erratic performer, Brenston was frequently booed off the stage. Unable to carry the responsibility of fronting a band, he fled back to his hometown, Clarksdale, Mississippi. The twenty-one-year-old Brenston missed the Delta town where Highway 49 meets Highway 61. Soon his performances were confined to the local juke joints. (It was from this same musically fertile atmosphere that Charley Patton, Robert Johnson, and Son House had introduced the Delta blues to the world, and where Muddy Waters, John Lee Hooker, and Eddie Born had grown up listening to it.)

By 1953, Jackie Brenston was playing saxophone in Lowell Fulson's band, his solo career at an end. Anyone who saw Brenston and heard his song couldn't get it out of their mind. Young Elvis Presley played "Rocket 88" many mornings before he went to school. Richard Berry, a Los Angeles rhythm and blues performer who gained fame with "Louie Louie," used "Rocket 88" as a model for his songwriting talents. Bob Geddins, a Texas bluesman relocated to Oakland, California, based many of his original uptempo blues tunes upon "Rocket 88." Bill Haley was a fledgling country artist with a penchant for rockabilly music when he first heard "Rocket 88." "It was one of those songs I couldn't forget," Haley remembered. Black and white artists alike were inspired to write new tunes by this seminal song.

After spending seventeen weeks on the charts and establishing the link between jump blues and rock and roll, "Rocket 88" and Jackie Brenston slipped into obscurity. Sam Phillips recognized the song's commercial potential and purchased publication rights to it for $910. Leonard Chess quickly licensed the publishing rights to Hill and Range, who hoped to re-release "Rocket 88" in the country market. A Bill Haley cover version on Holiday Records attempted unsuccessfully to cross over into the country and pop marketplaces.

By purchasing Brenston's song, Phillips made it clear that he was ready to enter the record business full-time. Over the next two years, Phillips began to explore the commercial possibilities surrounding the 78 rpm record, and the demand for recorded music. As a disc jockey, Sam was thoroughly aware of the sales statistics, and knew that there was now a large market for records. It didn't take long for him to look more closely at what the small labels were doing to make money.

Finally, the time to launch a small record label of his own seemed right. The rise of black radio stations, notably WEDR in Birmingham, Alabama, WSOK in Nashville, Tennessee, WERD in Atlanta, Georgia, and WDIA in Memphis had helped labels like Savoy, Jubilee, RPM, Modern, Flair, Duke, and Peacock reach new listeners. Sam Phillips envisioned his company as one that could compete with these small labels. There had already been an earlier try at launching a new record company in Memphis, Royal Recording, but it had failed to generate a profit. Sam had continued working at WREC as an announcer to keep the Memphis Recording Service alive, and his bosses at WREC ominously detailed the Royal failure and warned Sam that Memphis wouldn't support a recording enterprise. Phillips ignored the warnings. It was this wealth of local talent that buoyed Phillips' spirits during the hard times. "I opened the Sun label at the first of the year 1952," Phillips remarked to Martin Hawkins, "God, that was a frightening experience for me."

The presence of a successful record pressing plant in Memphis also gave him heart, and prompted him to pursue his dream. Plastic Products, founded by Robert E. "Buster" Williams in 1949, pressed records for a number of labels. Williams also pressed some records by artists he had signed off the Memphis streets. Not only was Williams a promoter and a record hustler, he was a consummate technology buff. He designed a sophisticated record pressing plant, and invented the compound from which the records he pressed were made. Sam Phillips and "Buster" Williams soon became good friends. When Phillips started the Memphis Recording Service, Williams provided the manufacturing credit and local distribution network that helped Sam establish his business. Later, by handling the warehousing and shipping for Sun Records, Sam was free to promote his products. There were others who helped the Phillips business venture. Buck Turner, a performer at WREC, provided a two-year loan and encouraged Sam to follow his dream.

In many respects, Phillips' Sun Records was a smaller version of the Bihari's Modern Record Company. Located in a two-story red brick building in Los Angeles' Watts neighborhood, Modern Records featured the blues sounds of Jimmy McCracklin, Lowell Fulson, and Lightnin' Hopkins. The Biharis, who had grown up in Oklahoma, early on recognized the gold mine of record talent in the South. As a result of their keen ability to judge musical talent, they were able to record such diverse talents as John Lee Hooker, Pee Wee Crayton, Elmore James, Jimmy Witherspoon, and Etta James. (The name Modern Records came from a jukebox from which the Biharis made much of their money. In black neighborhoods, they had a monopoly on supplying jukeboxes, and, as a result, they resolved to produce their own recordings of black artists in order to make even more.)

It was Les Bihari who made the deal with Sam Phillips to produce masters for Modern, and they released some Howlin' Wolf tunes. Many of the Howlin' Wolf songs that Phillips recorded were not released, however, because of arguments over songwriting credit. Like many record company owners, Jules Bihari insisted that he receive writing credit for many blues tunes. The pseudonym Jules Taub was used to take half the writing credit from a blues artist. Sam Phillips objected to this practice and the ensuing arguments were typical of those that ended Sam's business relationship with the Biharis.

Sam Phillips was also hostile to Jules Bihari's attitude about recording blues artists. "I don't think you have to be a genius to record blues. All you have to do is stick a microphone out there and let them play," Bihari commented in *Blues Unlimited* magazine. This remark ignored the long history of the blues and the difficulty that most record companies had in properly recording blues artists.

The record executive that Phillips believed understood the blues best was Leonard Chess. Like Phillips, Chess spent a great deal of time combing the South for blues talent. When Leonard Chess began doing business with Sam Phillips, there was a meeting of the musical minds. Chess was the single most important influence upon Phillips. From the day Sam Phillips met Leonard Chess, the cigar-chewing, fast-talking Chicago record mogul was Sam's inspiration. Chess spent hours talking with Phillips, and he offered to buy the acetate recordings that Phillips was making with local bands.

Since 1947, Chess had operated the Aristocrat Record label; in 1950, he changed the name to Chess Records. That summer, Leonard Chess traveled 5,000 miles throughout the South searching for new talent. He met Chester Burnett, the Howlin' Wolf, in West Memphis, Arkansas, and crossed the river to Memphis to talk to Sam Phillips. When Chess arrived in Memphis, he listened eagerly to Phillips' demo tapes. It was Leonard Chess who encouraged Phillips to release Joe Hill Louis,' "Gotta Let You Go" and "Boogie in the

Park." It was Chess' way of cutting out his competitors, the Biharis. Originally destined for the Bihari brothers RPM label, Chess shared enthusiasm for the two Louis songs convinced Sam Phillips to enter the record business. Chess also made a deal with Phillips to cut records that the Chicago-based record company would release.

Sam's first recording was released on August 30, 1950, on the Phillips label. It turned out to be the label's only release. The following month, Phillips Records passed into history. It was obvious that Sam Phillips had trouble merchandising his product. No more than three hundred copies of the first Phillips' release were pressed, and the record quickly faded from sight. On the positive side, Joe Hill Louis signed a contract with Columbia Records in September 1950. In less than two months, Columbia released a record by Louis, and Modern Records quickly bought four of his old master dubs from Sam Phillips. Wheeling and dealing in the record business made Phillips eager to release more of hIs own.

Early in 1952, Leonard Chess called Sam Phillips and told him he would not be purchasing any more master tapes. When Phillips asked why, Chess stated that the big-selling hits like Jackie Brenston's "Rocket 88" were no longer coming from the Memphis Recording Service. In reality, Leonard Chess, as the Bihari brothers would do later that year, was trying to save money by recording the artists in local studios himself. When Leonard Chess informed Phillips that he would not be purchasing any more master tapes from the Memphis Recording Service, Phillips reacted angrily. It appeared that his friends were forcing him out of the record business. "I knew what it was like to be cheated," Phillips remarked. He also told a number of musicians that he would survive. "Tenacity is one thing and I have that," Phillips opined. Sam Phillips felt betrayed. Realizing that he was close to alienating Phillips, Leonard Chess called back and attempted to save their friendship. It was too late.

Sam Phillips had learned a great deal from the Chess brothers, and he had watched enviously as Phil and Leonard Chess drove down from Chicago to sign local talent and buy the masters that Phillips recorded. The Chess brothers persuaded Howlin' Wolf, who worked in the fields near West Memphis, Arkansas, to move to Chicago. In addition to purchasing B.B. King's records, the Los Angeles-based Bihari brothers bought the rights to songs by Tampa Red and Sonny Boy Williamson. It was while producing these cuts for the Bihari brothers that Phillips experimented with Solomon Hardy's saxophone solos and Ford Nelson's piano riffs. These unknown musicians convinced Phillips to hire his own studio musicians.

The Bihari and Chess brothers provided early models around which Phillips organized Sun Records, and they often unwittingly alerted Phillips to local talent. Phillips was now even more determined to launch his own label. By the spring of 1952, Phillips' Sun Records label was in its formative stages, although there was more organization than product. Sam needed money.

In Jackson, Mississippi, Lillian McMurray and Johnny Vincent's Trumpet label was also recording many of the same artists that Sam employed. (On January 5, 1951, Lillian McMurray had supervised Rice Miller's —Sonny Boy Williamson II—initial recordings, launching her Trumpet label from a furniture store and record shop in Jackson.) Not only was the music similar to that recorded by Phillips, but the Trumpet label had great success in Southern markets. As he scouted for new artists, Sam Phillips visited McMurray and they talked at length about his legal and record problems. She told Sam that her own troubles came from a lack of money and the inability to judge all types of music. It was McMurray who ultimately convinced Phillips to bring a partner into his record business, advice that sent Phillips to Nashville to find one.

Sun Records

In February 1952, Phillips borrowed some money from Nashville record magnate Jim Bulleit to begin his Sun Records operation. Sam learned a great deal from Bulleit. The Bulleit label, a small but successful Nashville company, turned out blues records. Bulleit's company provided another model for Sun Records. Sam Phillips reasoned he could duplicate its success in Memphis. "I thought I could maybe make a go of a company that just recorded rhythm and blues numbers," Phillips recalled.

After entering into an agreement with Buster Williams' Plastic Products, Inc., at 1746 Chelsea Avenue, to do the pressing, Phillips hired Bill Fitzgerald to distribute the records. Fitzgerald managed a one-stop wholesale record distributor owned by Williams' Plastic Products. Judd Phillips was sent into the field to promote the records. Sam soon found out that there were two other Sun labels, one was the Sun-Ray Company of Albuquerque and the second was a Jewish folk song company. The Albuquerque company sued Sun Records, but lost the legal challenge and soon faded into obscurity. By the next year, Sun Records was on its way to success.

On February 25, 1952, Phillips recorded Walter Horton's harmonica and jug band virtuoso Jack Kelly, marking the beginning of the Sun Records venture. The session produced two songs, "Blues In My Condition" and "Sellin' My Stuff." Neither song was a commercial one, but Sam was excited about the tunes. He sent acetates from the master tape to Leonard Chess' Chicago-based label. When Chess showed no interest in the dubs, Phillips was depressed. Taking matters into his own hands, Sam made another set of dubs and sent them to WHHM in Memphis for airplay. (This country music radio station, located on Sterich Boulevard, had a play-for-pay policy, and a twenty-dollar bill inside the record cover guaranteed four on-air appearances.) The local reaction was positive, and Sam went ahead with his plan to release his first Sun Record.

For some reason, Phillips became disenchanted with the title "Sellin' My Stuff," which he retitled "Sellin' My Whiskey." The re-recorded tune, again backed with "Blues In My Condition," was originally slated to have been released as Sun Record's first release—number 174—with Jackie Boy and Little Walter Horton listed as the artists. By March 1, 1952, when Sun Records announced its first commercial release, the decision had already been made not to release it. Not everyone understood why Sam Phillips pulled this record at the last minute. It was probably due to fear of failure. "Sam couldn't get the saxophone solo out of his mind," Marion Keisker remembered. This record featured an alto sax duet with Johnny London providing an extraordinary lead, and was a perfect example of Phillips' ability to select blues music. Sam brought the sixteen-year-old black saxophonist back into the Sun studio, where London recorded an instrumental, "Drivin' Slow."

On March 8, radio station WHHM played the songs by Jackie Boy, Little Walter and Johnny London. It was the public response to these dubs which further persuaded Phillips to release Johnny London's "Drivin' Slow." By giving local disc jockeys acetate dubs of key songs, Phillips could estimate sales before he pressed copies of a record. In this way he could save money by pressing only those records he believed would sell. As a result of the response to various acetate dubs, on March 27, 1952, Sam Phillips pressed five hundred copies of Sun Record number 175, and promptly scheduled new recording sessions for Joe Hill Louis and Rosco Gordon. In the end, it appears that Phillips opted for a more mellow, middle-of-the-road record as Sun's first release. With pride in his eyes and a smile on his face, Phillips mounted Sun Record number 175 on his wall. The Sun sound, which would revolutionize rock and roll, was on its way. The Sun Record label was in business.

As Phillips began to experience some local success, he in turn was faced with the fact that other labels were signing his performers. Duke and Peacock were the chief culprits, with RPM/Modern also attempting to sign selected acts. Sam was learning some hard lessons about contracts. In late 1952, Meteor Records entered the blues and rhythm and blues field, further challenging Phillips' local hegemony. It was time for Sam to act.

In January 1953, using demo tapes intended for the Chess label, Sam Phillips planned his next record releases. Meteor Records had released Elmore James' "I Believe," and both the record and artist were successful. Phillips realized that the best blues musicians would flock to Meteor if he didn't move quickly. Reflecting on his new record company years later, Phillips remarked: "I don't know what made me take that very brave step which, from a strictly business standpoint, I'm not sure anyone in their right mind would have taken." As Phillips suggested, the blues and rhythm and blues records were part of a small, isolated market. Hobbyists, faddists, academics, and hopeless amateurs were turning out the music. Blues and rhythm and blues labels were invariably family affairs. It was common for a record company president to be the main salesman as well as the shipping clerk. When Chuck Berry walked into Chess Records in 1955, he was surprised to find Leonard Chess working at the receptionist's desk. Muddy Waters remembers Chess standing on Chicago's Maxwell Street one Sunday afternoon selling records. "I bought my own record from the man," Waters chuckled. "He wouldn't sell me a second copy." Making the records was the easy part. Selling them was another matter altogether.

There was already a great deal of payola in the music business, although it would be years before this became common knowledge. Payola was only one problem for the Sun label. The record business in general was full of conniving, manipulating con men who ran businesses that took advantage of the small record labels. The early one-stop distributors which handled Phillips' records often refused to pay for them. They returned many records and filed confusing claims. Fraudulent invoices were devised to avoid payment. Judd Phillips finally went to New York to learn how the big companies operated. He found out that they frequently paid disc jockeys to play their records, and the major labels had large expense accounts to wine and dine key industry figures. "The distributor in New York showed me what they were paying dj's. They had four dj's on the payroll...they could feel the difference in volume...," Phillips concluded. Like the major record labels, Sun reorganized its management and began to play the payola game. This resulted in a decline in artist royalties. "I never saw a dime in the early days," Rosco Gordon remarked. "But when you went back to see Sam, he would write you a check," Gordon concluded. As one of Sun Records successful black artists,

Rosco Gordon

Gordon often had to endure the indignity of someone else's name appearing as the co-songwriter on his records.

Most Sun Records' artists have commented that Sam Phillips did pay his artists a fair royalty. He was often late with the royalty payments, but this was due to the lack of available cash. During recording sessions, Phillips paid a small, but fair, wage to his session men. "My honesty and integrity are everything to me. I know what it is to be cheated...," Phillips recalled. To save money, Phillips listed only a few musicians on the Sun Record union contract. Others like Kenneth Herman, Marcus Van Story, Ronald Smith, and Doug Poindexter were not listed as being present during recording sessions. "I was mad as hell, not receiving recognition for playing on Elvis Presley's and Johnny Cash's records," Doug Poindexter later reflected. "Hell, I not only played on a number of them records, I helped arrange them." Sipping a glass of whiskey in his den, Poindexter turned to me, smiled and said: "There were so many guys helping Sam that them books couldn't list 'em all." It wasn't easy for Phillips to achieve success in this atmosphere.

By 1952, however, Sun Records was established as a legitimate business. The first two years were experimental ones as Phillips learned the ropes. It was necessary to turn a profit with vanity records to guarantee that enough money could be generated to continue the Sun Records operation. Once the company began, however, Phillips was confident that he could turn out successful blues and country music records.

It proved difficult to merchandise the early Sun material. Southern radio stations played the blues, but Leonard Chess, Jules Bihari, Huey Meaux, and other independent record companies had a corps of promotional men who bribed, cajoled, and flattered disc jockeys into playing their records—records on the Chess, Modern, RPM, Duke, and Peacock labels. Sam Phillips had no choice but to go on the road himself to promote his product.

Loading up his car with records, Sam drove to Shreveport, Louisiana, and through West Texas before returning to Memphis. It was not long before Sun Records had deals with Texas and Florida distributors. Sam always made sure a few extra records were included in the shipments for the disc jockeys. He emphasized his Southern roots, and appealed to the local musical pride of the djs. It worked. Sun Records steadily became a staple on most Southern radio stations.

While establishing the market for Sun Records, Phillips continued to search for new talent. He found a black gospel group serving time in the Nashville State Penitentiary. They were appropriately dubbed the Prisonaires. After a series of letters were exchanged between Warden James Edwards and Governor Frank Clement, and with the help of Jim Bulleit, Sam Phillips was allowed to bring his recording equipment into the prison. A few months later, under heavy guard, the Prisonaires were transported to the Sun studio for another recording session. In late 1953, the Prisonaires' "Just Walkin' in the Rain" (Sun 186) was a regional hit. The Prisonaires were not only a hit with country fans, but they were discovered by Northern black record buyers. *Ebony* magazine reported that "Just Walkin' In The Rain" sold almost a quarter of a million copies,

The Prisonaires.

and heaped praise on the Sun label. If Phillips was able to press 50,000 of this song he was lucky, but the publicity was important to Sun.

The Prisonaires' lead singer, Johnny Bragg, told a number of reporters that Elvis helped him with the lyrics to "Just Walkin' in the Rain," but this seems unlikely. Colin Escott and Martin Hawkins, in *Good Rockin' Tonight*, published in 1991, report Braggs' claim that Elvis was in the studio when the Prisonaires recorded "Just Walkin' In The Rain." It is unlikely that Elvis was hanging around Sun during the Prisonaires recording sessions. "It was hard to keep Elvis from the studio," Marcus Van Story remembered. "He loved the Prisonaires gospel sound." Despite this, Bragg's claim remains unsubstantiated. "I don't remember Elvis watching the Prisonaires record," Ronald Smith commented. The Prisonaires were nevertheless an important influence upon both Presley and Sam Phillips. Elvis was mesmerized by Bragg's vocals, and Phillips was intrigued by the crossover sound the Prisonaires produced.

Phillips found it impossible to continue the Prisonaires' success, however. As the follow-up record to "Just Walkin' in the Rain" Phillips selected "Softly And Tenderly." *Billboard* reviewed this release enthusiastically, but it failed to sell in large numbers. Sun Records then released two more pop Prisonaire records before the group faded into obscurity. There remain a number of unreleased Prisonaire recordings.

In fact, many of Sam Phillips' recordings remained in the vaults. He was a perfectionist with an ear for the right sound, and if the sound wasn't exactly right he shelved plans for the record. The key to Sun Records reputation and success was the quality of its product. From the beginning, Sun recordings had to be commercial in order to be released. At least that was the philosphy; Phillips often issued non-commercial records which he had assumed would sell, and also did the reverse—failing to release songs which might have done well. There was nothing scientific about the process. "Everything I recorded had to have a basic gut feeling to it," Phillips recalled. All of the early blues recording sessions, which took place at night because Sam was selling his products during the day, were supervised by Phillips because he didn't trust the instincts of those around him. It wasn't easy, but Sam Phillips was determined to put out the best music possible. A good early example of Phillips' critical approach occurred when he recorded Charlie Burse's "Shorty the Barber" and Sleepy John Estes' "Registration Day Blues" and "Policy Man." Why Sam Phillips never released these songs is open to speculation. Burse's record was considered too old-time, with its Memphis jug band influence, and the Estes' tunes were not only old-fashioned but dealt with difficult commercial themes.

When the Bihari brothers leased B.B. King's "Three O'Clock Blues" from Sam Phillips, it was because Sam and others hadn't realized that this tune could become a mammoth rhythm and blues hit. The Bihari brothers released B.B. King's seventh single a few days after Christmas in 1951, and shortly thereafter, in early 1952, the Lowell Fulson tune became a runaway hit. This song stayed on the *Billboard* rhythm and blues chart for much of 1952. Eventually King's recording reached the number 1 *Billboard* spot and remained there for fifteen weeks. With a national audience, B.B. King left Memphis and toured extensively. This caused Sam Phillips to brood intensely about his inability to produce another hit record on his own label.

In another case, a white, one-man band, Harmonica Frank Floyd, recorded two songs—"Rockin' Chair Daddy" and "The Great Medical Menagerist"—in July of 1951. The quirky singing style and strange musical accompaniment in Harmonica Frank's record prompted Phillips to delay its release. It simply wasn't a commercial recording. "Here was a musician I was very much into," Phillips remembered. "It was difficult to find a market for him." Playing it safe, Phillips instead released a country single—"Silver Bells" and "Blues Waltz" (Sun 190), by Ernest Underwood and the Ripley Cotton Choppers. They were a well-known local hillbilly band from Ripley, Tennessee, which was about fifty miles from Memphis. Phillips reasoned that their popularity would sell enough records to guarantee a small profit.

Not only was Phillips impressed with the Ripley

Sun's Harmonica Frank Floyd, looking as quirky as he sounded.

Cotton Choppers sound, but he also saw the seeds of a rockabilly musical style in the group. In 1954, Phillips approached the Cotton Choppers leader, Raymond Kerby, and talked about pairing Elvis with them. Kerby chuckled. He considered Elvis a musical oddity. The Ripley Cotton Choppers were committed to traditional country music and they let Phillips know their displeasure over the thought of appearing with Presley. Unwittingly, this attitude reflected some of the future criticism of Presley's music. Sam Phillips was undaunted by the Cotton Choppers reluctance to back Elvis, and instead signed Doug Poindexter and the Starlite Wranglers to a recording contract. They could release records in the country market while experimenting with a rockabilly sound.

The country record market was a sideline for Phillips, however. From 1951 to 1953, his strongest efforts were in the blues field, where he turned out some of the finest music in the South. He recorded or listened to B.B. King, Bobby Blue Bland, Big Walter Horton, Little Junior Parker, Willie Nix, Big Ma Rainey, Howlin' Wolf, Rosco Gordon, and Rufus Thomas among others. In Memphis, blues artists enabled Phillips to sell large quantities of records. Phillips paid the artist a fair price for the music and didn't interfere with their recording style. It was this widespread confidence in Phillips' production techniques that fostered a word-of-mouth reputation which brought the South's best blues acts to the Sun studio.

The business side of Sun Records was extremely frustrating to Sam Phillips. The most depressing incident occurred in 1953. In March of that year, Big Mama Thornton, a two-hundred-pound black female vocalist, had a hit record with "Hound Dog." Not only did it reach number three on the *Billboard* rhythm and blues charts, but the song, composed by two, twenty-year-old white Los Angeles songwriters, Jerry Leiber and Mike Stoller, appealed to both black and white audiences. It was in an effort to capitalize on the appeal of this song that Phillips released a parody record, "Bear Cat." After "Bear Cat" was released, Don Robey of Peacock Records in Houston sued Phillips for rewriting "Hound Dog." With his menacing sunglasses and two huge bodyguards, Robey, a nightclub owner as well as a record impresario, was a foreboding figure who scared anyone who came into contact with him. Robey's frightening physical presence bothered Sam Phillips and he never forgot how the Houston record mogul radiated an aura of power. It was not Phillips' style, but it was a wonderful lesson in another side of the record business. Most artists were skeptical of Robey's business dealings, but he knew the record industry better than anyone in the South. He also realized that he had a winning lawsuit.

A U.S. District Court ruled in Robey's favor, but much to Phillips' surprise Robey suggested that Phillips continue to merchandise Thomas' song. They could split the royalties. This was Sam Phillips' first lesson in the legal side of the record business.

Then there were problems with artists who were also under contract to other record companies. Howlin' Wolf, for example, would record for anyone, anywhere, for fifty dollars; this led to a great deal of legal action. The problems with artists like Howlin' Wolf and Little Junior Parker signing multiple contracts prompted Phillips to reorganize the business side of Sun Records. He decided to record as many artists as possible and, if they didn't have a hit record, he would simply move on to the next release. For the next few years, Phillips adopted a shotgun mentality. He would record and release as many records as possible by different artists. He never allowed an artist more than one release if they were not successful. Phillips reasoned that sooner or later a popular song would emerge. By 1953, Phillips changed this line of thinking, however. He now reasoned that it was necessary to slowly build and nurture a singer's career.

It was Little Junior Parker who finally showed Sam Phillips the road to commercial success. While he was growing up in West Memphis, Arkansas, Parker learned to play the harmonica with the Howlin' Wolf band. As a young performer on KWEM in West Memphis, Parker

Chester Burnett, the "Howlin' Wolf."

134

Little Junior Parker.

learned a great deal about the blues. Parker, though, was the archetypal crazed bluesman. Prone to heavy drinking and picking fights, Little Junior Parker could not be counted on to show up for a recording session. Contracts meant nothing to him. Soon there were legal and personal problems that shortened Little Junior Parker's career.

At this early stage in his career, although he found it difficult to get along with the mercurial artist, Sam found that Parker was willing to make concessions to cut a record. One of many acts Phillips experimented with in 1953, Sam recorded some fine songs with Parker. The second really commercial record for Phillips was Little Junior's Blue Flames' "Feelin' Good" (Sun 187), a classic that began Parker's Memphis career. (Junior Parker's recording of "Feelin' Good" was one that would greatly influence Elvis Presley.) The early records of John Lee Hooker provided the model for Phillips and Parker to craft early recordings such as "Sittin' Drinkin' and Thinkin" and "Fussin and Fightin." The pair sat in the Sun studio and listened to Hooker's unique boogie guitar style and driving vocals, and they attempted to re-create a similar sound.

"Feelin' Good" sold well in Atlanta, indicating that the Phillips brothers were successfully working the regional markets. In October 1953, Parker's record entered the rhythm and blues charts, and *Ebony* magazine featured a story on the Memphis blues artist. Capi-

talizing on his hit record, Little Junior Parker toured the South with Big Mama Thornton, Johnny Ace, and B.B. King.

What made Phillips most proud about working with Little Junior Parker was the fact that the Biharis had recorded him, with Ike Turner handling the production, without success. Little Junior Parker had his own unique style, but under Sam's tutelage Parker's guitar took on a much different sound. "He had this ability to make the guitar sound like two guitars," Phillips commented.

Other business moves balanced out the frustrations, however. In November 1953, Judd Phillips traveled to New York to talk with Broadcast Music Inc. about setting up a Sun Record publishing company. Hi-Lo Music was soon registered with BMI to publish Sun copyrights. A staff of excellent studio musicians, a dedicated one-person office staff, Marion Keisker, and the presence of new musicians expanded Sam Phillips' knowledge and horizons. Keisker, Phillips' secretary, was the perfect promotional-office staff person. A beautiful woman who combined a gracious manner with a tough-as-nails approach to business, Keisker was a liaison with the Memphis business community. She was able to help merchandise Phillips' records to skeptical locals. Once again, Sam Phillips reorganized his business and distribution network and slowed down the recording process. Also in late 1953, Judd Phillips convinced his brother that Jim Bulleit's interest in Sun Records was no longer an asset. In February 1954, Judd borrowed $1200 and bought Bulleit out. Sun was now free from outside interference, and Sam could negotiate his own business deals. This was an important turning point for Phillips. During the year, Sam frantically recorded numerous black acts. Judd Phillips helped sell the product by making a deal with a Shreveport, Louisiana, distributor, Stan Lewis, who agreed to get Sun Records played on local radio. The result was a regional hit for Rufus Thomas' "Tiger Man."

The fight with Little Junior Parker that had been smoldering for more than six months was temporarily set aside when Phillips brought him back into the Sun studio to record in March 1954. Parker and his band, the Blue Flames, cut three songs, including versions of "Love My Baby" and "Mystery Train"; the sessions were not successful ones, however. Parker had been touring with a package group of Duke Records' artists, and Don Robey was pursuing Parker to record for his label. The following month, Little Junior Parker broke his contract with Phillips and signed with Duke. Phillips sued Parker, won a $17,500 settlement from Don Robey, but found little personal gratification in it. Parker was an act he loved, and he had hoped to find him a hit record. But Little Junior Parker was forgotten as Phillips began looking for new talent. The business end was now complete, and the stage was set to find a superstar act. Amidst the controversy over Parker, young Elvis Presley came into the Sun Records fold.

Dewey Phillips

On the eve of recording Elvis Presley, Sam Phillips cemented his long-standing friendship with local disc jockey Dewey Phillips. Although Dewey was no relation to Sam, the two grew to be inseparable. In 1950, twenty-four-year-old Dewey Phillips went on the air over WHBQ with a radio program aimed at black listeners. Dewey was a student at the Memphis College of Music, and he worked in the record department at the W.T. Grant store on Main Street. He used these experiences to convince WHBQ to allow him to host a show called "Red, Hot and Blue." Dewey Phillips didn't originate the idea for this show, which was already on WHBQ, but he had a number of good ideas for updating it. The show went on the air from 10:00 to midnight nightly and from 10:00 to 1:00 on Saturday. It quickly became a Memphis favorite with both black and white listeners. When Dewey hosted "Red, Hot And Blue," an artist could be discovered or buried by his opinions. A man of proven judgment concerning records, Dewey was the most important radio voice in Memphis, so much so that Joe Liggins and the Honey Drippers once told a Memphis audience that they were going to record a song called "Phillips Sent Me."

Every night, Dewey Phillips was down on Beale Street or over in West Memphis at the juke joints. Not only was his knowledge wide, but he had the ability to pick out unique songs. When he first became friendly with Sam Phillips, Dewey was one of the key influences in the final decision to open the record company. Sam had had his doubts about the future of a small record label, and it was Dewey helped keep the dream alive. Sam basically had a silent partner in his new venture. Everyone knew that Dewey and Sam were involved in the record business, but few people realized how important Dewey's opinions were to young Sam.

Elvis Arrives

Everything was now in place for the first rock and roll musical explosion. Ultimately, it would be Elvis Presley who would benefit most from the groundwork laid down by Sam Phillips during the early Sun years: Elvis would make millions of dollars taking the blues sound and bringing it—albeit in a watered-down version—into the white marketplace. The significance of Sam Phillips to Elvis Presley's career cannot be exaggerated. Had it not been for Sam's continual bolstering of Elvis' confidence, Presley might never have succeeded as a touring act. At the Sun studios, Sam was equally important in crafting Presley's sound into a commercially acceptable product. The availability of Sam's business and Sam's openness to Elvis' presence there provided a musical education that allowed Elvis to grow and mature as an artist, surrounded as he was by the best blues and rockabilly musicians of his day. Sun Records artists were featured daily on local radio stations like WDIA, WROX, and KWEM, and Sam's reputation and his records drew new artists to Memphis like a magnet. "I came to Memphis to hear myself on the radio," Carl Perkins remarked. "Sam Phillips was the man we all wanted to record for," Jerry Lee Lewis stated. It was Elvis, to be sure, who helped all of these artists become mainstream acts by opening up a national audience to their music, but it must never be forgotten that it was Sam Phillips who made the records that created that music.

CHAPTER 8

The Early Sun Elvis, January-July 1954

In 1954, Elvis Presley's performing talent was to finally mature, a potent blend of all the sophisticated musical influences that pervaded his youth. Since his earliest days at Humes High, Elvis had searched eagerly for the right songs to make his singing style a commercially successful one. It was not until after he graduated from high school, however, that Presley had the confidence to experiment with an even wider variety of musical forms. As a result of his constant search for something new, Elvis developed a feel for what would ultimately become one of the most commercially successful sounds of his time. The merging of a number of musical styles—rhythm and blues, blues, and country —influenced the rise of rockabilly music.

Developing Style

In the year after graduating from Humes, Elvis worked diligently towards his goal of making a record. He hung out with Marcus Van Story, Stan Kesler, Paul Burlison, and Ronald Smith at Taylor's Cafe, next to the Sun studio, and talked about music. A great deal of Elvis' musical proclivity was an outgrowth of the Memphis scene. There was a vibrant, eclectic diversity among the local bands, whether their music was played in the blues clubs on Beale Street or the hillbilly bars on the outskirts of town. As he performed in small clubs, Elvis chose songs he believed the general public wanted to hear. During this period, it was Presley's knowledge of pop, blues, hillbilly, and rhythm and blues tunes that allowed him to effectively entertain local audiences, interpreting these tunes in his own unique rockabilly style.

As mentioned earlier, Elvis often sat in with Eddie Bond and the Stompers; young Presley was hired by Bond to perform the songs that Snooky Lanson and Giselle McKenzie were singing on the television program "Your Hit Parade." When they performed at places like the Home for the Incurables, a home for the physically handicapped which the band loved to play, it gave Elvis a chance to try out different types of songs. Ronald Smith and Kenneth Herman remember Elvis talking quietly about cutting a record after playing such shows. An avid radio and television listener, Elvis knew very well that pop songs sold millions of dollars worth of records.

Elvis matured and developed as a performer in small Memphis clubs, crafting his act in front of often very critical audiences. These crowds hooted and hollered and forced a performer to work hard. Ronald Smith, himself a dazzling young guitarist, spent a lot of time talking with Elvis about music, playing together with Elvis in the clubs, at the teen canteen near the Lauderdale Court, and at private functions. As Ronald and Elvis worked together, they not only continued a friendship that had matured since high school but, as independent-minded musicians, they delighted local audiences when they took country tunes and adapted them to a rockabilly tempo.

Like many other musicians, Elvis was basically just another unknown entertainer driving from one bar to another, looking for a performance venue. One of Elvis' favorite clubs was "Doc's" in Frayser. This small-town bar, ten miles from downtown Memphis, drew large crowds from nearby Millington Air Force Base. Every other Friday night, Elvis drove to "Doc's" and performed for five dollars. He dressed in a cowboy shirt and hat, and often wore a string tie. The four-by-eight-foot stage was barely large enough for Elvis and his guitar. After finishing his set, Elvis would walk down to the bar to buy the regulars a drink. As he sipped a cola, he would listen to criticism of his act. It was an invaluable experience. Doc's bar was typical of the small amateur clubs that Elvis worked in during 1953 and early 1954.

In these bars, Elvis talked with other singers who were recording vanity records and selling them. When Elvis played at Doc's, Charlie Feathers often came in on his way to another club or simply to relax. Feathers, born on June 12, 1932, outside of Holly Springs, Mississippi, was typical of the local artists who hoped to become recording stars. As noted earlier, Elvis picked up a great deal from this half-Irish, half-Cherokee artist. The crowd at Doc's was a blue-collar, beer-swilling one that liked country music, and Feathers suggested that Elvis perform country songs to please them. "Charlie loved hillbilly music," Ronald Smith reported, "he would sing those songs all the time." Charlie Feathers was simply educating Elvis in the fine art of survival in Memphis' honky tonk bars. Ronald Smith and Kenneth Herman remember Feathers giving Elvis much good advice. "Charlie Feathers never received the credit he was due for influencing Elvis' music," Smith remarked. "I remember Feathers spending hours with Elvis practicing new songs."

Since 1950, Feathers had developed a solid reputation playing his music around Memphis. His brother-in-law, Dick Stewart, worked for KWEM as the disc jockey, Uncle Richard. (In July 1954, Uncle Richard was one of the first djs to play Presley's "Blue Moon of Kentucky.") Since Stewart was connected to local musicians, he introduced Feathers to such bluesmen as B.B. King and Howlin' Wolf. It was not long before Feathers' music reflected the harmonica-guitar intensity and the growling vocal sounds of the blues.

Not only was Sam Phillips aware of Feathers' talent, but most local musicians would relate respectful tales of Feathers' musical prowess and songwriting ability. The word around Memphis was that Charlie could produce hit records. As a result, Phillips hired him to work as a songwriter, arranger, and demo singer. Ronald Smith remembers that when Chet Atkins came to town, he stopped at a guitar clinic to chat at length with Feathers. Atkins was eager to try out some of his musical ideas on Charlie. To most Memphis musicians, Feathers was a consummate professional far ahead of his time. Historians and biographers have generally ignored Feathers' substantial contribution to rockabilly music and to Elvis Presley's career. Although Charlie Feathers recorded for many labels, however, he never achieved commercial success.

Marcus Van Story was another of Sam Phillips' session musicians to greatly influence Elvis. At the time, in the early months of 1954, when Van Story was working for Phillips, he was also fronting his own band, which featured the best musicians in town. In Memphis, Van Story was regarded as an original talent, and was eagerly sought out by other performers. He could play bass, rhythm, or lead guitar as well as fiddle and violin. His harmonica playing was the finest in Memphis. Van Story would often encounter Elvis at Saturdays at Taylor's Cafe, where they would eat breakfast together. At first, as Van Story sat, eating his ham and eggs, Elvis was simply one of the many would-be singers asking questions. Not only did Marcus Van Story swap stories with Elvis, but he encouraged him to develop his own style. "I told Elvis he had to sound like himself," Van Story remarked. "He couldn't copy other people." On Friday nights, Van Story's band performed at a local hall, the Goodwin Institute. Sam Phillips had first heard Van Story at the Institute, and quickly hired him as a studio musician. Elvis came down to the Goodwin Institute and played with Van Story a number of times. "Elvis would wander in and we would do mostly country songs," Van Story remembered. "He had a real way with the crowd."

There were many artists who had an Elvis-type rockabilly sound. Ultimately, though, as Elvis honed his craft, it was he who became the model for a generation of singers. It was not just Elvis' music, but his clothes and style that mesmerized other fledgling rockabilly artists. A good example of one such performer in the Presley mold was a fifteen-year-old Mariana, Arkansas, singer named Jimmy Evans. He performed over radio station KXJK in Forest City, Arkansas, and the popularity of his rockabilly music eventually brought him to Memphis. Like many other singers, Evans hoped to sign a recording contract. Evans became an instant local celebrity in 1955 when his record "The Joint's Really Jumpin" (Clearmont 502) appeared on the Memphis charts. Evans' performing style and recording voice was so similar to Elvis' Sun sound that Dewey Phillips would in time dub him "Little Elvis."

Vanity Thy Name is Record

Soon the desire to record a professionally-produced song consumed Elvis, and he decided to take matters into his own hands. On Monday, January 4, 1954, Presley walked into Taylor's Cafe for a coke. Marcus Van Story was sitting at the counter and they talked. Elvis was going into Sam Phillips' Memphis Recording Service to cut a vanity record. Van Story agreed to go with him. "I told Elvis it would be fun to do a couple of songs," Van Story recalled. "To loosen Elvis up, I reminded him it was four dollars he was wasting to cut the song." Elvis laughed at Van Story's good-natured remark. As they entered the Sun Records building, Elvis remarked that there was an interesting sign on the studio wall. It read: "We Record Anything-Anywhere-Anytime." "I guess I'm in the right place, Marcus," Elvis commented.

Ever since Phillips founded the Memphis Recording Service to make some extra money, he had advertised his willingness to record vanity records. Initially, he recorded things like birthday parties, weddings, and bar mitzvahs, but by early 1954 Phillips' was making more money from the country and rockabilly musicians who hoped to cut a hit record. Chuckling at the sign, Elvis paid $3.98 to record a ten-inch, two-song acetate. As Van Story hung around the recording studio, Elvis, who was a little nervous, talked with Marion Keisker, Sam Phillips' secretary, which helped relieve his tension. Marcus also chatted with Keisker until Elvis invited him into the recording booth, where Van Story added some gentle guitar licks to the tunes. The two songs Elvis completed, "Casual Love Affair" and "I'll Never Stand in Your Way," reflected his pop musical tastes; Elvis also apparently recorded the song "Without You" at this session. They were both melodic ballads, and Joni James had recently placed "I'll Never Stand in Your Way (Little Darlin')" on the *Billboard* pop charts. Van Story, who liked the recording, urged Elvis to use some local musicians to strengthen his music. After the session, Elvis hoped to meet Sam Phillips, but the Sun Records owner was too busy to talk. Unfortunately, Phillips was selling his records and searching for new talent, and had little time to talk with Presley. Listening quickly to Elvis' vanity record, Phillips wasn't convinced that Presley's music would fit into either the country-rockabilly market or the pop field. His talent was much different than the singers that Sun released. Despite these thoughts, Phillips wrote a brief note to bring Presley back into the studio for an audition. Elvis was unaware of Phillips' interest. He was, however, elated with the professional-looking record. He immediately took it home to play for Gladys on the family's Sears-Roebuck record player. Elvis' mom loved it.

Elvis was persistent in his search for a musical career, a search not without setbacks. One such incident involved Clyde Leoppard, whose band performed at the Cotton Club in West Memphis, Arkansas. Leoppard's earliest band, the Snearly Ranch Boys, were musical legends. They recorded for Sam Phillips and played Western swing or hillbilly dance music. Ma Snearly, who ran a local boarding house, rented rooms and fed the musicians. Out of gratitude to Ma Snearly, the band used her name. Such important musical performers as Stan Kesler and Marcus Van Story played in this group. The band was typical of those playing in local bars, and they were used to back up new singers. By 1954, they were known as the Clyde Leoppard Band.

Leoppard was also the host of a popular Western swing radio show on KWEM, which came on the air prior to Howlin' Wolf's blues show. The music Leoppard played was uptempo hillbilly swing, and Elvis identified with it. Around the same time as his first recording session at the Sun studio, Leoppard informed Presley that he couldn't sing anymore during intermissions at the Cotton Club. "I can sing as well as anyone in your band," Elvis remarked. "Forget it, kid," Leoppard replied. Marcus Van Story couldn't figure out the reason for this exchange between Presley and Leoppard. Of course, it didn't help that the young girls hung around the bandstand when Elvis played. It was obvious that there was something about Elvis that irritated Leoppard. As it turned out, Leoppard had complained for months to Charlie Feathers that Elvis was doing his best to get into the band, and that he thought Elvis was a brash kid who needed more experience before he would ever play for him.

A more positive result of Elvis' interactions with Leoppard's band resulted from the fact that the group backed Earl Peterson, a country singer with a distinct rockabilly sound, whom Elvis saw performing at the Bon Air Club. Peterson, a twenty-seven-year-old from Lansing, Michigan, billed himself as "Michigan's singing cowboy." Like many artists, Peterson recorded songs on his own record label, Nugget. After limited success in Michigan, Peterson arrived in Memphis. A successful audition led to a Sun recording contract. In March 1954, Peterson's "Boogie Blues" (Sun #197) made inroads in the local country market. Although his record failed to achieve any degree of chart success, it was released nationally by Columbia in 1955. "Boogie Blues" was recorded with an infectious rockabilly sound, an upbeat tempo tinged with a blues feeling that highlighted Sam Phillips' production skills. Peterson's music was similar in style and technique to Elvis' early Sun recordings. In effect, after Phillips played "Boogie Blues" for Elvis, it became a training record. Elvis was quick to recognize the commercial potential in Peterson's sound, and incorporated a part of it into his act. When Presley's first Sun single, "That's All Right (Mama)" was released, it owed as much of its musical inspiration to Earl Peterson as it did to Arthur Crudup's signal version of the song.

Speaking of "Big Boy" Crudup, there were a number of his RCA Bluebird records that Elvis listened to during this period. One in particular, "I Don't Know It," became the model for Elvis' version of "That's All Right (Mama)." Originally recorded in Chicago on April 9, 1947, "I Don't Know It" was the first song Crudup recorded after "That's All Right (Mama)." Elvis simply copied the arrangement and musical direction of "I Don't Know It" when he made his own recording of "That's All Right (Mama)." It was Crudup's backup musicians, Ranson Knowling on bass and either Jump Jackson or Judge Riley on drums, who most caught Elvis' attention. In later years, Scotty Moore, Bill Black, and D.J. Fontana would be molded into a similar, if a little more upbeat, backup group.

Another black performer who influenced Elvis was a thirty-two-year-old blind blues singer named Howard Seratt. This obscure gospel artist combined an acoustic guitar, a harmonica, and a spiritual delivery into his own unique style. In many respects, Seratt's background was similar to that of Elvis. Both grew up poor and both were influenced by local musicians. Based in Manilla, Arkansas, Seratt began his career playing live over radio station KLCN in Blytheville. Seratt was known primarily for his gospel sound, but in concert he frequently performed uptempo blues songs, combining blues and country sounds while retaining a strong commercial pop tone. A local disc jockey took Seratt to Sam Phillips and, in 1954, Seratt's Sun recording of "Troublesome Waters" received excellent reviews in *Cashbox*.

When Sam Phillips released Howard Seratt's "Troublesome Waters," he quickly arranged a number of concert dates to promote the record. Seratt often appeared with Slim Rhodes, Hardrock Gunter, and others in country shows. It was during one of these performances that Seratt met Elvis Presley. Always willing to listen and learn, Elvis spent a great deal of time imitating Seratt's vocal phrasing. The combination of Seratt's innovative acoustic guitar and harmonica in "Troublesome Waters" (Sun #198) was another factor important in Elvis' early sound. The bluesy, gospel direction in Seratt's music, and the message of salvation in "Troublesome Waters" appealed to Presley. The two men became good friends, and Seratt taught Elvis a great deal about stage presence.

Dixie Locke

There was more to Elvis' life than music. Around the beginning of the year, he had started dating sixteen-year-old Dixie Locke. They both had strong show business aspirations, and shared a common excitement about music and acting. Dixie hoped to become a model or actress, and Elvis was able to easily discuss his show business aspirations around her. When Dixie laughed at Elvis as he did his Tony Curtis impersonations, he blushed. When he sang Dean Martin songs, Dixie would fake a disabling swoon. Locke, a junior at South Side High, attended the First Assembly of God church, which is where Elvis first met her in the spring of 1953. It was not until after Christmas 1953, however, when they became reacquainted at the Rainbow Rollerdome, that they started seeing each other more regularly.

Like most of Elvis' girls, Dixie Locke was shy and possessed of a subtle beauty. There was a light side to Dixie's personality that everyone liked. "She was always laughing, always enjoying herself," Elvis remarked. As typical Memphis teenagers, Dixie and Elvis met each week at the Rainbow to skate and talk. After the first night, Dixie told Vince Staten: "He took me home in his old Lincoln that night and we went out the next night and, you know, that was it."

Dixie spent a lot of time at Elvis' house, and had a chance to observe his relationship with his family and close friends. One of the Presley's neighbors, Rabbi Alfred Fruchter and his wife Jeanette, were friendly with Vernon and Gladys. Elvis was intrigued by Rabbi Fruchter's music, and he listened to the religious songs in Fruchter's collection. This was typical of Elvis' curiosity; he listened to every type of music possible. "He liked gospel music," Dixie remarked during an interview. "He also enjoyed blues songs. The movies were his favorite pastime."

Because of her strong church background, Dixie urged Elvis to sing gospel music. To further his gospel education, Elvis attended concerts at the Ellis Auditorium. He also spent a great deal of time listening to gospel records, and Ronald Smith remembers Elvis talking mysteriously about giving up country music in favor of gospel, doubtless because of Dixie's urgings.

Elvis' behavior around Dixie was hyperactive; he continually bit his fingernails, combed his hair, and raced his car's motor. Dixie Locke had a sense of compassion and character that soon prompted Elvis to confess his inner thoughts to her. Elvis finally revealed his misgivings about his father. He felt that Vernon had essentially abandoned the family by not even trying to earn an adequate living. When Vernon would leave the house in his fine clothes, bound for the local bars, Elvis would get enraged. On one occasion, his father came home with a diamond stickpin for his tie. Elvis screamed at his dad for spending the money on such a frivolous purchase. In quieter moments, Elvis confessed that his parents' economic problems were very serious. Dixie was understanding and encouraged Elvis to accept his parents' faults.

The catalyst to an increased social life, Dixie and Elvis went everywhere together. When they were not at the Presley's house, the couple drove out to Kay's Drive-In on Crump Boulevard to munch cheeseburgers and drink chocolate shakes. The trip was a ritual for them, because Kay's was the first place they had eaten after meeting at the Rainbow. The bargain matinee at the Suzore #2 theater was another favorite diversion for the couple. After the shows, they walked across the street to Charlie's, a dimly lit, pseudo-beatnik cafe that offered soft drinks in an atmosphere heavy with the sound of Charlie's favorite phonograph records. The owner had dropped out of Memphis State to pursue a poetry career in San Francisco. In less than a year, however, Charlie was back in Memphis serving up soft drinks in the dark room filled with music. Charlie also read his poetry. At the time, it was as close to being "strange" as was possible in Memphis.

Another spot that Dixie and Elvis frequented was a place near McKellar Lake known to some as the Teen Canteen. It featured a jukebox, but once in a while a band would appear. On more than one occasion, Elvis performed in this quaint little hall. Often after these dances, Elvis and Dixie drove down to Riverside Park to neck in his car. With a solidly middle-class family background, Dixie was a source of comfort for Elvis. She was also the first person to make Elvis aware of his parents' peculiar habits. Gladys was reclusive and appeared jealous. Vernon was away from home for days and ignored his family. Elvis' relatives were loud and abusive to one another, and they fought and drank excessively. Despite her personal misgivings about the Presleys, Dixie loved Elvis.

At South Side High, Dixie was one of the most sought after girls and Elvis, never confident with women or relationships, felt reassured with her on his arm. In February 1954, she agreed to a "trial engagement." Vernon and Gladys Presley loved Dixie because she radiated respectability. The Lockes, on the other hand, were one step up the social ladder from the Presleys, and Dixie's parents warned their daughter that her two goals—love and marriage—were not possible with Elvis. "I think Dixie was the one girl Elvis loved most in his life," Aunt Lillian remarked. This feeling was echoed by Vernon in an interview in *Good Housekeeping*: "I thought maybe they'd get married because Dixie was a mighty likeable girl."

As Elvis' first long-term love affair, and typical of Elvis' later behavior regarding women he loved, Dixie Locke was placed on a pedestal. When the English newspaper *New Musical Express* interviewed Elvis in West Germany during his tour of army duty, they inquired about Dixie Locke. With the Platters' "Smoke Gets in Your Eyes" playing on Elvis' record player, he commented: "She was kind of small with long, dark hair that came down to her shoulders and the biggest smile that I've ever seen anywhere." Elvis went on to praise Dixie's personality and suggested her goodness was monumental. "We were a big thing," Elvis continued. "I gave her my high school ring. For two years we had a ball." Although they finally split up, Dixie Locke remained the image of Elvis' sweet, perfect, virginal Southern girl. Problems between them developed when Dixie eventually complained about spending too many nights at Sun Records after Elvis made his second vanity record for Sam Phillips in January 1954. "There were so many nights we'd go over to the recording studio," Dixie later recalled. Her recollections are notable because they challenge the notion that Sam Phillips recorded Elvis with little preparation. Like many Memphis singers, Presley had caught Phillips' attention long before his first recording session.

The Road to a New Sound

Primarily in quest of a musical career, Elvis really didn't have time for a relationship that might lead to marriage, something which perhaps even he failed to recognize at the time. On weekends, Elvis drove around to the Memphis clubs hoping to find places to showcase his talent. Whenever he could, he sat in with the resident bands at the Eagle's Nest, the Bel Air or Bon Air clubs, or the Hi-Hat, or he frequented Beale Street. B.B. King remembers Elvis hanging around the blues clubs there. "He was a kid who wanted to learn," King remarked. It was on Beale Street that Elvis discovered Nate Epstein's pawn shop. A large rack in the center of the store featured the best pawned items from local dandies. While shopping at Epstein's, Elvis bought some of his first "hip" clothing.

When Elvis tired of the Memphis clubs, he drove

the ten miles to Doc's bar in Frayser, where he could get on stage any night he wanted to and practice his craft in front of what seemed to be generally disinterested audiences. Patrons at Doc's never forgot Elvis, however, and later showed up regularly at his Memphis shows. It was during this period that Elvis began experimenting with an uptempo version of Arthur "Big Boy" Crudup's "That's All Right (Mama)." Performing Crudup's songs at these country bars was quite natural, because of Crudup's rural country blues style. Primitive songs of this type were staples of the rednecks who frequented Memphis beer bars. At Doc's, Elvis sang five Crudup songs: "Rock Me Mama," "Hey Mama," "Cool Disposition," "Everything's All Right," and "That's All Right (Mama)." Few people recognized the songs when Elvis sang them, because they were performed in a very unique upbeat rockabilly style.

Elvis' direct road to a Sun Records contract unwittingly began on May 25, 1954, when Sam Phillips released Hardrock Gunter's "Gonna Dance All Night." Gunter's relationship with Sam Phillips had in many ways been an accidental one. While working as a disc jockey for WJLD in Birmingham, Alabama, Gunter became friendly with program director Jim Connally. When Gunter learned that Connally was Sam Phillips' brother-in-law, he quickly arranged for a Sun Records audition. Gunter was an established local radio and television personality who was performing on the Alabama hillbilly circuit, and Phillips hoped to cash in on this popularity by releasing one of Gunter's records. After

Hardrock Gunter.

141

cutting two tracks, Gunter sent them to Phillips, who issued them immediately as Sun Record No. 201, "Gonna Dance All Night" (originally recorded by Gunter in 1950 for Bang Records) b/w "Fallen Angel."

Since Gunter's records were played on regional radio and television shows, Elvis was exposed to them. "Gonna Dance All Night," despite its country direction, was a rock and roll tune, and the phrasing and upbeat musical delivery made it a natural for Elvis, who afterward attempted to mimic Gunter's rockabilly voice. Not only was it rock and roll-oriented, but the lyrics— "We're gonna rock and roll while we dance all night"—caught both Elvis' and Phillips' attention. The tune was a dance favorite on Memphis jukeboxes, although it ultimately didn't sell many records for Sun.

Sam Phillips attempted to persuade Gunter to move to Memphis so that Sun Records could promote his considerable rockabilly talent, but Gunter instead accepted a job with radio station WWVA in Wheeling, West Virginia. WWVA's prestigious country music show, "The World's Original Jamboree," offered Gunter excellent exposure. And so it happened that Hardrock Gunter never became a Memphis musical act. A song which fused blues and country music into a highly commercial blend, and an artist who can be identified as one of the important early influences upon Presley, turned down the opportunity that would soon be offered to Elvis.

The same day Sam Phillips released Gunter's record, he recorded two songs by Doug Poindexter and the Starlite Wranglers, "My Kind of Carrying On" and "Now She Cares No More for Me." Poindexter's band had everything it needed to play rock and roll, except that they performed in the country music tradition. One of the more hallowed beliefs among country artists was that drums were not necessary. "My Kind of Carrying On," for example, was recorded without drums, and primarily featured Bill Black's slapping bass and Scotty Moore's rockabilly guitar.

These two numbers included many of the elements that Phillips would soon use in Presley's recordings. As Poindexter pointed out, "Blue Moon of Kentucky" and "That's All Right (Mama)" owed a great deal to the Starlite Wranglers. Poindexter, an exceptional guitar player, was musically innovative. He tried everything to create a unique rockabilly sound. Poindexter's record sold only in the neighborhood of three hundred copies, prompting Phillips to once again look for more commercial material. The Starlite Wranglers were simply too country, and Sam made it clear that this sound was too risky.

A shy, quiet man, Poindexter remained in the background at Sun. The guitar sounds that Carl Perkins and Johnny Cash brought to the Sun studio were improved by Poindexter's deft instruction. Poindexter provided Sam Phillips with a number of important suggestions about Elvis' Sun recordings, working quietly in the studio without fanfare or credit. "I worked with all them boys and no one ever mentioned it," Poindexter explained. Although he was musically creative, Poindexter had neither the temperament nor the inclination to pursue a career as a professional musician. Once he married and began raising a family, he left the music business.

When Sam Phillips realized that Poindexter was going to work a full-time day job and give up music, he turned instead to the best musicians from the Starlite Wranglers. Not only were they a potentially explosive musical unit, but Bill Black's bass and Scotty Moore's guitar licks were exactly what Phillips hoped to employ in the studio to create hit records. Previously immersed in hillbilly and blues, Sam began to look in new directions, leading him into the fledgling rock and roll market.

Elvis and Sam Phillips Connect

When Phillips recorded street musician Harmonica Frank, Marion Keisker pointed out that Frank's song, "Rockin' Chair Daddy," was excellent, but his disheveled personal appearance made it impossible to merchandise the record. He was a one-man band, and the local clubs demanded a full band. Keisker's words resonated in Phillips' mind for a long time. She was convinced that Phillips spent too much time with old cow-

Marion Keisker.

boys. A shrewd judge of original talent, Marion opined for months that Sam was ignoring the best local singer, Elvis Presley. Since he was always in and out of the local clubs, Phillips had had occasion to see Elvis perform many times on amateur nights. He knew that Elvis was either loved or hated as a performer on the local scene. Sam considered recording Elvis as early as May 1954, but felt that Presley was too much of a new and untried act to waste time and money on in the studio. Elvis was so different from Phillips' other artists that it seemed a dangerous idea to even consider recording him. Aware that Elvis' talent was unique, Phillips was concerned about how to showcase it, and realized that an act like Elvis would need very special packaging.

Around this time, Peer Music, a Nashville publisher, sent a demo tape of a song called "Without You" to Sun Records. Written by a white inmate at the Nashville Maximum Security Prison, Sam had first encountered the song, in unpublished form, on a May 8, 1954, visit to see the Prisonaires. Their rendition of the tune had failed to interest Phillips, however. Eventually, a black singer was used by Peer Music to cut an acetate test pressing. In a cover letter, Peer pushed the tune as a natural for almost any Sun blues artist. It was common for music publishers to hire demo singers to make recorded samples of their songs, and because Peer executives realized that Phillips had a stable of excellent blues singers, they neglected to identify the black singer that did the demo. After listening to the song, however, Phillips couldn't think of a Memphis artist to record it. Executives at Peer were surprised, then, when Phillips requested the singer's name, a singer who bore a striking resemblance to Roy Hamilton. Peer Music, however, had no record of the vocalist.

For a week, Sam Phillips pondered the question of who could effectively provide the vocal on "Without You." Phillips constantly read the *Billboard*, *Record World*, and *Cashbox* charts, and these music industry publications offered a glimpse into changing consumer attitudes. Black singers were increasingly placing songs on the pop charts. This encouraged Phillips because it showed that white record buyers were eager to spend their money on black music, something which had not previously been the case.

Raymond Hill was one of the early black artists that Phillips believed could cross over to the white market. On October 6, 1952, Phillips had Hill record Arthur "Big Boy" Crudup's "My Baby Left Me." Hill, the saxophone player in Ike Turner's Kings of Rhythm, was from Clarksdale, Mississippi, and he blended rural blues with rhythm and blues influences. As a result, Hill's version of "My Baby Left Me" has a blues riff that was subdued but displayed a solid, Delta-guitar style. Hill's version of the song was not released because his vocal was too weak. There is an interesting Elmore James-style guitar on the recording provided by Willie Kizart, and the song suggests the future blend of Delta guitar solos with the Chicago blues. For Sam Phillips, however, Raymond Hill was not the artist who could sell records, and he abandoned the idea of taking Hill's exceptional talent into the white market.

There were a number of songs on the charts similar to "Without You." Phillips believed that it was as commercial as any song on the *Billboard* Hot 100. Although the tune had a black, bluesy sound, Phillips believed a white artist could cover it. A black artist, Phillips reasoned, simply could not generate enough airplay to guarantee a hit.

In 1954, the record industry charts were dominated by white artists, although black groups were crossing over. Although their beginning year was without commercial success, The Platters, formed in Los Angeles in 1953, were typical of the black groups crossing over to the white record buying audience. The following year, an L.A. songwriter and promoter, Buck Ram, took over the group and added a new lead singer, Zola Taylor. With Taylor's rhythm and blues vocal strength and Tony Williams pop leads, the Platters went on to place twenty-one songs on the *Billboard* charts between 1955 and 1959. The Platters became the prototype of the carefully-produced black groups singing carefully-crafted tunes sure to find a place on the *Billboard* charts. Such Buck Ram hits as "Only You," "The Great Pretender," and "The Magic Touch" contained none of the explicit sexual references or the subtle suggestiveness of unpolished rhythm and blues music. By blending innocuous cover versions of show tunes with syrupy originals, the Platters made themselves acceptable to white record buyers. In concert, they were dull and lifeless. Rhythm and blues performers such as Little Willie John, LaVern Baker, and Lloyd Price, among others, were what white audiences demanded in concert, but the Platters sold more records than any of these original black acts.

After spending considerable time trying to find the right black artist, Phillips instead began looking for a white artist to record black music. The decision was not a spur of the moment idea. Little Junior Parker had done a number of early Sun recordings with a hillbilly tinge. Since the early 1950s, many Memphis hillbilly singers had copied from black blues artists. For years Phillips had realized that white and black music was merging into yet another entirely distinct form, but simply had found neither the precise songs nor exactly the right singer to risk producing a record. In the end, it was a simple economic decision, one that had very little to do with the music itself.

It was Marion Keisker's continued urgings that finally prompted Sam to consider Elvis Presley. Sam

Phillips realized that Elvis, more than any other white singer he knew, sounded a lot like the black singers. Still, it took Phillips a month to bring Elvis into the Sun studio; the groundwork was carefully laid for Elvis' recording debut. As Greil Marcus has observed: "In the records Phillips makes you can discern something more than taste, something more like vision. He has cooked up a sound all his own...a sound to jump out of the jukebox." What Marcus is suggesting is that both Elvis and Sam Phillips had engineered their sound and style for some time, and that the result was not as spontaneous an event as Sam Phillips, Scotty Moore, and Colonel Tom Parker have suggested. Rather, Elvis' emergence was carefully rehearsed, one that depended upon a number of musical influences, and upon extensive planning by Sam Phillips.

On Saturday, June 26, 1954, Sam Phillips called Elvis' house. Gladys answered the phone, and she was amazed when Phillips asked her to send her son down to the Sun studio. Elvis was there in twenty minutes, and he went through half a dozen takes of "Without You." Something just wasn't right about Elvis, but Sam couldn't put his finger on the problem. Presley's vocals were uneven and Sam asked Elvis if he would like a coke. They talked at length about music, and Sam suggested that Elvis try another song. "You try one of your favorites," Phillips urged. When Elvis sang Dean Martin's hit "That's Amore," Phillips advised Elvis that he wasn't looking for a pop crooner. He lectured Elvis on the necessity of infusing emotion and raw feeling into his songs. When Phillips asked Elvis for a tune he was comfortable with, Presley settled on "Rag Mop," although not the Ames Brothers' 1950 hit, which wasn't Elvis' favorite version. As Sam Phillips talked to Elvis he realized that Presley had been influenced by Joe Lutcher's "Rag Mop." Phillips was astounded that Presley knew about the Los Angeles-based Lutcher, and even more surprised that Elvis had a working knowledge of artists on Modern Records. Phillips had leased material to Modern, and he was happy that Presley knew their type of music.

No one remembers exactly how much time Elvis spent in the Sun studio that day. The session was not recorded. There were no musicians in the studio and Phillips was simply testing Elvis' vocal talent. It seems unlikely that he spent much time there, but Elvis had finally sung for Phillips, and they agreed that Presley would record in a few weeks. Phillips had decided to try to capture "Rag Mop" using Presley as a demo singer.

Marion Keisker was always guarded in her comments about the late June session at Sun, although she acknowledged that Elvis had had a session that she called a "friendly audition" with Sam a few weeks be- fore the first Sun recording session on July 5. (It was Keisker who suggested that Phillips bring Presley into the studio during a "down time." "There was no time slower than just after July 4th," Keisker remarked with a whimsical smile.) Sam agreed that they would cut Elvis' first record the day after the July 4 celebration because the studio would be free of singers and late-night cowboys (the serious drinking on July 4 would keep the Sun studio vacant the next day).

To back Elvis at the session, Sam Phillips called upon Scotty Moore, asking Moore to also arrange for Bill Black to be there. Phillips respected Scotty Moore's intuitive feeling about musical talent, and Sam urged Scotty to set up an occasion a few days prior to the session where he could get to know Elvis. Scotty Moore recalls his first meeting with Presley: "Well my first meeting was naturally a couple of weeks before, or rather, no, it wasn't a couple of weeks before, it was a few days before our first actual session. I had been working with Sam for several months trying to come up with a record, an artist, a song, anything we could make a buck with and during this process Elvis' name came up and Sam gave me his number and I called him to come over to my house." What Moore failed to note or remember was that it was Sam Phillips who had instructed him to get to know Elvis before the first recording session, and not something Scotty had done just for the sake of making Elvis' acquaintance.

Scotty Moore.

At Sam's urging, therefore, Elvis, Scotty and Bill practiced a couple of songs in Moore's living room as Memphis prepared for its July 4 celebration. The fireworks made the evening celebration a festive one. Beale Street was crowded with tourists and the music blared from the clubs. The Bel Air, Bon Air and Crow's Nest were alive with country music, and the streets were filled with partygoers, a fitting setting for the night before Elvis' debut recording session.

When Scotty Moore later described the July 4 practice session, he remembered how wildly Presley had dressed that Sunday afternoon. Elvis had on a pink shirt, pink pants with a white stripe, and white shoes. "I thought my wife was going out the back door," Moore recalled. Once the shock over Elvis' clothes subsided, they practiced for awhile, doing two country songs and one ballad. Hank Snow's "I Don't Hurt Anymore" and Eddy Arnold's "I Really Don't Want to Know" were songs that Scotty Moore believed could break Elvis in the country market. Bill Black liked the way Elvis interpreted Billy Eckstine's 1951 hit, "I Apologize." This combination of country and ballad tunes, Black reasoned, was enough to guarantee Elvis some success. There was another side to Presley's music that neither Scotty nor Bill witnessed that afternoon, however. Since Elvis wasn't able to perform an uptempo song, they didn't realize his potential as a rockabilly singer.

Before too long, Moore's wife stopped the festivities and reminded everyone that, although the music impressed her, it was a holiday. No matter, as after they had gone through two or three different songs, Moore decided that Elvis was ready for studio work. After the session, Elvis left and Scotty and Bill talked about Elvis' performance. "The boy sings pretty good," Scotty remarked, "but he didn't knock me out." He then called Sam Phillips and stated that Elvis was ready to record. The Sunday, July 4, 1954, meeting at Moore's house established an instant rapport between Elvis, Scotty Moore, and Bill Black. Once they played some songs together, they recognized that they had similar musical roots.

In a number of interviews, Moore has suggested that the session planned for the next day, July 5, was really Elvis' first audition, an unrehearsed event that lead immediately to Elvis' emergence as an "undiscovered" talent. Either Moore was unaware of how much Phillips had observed, talked to, and worked with Elvis prior to that time, or he was attempting to perpetuate the legend that Elvis was an overnight sensation. The following year, Scotty Moore began to tell the revised story of how he first met and recorded with Elvis. This version, which surfaced in December 1955, bears the unmistakable influence of Colonel Tom Parker. The Colonel intended to preserve and perpetuate the myth

that Elvis was an original talent who simply walked into Sun Records off the street. A more plausible explanation is that Scotty Moore and Bill Black were brought into the studio to back Elvis because he was finally ready to record a commercially acceptable record, and that there was nothing accidental about Elvis' first recording session. Sam Phillips' goal was to achieve a regional hit record, a tactic he had used with many other artists, and the direction from which, it's safe to assume, he initially approached Elvis.

The July 1954 Sun Sessions

On Monday night, July 5, 1954, Elvis reported to Sun for his first recording session, arriving about eight o'clock. Elvis was nervous, so Sam Phillips suggested that they begin the session with an old standard, although not a favorite of Sam's, "Harbor Lights." (Elvis' version of "Harbor Lights" was inspired by Harry Owens and His Royal Hawaiians. The song contained guitar riffs similar to those used by Hank Garland, whose guitar style helped to develop a part of the early rock and roll sound.) There were five cuts of "Harbor Lights" completed during this session. The first cut was an instrumental to calm Elvis down and acquaint Scotty Moore and Bill Black with the musical direction that Phillips wanted. Only two of the cuts of "Harbor Lights" were strong enough to consider for commercial release. (Eventually, Elvis' two-minute and thirty-five-second version would appear on RCA's **Elvis: A Legendary Performer, Volume 2** in 1976. This cut featured a whistling bridge. There was also an alternate cut of "Harbor Lights" with a soft guitar bridge. After listening to these versions, Ronald Smith concluded that Elvis had even then crossed over into the pop market, a result of the fact that Sam Phillips recognized that Scotty Moore's guitar licks were a sophisticated mix of Chet Atkins' country guitar and Les Paul's electric city sound, a mix that was decidedly crossover.)

The soft ballad lyrics of "Harbor Lights" served to relax Elvis, and Bill Black suggested that they try recording Leon Payne's "I Love You Because." Elvis remarked that he loved Eddie Fisher's pop version of the song; the 1950 Fisher hit was one of Presley's favorites. Elvis told Phillips that he'd love to record it, but Sam initially rejected this suggestion because he wanted Elvis to attempt an upbeat, rockabilly number. But Elvis prevailed, persuading Phillips that it would be best to record a tune that he knew by heart.

Sam Phillips and Scotty Moore have both indicated that the Elvis' first recording session was a difficult one, primarily because of Presley's perfectionist nature. Although he was not in a position to make many demands during this first session, Elvis was not only critical of

(L. to r.): Elvis, Bill Black, Scotty Moore, and Sam Phillips in the Sun Records studio.

his own performance, but from the first moments in the studio he demanded excellence from Scotty and Bill. They were amazed by Elvis' professional manner, which was quick and self-assured.

This tendency toward musical perfection was demonstrated on Elvis' second song, "I Love You Because." Leon Payne, a blind composer who often appeared in concert with Bob Wills and the Texas Playboys, was too country for Presley, but Sam Phillips at first pressured Elvis to record the tune in Payne's mold. It was only after Elvis pointed out that he could cut a Fisher-type version that the song was completed. After five different takes, however, Sam Phillips abandoned the tune as commercially inviable. In 1956, Steve Sholes blended two of the cuts together into a master take, a strange mixture of Leon Payne's country version and Eddie Fisher's pop rendition. Elvis told Eddie Bond that he preferred the Fisher version precisely because it was pop. "Elvis loved those pop songs and knew them by heart," Bond remembered. It is therefore surprising that Elvis had difficulty recording the tune, which he had performed many times.

The next song Elvis tried was the one that was to thrust him into regional musical prominence, and turn Elvis' very first recording session into a hit-producing one. Arthur "Big Boy" Crudup's "That's All Right

(Mama)" was originally recorded on September 6, 1947, for RCA-Victor's Chicago-based Bluebird label. Elvis, again, had some difficulty recording Crudup's tune. Whereas most of the songs he sang tended to follow the same phrasing as the original performer or demo singer, his interpretation of Crudup's country blues song bore little relationship to the original. So, it was a moment of great creativity as Elvis interpreted "That's All Right (Mama)" in his own unique manner.

The trouble with the song developed as a result of the fact that Sam Phillips offered Elvis more freedom than he would subsequently experience in the RCA recording studio. At this stage, although practiced and professional when it came to songs for which he had an original basis—a "model," as it were—Elvis wasn't sure how to fully use a situation which gave him total freedom and creativity. As a result of this inexperience, Elvis' vocal on the first take of "That's All Right (Mama)" was labored. It was not until later, when they were all tired and had taken a short break during which Elvis began clowning around, that he broke into a faster version of the song that electrified Sam Phillips, who in turn hollered for Scotty and Bill to join in. The rest is history. Elvis Presley's recording career was on its way.

Delighted with Elvis' uptempo performance of "That's All Right (Mama)," Sam suggested they con-

146

tinue the session. Two of the takes of "That's All Right (Mama)" were strong enough to release into the growing rock and roll market; now Phillips had to come up with a b-side for Presley's record. This song had to be a country one, Phillips reasoned, to carry Presley's music in the Memphis market. A quick decision was needed, and Sam urged Elvis to consider recording a song by a well-known country artist. As a result, Bill Monroe's 1946 country hit "Blue Moon of Kentucky" was selected as the ideal companion tune to "That's All Right (Mama)." Elvis didn't feel comfortable recording the song, however, so he asked Sam Phillips to wait until the next recording session to do it. The July 5 session continued for yet another two hours, however. There were two attempts to record "I'll Never Let You Go (Little Darlin')." Between these two cuts Elvis sang a minute-long version of the gospel song "Satisfied." By this time, though, Elvis was tired, and these final cuts were also labored ones. Phillips set up another recording session for the following night to cut the songs that Elvis hadn't completed. (No permanent written record of this session exists. Not only did Sam Phillips not keep precise records, but he was very casual about dating his sessions. When Phillips collected the evening's recordings, he placed them in Scotch magnetic tape boxes. There were no numbers on the boxes, and they were simply stacked next to the production board. After Phillips shipped the tapes to RCA in November 1955, it was Steve Sholes who numbered the boxes; the songs from this session are probably from boxes 2, 12, 13, and 15.)

Elvis arrived at the Sun studio on Tuesday, July 6, at about seven-thirty in the evening. Already visibly nervous when he walked in, Elvis was then hit with Sam Phillips' announcement that it was his intention to release Presley's record within the next few days. Sam looked over at Elvis and didn't like the unsettling twitch exhibited by his new singer. "That's All Right (Mama)" was a sure hit, Phillips bellowed, and he told Elvis he couldn't wait to promote the record. Ronald Smith, who worked as a sometime session guitarist for Sun, remembers the excitement over the proposed Presley release. "I think Sam knew that he had something good," Smith recalled. "Some of the other boys weren't so kind toward Elvis," continued Smith. While many local musicians were instantly jealous, Elvis betrayed not a hint of arrogance or self-satisfaction; instead, he was astonished by all the fuss over his forthcoming record and very nervous about the prospect of personal appearances. After having worked diligently for a year towards making a record, Elvis confessed to Johnny Burnette that he was scared.

There was still the problem of selecting an accept-able song for the b-side. Sam Phillips believed that "Blue Moon of Kentucky" was the right tune for the country record buyer, especially since "That's All Right (Mama)" was perfect for the hillbilly, teen, and blues markets. Phillips reasoned that a country song was necessary for the b-side in order to broadly distribute and promote the record. As the July 6 session began, however, problems developed during the recording of "Blue Moon of Kentucky." The first take of Bill Monroe's song was only a minute long. Elvis' slow, labored vocal was out of sync with the musical accompaniment. Surprisingly, at the conclusion of the short take of "Blue Moon of Kentucky," Sam Phillips hollered: "That's fine, hell that's different, that's a pop song, nearly 'bout." Laughter followed and Sam began another song.

Then it was time for another take of "Blue Moon of Kentucky," which turned out to be only a one-minute and fifty-nine-second version. In Elvis' hands, however, it was this time turned into a strong rockabilly song, "country" enough for Phillips once on tape, and the perfect companion piece for the flip side of "That's All Right (Mama)." "Blue Moon of Kentucky" was completed in four takes, with Sam Phillips using a spoken bridge in one version. There was one breakdown, and one partially recorded version, leaving two complete takes that Phillips listened to before deciding that the rockabilly "Blue Moon of Kentucky" provided an excellent b-side.

Next, because Phillips had a nagging suspicion that the version of "I'll Never Let You Go (Little Darlin')" recorded the previous night was not suitable for commercial release, he had Elvis recut the song. The one-minute and three-second version of the old Jimmy Wakely tune was a warm-up for another song, "Blue Moon." Changing the style and musical direction of the session, "Blue Moon," a Rodgers-Hart song and a 1949 pop hit for Mel Torme, was a ballad suitable to Elvis' tastes. Phillips remembered how the girls swooned over the song when Elvis sang it at the Eagle's Nest. In the end, though, Sam considered the vocal on "Blue Moon" too inferior for commercial release. Although Elvis was exhausted, he finished off the second day of recording with versions of "Just Because" and "Tomorrow Night." Sam Phillips believed that, like "Blue Moon," "Just Because," or "Tomorrow Night" had no commercial potential. He placed these songs in the same category as "I Love You Because," "Tryin' to Get to You," and "I'll Never Let You Go," all of which Phillips was uncomfortable with. In November 1955, the tapes for these tunes were shipped to RCA when Presley's musical rights were purchased from Sun. "Just Because" was later released on Elvis' first RCA album, as well as on an RCA single.

After two days in the recording studio, Sam Phil-

147

lips had his first Elvis Presley record. Phillips told everyone at Taylor's Cafe that Presley's renderings of "Big Boy" Crudup's "That's All Right (Mama)" and Bill Monroe's "Blue Moon of Kentucky" was an unbeatable combination. He had worked with many performers, Phillips said, but he felt Elvis' vocal phrasing and timing was the best of any artist he had ever recorded at Sun. Phillips was confident that he had brought out the sound he wanted from Elvis. The raw, sexy inflection of "That's All Right (Mama)" and the rockabilly drive of "Blue Moon of Kentucky" was a unique product. Now it was time to market the Presley record.

On the Air in Memphis

The two sessions that Sam Phillips recorded with Elvis Presley were exciting ones. They also revealed how thoroughly Phillips was influenced in his decisions by past recordings. For example, he listened to a raw cut of Martha Carson's "Satisfied" during Presley's July sessions, convincing him that Elvis still had a way to go before he could record a commercial gospel tune. The original version of "I Love You Because" by Leon Payne was more soulful than Presley's cut, and Sam reasoned that Elvis' version would not be a competitive song. During these sessions, Phillips had Elvis listen to Bill Monroe's "Uncle Pen," but, although Elvis loved the song, he couldn't complete an acceptable take of it.

To gauge the commercial appeal of the two songs he had settled on for Elvis' first release, Sam Phillips pressed two acetate dubs of "Blue Moon of Kentucky" and a separate dub containing both songs. Since 1952, Sam Phillips and Dewey Phillips, the most popular Memphis disc jockey, had worked together to promote promising artists. Every Saturday night Dewey Phillips' "Red, Hot, and Blue" show on WHBQ featured the best of the new records. The audience, rock-oriented high school students, was young and eager for new rhythm and blues records. Sam Phillips believed "That's All Right (Mama)" was perfect for "Red, Hot and Blue." The other two disc jockeys that Phillips had close connections with were country-oriented. Uncle Richard on WMPA, and Sleepy-Eyed John Lepley on WHHM. Consequently, these disc jockeys were given only the copies of "Blue Moon of Kentucky."

In addition to being a popular disc jockey, Sleepy-Eyed John Lepley booked acts for the Eagle's Nest, so he was well aware of Elvis' talent. He envisioned a lucrative commercial future for Presley, possibly involving himself and his club, so he played "Blue Moon of Kentucky" every hour on his radio show. He began to court Presley, going out of his way to become friendly with the young singer. Sleepy-Eyed John had visions of managing Elvis, and he finally urged Presley to sign a management contract. Personally uncomfortable around Lepley, Elvis had no interest in signing with him. Elvis believed that Sleepy-Eyed John exploited the musicians at the Eagle's Nest. Lepley persisted, however. The following week, Elvis suggested that Scotty Moore sign him to a management contract. The agreement was not a real management deal; it was simply a means of keeping slick promoters like Lepley away.

On July 10, 1954, Dewey Phillips went on the air at WHBQ with his "Red, Hot and Blue" show. The 8:00 to 11:00 radio spot was a favorite of Memphis' young set. Phillips played any song his listeners requested, and also slipped in his own favorites. A flamboyant radio figure, Phillips drank openly both while on the air and in local clubs. It was a common sight to see someone hand Dewey a bottle of whiskey and a record through WHBQ's special booth at the Old Chisca Hotel on Main Street, from where the show originated. A local wild man, Phillips' arrests for drunkenness were as legendary as his show business successes. He was, however, the only man who could make a record an instant local hit. When Dewey Phillips agreed to play Elvis' "That's All Right (Mama)," it was due largely to his friendship with Sam Phillips. After one play, however, Dewey was an instant fan.

Dewey Phillips' show was popular because he talked to his listeners on the air. He seemed to be one of them. Irreverent. Loud. Brash. The twenty-eight-year-old Phillips vigorously defended the new music. He had an ear for the songs that kids liked. When Sam Phillips showed up to play Elvis' record, there was one minor problem. Dewey Phillips preferred playing black music, and it was primarily the black Sun artists who had been previously featured on "Red, Hot and Blue." Sam

Dewey Phillips on the air.

Phillips explained that Presley had a black sound. After this brief exchange and a few sips of whiskey, Dewey Phillips played the recording. The full impact of this night was immediately apparent to Elvis' friends. "We couldn't go anywhere with Elvis," Kenneth Herman remembered, "without someone hollering at us about his record."

In an interview in 1956, Gladys Presley recalled that Elvis was exceptionally nervous that Saturday evening. Before he left the house to go to the movies, Elvis instructed his mother not to move the dial from WHBQ's frequency. "Then he went to the movies," Gladys remarked. "I guess he was too nervous to listen."

At about 9:30, Dewey Phillips played "That's All Right (Mama)," and the phones began to resonate with a torrent of calls. The listener response to Elvis' first song was instantaneous. Local callers flooded the station with requests for more Elvis songs. It was common for Dewey Phillips' phones to ring like crazy for three hours anyway, but it was unprecedented for almost every caller to request another record by the same artist. Comically, a number of callers mispronounced Elvis' name. There were numerous black callers. Sam Phillips knew he had something special, and he convinced Dewey to interview Elvis on the air. Sam called Elvis' home to instruct him to come to the WHBQ studio. Gladys Presley informed Phillips that Elvis had gone to the movies. He was at the Suzore # 2 theater watching Red Skelton in "The Great Diamond Robbery" and Gene Autry in "Goldtown Ghost Riders," and had no idea how efficiently Sam Phillips had set the Sun Records promotional machine in motion.

Vernon and Gladys agreed to go down to the Suzore Theater and bring Elvis to the WHBQ studios. The Old Chisca Hotel was a hotel with a party atmosphere. A grand ballroom, a fine restaurant, and a bar full of people who mingled in the 1950s social-sexual atmosphere made the Old Chisca a promenade spot. When Elvis arrived at the studio, Sam Phillips whispered that there had already been fourteen telegrams and forty-seven telephone calls requesting replays of "That's All Right (Mama)." To make sure that listeners knew Elvis was a white artist, Dewey Phillips asked him where he had attended high school. When Elvis responded, "Humes High, sir," the listeners knew that the new sound was not a black one. Humes High was a white school.

Complementing the airplay on Phillips' popular "Red, Hot and Blue" show, Uncle Richard on WMPS was the first Memphis dj to play "Blue Moon of Kentucky," followed by Sleepy-Eyed John Lepley at the Sterich Boulevard WHHM studio. Lepley also spent an inordinate amount of time telling the listeners that he had played with Elvis at the Eagle's Nest. With the Presley phenomenon still a year away, Sleepy-Eyed John

was already attempting to get on the bandwagon. The three radio stations together filled the air waves with Elvis Presley's music, and the next day local record stores were swamped with requests for the recording. The only problem was that it hadn't yet been pressed for commercial release. "That's All Right (Mama)" was not officially released until July 19, 1954, to an immediate and growing demand for the record in Memphis.

Sam Phillips was knocked out by the enormous excitement over Presley's record, and quickly made plans to take advantage of this commercial phenomenon. Wink Martindale, another young disc jockey who was the morning man on WHBQ, was called into Phillips office to hear Presley's record. Martindale had begun working at WHBQ on April 20, 1954, and was struck by the wealth of local rockabilly musical talent. It was Elvis Presley, however, who was the most inspiring act. "I thought the guy was black," Martindale recalled, the reaction that Sam Phillips had wanted in order to test out the record. Phillips knew he could dismiss the record as just another obscure black singer if it failed, but if the record was popular, Phillips reasoned, he could take full credit for discovering Presley. Sam recalled for Martindale the response of listeners to the Dewey Phillips show. As a fledgling dj and aspiring actor, Martindale recognized that the reaction bespoke a unique musical talent. Martindale played Elvis' record on the air, later recalling: "The switchboard lit up like a Christmas tree." Another important observation in Martindale's reminiscences of the time is his recollection of how confident Elvis sounded during the interview with Dewey Phillips. Martindale believes that it

Wink Martindale.

was a false confidence; Elvis was so scared that he had no time to be nervous, and may have believed that it was a rehearsal, thus accounting for his relaxed manner.

There have been many descriptions of Elvis' interview with Dewey Phillips on the "Red, Hot and Blue" show, and no one other than Wink Martindale was able to guess the reason that Elvis seemed confident and articulate. Dewey Phillips himself provided what is probably the best description of the interview: "He sat down, and I said I'd let him know when we were ready to start. I had a couple of records cued up, and while they played we talked." Since he had performed in local clubs for a year, Elvis was at ease around Dewey Phillips and the people in the WHBQ studio. Elvis didn't realize that the interview had started, thus accounting for his relaxed manner. Under the circumstances, Phillips had little trouble coaxing an excellent interview out of Elvis. Listening to Presley, his ability to answer Phillips' questions demonstrated his early media charm, and there was no doubt that he had carefully planned his singing career.

Soon after the Elvis interview, Dewey Phillips began to be criticized by other local disc jockeys for praising Presley's music. "You can't believe how much criticism I got from my friends in the music business," Phillips remarked. Memphis record moguls and disc jockeys didn't like the way Elvis interpreted country songs. The thought of a rockabilly Bill Monroe in the sacred shrine of country music song was too much for the purists. "Elvis is worse than the colored singers," a country dj remarked to Phillips. "He lacks ambition; Elvis doesn't want to learn the country music craft," a reporter for the *Memphis Press Scimitar* commented privately to Dewey. Elvis was criticized for being too original. "It was then that I knew," Dewey Phillips recalled, "that young Elvis was a forerunner of a new sound."

In general, though, Memphis music critics were enthusiastic about Elvis' first record. One of the earliest critics to review Elvis' music was Jim Kingsley of the *Memphis Commercial Appeal*. Kingsley called "Blue Moon of Kentucky" the type of record that could "set the world afire." Another *Memphis Press Scimitar* staffer, reporter Edwin Howard, interviewed Elvis during a lunch break at Crown Electric on July 27, 1954. Elvis told Howard that he felt he needed only a minor break to become a mainstream musical act. Howard was intrigued by Elvis and wrote glowingly about his music. In 1956, Elvis told Carlton Brown: "When my first record came out I was a little leery of it. I thought everybody would laugh." There was no laughter in Memphis, however; after a few hours of airplay, Elvis was an instant star.

The commotion over Elvis' talent may have per-

suaded another music legend to pursue a career recording for Sun Records. On July 5, 1954, Johnny Cash returned to Memphis from a stint in the air force. Cash was in town the weekend when Elvis began his recording career. Like many other Southern musicians, Johnny dreamed of becoming a singer, and Elvis' spectacular rise to prominence made it seem possible for any singer to walk into Sun Records and walk out with a hit record. Cash listened intently to "Red, Hot and Blue," and loved every second of Elvis' "That's All Right (Mama)." He tuned into WMPA's Uncle Richard show and discovered "Blue Moon of Kentucky" being played in the country music marketplace. Cash's reaction was typical of Memphis record buyers: they wanted Presley's single. They also wanted to record for Sam Phillips' Sun label.

Selling Records

As a result of the demand for Presley's record, Sam Phillips drove over to Plastic Products to place an order for the Presley single. On Monday, July 12, 1954, Phillips ordered a thousand 45s and 78s of "That's All Right (Mama)" b/w "Blue Moon of Kentucky." The demand was so great for Presley's record in Memphis, Sun Records recouped its costs immediately. Popular Tunes on Poplar Avenue ran the first ad for Presley's single in Memphis, and the small record shop did a continuous business.

Since Presley quickly had an undeniable Memphis hit, Sam Phillips switched his concentration to opening up other Southern markets. Phillips single-handedly merchandised "That's All Right (Mama)"/"Blue Moon of Kentucky" in the areas outside of Memphis. Climbing into his car, Phillips drove through Arkansas, Tennessee, and Mississippi placing Elvis' records in small record stores, taverns, shoe shine stands, and radio stations. In Tennessee and Mississippi, the one-stop distributors were not convinced that Presley's record was strong enough to attract large orders from record stores. This forced Phillips to use direct sales techniques. He drove as far as Texas and Florida to drink whiskey with the one-stop distributors and convince them to take two to three hundred copies of "That's All Right (Mama)" on consignment. Before he approached the one-stop wholesalers, however, Phillips spent three days stopping at radio stations. The ever present bottle of whiskey, a few words of praise about the station, and a promise to share the profits brought Elvis' record airplay. Soon "That's All Right (Mama)" was on the Florida and Texas airwaves. Phillips quickly alerted distributors in the other Southern states to Presley's popularity; one-stop distributors couldn't resist ordering a record that was being played on the radio, and they ordered by the boxful. On July 23, 1954, Alta Hayes of Big State

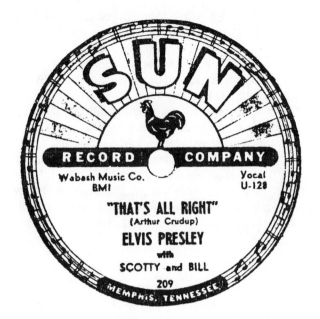 

Labels of Sun Records release #209: Elvis Presley's "That's All Right (Mama)" b/w "Blue Moon Of Kentucky."

Record Distributors in Dallas placed the first large wholesale order for Sun record #209. Dallas airplay was the reason that Presley's music broke throughout the Lone Star state, and it was not long before Elvis performed in Texas.

As indicated above, on July 12, 1954, Elvis had signed a management deal with his lead guitarist, Scotty Moore. It was a move designed to discourage Sleepy-Eyed John Lepley and a number of other slick management types, something recommended by Sam Phillips as an interim measure until a more experienced agent could be found. Sam Phillips hovered in the background as a friend, advising Elvis on his future. Although Phillips could have organized a management firm to promote Presley's career, he preferred to concentrate upon producing Elvis' records.

Scotty Moore received a ten percent booking fee. On all future concert dates, Elvis would receive fifty percent of the guarantee, with Scotty and Bill Black splitting the remaining money. In reality, the money was quite inadequate all around; the long drives and the low-paying concerts in barns, honky-tonk bars, and grange halls barely met expenses. To promote Presley's records, though, Sam Phillips urged that Elvis play anywhere, anytime, for any sum of money. This led to a series of high school gym engagements, honky-tonk bars, VFW halls, and country-western clubs where audiences were critical and demanding. The uncomfortable drives to such shows, the unpredictable circumstances, and the haphazard working conditions did have a beneficial side to them, however; the rigors of the road helped developed Elvis' musical discipline and style. He also

learned to deal first-hand with small-time promoters who hoped to make a quick buck from the emerging Presley phenomena.

At this point, Elvis, ragged and tired-looking during the first month of his professional career, continued to work a day job at Crown Electric. It was a dull, tedious job, and he was eager to quit. As Ronald Smith suggested, "Crown Electric had a rapid turnover in labor-type jobs." Despite the pressure of his schedule, Elvis also did whatever he could to promote his first Sun single. By playing local clubs, he created a demand for his record. He also spent time between shows convincing the audience to purchase "That's All Right (Mama)"—walking up to the bar, buying drinks for the locals, all the while pushing his first Sun single.

In September 1954, Roundman Knowland, a Greenwich, Mississippi, promoter, signed Elvis to appear at the town's American Legion hall. Local Legionnaires soon complained that Presley's record had too much of a "Negro sound," and, in what was the first protest against Presley's music, the American Legion club members demanded that Knowland book another act. The promoter succumbed to the pressure, and the Freddie Burns band was hired in Elvis' place, scooping up the $375 performance fee. Marcus Van Story, who was hired to play the Greenwich date with Elvis, was surprised that it was cancelled. "Elvis had a following down there," Van Story remarked. "It was his show that some people didn't like. I guess you could say this was the first protest against Elvis," Van Story chuckled. The reason that Roundman Knowland gave for cancelling the contract was that Presley's stage show was too raucous.

To be sure, Elvis, Scotty, and Bill were an energetic act on stage, and they excited the country crowds. Scotty and Bill never performed the same way, and Elvis always mixed his country songs with blues and rhythm and blues tunes. This was an approach to music that they all loved. Scotty Moore remarked at the time: "We played entirely by ear and feel was the most important thing to us." Happily, the same uninhibited pickup style spilled over into the recording studio. Sam Phillips didn't have the equipment to remix, splice, or over-dub recordings. He had a makeshift echo chamber and some standard recording equipment. The sound that Phillips produced was miraculously simple and hard-driving, the perfect elements for rock and roll music. He had simply needed the right artist to carry his musical conceptions to the general public, something he finally accomplished with the release of the first Elvis Presley Sun record.

On Monday, July 19, 1954, Elvis' first single was delivered to Memphis record stores. Stan Kesler delivered the first Presley singles to Charles Records on Main Street, and fifteen-year-old Eldene Beard was waiting for a copy. She told Stan Kesler that she had been waiting for the record since it was first played on Dewey Phillips' program. Miss Beard was typical of the young fans reacting to the new music. Some musicians also appreciated Elvis' revolutionary talent. Looking back upon the excitement created by Elvis' first record, Carl Perkins observed, "I think probably the first rockabilly record ever recorded was done by Elvis, which was Bill Monroe's 'Blue Moon of Kentucky'." In Perkins' view, rockabilly music was a convenient marriage between gospel music and traditional country tunes. "It wasn't Sam Phillips who influenced any of the artists," Perkins continued. "Everyone who went to Sam Phillips' Sun recording studio already had their own style developed." This may be true, but in Elvis' case Sam Phillips molded Presley's sound into a commercial product.

Enter Bob Neal

As Elvis worked on improving his music, local musicians became more and more impressed with the blend of musical influences reflected by his repertoire. "Elvis knew the blues, spiritual songs and rhythm and blues songs better than anyone in Memphis," Ronald Smith noted. Kenneth Herman suggested that "Elvis was one of those guys who felt the music." Despite this praise from fellow musicians, it was difficult to interest newspaper reviewers in Presley's songs that were not in the mold of his current hits. Sam Phillips was determined to publicize Presley's talent, so he began systematic visits to newspapers, and radio and television stations.

Alta Hayes of Dallas-based Big State Record Distributors, who had placed the first large order for Elvis' record, wrote to Sam Phillips and asked what Elvis' group was called. Phillips ignored the letter, but Elvis saw it and began thinking about a name for Scotty Moore and Bill Black. By late July 1954, Elvis' group was billed as the Blue Moon Boys, a tactic that allowed the group to advertise themselves as two acts. The general consensus was that Elvis Presley's early Sun sound was the result of a large backup band. Sam Phillips didn't attempt to dissuade anyone from entertaining this idea because he felt that once anyone saw Elvis and his two backup musicians, they would be doubly impressed with what could only be a very special and unique musical aggregate.

Elvis and the Blue Moon Boys.

On July 28, 1954, *Billboard* magazine reviewed "That's All Right (Mama)" and "Blue Moon of Kentucky." The review called Presley a "potent new chanter who can sock over a tune from either the country or the rhythm and blues markets." The review concluded with praise for "a strong new talent." On the same day, the *Memphis Press Scimitar*'s Edwin Howard, in his "Front Row Column," called Elvis an overnight sensation.

As July 1954 progressed, "That's All Right (Mama)" and "Blue Moon of Kentucky" received continuous airplay on four Memphis radio stations. Bob Neal, at WMPS, was one of Elvis' earliest admirers. Each day on his "High Noon Roundup," Neal played "Blue Moon of Kentucky." Invariably, a telephone call would come in asking why he wasn't also playing "That's All Right (Mama)." Neal realized that his predominantly country music audience apparently loved *anything* Elvis sang, and this intensified his interest in young Presley. Soon he was frequenting the Eagle's Nest to scout Elvis' act.

It was as a result of watching Elvis tear up the crowd

at the Eagle's Nest that Neal finally approached Elvis about a management contract. Not only did Elvis fill the cavernous Eagle's Nest, but he elicited a special response from the audience. "I'd never seen anything like it," Neal confessed to Dewey Phillips. Not one to keep a secret, Dewey Phillips told his "Red, Hot and Blue" radio audience that promoter Bob Neal was scouting Elvis Presley.

Overton Park Shell

In July 1954, as Dewey Phillips plugged the upcoming country music concert that was to take place in late July at the Overton Shell, he gave Presley's career yet another lift. Like a carnival showman, Phillips urged his Memphis listeners to come out and see the new local sensation—Elvis Presley. "That boy's talent is wonderful," Phillips screamed at his listeners. Publicity for the Overton show had at first featured Slim Whitman in an outdoor concert, and early posters didn't even list Elvis' name. There proved to be so much interest in Presley's music that his name was soon added to the bill. Ads in the *Memphis Press Scimitar* displayed Elvis' name prominently, although it was misspelled as "Ellis Presley" on one occasion. When his name finally appeared (apparently unbeknownst to Dewey, based on his later statements), it was due largely to Dewey Phillips' publicity and influence.

The giant country music extravaganzas at the Overton Shell were greeted with great anticipation in Memphis. "We loved those shows," Kenneth Herman remarked, "because we got to see the new musicians." The concerts also gave the country music moguls a chance to scout new singers. Bob Neal was one of the local promoters involved in the show, and it was he who signed Elvis for a special appearance with headliner Slim Whitman. Before placing Elvis on the Overton Shell show, however, Neal went over to Sun Records and talked with Sam Phillips.

It was clear that Neal's questions were directed toward a possible management contract. He asked Sam which distributors were selling Elvis' record. Phillips responded that one-stop wholesalers in Dallas and Atlanta had placed orders for 250 records based on the radio play of "That's All Right (Mama)." Phillips convinced Neal that "Blue Moon of Kentucky" was making inroads in the country market. In order to test Elvis' popularity further, though, Bob Neal booked him into the Overton Shell. Neal was interested in managing Elvis, but he wanted to make sure that young Presley was not a passing fad.

On Thursday, July 29, 1954, Elvis appeared at the Bon Air Club, and his band expressed some concern about the upcoming Overton Shell show. Scotty Moore

and Bill Black suggested that Elvis concentrate upon country songs. The audience would be a traditional country music crowd, and it would be good practice to perform some old country standards. At the Bon Air Club that evening Elvis sang his favorite, "Old Shep," followed with "That's All Right (Mama)" and "Blue Moon of Kentucky," and ending his brief set with "That's When Your Heartaches Begin." The Bon Air crowd was not particular about which songs he sang, giving him an opportunity to practice and get comfortable with the idea of doing only country tunes the next day. Backstage, Bill Black tried to further calm Elvis down about the Overton Shell show; Elvis was excited but also anxious about playing such a large arena.

By the time the two o'clock show approached on the afternoon of July 30, 1954, Elvis had become even more nervous than usual. Ready to go on stage, a large man from the musician's union suddenly confronted him. Elvis was told that he could not perform unless he joined the musicians union. After borrowing some money, Elvis quickly filled out a union card. The incident only served to further unnerve him; he perspired profusely, and felt sick to his stomach. Although stiff and nervous throughout the afternoon show, Elvis made it through a performance, which was a virtual repeat of the previous night's effort at the Bon Air Club. He left the stage to an indifferent scattering of applause, depressed about his performance. The butterflies had almost destroyed Elvis' stage presence. "My very first appearance after I started recording...was on a show in Memphis as an extra added single at an outdoor auditorium," Elvis remarked in 1956. "I came on stage and I was scared stiff." Throughout his career, Elvis never fully overcame his pre-performance fears. Although he was a master showman, Elvis was always as nervous as an amateur prior to going on stage. Following the first show, Elvis quickly left the Overton Shell. He was happy to have performed, but he didn't feel right with the country songs.

Before he performed during the evening show, Elvis had time to eat dinner. Depressed, he ate only one cheeseburger and drank half of his shake at a nearby truck stop restaurant. "You knew Elvis was upset when he couldn't eat," Ronald Smith remarked. Bill Black kidded Elvis about his loss of appetite. Excusing himself from Bill and Scotty, Elvis took a long walk around the Overton Shell. He thought about his future, and was determined to give an energetic performance in his evening show. After he had had time to critique his performance, Elvis decided that he couldn't stick solely with country songs. One of Presley's strengths as a performer was his awareness that it was always necessary to tailor a show to the audience. This was typical of Elvis' behavior during the Sun Record Company period.

When Elvis came out on stage at the Overton Park Shell shortly after eight o'clock on July 30, 1954, he was to create a signal moment in rock and roll history. With Scotty Moore standing to Elvis' right and Bill Black behind him to his left, he burst into "That's All Right (Mama)." After a few moments of silence, the young girls in the audience began clapping and screaming. An indication of Elvis' indefinable appeal, this wasn't the first time that Elvis' young fans had gone crazy. This time, however, it was on the largest scale he'd experienced. As Elvis recalled, "I came out, and I was doing a fast-type tune, one of my first records, and everybody was hollering and I didn't know what they were hollering at." This comment was typical of Elvis in 1954; he had no idea that his actions were creating a group of young rock and roll enthusiasts. "You'd see this frenzied reaction, particularly from the young girls," Bob Neal recalled. "We hadn't gone out and arranged for anybody to squeal and scream. For Elvis they just did it automatically."

When Elvis came over to Bob Neal's house the morning after the Overton Shell show, he was ecstatic. "This isn't just another singer," Helen Neal remarked to her husband, "this boy is different." Helen Neal urged her husband to manage Elvis. She pointed out that she could work until they made some money. Although they had five sons, Neal's radio job and the money he earned booking Elvis would be enough to get them through the hard times. Elvis liked the idea, because Bob Neal had a reputation for honesty and integrity. He was also the best-known promoter in Memphis.

There were other encouraging signs from the Overton Shell show. Everyone at the show agreed that Elvis was suited for hard-driving vocals. Before Memphis radio personality Dewey Phillips introduced Elvis during both shows, he urged him to sing uptempo rock songs. As Dewey Phillips recalled: "I introduced him and stayed on stage while he sang. He went into "That's All Right (Mama)" and started to shake and that damned auditorium just blew apart. He was nobody, didn't even have his name on the posters, but the people wouldn't let him leave." Although Dewey was wrong about Elvis' name being on the posters, he was right about the evening performance. It caused the crowd to go wild.

Malcolm Yelvington, another Sun Records artist, commented that the Overton Shell show firmly established Elvis' performing skills. Yelvington remembered that Elvis stole the evening from Slim Whitman. When Whitman walked off stage, Yelvington asked him what he thought about Elvis: "Well, if that young man keeps going someday he might make it." There was a twinkle in Whitman's eye, and Yelvington realized that he was happy about Elvis' instant popularity. (Yelvington also lies at the center of one of the myths among rockabilly

Malcolm Yelvington.

historians: that Malcolm Yelvington and the Star Rhythm Boys played with Elvis. Yelvington's music did influence Presley, but he denies that he and his band were ever Elvis' studio partners. In fact, the first record cut at Sun after Presley's "That's All Right (Mama)" was Malcolm Yelvington's cover version of the Sticks McGhee classic "Drinkin Wine Spodee-O-Dee." Another Yelvington tune, "Rockin with My Baby," was an uptempo rockabilly tune similar to Presley's Sun Records sound.)

Felton Jarvis was another important observer at Elvis' Overton Shell show. It was the first time Jarvis had seen Elvis perform, and he was intrigued by Presley's ability to manipulate the audience. The crowd came alive during Elvis' spontaneous performance, one in which a simple nervous knee jerk excited young girls to fever pitch. In later years, Jarvis produced a number of Elvis' records.

Scotty Moore and Bill Black were asked for years about Elvis' twitch, and they pointed out that he shook his leg on and off stage. It was simply a lifelong nervous habit. Once Elvis got used to performing, it was only natural that he shook his leg on stage. By 1956, the media was questioning Elvis constantly about his hip-shaking routine. Elvis often mentioned that the First Assembly of God church was the inspiration for his stage show. "The gospel choir and the preacher," Elvis remarked, "made me move with the music. I shook my leg as a natural reaction to the choir." In a conversation with Atra Baer, a *Cosmopolitan* reporter, Elvis called the wiggle "inbred." On a cardboard record accompanying an issue of *TV Guide*, Elvis once talked about the Overton Shell performance. He confirmed that he had started shaking his leg because he was uneasy during the evening show. Bob Neal told Elvis to go back for an encore and to shake his leg some more. "You know, like they say in advertising," Elvis told *TV Guide*, "it's the sizzle in the steak that counts." Whatever the reason for Elvis' wiggle, it was destined to change the course of rock and roll history.

Sam Phillips, after witnessing the afternoon show, had chided Elvis for being anxious about it. During a long, fatherly talk with Elvis, Phillips also urged him to put more fire in the evening show. "You've really got to move," Phillips lectured.

Chet Atkins attended the evening show at the Overton, watching in amazement as Elvis brought the crowd to its feet. "He moved different," Atkins remarked. "Instead of stomping his foot...when he'd sing, he'd wiggle his leg or his hip." Offstage, Marty Robbins watched Elvis from the wings; when he congratulated Elvis on a good show, he winked and told Elvis he was going to work up a version of Presley's record. Although not the first to cover the song, Robbins recorded "That's All Right (Mama)" on December 7, 1954. A few weeks before, Smiley Maxedon had recorded it for Columbia Records. There was obviously a great deal of interest in Elvis' brand of music, and the name stars were watching the young kid intently.

During the next six months, Elvis Presley developed into a strong regional act. He was not only ready

An early publicity photo of Elvis.

to pursue a rock and roll career, but he was in the right place at the right time. Popular musical tastes were changing, an army of teenage consumers were eager to purchase rock records, and Sam Phillips' Sun Records offered Elvis his best chance to make them. It was difficult to predict the impending rock revolution, because of the type of songs appearing on the *Billboard* charts (there were only a few rock and roll songs). But already there were signs of a revolution in the habits of music consumers.

CHAPTER 9

The Sun Beginnings, August-December 1954

By August 1954, rhythm and blues groups such as the Penguins, the Charms, the Moonglows, the Five Keys, and the Drifters consistently placed records on the *Billboard* charts. These black vocal groups all had one thing in common. Their records were generally produced by small labels and sold well to white record buyers. Major labels—RCA, Columbia, Capitol, and Mercury—were reluctant to sign black groups. When Mercury signed Dinah Washington, she was placed under contract because she had a strong appeal in the white, pop market. Sam Phillips' often remarked that his dealings with the major record labels reinforced the notion that they didn't know how to sell black music. This gave the small labels a virtual monopoly in the rhythm and blues field. Phillips, therefore, along with Chess-Checker Records owner Leonard Chess, Duke-Peacock magnate Don Robey, Imperial owner Lew Chudd, and Modern Record chief Jules Bihari turned out the majority of blues and rhythm and blues hits.

As Sam Phillips listened to stories from other record executives, he realized the cutthroat, competitive nature of the small, independent record business. In order to guarantee money for future record production, artist royalties were often not paid on a regular basis. Frequently, a record executive's name was listed as a co-writer of a song in order to further guarantee greater royalties for his company. Sam Phillips, though, emulated Atlantic Records owner Ahmet Ertegun. The only major record label to treat black artists fairly, Ertegun not only conscientiously paid royalties, but he treated his artists with dignity and respect, a policy that Phillips also followed throughout his career.

Some of the other smaller record labels went so far as to treat their artists like second-class citizens. Jimmy McCracklin, who recorded for Imperial, Checker, and Crown among others, remarked: "Imperial Records presented me with a $70,000 bill when I left them. I was paid fifty dollars a week, and told I was lucky to have a record contract." Fortunately, McCracklin, a multi-talented writer, retained the copyright to his songs, and he has continued to collect royalties from those he recorded for these labels. From time to time, McCracklin also produced hit records on his own labels—JMC, Art-Tone, and Oak City. To this day, however, Jimmy McCracklin is bitter about the way he was treated. "The white man took the money and the black man got nothing. The black man who did what the white man wanted continued to record," McCracklin concluded. Blacks who didn't tow the mark, it was clear, were simply passed over by the white establishment.

The Flip Records Experiment

The Sun Records studio, located near the corner of Walker and Union, had long been a hub of activity as countless unknown artists sought their first audition with Sam Phillips. Each day Sam's secretary, Marion Keisker, was besieged by country boys and city musicians alike who believed they had penned a hit record. At Taylor's Cafe, next door to Sun, hopefuls sat and talked about the unique sounds coming out of Sun. In addition to Sun Records, though, Sam Phillips had also founded another label to turn out records for local artists. The label, called Flip, which actually never even released a record until February 1955, was aimed primarily at the country market. Although he recorded a number of artists, Phillips ultimately released only four important songs on the Flip label. The most interesting Flip release was Carl Perkins' first record, "Movie Magg," backed with "Turn Around," songs recorded in December 1954 that became minor hits in the Memphis market. "Movie Magg" was a local jukebox favorite that was responsible for Perkins' initial rockabilly popularity. (Perkins' early success was later instrumental in Sam Phillips decision to sell Elvis' contract.)

In addition to releasing Carl Perkins' first record, Phillips also recorded country acts like Bill Taylor backed by Clyde Leoppard's Snearly Ranch Boys, Charlie Feathers, and the Miller Sisters. A number of significant black artists also recorded for Flip. Bluesmen Billy "The Kid" Emerson, Rosco Gordon, and Hot Shot Love turned out some excellent sides for the label.

Charlie Feathers had two rockabilly releases on Flip, "I've Been Deceived" and "Peepin' Eyes." Both songs made inroads in the country market and were Memphis hits. *Billboard* reviewed them and praised Flip for finding a major talent in Feathers. *Billboard* summed up Feathers' appeal: "'Peepin' Eyes' is a bouncy little item that should do business in rural areas." Eventually Feathers recorded a demo of "I Forgot to Remember to Forget," and Elvis used this recording when he cut the tune.

The Flip Records venture suggests that Sam Phillips was a gambler with a master plan. What Phillips hoped to accomplish with this strange mix of artists was a rock and roll hit record. Phillips read *Billboard* religiously, but was keenly aware of the changes in the record business due to rock and roll. Nothing short of a revolution was taking place in music. By 1954, Bill Haley and the Comets, Fats Domino, and Little Richard had placed their rock and roll songs on both the *Billboard* and *Cashbox* charts, leading to changes in radio airplay. (The following year Chuck Berry's "Maybellene" and Elvis Presley's "That All Right (Mama)" entered the rock music mainstream, the five Founding fathers of rock and roll had emerged, and the first Golden Age of rock and roll music was underway.) Sam Phillips recognized the commercial potential of rock and roll, and concluded from the immediate facts that apparently white and black artists alike could place records in the country charts, and that either could cross over into the fledgling rock and roll marketplace.

In retrospect, Flip Records can be seen as the misguided experiment resulting from Phillips initially faulty analysis of the music marketplace of his time. The problems that artists like Jimmy McCracklin experienced in the music business ultimately provided Sam Phillips with quite an education. The fighting between black artists and white record owners eventually influenced Phillips to radically alter some fundamental beliefs he held about music's commercial side: he came to realize, as noted in an earlier chapter, that the only way to reach a broader record-buying market was for a white artist to convincingly cover black songs of the type Sam was interested in producing, a conclusion that rested upon business as well as artistic considerations.

Certainly, by late 1954, the demand for *black music* had escalated. The number of black artists who placed singles on the *Billboard* Hot 100 was to increase from three percent to ten percent between 1954 to 1955. It was this increase in black music chart songs that further encouraged Sam Phillips in his idea of crafting one of his white artists into a black musical mold, once persuaded that the prospects for black performers, with a few notable exceptions, were relatively dim. Perhaps he could shape Elvis Presley's act so that it exemplified the best of black music. As a white artist, Presley could tour and appear in places where blacks were not allowed. White artists drew larger and better-paying crowds than blues performers. Television was reluctant to feature black artists, but many shows booked rockabilly musicians. These musicians had to have the right combination of looks, talent, and personal charm. Put simply, Sam Phillips was just one of many independent record label owners who had discovered that black hit songs sold better when recorded by a white artist. This fact changed Phillips' approach to recording and releasing as many black acts as possible. By 1954, Sam realized that only a few of the Sun blues recordings would ever become hits. After a time, he faced the fact

that there was just not enough money in recording black artists. If a black artist was signed after June 1954, it was because Phillips believed that he had broad commercial appeal. A shrewd promoter, Phillips realized that the time was right for a white rhythm and blues/rockabilly sensation to come to the fore, and Sam wanted to be the man to bring it off.

The early problems promoting and distributing the Flip label, however, persuaded Phillips to concentrate on Sun Records as a vehicle for success. Flip Records quietly went out of business two years later, but it had been an important testing ground for Memphis country artists.

The Hunt for More Publicity

From August through December 1954, therefore, Sam Phillips concentrated on grooming Elvis Presley to succeed in the rough and uncompromising music business. During the last four months of 1954, Phillips didn't release any key records by other Sun artists. The Sun Records label was fighting for survival, and Elvis was the label's first legitimate link to commercial success. Initially, it wasn't easy to promote Presley's music, because his records were played largely on country radio stations. "I honestly feel that I can know what it is to have a baby," Phillips remarked. "That's what Sun Records was to me." This was Sam Phillips' way of remembering how difficult it was to convince many disc jockeys to play Presley's records.

To the tradition-minded country disc jockey and musician, Elvis broke all the rules. He sang in a Negro dialect, he dressed like a city hipster, and he possessed a Yankee attitude. There was also mistaken belief that Elvis was arrogant, and this notion hampered his early career. The intellectually stagnant country music promoters viewed Presley as a short-term musical act. Despite his meteoric popularity in Memphis and other regional locales, few well-known country music managers were interested in handling him. He was thought of as a novelty act who would soon pass into obscurity. Few people realized the revolutionary nature of Presley's music.

Sam Phillips was one person who believed fervently in Presley's future. The owner of Sun Records not only predicted stardom for Elvis, but mortgaged Sun Records future to achieve the dream. As Elvis perfected his live act and radio play increased for "That's All Right (Mama)" and "Blue Moon of Kentucky," Phillips suggested that Elvis change his billing to "The Hillbilly Cat" or "the King of Western Bop," in order to capitalize on the growing popularity of rockabilly music. Phillips recognized that rockabilly music was a broad-based phenomenon and Elvis was the most commercial part of it.

Elvis and Sam in the recording studio.

Phillips formed this opinion when Sun artists like the Ripley Cotton Choppers, Earl Peterson, Hardrock Gunter, Harmonica Frank, Doug Poindexter, and Malcolm Yelvington sold records to buyers who were not traditional country fans. These artists, however, performed a hybrid of rockabilly and country music, and consequently never received the chance to sign with a powerful national label. The large-scale distribution and radio exposure necessary to bring rockabilly music into the commercial mainstream prevented Sun Records from selling these artists' recordings in large quantities.

Then, too, many of the Memphis rockabilly acts were too old for the teen-oriented rock music market. Their dress and stage manner was not suited to the burgeoning rock and roll culture. In Memphis clubs, Charlie Feathers and Warren Smith performed music similar to Elvis'. Feathers and Smith often drew larger audiences than Elvis at these clubs. They were part of the larger Memphis rockabilly explosion of bands and singers. "There were a lot of singers who performed like Elvis," Ronald Smith remarked. "It was the time; every young musician had that sound." Neither Feathers nor Smith suggested that Elvis stole their material, but the backup musicians in local bands believed that Elvis learned a great deal from these rockabilly pioneers. In particular, many Memphis musicians pointed out that Charlie Feathers had the same songwriting talent and musical direction that brought stardom to Elvis.

The problem with Feathers was that he didn't excite the crowds. He was a well-received local act but there was not a strong reaction to his music. Feathers had performed locally for too long, and his act was too

well known. As Feathers watched Elvis perform, he was frustrated by his own inability to elicit a strong crowd reaction. Elvis, on the other hand, had the looks and talent to expand beyond the South's regional market. The rhythm and blues tinge to Presley's voice had the potential to appeal to the enthusiastic minority who at the time delighted in the changing musical styles. Only one Sun recording artist fit the bill—Elvis Presley. The remainder were either too old, too country, or too unreliable. Phillips made the decision to push Presley's records with a great deal of energy and enthusiasm.

By August 1, 1954, after feverish efforts to garner publicity, radio time and distribution for Elvis' record, Sun Records reported that "That's All Right (Mama)" had sold more than six thousand copies. Sam Phillips finally had a strong regional artist. The sales of "That's All Right (Mama)" and "Blue Moon of Kentucky" so buoyed Phillips' hopes for a major country music booking, that he contacted the "Grand Ole Opry" to inquire about an appearance for Elvis.

Phillips made a call, but found that "Grand Ole Opry" chief talent scout Jim Denny was reluctant to book Presley. The reason for Denny's refusal remains a mystery. He was not the confirmed country purist that some have suggested. In fact, during the 1940s, Denny modernized the "Grand Ole Opry" by introducing new singing stars and de-emphasizing the old string bands that had dominated the "Opry." This ended the barn dance atmosphere of the "Grand Ole Opry," turning it into a highly commercial vehicle for country musicians. As a result of Denny's foresight, such country stars as Hank Williams, Webb Pierce, Ray Price, and Faron Young made their mark at the "Grand Ole Opry." Denny was always looking for new, undiscovered performers. He was a shrewd judge of talent, but Denny's decisions were often influenced by other musicians. Many Memphis musicians were critical of Elvis, and most of the country acts appearing on the "Grand Ole Opry" were hostile as well. Malcolm Yelvington, one of Elvis' strongest supporters, urged other musicians to leave him alone. When Yelvington and his Star Rhythm Boys played at the Eagle's Nest, he was impressed with Elvis' intermission sets. "I never played with Elvis, but I certainly admired him and his music," Yelvington reflected. Finally, however, although the negative opinions had severely prejudiced Denny, Phillips' perseverance paid off, and Denny agreed to audition Elvis.

On Monday afternoon, August 9, 1954, Elvis, Scotty, and Bill piled into Sam Phillips' car for the drive to Nashville. The trip was a pleasant one for Phillips, but he found the "Grand Ole Opry" talent department still had misgivings about booking Presley. They didn't like his musical style and believed that the country music purists wouldn't accept the young singer. Sam Phillips countered these misgivings by producing local record charts with impressive sales figures. He pointed out that country music fans were buying Elvis' record. Jim Denny was skeptical. He suggested that few people had seen Elvis in concert, and that his personal appearance and stage manner would determine the audience reaction. The "Grand Ole Opry" didn't care about record sales. They sold a brand of American music to a live audience, and the laughs or boos from a crowd could ruin a part of the show. After looking at Elvis, Denny told Phillips that they would have to rethink the idea of booking Presley. After reviewing the publicity surrounding Elvis' early shows, Denny told Sam Phillips to call him in a month if Presley's record continued to climb the regional charts. Denny then took the opportunity to tell Sam Phillips that he needed to bring some discipline into Presley's life. Elvis' clothing, Denny remarked caustically, was just one of his faults.

As Sam Phillips drove back to Memphis, he remembered that the "Louisiana Hayride" had given Hank Williams another chance when no one would book him. The "Hayride" had a reputation for booking unique acts. After spending a day cleaning up business in the Sun office, Phillips bade Marion Keisker good-bye and drove to Shreveport, Louisiana, to talk to Horace Logan, the talent coordinator for the "Louisiana Hayride." A quick side trip to Dallas and New Orleans had confirmed that local radio stations were still playing Presley's record. Elvis had a strong following in the area, and Phillips quickly made the "Hayride" executives aware of Elvis' drawing power.

Prior to the "Grand Ole Opry" audition, in order to gain more exposure, Elvis had headlined a show on August 7 at the Eagle's Nest with the Tiny Dixon band. Sleepy-Eyed John Lepley's club charged a $1.20 admission, and a sign on the wall proclaimed: "Don't wear a tie unless your wife makes you." It was a boisterous club with a large dance floor and a noisy, hard-drinking clientele. Elvis had trouble with his performance that night, according to Ronald Smith. The following day Elvis spent the entire afternoon at home practicing his stage moves in front of the bathroom mirror.

Many times Elvis appeared in more than one club in the same night. After he finished a spot at the Eagle's Nest, for example, Elvis drove quickly to the Bel Air Club at 1850 South Bellevue to sit in with Doug Poindexter and the Starlite Wranglers. Because of Elvis' popularity, Poindexter allowed him to appear as a guest vocalist. Poindexter realized that the future of country music was rockabilly-oriented. "I knew Elvis was something special by the way people reacted to him. We

drew a lot of people when Elvis sang," Poindexter observed.

When he reported to work on Monday, August 9, 1954, Elvis finally asked his boss, James Tipler, for two hours off that afternoon to audition for the "Opry." Elvis was feeling guilty about pursuing his off-hours career because Vernon Presley, despite the success of Elvis record, continually chided his son that a guitar man was "a no account drifter who would never make anything of himself." Despite the elder Presley's discouragement, there was a missionary zeal in Elvis, a commitment that led to more shows at the Eagle's Nest and other local Memphis clubs that drew increasingly larger crowds. The compulsive drive towards musical excellence was the key to Elvis' early success. Albert Goldman's biography, *Elvis*, ignores the time and energy that both Elvis and Sam Phillips committed to Presley's early career. The reason that many early critics dismissed Elvis at the time was that his only appearance on the "Grand Ole Opry" on October 2, 1954, failed to excite the audience. Goldman quotes a remark by Chet Atkins following Elvis' "Opry" debut: "I couldn't get over that eye shadow he was wearing," Atkins allegedly recalled. "It was like seein' a couple of guys kissin' in Key West." Atkins' comment is doubly surprising considering the more frequent complaint that Elvis was too aggressively heterosexual. No one else

Another early publicity photo of Elvis.

present at that show remembers Elvis wearing eye makeup; perhaps Atkins was just a little envious of the young amateur's dark good looks. Using flimsy recollections like this, however, Goldman not only distorts Elvis' image and music, but attempts to nullify the judgement of people like Sam Phillips that Elvis' raw talent was obviously that of a potentially major musical act.

Although he had no agent and only haphazard booking policies, Elvis' drawing power increased as he appeared in Memphis clubs. There was no need to advertise an Elvis appearance because he filled the local clubs with little advance publicity. A good example of an instant booking occurred on Monday, August 16, 1954, when Sleepy-Eyed John Lepley called Elvis at home. He wanted him to appear at the Eagle's Nest with the Jack Clement Band. Lepley offered Elvis $15 for the night. Since Elvis was paid $5 to $10 for most guest spots, he readily agreed. Doug Poindexter and the Starlite Wranglers were the Eagle's Nest house band that week, but Clement's band filled in on Monday nights. Clement hadn't drawn well and Lepley hoped that Elvis might attract a larger crowd.

Elvis also agreed to play two local benefits during the month. He appeared at the Kennedy Hospital, located forty-five minutes from the center of Memphis. The B'nai Brith Society benefit attracted a boisterous but appreciative audience. For almost a year, Eddie Bond, Kenneth Herman, and Ronald Smith had played at Kennedy Hospital. It was one of the easiest places to play, because they were always looking for free entertainment. Elvis was prepared to perform country songs, and he was surprised when a number of people requested "That's All Right (Mama)." Equally flattering was the fact that some of the patients had seen Elvis perform at Doc's bar in nearby Frayser.

The publicity from the Kennedy Hospital appearance prompted Elvis to agree to another free concert. On August 18, 1954, Elvis appeared at a benefit for an ex-Humes High student, Gene Marcotte. A number of musical acts preceded a baseball game at Bellevue Park, and Elvis' portion of the show brought the crowd to its feet with a rousing version of "That's All Right (Mama)."

On Friday, August 27, 1954, Charlie Feathers caught Elvis' act at the Eagle's Nest and couldn't believe the roar of the crowd. Elvis was the main attraction for a special ladies night dance, and Feathers remembered: "It was an event, but no one listened to Elvis' music." Ladies were admitted for fifty cents and the men paid one dollar and twenty cents. Elvis' Eagle's Nest show was the first where the women noticeably outnumbered the men. The reason for being there was simply to be close to Elvis, not to listen to him sing! Unwittingly, Elvis was instrumental in helping to develop the type of entertainment "event" that had little to do with people actually being able to hear a performer's music.

The day after Feathers watched Elvis perform, *Billboard* reported "Blue Moon of Kentucky" number 3 on its "Country and Western Territorial Best Seller" chart. Elvis was elated. There was a minor problem with success, however. Sam Phillips received five thousand orders for Presley's record, and he didn't have the money to press more copies. There simply wasn't enough money coming into Sun Records from the one-stop distributors. The wholesalers didn't pay Sun for ninety days, and then it was still difficult to fully collect the money.

"Louisiana Hayride"

Suddenly, Sam Phillips returned home from a promotional trip with a big surprise. Elvis, Scotty, and Bill were going to audition for the "Louisiana Hayride." Phillips mentioned that the "Hayride" booking agency had also secured two other club appearances, and the money earned from these jobs would pay for the trip. It didn't matter whether or not they were booked on the "Louisiana Hayride," the audition would result in at least two club dates. On Thursday, August 19, 1954, they drove the four hundred miles to Shreveport, Louisiana, and Elvis performed briefly before Horace Logan and the "Hayride" staff. It was an awkward moment. Elvis was extremely nervous, although he had no trouble singing "That's All Right (Mama)" and "Blue Moon of Kentucky." After the audition, Sam Phillips and Logan talked at length. The "Louisiana Hayride" agreed to an appearance by Elvis, but not until he performed at the other dates the "Hayride" had booked for him (the "Hayride" needed to book Elvis in nearby clubs to guarantee expenses). This was fine with Sam Phillips, who urged Logan to send observers to the dates the "Hayride" had booked for Elvis in Texas. That Saturday, August 21, 1954, Elvis appeared in Gladewater, Texas, and the following night at Magnolia Gardens in Houston. Although he was a virtual unknown, Elvis was cheered by the large crowd at the Magnolia Gardens and brought back for an encore. Elvis hadn't prepared for an encore, so he sang a shaky version of "Uncle Pen." Management at the Magnolia Gardens telephoned Horace Logan the next day and asked for Elvis to return within the next two months, confirming Logan's intuition that Elvis was a special act.

While in Dallas, Elvis became friendly with a number of djs who helped his fledgling career. Tommy Sands remembers Elvis hanging out late in the night with local disc jockeys at small hamburger joints. Elvis would eat two or three hamburgers, a double order of fries, and drink half a dozen Cokes. He was a friendly kid and local djs loved it. The girls always sought Elvis out, crowding around him. "He was the cat," Tommy Sands chuckled. "We called him that because he purred softly around the girls. Elvis had an enormous attraction," Sands recalled.

"Louisiana Hayride" management was impressed with the number of requests from local promoters for Elvis' services. Consequently, "Hayride" executives negotiated with Phillips over a one-year contract for Elvis to appear on the program. It would to be two months before an official agreement was worked out, and during this period Elvis' career prospered.

As Sam Phillips worked to further Presley's career, young Elvis enjoyed his limited fame and leisure. On Sunday, August 29, 1954, Johnny Burnette walked over to Elvis' house to talk about his upcoming show at the opening of the new Lamar-Airways Shopping Center, a small retail complex that Elvis was scheduled to appear at during the Katz Drug Store opening. Johnny Burnette's Rock 'n' Roll Trio, featuring Paul Burlison's lead guitar, were playing down the block at an Airways Avenue Chevrolet dealership. Johnny and Elvis talked a lot about their musical success, and Elvis proudly brought out the copy of *Billboard* with the comments on his record.

That afternoon Elvis and Johnny Burnette went to the Strand Theater to see the Dean Martin and Jerry Lewis movie "Living It Up." It was a rare moment for the two future rock stars as they ate popcorn, drank cokes, and Elvis sang along with Dean Martin. They chatted about how Burnette's Rock 'n' Roll Trio and Elvis and the Blue Moon Boys could extend their musical appeal. After the show, they walked to Ruben Cherry's record store, forgetting that it was closed on Sundays. Instead, they walked down the block for a hamburger and coke and continued to talk about rockabilly music.

On September 8, 1954, to commemorate its grand opening, Lamar-Airways Shopping Center ran a twenty-page advertising supplement in the *Memphis Press Scimitar*. This attractive advertising section not only included a picture of Elvis, but a feature headline: "Memphis' Newest Hit in the Recording Business." The following night, Elvis, Scotty, and Bill performed before more than three hundred people at a nine o'clock evening show. Playing from the back of a truck, Elvis sang "Old Shep," "That's All Right (Mama)," "Blue Moon of Kentucky," a Bill Monroe-inspired version of "Uncle Pen," "Crying Heart Blues," and "Tennessee Saturday Night." Peter Morton, manager of the Katz drug store, thanked Elvis for singing the country songs and paid him ten dollars. This appearance was an excellent tune-up for a recording session scheduled the next night at Sun Records.

Back to Sun Studio

As Elvis prepared for his second set of Sun recording sessions, Sam Phillips was optimistic. Although the "Grand Ole Opry" hadn't booked Elvis, he felt confident that the negotiations with "Louisiana Hayride" would make Elvis a regular. The "Hayride" was a show that appealed to a younger, rockabilly-oriented audience, so Phillips urged Elvis to record Lonnie Johnson's country blues song "Tomorrow Night," a tune well suited to Elvis' unique rockabilly style. When Johnson's "Tomorrow Night" appeared on the *Billboard* race charts in 1948, Phillips had been struck by its broader commercial appeal. Six years later, when Elvis walked into the Sun studio to begin another session, Phillips recalled the song; he was surprised to learn that Elvis was well aware of Johnson's music. Elvis knew that, in December 1947, when King Records released Johnson's original version of "Tomorrow Night," it had included a background chorus to enrich the sound. Presley had probably listened to LaVern Baker's recent Atlantic recording of "Tomorrow Night" (not only did Elvis keep up with Atlantic releases, but he performed Baker's hit "Tweedle Dee" in his act).

An important aspect of Johnson's music was that it was the product of his New Orleans environment. The vocal on "Tomorrow Night" features a far away sound from Johnson as the background singers come in to support his distant vocals. Elvis also admired Johnson's piano-guitar background on songs like "Working Man's Blues," and the plaintive guitar on another song, "Careless Love." Typical of Elvis, who was able to copy blues singers in a highly commercial manner, he urged Sam Phillips to use the guitar technique employed in Johnson's recordings, especially "Careless Love," as a model for his own version of "Tomorrow Night." After spending hours listening his favorite Lonnie Johnson songs, Elvis was ready to record. When they cut "Tomorrow Night" on Friday, September 10, 1954, however, the completed version was too rough for release; it sounded too much like Ivory Joe Hunter's music.

A big fan of Hunter's, Elvis suggested to Sam Phillips that they try and record a Hunter ballad. After a great deal of discussion, they selected Hunter's rendition of "Blue Moon." When Elvis was still at Humes High, Ivory Joe Hunter had had a minor hit with "Blue Moon," although it was not as popular as Billy Eckstine's 1948 million-selling rendition. Mel Torme also had a chart hit with "Blue Moon" in 1949, but Elvis was apparently unaware of this record. Elvis brought Hunter's MGM recording into the Sun studio and played it for Sam Phillips, remarking that Hunter had a country way with the blues. Elvis' own recording of "Blue Moon" was more in the Ivory Joe Hunter mold, a nice substitute for

Stacks of recording tape boxes surround Sam Phillips.

Elvis' botched version of "Tomorrow Night." He ended up combining Billy Eckstine's and Ivory Joe Hunter's versions, sounding like a cross between Dean Martin and Bill Monroe. Sam Phillips didn't like the results. He was disturbed by the soft, melodic style of "Blue Moon," and shelved it. He informed Elvis that it was too much like "Tomorrow Night." Ultimately, Phillips decided that neither song, in Elvis' hands, seemed suitable for the country music market.

There was tension and frustration as Phillips searched for the right tune for Elvis' second single. Since the Sun label had made inroads into the country music field, it was natural for Phillips to focus on releasing another country song. Phillips often had Elvis cut a familiar tune to calm him down; consequently, Jimmy Wakely's "I'll Never Let You Go (Little Darlin')" was recorded once again (Elvis had recorded the Wakely tune his first night in the Sun studio). The version was forced, however, and Phillips shelved it.

Suddenly, Sam Phillips had an idea. When he worked at the Peabody Hotel, Sam remembered, there seemed to be an endless stream of requests for Frankie Yankovic's polka hit, "Just Because," another song that Elvis knew by heart. Phillips reasoned that "Just Because" might be the perfect choice as the b-side for something like "Blue Moon." Although Sam Phillips fi-

nally did package the "Just Because"/"Blue Moon" combination from acceptable versions, it was not released until 1956 when RCA purchased the Sun catalog. Phillips just didn't have a strong feeling about the two songs at the time, and opted instead to have Elvis record a gospel song.

Martha Carson's Sun version of "Satisfied" was the model for Elvis' next recording. Carson, a gospel-influenced vocalist, blended traditional country music with a blues feeling. After Sam Phillips played her version, Elvis, Scotty, and Bill felt they could cover it. After two false starts, however, Elvis found "Satisfied" difficult to complete; he complained that gospel songs were hard to interpret. At this stage in his career, Elvis wasn't able to record a gospel song in his own style. He asked instead for an uptempo tune. Phillips, trying to calm Elvis, agreed, reasoning that a rocking rhythm and blues song was the solution.

One of Elvis' favorite r and b songs was "Good Rockin' Tonight." In 1947-48, Roy Brown and Wynonie Harris had both had hit versions of this song on the rhythm and blues chart. Their records were part of Elvis' personal collection, and he had performed the tune many times in local clubs. "Elvis knew all the recent records and loved to perform them," Eddie Bond remembered. "He prided himself in knowing rhythm and blue songs." Wynonie Harris' "Good Rockin' Tonight" (Deluxe 1093) was also one of Phillips' favorite songs, so he urged Elvis to cover it in Harris' jump blues style. (After the session, however, Elvis' "Good Rockin' Tonight" ended up owing more to Roy Brown's version.) As Elvis worked on "Good Rockin' Tonight," Sam Phillips realized that he needed to strengthen Presley's sound. Doug Poindexter, the leader of the Starlite Wranglers, was brought into the studio to revitalize the guitar parts. Although he was a country musician, Poindexter was thoroughly schooled in blues guitar licks. "I was always experimenting with my guitar," Poindexter remarked. "Sam asked me to add a blues touch to "Good Rockin' Tonight." Since Phillips listed only union members on the session sheet, Poindexter's contribution went unrecorded.

The September 10, 1954, Sun session concluded with Elvis cutting "I Don't Care If The Sun Don't Shine" in three takes. Buddy Cunningham was in the studio, and he produced a bongo drum sound by beating on an empty record box. Marion Keisker added a special verse to the song. Elvis recorded it so professionally that Sam Phillips decided to release it as the "a" or hit side on Presley's second Sun single, relegating "Good Rockin' Tonight" to the b-side. The decision was surprising, considering that Phillips normal process of gauging popular reaction to the songs should have suggested to him that he should do the reverse. With most Sun acts, Phillips proceeded slowly with a master of the song before he pressed the record in quantity. In order to measure the response to "Good Rockin' Tonight," Phillips persuaded Elvis to perform the song in several local clubs. At the Eagle's Nest, Bon Air, and Bel Air clubs, there was a strong reaction to it. Sleepy-Eyed John Lepley told Sam Phillips that Elvis' new tune was a sure hit. The careful previewing of Elvis' songs was typical of Sam Phillips; he carefully researched his listeners' tastes before releasing a record. Ignoring the evidence at hand, however, Sam proceeded with the idea that "Good Rockin' Tonight" should be the b-side, going with his initial gut feelings.

Just before Elvis' second Sun single was released, however, Phillips had what he felt was solid evidence that "Good Rockin' Tonight" would be successful in the Memphis market. Following a recording session at Sun, Sam suggested that Billy "The Kid" Emerson take Elvis over to the Flamingo Club on Hernando Street to see Pee Wee Crayton. "Pee Wee was good," Emerson remarked, "and Elvis learned about stage personality." Emerson remembered that Elvis didn't perform at the Flamingo, but young Presley did sing a couple of songs with Phineas Newborn. Emerson's interview with Jim and Amy O'Neil in the Spring 1980 issue of *Living Blues* suggests that several blues acts accepted Elvis' version of "Good Rockin' Tonight" with such enthusiasm that the reaction changed Sam Phillips' whole marketing strategy. Phillips immediately rewrote Sun's advertising to feature "Good Rockin' Tonight" as the hit single, and the reversed decision ended up being on the mark, as "Good Rockin' Tonight" quickly rose to number 3 on the Memphis charts. Phillips, concerned about placing Elvis' records on the country music charts, had initially misjudged the popular appeal of "Good Rockin' Tonight." In the end, however, the record quickly became one of Presley's strongest regional Sun hits.

Following release of the record, when singer Roy Brown played a series of dates in Mississippi in late September 1954, he was surprised to hear Elvis' version of his old song on local radio. More concerned with promoting his newly recorded songs, "My Gal from Kokomo," "Ain't No Rockin' No More," and "Black Diamond," Brown's interest was only casual, however. "I remember some local Tupelo station playing 'Good Rockin' Tonight'," Brown recalled. "It tickled me, but I didn't pay no attention to it."

"Grand Ole Opry" Relents

The increased radio airplay for Presley's first record had dramatically intensified Sun Records sales. Sam Phillips was very busy promoting his new discovery. On Saturday, September 18, 1954, as Elvis headlined at the Eagle's Nest Club with the Tiny Dixon band, Phillips sat in the back of the club. He was pleased with the crowd's reaction. The following Friday night, September 24, 1954, Elvis repeated the same show at the Eagle's Nest, and the next morning Phillips released Elvis' second record.

The release of "Good Rockin' Tonight" and "I Don't Care If The Sun Don't Shine" continued Phillips' pattern of combining an uptempo song with a country tune. Since it was necessary to constantly promote Elvis' records, Sam again took off in his car for Shreveport, Louisiana. For weeks, Phillips had been negotiating for Elvis to appear regularly on the "Louisiana Hayride." Elvis' August 1954 audition had prompted Horace Logan to keep track of the young singer. Finally, Logan and the "Hayride" management decided that the time was right to bring Elvis onto the show. Just as Sam Phillips was attempting to confirm a date with the "Hayride" management, the "Grand Ole Opry" called. Sam Phillips was ecstatic; the "Opry" was also interested in booking Elvis. The sudden appearance of "Good Rockin' Tonight" on the Memphis charts, and the general reaction to the record in the industry had finally convinced Jim Denny to showcase Presley. A contract specifying Saturday, October 2, 1954, as the "Grand Ole Opry" appearance date was mailed to Sam Phillips. He signed it and sent it back. It had been a real challenge to place Elvis on the "Opry," but apparently they were now ready to take the young singer seriously. Why Jim Denny decided to book Elvis remains a mystery. Not only was Denny hostile to Elvis' music, but he was personally abusive to Sam Phillips. Perhaps Denny just couldn't ignore the chart action of Presley's Sun recordings.

The "Grand Ole Opry" was an important opportunity for Elvis. Not only was the Nashville-based "Opry" the undisputed pinnacle of country music stardom, the mecca for country music performers, but record sales increased as a result of appearances on the "Opry." "Grand Ole Opry" was part of the WSM radio and television network, an NBC radio network affiliate. Since 1925, the "Opry" had evolved from a show featuring string bands to a showcase for the best country vocalists. Country audiences were loyal to the "Opry." The Saturday night show, broadcast over one of the strongest wave lengths in American radio, reached a massive audience. The success of the "Grand Ole Opry" prompted many imitations; the "Wheeling Jamboree" and the "Louisiana Hayride" were the two most popular second-line country music shows. Many "Opry" performers appeared on the other country music shows, and all of the shows together helped to sell large numbers of country records.

As they drove to the "Grand Ole Opry," Sam Phillips, Elvis, Scotty, Bill, and Marion Keisker talked about their expectations for the show. Elvis had diligently practiced a number of country songs. Ever since he was a little boy, Elvis had sung "Old Shep" and "Keep Them Cold, Cold Icy Fingers Off Of Me," and he believed these songs were appropriate for the Opry's audience. As the two-car caravan stopped for drinks midway in the two-hundred-mile journey, everyone was tired but excited. When Elvis arrived at the Ryman Auditorium, home of the "Opry," he was taken aback by its shabby appearance. Country music's premier music palace was a run-down building badly in need of repair.

Upon entering the auditorium, Sam Phillips determined that Elvis was to appear on Hank Snow's segment of the "Opry." The three-hour live "Grand Ole Opry" show began promptly at eight o'clock, and it was divided into carefully contrived segments to appeal to a wide variety of country music listeners. As Elvis nervously paced backstage, he met and had his first conversation with the legendary Hank Snow:

"What's your name?"

"Elvis Presley, sir," Elvis responded.

"No," Snow bellowed. "What name do you sing under?"

"Hello, Hank, I'm Sam Phillips, and this kid sings under a name that's dynamite."

Hank Snow walked away shaking his head. He chuckled to himself at the kid's mismatched, shoddy clothes. What was country music coming to when a new act couldn't afford boots, a hat, and a bright-colored country outfit? The kid wore a funny-looking sports coat accentuated by the strangest pair of pants he'd ever seen.

As Elvis prepared to go on stage, he looked at the script and saw that Kellogg's cereals sponsored his part of the show. During the two hours before the "Opry" show began, Jim Denny's role as the show's talent coordinator revealed his touchy, temperamental nature. Just before he went on, Presley was approached by Denny, who announced that Elvis could sing only songs he had recorded for the Sun label, something that Elvis had not planned for. Surprised by Denny's request and general attitude, it was Elvis' first introduction to the bullying manner of the powerful, Machiavellian entertainment promoter, and he was disturbed by Denny's arrogant, abrasive demeanor.

Hiding his disappointment, Elvis vowed to make the most of his appearance on the "Grand Ole Opry." Sam Phillips tried to reason with Denny. Some of Elvis' records, Phillips argued, were not suited for a country audience. If Elvis could perform traditional country songs, he would establish a broad base among country music fans. Bill Black jokingly suggested that Denny was out of touch with recent trends in country music. It was Black's way of letting Denny know that he had slighted Elvis. Denny insisted that he wouldn't allow an artist to sing a tune that he had not recorded. An example of the tradition-bound management that ran the Opry—which still had a ban on drummers because Denny and others believed that drummers belonged more to burlesque than country music—it was Elvis' first taste of conservatism and censorship in the country music world.

When Elvis finally appeared, he performed "That's All Right (Mama)" and "Blue Moon of Kentucky." Elvis wanted to sing "Good Rockin' Tonight," but Jim Denny believed that it was too raucous for the "Grand Ole Opry." When Elvis had asked Denny if he could sing it, the "Grand Ole Opry" talent coordinator responded, "We don't do that nigger music around here." Elvis had been nervous and stiff during his performance, and Denny reminded Elvis that he was still an amateur. Elvis' mediocre performance prompted Denny to suggest that Elvis go back to Memphis and continue driving a truck for a living. After this incident, Elvis was visibly fighting the tears back.

Normally a quiet person, Elvis was enraged over Denny's criticism. Enroute to Memphis after leaving Nashville, both cars stopped for gas. Elvis took his suitcase into the men's room and began brushing his teeth. After finishing, he flung the toothbrush into the toilet and left his suitcase in the men's room. Elvis' nerves were shot, and he was exhausted. The trip home was a quiet one.

Although he was busy in other states, Elvis continued to perform in local Memphis clubs. On Wednesday, October 6, 1954, he appeared during a ladies night show at the Eagle's Nest. Sleepy-Eyed John Lepley gave Elvis a rousing introduction, and mentioned his successful appearance on the "Grand Ole Opry." The disappointment over the "Opry" show had ended. Perhaps the "Opry" appearance was successful after all, Elvis reasoned. His friends told him it was well received.

The roaring approval of Memphis crowds inspired Elvis during this unsettled period. It was at the Eagle's Nest that Presley received his warmest welcome. The crowd always clapped loudly when Elvis sang "Good Rockin' Tonight." Sam Phillips was content to conclude that Jim Denny and the "Grand Ole Opry" staff had not accurately judged Elvis' talent. There was no need to point out the Opry's mistake; it was evident by the public's early hysteria over Presley's music.

The two performances at the Eagle's Nest, only a week after the "Opry" appearance, not only renewed Elvis' confidence, but these shows confirmed "Good Rockin' Tonight''s popularity. Not only was the song receiving extensive local radio play, but record sales were excellent in Tennessee, Texas, and Florida. There were also early signs that Elvis was much more than a local Memphis phenomenon. *Billboard* noted in its "Folk Talent and Tunes" column that Bob Neal of radio station WMPS in Memphis was organizing a tour with Elvis, the Louvin Brothers, and Jim Ed and Maxine Brown.

Back to the "Hayride"

As it turned out, only Elvis (and Jim Denny, of course) had viewed the "Opry" appearance as a disaster, however. Sam Phillips simply changed his plan to promote Elvis as a country star, and grew more determined than ever to find Elvis the proper exposure. The excitement over rockabilly and rock and roll music, and the financial support it promised, gave Phillips a chance to explore these markets. Nowhere was the cross between country, rockabilly, and rock and roll more evident than on the "Louisiana Hayride," where the reaction to Elvis had been much more positive. The acts looked and dressed country, but they had a new hard-driving sound. Horace Logan, talent coordinator for the "Hayride," liked the new musical hybrids emerging within country music. As Logan listened to Elvis' Sun recordings, he was impressed with Presley's voice.

Although the "Louisiana Hayride" had been on the radio for only six years, it had established an enviable reputation for discovering new talent. The critics dubbed the Louisiana-based show "The Cradle of the Stars," and it was the second most popular country radio program in America. In 1952, the "Hayride" garnered a great deal of publicity when Hank Williams returned to Shreveport. (He had shown up drunk on the "Grand Ole Opry," and was fired for this indiscretion. When the "Hayride" told Williams that he was welcome, it earned a somewhat undeserved reputation as the home of the maverick country musician.)

Due to their eclectic booking policies, the "Hayride" filled the 3,500-seat Shreveport Municipal Auditorium every Saturday night with a strange variety of performers. The large, barn-like showcase proudly proclaimed in three-foot-high bold letters: "LOUISIANA HAYRIDE." The three-hour show was divided into fifteen-minute segments, and each section had a regular host, and guest artists often read commercials. It was a free-flowing, wide-open show that periodically featured such country giants as Webb Pierce, Slim Whitman, Faron Young, Jim Reeves, and Hank Williams.

The "Louisiana Hayride" and Sam Phillips finally agreed upon terms to book Elvis as a regular; Horace Logan believed he had a bright show business future. The "Hayride" was a natural outlet for Presley, who appeared regularly on the Texas club circuit. It was an easy drive to Shreveport, and he could perform anywhere in Texas before or after an appearance on the "Hayride." Not only were the Saturday night shows a convenient layover for weekend concerts, but the exposure guaranteed future bookings.

Elvis' first appearance on the "Hayride" was scheduled for Saturday, October 16, 1954. Anxiously, he prepared for it in Memphis for an entire week. A perfectionist, Elvis spent hours in front of a mirror. He would curl his lip, wiggle his leg, and try to look like Tony Curtis. As Tommy Sands, another frequent guest on the "Hayride," remarked, "Elvis learned to work an audience. With his excellent voice and commanding stage presence, he became a local favorite." The "Louisiana Hayride" turned out to be a pleasant experience. As soon as Elvis, Scotty, and Bill walked into the Municipal Auditorium, Horace Logan made them feel at home. A tall, slender, grandfatherly gentleman, Logan had an intuitive feeling that Elvis was the forerunner of a new type of country music. As Elvis prepared for the "Hayride" show, Logan talked for almost an hour with him about the distinctive appeal of his records. There was no doubt this calmed Elvis prior his first "Hayride" show.

The freewheeling atmosphere at the "Louisiana Hayride" was a tonic for Elvis, and he gave his best

One of Elvis' many "Hayride" appearances.

performances on the show. When Elvis appeared on his first "Hayride" broadcast, the master of ceremonies, Frank Page, remarked: "Just a few weeks ago a young man from Memphis, Tennessee, recorded a song on the Sun label; and, in just a matter of weeks, that record has skyrocketed up the charts. It's really doing well all over the country. He's only nineteen years old. And he's a singer who's forging a new style—Elvis Presley." After a smattering of applause, a nervous Elvis remarked: "I'd like to say how happy we are to appear on the 'Louisiana Hayride.' We're gonna do a song for you we got on Sun Records that goes like this...." Elvis quickly began singing "That's All Right (Mama)," launching his career on the "Louisiana Hayride." Although everyone had been nervous about the debut show, the program format, the performances, and the music prompted the "Hayride" audience to explode with loud cheers.

The first show was an excellent one. Elvis' long nights in small clubs, the constant practice, and even the disappointment of the "Grand Ole Opry" appearance had all helped him evolve into an exciting performer. The "Hayride" audience loved him, and, after his first show, he was a local celebrity. The "Louisiana Hayride" contract called for forty-eight appearances a year with weekends off at the option of the "Hayride." The money was inadequate—Elvis received eighteen dollars a show, while Scotty and Bill were paid twelve dollars each—and the four-hundred-mile drive from Memphis to Shreveport and the lodging and food expenses made it impossible to live on the guarantee. But there were other reasons for signing the "Louisiana Hayride" contract. From October 1954 through December 1955, Elvis' music matured and his stage skills improved because of his many "Hayride" appearances. It was an excellent training ground for the fledgling musician.

Additionally, there was a lucrative concert market in Texas, Louisiana, Arkansas, and Tennessee. The "Louisiana Hayride" had its own booking agency and their agent, A.M. "Pappy" Covington, booked Elvis in nearby small clubs and high school auditoriums. One of Covington's first bookings took two days of phone negotiations with Lois Brown, owner of the Cadillac Club in New Orleans. After lengthy haggling, Brown refused to pay the $150 "Hayride" booking fee. Instead, she hired the Everly Brothers for $75. After more haggling with another promoter, Keith Rush, Covington was successful. For $75, Elvis and the Blue Moon Boys would appear at "The Old Barn Dance" in New Orleans, showcased in two separate musical sets.

When Elvis walked into "The Old Barn Dance" on Friday, October 22, 1954, he was surprised by the sparse crowd of about seventy-five people; the small crowd jeopardized Elvis' future bookings in New Or-

leans. The dance had been poorly publicized, and Elvis' records were just breaking in the area.

There were some high points during the week in Louisiana and Texas, however, as Elvis, Scotty, and Bill made successful appearances at the "Old Texas Corral" in Houston, and at a KSIJ radio concert broadcast from Gladewater, Texas. These Texas appearances developed a solid following for Elvis in Texas, where he experimented with new rhythm and blues tunes.

As Elvis prepared for his second appearance on the "Louisiana Hayride," "Blue Moon of Kentucky" was still climbing on the *Billboard* Country and Western territorial chart. There was also an increased demand for Elvis in concert. In fact, as Elvis came off stage after his second show on the "Hayride," Horace Logan gleefully informed him that he would appear the next night at the Lake Cliff Club in Shreveport with Hoot Rains and Curly Herndon. These two performers were regulars on the "Hayride," and the booking was designed to supplement Elvis' meager performance guarantee. After nine days in Louisiana and Texas, Elvis, Scotty, and Bill had just enough money for the trip home to Memphis.

Elvis' popularity was increasing daily. The October 23, 1954, issue of *Billboard* placed "Blue Moon of Kentucky" at number 6 in New Orleans and number 3 in Nashville. The *Billboard* Country and Western territorial chart for the week ending October 13 reported, for the first time, that Sam Phillips' campaign to promote Elvis' music outside of Memphis was succeeding. Record wholesalers in Dallas, Houston, and New Orleans were on the phone to Sun requesting larger and larger shipments of Elvis' first single, "That's All Right (Mama)" and "Blue Moon of Kentucky." Sam credited Alta Hayes of Big State Distributors in Dallas with breaking Presley's record outside of Memphis. "She told me that his record was interesting and she thought she could sell it," Phillips confided. Sam Phillips, however, still had the same old problem. He didn't have the ready cash to press more copies of Elvis' records.

During the week that Elvis was in Shreveport, there was a great deal of free time. Presley wandered down to the KWKH studios in Shreveport and recorded a number of songs. No tapes have surfaced, but several musicians remembered that Elvis taped "Give Me More More More (Of Your Kisses)," "Blue Guitar," "That's What You Gotta Watch," "Always Late (With Your Kisses)" and "Uncle Pen," songs that he is known to have practiced during 1954. He sang all of them in club dates, as they helped to fill out his live act, and it seems logical that he would use the time in the KWKH studio to further perfect these songs, and perhaps obtain a tape of them.

Backstage cameraderie of the kind that made Elvis'
"Louisiana Hayride" performances so important to him.

On October 30, 1954, as Elvis returned home from the "Louisiana Hayride," the *Memphis Press Scimitar* headlined: "ELVIS PRESLEY CLICKS." The accompanying article broke the story about Elvis' contract as a "Louisiana Hayride" regular. "The 'Hayride' specializes in picking promising young rural rhythm talent," the *Press Scimitar* noted, "and it took just one guest appearance last Saturday for the young Memphian to become a regular." That weekend, Elvis appeared at Sleepy-Eyed John's Eagle's Nest with Tiny Dixon and the Eagles, Chuck Reed, and Herb Jeffries. The homecoming weekend was a powerful tonic for Elvis. The crowds were larger than ever at the Eagle's Nest, and they cheered Elvis' every move.

Radio airplay had brought Elvis into the mainstream of the Southern record market. The popularity of the "Louisiana Hayride" prompted disc jockeys to increase Elvis' airplay. They provided Elvis with time on the air to explain his music, and this created strong record sales. On the way home after the week in Louisiana and Texas, Elvis, Scotty, and Bill talked about the future. They realized that they had to expand Elvis' repertoire. The next Friday, October 29, 1954, while appearing at Memphis' Eagle's Nest club Elvis sang "Blue Guitar" and "Uncle Pen." The reaction was positive and Sam Phillips

realized that Elvis was ready for concerts anywhere. His live act was perfected.

Defining a Career Direction

The main concern at this stage of Presley's career was selecting the songs he should record at his next Sun session. Elvis not only preferred blues and rhythm and blues tunes, but he continually brought his own records to the Sun studio. While he was on the road, Elvis bought and listened to hundreds of records. In late 1954, Elvis performed LaVern Baker's "Tweedle Dee" on the "Hayride" (the following year, he would also do Chuck Berry's "Maybellene" and Ray Charles' "I Got a Woman"). Charles Brown, a Texas bluesman who had moved to Hollywood, was an artist whose records Elvis discovered in a Shreveport record store. Brown's "Merry Christmas Baby" was one of Presley's favorite tunes. It was the smooth blues vocals that Brown delivered that impressed Elvis.

Lowell Fulson was another artist that Elvis emulated. A Texas bluesman, Fulson recorded "Reconsider Baby" in 1954 for Leonard Chess's Chicago-based Checker record label (Checker 804). Chess had close connections in Memphis with Dewey Phillips, and Fulson's records were played on Phillips' "Red, Hot and Blue" show. Destined to become one of Elvis' favorite songs, he had rushed out to buy "Reconsider Baby" at Ruben Cherry's record store. Elvis liked Fulson's sound so much that he often sang along with the song on the radio.

Although a relatively obscure blues artist at the time, Fulson had recorded songs like "Three O'Clock Blues" and "Everyday I Have the Blues" even before these songs became hits for B. B. King. Fulson often worked with the Arkansas songwriter Jimmy McCracklin, and they perfected a energetic jump blues style. From 1950 to 1954, Fulson became a minor star in the jump blues field, and Elvis listened to everything he could find by Fulson. During the summer of 1954, Fulson performed in and around Memphis. Elvis neither met nor talked to him, but he was able to watch the Fulson perform at the Club Handy. Elvis didn't perform "Reconsider Baby" publicly for some time after Fulson's version was released, and it was another five years before Elvis recorded the tune at RCA. No one was more surprised than Lowell Fulson when he was told Elvis covered it. "Sure did...I don't believe it," Fulson nodded quizzically.

Elvis' eclecticism bothered many of the tradition-bound country musicians. Bill Black, a country music devotee, urged Elvis to record country songs in a pop vein. Scotty Moore agreed with Black and suggested that a mainstream, pop sound guaranteed bookings and record sales. Ronald Smith told Elvis to follow his own interests. Elvis was uncertain about which musical direction to take, and he looked forward to leaving Memphis for the "Louisiana Hayride." In Shreveport, Elvis was a minor celebrity, and he had time to think about his future recording plans.

Back in Shreveport, Horace Logan urged Elvis to showcase his talent with ballads and sugar-coated country tunes. Lefty Frizzell, Hank Williams, Roy Acuff, and Bill Monroe were the artists that Logan urged Elvis to listen to during his spare time. Elvis countered by suggesting that Lowell Fulson, Lonnie Johnson, Arthur "Big Boy" Crudup, Charles Brown, Chuck Willis, and Billy "The Kid" Emerson were his musical influences. Logan blinked in amazement. He knew very little about this type of music. It puzzled Logan that Elvis didn't like traditional country ballads.

Elvis' second Sun record release helped to define his musical direction. There was a definite rock and roll tone in Presley's music. On November 6, 1954, *Billboard* praised "I Don't Care If The Sun Don't Shine" and "Good Rockin' Tonight." The "Louisiana Hayride" continued to help Elvis' musical popularity, and his appearances on the Shreveport-based show caught *Billboard*'s interest. It was not long before *Billboard* was paying very close attention to Presley's performances.

Most of these early shows were loose and fun. They highlight another side of Elvis' personality. On the November 6, 1954, show, for example, Elvis delivered a short commercial for Southern Doughnuts, which he described as "pipin' hot." He was nervous backstage. "I don't believe Elvis ever thought he'd do a commercial," Ronald Smith suggested. "Elvis was trying to catch the attention of the local disc jockeys," Smith concluded. It was not long before Presley's persistence paid off.

One week later, *Billboard*'s yearly disc jockey poll listed Elvis as the eighth most promising country and western vocalist. What made Elvis' eighth-place finish astonishing was the fact that his second record came out only five days before the balloting ended. "That's All Right (Mama)" was only a hit in Memphis, and this means the disc jockey's voted for Elvis on the basis of his reputation as a live performer and his very first recording. Sam Phillips had done an excellent job of publicizing Elvis, because most of the artists that Elvis was competing against in the *Billboard* poll were under contract to major record companies. As soon as "Good Rockin' Tonight" was released it jumped into the Memphis Top Ten. Immediately, one-stop record distributors throughout the South reported brisk sales of Elvis' second single. At WMPS, Bob Neal conducted his third annual poll of country and western artists; Elvis ranked tenth. On November 3, the Memphis ratings reported

Elvis' "Good Rockin' Tonight" number 3 on the survey, and two weeks later Elvis had two songs on the chart: "Blue Moon of Kentucky" at number 3 and "Good Rockin' Tonight" in the number 7 spot. Sam Phillips was promoting Elvis successfully in the country market, but he was also breaking Elvis' records in the rhythm and blues and rock and roll charts. Elvis Presley was a multi-talented performer, *Billboard* propounded, suggesting that Elvis' "style is both country and r. and b. and he can appeal to pop." In stultifying syntax, *Billboard* concluded that Elvis fit into all musical markets.

Bob Neal, the WMPS disc jockey, called Elvis in November 1954 and offered to manage him. (Scotty Moore, Presley's guitarist, was acting only as an interim manager to run interference for Elvis, as discussed earlier.) In addition to hosting a popular radio show, Neal owned a record store next door to the Warner Theater, as well as a booking agency—Memphis Promotions. It was Neal's Memphis Promotions that had booked the talent for the Overton Bowl show, and Neal believed that he could make Elvis more money by managing him. When Bob Neal offered his professional management services, Elvis readily accepted. It had been more than a month since Elvis quit work at Crown Electric, and the management deal made him feel like a real part of show business.

The contract with Bob Neal was for one year. (At first, Elvis agreed to it in principle only; he wanted to wait until January 1, 1955, to sign an official document. Elvis reasoned that he needed a couple of months to work with Neal. If things didn't go well, Elvis could refuse to sign the contract. In essence, Bob Neal was auditioning for the right to manage Presley.) To promote Elvis' career, an office was rented across the street from the Peabody Hotel. From this office, Elvis and Neal concentrated upon new ways to promote Presley's career. The management agreement stipulated that Neal receive a fifteen percent commission on all bookings. D.J. Fontana, the "Louisiana Hayride" drummer, had recently joined Elvis' group, and was paid a hundred dollars a week under the contract. The remainder of the money was divided between Elvis (fifty percent) and Scotty Moore and Bill Black (twenty-five percent each).

By now, Elvis had definite ideas about the management of his career. It was Elvis who convinced Neal to open the office across the street from the Peabody. Ronald Smith and Kenneth Herman indicated that Elvis shared with them his ideas about the future, destroying the myth that Elvis lacked a professional view of the music business. He realized the importance of promotion, and during his first few months with Sun Records he worked actively to publicize his career. Since Elvis was playing in country and western clubs, it was only natural that the general thrust of his career was initially in this direction.

During November and December 1954, Elvis was very successful in the country music market. Bob Neal's role was to increase the number of Elvis' concert appearances, and to bring in lucrative bookings. Elvis had discovered that he couldn't depend upon Sun Records for financial support. While the records were a commercial success, they didn't provide much ready cash. This fact was demonstrated on November 15, 1954, when Sam Phillips gave Elvis a check for $82.50, the royalty payment for "That's All Right (Mama)." Phillips presented the check to Elvis when he brought Presley back into the studio for another recording session.

New Sun Sessions

The November 16, 1954, Sun Records session was lengthy. Johnny Bernero was brought in to play drums and augment Scotty Moore's guitar and Bill Black's bass. That night Elvis recorded two full reels of "I'm Left, You're Right, She's Gone," a song that Stan Kesler and Bill Taylor had written expressly for Elvis. It was conceived as a country tune with a blues direction; Elvis also recorded it in a slow, bluesy version retitled "My Baby's Gone." The song has shown up on a number of Elvis bootlegs, and suggests the influence of the blues upon Presley's music. The session was long and quiet, and helped to polish Presley's studio sound. When the

Johnny Bernero's drums enhanced the November 16 session.

November 16 session ended, everyone was exhausted. (In 1987, RCA released the album **The Complete Sun Sessions**, which included takes 7 through 12 of "I'm Left, You're Right, She's Gone.")

Two nights later, Elvis performed at the Eagle's Nest with "Louisiana Hayride" artists Jimmy and Johnny. The place was packed with Elvis' fans, and the "Hayride" artists made numerous references to Presley's popularity. The energy that Elvis displayed at the Eagle's Nest was evidence of his zeal for a record career. The November 20, 1954 issue of *Billboard* again noted Presley's popularity, referring to his October 16 and 23 appearances on the "Louisiana Hayride," and mentioning that he had signed a contract to appear regularly on the show. *Billboard* also noted that such well-known entertainers as Slim Whitman, Johnny Horton, Red Sovine, Jimmy Newman, and Jim Ed and Maxine Brown among others were "Hayride" regulars, placing Elvis' name among illustrious contemporaries.

Sam Phillips' one-man campaign to merchandise Elvis' records was aided by Bob Neal's promotional skills. As a result of their combined expertise, Neal and Phillips persuaded the press to focus on Elvis' stage show. There was a strong demand for a new Presley record, prompting Phillips to schedule another recording session prior to Christmas. There was still no national recognition for Elvis' records, but the first two Sun singles had had strong regional success.

On December 8, 1954, Elvis attempted to record Bill Monroe's "Uncle Pen" and Lonnie Johnson's "Tomorrow Night." Neither song was satisfactory, and Phillips shelved the tape. They also failed to cover Rufus Thomas' "Juanita." While Elvis was recording, Sam Phillips informed him that Marty Robbins had just released a cover version of "That's All Right (Mama)." Ironically, Robbins' rockabilly cover, which owed little to Arthur "Big Boy" Crudup's blues version, outsold Elvis' tune. It was frustrating to Elvis that a country artist could bastardize a blues tune and have it sell so well. He didn't begrudge Robbins his success, but the episode served to intensify Elvis' search for unique material. He hoped to come up with a blues tune that would fit his style.

On December 11, 1954, Bob Strack, the disc jockey on the "Red River Roundup" show on KWKH in Shreveport, Louisiana, had Elvis as a guest on his program. He kidded Elvis about his music, remarking that Presley's records were very popular. Pointing his finger out the window, Strack laughed as fifty lovesick girls stared through the KWKH glass pane. Strack commented on other signs of Presley's popularity. The screams from

Elvis in December 1954.

girls in the audience at the "Hayride," Strack remarked, were not typical of the show. "You're something special," Strack informed Elvis. Strack also commented that phone calls requesting Elvis' music tripled when he performed in the Shreveport area. During the interview, Strack asked Elvis about his success: "I never had too high hopes or ideals, because...the circumstances of our lives didn't give room to dream too big...," Elvis responded. This humility was honest and characteristic of Elvis during his early years. He was still unaffected by show business.

While driving to appear on the Saturday, December 18, 1954, "Louisiana Hayride" show, Elvis thought a great deal about his upcoming recording session. In two days, he would be back in the Sun studio and it was important to record another regional hit record. Since blues tunes were important to Elvis, he searched for an obscure blues song, settling on a tune by a Georgia bluesman, Kokomo Arnold. After launching his music career in the South, Arnold had moved to Chicago and made his living bootlegging whiskey. Music was a sideline for him, but Arnold was still a historically significant bluesman who influenced many performers. (Arnold's "Sagefield Woman Blues" included the phrase "I be-

lieve I'll dust my broom," a line that inspired Robert Johnson's "Dust My Broom" guitar riffs and prompted Elmore James to make this tune his signature piece.) Arnold's Decca recording of "Milkcow Blues Boogie" had been covered by a number of country artists. In 1937, Decca released Cliff Bruner's version of the tune, and in 1941 Decca tried again with a country swing version by Johnnie Lee Wills. It was Moon Mullican's 1946 cover on King Records that most influenced Elvis, however. Mississippi Slim had played the record on his Tupelo show, and Elvis loved it.

On Monday, December 20, 1954, Elvis entered the Sun studio confident that "Milkcow Blues Boogie" was the song he needed in order to create a national audience for his music. Sam Phillips liked the idea of using "Milkcow Blues Boogie" because he believed that a rhythm and blues or blues tune coupled with a country ballad was still the best way to advance Elvis' career. The recording session was an excellent one. Elvis started slowly, then announced, "Hold it, fellas let's get real real gone." He then completed an extraordinarily vigorous version of the song. After listening to the cut, however, Sam Phillips had some reservations about "Milkcow Blues Boogie." He believed that Elvis' version lacked the ingredient necessary to become either a country or pop hit. Phillips suggested they try another tune.

On the next song, "You're A Heartbreaker," drummer Jimmy Lott was brought in to augment Elvis' sound. Lott was a well-known local drummer, but the use of a drummer was a major change for Elvis' music. No record was kept of which cuts Lott played on, but he probably also appeared on an alternate cut of the third song in this session, "I'm Left, You're Right, She's Gone." The versions of this song that Lott drummed on have appeared on a number of bootlegs as "My Baby's Gone." Also at the session was Doug Poindexter. The guitar licks heard in the latter song, similar to those used by the Delmore Brothers in a 1949 recording "Blues Stay Away from Me," were added by Poindexter. "I listened to the Delmore Brothers and they helped with guitar licks I used at Sun Records," Poindexter revealed.

When Elvis left the session, he was still very happy with "Milkcow Blues Boogie." Keeping with his time-tested procedures, Sam Phillips allowed that it was best to test the new tune before a live audience. Actually, all the ingredients for a mainstream rock and roll hit had coalesced during the recording of "You're A Heartbreaker." The echo used in the song, for example, contributed an eery, almost mystical quality to it, and the instrumental background was raw and energetic. Elvis was now *that* close to developing the unique sound necessary for his commercial success.

On Wednesday, December 22, 1954, Elvis appeared at the Eagle's Nest and performed an acoustic version of "Milkcow Blues Boogie." After the weak applause, Elvis was convinced that the song lacked commercial appeal. Sam Phillips was right. It was not what Elvis' fans wanted. He finished his brief fifteen-minute intermission stint that night at the Eagle's Nest with "That's All Right (Mama)," "Blue Moon of Kentucky" and "Good Rockin' Tonight." Discouraged, Elvis talked that night with Johnny Burnette about his preference for ballads. Dean Martin was still a strong influence, and Elvis crafted ballads like "Harbor Lights," "Blue Moon," and "I Love You Because" in Martin's inimitable style. Happily, Burnette encouraged Elvis to continue to perform rockabilly tunes.

On Christmas day, Elvis and his family celebrated at their new home at 2414 Lamar Avenue. Elvis' friends called to congratulate him. Johnny Burnette dialed 37-4185 and disguised his voice as a fan. Kenneth Herman called to ask if Elvis needed a new guitarist. Ronald Smith jokingly called with an offer for free guitar lessons. It was great fun. Elvis laughed and enjoyed the pranks. It was time to relax just before he left for a concert appearance in Houston, Texas.

The "Yuletide Jamboree" at Cook's Hoedown club in Houston was Elvis' last 1954 concert. Pappy Covington had booked the appearance, and about 150 people attended. The crowd was festive, and Elvis closed the show with an hour-and-a-half performance. When he was called back for an encore, Elvis surprised Scotty and Bill by closing with a cover version of LaVern Baker's "Tweedle Dee." It was Elvis' way of paying tribute to the rhythm and blues roots that had shaped his career.

Elvis South Side High friend Kenneth Herman (center) in 1986, flanked by Stan Kesler (left) and Ronald Smith.

The Elvis Presley mania that engulfed America in 1956 showed signs of emerging in late 1954. By December of that year, Elvis had established himself as a solid regional act. There were squeals of delight at country concerts, and public appearances at local radio stations attracted zealous, predominantly female crowds. He was a regular on the "Louisiana Hayride," and his concert appeal was strong. The Sun record sessions had produced recordings that guaranteed Elvis radio airplay. Sam Phillips was working hard at promoting Elvis' records, and Bob Neal's modern management techniques brought in bigger concert fees. Everyone agreed that 1955 would be a crucial year for Elvis.

CHAPTER 10
Building a Reputation,
January-April 1955

Elvis Presley's struggle for artistic recognition began paying dividends in early 1955. From January through April, Elvis worked at perfecting his performing skills while Sun Records continued to release his singles. The sales of Presley's 45s and 78s increased steadily due to careful selection of songs, and Elvis maintained his concert popularity. While still just a regional act, this period was the final stage in polishing Elvis' talent as he crafted his music for national exposure. Sam Phillips' promotional genius during the first few months of 1955 brought Elvis out of the Southern regional market and into limited Northern recognition. While the gains up North were not spectacular, there were also signs of interest elsewhere in the country.

In addition to Phillips' promotional work and Bob Neal's managerial skills, Elvis continued to be intimately involved in setting the course for his career. In his office across the street from the Peabody Hotel, Elvis was actively engaged in the publicity end of things. Indeed, it had been as a result of the difficulties he had previously encountered in this area that Elvis knew that he needed an experienced manager. Friends like Ronald Smith, who would wander down to Elvis' office where they would talk for hours about the future, and Johnny Burnette, who often came by the office, encouraged Elvis to sign with a well-known manager. In 1954, Memphis was a small town and everyone had a strong sense of community. If Elvis was to move into the mainstream of the music business, Ronald Smith remembered, he would have to be professionally promoted, and everyone agreed that Bob Neal seemed to be the man for the job.

Bob Neal Goes to Work

As a result of this quest for proper management, on Saturday, January 1, 1955, Elvis finally signed a contract with Bob Neal, who, as noted earlier, had been "auditioning" for the role for several months already. The details of this management deal had actually been worked out a few months earlier, and the well-publicized signing with Neal was designed more to promote Elvis' third single, "Milkcow Blues Boogie" and "You're A Heartbreaker," than anything else. Neal was not a well-known national figure, but he was regarded locally as an honest man with a solid Southern reputation. Kenneth Herman pointed out that Neal had the ability to inspire the acts he managed. Vernon and Gladys Presley

were impressed by Neal's honesty, and they felt comfortable with the genial Memphis disc jockey. Sam Phillips, Scotty Moore, Bill Black, and Marion Keisker, who all provided Elvis with opinions on topics ranging from music to clothes, also approved.

Those who knew Elvis best were aware that he read *Billboard* and other music publications religiously, although he never allowed anyone except close friends to see him read the trade journals. His record collection was large, but he was also very cautious about showing it to people. Combined with a great deal of humility and sincerity, there was also a deliberate intensity to Elvis' pursuit of a musical career that only a few trusted people knew about. "I remember how dedicated Elvis was to his craft," Tommy Sands remarked. "He was always concerned about management and business tactics." It is therefore not surprising that the new contract with Bob Neal was also a cautious one. Actually, it was the same one he had previously negotiated with Scotty Moore. Elvis received fifty percent of the income from concerts, Scotty Moore and Bill Black continued to receive twenty-five percent of the live performance fees, and D.J. Fontana was placed on a hundred-dollar weekly salary.

Using his gaudy Memphis Promotions Agency stationary, Bob Neal went to work earning his fifteen percent commission for Elvis' concerts. Immediately, Neal raised Elvis' concert fee from a range of $100 to $250 a night to $300 to $500. The problem was that Neal couldn't always secure good-paying engagements. As a result, Elvis often accepted lower-priced jobs. During 1955, however, under Neal's skilled guidance, Presley earned $55,000, an excellent sum for a regional artist.

With his trademark string tie, Neal looked more like a hog farmer than a music manager. He had a down-home, country boy personality, but beneath the "gee golly" and "oh boy" facade was a magnificent show business acumen. Neal's local reputation was based on the popularity of his "Farm Show" on WMPS each morning from 5:00 to 8:00. He also handled the "High Noon Roundup." It was the noon show that drew most of Neal's listeners; he told country jokes, strummed his banjo, and played rockabilly records. Neal also owned a small record shop that blended in nicely with his management agency. Basically, Neal was a poor man's Arthur Godfrey, and he loved show business.

Bob Neal had some important contacts in the Ten-

(L. to r.): Sam Phillips, Elvis, and Bob Neal form a team.

nessee-Mississippi area, and he was able to convince small-town disc jockeys to play Presley's records. Neal also arranged a number of radio interviews, which contributed to Elvis' regional success. A good example of Bob Neal's contacts was his close relationship with Lynn McDowell of WBIP in Booneville, Mississippi. After signing Elvis, Neal arranged for a radio interview with McDowell to promote an appearance at a local club. The WBIP interview was one of the first in which Elvis talked about his future, and he had a confident vision.

Neal insisted on calling Elvis the "King of Western Bop," but, happily, the title didn't stick. Eventually, Neal's advertising employed the phrase "The Hillbilly Cat." "I think Bob Neal picked up the term, the 'Hillbilly Cat,' from the musicians who hung around Elvis," Tommy Sands recalled.

Although people around Memphis fondly remembered Bob Neal's promotions, there were definite limitations to his abilities. He seldom promoted concerts more than 150 miles away from town. He had trouble booking supporting acts, and often paired Elvis with comedians, a mix that was not always appealing. Managers who handled the more popular country acts viewed Bob Neal as definitely small-time, and they paid little attention to his clients. A happily married man, Neal was seldom seen without his wife Helen or one of their five children. During the early months of 1955, he did a creditable job of advancing Presley's career. Ronald Smith reflected on Neal's management success: "Bob Neal helped Elvis, no doubt about it." Although he believed in Elvis' music and was totally honest, Neal would be unable to break Elvis into new markets. Despite his limitations, however, by simply continuing to build Elvis' solid regional reputation, Bob Neal would eventually help Presley to achieve national popularity.

Eagle's Hall, Houston

The first indication of Elvis' increased concert popularity occurred when he appeared on Houston's "Grand Prize Saturday Night Jamboree." The Texas radio show, aired on January 1, 1955, over KNUZ from 8:00 to 11:00, featured Tommy Sands and George Jones, but the large crowd was obviously there primarily to see "The Hillbilly Cat." Signs with Elvis' name on them were everywhere, and a number of people stopped Tommy Sands to ask him on which segment of the show Elvis would appear.

The Grand Prize jamboree was held at the Eagle's Hall, a large auditorium used primarily for country music concerts. There was no dance floor at the Eagle's Hall, and this agitated the crowd. That night it was filled with New Year's Day revelers, noisy and full of post-holiday spirit. The sold-out performance before a raucous, stomping crowd prompted Elvis to add a Ray Charles song to the show, "I've Got a Woman." It brought a standing ovation from the sea of cowboy hats, flannel shirts, and frilly women's dresses.

What made the Eagle's Hall show unique was the fact that not all of the Blue Moon Boys were with Elvis. At the last minute, Scotty Moore caught the flu and didn't travel to Houston. Scotty was home in bed with a 101° temperature. That night an extremely nervous Elvis Presley took the stage, fretting over his musical accompaniment. He didn't like the idea of performing without Moore. Still, Elvis felt good because his backup band had new clothes, and would otherwise make a good showing. Bob Neal had purchased Elvis, Scotty Moore, Bill Black, and D.J. Fontana gray sport coats, white

IN PERSON
Elvis
PRESLEY
SCOTTY and BILL
The Blue Moon Boys
For Dates—Write—Wire—Call
BOB NEAL
Exclusive Personal Management
160 Union Ave.   Memphis, Tenn.
Phone: Office 8-3667; Home 4-4029

shirts, and black bow ties. When Elvis took the stage in a dark suit, black shirt, and a silver-gray tie, there was a murmur from the crowd. The Eagle's Hall announcer, Ken Grant, introduced Elvis as "the Bopping Hillbilly," and Elvis began his set with a subdued version of "Good Rockin' Tonight." The show's master of ceremonies, Gabe Tucker, a local musician, filled in on guitar. It wasn't the show that Elvis' fans expected. Tucker's guitar work was limited, and his slow, country licks suffocated Elvis' rockabilly vocals. After he finished "Good Rockin' Tonight," Elvis introduced Bill Black and D.J. Fontana to the youthful crowd.

Next, Elvis began singing "Baby, Let's Play House." There were screams from the girls, and the audience shrieked with ecstasy. Elvis had some trouble with the mike, fumbling it. "Thank you, friends," Elvis shouted, breathing heavily. He followed with a forced version of "Blue Moon of Kentucky." "Ah, play it Gabe," Elvis hollered, and Gabe Tucker's guitar filled the break. Elvis toyed with the words "shaking" and "shouting" in "Blue Moon of Kentucky." After the song, he quickly left the stage but returned a few seconds later.

"Thank you very much, I was coming back anyway," Elvis remarked. "I'd like to do a little song right here that I hope you people like. This one's called 'little darling you broke my heart when you went away but I'll break your jaw when you come back'—did you ever hear that one? I'd like to do this little song here, it's called 'I Got A Woman'." The screams from the girls were constant during this song. Tommy Sands, who watched the early part of the show from backstage, was impressed with Elvis' stage presence. He had never seen such a visually exciting show. Sands remembered that young Presley was something special, and the Texas crowd was familiar with his music. A number of girls that Tommy Sands knew inquired about Elvis.

Tommy Sands

Many acts on the "Louisiana Hayride" were buried by Elvis' popularity. Other young men with good looks and a fine singing voice had a difficult time finding stardom as a result of Elvis' overpowering presence. Tommy Sands was a good example of an artist who was pushed to the side in Presley's rise to stardom. Like Elvis, Sands appeared regularly on the "Hayride." His sultry good looks and infectious rockabilly style appealed to the youthful "Hayride" audience. Since Sands was only seventeen years old, he still lived with his family. In 1954-55, Sands' parents moved to the Shreveport, Louisiana, area so that "Hayride" management could sign Tommy as a regular. Sands, like many aspiring performers, listened to many different types of music, but he most enjoyed rock music. Tommy never forgot how

Elvis handled rock and roll tunes. One of the reasons Tommy Sands recorded Chuck Berry's "Maybellene" and LaVern Baker's "Tweedlee Dee" was that Elvis performed these songs on the "Hayride." "I was amazed the way Elvis could take a black song and make it sound like it was his own," Sands noted.

"Rock and roll music was a part of the 'Hayride,' they encouraged it," Sands remarked. The "Hayride" staff understood and appreciated Presley's brand of rock music. Horace Logan, the "Louisiana Hayride" master of ceremonies, was, according to Sands, one of the shrewdest judges of musical styles in country circles. "Horace had a keen eye, he was aware of the country performers with a rock and roll orientation—Roy Orbison, Johnny Cash, and Bob Luman were acts that Logan liked." It was while performing at the "Louisiana Hayride" that Sands perfected his own rockabilly sound. Although he grew up with country music, Sands' earliest success was in the rockabilly market. In later years, his fame resulted from a cultivated teen idol image.

Although he was only seventeen years old, Tommy Sands had played local clubs in the Houston area since 1951. That year he met Colonel Tom Parker, who helped Sands launch his singing career. "The Colonel was like

Tommy Sands, RCA Victor recording artist.
(Photo courtesy Tommy Sands)

a father to me," Sands remarked. While still in high school, Colonel Parker drove Sands around in his car on summer tours with Eddy Arnold and Gabe Tucker. "The Colonel taught me a lot of tricks about show business. Not only did the Colonel drive me around," Sands remembered, "but he helped me learn the music business. The Colonel was always interested in stage presence and something different."

When Sands and Colonel Parker first heard Elvis on the radio, remarked Sands, "We thought it was a black guy." Tommy urged Colonel Parker to take a close look at Elvis' music, thereby becoming an important influence upon Colonel Parker by pointing out the unique aspects of Elvis' talent. Parker had first seen Elvis in New Boston, Texas, in November 1954, and came away very impressed with Presley's musical ability. The New Boston appearance was one of Presley's more spectacular. He performed in a small high school gym that allowed the fans to sit very close to him. The result was an intimate show that intrigued Colonel Parker and prompted him to monitor Elvis' future. Following the New Boston performance, Parker told Sands that Elvis had developed a new musical style. "It's one you ought to think about using, Tommy," the Colonel urged. They talked at length about Elvis' appeal. "Maybe we can get a record deal," Colonel Parker commented. Parker urged Sands to cut a demo tape in Presley's style. Sands would do well to come up with the same type of gimmick that Elvis had, Parker informed him. (Sands, commenting on a later period, also remarked that Elvis was happy with the Colonel all during the fifties. "The Colonel recognized something new in Elvis," Sands concluded, "and sold it to the general public.")

There was indeed a raw magnetism in Presley's music, and the crowds responded to it. Knowing there was a strong market for rockabilly music, Tommy Sands tried to cash in on it. Long an Elvis admirer, and with the urging of Tom Parker, Sands admittedly attempted to copy Elvis' act. "Elvis liked my musical style," Sands recalled. More than that, as discussed previously, he would soon employ the talents of none other than the Blue Moon Boys to back him. Sands believed that Scotty Moore and Bill Black were an integral part of Elvis' success because of the sophisticated brand of music that he played. "Scotty and Bill were innovative and highly skilled musicians. They were making rockabilly music long before Elvis." Sands believes that Bill Black's sense of showmanship was an important ingredient in Presley's shows. Black's clowning and ability to entertain the predominantly country crowds helped Elvis to develop a musical following. Scotty Moore's guitar work so skillfully blended with Elvis' vocals that most audiences believed that they had been playing together for years.

Because of Sands' rockabilly musical talent and per-

Tommy Sands, like Elvis, was a "Hayride" regular.
(Photo courtesy Tommy Sands)

176

sonal charisma, Scotty Moore invited him to appear with the Blue Moon Boys (Scotty and Bill Black) at a booking in Texarkana, Texas. Although a hit, the line-up was an indication of the level of hostility that had built up between Elvis, Scotty, and Bill. By now, Elvis was a familiar name in the territories—Texas, Louisiana, Arkansas, and Mississippi—partially because of his records and partially because of the reach of the "Louisiana Hayride" radio signal. It was easier to secure club bookings because of the popularity of the show, which everyone listened to. Not only were promoters able to advertise Elvis as a "Hayride" regular, but he worked for a relatively small guarantee. Crowds were large and the ticket price allowed everyone to make a nice profit. Elvis reveled in the glory. Girls were everywhere. Soon, however, the strain of touring began to show on Scotty and Bill. They didn't have the frenetic energy to keep up with Elvis, nor were they as well compensated. "After working twice with Scotty and Bill, I never did another Elvis-type show. It didn't feel right for me. I concentrated on becoming Tommy Sands. But I sure was influenced by Elvis," Sands concluded.

As Sands sat in Hawaii in the 1980s with this writer, reflecting on his friendship with Elvis, he talked at great length about Presley's impact upon the music business. Then, abruptly, Sands volunteered some observations about Elvis' personality.

"There is a story early in my career which shows what a gentleman Elvis was. One night in Houston, Texas, when I was appearing at the Eagle's Hall, Elvis was standing near the stairs leading up to the stage. After my set, I walked down from the stage and stood near Elvis. I was doing my best James Dean impression, just sort of standing there brooding. We sized each other up. Neither one of us said anything. Then Elvis broke the silence and talked about motorcycles, cars, James Dean, and karate. He was a tough guy, but he acted like a gentleman. He was kind to me at a time when I was trying to find my place in the business," Sands remarked.

Sands was impressed by Elvis' intensity and willingness to share musical knowledge. Many rockabilly artists kept to themselves, since the music was new and untried. "Elvis was warm and outgoing," Sands remembered. "Some of the other boys didn't want you to know what they were doing." Since they both had country music backgrounds, Elvis and Tommy talked at length about traditional country music. This led to conversations about the blues and rhythm and blues music. "Elvis had such a fine degree of musical knowledge, I could scarcely believe that he was beginning in the business," Sands concluded.

"He had a style that everyone hoped to develop,

and the girls loved his music. In fact, the girls loved Elvis so much it got me in trouble with him," Sands chuckled. "One night while I was performing on the 'Louisiana Hayride'," Sands recalled, "I met a girl that I had been dating in Houston for a long time. She teased me about sounding like Elvis, and the next thing I knew we were sitting out behind the 'Louisiana Hayride' in a car in the parking lot. She was talking to me about her sister, and then suddenly she kissed me," Sands exclaimed. "She was Elvis' date that night, and the next thing I knew Elvis was standing next to the car." Sands was nervous, because he had heard stories about Elvis' fistic skills. "I got out of the car very cautiously," Sands remarked.

"I want to see you in the men's room, now, Tommy," Elvis barked, pointing his finger at Sands. "*Now*, Tommy," Elvis hollered, as he walked rapidly away.

Sands broke out in a cold sweat. He was five-feet eight-inches tall and Elvis was five-feet eleven inches. There was also a considerable weight difference. The people milling around smiled knowingly at Sands—it was obvious that Elvis was angry and ready for revenge. Entering the men's room, Sands was startled when Elvis

Elvis, a serious student of karate, began his instruction in 1955.

walked over and put his arm around him. Elvis smiled and looked at him pensively.

"Tommy," Elvis remarked, "you made me look bad tonight. A man can't lose his woman, certainly not a guitar man." Elvis went on to make his point, all the while keeping his cool. "I'm sorry to have to call you out on this Tommy, but I've got my reputation to protect." Elvis was such a gentleman that Sands started feeling guilty. When Tommy tried to explain that the girl was a just a groupie, Elvis stopped him after he said a few words. "No need to explain about the girl, Tommy, she jumps from one to the next. I'll take her home, kiss her on the forehead, and she'll never see me again. They are like that in this business. Be careful my friend, and remember one thing—you're my friend Tommy, not hers." Then Elvis talked for almost half an hour—about his music and his future career, interspersed with compliments about Sands' own music. Finally, Elvis walked out of the bathroom. "When I saw Elvis after that incident, I knew we were friends for life. Few people realize how kind and generous Elvis was," Sands recalled. Tommy Sands never forgot Elvis' decency.

Cultivating the Crossover Sound

As noted earlier, one of Elvis' habits was to learn every song that any of his favorite artists had recorded, something he did faithfully with another contemporary black artist's music, that of Roy Hamilton. Although he was a mainstream pop act, Hamilton's records combined blues with pop. Most importantly, he produced hits.

Just as Elvis was becoming a well-known Southern act, Roy Hamilton's records broke nationally. In 1954, Hamilton had had a major hit with the inspirational "You'll Never Walk Alone," which proved enormously popular with white audiences. In January 1955, Hamilton's song "Hurt" was on the *Billboard* Top Ten, and Elvis used it to practice his own ballad style. Hamilton's gospel-tinged ballad sound was heavily influenced by the black church, a spiritual aspect that Elvis loved. It didn't surprise Sam Phillips to learn that Hamilton's background included a stint with the Jersey City Searchlight Gospel Singers. Like Sam Cooke, Jackie Wilson, and Clyde McPhatter, Hamilton had developed a gospel-trained voice as his ticket to major pop recording star status.

As a pop crooner, Roy Hamilton had more in common with Nat King Cole, Tony Bennett, and Frank Sinatra than he had with Roy Brown, Arthur "Big Boy" Crudup, or Lowell Fulson. In late July 1955, *Billboard* magazine reflected on the changing musical tastes when it headlined: "Negro Artists: Rise of Solid Pop Sellers." The crossover of rhythm and blues records into the pop market, *Billboard* noted, made records by black artists commercially acceptable among white audiences.

Elvis often copied or imitated the sound of the demo record singer, so it was only natural for him to select someone like Roy Hamilton to imitate during his non-recording singing sessions. During his recording career, Bill Black often caught Elvis singing along to Roy Hamilton's songs. Gospel tunes like "You'll Never Walk Alone" were the songs that had the most direct impact upon Presley. By fusing Roy Hamilton's gospel-tinged vocal style with the blues energy of artists like Roy Brown, Elvis created his own musical form, one that excited crowds during its earliest incarnation.

Throughout 1955, Roy Hamilton remained an enormous influence upon Elvis. The following year, "Unchained Melody" would continue Hamilton's success in the white market. During that year, when Elvis began recording for RCA, he methodically copied Hamilton's style on slow ballads. While he was on tour, Elvis spent a great deal of his time listening to Hamilton's music.

There is an amazing similarity in Presley and Hamilton's background. As Hamilton grew up in Leesburg, Georgia, and Jersey City, New Jersey, he gained a great deal of experience in local church choirs, and this resulted in an infectious gospel singing style. At the Central Baptist Church in Jersey City, Hamilton was a featured singer by his teens. When Elvis and Roy Hamilton finally met in January 1969 at American Sound Studios in Memphis, where Elvis was recording an album, they talked at length about their gospel roots. Elvis gave Hamilton a tune, "Angelica," that had been selected for Elvis to record. Sadly, just after recording the song, Hamilton died, a tragic end to a spiritual friendship that had grown out of Elvis background in black music.

The debt that Elvis owed to black music and musicians was something he always paid openly. In 1955, for example, he frequently attended radio station WDIA's "Starlight Review," held at the Ellis Auditorium in Memphis. One night toward the end of a show, Rufus Thomas brought Elvis out from backstage and introduced him to the predominantly black audience. There was a rush to get Elvis' autograph and, as Thomas explained, "There was a near riot; young blacks wanted to get a look at the boy who sounded like one of theirs." Thomas, who began his career in 1935 with the Rabbit Foot Minstrels, was a disc jockey on WDIA in Memphis and an early Elvis Presley fan. In the early 1950s, Rufus Thomas' records on Chess and Sun were minor rhythm and blues hits. In 1953, Thomas' "Bear Cat" was a big *Billboard* r and b chart record that helped Sun Records establish itself. Thomas not only played Presley's songs on WDIA, but defended Elvis' music in the black community.

As black audiences and performers listened to Elvis' early Sun recordings, they came to praise his ability to interpret blues tunes. "Elvis was what rhythm and blues needed," Rufus Thomas reflected. "Elvis took our rhythm and blues records and made them part of the white music." Rufus Thomas believes that while r and b music was an important influence upon Elvis as a Sun Records performer in 1954-55, it was Elvis, Thomas maintains, who paved the way for many black performers to enter the rock music mainstream. Thomas not only believes that Elvis broke down many early forms of segregation in the music business, but helped popularize blues and rhythm and blues records among white record buyers.

"Amateur nights on Beale, that's where B.B. King got started...," Rufus Thomas observed—it was also where Elvis picked up a great deal of musical knowledge and crowd-pleasing antics. Long before Elvis was twisting his body on stage, B.B. King used his guitar to excite crowds. Elvis never forgot how King manipulated the audience, and he worked diligently on finding his own means of pleasing patrons in local clubs.

One night in January 1955, after listening to performances by Rufus Thomas and B.B. King, Elvis and Johnny Burnette went to Chenault's, one of Presley's favorite Memphis restaurants, for a hamburger. They talked for a long time about black music. Elvis knew he had a unique sound grounded in rhythm and blues. It was obvious to Elvis, however, that he had to be as unique and different as possible in his delivery to win

Elvis and B.B. King, 1955.

over the fickle record-buying audience. That month, in a short note to Burnette mailed from Shreveport while he appearing on the "Louisiana Hayride," Elvis told Johnny that he was trying to put more fire into his show.

The January 16, 1955, radio interview with Lynn McDowell, a dj at WBIP, in Booneville, Mississippi, further demonstrates Elvis willingness to discuss his own talent as an outgrowth of black music. As they talked at length about his Tupelo childhood—Booneville was twenty-five miles north of Tupelo—Elvis used the interview to praise Mississippi's influence upon his music. Elvis talked about Arthur "Big Boy" Crudup's "Rock Me Mama," and how it changed his attitude toward the blues. (Crudup's 1944 song was the forerunner of "That's All Right (Mama)," combining uptempo blues with a rockabilly tinge. Like Presley, Crudup was an erratic guitarist whose voice covered his inability to play in any key other than E.) When Elvis left the WBIP studio, McDowell remarked that he had been given a history lesson in the blues. "I'm a country musician Elvis, but that blues stuff sure sounds good," McDowell remarked. Elvis, with characteristic humility, simply concluded: "Thank you, sir. It's my pleasure to be here." After they went off the air, Elvis again thanked McDowell for the chance to plug his record, and they continued to talk for almost an hour. There was a warmth and a genuine sincerity to Elvis' personality that came through in intimate exchanges of this type. Little wonder, concluded McDowell, that Elvis already had such an impressive following.

There were, of course, many Memphis music figures who were critical of Presley's music. A good example of hostility to Elvis came from David Gaines, the program director at WDIA. He not only didn't like Elvis' sound, but he believed that Presley had no talent. It was due solely to Rufus Thomas' insistence that Presley's records were played on WDIA. The arguments about the value of Presley's music among WDIA radio personnel is an interesting reflection of how revolutionary his sound was in the mid-1950s.

Taking Care of Business

The mainstream popularity of Elvis Presley was still a year away when Sun Records introduced his third single, "Milkcow Blues Boogie." The September 11, 1935, original recording by Kokomo Arnold was known as "Milkcow Blues No. 4," a typical country blues tune that appealed to Elvis because it told the story of a wandering soul who "was still in love with his milkcow." There was also a double entendre reference in the tune to the state of Tennessee and its women. The b-side, "You're A Heartbreaker," was a country tune with an echo that provided the perfect complement to "Milkcow Blues Boogie." The song, an old standard written by Jack Sallee, was a favorite of country music traditionalists. On January 8, 1955, *Billboard*'s "Folk Talent and Tunes" column reported that Bob Neal was managing Elvis, now a headliner on the "Louisiana Hayride." *Billboard* called the new Presley single an interesting record.

Following ten days at home in Memphis in early January 1955, Elvis was booked for a brief tour with Texas Bill Strength. The tour included guest artists Jim Ed and Maxine Brown, along with assorted members of the "Louisiana Hayride." On Wednesday, January 12, the tour began before a small crowd in Clarksdale, Mississippi, in a high school auditorium.

With a great deal of time on his hands between shows, Elvis continued to focus his energies on developing his music and his career. Backstage on the night of January 12, for example, Elvis listened to "Sincerely" by the Moonglows, marvelling at the Chess Records sound. Another good example of how he used his free time was demonstrated during three days off from the Texas Bill Strength tour. Having read about the Fontaine Sisters' "Hearts of Stone," Elvis quickly acquired a copy and realized immediately that he could cover it. Otis Williams and the Charms, a black vocal group, had released "Hearts of Stone" in November 1954, and the Fontaine Sisters' version was a pale imitation of the original. Reading record industry publications daily, Elvis continued to search through *Billboard* for new records. There was enough time between shows for Elvis to develop new songs for his act, any one of which could be quickly recorded in the Sun studio. It was just this mania for musical change and growth that characterized Elvis' approach to his career in early 1955.

On Thursday, January 13, 1955, Presley sang from the back of a truck in Helena, Arkansas, for twelve dollars. During this performance, he experimented with another new song, "When It Rains It Really Pours." The tune had just been released on Sun Records by Billy "The Kid" Emerson. The night that Elvis recorded "Milkcow Blues Boogie" in the Sun studio, he had listened to Emerson's record. It was the type of slow, bluesy tune that Elvis loved, and he had already told Sam Phillips that he, too, wanted to record it. Unfortunately, when Elvis performed it live, the audience did not respond very well. Elvis was surprised by the lack of enthusiasm, and, the next day, drove rather glumly to Shreveport for a Saturday night appearance on the "Louisiana Hayride."

Elvis looked forward to the "Hayride." After the show, there were always new girls to meet, old friends

to see, and Elvis basked in the celebrity status that accompanied his popularity. There were also people who loved to talk music, and this provided Elvis with the inspiration he needed to continue his drive to the top. A sense of reinforcement and a feeling of camaraderie, Elvis explained to Tommy Sands, overcame him when he appeared on the "Hayride." While Elvis had great faith in his ability, the truth is that the "Louisiana Hayride" provided support not readily available in other towns.

There were important insights into Elvis' character during the "Louisiana Hayride" days. D.J. Fontana recalled that "Elvis had barrels of energy. We'd get off a date at night and have to drive maybe four hundred to five hundred miles and he was so keyed up he'd wanna talk all night. So we'd stop the car at a restaurant and me or Scotty or Bill—whoever's turn it was—would walk him down the road a mile or so."

After appearing on the "Louisiana Hayride," Elvis was back on the road. From January 16 through January 19, 1955, he appeared in Booneville, Mississippi; Sheffield, Alabama; Leachville, Arkansas; and Sikeston, Missouri. The concerts were held in high school gyms,

Another "Hayride" appearance, 1955.
(Photo courtesy Tommy Sands)

VFW halls, and small honky-tonk bars. Shows were brief, but the crowds grew in size at each concert. Many country music fans were familiar with Elvis' records. From time to time they called out the titles. Local drunks often requested the same song many times over.

The nature of Elvis' audience puzzled many music industry observers. Exaggerated tales of jealous boyfriends who wanted to punch Elvis out had obscured the growth of a rabid Presley following early in his career. Put simply, the blue-collar, working-class audience identified with Elvis' music. There was not the split between the sexes that many historians of popular culture have suggested—both men and women liked it. Elvis, bit by bit, was becoming the musical touchstone for the tastes of a new generation. It was not long before local disc jockeys discovered that their shows had more listeners when Elvis appeared as a guest. Elvis would do as many interviews as possible to accommodate the disc jockeys. Quick to catch on, they in turn played his records while replaying older interviews. It was Sam Phillips who convinced Elvis to concentrate on doing radio interviews. "You can't buy better free publicity," Phillips lectured. Following his brief tour, Elvis returned for his usual Saturday night date on the "Louisiana Hayride."

On January 22, 1955, while preparing to go on stage for his "Hayride" performance, Elvis was informed by Horace Logan that Tom Perryman, a Gladewater, Texas, promoter, had booked Elvis for five dates in Texas and Alabama. It took Logan a great deal of time to negotiate the contract, because the "Hayride" wanted more money for Elvis' appearances. Perryman, a shrewd promoter, hoped to make a quick killing with this Elvis tour. Reluctantly, he agreed to a $750-a-night guarantee. The haggling over the price forced the promoter to blitz his concert sites with posters, newspaper ads, and radio jingles. Tickets sold out for these five shows within three days. Logan and the Hayride's management team were amazed by the ticket sales. Perryman, an astute judge of musical talent, failed to inform Logan that Elvis' records were being played more than any artist on East Texas radio.

Indeed, there was a great deal of interest in Elvis' music in Texas. The first Elvis Presley Fan Club, organized in Dallas, kept close tabs on the future King of Rock and Roll, helping him receive newspaper publicity. The club sent out postcards when Elvis appeared in Dallas, and were responsible for the many hand-lettered signs at his concerts. As early as December 1954, the Dallas Elvis Presley Fan Club printed membership cards and handed out advertisements on his Texas appearances. There were also special publicity sheets on Presley's "Louisiana Hayride" shows. Actually, Presley's records were popular throughout the state, selling in larger numbers in Houston and Dallas than in Memphis. Demand for Presley's personal appearances were constant throughout the Lone Star State.

When Elvis arrived for his first concert in Midland, Texas, a crowd of sixteen hundred filled the auditorium and another thousand people were in the streets. Although Elvis shared the bill with Billy Walker, he was the main attraction. Everywhere, there were signs sporting Elvis' name; buttons festooned the blouses of young girls.

The excitement surrounding Elvis' concerts attracted the Midland media. A producer for KMID-TV "Dance Party" approached Elvis to appear with Roy Orbison and the Teen Kings on the afternoon show. Elvis performed "Tryin' To Get To You" with the Teen Kings backing him. Colonel Tom Parker was in town and watched Presley perform on the show. Tommy Sands sat next to the Colonel, mesmerized by Elvis' ability to translate a rhythm and blues song into his own style. "The crowd at Elvis' show had seen the teen dance party, and you could tell they were waiting for the faster numbers. The biggest hall in town wouldn't have held Elvis' show that night," Sands remembered.

Due to the lack of good concert facilities, small but sellout crowds attended the concerts in Boston and Gladewater. Hundreds of people stood outside the halls, asking to buy tickets. The crowds milling around the front of these country auditoriums attracted local newspaper attention. In Boston, Colonel Tom Parker was once again backstage, watching the scene with great interest. A few days later, Elvis appeared in Lubbock with the Jimmy Rodgers Snow show, and Colonel Parker was again in town helping Hank Snow's son with his tour. The Colonel still wasn't sure about Presley's music. The boy had sex appeal, but would country music fans approve of his antics? Perplexed by Elvis' raw performing skills, he was just not sure that Elvis had a country music future.

At the Cotton Club in Lubbock, where Elvis shared the stage with the Jimmy Rodgers Snow, he found the crowd exceptionally quiet. This was surprising because Lubbock County was dry and the Cotton Club, located on the outskirts of town, had a reputation as a ribald spot, a place where you could buy set-ups if you brought your own liquor. There were fights every night between patrons who had brought in their own mixer. The crowd was an odd assortment of high school students who tried to look older and cowboys who tried to look younger. They all wanted to hear the new rock and roll songs.

Two Lubbock high school students, Mac Davis and John Denver, read the local newspapers while listening to Presley's records. Too young to go to the Cotton Club, they were still well versed about Elvis' exploits.

Someone who could attend the show, another young performer named Buddy Holly, showed up to hear Elvis. On his radio show in Lubbock, Buddy frequently plugged Presley's records. Amazed by Elvis' vocal style, Presley's performance was to prove a catalyst to Holly's own career. "As a young boy," singer Tommy Roe remarked, "I remember people talking about Presley's Sun Record tours. They were the highlight of local fairs," Roe concluded. Clearly, Elvis Presley influenced a generation of singers as he toured the small, backwater towns of the South in January of 1955.

The tension of performing each night in strange places took its toll on the band. They fought with one another over petty matters. Soon it was impossible to decide which new songs to place in the act. Scotty Moore, Bill Black, and D.J. Fontana were tired of touring, and communication between them broke down. "Hell we worked Texas for two years...before he got big," D.J. Fontana remarked. "We were always in Texas, Louisiana, or Arkansas because that's where the records were being played."

D.J. Fontana remembers these years with a nostalgic flair. "The better part of those two years," Fontana recalled, "were spent in a 1954 Cadillac that Elvis had built a wooden rack on top with a canvas to cover it." The energy that Elvis displayed kept the band going on the road. "He never got tired, but when he did, he'd

Another grueling tour. Scotty Moore, a soothing Coke in hand, relaxes against the trailer pulled by Elvis' Cadillac.

just crash eleven or twelve hours straight in those days," Fontana concluded.

The road was unending in early 1955. After seven months as a recording artist, Elvis was still a long way from being a star. When *Billboard* rated "Milkcow Blues Boogie" at the 80 spot and "You're a Heartbreaker" at number 76, it was an indication that Presley was finding only limited success. Ronald Smith continually reminded Elvis that he was, nevertheless, successful. As Smith pointed out, new artists were lucky to place one song on the *Billboard* pop listing. It was almost unheard of for a fledgling performer to have two songs on the charts.

Music industry publications continued to comment positively on Presley's singing. The January 29, 1955, *Billboard* labelled Presley's new release as a "slick country-style reading." It was the first Presley song to be placed in jukeboxes outside the South. In January and February 1955, although still primarily a regional artist, Elvis' music showed the first signs of breaking in other sections of the country. That night, as Elvis proudly read the *Billboard* review of his third record release to Bill Black, they prepared to appear again at the Eagle's Hall in Houston. The crowds were growing larger at each concert, and Elvis responded with longer performances. Pleasing his fans was Presley's primary goal.

Touring afforded Elvis the time to do just that, although it was an impulse that often led him down the path of dalliance. A good example of how close Elvis was prone to get to his fans occurred during the final stop on the tour that Tom Perryman booked for Elvis. This show was at the Creole Club in Mobile, Alabama, and it drew a hastily organized local fan club. Throughout this tour Elvis closed his show performing "That's All Right (Mama)," but during this show the fans screamed for another song, so Elvis performed "That's All Right (Mama)" twice. He laughed as he left the stage.

After the show, Elvis met a fan, Virginia Sullivan. She was a buxom, raven-haired beauty who had sent Elvis a titillating letter. Naturally intrigued, Elvis sent word to bring her backstage. When Sullivan arrived, she was wearing a tight blue dress that revealed her full figure. They spent half an hour talking as Elvis unwound. Elvis told her that it was important for him to stay in touch with his fans. After searching out her opinions, Elvis found that the fans often had strange ideas about his musical future. Virginia told Elvis that he should try to sound like Frank Sinatra. Politely, Elvis excused himself and apologized for having to drive back to Shreveport.

Because he loved beautiful women, Elvis was always vulnerable. While the brief encounter with Virginia Sullivan involved only conversation, Elvis had numerous relationships while on the road, many with young

While on tour, Elvis was never at a loss for female company.

mothers of small children. In this way, Elvis could act out his fantasies about being both a lover and a father. Some claims in this area, however, should be viewed with a skeptical eye. Lucy de Barbin, who alleges that she had a twenty-four-year relationship with Elvis, mentions that "he'd call from a small town" to talk. While he was in Lubbock, Elvis allegedly called de Barbin at her home in Monroe, Louisiana, for example. This wasn't typical of Elvis' behavior. Busy on the road, Elvis had little time to engage in telephone foreplay. Constant touring and the drive for a hit record consumed him. Girls were available at every concert, and it is inconceivable that Elvis would devote himself to maintaining a long-term relationship of the type suggested by de Barbin, especially one involving long conversations on the telephone.

Bob Neal Loses Favor

It didn't take Bob Neal long to realize that he could demand more money for Elvis while at the same time obtaining more prestigious bookings. In order to secure new concert venues, Neal flew to Shreveport to discuss the strategy for expanding Elvis' bookings with the "Louisiana Hayride" booking staff. At the "Hayride," it was the A.M. "Pappy" Covington who urged Neal to hold out for a minimum of $750 a night. This price seemed logical due to the increased demand for Elvis' music. As a result, Neal, determined to upgrade his client's earnings, produced a slick brochure extolling Elvis' musical triumphs.

In February 1955, Bob Neal sent out his elaborate new brochures advertising "Elvis Presley and the Blue Moon Boys." Filled with reviews of recent concerts and laden with pictures of Elvis on the "Big D Jamboree," a number of new clubs booked Elvis on the strength of the pamphlet. The bookings were often a gamble for

the clubs, because they were small concert venues. A higher-than-usual door charge and the increased sale of beer would bring the club to the break-even point, however, so it was worth the try. The owners were usually happy with this arrangement, because the artistic reception was positive. The crowd was pleased with Elvis' show, and returned to spend their money. As Elvis became popular, club owners shrewdly advertised that they had once booked the "King of Western Bop."

Many of the clubs were elaborate cocktail lounges that had not previously booked country music. The old dance bands and jazz combos were no longer popular, and clubs looked for new acts. A good example of this new type of club was the Town and Country Club in Donaldsonville, Louisiana. When Elvis appeared at this plastic-looking paradise on February 3, 1955, he was surprised by its "New York interior." The Town and Country was a large club with a recessed dance floor that had been remodeled by a shrewd businessman, Ralph Falsetta, who turned it into a bar to accommodate the hard-drinking locals. A special liquor permit allowed the club a great deal of latitude in selling hard liquor and beer to the general public. Eventually, Falsetta was elected Donaldsonville's mayor, and his club reflected the strong local economy.

When Elvis was brought into the Town and Country, it was to celebrate the club's new status. The best of the new country music acts played there, and the audience was young and critical. Elvis was a big hit, and he pleased the crowd with hard-driving, energetic sets. After a four-hour concert with two short breaks, Elvis, Scotty, and Bill drove to New Orleans.

In New Orleans, Elvis was again surprised by the venues. In this freewheeling city, many clubs had a black house band. On Friday, February 4, 1955, Elvis appeared in New Orleans at the Golden Cadillac Lounge on St. Claude Avenue. The admission price was fifty cents, and the club was packed. This booking paid three hundred dollars, lower than Elvis' usual fee. The $750 guarantee that Bob Neal promised Elvis was not always possible, and it was sometimes necessary to accept lower-paying bookings. The publicity to the contrary issuing from Bob Neal's office about how much money Elvis was making was show business window dressing. Happy just to be in show business, it was uncharacteristic of Elvis to complain about bookings, but he let it be known that was frustrated with the clubs he appeared in during early 1955. (Despite all his work and negotiations, however, Neal would ultimately fail to dramatically improve Elvis' earnings, something which inevitably opened the way for Colonel Tom Parker to purchase Presley's contract.)

More Studio Time

Following his appearances in New Orleans, Elvis returned to Memphis on February 5 for another recording session. He arrived tired and cranky. Sun studio was full of well-wishers and other people who inquired curiously about Elvis' road trip as he prepared for the session. The carnival atmosphere bothered him. After being on the road all day, he had trouble concentrating. With very little time to prepare for the session, Elvis decided to cut songs that he had recently performed in concert.

Elvis and Sam Phillips spent some time talking about song selection. They needed another hit record. Elvis thought that certain of his performance selections were more commercially appealing than others. As Elvis traveled from one concert appearance to another, he listened to the radio constantly. He often remarked to Bill Black that he hoped to record some of the rhythm and blues tunes he had heard on the radio. Charlie Feathers, Malcolm Yelvington, Stan Kesler, Doug Poindexter, Ronald Smith, Marcus Van Story, and other performers at Sun Records were intrigued by Elvis' constant talk about black music. Sam Phillips agreed that r and b material was admirably suited to Elvis' voice. As a result, the session, which was cut short because of Elvis' road weariness, produced two 1954 rhythm and blues songs: Arthur Gunter's, "Baby Let's Play House," and Ray Charles' "I Got A Woman." Elvis also completed a version of "Tryin' To Get To You."

In recording "Baby Let's Play House," Elvis had finally satisfied a desire to cut a record from his own

Arthur Gunter

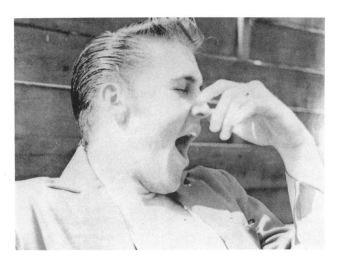

Though many thought Elvis was a tireless dynamo, he invariably experienced periods of total exhaustion.

collection. Gunter had first recorded his song in Nashville at Excello Records in late 1954. When Ruben Cherry's House of Records received a few copies from Ernie Young, the owner of the Nashboro Record Company, Elvis had eagerly purchased one. Like Cherry, Young operated a small record shop on the north end of Third Avenue in Nashville, and he frequently traded new records with Cherry. Just prior to Christmas 1954, Elvis picked up a copy of Gunter's record and loved its unique sound, Delta blues guitar combined with a country jump direction. Heavily influenced by white rockabilly artists, Gunter's husky voice was a good model for Elvis. Gunter had developed his style by listening to Blind Boy Fuller and Big Bill Broonzy. As Mike Leadbitter noted, "Arthur Gunter's music is a mixture of black and white traditions...," the very same blend of musical influences that Elvis experimented with in the mid-1950s.

An example of Elvis' dedication to rhythm and blues music was his recording of "Trying To Get To You." This tune, written by Rose Marie McCoy and Charlie Singleton, was a 1954 rhythm and blues hit for the Eagles. It was a tune that Elvis found in the bargain bin of Ruben Cherry's House of Records. Not only was it an obscure r and b hit, but it was a song that had a ballad inflection suited to Elvis' voice. Elvis was comfortable recording it, but after listening to a number of playbacks, Sam Phillips didn't feel that it was suitable for release. Elvis loved to perform "Trying To Get To You," and he had a chance to play it with Roy Orbison on KOSA-TV in Odessa, and KMID-TV in Midland, Texas. After these shows, Orbison began playing the tune, and he eventually recorded it for the Jewel label. It wasn't until RCA purchased Elvis' contract, however, that his version of "Trying To Get To You" was released.

The Hank Snow Jamboree

The day following this latest Sun session, Elvis appeared at the three o'clock and eight o'clock shows at the Memphis Auditorium. Faron Young, the headliner, was supported by Martha Carson, Ferlin Huskey, the Wilburn Brothers, and Elvis Presley was listed as the closing act. After performing three songs, Elvis went home for a much needed rest.

Meanwhile, Bob Neal had been looking for a large tour or a traveling country show that would give Elvis additional exposure. Due to Presley's popularity, the Hank Snow Jamboree considered booking him, but management were uncertain about his drawing power. Many music industry people viewed Elvis' act as a passing fad. One person who didn't necessarily subscribe to this view was Colonel Tom Parker. Since November 1954, Parker had watched Presley's career. He had also inquired about Elvis' personal life and found out that he had loving, Christian parents. While the Colonel made deliberate mental notes about Elvis' personal life and filed them away for future use, the immediate problem was to determine Elvis' commercial appeal, and then cautiously work him into Snow's tour.

Before he could even think of joining something like the Hank Snow tour, however, Elvis had to fulfill a few other concert dates. On February 11-12, 1955, he appeared at the Carlsbad, New Mexico, Sports Arena, and two nights later at the Legion Hut Dance in Carlsbad. People were turned away at the door, and the crowd cheered Elvis' every move. Significantly, the Carlsbad show had been booked with the cooperation with Colonel Tom Parker. Bob Neal had asked for the Colonel's help and, as Elvis watched Neal negotiate with Parker, he realized the full extent to which Bob Neal was basically the wrong person to guide his career. Parker demonstrated that he had connections among concert promoters that Neal just couldn't match.

On February 15, 1955, Elvis performed in a guest solo spot in Albuquerque, New Mexico, with Faron Young. The Albuquerque show was a disaster. Young treated Presley with contempt, and Bob Neal appeared more interested in getting autographs than in promoting Elvis' career. Following his appearance with Young, Elvis grew increasingly upset with Neal's management. Bill Black urged him to consider new options. The upcoming shows with Hank Snow, Black noted, would allow Elvis to see how Colonel Tom Parker organized and operated a package tour. Since Snow was a major country act, the tour would also test Elvis' ability to work a large, sophisticated country audience. Clearly, there was more to the situation than just the fabled machinations of the Svengali-like Colonel, sizing up Elvis

as a vehicle to making his fortune; young Presley was also considering the advantages of the Colonel's management. The stage was set for a business deal, and the Colonel and Elvis were about to join forces in one of the most legendary relationships in the history of the music business.

When Elvis caught up with the Hank Snow show on February 16, 1955, they were performing in Odessa, Texas. Elvis was brought in for two concerts. Snow had already completed a lengthy leg of the tour with dates in California, Arizona, New Mexico, and Colorado. His finely-tuned show included Jimmy Rodgers Snow, Charlene Arthur, and a comedian, the Duke of Paducah. Colonel Parker watched intently as Elvis excited the four thousand people in the audience. Following the show, the Colonel talked with Presley about his future. Tom Diskin, Colonel Parker's assistant, encouraged the Colonel to sign the youngster. (Diskin claims he was the first talent scout to spot Elvis in one of his 1954 Texas appearances.) Diskin informed the Colonel that Elvis had a special musical flair, and had been talking to the Colonel for months about Presley. For some reason, Parker, Diskin argues, was always hesitant about Elvis' appeal. A more plausible explanation is that the Colonel was not a hasty person when it came to signing new acts. Tom Parker not only listened carefully to Diskin, but also to Gabe Tucker and Tommy Sands. They all praised Elvis' music. For the Colonel, it was simply a matter of figuring out Presley's appeal—was it a long range one? Or was Elvis simply a local phenomenon destined to fade into obscurity?

Gabe Tucker, acting as a promotion man for Colonel Parker, had for years traveled a day ahead of the Eddy Arnold Show, plastering Parker's advertising all over the South. Apart from operating in the Colonel's shadow, Tucker himself dabbled with a number of musical instruments and wrote songs. In addition to playing the guitar, Tucker was adept with the bass and trumpet. He loved to jam with local musicians, and he was a marvelous promoter. Gabe Tucker and Colonel Tom Parker were so much alike that when they fought, they fought like brothers. Not only was Tucker a consummate hustler, but he was a regular in local pool halls. As a result, he had had ample opportunity to find out what the locals thought about Elvis Presley's music.

Tucker had been privy to the stresses and strains of the era when Colonel managed Eddy Arnold, and had negotiated a lucrative recording contract with RCA with the promise that Arnold would tour steadily. Colonel Parker, as noted in an earlier chapter, could never convince Arnold to tour as extensively as RCA and Arnold's music publisher, Hill and Range, would have preferred. Much of the trouble that Parker had with

Eddy Arnold stemmed from business disagreements. There is no evidence that Parker did not handle Arnold's interests honestly, but they ended their partnership due to a disagreement over business tactics. There was a snake-oil quality to Parker that Arnold disliked. The Colonel had a reputation for manipulating people for his own financial ends.

In January 1955, most people close to Colonel Parker believed that he had absolutely no interest in managing Elvis Presley. In truth, Parker was simply watching Presley's career unfold, mindful of his experiences with Eddy Arnold. Parker's inability to control Arnold had persuaded him that if he was to assume the role of personal manager again, he would demand that his next client—be it Elvis or someone else—never deviate from his instructions. Assuredly, there can be seen in all this an obsessive mania for total power. And while Gabe Tucker and Tommy Sands, strong Elvis boosters who believed Elvis had a bright show business future, certainly maintained Parker's interest, there can be little doubt that a businessman as astute as the Colonel approached the topic of managing someone like Elvis with anything less than a great degree of calculation and personal familiarity with Elvis' potential.

By the time Elvis completed the Hank Snow tour on February 18, 1955, in Monroe, Louisiana, he had delivered one of his strongest shows. The audience was younger, louder, and more responsive to the music. They asked for pictures of Elvis, but there were none to sell. Apart from the constant demand for his records, realized Tom Parker, a carnival-trained peddler, there was clearly an opportunity to sell pictures, trinkets, and junk merchandise at great profit. At the time, then, Parker viewed Elvis from the standpoint of a sideshow attraction, and probably had little understanding or appreciation for the exact nature of the appeal of Presley's music. The sound and substance of Elvis' act was a puzzlement, the results were quite clear, however—money could be made, and lots of it.

The stop in Monroe, Louisiana, is also pertinent in another way. Elvis had tried to break into show business in 1953 and 1954 by auditioning for a local Louisiana country music show. Richard Wilcox, sales manager at KWKA in Shreveport in 1953-54, remembers Elvis hanging around town looking for singing jobs. "The 'Hayride' bands would rehearse at the big studio," Wilcox told Dary Matera, "and Elvis would ride the bus from Memphis all night so he could watch them jam on Saturday mornings." This observation suggests how important music was to Elvis, and is another example of his obsessive-compulsive drive for success. It also suggests that the claims Matera and Lucy de Barbin made in their book *Are You Lonesome Tonight? The Un-*

told Story of Elvis Presley's One True Love—and the Child He Never Knew (1987), are again suspect. Elvis apparently didn't bother to search out de Barbin while he was actually in Monroe on this occasion; she doesn't even discuss the stop in her book. If she had been Elvis' secret love at this time, surely the Monroe concert would have had special enough meaning to be worth mentioning.

Elvis Breaks Outside of the South

On February 19, 1955, *Billboard* reported that Elvis' Eldorado, Arkansas, show had been a great success, something unusual, as it was not common for the magazine to report on small-town country concerts. *Billboard* also noted that Elvis was still a regular on the "Louisiana Hayride," and that his appearances had become the most popular part of the show.

Following his most recent regular Saturday night show on the "Hayride," Elvis had driven directly to Hope, Arkansas. There, on Tuesday, February 22, 1955, he appeared with Mother Maybelle and the Carter Sisters. That night Elvis faced an extremely tough country audience, composed largely of country purists. Nevertheless, Elvis charmed the crowd with renditions of "Uncle Pen" and "Old Shep." The next stop, Bastrop, Louisiana, was a small town with another country audience. Younger and more energetic, this time the crowd demanded "That's All Right (Mama)." The Bastrop audience responded so strongly that it was obvious that they had listened to the "Louisiana Hayride" broadcast, where Elvis had been the most applauded act.

After the Bastrop show, Elvis received a phone call from Horace Logan informing him that his next appearance on the "Louisiana Hayride" would be televised. Elvis had the luxury of a few days off between the Bastrop appearance and the televised "Hayride" show, so he worked on his stage mannerisms and consulted extensively with Sam Phillips about the type of songs to perform on live TV. As Elvis, Scotty, Bill, and D.J. drove to Shreveport, they were excited about appearing before a television audience. There is no doubt that TV was a major factor in success in the music world. There would be television scouts from the major network shows watching Elvis.

Following broadcast of the televised version of "Louisiana Hayride," Elvis set off on a five-day tour of Tennessee, Arkansas, Mississippi, Louisiana, and Missouri. In all of this, there were signs that Elvis' music was no longer a Southern phenomenon. Jukeboxes were now carrying Elvis' records in Northern cities, and his record sales were growing slowly, but steadily, in these areas.

The first major indication that Presley's popularity was spreading north occurred during a Circle Theater Jamboree concert in Cleveland, Ohio. Although he was scheduled to appear on the "Louisiana Hayride," Elvis was instructed by Bob Neal to fly to Cleveland for a country music jamboree. On Saturday, February 26, 1955, Elvis was one of many country acts in an 8:00 to 11:00 p.m. show. The show featured Faron Young, the Wilburn Brothers, the York Brothers, and Justin Tubb. The concert broadcast over WERE at last brought Elvis' music to a new radio audience. As a result, there were inquiries made to Sam Phillips from northern one-stop record distributors about the availability of Elvis' records. Places like Al Smith's Record Bar in South Bend, Indiana, ordered Presley's records and advertised them extensively. This mail-order house listed Presley's "Milkcow Boogie," the store's name for "Milkcow Blues Boogie" as one of their ten best-selling songs. In Hammond, Indiana, Elvis records were sold in a small shop as a result of the owner's trip to Louisiana. Having caught Elvis on the "Hayride," he had eagerly brought back early Presley releases to put on sale in his record/repair shop.

The March 1955 issue of *Country And Western Jamboree* was the first national magazine to recognize Presley's Sun records in a big way. This Chicago-based magazine featured a photo of Elvis, seated, with Sam Phillips and Bob Neal flanking him. *Country And Western Jamboree* had polled more than five hundred disc jockeys to analyze Presley's popularity. "Milkcow Blues Boogie" was featured in the magazine's "Movin' Ahead" section, and "I Don't Care If The Sun Don't Shine" was a top ten pick. The magazine also mentioned the first two Sun releases, and praised Presley's performing style.

There was an immediate impact from *Country And Western Jamboree*, as well as from an article in *Cowboy Songs*. Soon, Bob Neal's office was flooded with requests for concert fees and a future booking schedule. Sun Records sent promotional literature to disc jockeys in Ohio, New York, Pennsylvania, and the District of Columbia. There was a general curiosity about Elvis' music and, as a result of this interest, a Washington, DC, radio station contacted Bob Neal about an interview. Although there was still no firm indication that bookings outside the South were readily available, Neal was ecstatic over the prospect of media coverage in the North.

The "Town and Country Jubilee" in Washington, DC, flew Elvis in for the interview. During this radio talk with country singer Jimmie Dean, Elvis discussed rockabilly music with his host. The show, broadcast over WMAL-TV on Monday, March 14, 1955, at 5:30, provided important insights into Elvis' musical roots. There

was enough interest in Presley's future to attract New York television producers. After the show, Elvis took a train to New York and auditioned for the "Arthur Godfrey Talent Scouts" TV show.

The Arthur Godfrey talent coordinators were not accustomed to spending much time with new acts. They watched Elvis perform and quickly rejected him. Nervous and erratic, Elvis had made an unfavorable impression. Godfrey's talent coordinator told Presley that he was just not suited for national television. Much like the initial response at "Grand Ole Opry," Godfrey's program director made fun of Elvis' music. The executives who auditioned new acts were heavily influenced by Frank Sinatra, Perry Como, Nat King Cole, and Frankie Laine. If a singer didn't have the vocal affectations and stylings of pop crooners like these, it was difficult to secure a spot on the Godfrey show.

After the tiring week in Washington and New York, Elvis flew to Houston, Texas. On Saturday night, March 19, 1955, he appeared at the Eagle's Hall with the Grand Prize jamboree. Tommy Sands was the opening act, and, in recalling how Elvis performed, Sands felt that he appeared to have something to prove. "I could see a drive in Elvis that most of us didn't have," Sands remembered. "He knew what he wanted and went after it." Elvis pulled out all the stops, and the audience loved the show.

Management Problems

Unbeknownst to Elvis, an invitation from Colonel Tom Parker to join the Hank Snow Jamboree as a regular was just a couple of months away, but, in the confusion surrounding his future, Elvis reluctantly agreed to sign another contract with Bob Neal. There was a profitable concert market opening to Elvis, so it was financially expedient to buy out some of his appearances on the "Louisiana Hayride" to ensure his availability. It cost Elvis $400 a month to be freed from his regular Saturday night "Hayride" appearances, but the expense gave him the option of accepting more lucrative dates. Elvis was now approaching a concert market that guaranteed $500 to $750 a night, and there were plenty of good bookings available at that price. Despite a friendly agreement which freed him from the "Hayride," Elvis told Horace Logan that he still wanted to appear from time to time. Logan realized that Elvis had roots in the "Hayride," and he urged the youngster to come onto the show whenever possible.

In April 1955, *Billboard* reported that Elvis was booked solid. Few people knew that Elvis was unhappy with most of these bookings; many of the contracts had been accepted months before his meteoric success, and were held in cramped high school gyms or at honky-tonk clubs. Bob Neal—and Colonel Parker, who was still advising Neal—realized that the honky-tonk bars were actually excellent venues, because Elvis received the door from these shows. The Colonel's involvement resulted in the demand that the bars clear the place midway in the evening, then turn around and charge another entertainment fee for the second half of the evening, often resulting in gates of more than $1,000 a night. Still, it was sometimes difficult to collect the gate from those who sponsored these concerts, slick promoters who often vanished with the gate receipts. After spending a night performing in a smoke-filled room, Elvis hated to have to fight for his money, another aspect to many of the bookings that made them less than appealing.

Elvis in concert.

Then, too, such concerts were often unpredictable. At times Elvis drew small crowds due to inadequate promotion, while other nights people stood in line outside the hall. A good example of a small crowd occurred on Friday, April 1, 1955, when only 850 showed up in Odessa, Texas. The promoter failed to adequately advertise the concert, and it was a long, dull evening. Elvis was depressed. During the show, he performed with Floyd Cramer. They played country tunes. Most country artists didn't use drums, and the tradition-minded country crowd was curious about D.J. Fontana, whom Elvis had brought along. After the performance, Elvis once again reasoned that perhaps Bob Neal was not the right person to guide his career. Whenever Elvis felt depressed, he drove to the "Louisiana Hayride" to spend some time with his musical friends, so, by April 9, 1955, Elvis was back in Shreveport even though Bob Neal had bought the dates out. Elvis continued to appear on the show without pay, and members of the "Hayride" remember that Neal and Elvis fought about his future. It was now clear to many that Neal's inexperience was hurting Elvis. Sam Phillips, for his part, wor-

ried that Elvis' management problems might affect his concert appearances, which would in turn hurt his record sales.

Elvis headlined the "Big D Jamboree" in Dallas on April 16, 1955, appearing with Sonny James, Hank Locklin, and Charlene Arthur, among others, drawing the longest and loudest applause during his set. The Elvis Presley Fan Club was at the concert, holding up signs with Elvis' name printed with lipstick. The squeals and screams from the predominantly female audience made it difficult to hear the music.

The following Saturday, April 23, the "Louisiana Hayride" broadcasted a remote show from the Heart O' Texas Coliseum in Waco, and a crowd of five thousand filled the cavernous hall. While other performers watched in awe from backstage, the crowd was on its feet throughout Elvis' part of the show, screaming out the titles of their favorite Elvis rockabilly songs.

Previously, on April 25, Sam Phillips had released Elvis' fourth single, "Baby Let's Play House" backed with "I'm Left, You're Right, She's Gone." Phillips also launched an energetic promotional campaign to popularize the record. So quickly did it become a regional hit that when Elvis appeared on the April 30, 1955, "Louisiana Hayride," the single's b-side, "I'm Left, You're Right, She's Gone," was featured in the show. This concert was broadcast from Gladewater, Texas, where another small Elvis fan club made its home. As a result, he gave a rousing performance, and got a rousing welcome. When Stan Kesler heard about the crowd's reaction, he was tickled that one of his songs had gone over so well. Kesler, who wrote "I'm Left, You're Right, She's Gone," had convinced Sam Phillips to release the country-influenced version of his song, which Elvis had originally recorded in a blues vein, because he, Kesler, believed that the country styling was more commercial. It was. Kesler was also the one who urged Phillips to have Elvis debut the song on the "Louisiana Hayride," where the live crowd and the radio broadcast would lead to heavy record sales. The "Hayride" audience, Kesler argued, would prefer a country song, and other country stations would soon pick it up. Kesler was right again, as the tune showed up on playlists across Texas, Louisiana, and Arkansas.

Elvis, who had originally planned to debut "Milkcow Blues Boogie" on the Gladewater edition of the "Hayride," had had car trouble on the way to the show, and when he arrived his band was missing. Scotty and Bill had played another Texas date with Tommy Sands, and due to their own car trouble they also hadn't arrived at the arena. As a result, Elvis was backed by Ray Price's band, the Cherokee Cowboys. When Price suggested that his band didn't feel comfortable with

Elvis' music, Presley exploded, asking them if they had listened to any of his songs. The argument had more to do with Price's ego than with his band's musical interests. In the end, to Elvis' surprise, the Cherokee Cowboys provided excellent backing after he practiced "I'm Left, You're Right, She's Gone" with the band. When Presley announced that he would perform LaVern Baker's recent rhythm and blues hit, "Tweedle Dee," the band immediately broke into it. A country version of the song by Bonnie Lou was one of Ray Price's favorite tunes, and the Cherokee Cowboys played it superbly. James Clayton Day's steel guitar echoed throughout the auditorium as the Cowboys added a wild country twist to this rhythm and blues hit.

After the Gladewater show, Elvis talked at length with James Clayton Day about music. Not only was Elvis surprised about Day's broad musical knowledge, but he was intrigued by Price's flirtation with rockabilly records. Day, in turn, was impressed with Elvis' familiarity with the new music. There was also a great deal of talk about country music shows. Elvis discussed the "Midway Jamboree Show" in Gaston, Alabama, and laughed about his attempt to get on the show. Elvis didn't elaborate, and Day didn't inquire further. Then Elvis remarked how lucky he was to be a "Hayride" regular.

James Clayton Day wasn't the only one interested in young Presley. The Cherokee Cowboys as a group were intrigued by Elvis' musical interests. When Elvis talked about Little Walter's "My Babe" and Pat Boone's cover version of the Clovers' "Two Hearts," the Cowboys got a true picture of the extent of Presley's devotion to music. Elvis had discovered Little Walter in 1954 while going through a stack of records in Ruben Cherry's House of Records, and, in April 1955, Boone's tune was high on charts.

The period from January through April 1955 was transitional for Elvis. His career was attracting national attention. When Elvis' fourth single "Baby Let's Play House"/"I'm Left, You're Right, She's Gone" was released on April 25, 1955, it became the first Sun single distributed in the Northern and Western record markets. Sam Phillips pressed two thousand copies at Monarch Records in Los Angeles, and they were wholesaled in California, Oregon, and Washington.

The most significant change in Elvis' career was his increased concert activity. Every day new promoters were contacting Bob Neal or Sam Phillips about Elvis, and there was less and less haggling over money. Elvis was on his way to becoming a mainstream rock and roll act.

During this period, Elvis, himself a product of divergent influences, was already influencing a number of fledgling musicians. They watched him, liked his style, and got into the music business as a result of what they saw. In March 1955, Al Ferrier, a Louisiana rockabilly singer, cut his classic tune "No No Baby." In a session at Eddie Shuler's Goldband Studio in Lake Charles, Louisiana, Ferrier created a rockabilly sound which was very similar to what Elvis was recording. To promote the record, Ferrier was booked on the "Louisiana Hayride."

As a result of Ferrier's appearance on the "Hayride," he met and spent a lot of time talking to Elvis about music. After hearing Ferrier perform "Let's Go Boppin' Tonight," Elvis asked Ferrier if he could record it. "Send the song to Sam Phillips," Elvis allegedly remarked to Ferrier. After thinking it over, though, Ferrier kept the tune for himself. He reasoned that he might just as well turn it into a hit for himself. "That's one bad mistake I made by not letting Elvis record it," Ferrier later told Johannes Sipkema, Jr. During 1955 and 1956, Ferrier and his band toured constantly and recorded a number of songs in the Presley style. While he wasn't successful beyond the South, Ferrier is a prime example of the breadth of Presley's musical influence during the Sun years.

Within the same time frame, it was clearly Sam Phillips who prepared Elvis for stardom. By cultivating white musical tastes and developing an encyclopedic knowledge of black music, Phillips provided the intellectual and musical grist for Elvis Presley's act. The black blues music of the Delta was the backbone of rock and roll, but this sound had been around in one form or another since 1897 when a white bandleader, William Krell, published "Mississippi Rag" in Chicago. It was not until Sam Phillips founded the Sun Records company that Memphis was able to enjoy a local black music sound performed by white singers. The rise of rock and roll music was a complex phenomenon, but there is no doubt that Phillips and Sun Records established the regional popularity of Presley's rockabilly sound in the early months of 1955. Had it not been for Phillips' obsessive-compulsive desire to help build Elvis' musical reputation, the brand of Southern rock known as rockabilly would have had to wait a few more years for a national audience.

The tragedy during the January through April 1955 period was that Sam Phillips discovered that his success with one act made it difficult to run Sun Records. He devoted more time to Presley, and this led to a temporary decline in the marketing of other acts. Even as Elvis Presley's music traveled successfully up the Mississippi to Chicago, Detroit, and east to Cleveland, New York, and Philadelphia, Sam Phillips was forced to wrestle with the new challenges that grew out of these opportunities.

CHAPTER 11

Sun Mania,
May-August 1955

From May through August 1955, Elvis Presley's career continued to prosper in the Southern market. In July, Elvis' "Baby Let's Play House" and "I'm Left, You're Right, She's Gone" appeared on the *Billboard* Country and Western singles chart. As a result, Sun Records was deluged with requests for interviews by national magazines. The national news services and major television networks were monitoring Elvis, and this helped his career grow from a regional base into national prominence. To *Billboard* readers, of course, Elvis' name was already a familiar one because the music industry's bible had been closely following his career for some time.

The Colonel Makes His Move

Most significantly, Colonel Tom Parker made his first serious overture about a management contract in May 1955. The Colonel, too, had been reading *Billboard*, monitoring Presley's publicity, and inquiring quietly about his Sun record sales. The Colonel had discovered that a number of rackjobbers outside of the South were ordering Presley's records. Once Parker talked with the wholesalers, he realized that *Billboard*'s publicity was only one reason for the interest in Presley's Sun records. Most of the rackjobbers didn't keep up with new music. Waiting diligently for the next Frank Sinatra record, they paid little attention to new country, blues, or rock music releases. They were ordering Elvis' records, however, and they were ordering due to *demand*. Parker's assistant, Gabe Tucker, was assigned the job of analyzing Presley's sales, and he wrote many memos to the Colonel elaborately sketching out the breakdown of Presley's appeal.

As the Colonel's chief advance man, Tucker urged Parker to take a closer look at Elvis. Tucker, who had played guitar with Elvis one night during a "Big D Jamboree" show in Dallas, recalled how popular Presley was throughout Texas. Rockabilly singer Tommy Sands also continued to urge Parker to sign Presley. "I told the Colonel that Elvis was a super performer at least a hundred times," Sands remarked. "He had something that the rest of us lacked; I don't know what it was but he had it." Bob Luman echoed the same belief. "Elvis was ahead of the rest of us. He sure had a stage presence." Luman, who later had success as a country singer, remembered how wildly "Louisiana Hayride" crowds had reacted to Elvis.

There was still a major problem, however. Colonel Parker was faced with the prospect of having to buy out Bob Neal's share of Elvis' management contract. The Colonel had other ideas. Instead, he used his considerable country charm to convince Neal that Elvis needed management help. In May 1955, Parker drove to Memphis and talked with Bob Neal about Elvis' future. He also took time to visit Vernon and Gladys Presley. Jim Denson, a close friend of the Presleys, observed that "the Colonel had a hypnotic impact upon Vernon."

The Colonel spent most of his time with the Presley family for a reason. Parker realized that Vernon, a small-time hustler with big ambitions, could be easily impressed. The Colonel pointed to his own Christian roots and down-home Southern attitudes (Vernon and Gladys had no way of knowing that Colonel Tom Parker was an illegal alien from Holland), showboating a manner and style that befit successful businessman. The Colonel's large cowboy hat, flashy clothes, and cigar-chomping personality accentuated the image of the skilled country music manager. He was more down-home than anyone Vernon had talked to in his life. It was a wonderful charade, and Vernon fell for it.

By late May 1955, Colonel Parker had proposed a management contract to Elvis. He pointed out that Bob Neal was too inexperienced to promote Elvis nationally, and that he and Neal had been booking Elvis in kind of a quasi-partnership for some time anyway. "Colonel Parker was like a whirlwind, he never stopped," Tommy Sands remarked. "Bob Neal was slow, plodding, and careful," Ronald Smith stated. It was obvious to contemporary observers that Parker and Neal couldn't work together. "Everyone wanted the Colonel to manage them, including Elvis," Sands pointed out.

Sam Phillips was the only person who might have given Elvis some good advice, but he was too busy trying to sell Elvis' recording contract to a major label. Phillips already had a replacement in mind for Presley. Carl Perkins was in the Sun studio, and Phillips reasoned that Perkins could duplicate Presley's success. Not only were Perkins' roots similar, but he was a guitar virtuoso who inspired local crowds.

In January 1955, Phillips brought Perkins into the Sun studio and cut two songs: "Movie Magg" and "Turn Around." These tunes began Phillips' careful plan to nurture Perkins in the rockabilly market. As a result of Perkins' sound, Phillips used the same strategy that he had employed in developing Elvis' career. Memphis disc jockey Dick Stewart, known as Stuart Pinkham at KWEM, played Perkins' records, hyped his music, and eventually became Perkins' manager. Most of the other Memphis dj's also played "Movie Magg" and "Turn Around," and this went a long way towards convincing Phillips that Perkins could become as popular as Elvis. It made sense to cash in on the big money available for Presley's recordings, sell his contract, and reinvest the proceeds in a "new Elvis."

Sam Phillips talked with Bob Neal about Carl Perkins as Presley's replacement, and they quietly began lining up bookings to break Perkins into the country-rockabilly market. Phillips prepared an elaborate contract for Perkins with Stars, Inc., the management agency co-owned by Phillips and Neal. They hoped to place a Perkins' record on the *Billboard* Hot 100, and, in March-April 1956, this dream was achieved when Perkins' rendition of "Blue Suede Shoes" topped the national charts. Only a tragic automobile accident prevented Perkins from continued success.

Atlantic Records

As soon as Sam Phillips made clear his plans to find a replacement for Elvis Presley, major record labels began inquiries about Elvis' availability. Atlantic Records was the first major label to attempt to purchase Presley's contract. Ahmet Ertegun, the owner of Atlantic, offered Sun $25,000. Atlantic was a strong and productive rhythm and blues label, and Jerry Wexler, the label's legendary producer, believed its writers, arrangers, and studio musicians could add a great deal to Elvis' music. Not only did Ertegun have a plan for Presley, but he communicated these ideas to Sam Phillips. At this point, Phillips and Colonel Parker put their heads together. Phillips could sell Elvis' master tapes for a hefty sum, and Parker could negotiate a lucrative recording contract. Their assessment rested on Ahmet Ertegun's clear belief that Elvis was only a step away from mainstream musical success. As Phillips and Parker talked with Ertegun, they realized that the Atlantic Records chief was uniquely qualified to handle Presley's future.

Ever since Ertegun founded Atlantic Records in 1947 with his older brother Nesuhi and partner Herb Abramson, he had recorded some of the best rhythm and blues and rock and roll records in America. The label began unobtrusively when Ertegun sold a portion of his collection of more than 15,000 jazz and blues 78s to finance the operation. He at first used the money to record his favorite jazz musicians, but Atlantic Records quickly moved into the rhythm and blues field. Not only was Ertegun recognized as an exceptional mu-

sicologist, he specialized in the discovery and development of new musical talent.

In 1949, Ahmet took a trip through the South, and signed a songwriter-musical arranger, Jesse Stone, to a production contract. Stone, a close friend of Ertegun's partner Herb Abramson, had worked with National Records in New York, and Abramson convinced Ertegun of Stone's unique production talents. Stone already had a lengthy career in the music business. In 1926, his first band, Jesse Stone and His Blue Serenaders, began touring from their St. Louis, Missouri, base. In April 1927, Okeh Records released Stone's "Starvation Blues," and this began a recording career that moved into big band music. In the 1930s, Duke Ellington heard Stone's band and booked them into New York's Cotton Club. For the next fifteen years, Stone helped to lay the foundation for the blues and r and b musical explosion of the late 1940s and early 1950s. Ahmet Ertegun once remarked to British rock historian Charlie Gillett that "Jesse Stone did more to develop the basic rock and roll sound than anybody else."

In the early fifties, Jesse Stone wrote and arranged such Atlantic hits as the Drifters' "Money Honey," Ray Charles' "It Should Have Been Me," and Big Joe Turner's "Shake, Rattle and Roll." In late 1954, Stone heard Presley's "That's All Right (Mama)" and alerted Ertegun to Elvis' music. When Arnold Shaw and Bill Randle mentioned Presley's name to Ertegun, he remembered Jesse Stone's positive comments. It was not long before Ertegun was talking to Sam Phillips about Presley's contract. As Ertegun negotiated with Phillips, he had Jesse Stone in mind to arrange and produce Elvis' recording sessions. Had Atlantic Records signed Presley, Jesse Stone's genius would have provided Elvis with the backing he needed to push his personal talents far beyond RCA's limited vision.

In May 1955, eager to purchase Elvis' contract, Atlantic executives arrived in Memphis to take a final look at Presley. Ahmet Ertegun brought along a new writer and producer—Jerry Wexler. They visited Dewey Phillips' "Red, Hot and Blue" radio show with the idea of using Phillips' knowledge and influence to soften up Sam Phillips. By moving quickly and quietly, Ertegun hoped he could sign Elvis before the other major labels got wind of his intentions. But Ertegun was unprepared to deal with Dewey Phillips' maniacal behavior. When Ertegun and his entourage arrived at the "Red, Hot and Blue" show, they immediately noticed that Dewey Phillips was drunk. Phillips coughed and staggered around the studio. A burst of obscenities punctuated his speech, and he never sat down. When Ertegun and Wexler walked into the WHBQ studio at the Old Chisca Hotel, they couldn't believe Phillips was the on-the-air personality. To amuse himself, Phillips did push-ups on top of a picture of Marilyn Monroe taped to the studio floor.

Once he went on the air, it was sheer horror. With Ahmet Ertegun and Jerry Wexler standing next to him, Phillips growled to his audience: "I got these two crooks here from New York City, from Atlantic Records." Jerry Wexler stood up with a shocked look on his face as Phillips bellowed: "How you doin' all you Memphis chicks...and motherfuckers?" All Phillips could talk about was drinking and girls. Fortunately, after taking a big swig from a whiskey bottle, Phillips closed the mike.

"After the show, he took us down to a bar to meet Elvis in a little after-hours club next to the 'Home of the Blues,' Ruben Cherry's record store," Ertegun later recalled. Naturally, Elvis wasn't in the bar. Suddenly Dewey Phillips announced that he had seven or eight great-looking girls coming for a party. When a group of girls in high heels who looked to be fourteen to sixteen years old walked in awkwardly, Jerry Wexler turned red and mumbled that he was tired. Dewey Phillips would accept no excuses, and at three in the morning the group found itself in the Memphis State University gym watching the varsity basketball team practicing for a game in New York's Madison Square Garden.

It was not Sam Phillips' fault that Atlantic didn't purchase Elvis' contract. The night with Dewey Phillips drove Ertegun and Wexler right out of Memphis. Prone to bizarre behavior and eccentric attitudes, Dewey had treated the Atlantic people so poorly that they lost interest in Elvis. Dewey Phillips was the reason that Atlantic Records was unable to sign Elvis Presley to a recording contract. Even so, this well-publicized trip spurred interest within the music industry about the Sun Records sound. It was not just Elvis that the major labels were interested in; soon, talent scouts were looking for other rockabilly singers as well.

Hank Snow's All Star Jamboree

There was still the question of Elvis' long-term viability. Before he signed Presley to a personal services contract, Colonel Tom Parker wanted to watch him perform over the length of one more tour. Although Parker had been working with Elvis' manager Bob Neal, the Colonel wasn't yet ready to commit himself to a full-time management deal. Since Parker already managed Hank Snow, the easiest solution was to simply book Presley on Snow's upcoming tour.

At his headquarters in Madison, Tennessee, Parker invited Snow to his office. They talked a few moments about mundane things, and then Parker blurted out: "There's a boy around, Elvis Presley, and I think we should book him on the show with you. I think he'd

Colonel Parker, Elvis, Bob Neal and Hank Snow.

make us some money. The kids really like him."

"Be sure he behaves himself," Snow remarked. "I have thousands of loyal fans who I owe my best."

Snow didn't realize that the Colonel had hoodwinked him—he was less interested in enhancing the draw for Snow's tour than he was in the prospects for cementing a management deal with Elvis, whom he felt had great potential. While on the three-week tour, Elvis appeared before large crowds and demonstrated conclusively that he could compete with seasoned, professional musicians. It was impossible for another artist to follow him on stage. After the second night, Colonel Parker wisely switched Elvis to the closing act, a move which infuriated Snow. The Colonel also began to feature Presley's name prominently in the publicity releases for the tour.

"You must be crazy," Snow screamed at Colonel Parker. "This is my show and I am the star. I've been meaning to talk to you about that kid, anyway." What Hank Snow failed to appreciate was that Elvis was definitely a hot performer. "I don't even think we should be using him, jumping around like he does, shaking his butt around," Snow protested. Colonel Parker laughed, and assiduously ignored Snow's comments.

The Hank Snow tour performances proved a number of points to Colonel Parker. Most significant was that Elvis could be an appealing musical act *nightly*. The rigorous tour covered twenty-one concert dates, and the thirty-one performers included luminaries like Jimmy Rodgers Snow, the Wilburn Brothers, the Davis Sisters, Slim Whitman, and Hank Snow. At selected concert sites, Faron Young, Martha Carson, and Onie Wheeler also appeared as guest artists. Elvis still drew more applause than any performer on the tour.

Elvis was intrigued with Tom Parker, and asked his bass player Bill Black about the Colonel. Black was skeptical about the Parker's management skills. Recognizing that Parker was stingy with money, Black warned Elvis that money problems could easily result from the wrong kind of contract—he had heard horror stories about Eddy Arnold's unhappiness with Parker. A gentle, quiet man, Black warned Elvis to no avail; Presley was impressed with Parker. After four days on the road with the Jamboree, Elvis began talking about how well-planned he thought the tour was. "I think the Colonel has a special feeling for the crowds," Elvis commented. "No one can sell autographed pictures like him." Indeed, the carnival atmosphere surrounding the All Star Jamboree was evident during the long intermission between the two segments of the show—an intermission that lasted longer than the performances. Colonel Parker had set up the extravaganza to separate the locals from as much money as possible, and there were continual references to the souvenirs available for purchase. "He's too slick," Black intoned. Bill Black had been in the music business a decade longer than Elvis, and was uneasy about quick-buck promoters. "Be careful, Elvis, this business is a rough one," Black warned.

When the show stopped in Daytona Beach, Florida, Elvis picked up the May 7, 1955, issue of *Billboard*, and read that Arnold Shaw had just been named general professional manager of the Edward B. Marks Corporation, one of New York's major booking agents. As Elvis' first booster in New York, Shaw was to become an important ally. Sam Phillips had talked to Elvis about Arnold Shaw's intimate knowledge of the rock music business. He let Presley know that Shaw could help his career. Neither Elvis nor Sam Phillips had yet met Shaw, but Sam hoped to play Elvis' music for Shaw during the New Yorker's upcoming visit to Memphis. Phillips desperately needed the opinion of a well-known, respected New York agent if he was to sell Elvis' recording contract. In addition to being a booking specialist, Shaw was an honest critic and a friend of the new rock music. Shaw would not visit Memphis until late in the summer of 1955, but Phillips was in constant touch with him. Elvis' music was known in New York by May 1955, and there was already an undercurrent of interest in his recording future among the major record labels.

The Colonel is Convinced

As RCA, Columbia, Decca, Mercury, Capitol, and Atlantic Records grew familiar with Elvis' music, Colonel Parker was busy molding his future protege into a mainstream musical act. The Colonel was impressed with Sam Phillips' regional success in merchandising Elvis' records. Not only were the Sun discs selling well, but they were purchased by a diverse mix of white country fans, young rhythm and blues devotees, and black people.

As a result of Elvis' unique pattern of record sales, Parker paid more attention to the concert audiences, and the way the fans reacted to Elvis' music. During his years in the country music field, Parker had always been intrigued by the changes in audiences. He recognized that Elvis was a unique act, and during the Hank Snow tour he decided that Elvis' special performing qualities, including his sex appeal and swaggering musical gyrations, were the outlandish key to his exceptional appeal. Parker had an old-fashioned sense of burlesque, and he urged Elvis to exploit his stage mannerisms, suggesting that Elvis add even more energy to his stage show.

Just the kind of on-stage antics that the Colonel —and Elvis' fans—loved to see.

There were a number of concerts that finally convinced the Colonel of Elvis' commercial potential. One of Elvis' earliest successes occurred on May 10, 1955, when a young crowd of almost three thousand attended a concert in Ocala, Florida. The females in the audience squirmed and squealed, and the loud applause for Elvis again outstripped the reception for Hank Snow, the Wilburn Brothers, and Faron Young.

The Colonel had printed up large quantities of hats and pillows to sell to the throngs, and the young crowd spent huge sums of money on Parker's plastic souvenirs. The newspaper and radio people received pillows with the "Hank Snow All Star Jamboree" printed in garish red. Through intensive advertising in local newspapers and with live spots on radio stations, Parker had succeeded in creating a raucous carnival atmosphere. There were a number of acts to publicize and the Colonel urged the media to spotlight the best of them, but it was not accidental that Parker placed Elvis in the closing spot on each show. He also blitzed the press with publicity handouts about Presley. No one was surprised when Elvis garnered more media attention than Hank Snow. Clearly, the Colonel was up to something. Although Parker was playing favorites, something which created tension between the performers, neither Presley nor Snow were curt to each other. Hank Snow was a professional entertainer, and he realized that Elvis was appealing to a whole different audience.

On Friday, May 13, 1955, whatever doubts Colonel Parker may have possessed were eased when the Jamboree played in a baseball park in Jacksonville, Florida. A capacity crowd of fourteen thousand fans cheered so loudly for Elvis that no one could hear his songs. In an hour, all of Parker's schlocky trinkets were sold out. The crowd took advantage of the freedom of movement afforded by the layout of the baseball stadium, and darted through security guards in search of Elvis. The Colonel watched the scene with amusement. There was no danger to Elvis or the other entertainers; a large crowd of young girls simply wanted to see their idol. Suddenly, Colonel Parker had an inspiration. He would concoct stories of a riot—or at least a disturbance! The press, hungry for news about Elvis, dutifully reported that the fans' actions had grown to excess. Actually, reported a certain young man named Johnny Tillotson, who was in the stadium dugout waiting to interview Elvis, the crowd "was well behaved but playful. There was no danger to anyone." What Tillotson remembers is an appreciative crowd who had found a new sound. Tillotson noted, however, that—with the Colonel's blessing—"The press couldn't wait to report that Elvis was causing riots."

There were some minor events that made the otherwise relatively tame "riot" into national news, however. The Jacksonville crowd wrote phone numbers and messages in lipstick on the side of Elvis' Lincoln Continental. There were scratches on the paint, and large lipstick and nail polish drawings all over the beautiful new pink car. Elvis was upset. His car was a status symbol. Colonel Parker laughed and told Elvis that crowds like that would enable him to buy two or three new luxury cars. That night, a large number of fans showed up at Elvis' motel and stormed the parking lot. Elvis came to his motel room window and took his shirt off for the adoring crowd. Five Memphis friends traveling

with Elvis were swept up in the ribald atmosphere. There was gold in this type of pandemonium, and Tom Parker reassured Elvis that the screaming, panting teenage girls were his ticket to stardom, a stardom that was now clearly rushing towards Elvis.

After the Jacksonville concert, record sales increased even more dramatically. Earlier, Sam Phillips had persuaded a Florida one-stop record distributor to handle all of Elvis' Sun releases, and the distributor heavily influenced local radio play. For the preceding six months, Elvis' music had played daily on key Florida radio stations, prompting the strong demand for Presley concerts. Black rhythm and blues stations that played the new rock and roll discovered that their listeners were turning to white stations playing Presley's music. As a result, black radio stations in Florida added Elvis to their playlists. There were no longer any doubts; Colonel Parker decided to sign Elvis to a management contract as quickly as he could.

There was a potential problem, however. Because Hank Snow and Colonel Parker were still partners, Parker had to offer Snow a chance to share in the Presley management deal. Snow, a shrewd businessman, had built his following upon an image of purity and intelligence. He neither drank nor smoked publicly. A small man at five feet, four inches tall, Snow had a Napoleonic complex, a short person's self-doubt coupled with a power mania that prompted him to strut around in custom tailored suits and shoes in an attempt to create the illusion of being taller than he was. Tom Parker knew that the thing to do was to bluff the insecure Snow.

"Hank," the Colonel said, "tell you what let's do. You put everything you make and I'll put everything I make and we'll sign up this boy's contract and we'll manage him." Looking with disbelief at the Colonel, Snow refused the ludicrous suggestion, freeing the Colonel to sign Elvis to Hank Snow Attractions himself, and to cement a personal arrangement with Elvis that essentially excluded Snow from sharing in the results. As their negotiations had been carried out quietly, very few people were aware of just how close Colonel Tom Parker was to managing Elvis Presley.

By the time the Hank Snow Jamboree appeared at the Mosque Theater in Richmond, Virginia, on May 16, 1955, there was a great deal of internal conflict centering around Elvis' popularity. Scotty Moore and Bill Black were fighting with one another, and harsh words were exchanged between Colonel Parker and Hank Snow. It was obvious that everyone needed a rest.

After a day of sightseeing, Presley and his band were scheduled to appear in nearby Roanoke, Virginia. On May 18, 1955, Elvis spent the day walking around town before he performed in 7:00 and 9:00 o'clock shows at Roanoke's American Legion auditorium. The performers were booked into the Hotel Roanoke, across the street from the auditorium. Since there was plenty of free time, Elvis went downtown to the Roanoke Record Shop at 116 W. Church Avenue to search for some rhythm and blues records. Mrs. Viola Bess, owner of the shop, had been the one who had booked the Roanoke concert, and she was working in the store when Elvis arrived. They talked at length about his music, and Elvis made it clear that he depended upon the new black sounds to supplement his musical act. After searching through the store's record bins, Elvis walked back to the Hotel Roanoke for lunch.

The serious side of Elvis' personality became very evident to those who met him in Roanoke. Before the first show, he sat backstage on a small chair and chatted with two local reporters and a half dozen disc jockeys. One of them, King Edward, a local radio personality on WSLC, described Elvis as "a comic." King Edward was very polite, but clearly viewed Elvis as a nice kid who had a lot to learn. Although, like many Southern djs, King Edward didn't realize the full potential of Elvis' innovative musical style, he did remember that Elvis' was very serious about his music and his performances. Feeling that the country-western market was just too restrictive, Elvis made it clear that he believed that he couldn't continue to work in it, and that his records had to appeal to a wider audience. Since Elvis was very deliberate about plotting his future musical

career, it was not surprising that he asked for advice. "He'd often take the time to ask other artists if they liked what he was doing," King Edward noted, "or if they thought he looked silly."

Not only was Elvis concerned about his stage appearance, but he was continually re-examining his repertoire. Alvin Hudson, an officer with the Roanoke police, also chatted with Elvis for a long time. Since Presley closed the show, he had a lot of time to talk with Hudson. When Elvis went on stage, Hudson was astonished by the crowd's reaction. "Elvis sang only a couple of songs—'Blue Moon of Kentucky' was one. People rushed from their seats and stormed onstage," Hudson remembered. The reception was an indication that Elvis was right, that it would be very difficult for him to remain with the rather staid country music tours, especially considering the conflicts that lay just below the surface on the present one.

Two days after the Roanoke appearance, Elvis closed out the Hank Snow Jamboree tour in Chattanooga, Tennessee. The normally sedate local audience howled from the beginning to the end of Elvis' portion of the show. Colonel Parker, who was making final preparations to sign Elvis to a management contract, began designing new Elvis merchandise.

Post-Jamboree Appearances

Once the Hank Snow Jamboree completed its tour, Elvis returned to the "Louisiana Hayride." He no longer needed to perform on the "Hayride," but he missed the camaraderie and interplay between the musicians. On the "Hayride," Elvis could also try out new songs. A good example of this occurred on May 21, 1955, when he sang Big Joe Turner's "Flip, Flop and Fly," a rhythm and blues standard that Elvis was working into his act. When Elvis played the Turner song backstage, Onie Wheeler suggested that it was inappropriate for the "Hayride" audience. Elvis tried it out anyway. (Throughout 1955, Elvis performed the tune intermittently, and the following year, during Elvis' third appearance on the Dorsey Brothers' television show, he sang a truly inspired version of "Flip, Flop and Fly.")

The day after this "Louisiana Hayride" show, Elvis drove with Onie Wheeler to Houston to appear at the Magnolia Gardens. This appearance allowed Elvis to talk at length with Wheeler about musical trends. They agreed that country music was in transition, and that there was a shift toward rockabilly sounds. The hostility of traditional country stars during Elvis' concert appearances prompted Wheeler to speculate on the reception Elvis would receive at the upcoming Jimmie Rodgers celebration.

When Elvis had been booked to appear at this yearly

A duet with the King.

The Elvis Presley unit, with Onie Wheeler, appears with "Louisiana Hayride," Shreveport, next Saturday (21), and the following day stops off at Magnolia Gardens, Houston. From there the unit members will hop into Meridian, Miss., for the Jimmie Rodgers' celebration. The Presley group appears with "Big D Jamboree" Dallas, May 28.

A trade news item about Elvis' activities.

country music gathering, Bob Neal reasoned that it would give country music purists a chance to judge Presley's talent first hand. Sam Phillips cautioned that the crowd might be hostile to musical innovation, because Rodgers' fans tended to be no-nonsense, uncompromising types. Upon arriving at the Third Annual Jimmie Rodgers Memorial Celebration in Meridian, Mississippi, Elvis was surprised by the large and vocal audiences. The two-day event, held to honor Rodgers, brought out a large number of country musicians, including Slim Whitman, Ernest Tubb, Jimmy Newman, Jim Reeves, and Johnny Horton. The other acts shied away from upbeat, rockabilly music, but on Wednesday, May 25, 1955 Elvis performed his standard set, mixing blues, rhythm and blues, and country tunes. As predicted, it was not a well-received performance. As part of the celebration, Elvis rode in the parade down the main street of Meridian, only to be booed lustily by the large crowd. Many Mississippi country music fans disliked the way that Elvis performed. The overall reception explains why Elvis cut his stay short and never again accepted a return invitation.

After his brief appearance in Meridian, it was back to Dallas for a Saturday, May 28, performance on the "Big D Jamboree." Elvis felt relieved to be back amongst his most rabid fans. Crowds were becoming increasingly difficult to control, however, and the reaction to Elvis' act throughout Texas was reaching an undeniable level of pandemonium. The following afternoon, Elvis appeared at Fort Worth's Northside Coliseum at 3:30 p.m., then quickly drove back to the Sportatorium in Dallas for an 8:30 evening show. The afternoon concert in Forth Worth had drawn seven thousand people. The show's high point was Elvis' rendition of "Tennessee Partner." The Fort Worth Star-Telegram reported that Elvis was "utterly fantastic."

These three Texas shows garnered Elvis a tidy

$1,500. The promoters was delighted that there was still plenty of money left from the gate to pay Ferlin Huskey, Jim Ed and Maxine Brown, Martha Carson, and Onie Wheeler's excellent guarantees. The word was spreading that when Elvis performed, the box office receipts were double the take whether it was in a honky-tonk bar or in a country music coliseum. In the bars, door receipts were so large that club owners tried to book Elvis for the successive evenings, something that was no longer possible because the demand for Presley's personal appearances had already resulted in solid bookings elsewhere. By May 1955, promoters in the larger coliseums were often willing to pay an extra $200 to $300 to book Elvis. The fact that promoters persistently made these offers underlines the fact that Elvis' popularity was enormous.

The steady stream of special financial considerations was not lost on Colonel Parker. He recognized that Elvis' drawing power put him in the driver's seat, and the Colonel manipulated Elvis' future bookings to great advantage. Although Bob Neal was still in charge of bookings, the Colonel advised Neal which ones to accept. Quietly, behind the scenes, Parker showcased Elvis in the best possible concert and club venues in the South. If a high-paying club appearance wasn't available, Colonel Parker convinced Elvis to work a small club for a percentage of the door, reasoning that Elvis was a solid draw, and there was no need for a big guarantee. (Normally, a percentage of the door worked to the advantage of the owner or promoter who was unsure of an act's drawing power; since the Colonel knew what Elvis' draw was going to be, the percentage was more usually more advantageous to Elvis than a guaranteed fee.) Parker's strategy of playing for the door was evident from May 30 through June 3, 1955, as Elvis performed in Abilene and Odessa, Texas, Guymon, Oklahoma, and then in Amarillo and Lubbock, Texas. Lubbock's Cotton Club was typical of the venues that Parker helped book. Since the club drew large crowds, most entertainers were happy to work there. It was not only Lubbock's leading country dance hall, but it was a well-known venue booking the best traveling country acts. That night at the Cotton Club, Elvis' share of the door was more than $100. Although this was not a large sum, Elvis was only one of many acts. The Lubbock show also included Ferlin Huskey, Martha Carson, the Carlisles, the Browns, George and Earl, and Onie Wheeler.

Buddy Holly and Bob Montgomery, performing locally as Buddy and Bob, came to hear Elvis' sing his rockabilly songs that night. (An interesting sidelight to Holly's visit involved the fact that a friend of his shot a minute of movie footage of Elvis; the small movie camera caught the growing confidence and professional stage presence that was to soon make Presley the hottest "unknown" musical act in America.) During Elvis' appearance, Buddy Holly walked over during the intermission and chatted with Presley. Holly later told his business manager, "Hi Pockets" Duncan, that Elvis offered a great deal of encouragement. The next day on Holly's radio show over KDAV, he performed a number of Elvis' songs.

There were others noticing Elvis' talent. On June 4, 1955, *Billboard*'s "Folk Talent and Tunes" column quoted Cecil Holifield, the owner of record stores in Midland and Odessa, Texas, on Elvis' local popularity. "He is the teenagers' favorite wherever he appears," Holifield remarked. Colonel Parker eyed the *Billboard* story, an encouragement to pursue future Texas bookings for Elvis.

As Elvis criss-crossed the South in June 1955, Sam Phillips persuaded Colonel Parker to book Carl Perkins and Johnny Cash into selected concert sites with him. There were two reasons for Phillips' action. Because of the pressures of touring, Sam Phillips just wasn't sure how long he could hold Elvis and the Blue Moon Boys together. Having already had the foresight to realize that he'd probably need to fill Elvis' slot as a Sun artist in the near future anyway, Phillips hoped to expose his new talent to the same audiences that applauded Presley's music. By encouraging performers like Cash and Perkins to emulate Elvis' style, Sam hoped to guarantee future record sales as well.

On June 7, 1955, Perkins and Cash appeared with Elvis in Marianna, Arkansas. Johnny Cash nervously opened the show, and was rather tentative on stage in his brief performance. Carl Perkins, on the other hand, was relaxed and outgoing. When Elvis came on stage, the crowd of a thousand roared its approval. Following the show, the three Sun artists went out for something to eat, and they talked about music late into the night. The next day, Elvis rejoined the lineup of the Hank Snow Jamboree.

When Elvis arrived at the National Guard Armory in Lawton, Oklahoma, the Jamboree shows for June 9-10, 1955, featured Ferlin Huskey, Marty Robbins, Sonny James, the Maddox Brothers, and the Belew Twins. Elvis spent a lot of time backstage talking with Marty Robbins, and was surprised to find out the extent to which Robbins loved his music. On December 7, 1954, Robbins had recorded "That's All Right (Mama)" using Elvis' Sun recording as his model. In fact, Robbins' version was a virtual copy of Elvis' record, the only difference being a fiddle bridge. Robbins was apologetic for his song's similarity, but Presley was flattered that someone else had recorded it in his style. Robbins told Elvis that he, too, hoped to cross over from the country field into a broader pop market, and he expressed a desire to record rock and roll. After spending two days together in Lawton, Elvis and Marty had established a special bond between one another.

The days that followed were filled with personal triumphs for Elvis, coupled with signs of total exhaustion. During Elvis' June 11, 1955, appearance on the "Louisiana Hayride," he lacked his normal energy. After Elvis closed the show with "That's All Right (Mama)," he complained to Scotty and Bill that he was tired. The Blue Moon Boys and Elvis were scheduled to perform twenty of the next twenty-five nights. Bill Black complained that they were musically ragged because of the heavy tour schedule, but everybody knew that the road was necessary, especially Elvis, who had just purchased a new pink Cadillac and had car payments to make.

Large crowds turned out when Elvis appeared in Bruce, Mississippi, on June 13, 1955, and again the following night in Tupelo. It was good to see old friends, and Elvis spent a great deal of time visiting with his former neighbors. For these concerts, Elvis sent for Ronald Smith and Kenneth Herman to act as his musical backup band. Scotty Moore and Bill Black wanted to take a short break from the hectic touring schedule, and so had driven home. Smith and Herman played the two dates, and it was like old times back in the small clubs. Afterward, Ronald and Ken went back to Memphis, and Scotty and Bill rejoined Elvis for a brief Texas tour.

As they drove South, there was constant wrangling between Elvis, Scotty, and Bill over money. Then, tragedy struck. After four concert dates, Elvis' pink Cadillac caught fire and was completely destroyed. Scotty and Bill, following in a second car, managed to save the musical instruments, but in order to get to a concert in Stamford, Texas, they had to charter a plane. Elvis considered the fire an ill omen. Everyone laughed and encouraged him to forget his bad luck.

From June 17 through 22, 1955, Elvis continued to appear in Texas. The shows were monotonous for him because he hadn't had time to develop any new songs. It was difficult to appear spontaneous performing the same musical set night after night. The media continued to run notices about Elvis, and he was frequently mentioned in *Billboard* and *Cashbox*.

Rockabilly Comes of Age

Presley's favorable publicity was paralleled by growing acceptance and popularity of rockabilly music. This new form of American music had by now attracted a sizable number of new followers. From July 1954 onward, *Billboard*'s record reviews had praised Elvis, and Paul Ackerman, *Billboard*'s music editor, was one of Presley's staunchest supporters. One of the first copies of "That's All Right (Mama)" was special-delivered to Ackerman by Sam Phillips.

Since 1953, Dewey Phillips had used the term rockabilly on his "Red, Hot and Blue" show on WHBQ. It was a designation that separated uptempo country songs from traditional hillbilly music. It was not until June 1955 that the term was commonly used by major record executives to identify hillbilly bands who employed a rock and roll orientation. The rockabilly sound clearly excited the crowds, and RCA-Victor, Atlantic, Decca, and Capitol records eagerly signed rockabilly artists. All the major record labels had focused on Elvis as the future king of the rockabilly sound.

The ascendancy of rockabilly music was evident at a Presley concert on June 23, 1955. Elvis appeared in Big Springs, Texas, with Leon Payne. The young crowd demanded encores of "That's All Right (Mama)" and "Baby Let's Play House." This appearance with Payne was also an important one for Elvis because of Payne's songwriting skills. After having recorded Payne's "I Love You Because," Elvis was eager to talk with the singer. For a short time, Payne had toured with Bob Wills, and Elvis hoped to learn as much as he could about Payne's experiences with Wills and the Texas Playboys.

So far, June 1955 had seen a continuation of Elvis' endless and exhaustive blur of one-night stands, broken up by appearances on the "Louisiana Hayride." Elvis told Bill Black that he depended upon the "Hayride" to maintain his ties to country music. On June 24, 1955, Elvis appeared in a high school gym in Altus, Oklahoma. This show featured Elvis and the Blue Moon Boys, as well as two local singers. Since Presley's group was on stage longer than usual, they were able to play some new songs. The audience clapped loudly when they completed a cover version of Jean Shepard's "Satisfied Mind." Two nights later, Elvis appeared with Marty Robbins and Sonny James in Biloxi, Mississippi. A Mississippi town with a resort atmosphere, Biloxi was filled with pretty girls and hard-drinking vacationers.

While performing in Biloxi, Elvis met a local girl, June Juanico. She was typical of Elvis' women; a dark-haired beauty with lithe features and a quiet, understated personality. The auburn-haired, blue-eyed receptionist followed Elvis around Biloxi like a puppy dog. They dated for a year. It was the perfect relationship for Elvis, because June Juanico was Southern, beautiful, submissive, and enthralled with show business.

On June 29-30, 1955, Elvis appeared at the Radio Ranch Club in Mobile, Alabama. This club, owned by Curtis Gordon, a local country music artist, featured Gordon's Radio Ranch Boys, who unfortunately had to leave the stage early because the crowd demanded Elvis. The clamor for Elvis was helped by his record "Baby Let's Play House," which was also on the country and western charts in Houston, New Orleans, Richmond, and St. Louis. Another Presley song, "I'm Left, You're Right, She's Gone," was #4 on the local Memphis C & W charts.

National media recognition for Elvis continued in June 1955 when a *Cowboy Songs* article, "Sun's Newest Star," praised Elvis. Though brief and impressionistic, this glimpse into Presley's career helped the concert gates. Although the money increased for Elvis, Scotty, and Bill in some concert venues, they continued to play for small guarantees if they had time. On most weekends, however, Elvis and the Blue Moon Boys generated $300 to $500 a night, with weekday concerts bringing in $50 to $200. For the first time in his life, Elvis had plenty of spending money, and he bought clothes and records in abundance.

Also in June, Elvis rented a home for his parents at 1414 Getwell Street. The house was a relatively simple one on a busy street. Despite his popularity, Elvis' phone number, 48-4921, was listed in the Memphis phone book, and he was generally accessible to his fans and loved the fame and adulation. Marty Lacker, a future member of the so-called "Memphis Mafia," remarked that Elvis loved to cruise around downtown when he was not on tour. At this point in his life, neither Elvis nor anyone else thought of him in mythic terms—when not on stage, he was basically no different than his fans.

To some observers, there were signs of change in Elvis' life, however. Ronald Smith remembers Elvis' circle of friends tightening. "One night Elvis wanted to go

Fans everywhere greeted Elvis with adulation, encouragement, and respect—here he is on the way to a movie with a date.

roller skating. It was too hot and muggy," Smith recalled. "So Kenneth Herman and I decided to do something else. Before we left, George Klein stared hostilely at us." Smith was perplexed. Klein seemed abusive and aggressive. "If Elvis wants to go roller skating, guys," Klein stated, "then we go roller skating." In disgust, Smith and Herman left Elvis' inner circle—they couldn't believe the sycophantic behavior of some of Elvis' superficial friends, and were annoyed about the way Elvis' so-called friends were simply using him to meet girls. "Elvis also had a dark side," Smith recalled. "He was a wonderful guy, but the pressure from his friends changed him."

Smith also remembered the constant pressure placed upon Presley to deliver superb concert performances. Elvis never seemed to be off stage. His closest friends noticed that he was consumed with show business. When he came home, Elvis continually practiced his stage act in front of a floor-length mirror. Elvis purchased the mirror in a Memphis store one day after watching Lowell Fulson use a backstage mirror to perfect his moves in the Club Handy. (Elvis had originally gone to the Club Handy with Billy "The Kid" Emerson, and he remarked to Emerson that he was intrigued by Fulson's practiced stage mannerisms.) On the few days a month that he could return to Memphis, it was difficult for him to relax and sleep, and he spent long hours walking and talking before finally going to bed. To Smith and Herman, the changes encircling Elvis were not healthy ones. A new group of friends had begun to exert an influence and control over many aspects of his life, and this in turn altered his personality.

The most relaxing part of Elvis' life seemed to be his daytime visits at home with his mother and father. During the early summer of 1955, as Elvis and his parents relaxed at 1414 Getwell, they enjoyed feelings of family closeness that had eluded them for much of their lives. Elvis was making good money, and his music was becoming more popular each day. After a year in the music business, constant touring had taken a toll, and Elvis desperately needed a vacation. Despite his pleas for some time off, Bob Neal and Colonel Parker made it clear that Elvis had to continue his frenetic schedule. The only way to build Elvis' following and sell his records was to tour, they told him. As Colonel Parker suggested, it was the fans first and the media second that was making Elvis a hot act. It was important to please the fans while continuing to build goodwill with the press. Eventually, Colonel Parker and Bob Neal relented and allowed Elvis to take a two-week vacation—Elvis not only performed energetically for the next few days, but he cooperated eagerly with the press—but it was the haven of home that provided him with the few brief moments of respite he otherwise enjoyed.

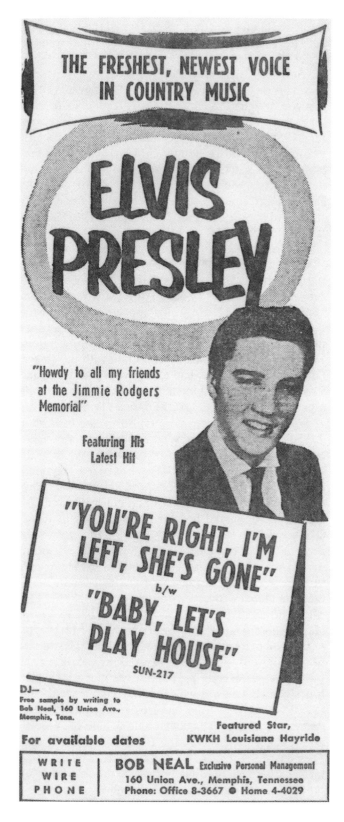

One of Bob Neal's publicity efforts, complete with a reversal of the song title "I'm Left, You're Right, She's Gone."

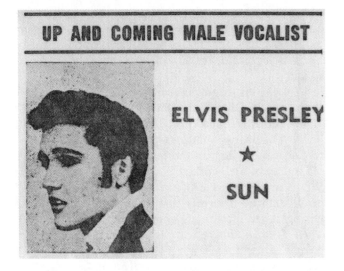

UP AND COMING MALE VOCALIST

ELVIS PRESLEY

★

SUN

After appearing on July 1 at Lou Millett's club in Baton Rouge, Louisiana, Elvis drove to Waco, Texas, for a radio interview. The music industry weekly *Cashbox* had just selected Elvis as the best "Up and Coming Male Vocalist" in the country music field. When Elvis performed in Waco, he was only one of many acts at an Independence Day weekend gospel concert. Since gospel music was Elvis' favorite, he was eager to perform with the likes of the Statesmen and the Blackwood Brothers. The Sunday, July 3, 1955, concert in the park was a warm up for a gospel jubilee the following day, when Elvis headlined two Fourth of July celebrations. After the Waco performance, he drove twenty-five miles to Stephenville, where, teaming that afternoon with Slim Willet and the Farren Twins, Elvis delivered an unusually energetic show. The day-long celebration in the City Recreational Building and the local rodeo grounds also featured the Deep South Quartet, the Stamps, and the Stamps Ozark Quartet. That night, he sang again with the Blackwood Brothers and the Statesmen in a park in DeLeon, Texas. Gospel music always inspired him most of all, and he went all-out to show his talent. It was not just that Elvis loved gospel music; he got emotionally high performing it.

Driving back to Memphis for his two-week vacation, Elvis was happy that *Billboard* had rated "Baby Let's Play House" number 15 on the "Country Best Sellers in Stores" chart. The record remained on the chart for ten weeks, peaking at number 10 in late July 1955, another sign that Elvis' hard work and constant touring was paying off. To capitalize on the *Billboard* listing, Colonel Parker prepared a late summer, early fall booking schedule.

"Mystery Train"

There was great demand for Elvis to produce a new record to keep the ball rolling, so it was necessary to return to the Sun studio to record some new material. Sam Phillips spent a great deal of time preparing for Elvis' July 11, 1955, recording session. Elvis and Sam talked at length about the type of songs that were best-suited to him. One tune that had stuck in Phillips' mind was Little Junior Parker's 1953 recording of "Mystery Train." After Elvis, Sam, and Scotty listened to Parker's version, they flipped it over and played the b-side, "Love My Baby." Scotty Moore listened intently to the instrumental virtuosity of black guitarist Pat Hare, whose guitar work had more in common with Delta bluesmen than with country musicians. It took half-a-dozen attempts before Scotty learned Hare's guitar licks from "Love My Baby." Moore used them on "Mystery Train," a re-combination of elements from the record that transformed Elvis' "Mystery Train" enough to make it popular among both country and rock music fans.

Sam Phillips was tickled with the results. Revenge was also a motive for recording "Mystery Train." As noted in an earlier chapter, Don Robey, owner of the Duke-Peacock labels, had come to Memphis in 1953 to listen to Little Junior Parker, and it was not long before Parker left Memphis to tour with the Johnny Ace Revue. After Johnny Ace's bizarre death, Parker toured with the Blues Consolidated Show featuring Bobby Blue Bland. Robey, himself a prosperous nightclub owner, was able to book his acts into the best clubs. In 1953, however, Parker had been one of the first major artists for Sam Phillips' Sun label. When Phillips recorded Little Junior Parker, he was able to give Parker's country blues a sophisticated urban direction. A highly commercial city blues sound made Parker a strong club attraction, and Sam Phillips pointed out this would have been impossible without the Sun sound. Phillips was angry that Little Junior Parker had left Sun to sign with Don Robey's Houston-based Duke-Peacock firm. Sam filed suit in a Texas federal court against Don Robey for infringing upon Sun Records' rights to Little Junior Parker's records, and, in a federal district court in Texas, Judge Connolly ruled in Sam Phillips' favor. It proved to be a hollow victory because no damages were collected from Robey, and Junior Parker continued to record for Robey with limited success until 1966. Phillips, in response, refused to release any of Parker's Sun recordings.

Unwittingly, this scenario aided Presley's career when Phillips had Elvis record "Mystery Train," which he might not have done had there not been the personal differences between Sam Phillips and Little Junior Parker. Not only was Phillips determined to find another top flight blues act, but he had promised himself to re-record some of Parker's songs. It had been Phillips who had molded Parker's raw blues into a highly commercial product, and he was furious when the diminutive musician had demanded more money, and had then abruptly left—he would show Little Junior Parker that it had been a mistake to leave the Sun label.

It had been almost two years since October 3, 1953—when Little Junior Parker's "Feelin' Good," entered the *Billboard* rhythm and blues chart—and Sam Phillips was primed to take his revenge through Elvis. In addition to Little Junior Parker's "Mystery Train," he had Presley complete three more songs: "I Forgot to Remember to Forget," "Tryin' to Get To You" and "When It Rains It Really Pours," the commercially strongest of which was Stan Kesler's "I Forgot to Remember to Forget." Kesler wrote and produced the song while going through a painful divorce. Although Charlie Feathers is listed as the co-writer, Kesler made it clear that he alone wrote the song. "Charlie did all the demo tapes and I thought it was only fair to give him half the song. We had an agreement to pool our talents," Kesler remembered. Since Kesler didn't like to sing, he depended upon Feathers to make the demonstration tape. "I think we worked together pretty well," Kesler noted. "We all knew that Elvis was bigger than the local scene," Kesler concluded, "and it was only a matter of time before he was a star." Part of the magic that facilitated that stardom was provided for Elvis by people like Stan Kesler. At the July 11 session, Kesler, an accomplished country musician, persuaded Sam Phillips to augment Elvis' sound with a piano, and Frank Tolley, a member of Malcolm Yelvington's Star Rhythm Boys, was brought into the recording studio. Not only did Tolley's piano virtuosity provide a new energy for Presley's recording, it helped break them into the mainstream country market.

Rufus Thomas

After a year with Sun Records, Elvis was a Memphis entertainment phenomenon. The extensive publicity, the record sales, and the reaction to Presley's public appearances prompted local singer and disc jockey Rufus Thomas to invite Elvis to one of the live shows that he hosted at the Palace Theater on Beale Street.

Since 1953, when Sun released Thomas' record "Tiger Man," he had evolved into a strong local blues act, and was one of the first black artists to cross over into Memphis' white market. Rufus Thomas first met Elvis when Presley had come to the Flamingo Club with Billy "The Kid" Emerson, and he had played Presley's music on his radio show on station WDIA. David James, WDIA's program director, had complained that the predominantly black audience didn't want to hear Elvis. "I didn't agree," Thomas remembered. "I have always been able to feel music, and I knew our audience wanted

songs like Elvis sang." On Thomas' show there were numerous phone requests for Presley's tunes. Not only did Elvis' music light up the WDIA switchboard, but, as Thomas suggested, Presley was the forerunner of a new sound.

During his lengthy career, Rufus Thomas had four shows over WDIA: "Sepia Swing Club," "Cool Train," "Hoot n Holler," and "Boogie for Breakfast." Some of Rufus Thomas' popularity was due to the fact that he replaced B.B. King on the radio. He picked up B.B.'s old audience and worked it skillfully. When King left WDIA and Thomas took over the "Sepia Swing Club," he introduced a format that appealed to both white teenagers and traditional country music fans. In 1953, when Thomas' hit record "Bear Cat" (Sun 181), appeared as an answer song to Big Mama Thornton's "Hound Dog," Elvis listened eagerly to it. In 1954, when WDIA went to a twenty-four-hour broadcast schedule, Thomas was its main air personality. Elvis complained to Bill Black that he missed Thomas' show when they played out-of-town venues.

Not only was Thomas a creative force on the Memphis music scene, he also recognized and championed the revolutionary changes that Elvis brought to American music. Once Presley's records were released, Thomas plugged them on his radio show. It was not yet common for a black dj to play a white artists' material. "Elvis crossed the color line," Thomas remarked. "He was white but sounded like us. Johnny Otis was another one like Elvis, but Johnny lived the Negro's life." Hosting his weekly amateur show at the Palace Theater while working days for the Memphis Luggage Factory, Thomas was a keen observer of musical trends. In Thomas' view, Elvis was a musical pioneer who brought black sounds to a white audience. "Elvis gave an injection to black music that no black artist had ever done," Thomas remarked. The reason for this opinion was the reaction that Rufus Thomas had witnessed during the Sun years. "He wasn't known up north," Thomas continued, "but he sure did set our part of the country on fire."

In fact, black record buyers did purchase Elvis' Sun recordings in large numbers. Elvis was very well known in the black community, and the excitement over his music erupted spontaneously one night at the annual "Starlight Review" show at the municipal auditorium. This July 1955 extravaganza used local talent to raise funds for charity, and Thomas had invited Elvis backstage for this event. When Presley arrived, he was surprised to find Thomas dressed as an Indian. "You sure don't look like the Rufus Thomas I know," Presley remarked. A gentle smile and friendly wink made Thomas feel at ease. They talked about the music scene, and Thomas invited Elvis on stage for a few numbers. There was a hushed silence as Elvis Presley and Rufus

Thomas walked out to center stage. Approaching the microphone, Thomas said, "Ladies and gentlemen—Elvis Presley." There was loud applause and frenetic squealing. The crowd was unexpectedly vocal, and members the audience rushed the stage. The pandemonium made it impossible for Presley to perform, and he was quickly escorted backstage. Elvis never forgot that night with Rufus Thomas.

As a popular recording artist, Rufus Thomas did not last long with Sam Phillips because he was erroneously perceived as a novelty act. Thomas cut only one other record for Sun after "Bear Cat." "When Elvis and Carl Perkins and Johnny Cash came along," Thomas remarked to Peter Guralnick, "Phillips just cut us off and went to white." Surprisingly, there is no bitterness evident in Thomas' attitude. In his own way, Thomas was influential in Elvis' career. As the emcee for amateur nights at the Palace and Handy theaters—many Memphis teenagers attended these shows—Thomas nurtured a great deal local talent just like Elvis.

Arthur Gunter

The figure of Rufus Thomas highlights the growing connection between hillbilly and black music in the mid-fifties South. As Elvis and other young whites listened to Thomas on WDIA, they sang along with blues songs using their "country" voices. A good example of the result of the marriage of such diverse elements is evident in Presley's recording of "Baby Let's Play House." When the song was released, few people connected it with obscure blues singer Arthur Gunter, even though the song had been a hit for him. Once Elvis recorded it,

ELVIS PRESLEY
Baby Let's Play House 77
 SUN 217—A highly distinctive country effort, this is patterned after primitive Southern blues. Great rhythm effects and trick warbling. Should get played. (Excellorec, BMI)
I'm Left,
 You're Right, She's Gone....71
 Presley has the maracas loaded for this unusual, rhythmic country chant. But the content fails to keep pace. (Hi-Lo, BMI)

The May 14 *Billboard* review of "Baby Let's Play House" b/w "I'm Left, You're Right, She's Gone."

however, the song became a mainstream Southern rockabilly hit, the popularity of which was evident on July 22, 1955, when Elvis appeared at the Pioneer Jamboree in Odessa, Texas. The predominantly country crowd—Ferlin Huskey, the Browns, and Sonny James were among the other acts on the bill—continually hollered out for "Baby Let's Play House." Few people in the audience realized that a black singer was the source of Elvis' latest hit. Previously, on May 14, 1955, *Billboard*'s review of "Baby Let's Play House" rated it 77, while the b-side, "I'm Left, You're Right, She's Gone" was listed at 71. Both songs were praised for their distinctive *country music* direction. One of the ironies of Elvis' entire early career, in fact, is that his black musical roots were not recognized by his fans, even though he openly discussed and acknowledged them.

Arthur Gunter's version of "Baby Let's Play House" had been released by Excello Records in 1954. Excello was typical of the small labels that Phillips and Presley followed as they looked for new songs. Interestingly, there are amazing similarities between the Excello Record label founder, Ernie Young, and Sun Records magnate Sam Phillips. Both appreciated black music, and both had a vision of its future in a white market.

Excello Records was typical of many newly-formed small record labels of the time. In 1951, Ernie Young, the owner of a record shop on the northern end of Third Avenue in Nashville, founded a small mail-order record label, Nashboro Records. Young was closely connected with local disc jockeys, which enabled him to garner radio airplay for his blues and hillbilly artists. In a scenario that was a carbon copy of Sun Records, Young recorded local talent like Kid King (Skippy Brooks), Louis Brooks, and Arthur Gunter. Young had the same problems as Sam Phillips: the number of black music labels in Nashville was minuscule, the dominance of the "Grand Ole Opry" broadcasts made country music king, and few people paid attention to the blues. Young, like Sam, founded Excello Records to record black artists and serve the needs of local blues buffs but, again like Phillips, Ernie Young hoped to cross his artists over into a mainstream record buying market. Young was also interested in country music and urged black artists to listen to it. The results of Young's encouragement were amazing. In January 1955, Arthur Gunter wrote "Baby Let's Play House" after listening to Eddy Arnold's 1951 country hit, "I Wanna to Play House With You." He used the barrelhouse piano player Skippy Brooks to add some blues piano chords to the song. Gunter had listened studiously to white rockabilly music, and the resulting songs were a far cry from the traditional blues that permeated local black clubs. Many of his songs were influenced by the music of Blind Boy Fuller and Big Bill Broonzy.

Unfortunately, Arthur Gunter recorded for a small label and was destined for musical obscurity. When his brother and fellow band member, Little Al Gunter, was killed in a barroom brawl, Arthur moved to Michigan and went to work for the post office. Ernie Young bought the rights to "Baby Let's Play House" and collected the royalties. "I got more money from Elvis in royalties than I did from Arthur's record sales," Young noted. Excello Records, like most small labels, had purchased Gunter's songs outright. Young paid Gunter $500 for "Baby Let's Play House," and it was the smartest investment Ernie Young ever made. In hindsight, one of the tragedies of early rock and roll music is that many talented black songwriters and performers wound up broke and forgotten as a result of lopsided deals like these, although at the time they were the norm and apparently perceived, under the pressure of making a living, as lucrative enough to the artists concerned.

Back to Touring

At the time that Elvis recorded "Baby Let's Play House," he had been spending a lot of time with Johnny Burnette. Although he was on the road a good deal, Elvis had several opportunities to share his musical ideas with Johnny. Once Elvis' recording became popular, Burnette's group, the Rock and Roll Trio, began playing a song they called "Oh Baby Babe," an exact copy of Presley's "Baby Let's Play House." The Rock and Roll Trio recorded the tune on May 7, 1956, for Coral Records. Just a year earlier, in July 1955, as Elvis prepared for the "Big D Jamboree" in Dallas, the Rock and Roll Trio was practicing for an appearance on the "Ted Mack Original Amateur Hour."

At the "Big D Jamboree" on July 23, 1955, Oscar "The Baron" Davis, an advance man for Colonel Parker, realized early on that the youthful crowd was there primarily to see Elvis perform. Held at the Sportatorium, the admission for the show was sixty cents for adults

and thirty cents for the kids. The Dallas city government booked the Presley concert to promote a free bus ticket program for those who came by public transportation. A special newspaper ad read: "you get a FREE bus ticket home...if you COME by BUS!" Elvis' show prompted a Dallas newspaper to remark that he was "one of the brightest new stars."

Elvis' crowds were not always young and enthusiastic. The night after the "Big D Jamboree," he appeared at the Round-Up Club at 2005 S. Eryay in Dallas. A boisterous gathering of adult country music enthusiasts greeted Elvis, who altered his song selection to include traditional country tunes. Elvis was as readily accepted by the older, hard-drinking crowd as he had been by the kids at the Jamboree. The Round-Up Club, a typical Texas honky-tonk bar, forced an entertainer to meet its demands. If they didn't like your music, you couldn't be heard in the beer-bottle-clanking atmosphere. Fistfights were common. If the crowd behaved, it meant you had probably established your musical reputation, and that people wanted to listen.

To follow the Dallas appearances, Colonel Parker had booked a well-publicized, five-day tour of Florida to showcase Elvis' talent. The Colonel realized that it was important to book these concerts with the best country talent and do everything possible to make Elvis the tour's star. As Elvis prepared for the tour, he was nervous about the opening concert in Tampa. Not only had it been Colonel Parker's hometown, but Tampa had a reputation as a tough place for new entertainers to succeed. The first stop also made Elvis anxious because the Colonel's publicity had created a circus-like atmosphere that Presley disliked.

The Florida tour included some of the biggest names in country music. Elvis looked forward to it because he would perform with entertainers he admired: Andy Griffith, Ferlin Huskey, Jimmy Rodgers Snow, and Marty Robbins. There was a great deal of speculation about how well Elvis would be accepted outside of the Tennessee-Texas-Alabama circuit that had responded so well to his music, and while this didn't bother Elvis, he was aware of the possible results of poor publicity. Happily, one-stop record distributors had ordered hundreds of Elvis' Sun recordings and, due to jukebox play and small record store sales—his records had received strong airplay for a year in the area, and the ground swell of public curiosity boosted ticket sales—Elvis sailed through the Florida dates.

When the news got around that he would open in Tampa on Monday, July 25, 1955, at the 116th Field Artillery Armory, there was considerable excitement. The ground swell of interest in Elvis was not lost on the show's sponsor, the Seratoma Club. The organization flooded the Tampa area with attractive handbills advertising Presley's appearance, and, as a result, the crowd was so large that the armory filled in less than an hour. The next two concerts in Orlando, Florida, followed the same pattern. During the Wednesday, July 27, Orlando show, *Billboard* dispatched a reporter who would later describe Elvis as "stealing the show." The Florida press also followed Elvis' performances enthusiastically. After the triumph in Orlando, Elvis moved on to Jacksonville for two nights, where he planned to add Rufus Thomas' "Juanita" to his concert repertoire. A few years later, when Thomas recorded "Juanita" for Sun Records in April 1957, Sam Phillips didn't believe in its commercial possibilities. As a result, it had been sold to Chess Records. It failed to make the charts. "Sam Phillips sold me the damned song to get even with me," Leonard Chess recalled. Why Elvis selected the song for his act is a mystery. Rumor has it that Elvis watched Thomas perform "Juanita" in local clubs. Combined with that, it probably was simply due to his penchant to experiment with rhythm and blues songs, coupled with the fact that he had just visited with Thomas in Memphis.

On Friday, July 29, 1955, as Elvis prepared for the second night in Jacksonville, the crowd was boisterous and unruly. Two new promoters, WQIK dj Marshall Rowland and Mae B. Axton, had brought the show to the Jacksonville minor league baseball park. They nervously watched the large throng milling around the small stadium. It was an awkward venue for the performers, who dressed in the baseball clubhouse and came on stage through the dugout.

Johnny Tillotson, then a high school disc jockey on WWPF, wanted to interview Elvis, as he had tried to do in May. When Tillotson arrived at the ball park, there was a great deal of excitement. Hundreds of people were walking around under the baseball stands, and a crowd of about thirty people had surrounded Elvis. As Tillotson pondered the strategy he'd need to get his interview, Elvis began to walk toward the baseball dugout. Realizing that he might not be able to get to Elvis, Tillotson decided on a unique strategy. In order to get Elvis' attention, Tillotson began parroting Elvis' version of "Baby Let's Play House." Elvis, standing with Scotty Moore, Bill Black, and other musicians in the dugout, yelled out: "Hold it! What's that?" Presley smiled and cast a quizzical glance at the diminutive high school student. "I introduced myself as a local singer that needed to interview him, because I had promised my listeners the interview," Tillotson remarked. "If I hadn't been able to complete the Presley interview, my listeners would have deserted me." When Johnny told Elvis that his radio future depended upon an interview,

Elvis smiled and sat down for a quick chat. The amiable Tillotson made Elvis very comfortable, and they actually talked for quite some time.

Afterward, as Johnny Tillotson—who, in a few years, would score with hits of his own ("Poetry In Motion," "It Keeps Right On A-Hurtin' ")—watched Elvis' show, he was impressed by Elvis' concert because of the broad cross section of people who attended it. He also picked up some subtle points about working a crowd. A number of accounts have described this night as one in which a riot ensued, but Johnny Tillotson doesn't remember a riot at any of Elvis' appearances in Jacksonville. "Riot isn't the correct adjective to describe the crowd's reaction to Elvis," Tillotson remarked. "The response to Elvis' music was a very positive, enthusiastic, totally spontaneous happening of the audience. They were simply leaving their seats to acknowledge Elvis' performance, there was no violence," Tillotson concluded. After the concert, Elvis left for a local motel.

On Saturday, July 30, 1955, Johnny Tillotson aired the interview over WWPF, and it was an in-depth analysis of the reasons for Presley's success. A combination of high energy and a raucous blues musical style, Tillotson told his listeners, had made Elvis a very special act. Blues and rhythm and blues songs, Elvis emphasized, were key to his musical appeal to a wide variety of young people.

When the Florida tour closed on July 30 in Daytona Beach, Elvis was ready to go back to the quick, backbreaking one-night stands. In fact, the day after closing the tour, he appeared with Johnny Cash, Webb Pierce and Wanda Jackson, among others, at the Community Center in Sheffield, Alabama. The night was an interesting one because a number of local bands wanted to play with the touring groups. The Sheffield Community Center was brimming with a musical enthusiasm and a blend of raucous sounds that would soon give way to rock and roll music. The Sheffield concert, where twenty-eight hundred people waited for him to come on stage, would highlight Elvis' drawing power. In a series of concerts that also included Little Rock and Camden, Arkansas, and Tupelo, Mississippi, Elvis drew more than fifteen thousand customers. Had the halls been larger, Elvis would probably have drawn another five thousand. In Little Rock, for example, more than one thousand fans were turned away.

The Sheffield concert was held in an area that included the towns of Florence, Tuscumbia, and Muscle Shoals. Later, in the sixties, the Muscle Shoals recording studio would blossom in the area, as would the Florence Alabama Music Enterprises—the FAME studio. A decade later, Muscle Shoals had become part of the Southern soul triangle, which included Memphis and

Macon, Georgia. At the time Elvis visited the Muscle Shoals area in 1955, Dan Penn, Rick Hall, Billy Sherrill, Spooner Oldham, and Buddy Killen were just local boys coming of age or working quietly in the music industry. Like many locals, they went to see Elvis' Sheffield show, which was a longer one than usual. This was due to the fact that Sheffield had a population of 100,000 people with a reputation for hard-drinking, music-loving, country hijinks. W.C. Handy and Sam Phillips were from Florence, and the area teemed with musicians. There was a strong gospel tradition, and country bands like Carmol Taylor and the Country Pals and Benny Cagle and the Rhythm Swingsters played in local clubs. At the Sheffield Hotel, thirteen-year-old Arthur Alexander was then a young bellhop. A few years later, Alexander would write "You Better Move On" and "Anna," providing the Rolling Stones and the Beatles respectively with two of their early songs. All the elements of a creative musical blend, which included the blues, gospel music, and country songs, were present in Sheffield's rich environment. There is no doubt that Elvis picked up a good deal of his Southern soul sound at concerts in places like Sheffield.

The Dotted Line

Elvis continued to appear night after night in a grueling concert schedule to increasingly appreciative and boisterous crowds. It was still difficult for the Presley management team to move him into the larger arenas, however; there had to be a permanent business arrangement between Elvis and the Colonel to facilitate the disposition of greater sums of money. At this point, Elvis was eager to sign with the Colonel, and the pair met again in Little Rock, Arkansas, to continue their negotiations for a management deal. After two days in Little Rock, Elvis returned to Memphis and talked with Vernon and Gladys about Colonel Parker.

It was not long before Parker followed Elvis into Memphis. He spent two days with Elvis' parents, and made it very clear that he would sign Elvis to a contact only if he believed that a series of high-priced deals could be negotiated with a major record label. Vernon Presley was impressed by the Colonel but, at this point, Gladys had grown uncertain about his intentions. There was something about the Colonel that Elvis' mother didn't like, although she could never adequately express it to her friends. She just didn't trust him. One day, Delta Mae Biggs, Vernon's sister, walked into the Presley's home. Gladys was screaming.

"That damned Col. Parker's drivin' me crazy."

"What?" Delta intoned.

"That man in the funny hat, he's after my boy."

"Calm down, Gladys."

"Yourself," Gladys bellowed, and walked away.

This scene was apparently repeated hundreds of times in 1955. "We quit going around the Presley's house," Ronald Smith and Kenneth Herman remarked. "There were too many arguments." Elvis, however, was too busy performing to notice the strain.

On Friday, August 5, Elvis appeared in Bob Neal's "Eighth Anniversary Jamboree" at the Overton Bowl. In addition to Webb Pierce, Red Sovine, Wanda Jackson, Sonny James, and Johnny Cash, Neal also booked rockabilly singer Charlie Feathers. While waiting to go on stage, Elvis and Feathers talked about the show. Feathers pointed out that *Billboard* had sent a reporter, a prospect that excited Elvis because Sam Phillips was preparing to debut Presley's latest Sun record. (When *Billboard* later included "I Forgot To Remember To Forget" in its "Review Spotlight" in its August 20 issue, the music industry bible stated that Presley's song would "get strong initial exposure." They called the record's flip side, "Mystery Train," a "splendid coupling.")

The day after Bob Neal's "Eighth Anniversary Jamboree," Elvis' fifth and last Sun single, "Mystery Train" b/w "I Forgot to Remember to Forget" was released. "Mystery Train," the rhythm and blues a-side, was the one that Sam Phillips believed would be a hit. Just prior to pressing copies, Johnny Bernero's drums had been added to the b-side to enhance the country music feel. Bernero, discussed in an earlier chapter, worked across the street from the Sun Studio at the Memphis Light, Gas and Water Company, and he had sat in for Phillips on numerous occasions. Although he was at first uncertain about adding the drums, Phillips liked Bernero's

Meeting fans at a record store autograph session.

light touch and went ahead with the new version. To promote his new record, Elvis returned to Texas on August 8, 1955, for concerts in Gladewater, at the Texas State Fair in Dallas, and in weekend appearances in San Antonio and Houston.

On Monday, August 15, 1955, Colonel Tom Parker officially signed Elvis to a one-year management contract. Sam Phillips was so busy with Presley's new record that he paid little or no attention to Elvis' management change, but Bob Neal was included as an adviser to Elvis on the agreement. There were two one-year options in the contract, and some other strange provisions favoring Colonel Parker. Elvis was required, for example, to pay Parker $2,500 in five installments and play 100 concerts for $200—including the backup musicians' wage—during the contract's first year. In other words, Elvis was in debt to the Colonel for $2,500 the moment he signed the agreement, which basically guaranteed Colonel Parker compensation for managing Elvis even if Elvis abruptly refused to honor the contract for some reason.

On the reverse side, negotiations for their first contract do reveal that the Colonel was apparently not as shrewd in analyzing Elvis' earning power as some books have suggested. Parker had no idea that Elvis had earned slightly more than $50,000 in 1955, even without decent management or good road guarantees for the full year. When Elvis did receive a guaranteed fee, the bookings were usually from $200 to $500 a night, and with two-hundred-plus nights on the road, Presley earned a good living. A great deal of money also came from less well-paying agreements with small clubs, where Elvis would personally receive the door receipts, all of this supplemented by small royalties on sales of his records.

On Wednesday night, August 31, 1955, Elvis appeared with Scotty Moore and Bill Black on Bob Neal's Memphis radio show over WMPS. The interview had originally been set up to publicize an appearance that Friday evening in Texarkana, Arkansas, but Elvis spent most of the time talking about Colonel Tom Parker's plans for his career. There was a sense of urgency and a gleeful tone in Elvis voice as he excitedly described his bright future. The new management agreement put Colonel Parker firmly in charge. Parker was already negotiating with the major labels, and by the end of the year Elvis would be signed to RCA-Victor and on his way to becoming a major star. Unfortunately, the Sun sound, so instrumental in his rise to fame, would soon fade into obscurity for him, and the rewards that flowed from the constant striving for commercial success would ultimately lock Elvis the performer into a predictable mold. Ironically, Elvis would reach the pinnacle of rock and roll fame by recording songs that he loved, but once there would retreat into a world of safe, well-produced, more commercial songs, many of which he hated.

CHAPTER 12

Sun Rise,
September-October 1955

In September and October 1955, regional phenomenon Elvis Presley was an entertainer with a hot future. As rhythm and blues records in general enjoyed increased sales and radio airplay, so did Presley's Sun singles. Presley's five recordings were strong in the South, but since June 1955 his music had received steady airplay on key stations in Cleveland, Chicago, Detroit, and Los Angeles. It might be well to recap the various factors in Elvis' career that, in a scant eighteen months, had brought him to this point—a star about to burst upon the national scene.

Why was Elvis Presley's music so popular? At the center of several converging elements is, of course, Elvis himself. During his first year-and-a-half as a professional entertainer, Elvis swiveled his hips, danced about the stage, and freely expressed himself in a manner that befitted the first truly remarkable rock and roll personality. The central reason for his success, then, is that he insisted on having a great deal of personal recording and performing freedom. In the studio, Sam Phillips had deftly used this innate free-spiritedness to bring out Elvis' unique interpretation of rhythm and blues, blues, and country tunes. Elvis' talent and Phillips' vision, as primary as they were, could not have succeeded without the existence of certain other individuals who either aided or acted as counterpoints to Elvis, nor without certain events or trends which clearly played a crucial role in what occurred exactly at this time.

Bill Randle and Arnold Shaw

In September 1954, when Bill Randle at WERE in Cleveland began playing Elvis' records, he became the first northern radio personality to play Presley's music. In doing so, he alerted the music industry to Elvis' commercial potential. The question of Bill Randle's influence upon Presley's career is an important aspect of the latter Sun days. Just as Elvis began making inroads into northern markets, Randle contracted with Universal Pictures to produce a movie called "The Pied Piper of Cleveland: A Day In the Life of a Famous Disc Jockey." With Bill Haley, Pat Boone, and the Four Lads committed to the movie, Randle looked for a young newcomer to fill out the bill. Elvis was his choice. (Randle and the details of his film will be further discussed later in this chapter.)

As Bill Randle's position in the radio field increased in prestige, his support for Presley convinced many industry insiders to give close consideration to Elvis' music. Randle's scholarly demeanor, complete with horn-rimmed glasses, radiated intellectual seriousness, prompting many record executives to take a second look at all the new rock music artists. One of the people Randle impressed was Arnold Shaw, the general manager of New York's Albert B. Marks Music Corporation. Shaw, a brash, fast-talking New Yorker, was the opposite personality type, but he was equally adept at challenging critics who debunked rock and roll. When station director Norman Furman of WBMA in Boston instructed his djs not to play "record hop" music, Shaw spoke out against Furman's short-sighted tirade against rock music.

At the time, the influence that New York-based dj Alan Freed—who continued to reign as the King of Rock and Roll disc jockeys—had on the rock music industry was disintegrating. Shaw, who hated Freed (who had also made a name for himself in Cleveland), set out to persuade Randle to come to New York and host CBS's Saturday morning radio show. Eventually, Randle agreed and was imported to New York as pretender to Freed's throne. The move allowed Randle to play Elvis' music in both the Cleveland and New York markets, so that he also became the first to break Elvis nationally.

Both Randle and Shaw were significant supporters of Presley's music, and helped form Elvis' musical mystique. Due to their efforts, further discussed later in this chapter, the music industry became much more aware of the extent of the changes in taste that were occurring in the area of popular records.

Pat Boone

In 1955, the title of an article in *Billboard* trumpeted: "The Year R & B Took Over Pop Field." There had been a staggering two hundred percent increase in rhythm and blues record releases. Small labels and unknown artists popped up on the charts with amazing regularity. While the sale of rhythm and blues didn't yet equal pop record figures, nonetheless, the new music was an astounding commercial phenomenon. Pat Boone is a prime example of an artist who cashed in on the burgeoning popularity of black music. Covering several rhythm and blues hits in 1955, Boone placed his first three Dot Records releases on the *Billboard* Hot 100 Pop chart. Boone's first Dot release, a syrupy remake of Otis Williams and the Charms' "Two Hearts," reached number 16 in April of that year.

Boone's image made him more acceptable to adults, a deliberate Dot Records marketing strategy. The white buck shoes and white cardigan sweater that Boone wore in his public appearances were in sharp contrast to the black leather jackets, pegged pants, and motorcycle boots of many teenagers. Boone next scored with cover versions of the El Dorados' "At My Front Door," a number 7 *Billboard* hit, and then one of Fats Domino's classic rockers, "Ain't That a Shame," reached number 1 on the *Billboard* pop chart. Pat Boone became a legitimate teen idol, and was the first national rock star to benefit from a sophisticated national marketing campaign. The publicity department at Dot Records shrewdly portrayed him as a New York-based Columbia University student studying to become a high school English teacher. In industry circles, Boone was referred to jokingly as "the hip-swiveling grammarian." Both Colonel Tom Parker and Sam Phillips watched Boone's career closely and, being friends of Randy Wood, the owner of Dot, they talked with Wood at length about his rock music marketing successes.

The Pat Boone story mirrors the success that a small record company could achieve in the 1950s. When Dot Records was founded in 1951, Randy Wood had run the operation out of his home. A smiling, auburn-haired, easygoing young man, Wood was an excellent businessman with a clear grasp of the record industry. Like many small record label magnates, he realized that black music was crossing over into the mainstream pop record-buying market. In conversations with his artists, Wood contended that white musicians could better sell black music. At first, Pat Boone was surprised by Wood's selection of rhythm and blues material but, once Boone actually recorded the songs, he realized their commercial appeal. When Alan Freed refused to play Boone's cover versions of black music, magazines and newspapers vehemently defended Boone's covers. Peter Potter, the host of Hollywood's "Juke Box Jury," remarked, "All rhythm and blues records are dirty and as bad for kids as dope," an attitude that helped Randy Wood and Pat Boone sell Boone's recordings as real rock and roll music.

The financial success that Pat Boone enjoyed prompted Colonel Parker and Sam Phillips to try and get Elvis to adopt a more clean-cut image. It was not an easy task to clean up Elvis' dress and performing style. He wore his clothes in an exaggerated manner, and his aggressive stage antics often got out of hand. Yet, personally, Elvis was polite and articulate. It was a long and painful process to craft Elvis' live performances into a mainstream mold. Elvis had found it difficult to record a rhythm and blues or blues song in a watered-

Pat Boone never dressed—or moved—like this.

down manner. His reactions to r and b lyrics and music were every bit as elemental as those of the black artists he so admired. Apart from trying to appeal to several markets with one record, this is why Sam Phillips also had Elvis record country tunes with a rockabilly feel—at least part of Elvis repertoire was a little more sedate than the "Negro music."

The Role of Radio

Station managers in the 1950s did not depend on a particular rating method to establish their playlists; instead, music radio revolved around individual dj personalities, many of whom were strong enough to carry the station to popularity. Independent-minded disc jockeys dominated the airwaves and played whatever type of music they liked. It was still a time of decentralized, independently-owned broadcasting stations, and this worked to Elvis' advantage because many of the popular djs were often intrigued by Elvis' music. Unlike some of their peers, these knowledgeable disc jockeys would talk at great length about Elvis' black roots, rhythm and blues music, the blues, and the rise of the "Negro sound." (A generation of young rock enthusiasts grew up listening to djs who they believed were black, but who were in fact white radio personalities who simply loved the blues—including the likes of Alan Freed at WINS in New York and Wolfman Jack at XERB in Del Rio, Texas.) At the same time, much of radio programming was still controlled by a small group of radio station owners and managers with contrary attitudes, and not all new artists received extensive airplay on those stations, including Presley.

In New York City, for example, Martin Block hosted the "Make Believe Ballroom," a Saturday night program aired over WNEW that announced the week's hit songs. A supporter of Elvis, Block was opposed in this by New York's Alan Freed, WINS's evening rock and roll anchor from 7:00 to 11:00 p.m., who resisted playing black music recorded by whites. Maintaining that Elvis was one among many that were making money off the talent and creations of black artists, more than one promoter and RCA executive were informed by Freed that Presley was not an accomplished artist.

Freed was merely prominent among a number of other djs who were critical of Elvis. As a joke, for example, one Midwestern dj organized a "Music for People Who Don't Care Much for Elvis" club. When more than five thousand favorable responses flooded the radio station, the anti-Presley spoof got lots of publicity. In Ann Arbor, Michigan, Dave Pringle advertised membership cards for the "I Hate Elvis Presley Club," a tongue-in-cheek spoof offering a membership card that read: "He makes me feel surgical—like cutting my throat." A razor blade was attached conveniently to the card.

There were other, more serious protests directed at Elvis' records. Terry McGuire of WCMC in Wildwood, New Jersey, objected to Presley's music on religious grounds. Soon local Catholic priests were pillorying Presley from the pulpit. Bob Day of WNIX in St. Johnsbury, Vermont, voiced similar sentiments, and characterized Presley's music as fostering "bad taste." In Seattle, Pat O'Day of KJR didn't play Presley's music because he feared he would lose his audience.

Presley's unacceptability to some came to form the basis of a competition in which some djs used Presley's music to build up an audience. Some capitalized on the controversy by playing his records continuously. On the flip side, some radio moguls believed that by attacking Presley their ratings would improve. Some stations conducted call-in polls to decide whether the listeners preferred Pat Boone's antiseptic rendering of rhythm and blues tunes to Elvis Presley's raucous versions. In southern California, for example, Chuck Blore at KFWB was typical of the dj who asked his listeners to decide who

Elvis with Memphis dj Dewey Phillips.

should be deported from America—Pat Boone or Elvis Presley. Bob Rickman of WPGC in Washington, DC, established the Society for the Prevention of Cruelty to Elvis, while Norman Prescott of WBZ in Boston gave away pieces of Elvis' hair to his fans. Most of it was all in good fun.

On balance, there were many more djs like Dewey Phillips, who improved his ratings in the Memphis market with rock and roll. When Phillips interviewed Elvis on the radio in July 1954 just as "That's All Right (Mama)" was released by Sun Records, his "Red, Hot and Blue" program received its highest-ever rating. (Phillips' collaboration with Sun Records' owner Sam Phillips was essentially a form of the payola, an indiscretion for which Alan Freed was ultimately banned from the airwaves. When Norman Prescott, the first witness in the 1960 payola hearings before the U.S. House of Representatives, was called to testify, he pointed out that payment for radio airplay was by then merely a time-honored practice.) Later, at KLIF in Dallas, Texas, a street reporter asked local citizens if they liked Elvis Presley's music. When these street interviews came back positive, and revealed that Elvis performed regularly in the Dallas area, KLIF played his music as if he was a local act. The Dallas-based "Big D Jamboree" in turn drew larger crowds due to the radio airplay, and Elvis' cooperation with the media increased his record sales. Elvis, in effect, became a barometer for rock and roll radio wars.

Such radio wars were in turn just a barometer for a growing national debate over the future of rock and roll music, however. In addition to djs like Freed, there were numerous adults, civic organizations, and church groups who complained about what they regarded as Elvis' lurid music. People outside radio were either influenced by critical djs, or themselves sparked wariness in local radio personalities by loudly voicing their own antipathies. Lawrence Whipple, the police commissioner of Jersey City, New Jersey, made headlines when he went so far as to stop one of Alan Freed's rock and roll stage shows. Monsignor John B. Carroll, the director of Boston's Catholic Youth Organization, complained that "rock and roll has left its scar on youth." Rock music pointed in the wrong moral direction, the archbishop of Boston opined, and he urged radio stations to stop playing it. In Houston, Texas, John Orman, the juvenile delinquency and crime commissioner, expounded on the dangers of rock music in lengthy interviews. Even Jimmy Rodgers Snow, a former friend of Elvis', took to the pulpit and critized Presley for allowing rock and roll to destroy American youth. "I have seen what rock and roll can do to your soul," a Bible-thumping Snow bellowed. Once the moral issue was introduced into the rock and roll debate, an aggressive and emotional attack upon the music began. Everywhere in America there were opinions about the negative impact of rock music upon young people. Few, however, seemed to understand exactly or were able to articulate exactly what it was that made rock and roll so dangerous.

During this time, there were other important changes in radio programming that would directly influence the course of Elvis' career. A veritable revolution occurred in radio one day in the mid-fifties in Omaha, Nebraska, when Todd Storz, the owner of KOWH, went out for an afternoon of drinking with his program manager, Bill Stewart. As they sat in a small bar arguing about what songs to play on the radio, a cocktail waitress continued to play the same songs on the jukebox over and over again. In the course of their marathon drinking session, Storz finally realized that the same seven or eight songs had been playing repeatedly, apparently to the delight of the most of the patrons in the bar. After the bar closed its doors to incoming customers, Storz noticed that the waitress used her own money to continue playing the jukebox as she and the bartender cleaned up. Todd Storz would return to his job at KOWH with a new idea. If a cocktail waitress and her patrons wanted to hear the same tune again and again, why wouldn't a radio station format based on a repeating playlist work—a list of the forty most popular songs, for example. Out of that list, the eight most popular songs would receive the most airplay. Thus, unwittingly, Top 40 radio was born at precisely the time that Elvis

Presley's records were being favorably received on the *Billboard* charts. New York's WINS radio was one of those which converted to the Top 40 format. When the station brought in Mel Leeds from a Kansas City station, Leeds placed Presley's music in the mainstream rotation. Ultimately, because he invariably had two or three songs in the top ten, Elvis would benefit immeasurably from the Top 40 radio format (although even at stations not using that format, Elvis proved to be a favorite). Between 1956 and 1962, it helped Elvis to thirty-one out of RCA's thirty-nine million-selling singles.

The Effect of Changing Attitudes

In 1954-1955, then, radio was of paramount importance to the rock and roll revolution, the veritable key to promoting new rock songs. The irony of attacks on rock music in general, and on Elvis in particular, was that the controversy they created only resulted in higher record sales. Suddenly, too, the public was eager to spend its money on live concerts, leading to yet another area of commercialization for rock music.

As the carnival atmosphere surrounding the new music and Elvis increased, Colonel Tom Parker saw an opening to exploit the situation by packaging Elvis as "the man who invented rock and roll." A gimmick that was helpful at the moment, it was always the Colonel's intention to cross Elvis over into a mainstream pop music market, of course, envisioning a larger audience than just the country, blues, rhythm and blues, and rock enthusiasts who then embraced Presley's music. In 1955, Colonel Parker pointed out to Elvis that there were only a few rock and roll songs on fledgling Top 40 radio, and he urged Elvis to broaden his repertoire of songs.

Rick Sklar's book, *Rocking America: How the All-Hit Radio Stations Took Over*, contains an appendix of rock songs rated by radio stations as suitable for station playlists. In 1955, for example, Bill Haley and the Comets' "Rock Around The Clock" was the only mainstream rock and roll song on the list. The Top 40 playlist included the McGuire Sisters' "Sincerely," Georgia Gibbs' "Tweedle Dee" and "Dance with Me Henry," the Fontaine Sisters' "Hearts of Stone," and Pat Boone's "Ain't That a Shame." Sklar points out that the cover versions of these rhythm and blues hits dominated the market because white record producers could easily copy the black arrangements, tone down the musical background, and render the vocals antiseptic enough to be suitable to mainstream America.

The Roy Brown story is one of the tragic, but typical, tales of the music business, and serves as an example of how black artists were treated. Brown, one of the hottest rhythm and blues acts in America, like many black artists, didn't receive proper royalty payments. "They treated me like a little colored boy," Brown remembered. "I could never convince them that I had both talent and brains."

Brown began his career in Shreveport, Louisiana, with a weekly engagement at Billy Riley's Palace Park. Brown sang old standards like "Stardust" and "Blue Hawaii." "I was a black guy who sounded white," Brown remarked. "For the time I was a real novelty act." It was a story that Elvis would recreate in reverse at Sun Records.

From his earliest days with the Houston's Gold Star label, Roy Brown was a recording and performing genius, although, initially, his audience was limited to the black or so-called "race" charts. Brown was one of the first black acts in Houston to escape the relegation of most blacks to performing in small clubs located on "the other side of town." He was a strong nightclub draw, and it was not long before white club owners booked him in Texas's better night spots. Unfortunately, Brown had to leave Texas in a hurry when he was discovered making love to a club owner's girlfriend.

Cecil Gant encouraged Brown to take his act north. Gant introduced him to Jules Braun, the owner of Cincinatti's DeLuxe label. In 1948, Brown wrote and recorded "Good Rockin' Tonight" for DeLuxe and became a rhythm and blues superstar. In 1950, the prestigious King label bought out Brown's contract. His records were eagerly bought by a new generation of r and b aficionados. Soon Brown's singing style influenced such diverse talents as Little Richard, Buddy Holly, Chuck Berry, Bobby Blue Bland, and Elvis Presley. As one of the first rhythm and blues singers to sell to white record buyers, Brown was in an enviable position. He was not only an established black act, but he had his music covered by white artists.

Unfortunately, Roy Brown wasn't able to continue his career because he challenged the way black artists were treated within the industry. He had the audacity to file a protest with BMI over the payment of songwriting royalties. It had always been understood among black artists that if they complained about such payments, they simply wouldn't work or record anymore, so it took great courage to speak out against this racist system. In 1951, therefore, when Brown complained that his manager, Jack Pearl, had cheated him, the musicians' union investigated, Pearl's management license was suspended, but thereafter no booking agent would touch Brown. By challenging the manner in which the booking agencies and record companies treated black artists, Brown had destroyed his promising future.

In order to continue as a performer, Brown was forced to change his career strategy. To survive financially, he had to act as his own booking agent, leaving the North to play in small Southern towns. Tupelo was typical of these concert sites. The Tupelo sheriff and an assortment of local businessmen made good money promoting community dances, affairs where racial lines were dropped for a night and everybody enjoyed the music. In a lengthy interview in San Francisco before his death, Brown recalled that: "Tupelo had a code; the black people on one side of town and whites on the other; however, at the dances everyone came together." It was common for a black and white audience to mix quietly over the music, some bootleg alcohol, and a little gambling. The presence of segregation in the schools, on the job, and in residential neighborhoods just didn't prevail at such nighttime affairs.

Vernon and Elvis Presley were among those who attended these dances, as well as other small town affairs at which Brown played. In an interview with John Broven, Brown remembered that "Elvis was on the bandstand singing" on a number of such occasions. "I used to play for the high sheriff; it's a dry town and Elvis would come around, he wanted to sing." When Elvis found out that Brown's guitar player, Edgar Blanchard, loved to drink, he brought him some of Tupelo's finest moonshine straight from Shakerag. The moonshine allowed Elvis to get on stage with Brown's band. "That boy said he was on vacation," Brown remembered. "He sure didn't live in Tupelo, but he was down there seeing family."

Roy Brown couldn't date the times that Elvis played with him, but it is known that Elvis played and loved Brown's "Hard Luck Blues." Brown originally recorded the tune in Cincinnati at King Records, and it was his last hit before he was blacklisted. Elvis Presley apparently came to the Tupelo concerts regularly, however. Apart from dances in Tupelo, Elvis got to see Brown at Memphis club dates. The Flamingo Club was typical of these hangouts, and it is known that Elvis saw Brown perform there a number of times between 1952 to 1954. Roy Brown remembers Elvis hanging around both his Tupelo and Memphis appearances. "Elvis loved the music and he was everywhere. We thought he was just another nice white kid," Brown chuckled. Brown was surprised when his bass player, Tommy Shelvin, brought a copy of Elvis' Sun recording of "Good Rockin' Tonight" to a Hollywood club date. Brown sat in the dressing room listening to Elvis' version. "It was a fine blues song. I couldn't believe it." Elvis' rendition, of course, eliminated the sexual innuendos that prevented Roy Brown and Wynonie Harris from having crossover hits of the song.

It would not be long before Elvis took virtually all the elements of a "Negro act" into every important auditorium and ballroom in the nation. At the time, however, it was still difficult for him to obtain radio play in certain parts of the country precisely because his act was considered "Negro." Although Presley collared five of the top fifteen hit records in 1956, he remained unacceptable to most industry people. The reason was simple. Radio and recording executives viewed rock and roll as a temporary phenomenon filled with unacceptable types. The poor treatment of black artists was reflected even in the pages of *Billboard* and *Cashbox* magazines, which followed the current practice of segregating records by race. They also reported on black music in a special section.

When Ahmet Ertegun, the owner of Atlantic Records, began producing and releasing hit records for the Clovers, the Orioles, Ruth Brown, Ray Charles, the Cardinals, and the Drifters, he signed a distribution deal with Columbia Records. The Columbia executive who negotiated the deal was amazed that Atlantic was paying a "three to five percent royalty" to its acts. The startled Columbia executive remarked, "So it's you that's been spoiling it for everybody." The major record companies—Decca, Columbia, and RCA—were paying black artists minuscule royalties. They simply told the black performers that they had to make their money from concert dates. "By offering the black artists the same kind of terms that RCA would be offering to their top white artists, we were able to draw good performers," Ahmet Ertegun recalled. Atlantic Records led in the realization that musical tastes were changing and that the most important consideration for a businessman was to meet the consumers' demand for the music they preferred.

By late 1955, however, the distinction between rhythm and blues and pop music, based exclusively on race, had at least begun to fade as r and b and pop tunes blended into the charts. It was now possible for either a black or white artist to cross from the rhythm and blues or country charts into the pop music ranks. The right record release could hit on all charts: r and b, country, and pop.

Changes in the Record Business

As Elvis prepared for his final assault upon fame and fortune, aided by Sam Phillips' fine Sun recordings, he also helped his career by developing an unusually cooperative attitude with the press. The media's importance was not lost on Elvis, Colonel Parker, or Sam Phillips—all fully realized its role in musical popularity. The time was coming when Elvis' music and radio interviews would be played extensively in northern markets.

After all, what had caused Elvis' mass popularity

in the South? Undoubtedly, it was the radio broadcasts of the "Louisiana Hayride" on KWKH that made him a regional star. Had it not been for his appearances on the "Hayride," Elvis would not have been able to travel throughout the South performing in high school auditoriums, honky-tonk bars, and the fair circuit. It was the strength of the radio signal that KWKH beamed from Shreveport, Louisiana, that prompted a generation of teenagers and country music buffs to demand that Elvis be booked into local halls. Long before his fans saw Elvis in concert, they had heard his music on KWKH.

As a result of these appearances on the "Louisiana Hayride," of course, Sam Phillips could not keep Elvis' records in stock. It was this explosion in record sales that added yet another dimension to Presley's success. For years, the major record labels had distributed their records to stores through factory-owned branches. The rise of small, independent labels led to the birth of what came to be called "one-stop" record distributors, which also carried singles from small companies like Sun. Not only did the one-stop wholesale its product to jukebox operators, but they often influenced radio airplay. Elvis Presley was one of the artists to benefit from the proliferation of one-stops—which aided the sale of his Sun singles not only in the South, but in states like California where the abundance of small labels served as an inducement for such distributors to carry a wide variety of records.

There was a weakness in the one-stop system, however. Sam Phillips couldn't keep up with the demand for new records. The reason that Phillips wasn't able to meet the onslaught of orders for Presley records was due to the time that wholesalers took to pay off their debts. Phillips was never able to accumulate the money needed to adequately press enough 45rpm records or to put out a long-playing Presley album. Sun was a small operation, and the irony of Sam Phillip's success is that it nearly destroyed his business. A major record label was needed to press, publicize, and distribute Presley's material, one for which cash flow—or the lack of it—was not going to be a problem.

The New Performance Styles

Acceptance of the frenetic style of performing rock and roll was another factor that aided Elvis' career. Little Richard's wild piano performances, Chuck Berry's duck walk, and Bill Haley's saxophone soloist, Rudy Pompelli, bending to the floor while the bass player rode his instrument were examples of the new visual impact of rock music. When disc jockeys used the term "Big Beat," it helped young people to identify with the music. Suddenly, rock musicians were a role model for a new generation. As he performed in dingy auditoriums, small honky-tonk bars, and well-lit high school gymnasiums, Elvis employed all the performance antics of rock and roll music that would ultimately win over a new generation of fans. After a wild and exciting show filled with "animal gyrations," however, Elvis was polite, calm, and clean-living off stage. He was a press agent's dream—a poor boy who could entertain with skill and then talk to reporters conservatively and politely. In many respects, Elvis mirrored the contradiction of rock and roll music. It was a wild, primitive musical form that frightened people who were not used to its dynamic visual impact. Yet, after people listened to rock music without prejudice, they embraced it.

The manner in which Elvis exploited the changes that rock music brought to show business was demonstrated in his selection of songs. He performed tunes that excited his audience. Elvis realized that it was necessary to work the crowd. He had learned this lesson long ago at the Eagle's Nest and other small clubs in Memphis. He wasn't content to simply stand there and sing. Elvis had to create an event that everyone remembered.

A good example of Elvis' impact upon his fans occurred in New Orleans, Louisiana, on September 1, 1955, when he appeared at the Golden Cadillac Lounge on St. Claude Avenue near Poland Avenue. The Cadillac was a white club with a black band. Danny White and the Cavaliers were the house band during its heyday. The booking agent, Keith Rush, was a wheeler-dealer on the New Orleans music scene, and he envisioned big profits because of the popularity of Presley's records. Local New Orleans music fans looked upon the Cadillac as a rhythm and blues meeting place, so they eagerly anticipated Presley's performance because they knew he would cover r and b hits.

The night that Elvis appeared at the Golden Cadillac, it was filled with excited spectators. His show was truly unique. After opening with "That's All Right (Mama)," Elvis interspersed r and b songs with his Sun recordings. Elvis knew that the audience was an r and b one, and he tailored his song selection to include tunes like "Shake a Hand" and "What'd I Say." A local New Orleans r and b singer, Bobby Mitchell, was in the audience. Mitchell was stunned by Presley's "black sound."

The night at the Golden Cadillac is a microcosmic example of how Presley's small club dates helped to sell his records. Responding to customer demand, Johnny Vincent, the owner of Ace Records and distributor for Sun Records in New Orleans, immediately told his chief employee, Joe Corona, to order more Presley records. At Joe Assunto's One-Stop Record shop, there was a run on Elvis records. RCA and Mercury Records had distribution arms in New Orleans, and their local executives wrote to the parent companies that Presley's music was hitting the charts in a big way. It was as if the Golden Cadillac Lounge date had touched a nerve with New Orleans music fans. Presley's records were selling in unprecedented numbers.

Cosimo Matassa, founder of the legendary J and M Recording Studio, recalled the drawbacks to Elvis' popularity, however. As someone with a business developed much along the lines of Sam Phillips' early Memphis Recording Service, the success of Elvis and other whites "made it difficult for us to sell black artists. Elvis was popular among the people who bought black music." "The biggest impact Elvis had on us in New Orleans and me personally was a negative one—he took away part of our market," Matassa added. As he recalled the history of New Orleans radio, Matassa remembered how the disc jockeys played Presley's music after he appeared at the Golden Cadillac Lounge. On WJMR, WNOE, and WWEZ, Elvis' Sun records were carving a territorial niche for his music.

The time was clearly ripe for Elvis Presley. His regional success had brought him to the attention of national players in radio and recording industries at a time of great societal and musical upheaval. Things were changing. A white artist whose performance delivery and repertoire looked and sounded black—especially

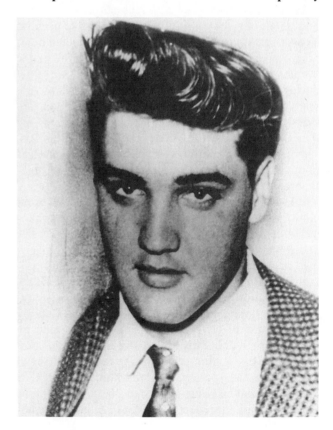

if his music was genuine as well as good—couldn't avoid being the center of controversy. The controversy surrounding Elvis would hereafter not only propel him to national stature, but would in its own way fire the engine of further social change. With the preceding as background, let us now return to the two months of activities precedent to the next major change in Elvis' life—signing a recording contract with RCA-Victor.

Early September 1955

The New Orleans club scene was one that Elvis loved, and following his show at the Golden Cadillac he took some time out to enjoy a little of New Orleans' night life. As usual, as a result of his uncontrolled energy and passion for music, Elvis combined his performing with the interests of a fan, and so drove out to Rampart Street and looked in on the Astoria, Blue Eagle, and Tiajuana clubs before calling it a night.

On Friday, September 2, 1955, while driving to Texarkana, Arkansas, he was ticketed for speeding. A few hours later, Elvis was involved in an automobile accident that resulted in more than a thousand dollars in body damage to his 1955 pink Cadillac. When the distraught Presley appeared on Friday, September 2, at the Arkansas Municipal Auditorium and performed in two shows at 7:00 and 9:00 o'clock with Johnny Cash, Charlene Arthur, Floyd Cramer, and Jimmy Day, he informed the crowd: "I've had a few surprises recently, now here's one for you...." Elvis then began to perform a cover version of Faye Adams' 1953 rhythm and blues hit, "Shake a Hand." An interesting sidelight to the evening is the fact that Floyd Cramer played the piano during Elvis' appearance. The show, however, was generally lackluster, with Elvis showing signs of fatigue. Obviously under great strain, he complained to Johnny Cash that the price of sudden fame was becoming burdensome. As his tour continued, Elvis betrayed visible signs of the strain brought on by constantly being in the public eye.

That night in Texarkana, Elvis and Bill Black went out for something to eat. It was unusual for Elvis to hang out with Black, and it was obvious that young Presley had something on his mind. Elvis was having misgivings, and wondered if he was headed in the right musical direction. Tired and anxious, he asked Black whether country music was the road he should follow, or whether he should continue to mix his songs. Country music audiences were often critical of Elvis, and he was concerned about his future. Bill Black did his best to reassure Elvis. After telling young Presley a string of jokes, Black had a serious talk with him, advising Elvis to just perform his songs and forget about the opinions of other people. In effect, Bill Black became a tempo-

rary surrogate father figure and helped to nurture Elvis through a difficult period. Ronald Smith and Kenneth Herman, too, recalled that Elvis was reassessing the state of his career after returning from his September dates.

The following night, Elvis appeared on the "Big D Jamboree" in Dallas, and Tommy Sands remembered that he looked worn out. Elvis discussed his feelings with Sands, and went on at length about Black's idea that Elvis should record more country songs. "Elvis had a weary look to him," Sands remarked. "The strain showed in his face and his clothes hung on his thin frame. Elvis weighed about 160 pounds and appeared haggard in concert," Sands noted. When he graduated from Humes High, Elvis had weighed 185 pounds. The road was taking its toll, but he drove on relentlessly in pursuit of stardom.

There is no way to accurately determine Elvis' earnings in 1955. The figure that Bob Neal gave out in interviews—$55,000—is probably close to the truth. This money was earned largely through long, backbreaking concert schedules. It was difficult to make large sums of money due to the limitations of the live concert business. At the "Big D Jamboree," for example, the sixty-cent admission for adults and thirty-cent fee for kids was a real bargain. Performers received only a small percentage of the gate. Yet, live appearances were essential to Elvis' popularity. Attracting a youthful crowd, the large number of pubescent females who cheered Elvis' every move were all potential record buyers and repeat concertgoers. There was a great deal of publicity to be had in local Texas newspapers, and this made Elvis an instant celebrity. (Following such concerts, many of Elvis' admirers mingled with him at his motel or in a nearby restaurant. The number of young girls who had liaisons with Elvis was numerous, although the vast majority refused to speak or write of their involvements, largely to protect him. Everyone realized that any hint of scandal or excessive sexual activity would hurt his career.)

As he toured small and large towns alike, a rapidly growing following cheered his every move. A typical Elvis tour was concluded from September 5 through 9, 1955, when he performed in Forrest and Bono, Arkansas, Sikeston, Missouri, as well as Clarksdale and McComb, Mississippi. The shows were all sellouts. In Bono, the town's 311 inhabitants geared up for an influx of people who came from throughout the county. When 1,152 people showed up at the rodeo grounds, it was clearly due to Elvis' Sun recordings, which were hot among the country music enthusiasts.

The sale of Presley's records continued to grow stronger. In Florida and Texas, for example, there were more orders from one-stop distributors than Sam Phillips could fill. Every two weeks, the Binkley Distribution Company of Jacksonville, Florida, ordered fifty copies of each of his Sun 78s as well as a hundred 45s of each of his records. A full year after Elvis' first record was released, Binkley Distribution ordered three hundred copies of "Baby Let's Play House." As a result of his Texas appearances, Big State Record distributors in Dallas ordered five hundred copies of "Baby Let's Play House," and back-ordered three hundred copies of each of the remainder of Elvis' records. The local charts in Texas, Florida, Louisiana, Alabama, Arkansas, and Tennessee clearly reflected Elvis' enormous appeal.

On September 4, 1955, Elvis appeared at the Round-Up Club in Dallas, Texas. There was often virtually no profile of his audience available to Elvis when he was booked into new places like the Round-Up Club until he arrived, although this ended up being an important part of his musical training. Adapting to the crowds, which were now invariably large, continually tested the limits of his versatility. Changing his song selection, he experimented on this occasion with some old country standards—"Old Shep" and "Uncle Pen."

During the period discussed above, September 5-9, old Memphis friend Eddie Bond shared some dates with Elvis. Since his days at Humes High, Elvis had played music with Eddie (who eventually recorded songs in Memphis that were leased to the Hollywood-based Ekko label). He also was friendly with Bond's father, who financed and produced Johnny Burnette's first record for the Boone, Mississippi-based Von label, "Go Mule Go" b/w "You're Undecided."

With Bond was an aspiring guitarist named Eddie Cochran. A virtual unknown at the time, Cochran went on to become a mainstream rock act with such hits at "Summertime Blues," "Sittin' in the Balcony," and "Twenty Flight Rock." The sixteen-year-old Cochran began his professional career as a backup guitarist for hillbilly singer Hank Cochran. After a time, they appeared as the Cochran Brothers, although they were not related. When he met Elvis, Cochran had recently moved to Dallas to pursue a country music career. In the midst of this exciting atmosphere, Eddie Cochran could not help but be impressed with Elvis, and Cochran's early records—"Mr. Fiddle," "Guilty Conscience," and "Your Tomorrows Never Come"—were authentic rockabilly tunes that bear Presley's unmistakable influence. Later, in 1959, Cochran recorded "Milk Cow Blues" at Goldstar Studios in Los Angeles, and his rendition demonstrates an uncanny resemblance to Presley's Sun Records version.

RCA Enters the Picture

Just as Elvis was concluding the September tour, *Billboard* positioned "Mystery Train" and "I Forgot to Remember to Forget" in its "This Week's Best Buys" section, inspiring Sam Phillips to offer Elvis to Decca Records for $5,000. Owen Bradley, a well-known country music producer, pointed out to Sam that no one paid that kind of money for an unknown. Phillips, undeterred, then offered Elvis to Randy Wood at Dot Records for $7,500. Wood walked away without responding. Sam Phillips decided the only thing to do was raise his price again. Phillips reasoned that a higher asking price for Presley's Sun record catalog would create interest. He was right. Once Phillips announced that Elvis' contract would be sold for no less than $20,000, there were inquiries from Columbia and Decca Records.

The reason for the change in the attitude of New York companies was industry gossip about Presley's future. During the summer of 1955, Arnold Shaw, discussed earlier, visited Memphis and Nashville, where he quickly recognized Elvis' breakthrough talent. Not only was Shaw an important figure in the music business but, as the director of the creative department of the Edward B. Marks Music Corporation, Shaw was in a position to influence record moguls. His office, located in the RCA building on what is now the Avenue of the Americas, was a place where he frequently exchanged opinions with RCA executives. After five o'clock, when the workday ended, Shaw and RCA's younger record

Eddie Cochran (above) was introduced to Elvis by Eddie Bond.

heads often stopped off at Manhattan bars and discussed emerging performers like Elvis Presley. Shaw talked at length about Elvis' obvious talent, and relayed his stories about his trip to Memphis. Shaw beamed as he described listening to the recordings of Elvis' music that Sam Phillips had played for him. The respect and integrity that Arnold Shaw commanded in the recording industry prompted RCA executives to sit up and listen. When Shaw described Elvis as a crossover artist who could sing pop tunes as well as the new rock music, record moguls paid attention. Had it not been for Shaw's enthusiasm, RCA might have continued to ignore Elvis.

Bill Randle, as noted above, had be instrumental in acquainting Shaw with Elvis' music. There is no way of measuring Randle's influence, but he also helped to break down the reluctance of New York music executives to consider Presley's music. Initially, New York critics dismissed Elvis' records as hillbilly tripe. Alan Freed refused to play Elvis' "Good Rockin' Tonight" because he considered Presley similar to Pat Boone—white poseurs, according to Freed, who didn't deserve New York airplay. It was only after Bill Randle was brought to New York by Shaw that Elvis' records were played in America's largest market. Since Randle was being groomed to replace Freed, his opinion mattered. Once in the Big Apple, Randle unabashedly extolled Elvis' musical talent, prompting a number of inquiries to Sun Records about Presley's availability. RCA, too, believed that Randle was extraordinarily perceptive when it came to youthful musical interests, and added his observations to those of Arnold Shaw.

In addition to Shaw's and Randle's kind words, a few early rock stars extolled Elvis' commercial musical virtues. Bill Haley, 1955's premier rock artist, riding high with "Rock Around the Clock," praised Elvis' potential. "I went to Bill Randle," Haley remarked, "who was the top disc jockey in Cleveland at that time on WERE, and I started telling him how good Elvis was...." Following their August meeting in Ohio and a round of performing in the Midwest, Bill Haley summed up his feelings about Elvis' talent. "I told him," Haley remarked, "you're leaning too much on ballads....You've got a natural rhythm feeling, so do your rhythm tunes." There is no concrete record of Elvis' reaction to Haley's suggestions, although, generally, from the summer of 1955 on, Elvis was more of a rock singer than a ballad artist. Ronald Smith recalls that a number of musicians appearing with Elvis urged him to take the shackles off his singing and use the raw energy that excited fans on the "Louisiana Hayride." It was not common for entertainers to praise one another, and Haley's comments were typical of those by other recording artists which reflected the level of professional appreciation for

Rock legend Bill Haley.

Presley's talent.

Jackie Wilson was another artist who recognized Elvis' crossover appeal. After taking over as the lead vocalist in Billy Ward and the Dominoes, Wilson grew tired of the monotonous ballads and rigorous tours that Ward demanded. As Wilson listened to Elvis and watched blues singer Roy Brown perform, he crafted his own music into a crossover sound. "What people often forget," Wilson remarked in 1955, "is that black performers wanted to cross over into the pop field. Elvis showed us how to do it."

The following year, Elvis was performing for two weeks at the New Frontier Hotel in Las Vegas at the same time that Jackie Wilson was in town appearing in a local lounge with Billy Ward and the Dominoes. Shortly after Elvis opened on April 23, he went to see Wilson sing "Don't Be Cruel." Elvis was amazed by the manner in which Jackie Wilson interpreted the song, and accorded Wilson a fine honor by remarking "...he sang the song better than I did. I went back four nights straight to see Billy Ward and the Dominoes."

The confidence-building comments by other musicians were also an important asset to Elvis because their highly publicized statements allowed Sun Records to make it look as if it was turning down offers to buy Presley's contract. When Randy Wood, the president of Dot Records, re-entered the Presley sweepstakes and bid $10,000 for Elvis' contract, Sam Phillips leaked the Dot Records offer to other labels, attracting even more interest. Most of all, Phillips was attempting to interest Columbia Records in Elvis, because Columbia's prestige would bring every other major record company into the bidding. Much to Phillips surprise, however, Mitch Miller, Columbia's chief talent scout, indicated that Phillips' $20,000 asking price was too high for "the unknown Hillbilly singer." Quietly, though, Miller offered $15,000. At the same time, Dee Kilpatrick of Mercury Records bid $10,000. After being rebuffed, Kilpatrick wanted to increase the bid, but he couldn't convince the label's key executives of Presley's worth. It was at this point that Colonel Tom Parker seriously entered the negotiations. He had been aiding Phillips unofficially for some time. Phillips simply could not complete the transaction, because there was still a great deal of indecision about Elvis' show business future.

Colonel Parker recognized that only a trip to New York would move things along, as the Big Apple was *the* market in which to merchandise Elvis. The Colonel flew to New York and, after settling into the Hotel Warwick, called Arnold Shaw to discuss the a strategy to attract a major label. Shaw was convinced that RCA could be persuaded to sign Presley. The Colonel had managed Eddy Arnold and Hank Snow when they signed with RCA, and everyone made money. The difficulty in shopping Elvis' music around New York was that his records were neither played nor did they sell well as yet in the East. Rock and roll music was different.

Parker also hoped that Ahmet Ertegun's Atlantic label would reconsider purchasing Elvis' Sun contract. As an independent recording company with major distribution ties and a string of hit records, Atlantic tended to sell its product more quickly than other labels. Ertegun had a reputation for honesty and integrity that was rare in the record business. He not only paid his artists royalties, but he personally supervised many recording sessions. Using the pen name A. Nugetre, Ahmet Ertegun wrote some of the label's classic hits—most of the Clovers' early hit records, for example, were A. Nugetre compositions. Ertegun had expressed interest in purchasing Elvis' contract as early as March 1955 but, as related earlier, had run afoul of Dewey Phillips on his fact-finding trip to Memphis. Over the years, Ertegun has never discussed why he didn't pursue Elvis' contract with greater intensity. Eventually, Ertegun offered $25,000, but then dropped out of the bidding when the figure spiraled even higher.

In September 1955, *Country Song Roundup* published a nationally-circulated article on Elvis entitled "Folk Music Fireball." The article was a complimentary piece of journalism extolling Elvis' unique talent,

and helped to break his music in a number of northern markets. The piece presented the picture of a wholesome, boy-next-door entertainer who had a talent which excited his audiences. The article, which included a photo of Dixie Locke seated next to Elvis during the interview, was followed by a 1955 Hillbilly popularity poll. The feature article was "Hank Snow's Journey to Fame."

Colonel Parker and Hank Snow had been instrumental in setting up this piece of publicity, hoping that it would promote increased ticket sales for Elvis' upcoming tour with Snow. The magazine, distributed widely in the East and Midwest, did just that, but also helped "Mystery Train" to creep onto playlists in Chicago, Detroit, Boston, Cleveland, and Philadelphia. At WPWA in Chester, Pennsylvania, where Bill Haley had once been a disc jockey, there were calls for "Mystery Train" soon after the piece appeared, and local djs began to talk busily about the Presley phenomenon. The migration of Southerners to the factories in Pennsylvania, Illinois, and Michigan was also instrumental in the spread of Elvis' music northward.

Suddenly, more West Coast radio stations were playing Presley's records. In Seattle, KJR not only hyped "Mystery Train," but held a contest to determine Presley's future star appeal. In San Francisco, KSAN disc jockey Jumpin' George Oxford played all of Elvis' Sun recordings. Oxford often presided over shows at Jimbo's Bop City, a jazz club in San Francisco's black section, which featured Monday night rock and roll sessions.

The Last Jamboree

On September 11, 1955, Elvis began his last tour with the Hank Snow All Star Jamboree, starting in Norfolk, Virginia. Sheriff Tex Davis, who co-authored "Be-Bop-a-Lula" with Gene Vincent, promoted the date. Davis broadcast the first night's show over WCMS. (He also played Presley's records extensively on his radio show and conducted a call-in contest to judge whether Elvis or Pat Boone was more popular. Elvis won easily.) The tour's supporting acts included Cowboy Copas, the Louvin Brothers, and Jimmy Rodgers Snow. An easygoing atmosphere was evident during the early performances, and this encouraged Elvis to experiment with his song selections. During the tour, Elvis tried out "Blue Guitar," a 1954 song written and recorded by Sheb Wooley. It is likely that Elvis recorded a demo of "Blue Guitar" at Sun, but a tape has never surfaced.

Gene Vincent, recently released from the hospital after suffering a broken leg, attended the Jamboree show both nights. Vincent was impressed with Presley's performing energy. "I wasn't influenced by his voice,

Gene Vincent.

There was an air of excitement on September 15, 1955, when the Jamboree opened in the American Legion auditorium. A benefit for the city's sandlot baseball program, it was an event that brought out many local would-be musicians. The *Roanoke Times* and the *Roanoke World-News* had taken to calling Elvis "the Hillbilly Frank Sinatra." Elvis' name, appearing last on the concert's advertising cards, stood out in large letters as big as Hank Snow's name. There were whispers backstage that Snow was unhappy with the way that Elvis had upstaged him during the tour. It was to Colonel Parker's benefit to initiate bad blood between Elvis and Snow. Since Snow was a fifty-fifty partner with Parker in Hank Snow Enterprises, he would be entitled to half of Elvis' future royalties if young Presley signed with their company rather than going with Parker personally. During the tour, much to Parker's satisfaction, it was very uncomfortable backstage. There was also common agreement among the performers that the crowds turned out to see and hear Elvis.

The *Billboard* charts for the first week of September 1955 had placed "I Forgot to Remember to Forget" at number 1 in Memphis. "Mystery Train" was number 4 in the Dallas-Fort Worth area and number 5 in Houston. The chart gains were due to the promotional efforts of the Big State Record Distributors, which concentrated upon Tennessee and Texas, where Elvis was a strong regional act, but also had field representatives in Louisiana, Missouri, and Virginia, something which paid off in large record sales in these areas. In New Orleans, "Mystery Train" was number 8 on the local charts. "Baby Let's Play House" was number 4 in St. Louis, and number 8 in Richmond, Virginia. *Billboard* placed "Mystery Train" number 14 and "Baby Let's Play House" number 15 on the country and western charts. In terms of radio airplay, "I Forgot to Remember to Forget" was rated 10, and "Baby Let's Play House" number 15.

Also by September, Music Merchants in Philadelphia had inquired about Presley's records. Since 1952, Elliot Wexler's Music Merchants had been one of the premiere record jobbers in the country, setting up record racks in drug stores, supermarkets, and variety stores. Given a small amount of space, Music Merchants guaranteed local stores a profit. After ordering a small quantity of "Mystery Train," they began marketing it in Pennsylvania, Maryland, and Virginia, where it sold well. Safeway and Woolworth stores, two of the chains that Music Merchants serviced, sold Presley's records in large numbers. After signing a management agreement with Elvis, Colonel Parker kept in touch with Elliot Wexler, from whom he learned a great deal about merchandising.

except that he was obviously young like me and I was encouraged by this, 'cause I was just a shy kid." There is no doubt that Elvis affected Gene Vincent's career. Much like Eddie Cochran, Vincent saw his own rock and roll future after watching Presley's stage show. Gene Vincent's band, the Blue Caps—Jack Neal, Cliff Gallup, Willie Williams, and Dickie Harrell—also watched Elvis, Scotty Moore, Bill Black, and D.J. Fontana with great interest. Impressed with Elvis' band, they felt reassured that they, too, had a future in the music business.

As the Hank Snow tour progressed, Elvis' charismatic touch was repeated in city after city. There were signs at all the concerts of a special feeling between Elvis and his fans, who threw flowers, notes, and assorted gifts onto the stage. The feeling of love and identification with the music seemed to go far beyond previous concert scenes. Such a feeling was evident between September 11 to 22, 1955, as crowds grew larger and more boisterous, and audiences cheered Elvis while ignoring the other acts. This led to some changes in the order of appearance when the troupe performed at Roanoke's American Legion auditorium, after only two shows in Norfolk. A new concert handbill was distributed featuring Elvis as an "extra attraction by popular demand." Colonel Parker reasoned that this type of advertising would sell more tickets. The result was that the promoter who brought the Jamboree to town—who was also the owner of the Roanoke Record Shop and was not only unable to keep Presley's records in stock—quickly ran out of dollar concert tickets as well.

On September 22, 1955, while performing with Cowboy Copas in Kingsport, Tennessee, Elvis opened his portion of the show with Bill Haley's "Rock Around the Clock." In August, when Elvis had met Haley during his appearance in Cleveland with Bill Randle, they spent a great deal of time backstage talking about rock music, and had sung "Rock Around the Clock" together. Colonel Tom Parker also talked at length with Haley's manager, Lord Jim Ferguson, prompting the Colonel to recommended that Elvis record songs that local audiences were purchasing. Bill Haley also urged Elvis to develop his stage personality to its fullest. When Haley went on stage that August night, Presley watched him closely and reflected upon their conversation. Haley was a dynamic performer and the audience responded with vigorous applause. It was as if Bill Haley was rising to the challenge that he knew was coming from young Elvis Presley. For his part, after thinking about the positive reaction to "Rock Around the Clock" that he had witnessed, Elvis began to include Haley's signature song in his own act.

Negotiating With RCA

When Elvis returned to Memphis on September 23, 1955, he found that Colonel Tom Parker had been working diligently to secure a recording contract for him. Elvis called the Colonel shortly after coming home to inquire about negotiations with the major record labels. The Colonel didn't have good news. It appeared that many of the labels were still unsure about marketing Elvis, although there was strong interest from RCA-Victor.

Contrary to popular myth, it was not easy to sell Presley's contract. Colonel Parker had to negotiate long and hard to make a deal. There was concern about the

Elvis at home with Gladys, who thought the Colonel
would do her son no good.

accuracy of the count for sales of Elvis' Sun recordings. Had these records sold in the quantity that Sam Phillips suggested? Was Elvis simply a flash in the pan? How accurate were the reports of Elvis' regional success? These questions perplexed the recording industry, but they had to be answered before anyone bought the rights to release Elvis' future recordings. After a great deal of thought, however, key RCA executives concluded that the reliability of Sun's record sale numbers was inconsequential. It was simply impossible to analyze Elvis' impact in the northern market based on his existing track record, so that if Elvis was signed he would in any case have to be publicized in an expensive ad campaign. Considering the money involved, RCA believed that it had to proceed slowly.

There were two people who changed RCA's worrisome attitude. One was Arnold Shaw, the New York booking agent and publishing house magnate discussed above, who disputed this pessimistic attitude in discussions with RCA's key executives. The other was Steve Sholes, a Nashville-based veteran country music producer for RCA, who argued that Elvis definitely had a new sound. Sholes, who had previously produced only traditional country music, believed a tune like Elvis' "Baby Let's Play House" was a potential crossover song. Since Sholes was one of the most respected producers in Nashville, his opinion mattered to recording executives, and he was brought into RCA's front office to help in the negotiations to purchase Elvis' recording contract.

In an attempt to downplay Elvis' importance, a number of key RCA executives suggested that Colonel Tom Parker had himself had second thoughts about managing Elvis. They argued that the contract between Elvis and Hank Snow Attractions, which was signed on August 15, 1955, demonstrated that Colonel Parker was not interested in spending large sums of money to publicize Presley, an indication that Parker was still uncertain about Elvis' future. Further complications arose as a result of the continual disagreements between Hank Snow and Colonel Parker over Elvis' contract. No one has yet revealed what the arrangements were between Snow and Parker, but it is known that Hank Snow personally wanted no part of Elvis Presley when Parker had signed him. Thereafter, Colonel Parker seized every opportunity to rile Snow by telling him, for example, about how "the girls are tearing off that boy's clothes in Florida and Georgia." Snow fumed over these asinine comments, and blanched when the Colonel mentioned "Elvis' obvious sexual appeal." One day, in a fit of rage, Snow hollered: "Good, god-fearing Christian people love me, Colonel, I can't let that hillbilly ruin my act." By agitating Hank Snow, Colonel Parker had guaranteed that a distance would be maintained between Snow and Elvis, and that Snow would not be prepared to pursue any contractual rights he might feel he was entitled to in connection with Presley. Having carefully separated Snow's financial interests in Hank Snow Attractions from his personal management of Elvis, Parker was able to virtually guarantee that Snow would not create a barrier.

In order to better analyze Elvis' musical appeal, RCA executives spent time talking to Sam Phillips. After lengthy discussions, RCA concluded that Elvis had a bright commercial future. In the course of the discussions with RCA, Phillips went so far as to claim that "That's All Right (Mama)" had sold twenty thousand copies. If Elvis had sold that many records, RCA wondered, why did Phillips wanted to sell his contract? The answer was a simple one. Sam Phillips was broke. Phillips already had another brilliant musician, Carl Perkins, under contract. Everyone around Memphis believed that Perkins had as much talent as Elvis. What Sam Phillips didn't fully appreciate was the degree to which animal magnetism made Presley a more commercial property than Perkins would ever be. Since Phillips had sold thousands of records by many different artists, he believed that, for his purposes, Elvis could be easily replaced.

Even with Colonel Parker in the fray, Sam Phillips had a great deal of trouble selling Elvis. From the beginning, RCA and the recording industry in general was skeptical about Presley. "In practically all of 1955 there were negotiations of one sort or another going on," Bob Neal recalled. Neal remembered that he would get calls from record companies inquiring about Elvis, and he would put them off while he talked with Colonel Parker or Sam. "I don't think Sam believed that we could sell Elvis," said Neal, "he was frustrated with the larger labels who wouldn't commit themselves to a price. Everyone seemed to want Elvis for nothing," Neal concluded.

It was this inability to come to a common agreement on the price for Elvis' contract that ultimately worked to Colonel Parker's advantage, however, because it gave him time to persuade his close friends at RCA—Steve Sholes, the head of the Nashville a & r department, and Frank Folsom, RCA-Victor's president —of the value of signing Presley. Parker had known these influential musical figures for years, an association which had resulted in RCA contracts for Eddy Arnold and Hank Snow. The Colonel certainly had the right contacts in the industry. All that was necessary was to convince RCA that Elvis' music was the wave of the future. Steve Sholes and Frank Folsom were the only ones at RCA who believed in Elvis, but in the end the opinion of such key executives tipped the scales.

Not long after receiving the advice of Sholes and Folsom, RCA agreed in principle to sign Presley. Sam Phillips flew to New York to settle the details. Throughout October 1955 there were serious negotiations, and the prolonged dealings served only to heighten interest in Elvis within the industry. This again worked to Colonel Parker's advantage, because he dutifully alerted RCA to the overtures he had received from its potential competitors. Despite the pressure, there was the problem of finding suitable financing for Elvis' contract as far as RCA was concerned. The $40,000 purchase price that Sam Phillips had asked RCA to pay included a $5,000 bonus to cover past royalties owed Elvis by Sun. Initially, RCA management balked at this high price. The figures were bandied about for the press by Colonel Parker, but RCA wouldn't settle. A means had to be found to raise the money for Elvis' contract.

Hill and Range

It was at this point that Jean and Julian Aberbach, owners of Hill and Range music publishers, entered the Presley contract negotiations. The Aberbach's were among the shrewdest business people in the industry. They were a Viennese Jewish couple who had entered the music publishing business in Berlin during the days of cabaret entertainment. After immigrating to America, they displayed a brilliant musical sophistication in the country music field, where they had a knack for picking out hit country songs. The important part, of course, is that they also obtained the publishing rights to these songs. The name Hill and Range was intended to signify country (Hill) and western (Range) music. It took only a few years for the Aberbachs to become respected and wealthy.

It was Hill and Range who had signed a contract with Colonel Parker for Hank Snow's songs. Apart from links with Colonel Parker, the Aberbach's were fully aware of the stir that Elvis was creating—that Bill Randle at WERE in Cleveland, for example, was playing Presley records an average of five times a day. Hill and Range had monitored audience reaction to Presley's music for some time, and they let RCA know that they were willing to publish Elvis' music. More than that, the Aberbach's quietly offered to advance a portion of the money RCA needed to sign Elvis. Hill and Range wanted total secrecy about its monetary contribution to Presley's contract, however. The Aberbachs were concerned about angering Hank Snow and perhaps losing his music publishing rights. They also worried that a larger music publisher might approach Elvis before their offer was accepted. The significance of the Aberbach's actions is that their involvement convinced RCA that Elvis was a potentially blockbuster musical act.

There was still the question of Hank Snow's financial ties to Elvis, however. Colonel Parker had laid the groundwork for Snow's ready acceptance of Elvis departure, but that did not mean that Snow was as willing to relinquish rewards he might feel were due him as a partner in Hank Snow Jamboree Attractions. Indeed, Albert Grossman's Elvis biography suggests that Hank Snow "hoped to profit" by himself introducing the Aberbachs to Presley's music, although Snow's claim that he was instrumental in making the Aberbachs aware of Elvis is a totally erroneous one. The people at Hill and Range were aware of Elvis long before Snow suggested they sign him. What bothered the Aberbachs was Snow's sudden and intense financial interest in Elvis. When Gordon Stoker, a member of the Jordanaires, met Hank Snow at the WSM jamboree, Snow remarked that "Elvis was really tearing up wherever he played." Stoker was puzzled, as Snow had previously displayed little interest in Presley's management. Stoker, of course, could also not be aware of the open hostility to Elvis that Snow evidenced in conversations with Colonel Parker.

To guarantee that they would not end up losing Snow's contract with Hill and Range, therefore, the Aberbachs insisted that their interest in Elvis be quietly negotiated with the Colonel and RCA. Both Colonel Parker and Hill and Range also took steps to convince Snow that Elvis was a temporary musical phenomenon, a minor player unworthy of his concern. Coupled with his dislike for Elvis as a performer, the conclusion of people he knew and trusted that a share in whatever deal involving Elvis was being negotiated should be of little consequence to him, Snow basically took himself out of the picture. Had Hank Snow bothered to pay close attention, he would have realized that "Mystery Train" was a minor hit. Even though the song lacked proper distribution, had little advertising, and only sporadic airplay, Elvis' fifth Sun single was holding steady at the number 15 position on the *Billboard* Country and Western singles chart. After playing "Mystery Train" the first time, Bill Randle remarked to Arnold Shaw, "My phone hasn't stopped ringing and I haven't been able to stop playing the record. Take my word...he's [Presley] gonna bust wide open into the biggest thing that ever hit the music business." Conversations like these were repeated many times in the press and, although they apparently escaped Snow's notice, coupled with public reaction to "Mystery Train," they helped change RCA's mind about Elvis.

Elvis Keeps Busy

In the midst of the lengthy negotiations for a recording contract, Elvis continued to perform. The last week of September 1955 was an exciting one for Presley as he toured Texas singing rockabilly songs with a group of country musicians. On Monday, September 26, the West Texas tour with Johnny Horton, David Houston, and Tillman Franks, among others, began in Wichita Falls. Horton was from Tyler, a town in East Texas, and had a rabid local following. Like Elvis, he also appeared on the "Louisiana Hayride," and was an accomplished honky-tonk singer. Horton's vocals featured a growl borrowed from T. Texas Tyler, and his rockabilly signature song, "Honky Tonk Man," was a crowd pleaser.

Rising to the challenge, Elvis unleashed Scotty Moore's strong, angry electric guitar for some extended solo play. Moore's guitar licks, like Horton's, borrowed elements of Onie Wheeler's lead solos. Elvis smiled at Horton as he left the stage; the healthy competition added some spice to the evening's routine.

Although he was relatively unknown at the time, Johnny Horton's abilities were not lost on Elvis. With a style similar to Onie Wheeler's, Horton employed primarily acoustic instrumentation, but from time to time he used a driving lead guitar hook-up in his rockabilly songs. "Honky Tonk Hardwood Floor" was the best example of how Horton could harness a growling electric guitar. Elvis thought that Horton's sound was too hillbilly, and opted for straight-ahead rockabilly. An exceptionally egotistical performer, Horton simply ignored Elvis' comments about the young audiences' preferences for hard-driving rockabilly music.

Billie Jean Williams, Hank Williams' ex-wife, had married Johnny Horton in 1954, and she was along on the tour. Billy Jean had given Elvis some food money during one of his earliest performances on the "Louisiana Hayride," and they remained close friends. She

On the "Hayride" with the Jordanaires.

told Elvis to just ignore her husband back, and tried to ease Elvis' mind about the course of his career, explaining how Hank Williams had worked for years around Nashville before he became a country music sensation.

By this time, Elvis was convinced that southwestern Louisiana and east Texas rockabilly music was the forerunner of a major new style, a sound that would become an integral part of rock and roll music. On this tour, it was Elvis who suggested that Scotty Moore not only employ a stronger electric guitar, but that he also develop a more visible role on stage as a way of working more music by the Blue Moon Boys into the shows. As a result, there was a definite increase in the amplification of Elvis' music. The changes produced conflict between Elvis and Scotty, however, who also argued over money, hotel accommodations, and even food. It was a hectic, confusing time for Elvis, what with the strain of constant touring and the uncertainty of a major recording contract plaguing both Presley and his backup musicians.

Elvis tried to ignore the stress by flinging himself into a frenetic schedule of performing and conducting interviews. When he had spare time, he spent it in local drive-ins and greasy-spoon restaurants. The availability of pretty, young Southern girls meant the nights were seldom dull. Although he didn't drink or smoke, his diet, sleeping habits, and personal hygiene were not conducive to a healthy life. Elvis was young, however, and able enough to withstand the rigorous life on the road. Despite all the touring distractions, Elvis' efforts to shape a new sound were unrelenting. By the time the week-long tour of Texas had ended, following stops in Bryan, Conroe, Austin, and Gonzales, Elvis had succeeded in adding more of the basic elements of rockabilly to his act.

As Elvis headed back out on the road in early October 1955, the signs of musical change were everywhere—suddenly, performers like Fats Domino, Little Richard, Bo Diddley, Chuck Berry, LaVern Baker, Roy Brown, the Platters, Johnny Ace, the Penguins, Etta James, Ray Charles, and numerous other rhythm and blues acts succeeded in convincing even the most disdainful Americans that a new, raw, energetic music was exploding on the horizon. Elvis, as noted above, had already begun exploiting these changes in the music world. Now a recognizable if minor national phenomenon, Elvis' limited regional success was clearly ending by late 1955.

Elvis began headlining his own jamboree on October 11, when a program billed simply as the "Elvis' Jamboree" started on a one-week Texas tour. After opening in Abilene, the group moved on to Midland, Amarillo, Odessa, and Lubbock. Jimmy Newman, Johnny

Cash, Floyd Cramer, Porter Wagoner, Jean Shepard, Jimmy Day, Bobby Lord, and Wanda Jackson were supporting acts. With that many performers, Elvis was through with his own October 15 Lubbock show by eleven o'clock, which allowed time for a late night appearance at the Cotton Club, arranged by Bob Neal for a fee of $400. Colonel Parker was also making the most of Elvis' drawing power as a headliner, pointing to the reaction to this tour as convincing evidence that Elvis was a hot property. RCA took note.

Earlier that day, as the Elvis Presley jamboree lineup prepared to go onstage at the Fair Park Auditorium in Lubbock, Buddy Holly and Bob Montgomery —Lubbock's own "Buddy and Bob," mentioned earlier—had opened the show. Bob Montgomery was a country music star and industry figure with limited success, and Holly, of course, was destined to become a rock and roll legend. At the time, though, Buddy and Bob were simply another act looking for a record contract. Hi Pockets Duncan, a country dj on KSEL, remembers that the weekend was an exciting one for Holly. Not only was he able to play on the same bill with his idol, Elvis Presley, but Buddy had played with Bill Haley and the Comets the night before Elvis came to town. Dave Stone, the owner of KDAV, allowed Buddy Holly to open the Haley show. Jimmy Rodgers Snow, Hank's son, was one of the acts appearing with Haley, and he spoke glowingly of Holly's talent. A Nashville talent agent, Eddie Crandall, accompanied Snow, and was struck by the commercial possibilities of Holly's material. In fact, Crandall was so impressed with Holly that he began negotiations that led to a Decca recording contract.

Rock music dominated young people's lives in Lubbock. The local radio station, KSEL, played an hour of rock and roll each afternoon after school was dismissed. On Sunday afternoons, KDAV, a radio station located in the barren country south of town, opened its studio

After Buddy & Bob: Buddy Holly and The Crickets.

224

to young people, who drove out to request songs and watch local performers singing in the glass-paneled studio. It was a wonderful way to spend a lazy Sunday afternoon, and it allowed singers like Buddy Holly to refine their talents. Elvis Presley, "the Hillbilly Cat," was the most requested artist on the station's playlist. Many of the live performers emulated Elvis' style, right down to his dress and stage manner.

Apart from headlining his own tour, the Lubbock date was a major turning point in Presley's career because it was the first time he was threatened with physical violence. Just after he arrived in town, he received an anonymous call at his motel. The caller, a gruff-talking man, informed Elvis that he would be assassinated while on stage. This was the first of many death threats would receive in his career, and no one knew how to handle it. The call not only frightened Elvis, but it sent cold chills down the backs of Scotty Moore and Bill Black. "We couldn't believe it," Black remarked. "There were often barroom fights, but no one talked of killing." Because of the death threat, two sheriff's deputies were assigned to Elvis. They spent the entire day walking around Lubbock with him. Finally, after the concert, as he headed off for a show at a small honky-tonk bar, thinking the security was probably unnecessary, Elvis urged the two sheriff's deputies to go home with his thanks. After the set at the bar that night, Elvis was walking to his car when a friendly stranger hollered for an autograph. Elvis agreeably walked over, only to have someone punch him in the face. An angry Elvis forced Bob Neal to drive him around Lubbock all night looking for the assailant. "He was determined he was going to find somebody and fix him up," Neal remarked.

On Sunday, October 16, 1955, Elvis closed out the Lubbock weekend by appearing at Hub Motors, a local Ford dealership, singing from a hastily constructed stage on the used car lot. The subdued crowd of curious onlookers was thoroughly entranced. Mac Davis, then a young high school student, had seen Elvis on Presley's previous trips to Lubbock. Inspired by what he saw, Davis wrote his first song, "Mau Mau Mary," complete with Elvis Presley's rockabilly inflection. Following the show, Elvis left for a performance in Arkansas. After performing at a Jaycee stage show in El Dorado, Arkansas, Elvis drove his pink Cadillac to Cleveland, Ohio, for two shows with Roy Acuff and two daytime high school performances that were being filmed for a movie. Little did Elvis know that his drive to Cleveland probably represented the last moments of privacy and obscurity in his career.

The focus of the daytime Cleveland concerts was not on the music, but rather upon a Cleveland disc jockey Bill Randle, mentioned earlier. Randle's show on

WERE was similar to Alan Freed's New York-based rock revue. Although Randle was dull and lifeless on stage during shows, he had a sure knowledge of what made a hit record. As Arnold Shaw suggested, Randle "was one of a select group of personality deejays who had demonstrated a rare and consistent ability to 'break' records."

It was to help publicize Randle's career that Universal Studios contracted with Elvis to appear in the movie, "The Pied Piper of Cleveland, or a Day in the Life of a Famous Disc Jockey." In addition to Elvis, musical talent for the film included Bill Haley and the Comets, Pat Boone, and the Four Lads. The primary reason that Elvis was on the show was because Arnold Shaw had convinced Randle that Presley could boost his credibility as a dj. Universal hoped to use this short promotional movie to break rock and roll music in its films as well as aid in shifting Randle's popularity to the lucrative New York market, where he aspired to become the heir to Freed's rock and roll crown. (Universal also came away with an unexpected preview of Elvis' screen talent, something which it was not to capitalize on until fourteen years later, however, when it released "Change of Habit" in 1969.)

On Wednesday at noon, October 19, 1955, the first show was held at the St. Michael's High School auditorium. It was followed by a show later that afternoon at Brooklyn High School. After the second concert, Elvis met Pat Boone backstage and they talked briefly about their musical interests. Boone's first impression of Elvis was "real slinky, you know, with his coat a little too big and his pants a little too long."

The two performances were to be spliced into a short documentary. During each show, Elvis sang "I Forgot to Remember to Forget," "That's All Right (Mama)," "Blue Moon of Kentucky," "Mystery Train," and "Good Rockin' Tonight." Both shows were among Elvis' tightest live performances. This was largely due to director Arthur Cohen, who not only handled the assignment professionally but tried to impart some key tips to Presley. When Elvis refused to listen to Cohen's advice, Cohen recommended that the filming be suspended. Bill Randle stepped into the hostile situation and calmed everyone down. After restoring a sense of order, the film was completed, and Randle paid the camera people and the crew.

The Cleveland movie was never released due to a technicians' strike and to a change in Universal Studio's attitude concerning the commercial value of rock music. When the movie was shelved, everyone breathed a sigh of relief. Both the camera crew and the director had had no idea how to film the concert portions of the show to best effect. Colonel Parker, worried that a poorly made movie might expose the flaws in Presley's musical act, was not unhappy. Bill Randle tried vainly to edit the footage, and a brief clip of it aired in 1958 on WEWS-TV, but the complete film was doomed without the fourteen union clearances it needed qualify for release.

In addition to performing at the high school assemblies, Elvis also appeared that night at Cleveland's Circle Theater in a country music jamboree. In Cleveland, three country music clubs vied for the attention of local crowds. Cleveland's best country palace, however, was the Circle. *Billboard* had just reported that Mike Michaels of KDMS in El Dorado, Arkansas, called Elvis "just about the hottest thing around these parts. His style really pleases the teenagers." This comment certainly described Elvis' performances at the Circle Theater, where the young crowd was louder that evening than during any previous country music show. Although he was unaware of it at the time, Elvis' Cleveland performances were witnessed by a number of recording company executives and television talent scouts, as well as covered extensively by local newspapers. The Circle Theater concert persuaded the "Arthur Godfrey Talent Scouts" television program to grant Elvis another audition. While Elvis performed in Cleveland, Bob Neal placed a number of ads in trade publications to solicit bookings. The ads resulted in a series of new concert dates, and served to further publicize Elvis' growing popularity.

This was a period in which Elvis was given a great deal of advice about his singing career. Bill Haley, as noted earlier, believed that Elvis was too heavily influenced by ballads. He urged Elvis to sing faster rockabilly songs. Pat Boone commented that Elvis' enunciation was weak. Roy Acuff, although he praised his interpretation of Bill Monroe's "Blue Moon of Kentucky," urged Presley to accentuate his songs with a country twang. Eddie Bond, like Bill Black, told Elvis to be himself and ignore the critics. "I told Elvis to sing what he liked, the way he liked it," Bond recalled. "Elvis was a pop singer and I told him not to be ashamed of his musical tastes." Despite the turmoil and conflicting opinions surrounding his talent, Elvis remained poised and polite. Ronald Smith remarked, "Elvis was under a lot of pressure, but he remained his own person."

The observations of Pat Boone are particularly interesting, inasmuch as the press attempted to make much of the differences between the two singers. Boone remembered that Bill Randle predicted quick stardom for Presley, although Boone himself wasn't so sure. He could hardly understand Elvis, and was skeptical about his clothing. Boone quickly became a Presley booster, however, and the two singers became fast friends. Both were Southern boys rising in the ranks of Yankee-dominated rock and roll, and this provided a lifelong bond. "Elvis was just starting to prove himself up north, when we became friends," Boone recalled.

The next stop for Presley was in St. Louis, Missouri. On October 21-23, 1955, the Roy Acuff show moved to St. Louis, where they performed for an audience of recently-migrated Southerners. Judd Phillips, aside from being an equity partner in Sun Records, was a promotions assistant to Acuff, and was the key to Elvis' participation in the show. Elvis spent the afternoon listening to KATZ radio, and was surprised that the station broadcast local concerts from small clubs. Following his performance, Elvis went to the Cosmopolitan Club in East St. Louis to listen to the local musicians. The area, in the center of St. Louis' burgeoning black music community, was the same in which Chuck Berry had started his career. A shrewd student of the rock music industry, Berry realized early on that the right image and a mainstream interpretation of pop songs was the way to fame and fortune, a fact that Elvis was just becoming used to.

Elvis was fully aware that Bob Wills and the Texas Playboys' song "Ida Red" had provided Berry with his inspiration for "Maybellene," his first hit. While in St. Louis, Elvis also heard the flip side of "Maybellene," a song entitled "Wee Wee Hours." It was a blues song that Elvis came to love, and one which prompted him to remark on one occasion that Berry was more of a bluesman than a rocker. Since Berry and Presley began their careers at the same time, it is a tragedy that they never really got to know one another.

Bill Haley and Elvis in Cleveland.

FOLKS IT'S MONDAY NIGHT
AT THE SILVER MOON

Get a party together now – Call the Silver Moon and make your reservations to join in the fun MONDAY night. Hear Elvis Presley in PERSON.

IN PERSON

Elvis PRESLEY
SCOTTY and BILL

"That's All Right, Mama"
"Blue Moon of Kentucky"
"Good Rockin' Tonite"
"Heartbreaker"

FUN! MUSIC! JOKES!

If you like GOOD Western Music (and who doesn't) You'll enjoy Elvis Presley and the Moon Lighters singing and playing your favorite western tunes.

POPULAR RECORDING STAR
ELVIS PRESLEY
With the "MOONLIGHTERS"
9 til ? – Mon. Oct. 24
$1.50 per person
HIGHWAY 67 – N
SILVER MOON

One of Elvis' late October 1955 club dates.

When Berry later wrote "Johnny B. Goode" and "Bye Bye Johnny," admittedly autobiographical tunes about Berry's own life, they contained more than a passing similarity to Elvis' career. Berry, born on Goode Street in East St. Louis, slyly referred to Elvis' career in his song "Johnny B. Goode"—the country boy in the song who never learned to read or write so well could easily have referred to Elvis, or at least to the incomplete public image of him and his educational background. When Berry made reference to his fictional performer carrying a guitar by a railroad track, it could have been a direct reference to the Mississippi-Alabama State Fair at which Elvis hung out as a young man with his guitar. Berry's song further proclaimed that his singer's mother (Gladys?) told him that some day he would be a man, as well as the leader of his own band. In February 1960, Berry's "Bye Bye Johnny" carried Johnny B. Goode's story to Hollywood at precisely the moment Elvis was resuming his own post-army movie career with "G.I. Blues." Berry's lyrics also mentioned how Johnny B. Goode built his mother a mansion by the railroad tracks once he became a wealthy movie star. (Berry also made a series of rock and roll movies, but suggested that only

"white performers" could continue their Hollywood successes.)

After his visit to East St. Louis, Elvis was confident that his music was moving in the right direction. The jukebox at the Cosmopolitan Club had "Mystery Train" inside, and it was not Little Junior Parker's version—the playlist credit clearly read "Elvis Presley." "Curiosity provoked me to lay a lot of country stuff on our predominantly black audience," Chuck Berry recalled about his own days at the Cosmopolitan. He remembered overhearing the idle talk about him on the street—"Who is that black hillbilly at the Cosmo?" What Berry's comments suggest is precisely the reason that Elvis and other musicians were drawn to the Cosmopolitan Club: black blues and rockabilly music were merging into something else, something that sold records.

Following his stay in St. Louis, Elvis drove leisurely to Alabama, where he was scheduled to begin a rigorous month of concert appearances. Although his popularity had brought him to the brink of stardom, many of Elvis' concert venues were still small and relatively insignificant. The latter months of 1955, in fact, were spent in obscure dance halls, small clubs, and local fairs. To Elvis, however, the October-November concerts were just one last chance to polish his stage act. Although he knew that a recording contract with RCA was very close, he could not have known at this point that it was absolutely assured, nor that, after signing with RCA, he would receive enough television work in early 1956 to make him a superstar on the national entertainment scene.

From October 26-28, 1955, Elvis appeared for three nights at a fair in Prichard, Alabama, for promoter Jack Cardwell, a WAIP dj. Before these concerts, Elvis submitted to a lengthy radio interview plugging his latest Sun release, "Mystery Train." During this interview, Elvis talked about his future with a major record label. There was no doubt that Elvis knew that Colonel Parker was on the verge of closing the RCA-Victor recording contract. In a relaxed manner, he talked about black music and its impact upon his style. Returning on Saturday, October 29, 1955, to the "Louisiana Hayride" in Shreveport, Elvis sang Chuck Berry's "Maybellene."

A small but important step towards finalizing the sale of Elvis' contract also occurred in late October 1955. Colonel Parker began to threaten suit against Sam Phillips if Elvis' back royalties weren't paid. As a result, Sam, who had just paid Judd Phillips $1400 for his partnership interest in Sun, thereby making Sam the sole proprietor, didn't have the cash or the time he'd hoped for to continue holding out for the top-dollar figure currently being considered (and rejected) by RCA. The urgency for Colonel Parker was that Bill Randle had been attempting to intercede in hopes of making a record deal for Elvis himself, thus undermining Parker's position. As he was determined to keep total control of Elvis' recording and touring career, Colonel Parker pressured Phillips with a suit in order to get Sam to lower his asking price. The logjam finally broke due to a number of factors, of course, and the stage was set for Elvis to enter the rock music world as its first superstar act.

CHAPTER 13
Sun Burst,
November-December 1955

During the first week of November 1955, RCA quietly finalized arrangements with Colonel Tom Parker and Sam Phillips to purchase Elvis' Sun recording contract. RCA then set its publicity machinery in motion to make Elvis into a superstar. On top of all the other factors influencing RCA's decision to sign Presley, there was finally a corporate consensus that he could be a moneymaking act. It was becoming clear that rock and roll music was bursting onto the scene with such vitality and intensity that the profits from a standout exponent of this new musical form were potentially enormous. All the major record labels were aware of this trend, and were eagerly seeking out new rock tunes.

Rock Music Comes of Age

The vast sums of money that could be generated from rock music first became apparent when Alan Freed began promoting profitable theater concerts. New York entertainment moguls paid close attention to these widely-publicized rock and roll shows. A number of key RCA executives attended Freed's week-long back-to-school concerts from September 2-9, 1955, at Brooklyn's Paramount Theater and came away impressed. Not only did Freed's shows draw large throngs, but the profits exceeded $125,000.

When Freed's "Big Rock 'N' Roll Show" was first announced, Tony Bennett was the headliner. Bennett came down with a cold after only one show, although no one seemed to notice as the other acts turned out to be more popular with the kids. Freed's show was heavily weighted towards rhythm and blues acts—the Harptones, the Moonglows, Nappy Brown, the Cardinals, and the Nutmegs, among others, joined Chuck Berry in a concert that had ticketbuyers standing in a line that stretched around the corner. The *New York Times*, normally a staid and reserved newspaper, sent a reporter to interview the delirious concertgoers, and radio and television reporters added to the hype—rock music had become a media phenomenon. Freed's show and the attendant media coverage had a dramatic effect upon Elvis Presley's future with RCA, because it further alerted company executives to rock music's commercial potential.

When Chuck Berry arrived in New York for the show, he checked into the Alvin Hotel and went over to Manhattan to meet Alan Freed. It was from Freed that Berry heard the gossip about Elvis Presley. Berry told Freed that he was already aware of Elvis. Not only had Elvis played St. Louis, Berry's hometown, but Chuck had heard about him all over the South.

The conversation about Presley was all but forgotten as Berry performed his first show at the Paramount. It was a noon concert, and Chuck had been surprised to see Nat King Cole and Dizzy Gillespie chatting on a street corner as he entered the theater. As Berry recalled, he wanted to "look sharp for New York," so he had purchased three pairs of brown suede shoes and three rayon suits for his backup group.

Berry's first hit, "Maybellene," had finally allowed him to graduate from the small blues clubs to larger concert halls such as the Paramount. The crossover popularity of Berry's music was further demonstrated when "Maybellene" was covered by such unlikely groups as the Johnny Long and Ralph Marterie orchestras. Indeed, a number of white singers and established orchestra leaders were looking to rock music for new material. Chuck Berry was surprised at the number of jazz and big band artists that liked "Maybellene." "I realized during those shows that my music and Elvis' records were creating a new sound," Berry concluded.

Jimmy Beasley, a recording artist for Crown Rec-

Chuck Berry in the mid-1980s.
(Photo courtesy Johan Hasselberg)

ords, played in Freed's house orchestra. Beasley was one of many black artists who later crossed over into the white marketplace. "You wouldn't believe the crowds in those days. I loved it." Beasley went on to explain that the musicians talked about "that young kid from Memphis" and his success with a black sound. "The interest that Presley brought to black music was important. He made it possible to sell records in the white market," Beasley noted.

Jimmy Beasley also remembered that many of the artists had first read about Elvis in *Billboard* after listening to industry gossip. "We all knew that Southern boy was destined for greatness." "My hits were minor ones, but without Presley's success I wouldn't have had a chance," Beasley speculated. In 1956, Crown Records had success with Beasley's "Don't Feel Sorry for Me" and later with "My Happiness." (Elvis, too, had recorded "My Happiness" in 1953 as a demo at the Memphis Recording Service. For years this ten-inch acetate was in the possession of one of Presley's high school friends, Ed Leek, amidst rumors that it had been lost. "He brought it over to play for my grandparents," Leek recalled, "and I wound up with it." It was typical of Elvis to give his old friends such gifts. Leek asked Elvis if he wanted the record back and Presley didn't seem to push for it. It was eventually sold to RCA and released in August 1990 to mark the thirteenth anniversary of Presley's untimely death.)

Good Sounds Made Better

There were important technological advances in the recording industry beginning around this time. When Atlantic Records decided to record an obscure New Orleans jazzman, Wilber de Paris, in "binaural" sound, the industry responded with disbelief. Ahmet Ertegun and Jerry Wexler, the creative forces behind Atlantic, appeared to have lost their minds, as the binaural process required a record player with two needles. The record was not a hit, but Ertegun and Wexler ultimately had the last laugh; realizing that recording technology was on the verge of vast improvement, they led the way in experimenting with a fuller sound despite the naysayers, and garnered the attention of many innovative and creative musicians as well as a great deal of favorable publicity.

The ingenuity displayed at Atlantic was typical of the smaller- and medium-sized record labels, which could afford to take a chance with rock music. When Elvis Presley recorded with guitarist Scotty Moore and bassist Bill Black at Sun, the records they produced were also an experiment, one made possible by Sam Phillips' ability to manipulate the recording process—an attempt to make three musicians sound more like a full band.

This experimentation with sound came just at the right time, and was another timely aspect of the changes that benefited Elvis as he came to the fore. The American public had entered the era of the "hi-fi" craze, and consumers spent thousands of dollars on new equipment. A flood of amplifiers, preamplifiers, FM tuners, and speakers with sophisticated woofers and tweeters created a new industry. Interest in the 78rpm recording evaporated as quickly as the interest in vinyl did when compact discs were introduced decades later. In June 1955, Columbia Records totally abandoned 78s to concentrate upon long-playing albums and 45rpm records. Having anticipated the developments in hardware, Atlantic Records made a fortune in this market. The business of rock and roll was on its way to immense profits as a result of the new recording technology.

The Role of Television

Another important aid in the rock music revolution was the increasing interest on the part of major national television shows in featuring rock music acts. By 1955, Ed Sullivan's television show, the "Toast of the Town," was drawing a large viewing audience with one rock and roll act after another. Such performers as LaVern Baker, the Five Keys, and Bo Diddley were televised all over America, extending rock and roll's reach as an increasingly popular national phenomenon.

Some television executives found that working with rock and roll acts was not easy, however. When Ed Sullivan's producers attempted to force Bo Diddley to sing Tennessee Ernie Ford's hit "16 Tons," they were surprised by Bo's fierce independence. He sang "16 Tons" at the dress rehearsal, but came out during the show to perform his hit, "Bo Diddley." The producer was dumb-struck. When asked why he didn't sing "16 Tons," Bo replied: "That's how '16 Tons' sounds to me." The story is typical of some of the resistance that television "standards and practices" faced from contrary rock musicians. Many television executives were forced to turn a blind eye and ignore these acts of defiance, basically because they had no choice but to comply with the most important factor in television program-ming—public demand.

Locally, of course, many towns large and small aired after-school shows with a dance party format. In Philadelphia, "American Bandstand," hosted by Bob Horn, was typical of the local programs aired in the Eastern market. In late 1955, while Horn was on vacation, a young disc jockey named Dick Clark stepped in as a substitute host. In the spring of 1956, when Horn was arrested for drunk driving, Clark took over the job permanently. The twenty-six-year-old Clark looked as young as his audience, but he had a sure grasp of the music. He also had an ingratiating and confident manner, one that endeared him to his audience as well as to the guest artists appearing on the show. Although "American Bandstand" didn't become an ABC network show until August 5, 1957, it did help define the economic power of rock music. When artists appeared on "American Bandstand," their records sold in larger numbers within locales reached by the show. Smaller record labels, of course, were especially keen to see their artists appear on Clark's show. "I appeared on American Bandstand's afternoon show when 'The Walk' hit the charts," Jimmy McCracklin remarked. "That show sure did help my record."

Television had begun its climb to parity with radio as a key factor in breaking rock music into a broader commercial marketplace. The product was easily sold once it was previewed on national television. In 1955, there were twelve million teenagers in America who had an income of at least nine dollars a week. It was the new record-buying habits of these teenagers that convinced many the music industry to ignore the antics of wild rock performers and to sell a type of music they personally considered repugnant. The six major pop-oriented record labels—Capitol, RCA, Decca, Columbia, MGM, and Mercury—had little interest in rock music, but they were interested in money.

Bill Haley

The musical tastes of teenagers had come under increasing scrutiny by record company executives. Research demonstrated that half the young people purchased at least one record a month, and another twenty-five percent bought two a month. Demographic studies indicated that in urban areas there was a rush to purchase new small-label releases. Rhythm and blues and rockabilly records were proving extremely popular among young people.

The band that is a case study in the power of blues and rhythm and blues music is Bill Haley and the Comets. Before forming the Comets, Haley had been a country musician. After growing up in Michigan, he moved to Pennsylvania where he was heavily influenced by black music. From 1948 to 1950, Haley recorded country songs for Cowboy, Center, and Keystone Records with little success. Haley looked, dressed, and acted like a drugstore cowboy, but he loved black music. "Bill would sneak out to the black clubs and raise hell till all hours in the morning," Marshall Lytle, a member of the Comets, remembered. This infatuation with black music ultimately prompted Haley to record a cover version of Jackie Brenston's "Rocket 88" for Holiday Records, beginning a total change of direction in his career.

In 1952, Haley signed with the Philadelphia-based Essex label and recorded an uptempo song, "Rock the Joint." It was a moderate hit and Haley, with his new group the Saddlemen, began playing clubs in the East and Midwest. One night, Haley found himself, of all places, in a black blues club in Chicago. The audience response was so positive that it made it easy for Haley to turn in his cowboy outfits for "cat" clothes. After a number of other minor hits, Haley recorded "Rock Around the Clock," which came to be the featured song in the movie "Blackboard Jungle" as well as becoming the national anthem of rock music.

Haley's style drew upon the same musical influences as those which had shaped Elvis Presley, and in many ways he helped pave the way for the success which Presley was to enjoy. In the end, it was Elvis' raw animal magnetism and youthful performing energy that caused him to eclipse Haley's talent. Elvis was rock and roll. He was raw, rough, energetic, and possessed a feel for the music that Haley, for all his talent, lacked.

The Mythos of Rock 'n' Roll

The first rock and roll myth was born during Elvis' last year at Sun Records. During a 1954 Christmas Eve show at Houston's City Auditorium, a series of performances by artists from Don Robey's Duke and Peacock record labels erupted into front page news when a young blues singer, Johnny Ace, allegedly killed himself playing Russian roulette backstage. This seemingly insignificant incident had a definite impact upon the rising popularity of rock music—Ace became the first symbol of the more tragic aspects of the rock and roll lifestyle.

The rise of rock brought with it confusing contradictions. Dark images of moral decay were offset by ever-growing respectability. Elvis—damned by many—appears here with Memphis city officials anxious to claim him as their own.

The press, however, failed to mention that Ace, a rhythm and blues performer, wasn't strictly a rock singer.

The Johnny Ace story is an important one. He was one of many Southern artists signed by Don Robey. After his death, Robey greased the publicity wheels and sent Ace's "Pledging My Love" to number 1 on the *Billboard* rhythm and blues chart—a posthumous hit that helped romanticize the tragedy of his death.

Willie Mae "Big Mama" Thornton was backstage in the dressing room with Ace and his band at the time. She remembers that, yes, Ace had been playing Russian roulette—he'd made a hundred dollar bet, and won. Everyone then went about their business, including Johnny Ace. "We all left the room and we went back and found Johnny dead," Big Mama recalled. "Word was some gangsters killed him." Whatever the cause of death, Elvis was intrigued with the Johnny Ace affair. He talked about Ace for years after the incident. Ironically, when Elvis died in August 1977, his cover version of "Pledging My Love" replaced Charlie Rich's "Rolling With the Flow" as the number 1 tune on the *Billboard* country music chart. Presley's lifelong obsession with Ace had added another strange twist to the story of his career.

The "tragic" side of rock music was built up even further by the death of James Dean in a fiery automobile crash in late 1955. The emotional reaction to young Dean's death—his screen image, established in "East of Eden," was that of a rebellious, troubled and misunderstood teenager—caused him to be viewed in the same way as if he had actually been a rock music personality. In March 1956, RCA tried to capitalize on Dean's untimely death with a folksy record called "The Ballad of James Dean," by Dylan Todd. At this point, RCA was in the midst of selling Elvis Presley, and the James Dean gimmick—on the heels of Dean's untimely death and the release of his second movie, "Rebel without a Cause"—was simply another road to commercial profit.

RCA had also learned a great deal from an earlier movie, "Blackboard Jungle." By May 1955, the movie and its soundtrack had helped to popularize rock and roll. The title song, "Rock Around the Clock," not only made Bill Haley and the Comets a hot rock act, but made all of the movie's music a focal point for teens. As kids flooded into record stores to purchase "Rock Around the Clock," they searched eagerly for other rock and roll records.

Also in 1955, "Unchained Melody" by Roy Hamilton on Epic, Al Hibbler on Decca, and Les Baxter on Capitol was a top ten hit for all three artists. While not a rock song, the popularity of "Unchained Melody" was again due to teenage record purchasers who wanted to buy the record because it was featured in the movie

"Unchained." Increasingly, record companies saw the movies as a means of popularizing rock records. (After watching Elroy "Crazy Legs" Hirsch and Barbara Hale in the movie, Elvis himself was still singing "Unchained Melody" in his dressing room as much as two years later—friends said he used the tune to warm up his voice.)

Some in the record industry found it difficult to come up with other white artists in the mold of Bill Haley and Elvis, and made the mistake of signing a pop groups or crooners to turn out "rock" recordings—the kids didn't buy it, and the move had the effect of selling even more of Presley's records. Most "rock" songs of the era were little more than industry-contrived cover versions of black songs. A good example of this phenomenon is evident in the career of the Crewcuts. A pop quartet from Canada, the Crewcuts placed nine songs on the *Billboard* pop chart in 1954-1955. Their hits included cover versions of the Chords' "Sh-Boom," the Nutmegs' "A Story Untold," the Penguins' "Earth Angel," and Nappy Brown's "Don't Be Angry." When Chicago-based Mercury Records released the Crewcuts' long-playing album **Rock and Roll Bash** on its Wing label, there was strong resentment among black musicians. "There were a lot of white artists who recorded black songs strictly for the money," Jimmy McCracklin observed. "Most of them didn't sound like the black man; those who did made money." McCracklin's wry comments suggested that the time was ripe for a white man who sounded black to be packaged by a major record label, and indeed it was.

Life on the Edge

Elvis continued to travel and play in small towns while Colonel Parker negotiated a recording contract for him. To some, one of the mysteries of latter stages of Presley's Sun-era career was why he continued to play low-paying jobs even as he approached the brink of stardom. While this is a valid question in hindsight, it should be remembered that despite all the industry interest, the positive signs, the public acclaim, nothing regarding the course of Elvis' future was yet absolutely certain.

A good example of a less than opportune booking occurred between October 31 and November 5, 1955, when Elvis played the NCO Club at Keesler Air Force Base in Biloxi, Mississippi. When Elvis arrived in Biloxi, he found himself a cheap motel room. The six nights at the NCO Club paid only $85, so Scotty Moore and Bill Black had returned to Memphis, leaving Elvis to play the engagement as a solo act. Actually, it was much like playing the Eagle's Nest in Memphis. As Elvis walked

into the bar he met Jim Russell, the person who had booked the previous week's act, Bill Bennett. Russell, who had recently moved to New Orleans from Pittsburgh, was a thirty-six-year-old disc jockey/promoter who had once worked with Alan Freed. Upon his arrival in New Orleans, Russell had founded his booking agency, making some extra money diverting acts from nightclubs, dance halls and auditoriums to NCO Clubs like the one in Biloxi.

"I'll never forget Elvis when he walked into the NCO Club," Russell remarked, "he looked and dressed poor." Russell lent Presley five dollars so he could buy some food. "Elvis complained that he lacked good management," Russell remembered, "he hinted around to me about managing him. I turned him down cold." There were eighteen people at the NCO Club that night, and Russell recalls that only four of them sat directly in front of the stage and watched Elvis perform. "There were two tables playing cards and another group at the pool table. The four girls in the club watched Elvis, I should have known then what he had," Russell chuckled.

While he was in Biloxi, Elvis spent the week with June Juanico. Elvis had met Juanico on June 26, 1955, during a previous Biloxi show. She was a singer, dancer, and model who had the same show business aspirations as Elvis. They spent an idyllic week. As they rode

horses and went swimming, Elvis unburdened himself to her. He was wary about the future success of his career, and he again complained about his management. Elvis was especially needful, as he had just learned that Bob Neal had been involved in an auto accident. The record deal with RCA was still up in the air, and Presley's nerves were shot. "I never saw anyone so insecure," Jim Russell recalled. "That boy had a lot on his mind." Russell remembers that Elvis felt all but abandoned by Parker. "If I had realized how close the Colonel was to a recording deal, I would have moved in on Elvis," Russell lamented.

When Russell returned to New Orleans, he began to take more account of the mentions of Presley's name in local music circles. Keith Rush, a promoter who had a radio show on WSMB, played Elvis' records heavily, and pushed his music enthusiastically in the Crescent City. Elvis' Sun singles were played on a variety of New Orleans radio stations that November, and there was a great deal of action in local record stores. "I couldn't believe how well Presley's records sold," Russell remarked. "They were gone from the stores in a few days and Sam Phillips couldn't get anymore for a long time. I don't think Sun Records kept its financial accounts straight. They never seemed to have any money," Russell concluded.

Johnny Vincent, the owner of Ace Records, had a one-stop distributorship in New Orleans and he wholesaled Sun records to local stores. "The problem was getting Sam Phillips to get us the records," Vincent remembered. Other distributors echoed the same sentiment. Phillips had a prime product that was just too big for his operation.

Joe Banashak was another New Orleans music figure who recognized Presley's importance early on. Banashak owned a record label called Band, as well as other small labels that specialized in carrying some of the best local rhythm and blues music. Originally a Dixieland fan, he became intrigued with New Orleans rhythm and blues music in the mid-fifties. In 1955, Banashak, who had recently left the record business to work for the Admiral Corporation, was approached to take over A-1 Record Distributors in Oklahoma City. As Banashak told Jeff Hannusch, "I said no at the time because I was quite successful out of the record business." The regional success of Elvis Presley was one of the reasons that Banashak ultimately took over A-1 Record Distributors, however. "I loved Elvis' sound," Banashak remembered, "it was exciting to merchandise his music. It was also quite profitable."

When RCA's regional representatives had checked with Banashak over drinks and dinner, he had told them he knew all about Elvis Presley. Banashak found it interesting that the record stores that ordered hit records by local rhythm and blues acts like Roy Brown, Fats Domino, Shirley and Lee, Guitar Slim, and the Spiders also preferred Presley's music. Banashak believed that Elvis paved the way for the next generation of New Orleans musicians, which included Clarence "Frogman" Henry, Ernie K-Doe, Irma Thomas, Aaron Neville, Benny Spellman, Jessie Hill, and Chris Kenner, among others. Elvis was not the sole reason for the rise to prominence of New Orleans rhythm and blues, but he influenced the mainstream popularity of the music.

As Jim Russell suggested: "New Orleans was ready for a musical explosion. The talent was there, the people to produce the songs were waiting and the record buying public was looking for a product." Russell went on to suggest that Sam Phillips' Sun singles had a big impact upon the local music scene. "Sam was around New Orleans in 1955 and people were impressed with his operation. A lot of our people hoped to duplicate it."

Like many promoters who saw Presley in his early years, Jim Russell occasionally had second thoughts about his music. Elvis invited Russell to come to Amory, Mississippi, to watch him perform with Johnny Cash and Carl Perkins. "We heard a lot about Carl Perkins in New Orleans and I heard through the musicians' grapevine that Elvis tried to pick up some licks from him. I don't think Elvis ever did."

Carl Perkins

As touched on previously, Carl Perkins began his Sun Records career during Elvis Presley's eighteen months at Sam Phillips' Sun label. In some respects, Perkins' background and early career was very similar to Elvis' own. He was born into a typical country music setting near Tiptonville, Tennessee, in April 1932. As he grew to maturity, Perkins was influenced by traditional country music, the blues, and rockabilly, and evolved into a country singer with a black rhythm and blues sound. By the time Elvis emerged as a Sun recording artist in 1954-55, Perkins was just beginning the early stages of his own career.

Although he was still a young man, just three years older than Elvis, Perkins was balding, married, and already raising a family—not someone cut out to be a teen idol. What is important about Perkins, contrary to Jim Russell's conclusion, is how his rockabilly style influenced Elvis. Perkins was a rural rock poet much in the same way that Chuck Berry was an urban poet. Perkins' more obscure songs—like "Pop Let Me Have the Car," an example of his songwriting skills—evoked images of teenage America. Carl had the commercial touch in his music down to a fine point, but his personal appearance, background, and place at Sun Records worked against him.

A wild and energetic performer, Carl Perkins epitomized a distinct part of the Southern musical tradition, one different from Elvis' heritage. There was a whiskey-soaked barroom intensity to Perkins' records. His rockabilly sound was raw and original, and not as sophisticated as Presley's. A Southern sound for the rural working man echoed in Perkins' voice and guitar.

In the summer of 1954, Carl Perkins was earning thirty dollars a week in the honky-tonk bars around his home in Jackson, Tennessee. He had moved his family into a government housing project, the Parkview Courts, and was energetically pursuing a show business career. When he first heard Elvis singing "Blue Moon of Kentucky" on the radio, he immediately decided to approach Sam Phillips at Sun Records for an audition. "Presley's song," Perkins remembered, "was exactly what I was doing. I knew I could make hit records." It was not long before Elvis and Perkins would meet.

In September, Perkins and his band were booked into a honky-tonk club in Bethel Springs, Tennessee. They got permission to start their gig at ten o'clock, so they went to see Elvis perform at a local high school dance. They were hooked by Presley's energetic stage show. "Elvis was playing and doing things on stage like us," Perkins remembered. Elvis talked with Carl after the show and they exchanged some ideas on music, further encouraging Perkins to travel to Memphis.

In September and October 1954, Perkins and his band began to turn up outside the Sun studio. They frequently came into Taylor's restaurant for dinner. "I think Carl was a little shy in those days," Marion Keisker remembered. "He would sit in Taylor's and drink coffee and smile at me when I came in for some food." A nice lady who was sometimes overly protective of her boss, Keisker discouraged Perkins and prevented him from talking to Sam Phillips. It was nothing personal; she was just running interference in an atmosphere filled with would-be hitmakers all scrambling to get Sam's attention. Finally, however, Carl got up the nerve to approach Sam Phillips directly. One day, as Sam drove up and parked his Cadillac in front of Sun Records, Perkins was waiting with his spiel for a recording contract. He was immediately taken aback by Sam's snappy clothes. "I had never seen a better dressed man," Perkins remarked. "Even his tie and socks were the exact color of the Cadillac."

Surprisingly, Phillips invited Perkins into the studio, where the two talked about a recording contract. Phillips let Perkins know the facts. If he wanted a record deal, he would have to write his own songs. If Perkins could write some original songs, Sam might consider recording them. Furthermore, Sam was not impressed with the other members of Perkins' band. Carl's brothers, Jay and Clayton, Sam remarked, were sloppy Ernest

Tubb impersonators. They had no place in rock and roll music.

To strengthen his band's sound, Perkins brought in W.S. "Fluke" Holland, a drummer from Saltillo, Tennessee. Holland had begun playing with Perkins at a Bethel Springs concert in September 1954, and was a steady, if unspectacular, artist who added a great deal to Perkins' act.

As noted, Perkins had picked up his black sound as a farmboy. "I was the only white sharecropper among them," Perkins recalled, "and I learned much from them." Tiptonville was located in a tri-state area of northwest Tennessee where Arkansas, Missouri, and Tennessee meet, an environment that spawned white kids who loved black music, white kids who ended up playing a form of hillbilly rock and roll replete with corny lyrics and hard-driving guitar riffs. Too corny for Sam Phillips, who urged Perkins to develop a more sophisticated style. What amazed everyone about Carl Perkins, however, was the way he could cover John Lee Hooker's or Muddy Waters' songs, yet still display an affinity for Bill Monroe-style country blues. Sam Phillips was quick to notice something else: Elvis sounded black, and so did Perkins.

In October 1954, when Perkins recorded his first song at Sun, Elvis was hanging around the studio. "Honky Tonk Gal" was a tune straight out of the misery of the juke joints and hillbilly bars. Elvis chuckled. It reminded him of the Eagle's Nest. There was also a hint of Hardrock Gunter's music in it. As a fledgling songwriter, Perkins was clearly influenced heavily by such classic Gunter tunes as "Boogie Woogie on a Saturday Night" and "Honky Tonk Baby."

Sam Phillips, who hadn't seen anything from Perkins up to that point to change his mind, still viewed Carl as a country singer. Gradually, however, as Sam drove his car through Tennessee and Mississippi he began to hear intriguing tales about Perkins' guitar virtuosity. There was enough notice of Perkins' music to keep Sam interested—Carl had a well-deserved reputation as a first-rate performer—but it was not easy to sell the early rock acts, which had to be young, energetic, pop, and good looking, and as a performer Perkins was none of these.

The first really commercial song that Perkins wrote was "Movie Magg," a rockabilly tune that prompted his barroom audiences to get up and dance. After listening to it, Sam Phillips was hesitant no longer, and promised the young singer a contract if he would come up with another song. "I saw Carl then as possibly one of the great plough heads in the world," Phillips confessed, "there was no way Carl could hide that pure country in him. Pure country can mean an awful lot of soul." Phillips was surprised when Perkins promptly returned with another new song, "Turn Around." True to his word, Sam signed Carl to Sun, and it was not long before Perkins was out on the road working the small dates that Sam Phillips believed were essential to selling records.

The next step was to team Perkins with other fledgling Sun acts. Perkins, Johnny Cash and Elvis were sent out on the road together to pump up record sales, as well as to give Carl a little seasoning. In concert, Perkins was more often a hillbilly than a rockabilly singer. He appealed to an older, hard-drinking crowd. There were some strengths in Perkin's act that Elvis lacked. In particular, Perkins could sing and play lead guitar at the same time. Elvis depended upon Scotty Moore's lead guitar riffs and Bill Black's infectious bass. When Carl and Elvis performed at the same concert, they brought out the best in each other, however.

A good example of their friendly rivalry occurred in an Amory, Mississippi, concert. Johnny Cash opened the show with excellent versions of "Cry, Cry, Cry" and "Hey Porter." After acknowledging the applause, Cash continued with traditional country songs. Carl was the next act, and he sang "Let the Jukebox Keep on Playing" and "Gone, Gone, Gone." The former was a hillbilly song, while the latter was classic rockabilly. The audience loved it. When Elvis came out to finish the show, he took up the challenge offered by his Sun Records cronies. He did ten songs over the course of the next hour in a set that left the audience in ecstasy. Elvis received the loudest applause of the evening, and the crowd left delighted with the show.

It was at the same concert in Amory that Perkins showed the music for "Blue Suede Shoes" to Elvis. Perkins told Presley that he had written the song on the back of a potato sack while at home in Jackson. As Carl sang the song for Elvis, Presley paid close atten-

Audience reaction to Elvis was unparalleled.

Elvis in Memphis, late 1955.

"Heartbreak Hotel"

On November 10, 1955, Elvis left Memphis with Bob Neal and drove to Nashville for the annual Country Music Disc Jockey Convention at the Andrew Jackson Hotel. From Florida, Mae Boren Axton drove to Nashville with a new song in hand, "Heartbreak Hotel," a tune co-written with Tom Durden after he had read a poignant newspaper article in the *Miami Herald*. Under with a headline: "Do You Know This Man?" was a story describing the suicide of a man who had scrawled a one-line note before his death: "I walk a lonely street." The line became the lyrical focal point for "Heartbreak Hotel," and it was not long before the song was a crucial part of Elvis Presley's contract talks with RCA.

A friend of Mae Boren Axton, Colonel Tom Parker had hired her as a publicist during a number of Hank Snow's tours. She had also been responsible for booking Elvis in Jacksonville, Florida, a number of times. "Mae was a well-known and respected figure in the music business," Johnny Tillotson remarked, "it was only natural for her to approach Elvis with 'Heartbreak Hotel'." Axton had witnessed the reaction to Elvis' music, and realized that Presley held the ticket to great wealth. Johnny Tillotson remembers how excited Axton was over the prospect of Presley recording her song. "She realized early on," Tillotson remarked, "that Presley was going to be a huge act."

By the time Axton brought "Heartbreak Hotel" to Nashville, a demo of the song had already been turned down by the Wilburn Brothers. They thought it was weird. After listening to country singer Glenn Reeves' demo tape of the tune, Elvis told Axton that he loved it. As Elvis practiced it, Tom Durden noticed that Presley was copying the demo singer's style exactly. "Elvis was even breathing in the same places that Glen did on the dub," Durden remarked. "Heartbreak Hotel" was an important song for Elvis; he needed original songs, and it definitely fit his style.

To make sure that this song was right for Elvis, however, Colonel Parker played the demo for a number of music people. They all agreed it was excellent. The Colonel wasn't convinced, and Axton and Durden were about to take the song elsewhere when Glen Reeves convinced Parker that the song had enormous commercial potential. The Colonel believed that Reeves had an ear for hit songs and the deal was consummated. To sweeten the deal, Axton and Durden agreed to give Elvis a share of the songwriting credits, a common practice in the music industry in the 1950s. Although Elvis didn't pen one word of this tune, the fact that Axton went so far as to offer Elvis a third of the songwriting credits if he would record it helped increase Colonel

tion to the way it flowed, later allowing him to record one of the most soulful and commercial versions of "Blue Suede Shoes"—modelled on Carl Perkin's demonstration performance! Indeed, after Elvis first heard "Blue Suede Shoes," he told Ronald Smith that he felt like the song had been written for him, so taken with it was he.

For six months, Sun had Perkins tour with other acts, his talent gradually developing into a box office draw that could stand on its own. Sam Phillips had big plans for Perkins, but he had to be convinced that Carl's songs could sell. Sun was so busy pushing Presley's embryonic career that Perkins almost got lost in the shuffle, but finally, when "Movie Magg" b/w "Turn Around" was released on the Flip label in the spring of 1955, it was immediately clear that Perkins could catch the attention of record buyers. After years of playing honky-tonk bars around Jackson, Carl Perkins toured the Southern bar circuit with great success. His songs were naturals for the expanding rockabilly market because they combined energetic guitar riffs with poignant country lyrics. "Turn Around," for example, was a maudlin country tune filled with simplistic moral overtones so typically beloved by inhabitants of the rural South.

Parker's enthusiasm for the song.

For his part, the deal made Elvis nervous because he prided himself on his artistic integrity. Colonel Parker was proving to be too manipulative even at this early point in Presley's career, pressing Elvis to record songs that would add to his royalties. To woo his singer, Colonel Parker expressed confidence that "Heartbreak Hotel" had a special quality, musically speaking; the real reason behind his interest in the song was the extra royalty money that Elvis would collect. In the end, Elvis accepted the Colonel's plea that they had to work with songwriters who would allow them to share in the royalties.

As significant as the drama surrounding the acquisition of "Heartbreak Hotel" for Elvis was, the RCA deal overshadowed the events of the day. As negotiations over the song went on quietly and without fanfare, there were rumors everywhere at the Andrew Jackson Hotel that Elvis Presley was about to sign the most lucrative recording contract in history, rumors which would obscure the fact that the deal Colonel Parker negotiated for his young protege was really rather average.

RCA Signs Elvis

Just as the negotiations to record "Heartbreak Hotel" were concluded, RCA announced to the Nashville convention that it had purchased Elvis' recording contract from Sun Records. In addition to recording new material, RCA would distribute his five Sun singles from that point on.

To reach this point, negotiations between Colonel Parker and RCA's management team had gone on around the clock for ten days. In another ten days, on November 20, Elvis and RCA would sign the final agreement, and the next day an internal company bulletin would announce Presley's three-year contract. The memo further outlined a clearcut and aggressive campaign to promote his RCA record releases—a blitzkrieg advertising campaign designed to sell his five existing Sun singles (on the RCA label) quickly in a number of markets. The message was upbeat—there was potentially big money in Elvis' future. It would be quite surprising if there was really anyone who knew just how big at the time, however.

Early in November, *Billboard* had reported that Sun's "Mystery Train"/"I Forgot to Remember to Forget" had garnered the disc a number 7 position on the country western charts. The record was also number 9 on jukeboxes, and number 12 in radio airplay. This announcement came a day after marathon negotiations had started, and couldn't have come at a better time. If Elvis' rock and roll popularity faded, RCA reasoned,

the country market would obviously sustain him. RCA was counting on Elvis to bring the label its initial rock music prominence, but they also realized that Presley had a country and pop appeal that would probably bring him a wider range of fans.

Steve Sholes, the head of Specialty Singles for RCA, and Bill Bullock, the Singles Division manager, were the key executives who completed the negotiations with Colonel Parker. It was Sholes who had scouted Elvis when Presley appeared on the "Louisiana Hayride." Sholes immediately recommended signing Elvis, although he realized Presley's music would take a special promotional push. This had less to do with the quality of Elvis' songs, and more to do with the changes in music tastes. Sholes was concerned that Elvis would alienate tradition-minded country music audiences, although news like the *Billboard* chartings helped allay his fears. In a memo to RCA management, Sholes expressed every confidence that Colonel Tom Parker's management skills would help break Presley's music into the mainstream.

After signing Elvis, RCA would release his five Sun singles within a few weeks. Suddenly, inasmuch as Sun was able to continue merchandising its final batch of records, Elvis found himself in the enviable position of having two record companies selling his records. RCA's star-making machinery so expertly hyped the news of Presley's lucrative recording contract with the company that it boosted his popularity, created a hot market for Sun singles, and advertised present and future RCA releases in a single stroke. The greening of Elvis Presley was in its formative stages, and it would not be long before Presleymania burst upon the national scene.

Elvis Presley, RCA recording artist.
(L. to r.): Colonel Parker, Gladys, Elvis, Vernon,
RCA legal representative Colman Tilly III, and Bob Neal.

Trouble in Paradise

At the time, few people were privy to the details of the intricate relationship between Colonel Tom Parker and Elvis Presley. When RCA purchased the Sun Records catalog, the media and general public were more intrigued by what appeared to be a spectacular contract paying $40,000 to a relatively new performer for a recording future with an established and respected label. (As we have seen, RCA actually paid only $25,000 of the money, with Hill and Range, Presley's music publishing company, contributing the remaining $15,000. With no sign of humility, RCA announced that it had paid this astronomical sum because the company believed in Presley's future; in actuality, although it was of course obligated to keep the role of Hill and Range under wraps, the simple truth is that RCA had not felt Presley worth the asking price.)

In any case, by late November 1955, Colonel Parker was already plotting Elvis' future in detail. Bob Neal continued to handle the mundane day-to-day details necessary to keep Presley working, while Parker, who couldn't be bothered with the small and insignificant dates that Elvis had been contracted to play, focused on the national audience that he was gearing up to attract.

In a confusing series of legal moves, Colonel Parker and Bob Neal signed a contract that specified that Neal would continue to act as Elvis' co-manager. Another contract (text reproduced opposite) was signed with Elvis placing Parker in total control of Presley's future musical career, however. Colonel Parker used a layered or multiple contract system to perpetuate his management control, shrewdly signing an agreement with Neal that limited the amount of money that the Colonel would have to pay him. Despite the fact that the original management contract that Neal signed with Elvis did not expire until March 15, 1956, the Colonel's maneuverings essentially resulted in Neal receiving a reduced commission.

The perplexing question is why Bob Neal agreed to all this, and why he advised Elvis to sign the contract with Colonel Parker. Until Neal's contract with Elvis expired, he was guaranteed twenty percent of Presley's earnings. The underlying reason for his acquiescence seems to be that, over the long run, Neal ended up receiving a substantial cut of Elvis' new earnings by simply continuing his business relationship with the Colonel for many years thereafter. Neal believed that he had done all he could for Elvis, and saw the Colonel as the logical promoter for Presley's talent. Bob Neal clearly prospered from his continuing association with Colonel Parker, and never had an unkind thing to say about their dealings.

AGREEMENT

"SPECIAL AGREEMENT between ELVIS PRESLEY, known as artist, his guardians, Mr. and/or Mrs. Presley, and his manager, MR. BOB NEAL, of Memphis, Tennessee, hereinafter referred to as the Party of the First Part, and COL. THOMAS A. PARKER and/or HANK SNOW ATTRACTIONS of Madison, Tennessee, hereinafter known as the Party of the Second Part, this date, August 15, 1955.

COL. PARKER is to act as special adviser to ELVIS PRESLEY and BOB NEAL for the period of one year and two one-year options for the sum of two thousand five hundred dollars ($2500.00) per year, payable in five payments of five hundred dollars ($500.00) each, to negotiate and assist in any way possible the build-up of ELVIS PRESLEY as an artist. Col. Parker will be reimbursed for any out-of-pocket expenses for traveling, promotion, advertising as approved by ELVIS PRESLEY and his manager.

As a special concession to Col. Parker, ELVIS PRESLEY is to play 100 personal appearances within one year for the special sum of $200.00 (Two Hundred dollars) including his musicians.

In the event that negotiations come to a complete standstill and ELVIS PRESLEY and his manager and associates decide to freelance, it is understood that Col. Parker will be reimbursed for the time and expenses involved in trying to negotiate the association of these parties and that he will have first call on a number of cities, as follows, at the special rate of one hundred seventy-five dollars ($175.00) per day for the first appearance and two hundred fifty dollars ($250.00) for the second appearance and three hundred fifty dollars ($350.00). San Antonio, El Paso, Phoenix, Tucson, Albuquerque, Oklahoma City, Denver, Wichita Falls, Wichita, New Orleans, Mobile, Jacksonville, Pensacola, Tampa, Miami, Orlando, Charleston, Greenville, Spartanburg, Asheville, Knoxville, Roanoke, Richmond, Norfolk, Washington, D.C., Philadelphia, Newark, New York, Pittsburgh, Chicago, Omaha, Milwaukee, Minneapolis, St. Paul, Des Moines, Los Angeles, Amarillo, Lubbock, Houston, Galveston, Corpus Christi, Las Vegas, Reno, Cleveland, Dayton, Akron and Columbus.

Col. Parker is to negotiate all renewal on existing contracts."

As for Elvis, his decision to sign with Colonel Parker was due in large part to the influence of Vernon Presley. The Colonel was Vernon's choice to manage Elvis. After all, hadn't Parker masterminded Eddy Arnold's and Hank Snow's careers? When Parker showed up at the Presley home with hundred-dollar bills for Vernon, he made a friend for life. Vernon would run down to the local beer joints and wave the one-hundred-dollar bills in people's faces. Jim and Jesse Lee Denson watched Vernon's antics and couldn't believe their eyes. Vernon wasn't the same man who had shown up at Jim's father's mission. The regulars in the local beer halls talked a lot about Vernon Presley's personality and his constant need for ego reinforcement. Colonel Parker understood this character trait and made the most of it. Vernon not only admired the Colonel as a businessman, but was smitten by Parker's flamboyant personal manner. Little did Vernon know that Colonel Tom Parker prided himself on convincing country bumpkins like Vernon Presley that he was as pure as the driven snow.

Vernon, as a result, badgered Bob Neal for months to give up his interest in Elvis. An honest and ethical man, Neal finally agreed with Elvis' dad that the Colonel was more experienced and better connected in the recording industry than he. The probability is, however, that had Bob Neal been privy to the details of the agreement between Elvis and Colonel Parker, he would have recommended that Elvis not sign the document.

The contract was ultimately signed by Vernon and Elvis, although Gladys refused to endorse it. Tom Diskin witnessed the signatures and Colonel Parker signed for Hank Snow's Jamboree Attractions. Gladys Presley took a dim view of Colonel Parker and his business methods. She once compared him to a well-known Tupelo farmer who sold his land over and over again to the same people. This obvious comparison to Orville Bean bothered Vernon, and he hollered vociferously at his wife. "Mind your own business, Gladys," was a common refrain. Vernon loved Elvis' stardom and he didn't want anything to interfere with it, so Gladys' complaints went unheeded. Gladys simply didn't trust the Colonel to fairly divide up Elvis' money. "The Colonel always gave Vernon one-hundred-dollar bills when there was a problem," Jim Denson remarked. "The hundred-dollar bills were flowing like water when the contract was signed."

In time, Parker again appealed to Vernon's vanity in order to have him convince Gladys that he was a good Christian man. While Gladys didn't approve of the contract negotiations, she was reticent to step in and force her son to terminate his agreement with Parker. As Tommy Sands remembered, "A lot of people wanted the Colonel to manage them. Elvis was very happy with the early contract." The common industry view that the Colonel was an honest man eventually placated Gladys. At least this is the public relations view. (The original contract between Colonel Parker and Elvis would be modified and a new agreement signed on March 15, 1956. Like the first contract, however, the modified agreement tied up Presley's show business future. It was a no-risk agreement and Colonel Parker was firmly the mastermind of Elvis Presley's career (more about this in Chapter 15).)

The contract between Colonel Parker and Elvis was a non-specific agreement that bound Elvis to Parker in a form of medieval servitude. No one knew the extent of Parker's share of the profits from the agreement. One rumor in the entertainment industry suggested that Parker received the enormous sum of twenty-five percent. A number of "Grand Ole Opry" regulars remember Tom Diskin bragging that the Colonel received half of Elvis' wages. Regardless of the Colonel's cut, the contract was one-sided and unfair to Elvis.

The agreement required Presley to work a specific number of concerts each year for a small fee. A clause in Elvis' contract clearly spells out the Colonel's power. "As a special concession to Col. Parker, ELVIS PRESLEY is to play 100 personal appearances within one year for the special sum of $200.00 (TWO HUNDRED DOLLARS) including the musicians." The contract goes on to specify that if "ELVIS PRESLEY and his manager and associates decide to freelance, it is understood that Col. Parker will be reimbursed for the time and expenses involved in trying to negotiate the association of these parties and that he will have first call on a number of cities...." It was further specified that Elvis must work three concerts for fees of $175 for the first appearance, $250 for the second concert, and $350 for the third engagement in forty-seven cities, so that even if Elvis broke his contract, Colonel Parker was guaranteed 141 Elvis concerts at a minimal cost.

The contract with Elvis was good business for Tom Parker. It allowed him to make deals for Elvis' services without even consulting his client. The way it was written, Elvis never knew from one day to the next what his future held, something that made for the type of psychological stress that later placed Presley on an emotional roller coaster. In 1955, the contract was not that important, of course, as things were just beginning, and comparatively little was at stake. It was in later years that it hurt Presley's career. The worst immediate effect that it did have was that it influenced Elvis' choice of material to record. Parker used inexperienced, unknown songwriters to pen sometimes syrupy commercial ditties that Elvis hated, and went on to make movie deals based on mediocre scripts that eventually unnerved Elvis. The Colonel was also instrumental in preventing Elvis from changing his movie image in later years. When Barbra Streisand offered Elvis the lead in a remake of "A Star Is Born," the Colonel turned it down, ostensibly over salary and billing. Elvis wanted desperately to do the movie, and would have been perfect for the role of an over-the-hill rock and roller eventually played by Kris Kristofferson. Parker's status as an illegal alien is also cited as the reason Elvis never toured internationally. From day one with the Colonel, then, Elvis was basically confined in a career straight jacket.

Colonel Takes Control

The myth has grown up around Elvis Presley that he and the Colonel worked together solely on a handshake. For years the press reported that Tom Parker committed himself to Elvis' career without a written agreement. While this gave the Colonel the appearance of an honest good-old-boy, an image which he played to the hilt, nothing could be further from the truth. Basically, the press just never took a really close look at the relationship; the media view was that they were just two hillbilly entertainment figures who deserved one another, an image which prevented most writers from approaching Elvis as a serious entertainer for quite some time.

The true extent of Parker's dealings with Presley became apparent after Elvis died, however. After years of gossip and whispering around Memphis, a local probate court appointed Blanchard L. Tual as Lisa Marie Presley's legal guardian in May 1980. For years, lawyers and judges who drank at the Peabody Hotel bar had discussed the Presley estate. There was an uneasiness in the legal community over the manner in which it was administered. The purpose in appointing Tual was to find out if Parker had "violated his duty to Elvis and to the estate." The probate court ordered all payments from Presley's estate to Colonel Parker to cease. In an unusual legal move, the Memphis court instructed Tual to file suit against Parker. As a result, on September 29, 1980, a lawsuit was brought, with Tual acting for Elvis' daughter, requesting that the original contract between Presley and Parker be nullified because the Colonel had not acted in Elvis' best interests.

Tual filed a second suit on July 31, 1981, in the Shelby County, Tennessee, probate court. When the court finally heard *Presley v. Parker* in 1981, the first inside revelations of the business relationship between Elvis and the Colonel surfaced. An analysis of this agreement indicates that Presley's career was hamstrung by a shortsighted management attitude, and that the Colonel acquired great wealth by taking advantage of Elvis with an insider's knowledge of the music business.

The specific revelations that Tual's suit brought out were that Parker received an unprecedented fifty percent fee for handling Elvis' business. "From the documentation, there can be no shadow of doubt...that the Colonel did not respect his fiduciary role with Elvis Presley...," Tual charged. The most glaring management error, according to Tual's suit, was the decision to sell all of Elvis' previous recordings to RCA. In March 1973, Colonel Parker sold Presley's entire record catalog for $5.4 million, giving RCA more than seven hundred recordings at a bargain basement price. Since Elvis was only thirty-eight years old at the time, he effectively lost millions of dollars worth of future song revenues. (It was widely felt throughout the recording industry that Presley's royalty rate was a low one to begin with.) Perhaps the Colonel realized that Elvis' declining health and personal problems foreshadowed an early end? In any event, the deal specified that Elvis had to split the sales fee with Colonel Parker. Since Presley had no significant tax shelters, he ended up netting approximately $750,000 from the deal. In a separate business agreement with RCA, the Colonel was paid $1,550,000 for helping to arrange the sale and cooperating with RCA in promoting Elvis' tours.

Presley v. Parker revealed other examples of the Colonel's personal manipulation of Elvis' career. The allegations against Parker were serious. Few were made public, however, and the Colonel voluntarily gave up his interest in Elvis' future affairs in return for not being prosecuted. The Elvis Presley estate was pleased with the arrangement because it avoided nasty publicity that would have only served to further tarnish Elvis' reputation. In his later years, the Colonel has remained as enigmatic as he was during his heyday. The lawsuit simply ended a chapter in the Presley story and allowed Parker, with a wave of his hand and a big smile, to retire to Madison, Tennessee, and Palm Springs, California, with his memories and his money.

Over time, the mystery behind the failure of Atlantic Records to pursue Elvis' contract was also traced back to the figure of Colonel Tom Parker. Indeed, the Dewey Phillips fiasco had gotten things off to a bad start, but it turned out that it was the involvement of Parker that Ahmet Ertegun most objected to. Simply put, Ertegun had stopped his bid for Presley's services because of Parker's business practices. "I didn't feel comfortable with the Colonel, so we parted company," Ertegun commented. At the back of Ertegun's mind, too—yet another reason why he soured on Elvis—was the financial condition of Sun Records. Sam Phillips had demanded $5,000 just to pay Elvis' back royalties, which prompted Ertegun to wonder, if Elvis' record sales were that good, why Sun Records was in a desperate financial condition.

Ertegun had originally been very serious about Presley, however, and was amazed how little faith RCA had in their new superstar. Steve Sholes admitted to Ertegun that, while enthusiastic about Elvis' music, he was not entirely happy to have Presley as an RCA recording artist. "Sholes thought Elvis was undisciplined," Ertegun remarked, "Maybe Presley was too damned talented for RCA."

Ironically, as it turned out, Ertegun and Jerry Wexler discovered a gold mine of recording talent in Memphis during the Presley negotiations, something that made the whole debacle worthwhile in the long run. Atlantic came away with the music that led to the Stax-Volt sound, a sound that it successfully promoted throughout the sixties. "Without the fight for Elvis," Ertegun remembered, "we would never have found the other music." Cosimo Matassa, the J and M Recording studio boss, remembers that Wexler and Ertegun's visit to New Orleans was filled with tales about Memphis, Sun Records, Sam Phillips, and Elvis Presley. "When Ertegun and Wexler came to New Orleans, they listened to hundreds of my songs and only took a couple records. Those songs turned out to be big hits," Matassa chuckled. From developing acts in Memphis and New Orleans, Atlantic Records reaped all the benefits it aspired to when its executives came South, and it became one of the most progressive labels of the next decade.

Sun Records: The Aftermath

Back in Memphis, more than one observer was amazed that the success of the sale of Presley's five Sun singles to RCA seemed to place more of a financial strain on Sam Phillips than it did to alleviate his problems. "Sam could never collect his money on the records, he was always driving around leaving records here and there and he just couldn't come up with enough

Elvis and Sam Phillips at Sun recording studio—Presley's success was no cure for Sam's problems

money. Plain and simple, he was a bad businessman," one of his early artists remembered. This comment was not typical of Sun artists, but it points out that Sam may not have fully realized the value of the wealth of material he controlled at Sun Records. When RCA purchased the master tapes for all of Elvis' records from Sun, for example, it obtained all the alternate takes as well, including a number of unreleased songs and many breakdowns with studio conversation amongst the musicians and Sam Phillips. Of course, such a judgment is easy to make in hindsight after values have become crystal clear, and far more difficult an assessment to make with certitude in the face of pressing financial needs.

The fifteen boxes of tapes that were reportedly sent to RCA by Sam Phillips are the major historical source for Elvis' early music. Few people at RCA could have realized the historical importance of the Sun tapes at the time, of course. Eventually, having no idea what to do with them, they were simply stored for future reference. Stacked in a warehouse with no labeling, no filing system, and no way of analyzing the contents, the company simply ignored and neglected a rich piece of musical history. From time to time, RCA finds and releases alternate, unfinished, and studio breakdown cuts, but to this day it has no idea where all its Presley tapes are stored.

In the 1970s, some of Elvis' best Sun recordings appeared on bootleg albums and 45s. These apparently came directly from the RCA archives, allegedly from tapes *discarded* by the label. There have also been rumors that RCA has taped over some of Elvis' outtakes and unreleased tunes. A California bootlegger alleges that RCA threw away what it regarded as damaged tapes, and lost or misplaced other Presley recording sessions. "I had a janitor bring me tapes from RCA. He sold them to me and I put out the bootlegs. The janitor bought a big Cadillac or we would have never been caught."

RCA refused comment on these allegations, but the drive to crack down on bootlegging in the 1970s and 1980s would have been impossible without the monetary contributions it made, a signal that it was well aware of the proliferation of bootleg Presley material. One conclusion is inescapable: RCA had little idea of the value or historical significance of Elvis' Sun recordings and, coupled with the unsystematic records kept by Sam Phillips, no one will ever know the full extent of the archival material transferred from Sun to RCA.

In order to gauge the depth of what has been salvaged and what may have been lost, it would be worthwhile at this point to examine the material contained in some key bootleg LPs featuring Sun-era material, as well as a few legitimate RCA releases from the period.

Released in Holland, for example, a bootleg album called **Elvis Presley: Good Rockin' Tonight** featured a number of alternate Sun tracks, false starts, and studio conversation. There were such gems as a take of "Blue Moon of Kentucky" followed by Sam Phillips' enthusiastic comment, "That's real fine. That's a pop song now!" This LP also included a version of "I Don't Care if the Sun Don't Shine" which has two false starts and an extremely strong bass rhythm sound. In fact, Bill Black's bass dominates the alternate takes, apparently the reason why RCA was reluctant to release these cuts. Another gem on this bootleg is a slow bluesy version of "I'm Left, You're Right, She's Gone" called "My Baby's Gone." Because of the overtly spiritual inflection in Elvis' voice as he sings the song, Sam Phillips considered this recording too soulful for immediate release.

Copies of the slower, unreleased version of "I'm Left, You're Right, She's Gone" were circulated to Memphis radio stations, including one to Dewey Phillips at WHBQ.

In 1984, RCA released **Elvis—A Golden Celebration**, a six-record set issued to commemorate Presley's thirtieth anniversary as a recording artist and his rapidly approaching fiftieth birthday. This long overdue package was viewed by many as a grudging tribute to bootleggers, who had already released the material in better packaged albums with historically accurate liner notes. On side 1 of the first record, the material was entitled, "The Sun Sessions—Outtakes, Memphis, Tennessee—1954 and 1955." "Harbor Lights," recorded during Elvis' first Sun recording session, and an unreleased version of "That's All Right (Mama)" are the first two cuts. They are examples of the pure coun-

try and blues sound that Elvis brought into the Sun studio. These songs are followed by a slow take of "Blue Moon of Kentucky," an unreleased cut of an old Bill Monroe song that suggests that Phillips' influence was pivotal in developing Elvis' sound. The version is labored to the point of being sluggish, and is far too brief for commercial release. It is, however, an important addition to the Elvis collector's file, doubly so because it includes Phillips' comments at the end of the take showing clearly what he and Elvis were working for. Another interesting cut is a false start of an unreleased version of "I Don't Care if the Sun Don't Shine," which highlights Presley's strong voice and demonstrates Phillips' considerable production skills.

The take of "I'm Left, You're Right, She's Gone" is an example of a blues-inspired Presley song that neither Sun nor RCA would release thirty years before. Written by Stan Kesler and William Taylor, the song demonstrates Elvis' volatile and uncontrolled energy in the studio. When Scotty Moore remarked that "Elvis was always on the go. He just couldn't stop," he was referring to a performance like this one. Bill Black remembered that "Elvis wanted that extra little something in his songs, he tried everything in the studio," and this one proves it.

Another interesting song in this LP collection is a short version of "I'll Never Let You Go (Little Darlin')" from the January 1955 session, although it is unfinished and hurried. The final tune on this side is the most significant one in the box set, however. It is a previously unreleased cover version of Billy "The Kid" Emerson's "When It Rains, It Really Pours." The song is interesting because there are breakdowns and conversation right in the midst of a straight-ahead attempt to finish the take. Elvis' version of Emerson's song demonstrates the influence of Memphis blues artists on Presley's singing, and there is a blue-collar, workingman's approach to the tune. Ironically, Sam Phillips released Billy Emerson's version of "When It Rains, It Really Pours" on January 8, 1955, the same day he released Elvis' "Milkcow Blues Boogie"/"You're a Heartbreaker." Perhaps Elvis picked up a copy of Emerson's tune that very day, and felt he had to record it. No one really knows for sure when the lightning struck, although it is known that Elvis talked extensively with Emerson and loved the tune.

An interesting sidelight on RCA's knowledge and use of the Sun tapes occurred on January 11, 1956, the date of Elvis' first recording session for his new label (an event that will be discussed in more detail in the next chapter). It began with Steve Sholes in the control booth. Next to Sholes were piled many of the soon-to-be-forgotten Scotch magnetic tape boxes of Presley's

Sun recordings. It was Sholes' job to go through the boxes and select the Sun material that he felt might be appropriate for Elvis' first RCA album. "I figured it would be good luck to have Elvis' early songs near us," recalled Sholes.

One of the most interesting decisions made that day revolved around Sholes' judgment that they should probably skip another attempt at "Harbor Lights," which was on a Sun tape in a container labelled Box 15, but which was too raw for commercial release. (Box 15 included two completed takes of "Harbor Lights" as well as three breakdowns and an instrumental version. The first completed cut was 2:27 and the second was 2:35, and both were noted as "N.G." (for "no good"). Sam Phillips had felt that neither version was commercial.) It was a perfect, middle-of-the-road pop song with an uncomplicated musical arrangement, but Sholes decided after listening to it that Elvis probably couldn't sing it to good effect. Actually, the song was in Box 15 of the Sun tapes because Steve Sholes had numbered the pile of boxes from the top down after he received them from Phillips. Therefore, what seemed to Sholes to be a recent example of Elvis singing "Harbor Lights" was actually the first tune on the very first tape that Phillips had made of Elvis, and was not representative of what Elvis was capable of doing eighteen months into the future.

Sholes made a series of notes on "Harbor Lights." He felt that Elvis' vocal was labored and too country. The sound quality was grainy and he didn't care for the musical background, so utilizing the Sun recording itself was out of the question. RCA hoped to break Elvis in the rock market, but since he sounded demonstrably like a lovesick hillbilly on "Harbor Lights," there was no point re-recording it. Sholes suggested that the song be shelved, and once he spoke negatively about it, RCA executives nixed it. Apparently, although RCA was the acknowledged kingpin of American record companies, the methods for finalizing the selection of Elvis' early record releases could have benefited from some fine tuning.

The Carnival Begins

In early 1956, while Elvis spent his time preparing his first releases for RCA, Colonel Parker would start busily arranging concerts and merchandising his special products. The Colonel had little time to be concerned with music—any type of Elvis record would sell, so why worry about it. Parker's attitude meshed well with the corporate sense and organizational mania to cash in on Elvis' surging popularity that was rife at RCA.

If must be admitted that, if only money is considered, Colonel Parker chose wisely when he signed with RCA, the industry giant. Not only did RCA consistently conduct the best advertising campaigns, but they excelled in distribution. For years RCA had engaged actively in licensing subsidiary products, a practice that was in line with the Colonel's ideas about promoting Elvis. A sophisticated New York corporation, RCA was well aware of the fans' desire for memorabilia. It was not long before RCA began licensing such special products, thereby flooding the Presley market and setting the stage for Colonel Parker to merchandise hundreds of pieces of fan paraphernalia. Even at this early stage, however, a number of record industry insiders believed that there was too much emphasis upon Presley's non-musical side, however. There were too many schemes flowing from Colonel Parker involving the sale of pillows, pins, teddy bears, and fan-oriented memorabilia. The music got lost in the scramble to maximize profits.

The number of internal memos circulated within RCA concerning Elvis' career chronicles the degree of concern over his continued success. These memos detailed exactly how to handle the publicity surrounding Presley's records. As far as the re-release of the Sun singles, RCA intended to advertise each song in the market where it had first sold. Most RCA staffers looked for Presley to chart his records in the country music marketplace.

What is most intriguing about the internal mechanics at RCA is contained in a series of memos dated from July to November 1955. Long before signing Elvis, RCA clearly had taken great care to monitor his career. A good example of RCA's early interest in Presley occurred at the time of his final Sun Records recording session. Not only was an RCA talent scout eating breakfast in Taylor's restaurant next door to Sun when Elvis recorded "I Forgot to Remember to Forget" in July 1955, but RCA promotion men were accumulating opinions of Elvis at Southern radio stations. Were Presley's records simply country ones with a beat? Memoranda reveal that they were worried that Elvis' recordings would not climb the *Billboard* pop chart. Some of Elvis' songs, RCA reasoned, could simply be covered by more prominent pop artists. As Elvis entered the RCA recording studio, for example, Toni Arden covered "I Forgot to Remember to Forget" (RCA 6346), and it was released in January 1956 to test the *Billboard* pop charts. RCA reasoned that other artists might just as easily make hits with Presley tunes. Although it was five months before they would sign Presley, RCA already had a vision for his future, but a rather shaky and uncertain one it was. Because there were some who were nervous about exactly what to do with Elvis, there were early press releases that indicated that RCA would carve out a highly commercial Nashville sound with Elvis at its center. "I don't think Elvis liked recording in Nashville," Ronald Smith remarked. "He didn't feel comfortable in that big old church that RCA used as a studio." (Actually, as we shall see in the next chapter, it was an office building once owned by the Methodist Church, and Elvis kind of liked it.) Certain that RCA could never duplicate the Sun sound, most other Sun artists and Memphis friends echoed the same sentiment.

Despite RCA's inability to understand Elvis' musical direction and artistic qualities, there was no way anyone could criticize his record sales. From 1956 to 1962, Elvis accounted for thirty-one of RCA's thirty-nine million-selling singles. Despite this success, resistance to Presley's music within RCA's management ranks was to persist. Rather than allowing Elvis to select and produce his own songs, RCA increasingly insisted upon firmer controls. After all, they knew best what it took in the music business to make gold records.

Not long after Presley's initial successes, RCA began shifting its marketing away from Elvis' loyal fans. Dedicated fans, after all, would buy the records no matter how they sounded or were produced. It was a can't miss corporate opportunity to broaden Elvis' appeal. Sadly for Elvis (musically speaking), despite weak song selection, his LPs sold just as RCA handlers thought they would, with disheartened loyalists and newfound listeners buying enough records to account for nine of RCA's forty gold albums between 1958 to 1960. And it never occurred to RCA management that Presley's astonishing sales figures could have been increased many times over with a little more care and special packaging.

By the time Presley would return to civilian life after two years in the army, 1958-60, RCA had decided to accelerate its market-broadening strategy, one that involved presenting a new Elvis in the mold of Frank Sinatra. Clearly, RCA had no idea how to handle a rock music act. When the Beatles invaded America in 1964, for example, RCA talent scouts ignored the group, suggesting that the Beatles were just a passing fad. Elvis wanted desperately to update his music, but RCA refused to change the time-tested method of cutting two- or three-minute-long formula records. His career had been reduced to a succession of songs in which the music was bland, the words innocuous, and the production tired. As a recording artist, Elvis reached an early grave by the mid sixties. He would make a spectacular comeback in 1968 on national television singing the music he loved, but throughout the rest of his career he faced an unyielding RCA corporate mentality that slowly strangled his creativity, a burden which, tragically, he bore quietly.

The lack of vision surrounding Elvis' career was

directly attributable to the then president of RCA, George Marek. An opera buff, Marek was uncomfortable with Elvis as a performer from the outset. His staff was instructed never to refer to Elvis as "the Bopping Hillbilly," doubtless a real tooth-grinder of a tag. Marek became visibly angry when RCA executives praised Presley's talent. For years Marek instructed RCA not to sign any more rock music acts. When Sam Cooke was brought to RCA, he, too, was forced into a pop mold and asked to work with two producers who turned out schmaltzy tunes.

The problem of poor song selection was not lost on record bootleggers. A bootleg album entitled **Elvis' Greatest Shit** was released in 1980 and featured twenty-two of Presley's worst songs. This parody LP, appropriately issued on the Dog Vomit Records label, included an unflattering picture of Elvis which had appeared on the cover of the *National Enquirer*'s September 12, 1977, issue. Not only did this record feature such dreary tunes as "Fort Lauderdale Chamber of Commerce," "There's No Room to Rhumba in a Sports Car," and "The Walls Have Ears," but the album also contained a pseudo-prescription written by Dr. George Nichopoulos. Despite its poor taste, **Elvis' Greatest Shit** made some serious points about RCA's stranglehold over Elvis' records.

It was the improper packaging, inconsistent promotion, and watered-down material that ultimately destroyed Elvis' career. By the late 1950s, to be sure, he had already complained to close friends about the songs RCA had him record. More significant was the fact that the whirlwind success that had accompanied his early record sales had prevented him from questioning the wisdom of a long-term contractual arrangement with RCA and Colonel Tom Parker. Looking back on his career after he got out of the army, Elvis told a longtime Memphis friend that he was certain that he had made a mistake by agreeing to the management terms proposed to him by Colonel Tom Parker.

Hill and Range Prosper

Oddly enough, it was Hill and Range, Elvis' music publishers, which profited the most from his RCA contract compared to what they invested in it. Part of Hill and Range's business strategy was to purchase songs from unknown writers. These composers guaranteed Elvis a portion of the writer's credit, a standard industry practice in the 1950s. Once Elvis' name was placed on a song, he collected a royalty through either Presley Music (BMI) or Gladys Music (ASCAP). There were few complaints. The young and generally unknown songwriters were happy with the arrangement, which after all allowed them to make at least a subsistence living by having their songs published, particularly when an artist as popular as Elvis Presley was involved.

Hill and Range received enormous profits because it was guaranteed fifty percent of all of Presley's publishing income. The large sums of money collected by Hill and Range were justified by pointing to the voluminous paperwork and business skills required to maintain a major music publishing firm. It was not long before Hill and Range became the largest independent music publishing house in the world. Hill and Range had been in business for eleven years, but it was not until they made a deal for Elvis Presley's music that they became a multi-million-dollar music conglomerate.

From the beginning, Elvis had been uncomfortable with the Hill and Range agreement. Presley didn't like the idea of receiving writing royalties for songs in which he had had no input. Consequently, he never filled out the paperwork required to collect his share of the songwriting money. This was a silent protest on Elvis' part. He couldn't take advantage of young, unknown songwriters. "Elvis did his best to stop Colonel Parker from saying that he wrote some of his own songs," Ronald Smith remembered.

Owing to the significance of the agreement between Colonel Parker, Sun Records, RCA, and Hill and Range, we have spent several pages analyzing the events which followed the announcement of the agreement on November 10, 1955, often ranging quite far into the future in an attempt to put some perspective on them. It might be well to resume our chronicling of Presley's early career at this point, bearing in mind that Elvis, of course, had yet to sign onto the deal.

Closing Out the Year

Elvis was on the road almost every day in the last months of 1955 playing concerts, appearing at radio stations, signing autographs in record stores, or talking to music people. The skyrocket that was Presley's career became apparent on November 12, 1955, when *Billboard* announced that he ranked number 1 as the "Most Promising Country and Western Artist" in the magazine's annual poll. He was also listed as number 13 on the "Most Played C & W Artist" poll, and number 16 in the "Favorite C & W Artists" category. Yet, although *Billboard*'s stamp of approval clearly illuminated his road to stardom, Elvis' backbreaking tour schedule left little time for idle moments.

A good example of Presley's exhausting schedule commenced on Saturday afternoon, November 12, 1955, when he performed in Carthage, Texas, only to immediately jump into his car for a drive to an appearance

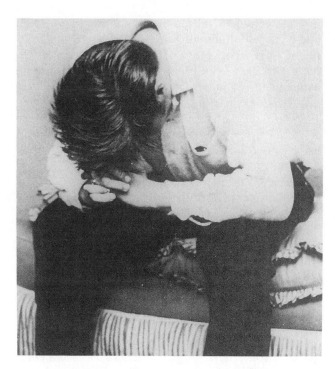

A recording contract was still no cure for exhaustion.

on "Louisiana Hayride." The drive from Carthage, a small Texas town a hundred miles from Shreveport, seemed to pose no problem for him, however. When he walked onto the stage at the "Hayride," Elvis had more energy than any two performers. "I never saw anything like the frenetic performing skills of Elvis," Tommy Sands remembered, "and when I found out he finished a two-hour drive before walking on stage I was amazed." Sands remembered that Elvis talked about finishing his Carthage show with "Uncle Pen," the 1951 hit by bluegrass artist Bill Monroe that Elvis loved to perform. "Elvis wanted to give the country folks what they wanted," Sands remembered, "and he glowed when he told me how the Carthage crowd clapped for his last song."

After the "Louisiana Hayride" show, Elvis, Scotty, and Bill got up early the next morning and drove four hundred miles back to Memphis. They arrived in time to appear in two shows at the Ellis Auditorium with Hank Thompson, Carl Smith, Charlene Arthur, and Carl Perkins. It was in the course of these shows that Elvis sang "Satisfied" in an impromptu backstage duet with Charlene Arthur. (For some time, Elvis had talked about having recorded the song at the Sun studios. Allegedly, he did so on September 10, 1954, between takes of "I'll Never Let You Go (Little Darlin)." However, a recording has never surfaced. Sun insiders claim that it was destroyed shortly after Presley cut it, although there is some speculation that RCA may have lost the master at a later date.)

Charlene Arthur dated Elvis for a few weeks during this period. Arthur, a buxom, exciting performer, had a gospel-influenced voice. She was also quite different from Elvis' other dates. Unlike the quiet, demure girls that Elvis preferred, Arthur was a woman with a mind of her own, something that made a permanent relationship with Presley impossible. During a late 1955 farewell performance for Texas Bill Strength of KWEM—Strength was taking a job in Minneapolis, where, as Strength told the audience, he would introduce the Yankees to real country music—Elvis and Charlene Arthur parted company.

Following the Bill Strength farewell, Elvis and many of the supporting acts left Memphis and toured for a week, appearing in Forrest City, Camden, and Texarkana, Arkansas. They concluded this short tour with stops in Sheffield, Alabama, and Longview, Texas. These performances were among Elvis' best because Carl Perkins was on the bill. It was not just the challenge that Perkins' act posed for Elvis; Carl was a good friend who helped to polish Presley's stage show.

Elvis' response to Perkins' friendly rivalry was to perform some new songs. Presley's love affair with rhythm and blues was demonstrated when he included LaVern Baker's hit "Tweedle Dee" in his act. Since late 1954, Elvis had listened to and sporadically performed some of Baker's songs. After doing "Tweedle Dee" on this mini-tour, Elvis also performed it on the "Louisiana Hayride." During this period, Elvis also worked a country tune, "Tennessee Saturday Night," into his concerts. After performing it on the "Hayride," Elvis told Bill Black that he felt that they just had to do it in the studio. Indeed, at some point in 1955 Elvis did record this tune, although it, too, was never released commercially. Eventually, a bootleg single featuring the song was released as bogus Sun Record 252.

On November 19, 1955, Elvis' appearance on the "Louisiana Hayride" was one of the most exciting performances of his young career. In a playful mood, he used a rhythm and blues approach while performing his songs. The "Hayride" was broadcast that night from Gladewater, Texas, and Elvis inspired the crowd with a ripping version of "Tweedle Dee." In a jubilant mood, he flew to Nashville after the show. Colonel Parker had sent word that recording contract negotiations had been completed.

The following day, Sunday, November 20, 1955, Elvis signed a three-year contract with RCA. There was nothing unique about the agreement Presley signed—it was a standard recording industry document. He also inked a music publishing contract with the Hill and Range. Colonel Parker had convinced Elvis that a long-term publishing deal was to his financial advantage. The Colonel advised Elvis to set up Elvis Presley Music, Inc.

(BMI) and Gladys Music (ASCAP) to hold the copyrights to his songs, and to designate Hill and Range as the administrative agent to collect his royalties. It was an attractive business deal for Hill and Range, which, as noted above, was paid fifty percent of Presley's royalties in return for acting in this capacity. To increase Presley's earnings, Hill and Range hired six salaried songwriters to pen tunes for him, supplementing, as previously mentioned, the pool of songs it was acquiring from lesser lights. The company's star team included Jerry Leiber and Mike Stoller, the California team who had written many hit rhythm and blues classics together. The word on the street was that Leiber and Stoller had their ears attuned to the teen marketplace. Ben Weisman, a Brooklyn-trained classical pianist who had apprenticed under Irving Berlin, was brought in to write "hillbilly songs." As Weisman remembered, "I was a city guy writing country tunes for big money." Combined with all this was a stable of RCA songwriters, and the whole would soon mesh with Presley's talent to create a fiscal revolution unprecedented in the music business.

Hard on the heels of the finalization of the RCA deal, the decision was made to seek national television exposure. Colonel Tom Parker negotiated for bookings on major network shows. "I think the Colonel was given too much credit for Presley's 1956 television success," Marion Keisker remarked. "We could all see it coming; the Colonel wasn't so sure." Still nervous about Presley's future, Parker encouraged him to continue to refine his act with local audiences.

A Taste of Things to Come

In 1956, Elvis Presley would sell ten million singles, the largest number ever sold in one year by a single performer. During the first half of 1956, Elvis' record sales accounted for half of RCA's total revenue. "Don't Be Cruel" sold six million copies while it was on the *Billboard* charts. "Love Me Tender" was the first record in industry history to ship gold. When "Heartbreak Hotel" was released, it sold thirty-eight million records over the next five years. During his first decade at RCA, Elvis Presley accounted for 115 million record sales. At the time, these figures were absolutely astonishing; looking past the numbers, however, the more astute critics also praised the quality of the music. Indeed, during the first six months of 1956, Elvis made some of the best music of his career. While the transition from Sun to RCA was not a smooth one, nevertheless, the music that Elvis produced during his early RCA years was exceptional. To be sure, this was more due to Elvis' raw talent than to RCA's production skills.

Elvis' critics have suggested that his later music failed to capture the intensity and innovative sound of the

Christmas 1955.

pared for Elvis Presley," Guralnick writes. "The violence of its reaction to him testifies to this...." Elvis was the Tony Curtis forelock and ducktail, the Marlon Brando sneer, the James Dean cynicism all wrapped up in one musical package, and it caused a sensation. Elvis was the ultimate contradiction; half rebel and half solid citizen—a God-fearing, flag-waving, down-home American boy. Presley's personality mirrored all the conflicts and frustrations of the 1950s. One of the most important contributions he made during this phase of his career was the ability to just be himself, something which allowed many other performers to identify with his music, his personality, and his devil-may-care attitude.

Waylon Jennings remembers that Elvis was "like an explosion." Buddy Holly remarked that "without Elvis, none of us would have made it." Johnny Tillotson called Elvis "the hurricane that brought in rock and roll." Gene Vincent labelled Elvis "the guy who made me think I could perform." These tributes continued into the sixties, when John Lennon, Mick Jagger, and Pete Townsend, among others, credited Elvis with inspiring a generation of British rock musicians. He was truly the King of Rock and Roll, the musical genius who gave birth to mainstream commercial rock music.

early Sun recordings, and certainly as Elvis' control of his career slipped ever further from his grasp, this is very true. "There was something about the looseness at Sun that rubbed off on the recordings," Phillips recalled. Marion Keisker pointed out that "Elvis never rehearsed, he sounded like a jukebox. That's why his records were so good." Sam Phillips hit home when he suggested that the people at RCA just didn't understand Elvis or his music. Phillips does claim that he never said: "If I could find a white man who had the Negro sound and the Negro feel, I could make a million dollars." Whether or not he actually uttered these words is a moot point; the course Sam Phillips took at Sun could only have occurred as a result of the realization of the truth carried within them.

Author Peter Guralnick has come closest to defining Presley's early appeal. "The world was not pre-

As his time at RCA progressed, Elvis would have little freedom. He would be saddled with heavy-handed producers, tight budgets, and meddlesome corporate executives. In a few years, his RCA career would turn into a nightmare, and he would begin going through the paces to fulfill his contract obligations. From the outset, RCA just couldn't get acclimated to having an act known as "the Bopping Hillbilly," so they did their best to create a new and more sophisticated Elvis Presley. The end of the Sun Records era was a watershed in Elvis Presley's personal and professional life, and by examining the first six months at RCA in the chapters which follow, it will become possible to see the effects of the changes that would so dramatically alter his life. He was now a prisoner of fame and fortune, and the cold, cruel world of corporate capitalism would slowly and inexorably chart his destiny.

The New Elvis,
January-February 1956

On Thursday, January 5, 1956, Elvis Presley arrived in Nashville for his first RCA recording session. The drive to Nashville was unpleasant due to cold weather and a slick highway. Although it would be another five days before Elvis actually started taping, he wanted to do some planning for this all important session. Nervous because of what he viewed as his earlier initial failure on the "Grand Ole Opry," it was important for Elvis to bring off an impressive first recording session with his new record company. With the enormous financial investment in Presley's career, RCA was equally determined to obtain commercially successful music from Elvis.

Nashville

RCA's Nashville studio had a dark, eerie quality to it. Located at 1520 McGavock Street, it was a dilapidated old building—the Methodist Television, Radio and Film Commission building—with a rickety stairwell leading to a vacant second floor. A facility generally used by new acts, the building's poor condition reflected RCA's unwillingness to spend money on a sophisticated recording studio. Yet, to the astonishment of industry figures, the studio produced an excellent sound, and, oddly enough, Elvis particularly loved the rear stairwell, which doubled as an echo chamber. Sam Phillips' Sun recordings had employed an echo, an effect favored by most rockabilly musicians, and Elvis hoped to recreate it in the stairwell.

The RCA sessions were to be produced by the best-known producer in country music, Steve Sholes. Few people realized the extent to which Sholes had been monitoring Elvis' Sun recordings over the previous months; as a result, he would go on to create some of Presley's finest records. For his part, Sholes believed that the equipment, building, and ambiance of the Nashville studios made fledgling artists feel comfortable, and that RCA couldn't have selected a recording site better suited to Presley's talent. "Elvis walked into the studio and smiled," Sholes remarked, "then he started tapping his foot as he looked around the room." Sholes felt like Elvis was comparing the RCA studio to Sun. "What Elvis was doing," Bill Black remarked, "was trying to figure out if RCA could sell his product."

In preparation for Elvis' recording session, the RCA publicity department cranked out a series of press releases lauding Presley's talent. They attempted to generate controversy by suggesting that Elvis was going to record some "Negro" music, more than a passing reference to the fact that Elvis favored rhythm and blues tunes at a time when it was considered commercially risky. When Elvis performed a medley of Joe Turner songs—featuring "Shake, Rattle and Roll" and "Flip Flop and Fly" on the Dorsey Brother's "Stage Show" later in the month, the New York critics reacted harshly. Elvis was perplexed over their vengeful prose. He had performed this medley all over the South for almost two years. It was a natural extension of his rhythm and blues roots. To America's youth, who revelled in the fact that adults squirmed and fretted over Presley's act, the medley made him a hero, and was one of the reasons for his immense popularity.

Before Elvis went into the RCA studio, however, he sought out Charlie Feathers for some advice. For years Elvis had been aware of the respect that fellow musicians accorded Feathers. "I was with Charlie Feathers at a park where he was playing," Ronald Smith remembered, "and Chet Atkins showed up to listen. Atkins showed open admiration." Feathers' effect on Elvis was a tonic. They laughed and joked, and Elvis' anxieties were calmed, helping him a great deal.

On Thursday afternoon, Elvis met with Steve Sholes and Chet Atkins to discuss preparations for the session. Atkins was RCA's A & R man for country music, and Sholes requested his opinions on Presley's future repertoire. Neither Sholes nor Atkins were impressed with Elvis' interest in rhythm and blues; rather, they hoped that there was a country hit in him. They were concerned that the rhythm and blues and blues tunes which Elvis favored might hurt his commercial appeal. Eventually, though, Sholes and Atkins agreed to let Elvis record songs that he felt most comfortable performing. After all, this is what made Presley's Sun recordings sell so well, so there was no sense fooling with a proven formula.

After two days in Nashville, Elvis returned home to Memphis on Saturday, January 7, 1956, to rest before returning for the recording session. On Sunday, Vernon and Gladys held a twenty-first birthday party for him. There was a subdued atmosphere among the guests, however—everyone was nervous about the impending RCA recording sessions. "I could see the tension in Elvis," Ronald Smith remarked. "He wasn't the same person."

Elvis in early 1956—on the way with RCA.

It was already difficult for many of Elvis' old friends to see him. They tried to call and couldn't get through on the telephone. When they dropped by Elvis' house, he wasn't home. Not surprisingly, an air of tension surrounded young Presley—the stakes were mammoth ones. His entire future as a recording artist rested on the success of these sessions.

Even at this early stage, Elvis openly complained about RCA's unwillingness to define his musical future in terms he could accept or understand. In a few days, a host of middle-aged recording executives would come in to shake his hand at his first recording session, but it was soon apparent that they had little knowledge of his music. They stared at Elvis, and he fidgeted uncomfortably. Few of them were familiar with rock and roll music, and there were moments of awkward silence. Down-home, good-old-boy backslapping was a thing of the past.

But RCA did have a plan. They were intent on recrafting Elvis' "hillbilly cat" image into a mainstream commercial mold. RCA had Frank Sinatra's career in mind when they worked on Elvis' transformation. Hadn't Sinatra started his career as a bobbysox idol? Wasn't the next step a more sophisticated musical direction? Perhaps a movie career was in the works?

The Role of Steve Sholes

As noted above, Steve Sholes, the forty-five-year-old head of RCA's artist and repertoire department, was placed in charge of Elvis' early recording sessions. Originally from New Jersey, Sholes had worked for RCA since graduating from high school. While in college and working part-time for RCA, he received an extensive musical education. He had a keen ear for both country and rock music, and had witnessed the rise of jump blues and the popularity of rhythm and blues tunes in the early and mid-1950s.

In Nashville, Sholes was a respected producer who supervised hit records for Hank Snow, Pee Wee King, and Johnny and Jack. Many of Sholes' hit songs were recorded at Brown Brothers' Transcription Service, and it was in this primitive facility that Sholes learned what it took to make a hit record. He also knew how to fit into the country music establishment.

A large, heavy man who seldom lost his temper, Sholes was tested by many of the top country stars, the most famous of which was Hank Williams. At the time, Sholes was producing hit records for Hank Snow, and decided to cut a Hank Williams tune, "You Better Keep It on Your Mind." Initially, Sholes believed that the Williams song would fit Snow nicely. After listening to it, however, Sholes didn't believe that it was right for Snow and abandoned the idea. One night at the "Grand Ole Opry," Williams angrily confronted Sholes. "Listen you fat Jew," Hank bellowed, "don't ever let me hear you saying my songs are low-class again." Sholes glowered at Williams and said nothing. This story typified the pressures placed upon Sholes, and demonstrates how ably he controlled himself. There was a feeling among many of Nashville's country music elite that Sholes was an outsider, and there was more than a little jealousy generated between many performers over his power to choose from RCA's stable of artists.

An exceptionally literate man with a degree from Rutgers University, Sholes basically had an ear for significant lyrics and demonstrated a knack for producing hit records. As mentioned, Sholes brought in guitarist Chet Atkins to help with the studio work; Atkins' versatility enabled Sholes to bring many of his musical ideas to fruition. From the time Sholes had first established himself in Nashville, he had relied heavily upon Chet Atkins' advice. They talked at great length in the recording studio, and it was Atkins who organized the recording sessions. Atkins worked with Perry Como and Al Hirt as well as Elvis Presley. Sholes recognized what an asset he had in Atkins as far as producing Presley's early RCA records, and so placed no stylistic limits upon his production techniques. Had Steve Sholes not recognized Atkins' production ability, Presley's records might not have been as strong. Sholes knew that Atkins saw the link between rockabilly and black music, and could help coax the right sound out of Elvis. A knowledge of the music of Jimmie Rodgers and Bob Wills was clearly evident as Sholes and Atkins attempted to craft Elvis' early RCA sound.

As one of the key RCA figures who had pushed to sign Elvis to a recording contract, Sholes was determined to create a masterful new sound. He felt the best way to tailor the sound to the artist was to analyze Presley's style. He spent hour after hour listening to tapes of Elvis' Sun recordings, scribbling copious notes. He came to believe that while Scotty Moore, Bill Black, and D.J. Fontana were fine musicians, their recording abilities with a view to strengthening Elvis' sound were questionable. Additionally, it troubled Sholes that Moore and Black bickered with one another so much over their music. D.J. Fontana, the drummer, was quiet, remaining in the background. The noticeable dissension within the group made Sholes anxious, however. Elvis' best sound could not be produced in such an atmosphere.

After days of listening to the fifteen boxes of tapes from Sun Records, Sholes divided them into two piles. There were five tapes containing recordings which he deemed had commercial potential; the other ten that were placed in a pile he labelled "Needs work." What happened to these tapes, as noted in the previous chapter, remains a mystery. Once Sholes finished with them, he turned his attention to Elvis, with whom he spent many long hours talking.

As he talked with Elvis about producing a hit record, Sholes concluded that musicians other than the Blue Moon Boys were needed. The piano was a natural instrument for Elvis, but he couldn't play it well enough in a recording studio, so Sholes hired Floyd Cramer to do the job, an excellent choice. For six months, Cramer had played alongside Elvis on the "Louisiana Hayride," where they first met, and they had also appeared on concert bills together. In October 1955, Cramer toured with Elvis as part of the Jamboree tour that began in Abilene, Texas, and concluded in St. Louis, Missouri. Elvis was at ease with Floyd, and respected his musical skills. Only two years younger than Elvis, Cramer was an easy-going country boy from Shreveport, Louisiana.

Because Scotty Moore was to be left out, Elvis also needed another guitarist, so he was elated with the decision to hire Chet Atkins. "Elvis was worried his sound wasn't professional enough," Ronald Smith remembered, so when Atkins was hired to strengthen the guitar parts, Elvis couldn't have been happier. Important decisions like these—Atkins was featured on four of the five songs cut during the January sessions—had a direct effect on the quality of Elvis' first recordings.

The session musicians also included the Speer brothers, Ben and Brock, and Gordon Stoker, who provided spiritual-based background vocals. Unlike many RCA executives, Sholes was determined to avoid turning Elvis into either a country act like Eddy Arnold or a pop crooner like Frank Sinatra. There was a freshness to Presley's music, and Sholes believed Elvis could, within reason, do just about anything he asked of him with the right backup. The fifteen boxes of Sun tapes had yielded only a few commercially acceptable tunes, but Sholes still liked the primitive nature of these recordings. He reasoned that Elvis' blend of raucous blues tunes with traditional pop songs could easily make him a commercially successful artist.

During his college years, Steve Sholes had developed the habit of keeping careful notes, a practice which he continued during his years with RCA. Like many record industry executives, however, Sholes was suspicious of producers, managers, and other record company types, so that his notes were usually cryptic, crude scribbles that only he could decipher. When Elvis' career skyrocketed in early 1956, Sholes' notes became a much sought after item by bewildered RCA management types looking for the reasons for Presley's enormous record sales. As more and more people within RCA requested Sholes' notes, he revelled in the praise and adulation. He loved power, and his notes came to be viewed as the stone tablets which held the keys to a mystery—much like the Rosetta stone or the Mosaic commandments. Sholes often teased people with the pronouncement that he was in charge, and he duly waved his notes to prove it. When he died, Joan Deary, Sholes' assistant, kept the notes evaluating Presley's Sun sessions. They are an important source in analyzing Sholes' careful approach to the recording process. Yet, their cryptic nature has kept secret the complete details of exactly what Sun Records transferred to RCA. The full extent of this material may never be known, although bits and pieces of the Sun puzzle have surfaced since Presley's untimely death.

Early in his relationship with Elvis, Sholes realized that Colonel Parker's only interest was in the money end of the business. The Colonel had little concern for the music. Once in a great while, Parker selected a song for Elvis to record, but invariably there was a special deal or songwriting credit involving money to explain his actions. Sholes was relieved that Parker did not care to participate in the recording sessions more than he did.

As an insurance policy against Parker's interference, Sholes spent long hours convincing the Colonel that he was crafting Elvis' music into a highly commercial sound, one that would guarantee Presley superstardom. In addition, RCA had a hefty advertising budget to promote Elvis' records. No expense was to be spared in making Presley a major star in the record world. Because he understood the pecuniary motive that drove the Colonel, Steve Sholes was one of a very few people who could reason with Parker, and it was Sholes who convinced Parker that RCA was pushing Presley's music in an unprecedented manner.

The first signs of RCA's promotional hype were evident on Saturday, January 7, 1956, when Sholes and Colonel Parker met to discuss a full-page advertisement RCA purchased in the December 3, 1955, issue of *Billboard*. The impressive display ad prominently featured Elvis among RCA's leading country artists. In a series of meetings with RCA's Nashville publicity department, Sholes pointed out that this advertising guaranteed that RCA would recoup its initial investment. The country music market, Sholes argued, was highly profitable. Presley's records could be sold by identifying his music with key musicians. Using his notes to accentuate his argument, Sholes read off a list of musicians who would help sell Presley's music. Chet Atkins'

An early RCA publicity photo.

guitar and Floyd Cramer's piano, Sholes argued, were essential in convincing country fans that Elvis was an important new country property.

What Sholes failed to mention to Colonel Parker at the time was that he was worried about Elvis' vocal range. Sholes confidence in Elvis' voice was less than complete, and he had concentrated almost solely on his performing style. He believed that Presley's vocals were weak, erratic, and lacked a distinct direction. By adding the musical punch of backup vocalists and extra musicians, Elvis' records would sound much stronger. This explains Sholes' use of Ben and Brock Speer to sing lead tenor and baritone to highlight Presley's vocals, and the Jordanaires' Gordon Stoker to sing first tenor—all designed to further strengthen Elvis' studio sound.

Gordon Stoker has admitted that he was a little uncertain about Presley's future after these sessions. Elvis, on the other hand, was so impressed with the Jordanaires that he promised Stoker that if his records continued to sell, the Jordanaires would be included on future records and in concert tours. Stoker was frankly skeptical. "We didn't think they'd go big," Stoker remarked about Elvis' records. "We didn't even remember Elvis' name." Those words soon returned to haunt Stoker as Elvis became the biggest name in show business. True to his word, Elvis included the Jordanaires in his future recording sessions and concert dates for many years thereafter.

As the development of rock and roll as a musical style came into sharper focus, Steve Sholes quickly realized that it was destined to be highly commercial. Unlike many Nashville producers, Sholes believed that Elvis was the perfect practitioner of the new art. The popularity of early rock and roll music and the rock revolution prompted Sholes to mix songs like "I Got a Woman" and "Money Honey" with traditional country and pop songs.

Sometimes, it seemed like everybody had an opinion. Gabe Tucker, Colonel Parker's publicist, remarked that, "Sholes found Elvis loud and boisterous and tried to pound him into the conservative RCA mold," but this comment fails to recognize that Sholes fought top RCA management to allow Elvis to record tunes like Ray Charles' "I Got a Woman." The truth is that, much to his credit, Sholes resisted the tendencies of RCA executives to seek to mold Presley into solely a pop singer. In these very early days, Sholes often found it difficult to convince these same executives that he was pursuing the right course with Elvis.

As a result of Elvis' Sun Records success, Sholes was expected to continue turning out hits. There were such heavy corporate pressures brought about by RCA executives that Sholes even briefly considered leaving the music business. There is no doubt that his rapidly expanding waistline reflected his frustrations. A year before he died in 1968, Sholes told David Dalton, "The money we paid [for Elvis]...was pretty big...and [RCA] wanted me to assure them that they would make their money back in the first year." Sholes complained about his dilemma as early as 1956, but later had a good chuckle over Presley's success during the next decade. Even Hill and Range, Elvis' music publishers, wanted him to record two songs from their catalog and were upset when Sholes' judgement prevailed. But the local music powers would not leave Sholes alone, and they gossiped about him in every conceivable way.

Sholes was not without his detractors outside of the Presley team, as noted above. A great deal of criticism was directed toward the records he produced for Elvis Presley. Many of Nashville's producers had trouble understanding the changes in American music. The period from 1956 until his death in 1968 was not an altogether pleasant time for Sholes. In Nashville, a network of good-old-boys carried insidious tales from one record label to another. This group of gossip-mongers hit hard at Sholes' credibility, and made nasty remarks about his song selection. "Hell, we thought Sholes was queer for Elvis," one record company official remarked. "You have to realize it was hard for us to accept that boy's music."

More often than not, the nasty remarks were made about Sholes' New Jersey origins, but in reality it was not just disdain for a Yankee, but the negative reaction to Elvis that prompted the vicious gossip. With his peculiar dress and exaggerated hairstyle, Presley was the antithesis of everything that the RCA corporate executive or the country music traditionalist valued. In early 1956, Charlie Lamb, the publisher of *Music Reporter*, presented an award to Elvis for his record sales, and Lamb told Colonel Parker that he had never seen a young man who was so unusual. When pressed to explain his remarks, Lamb stuttered and wandered away from the Colonel. Like most record industry figures, Lamb could not put his finger on what made Elvis different. Perhaps, Lamb speculated, Elvis couldn't turn out the type of records that generated a stable, clearly-defined audience. If this was the case, it was the kiss of death in the country music field.

The First RCA Session

When Elvis first arrived in Nashville to record, he announced that he was happy to be an RCA artist. It was difficult for him to adjust to the complex RCA recording system, however. Always polite and friendly, Elvis was too young, too green, and too eager to comprehend the petty politics and cynical machinations of the recording industry. He was used to walking into the Sun studio and cutting his tracks in a relaxed atmosphere, one bereft of innuendos, backbiting, and gossip. "I don't think Elvis was happy in those early RCA sessions," Marion Keisker remarked. "He couldn't understand those folks, so he put on his friendly good ole boy face." An idealist with a strong sense of his own commitment and goals, Elvis was hurt by the pervasiveness of these attitudes. His only solace came in his work.

It was fortunate, therefore, that Elvis still had concert commitments to fulfill while he was preparing for his first recording session. The "Louisiana Hayride" was still important to Elvis' overall popularity, and he continued to drive to Shreveport to appear on the show. The upcoming two-day recording session was a watershed in Elvis' fledgling career, and he realized that it might make or break him. The drive to and from Shreveport was a tonic for Elvis. He could always think better while on the road.

On Saturday, January 7, 1956, just three days before his first recording session, he appeared on the "Hayride" and performed "I Got a Woman," hoping soon to be able to record it. Many of the regulars on the "Hayride" slapped Elvis on the back after he covered the Ray Charles tune. They loved the way he could take a rhythm and blues tune and perform for country fans. Tommy Sands, who also recorded for RCA, noticed that it was difficult for Elvis to hide his anxiety.

On Tuesday, January 10, 1956, Elvis reported to the studio. He was nervous and paced for at least ten minutes around the room. Finally, Steve Sholes suggested that he do something to calm himself down. Elvis sat down next to Floyd Cramer and started playing the piano. Cramer got up and went to the bathroom. Elvis began singing spirituals. After breaking into "I'm Bound for the Kingdom," Elvis continued with "I'll Tell It Wherever I Go." Gordon Stoker of the Jordanaires joined in, and Ben and Brock Speer added their voices. The tension was broken.

During the next two days Elvis would cut five songs. The January 10 session began at two o'clock and lasted until five in the afternoon. Following a two-hour dinner break, the entourage returned for three more hours. By ten that night, Elvis' first RCA recording session had ended. The following day, a second session from four to seven concluded Elvis' initial studio venture. It was a memorable two days marked by both highs and lows.

The lows grew out of the newness of the situation, the departure from the old, comfortable ways. When Elvis later reflected on his first RCA session, he recalled how much different the process had been at Sun.

In the RCA recording studio.

Ronald Smith and Kenneth Herman often wandered in to joke with Elvis. Marcus Van Story would pull out his harmonica and play some blues riffs that relaxed Elvis. Ronald Smith would grab a guitar and imitate Scotty Moore's sound. Kenneth Herman would add some uptempo rockabilly sounds on his steel guitar. Eddie Bond dropped in to talk about his future plans, something which not only inspired Elvis, but made him feel at ease. There was a sense of family in the Sun office, and the presence of large numbers of creative people filled Elvis with electricity.

At the RCA studio, in contrast, a steady stream of corporate businessmen in their business suits made Elvis nervous and anxious. He would watch RCA executives stare at him, something that made him very uneasy. The psychological pressure placed upon him was tremendous. At RCA it was all business, and Elvis quickly grew depressed over the lack of a creative atmosphere. He tried to combat it. Playful remarks, practical jokes, and humility were devices that Elvis employed to rid himself of the insulting looks and remarks. Every Sun Records artist interviewed about Presley's success vividly remembers how he complained about the early RCA sessions. "My music wasn't the same after Sun," Elvis remarked to Ronald Smith.

Gone was the friendly face of Stan Kesler, who sat in his control booth and helped to arrange the music. Kesler, a young man, had a fatherly relationship with Elvis. A man with a sure musical sense, Stan was someone who worked unobtrusively and diligently, and Elvis often talked about Kesler's deft musical touch.

Doug Poindexter no longer sat around the studio running paper through his guitar strings to get the right type of rockabilly sound. A large, quiet man, Poindexter was a guitar virtuoso that everyone respected, and he shared his extraordinary knowledge with many other musicians. Elvis had been one of Poindexter's most interested students.

Charlie Feathers no longer fiddled in a nearby corner with arrangements and innovative guitar breaks.

Paul Burlison no longer dropped in to look over the scene.

The hordes of hopeful rockabilly singers carrying their songs around were no more.

Instead, Colonel Tom Parker and his penguin-shaped assistant, Tom Diskin, were in the RCA control booth. The Colonel loved to hang around the recording studio—it gave him a feeling of power, and he loved to wave his cigar in the air and talk noisily. Diskin was like a puppy, hanging on Parker's every word. While the Colonel was in his element, Diskin confessed that he, too, missed Sam Phillips and the informality of the Sun sessions.

Fortunately, Steve Sholes instantly recognized Elvis' problem. He walked over and put his arm around Presley's shoulder. They talked quietly at length. To get Elvis into the proper mood for this session, Sholes suggested that he pick the first song to record. This surprised Elvis, but it was an important ploy. For once Elvis felt that at least one RCA executive understood him. There had been talk about covering a Ray Charles song. Elvis had performed Charles' "I Got a Woman" on the "Louisiana Hayride," and the idea of recording the rhythm and blues song as his first RCA cut definitely appealed to him.

Once the recording session began, there was pandemonium. Elvis danced around the room, and Sholes was forced to halt the taping. He explained to Elvis that the new technology required precise recording techniques. An artist must stand at a predetermined spot, a large "X" taped on the floor. Elvis sheepishly followed Sholes' instructions. The next cut was a disaster, and Sholes, quick to improvise, wisely remiked the studio. Elvis could now dance and sing to his heart's content. During the first hour of Sholes' initial recording session, he demonstrated patience, flexibility, and the ability to adjust to Presley's unique musical style.

Elvis, in contrast, didn't change at all. He took his shoes off for comfort, and then accidentally cut his finger on a guitar string. When Steve Sholes suggested that they take a break, Elvis refused. The drive toward stardom wouldn't abate. Elvis was enormously serious—he wanted to be a superstar. Rather than taking a break after the lengthy process of cutting the first song, the session continued.

It was the second song that was special for Elvis— "Heartbreak Hotel." There were many who believed that the song was a disaster. Colonel Tom Parker was unusually quiet during the taping. Steve Sholes rubbed his neck nervously. The musicians looked bored. No one realized that they were making history. Sam Phillips later remarked to a New York *Post* reporter that "Heartbreak Hotel" was so poorly recorded that "only a damned fool would release it." Phillips, however, was a proud man trying to make a point: he was the only person who could effectively record Elvis Presley.

After "Heartbreak Hotel" was completed, Sholes ended the session with a raucous version of Clyde McPhatter and the Drifters' "Money Honey." This Jesse Stone song was one of Presley's favorites. It was the Drifters' debut record with Clyde McPhatter as the lead singer, and had been a major *Billboard* rhythm and blues hit in March 1954. Like many young people, Elvis purchased "Money Honey" and spent hours listening to it. Presley's vocal styling on this rhythm and blues song is classic, a tribute to McPhatter's own effort, which had inspired Elvis to record it. After Presley completed "Money Honey," the mood in the studio quickly changed. Elvis had electrified the small audience with his vocal intensity. In fact, the musicians suddenly believed that they were making excellent progress.

It was precisely events of this type, growing directly out of the infectious nature of Elvis' persona, which had made the Sun years so exciting. There were strong emotions—moods ranging from total despair to overwhelming elation—during many of Presley's recording sessions, emotions that invariably inspired the musicians and created a euphoric studio atmosphere, one that drove the session players to new artistic heights. Some of the best musicians in Nashville would soon eagerly anticipate playing with Presley. The word would get around that he was different, but according to Hank Garland "good as they come in the recording studio."

Hank Garland was one of the observers at Presley's first RCA session. Considered to be Nashville's most innovative guitar player, Garland toured with Elvis sporadically from 1956 through 1958 and played at Presley's 1958 Nashville session, which produced such hits as "I Need Your Love Tonight," "A Big Hunk of Love," "A Fool Such as I," and "I Got Stung." At Elvis' first recording session, Garland was struck by the innovative nature of Presley's music. He recognized that Elvis had an ability to improvise, a trait that also distinguished Garland's music. After the session, Elvis and Garland went out for something to eat, and then walked back to the RCA studio together to talk with Steve Sholes.

Garland recalls that two hours after the first recording session ended, at midnight, Steve Sholes was still in the studio making notes. He was scribbling his impressions of "Heartbreak Hotel" on two napkins. It was not only the song that launched Elvis' national career, but it was also a tune that Garland believed was a perfect hit record. Hank Garland recalled, however, that there were a lot of nay-sayers, and that almost no

one was sure about the record's eventual b-side, "I Was the One."

Sholes had been open to suggestions about the flip side to Presley's record. Chet Atkins and Hank Garland believed that a country ballad was the perfect complement. As the session continued, Gordon Stoker and the Speer brothers played a more prominent role in the recording process. Their opinion helped Sholes to select "I Was the One," a plaintive, wailing ballad that had a special feeling to it. The arrangement was purposely set so that the song had a melodramatic quality, one that both listeners and critics appreciated. The song went a long way to making Elvis appear like a two-sided hit artist.

An unsung heroine from Elvis' first recording session was a young female assistant named Ginnie, who saved the day by mentioning how much Presley's music appealed to her. As one of RCA's office workers, her job was to go out for coffee and take the paperwork to its appropriate station. Being in the same studio with Elvis excited the young girl; she talked about his ability to inspire. It was her impassioned defense, after listening to a number of the executives complain about the intense emotion in "I Was the One," that led to their reconsideration of the song. Ginnie, short for Virginia, was typical of the young female fan who loved Presley's music.

Because of the hoopla surrounding Presley's first recording session, it was difficult to record a large number of songs. The only other tune completed that day was "I'm Counting on You." This song, included on Elvis' first RCA album, was not released as a single until August 31, 1956.

The Dorsey Brothers Television Shows

While RCA made plans to release new Presley material, Elvis continued to travel and perform with Scotty Moore, Bill Black, and D.J. Fontana. After a year-and-a-half on the road, the group fought incessantly. Bill Black was drinking too much. Scotty Moore was spending large sums of money. D.J. Fontana sulked in the corner because he felt that he wasn't really a part of the band. Colonel Parker solved this problem by housing Elvis away from the other band members. When Jim Denson went to New York to visit Elvis in late January 1956, he was shocked by how carefully the Colonel had isolated Elvis from his old friends. "We went to Central Park a day before Elvis did the Dorsey Show," Denson remarked, "and Elvis was just about to cry. He was lonely and wanted to be with his old friends." (The fact is that Colonel Parker had been embarked on a strategy of separating Elvis from his friends and early musical influences for some time. Old and trusted friends like Ronald Smith, Kenneth Herman, and Eddie Bond were replaced by the sycophantic personalities of Red West, George Klein, Marty Lacker, and Junior Smith, good-old-boys who made a career out of Presley's fame and were responsible for an unrealistic atmosphere which surrounded Elvis until his death.)

Although Elvis continued to make good money doing moderately-sized concerts, the long drives to out-of-the-way venues were reducing profits. Immediately following the conclusion of the RCA agreement the previous November, Colonel Parker had decided that Elvis needed to start appearing in major forums and, unlike the average country music promoter, the Colonel was not afraid of the Yankee concert market. The Colonel realized that it would be difficult for a country singer to sell his product through isolated appearances in New York, Chicago, or Los Angeles, but he had an idea how Elvis could make his mark above the Mason-Dixon line in a big way. To break Elvis in the North, he needed television exposure.

As a result, on December 17, 1955, the Colonel had booked Elvis for four appearances on the "Tommy and Jimmy Dorsey Stage Shows." At a guarantee of $1,250 a show, Elvis was impressed even before Parker, always dealing, increased the total number of appearances to six. Jack Philbin, the Dorsey executive producer, had later agreed to more appearances on the strength of "Heartbreak Hotel," which he felt would be a mammoth hit. As a result, Philbin insisted that Elvis perform it as often as possible on the Dorsey broadcasts. RCA, of course, was happy to oblige, because the Dorsey show would be Presley's first national exposure. During the week prior to the first broadcast, Elvis and his band practiced nightly, understandably nervous about appearing in New York for the first time.

On Friday, January 27, 1956, the day before Elvis' first appearance on the Dorsey brothers' show, "Heartbreak Hotel" was released. The poignant lyrics of "Heartbreak Hotel" created a musical drama that especially appealed to young people. The song reeked of teen agony. Loneliness, desperation, and psychodrama blended powerfully in an appeal to the adolescent heart. When Elvis wailed "I'm so lonely I could die," thousands of teenagers identified with his alienation.

By mid-1956, of course, the older and wiser heads among the music and entertainment critics would be making fun of Presley's lyrics—Jack Gould of the *New York Times* called Elvis' music a variation of the hootchy-kootchy. In Gould's view, Presley was a fraud. Jack O'Brien, the *New York Journal American* columnist, compared Presley to Georgia Southern, a well-known burlesque performer. Jerry Marshall of WNEW in New York criticized Colonel Parker for not building Presley into a Sinatra-type performer. Much like the tradition-

alists in the record business, few of these people realized that there was a market for teen-oriented lyrics, "Heartbreak Hotel" would become a smash hit. It would not be until February 22, 1956, that the song would chart at number 68 on the *Billboard* Hot 100, however, from which point it began a slow, steady climb to the number 1 position. By the time "Heartbreak Hotel" peaked on the *Billboard* charts on April 25, Elvis Presley was a national star, in good measure because of the exposure he received as a result of the Dorsey shows.

His first appearance on January 28 featured exciting live versions of "Shake Rattle and Roll," "Flip Flop and Fly," and "I Got a Woman." During his second appearance on February 4, Elvis performed "Baby Let's Play House," and closed with a theatrical version of Little Richard's "Tutti Frutti." Elvis was betrayed by the sound system, however. The Jordanaires sounded like they were singing in a tunnel, and Scotty Moore, Bill Black, and D.J. Fontana were barely audible, problems which, unfortunately, would continue throughout the remainder of the broadcasts. On the third Dorsey show, February 11, 1956, Elvis was introduced by nationally known disc jockey Bill Randle, and he performed "Blue Suede Shoes" and, finally, "Heartbreak Hotel."

The effects of Elvis' appearances were not immediately apparent, although in the long run, as noted above, they must have provided a measure of recognition as record buyers were drawn in growing numbers to "Heartbreak Hotel." As usual, the "Perry Como Show"

Elvis flanked by Tommy and Jimmy Dorsey.

256

attracted almost twice as many viewers as the Dorsey show, although *TV Guide* noted that Elvis' appearances on the Dorsey shows had attracted increasingly larger audiences. (Just before Elvis' first Dorsey appearance, a cold January night, it was virtually impossible to give tickets away, for example. Elvis' name was on the marquee, but it meant nothing to passers-by. The crowd applauded loudest and longest for singer Sarah Vaughan. The audience at Elvis' third show was even less enthusiastic. They sat quietly and glared at Elvis like he was from outer space. One of the reasons for the unresponsive audiences was the theater from which the Dorsey show originated. The small venue, situated in the West Fifties, New York's theater district, was an uncomfortable little cracker box, one fitted, as a contemptuous television executive remarked, to a "cracker box performer." Located in mid-Manhattan, it was not usually the site of a rock and roll music performance. The audience was predominantly middle-aged—servicemen, tourists, and a few brave New Yorkers showed up to catch the shows.)

The height of Presleymania was still six months away, but the Dorsey shows introduced Elvis to large, appreciative national audiences. While Elvis' exceptional manners, rugged good looks, and down-home sincerity charmed the public, however, they didn't tame the New York critics, who continued their acerbic writing. Most TV executives, too, treated Elvis' Dorsey performances as a curiosity rather than a significant musical turning point. The exception was Arnold Shaw, the general manager of one of New York's most important booking agencies and publishing houses, who, as we have seen, had been praising Elvis for six months. Shaw believed that young Presley was the forerunner of a new kind of music, and his comments were all positive, like those of Dorsey show executive producer Jack Philbin. When Philbin suggested that Elvis was "a guitar-playing Marlon Brando," Shaw readily agreed. This sentiment was echoed across the nation in small-town newspapers.

As reporters pressured Elvis for interviews, petty jealousies surfaced as Scotty, Bill, and D.J. felt left out. National television critics observed that there were problems with Presley's act. Indeed, Elvis' backup band just didn't perform confidently before Northern audiences. Scotty Moore was quiet and determined to find his own niche in the music world. D.J. Fontana simply smiled, and looked forward to returning home. Only Bill Black's sense of showmanship—as he rode his bass and clowned onstage—kept the group alive. Black was confident of his performing skills; he also was a critic of the star system. "I didn't have any real differences with Elvis," Black remarked, "it was the times. We were too busy and underpaid." The band simply didn't rel-

ish their appearances on the Dorsey shows. They weren't used to the aggressive crowds, the adulation, or the hype of superstardom—fame did not sit well with these Southern boys, and it was not long before internal friction turned into outright hostility.

Despite all the drawbacks, however, the six Dorsey stage show appearances were not only a catalyst to more television offers, but they initiated a debate about the artistic value of rock music. No one was really prepared for Elvis' initial appearance on the Dorsey stage show. One flabbergasted observer of Presley's performance was Big Joe Turner. "I was getting ready for a gig," Turner recalled, "and I saw this crazy-looking white kid on TV. I knew he had something special." Such comments were echoed by any number of blues singers.

Adding Fuel to the Fire

During 1956, *Billboard* magazine polled 179 radio station managers and disc jockeys about the future of rock and roll music. *Billboard* was flooded with comments like "It's the worst influence ever to hit the music business...." The poll revealed the song "Moonglow" from the movie "Picnic" was rated as 1956's top tune. Only three of the twenty-one top songs picked by the djs were rock and roll numbers, and they picked Pat Boone as the top rock and roll artist. When RCA released Kay Starr's "Rock and Roll Waltz" in December 1955, it remained on the *Billboard* pop chart until June 1956, a success which prompted other record companies to turn out exploitation singles of the same kind. Sunny Gale's "Rock and Roll Wedding," Gale Storm's "Teenage Wedding," and the Chordettes' "Teenage Goodnight" were examples of traditional pop artists recording what the major labels believed was rock and roll music. Clearly, "easy listening" music was still the most popular type in America.

Reaction to the *Billboard* article created a wave of rock and roll enthusiasm—small radio stations, independent record labels, and obscure artists responded vociferously to the *Billboard* story. When the real thing was available on a level playing field, they argued, "copy" artists and their insipid renditions would vanish. Leonard Chess complained that *Billboard* often ignored Chess' best records. Huey Meaux of Duke-Peacock Records suggested that some of the best rhythm and blues songs didn't have a chance due to the structure and practices of the charting services.

In the face of an intractable establishment, however, public tastes were nevertheless changing the way things were. Increasingly, Little Richard, Chuck Berry, Fats Domino, and other black artists were selling their product to white record buyers. Alan Freed had turned into rock and roll music's superpromoter. Successful

Freed rock and roll shows in New York foretold the time when these extravaganzas went out on the road. Rock and roll had arrived as a commercial musical form. The controversy over lyrical content, and the argument over the good- and bad-taste elements of rock music acted as a commercial catalyst for the music. Controversy sold the product, and at the center of the debate were Elvis Presley's television appearances—some white performers were actually doing the "Negro" music, and not just "tasteful" pop caricatures of it!

RCA—now throwing caution to the winds—was delighted by the furor over Elvis' music, as they hoped to capitalize upon it. The first Dorsey appearance had created an increased demand for Presley's records, so that the selection of songs for Elvis' upcoming recording session was now a doubly important consideration. RCA had scheduled the next session for its New York City studios. Suddenly, a serious debate erupted among RCA executives, many of whom had initially dismissed Elvis, over Presley's musical direction. Another important consideration was the mail coming into RCA's offices. Overwhelmingly the fans loved Elvis' rock and roll numbers. Many of the letters asked where they could buy cover versions of Elvis singing "Shake Rattle and Roll" and "Flip Flop and Fly," which Elvis had sung on the first Dorsey show. It was apparent that cover records would sell—despite the fact that people like Alan Freed belittled white artists who covered black songs, the popularity of Pat Boone's cover records clearly indicated there was a strong market for such product.

The decision was made. The Sun sound had created Elvis' first musical popularity and, consequently, RCA's more enlightened New York executives prevailed, reasoning that they shouldn't try to alter it. There was no need for an impressive array of studio musicians. Elvis' original backup musicians were the best in covering black songs, so RCA decided to retain them for the New York recordings. As a result, Scotty Moore, Bill Black, and D.J. Fontana would join Elvis in the studio, along with black piano player Shorty Long. (Long, of course, would go on to Motown's Soul label in the early sixties, and is best remembered for penning and recording songs like "Devil With the Blue Dress" and "Here Comes the Judge.")

The two-and-a-half week wait between recording sessions was a busy period for Elvis. He prepared for upcoming performances on the Dorsey show even as he continued to appear on the "Louisiana Hayride." Nevertheless, the time was valuable as it gave him the chance to select songs for recording that he felt comfortable with. Such tunes as Carl Perkins' "Blue Suede Shoes," Little Richard's "Tutti Frutti," and Big Joe Turner's "Shake Rattle and Roll," among Elvis' favorites, came to mind. An industry insider remarked that Elvis was

given some control at this point because RCA personnel had no idea how to select songs for a rock and roll performer. As a result, except for Steve Sholes, no one at RCA had any idea what songs Elvis would record at his next session.

The question of which songs to record was answered during Elvis' trips back to the South. There were a number of concert performances before the RCA sessions that helped him make his final decisions. After each successive concert, he spent an inordinate amount of time finding out what songs they wanted him to record.

On Saturday, January 21, 1956, Elvis had appeared on the "Louisiana Hayride." After the show, he went back to the Al-Ida Motel where he rendezvoused with a long-time local girlfriend. Since his first visit to the "Hayride" in 1954, Elvis had been befriended by a raven-haired local beauty, and he valued her opinion about his music. Married to a local businessman, she had to see Presley on the sly. The girl, known only as "Cookie" to Elvis, was an important source of confidence, and was able to soothe young Presley's ego. He talked to her at length about doing "the right songs." It was important to him to find songs that were acceptable to his fans.

Presley's close friend Tommy Sands also listened to Elvis' musical concerns. "Elvis knew rhythm and blues music, and he was determined to make the best of his early RCA recording sessions," Sands recalled. "The Al-Ida was across the river and it was a symbolic ritual for Elvis to escape to this safe, warm spot. It wasn't just the music that Elvis talked about, but he reflected on his future," Sands added. In an astonishing personal show, Elvis ran through the entire repertoire of songs he wanted to record in the RCA studio. "I sat in that motel and watched Elvis perform his songs from memory. It was an extraordinary experience," Tommy Sands remembered. No one at RCA ever knew that Elvis' licks were being perfected in places like the Al-Ida Motel, and probably a good thing at that.

The following Friday night, January 27, 1956, Elvis appeared in Austin, Texas, where he performed, in another tune-up for his recording session, "Blue Suede Shoes," "Tutti Frutti," "Shake Rattle and Roll," and Lloyd Price's "Lawdy Miss Clawdy." The next morning Elvis, Scotty, Bill, and D.J. drove to Dallas and boarded a plane for New York for their January 28, 1956, Dorsey show appearance, after which they were scheduled to return to the recording studio. Because of Colonel Parker's ceaseless booking activity, however, Elvis didn't have an opportunity to relax before the recording session. On Sunday, January 29, 1956, Presley flew to Richmond, Virginia, for a quick concert appearance. Aside from the stress induced by the flight, he was forced to wait almost an hour for transportation to the local auditorium, all of which wore Elvis down and made him nervous. On top of everything else, he was told during the Richmond concert that his RCA recording session would begin at eleven o'clock the next morning. This further distressed him, as he was definitely not a morning person. That night, Elvis spent a few sleepless hours talking to the owner of a local record store, and at 5:00 a.m. he left the motel and went to the airport for the flight back to New York. Stopping in a local coffee shop for a bite to eat, he finally decided to slow down and take his time as a way of relieving the tension.

Round Two

When the musicians arrived at 155 East 24th Street on the morning of January 30, 1956, the New York RCA recording center was empty. Elvis was on his way from the airport, and it was decided that Presley would probably need some extra time before he could begin. As a result, RCA changed the session times and, when Elvis arrived at eleven, he learned that the set had been put off until three o'clock. He returned at two, recorded from three to six o'clock and, since the studio was otherwise vacant, the session continued on into the night.

Due to the extra hours added to this recording session, Elvis was able to include some new songs in his repertoire. He loved Carl Perkins' "Blue Suede Shoes," had performed it many times in concert, and so recorded a cover version (having no idea that it would outsell Perkins' original hit when released). Elvis' rhythm and blues roots exerted themselves when he picked Arthur "Big Boy" Crudup's late 1940s rhythm and blues tune "My Baby Left Me" as one of the session's selections. (Originally a country blues song, Crudup himself had recorded "My Baby Left Me" for RCA. After Steve Sholes previewed Crudup's renditions, he decided that Presley's vocal style was perfect for Crudup's material and urged Elvis to record several of them.) Although any number of Crudup's songs were excellent ones for Presley, it was difficult to decide which ones to record. As a result, apart from "My Baby Left Me," a few relatively uninspired versions of "One Sided Love Affair" and "So Glad You're Mine" were also completed.

All in all, the session was an uneven but an eventful one. Clearly, Elvis needed more time in the studio to produce hit records. Steve Sholes convinced reluctant RCA executives to pursue increased studio time amidst a more relaxed atmosphere. Unfortunately, Sholes couldn't change recording hours to the evening, so studio time was set up for the next day. "They didn't realize Elvis was a night person," Sholes remarked, "they said it was his job to come in during the day." This

proved to be a mistake.

When Elvis returned to RCA's studio the following day at midday, he was not feeling well. The year-and-a-half of constant touring had taken its toll, on top of which the RCA sessions were nerve-wracking. As a result, Elvis completed only two songs during the noon to three session. The most successful effort was a cover version of Little Richard's "Tutti Frutti." The other song, "I'm Gonna Sit Right Down and Cry (Over You)," was one that Elvis was unfamiliar with, and this made it difficult to record. It was just too early in the day, and Elvis was not at his best.

Elvis spent the next few days relaxing in New York. Although he stayed at the bustling Warwick Hotel, Colonel Parker limited his visitors. There was time for him to walk the New York streets, as he was still unrecognized by most people, especially in the Northern bastion on the Hudson. But Elvis felt lonely, so he spent a great deal of time on the phone calling old friends in Memphis.

There were subtle, yet pervasive, signs in the press concerning Presley's imminent stardom. As Americans discussed rock and roll music, the young singer from Memphis, Elvis Presley, was at the center of the national controversy. RCA hired a fan-mail secretary just to handle letters to Elvis and the increasingly bothersome phone calls to the RCA offices. On one occasion, a secretary at the New York office opened a letter containing a picture of Elvis in front of the Al-Ida Motel. It was from a Louisiana Baptist minister, and it questioned Presley's morality. RCA began a publicity campaign to nullify the criticism. The dollars were rolling in, and RCA didn't want anything to jeopardize its new star's growing popularity.

His heavy work schedule kept Elvis from a full awareness of the impact his music was having. Preparing for television shows, completing as many radio interviews as possible, or playing concert dates, there was never a quiet moment, and the busy schedule obscured the changes in the Presley organization. "We never saw any newspapers," Scotty Moore remembered. "We didn't know we were getting big write-ups." The tightly controlled schedule Colonel Parker forced upon Elvis, however, was slowly strangling his creativity. There were important changes in Elvis' daily routine. No longer did he have free time. The casual, carefree days of playing the "Louisiana Hayride" and driving to small concert dates was a forgotten luxury. The success at RCA had brought a breakneck character to Elvis' life. Even as Elvis' music broke nationally, he had little awareness that he was becoming a major record star. Kenneth Herman remembers Elvis returning to Memphis perplexed over the hysteria associated with "Heartbreak

Hotel." "Elvis was a simple guy," Herman related, "who couldn't believe the screams and squeals over his music. To the media, he appeared confident and in charge. To his friends, Elvis was still a nice guy who was amazed by his success."

Later in February 1956, *Billboard*, the bible of the music industry, would comment on Elvis' popularity: "Presley is riding high right now with network TV appearances." The music trade publication remarked that the sales of "Heartbreak Hotel" had "snowballed." Praise from *Billboard* created excellent publicity in other magazines and newspapers.

Meanwhile, to cash in on this snowballing effect already apparent to RCA executives, Elvis was brought back into the studio. Unfortunately, they still weren't listening to their artist and couldn't have picked a worse time—the February 3, 1956, session was scheduled to begin at 10:30 in the morning, an early hour that made it difficult for Elvis to be at his best. Happily, the songs selected for this session inspired him. A cover version of Lloyd Price's "Lawdy Miss Clawdy" allowed him to play the piano. Not only did he record Price's song with feeling, but the piano enhanced his vocal. Elvis was loosening up. The next tune, "Shake Rattle and Roll," evoked a performance modelled on Big Joe Turner's classic version. The song contained a line about a woman's dress, to which Elvis added the phrase: "see the sun come shining through...." Everyone in the studio laughed, and Elvis knew that his discomfort with his new surroundings was beginning to dissipate.

The February Thaw

The day after Elvis had completed his January 30-31 RCA sessions and interviews, he had begun to prepare for his second appearance on the Dorsey Brothers' "Stage Show." RCA did everything possible to make this appearance a success, hoping to recoup some of the money that they had spent purchasing Elvis' contract.

When Elvis appeared on the February telecast, he hoped to counter the negative newspaper publicity that RCA predicted New York's newspaper critics would surely generate. RCA persuaded a number of local radio stations to increase Elvis' airplay; Bill Randle and Arnold Shaw were important factors in this radio blitz. Respected figures in the music industry, they had always championed Elvis' talent.

The manner in which RCA trumpeted Elvis' appearances on the Dorsey show left no doubt that it was settling into the role of the first major label to find and foster a rock and roll singer. Yet, the main reason that they hoped to sell Elvis to the general public was still financial. RCA had little interest in the music. The success of Elvis' five Sun singles in the early months of

1956, a clear indication of his potential popularity, never persuaded RCA that it should try to achieve a sound close to the Sun sound. Ultimately, with no real feel for Presley or his music, the philosophy boiled down to capitalizing on whatever worked in the marketplace and making Elvis sing *that*, like it or not.

Despite his record sales and the positive reaction to his concerts, a number of RCA executives still believed that Presley was primarily a country music act. Small wonder then that, in February 1956, Elvis was featured in *Country Song Roundup*. The article, "The Elvis Presley Story," was a brief, but convincing, feature story that predicted future stardom. Since RCA was an important advertiser, *Country Song Roundup* assembled its story largely from RCA press releases. No one bothered to interview Elvis. As a result, the article revealed that RCA had serious gaps in its knowledge of Elvis' career. Working at cross-purposes with those at RCA pushing Elvis' country appeal, the Colonel, it seems, had been instrumental in conveniently leaving out the country music fan's reaction to Elvis on the "Louisiana Hayride," preventing RCA from publicizing his "Hayride" successes. Parker believed that the "Hayride" was too hillbilly for the sophisticated Northern consumer.

Many of the legends that grew up around Presley's career, for that matter, were perpetuated by RCA's inaccurate publicity statements, and—so long as RCA's efforts didn't affect the Colonel's own agenda—it didn't matter to the Colonel whether or not RCA had the facts straight. Colonel was too busy making deals. Generally, these myths centered around the barely literate hillbilly background of the Presley family. Elvis' dad, it turned out, was the source of much of this publicity. Vernon Presley continually told reporters that he was an orphan. RCA further obliged Vernon's fantasy by suggesting that he was a strong, self-made man. As one

Elvis and Vernon.

RCA press release after another praised Vernon for raising his family from the depths of abject poverty, he reveled in the adulation. Vernon went so far as to suggest that he had been an elder in the Tupelo First Assembly of God, and a picture of Vernon with church elders was circulated to verify this bogus claim. (Donald L. Dunavent, pastor of the East Heights Assembly of God church in Tupelo, went back through the church records and found no evidence of Vernon's selection as an elder.) Some Memphis residents remarked that Vernon himself had ended up believing RCA's fictional press releases.

Elvis dearly loved his dad, but Vernon was an enduring burden to him. If there was a hillbilly heritage in the Presley family, it was certainly Vernon who kept it alive. In later years, his one driving passion was to spend Elvis' money as rapidly as possible (and make sure that everyone else—Elvis, his wife, his employees, and his friends—got as little as possible to spend on things Vernon considered frivolous). In addition, a number of Elvis' girlfriends have remarked that Vernon asked them for dates after Elvis was through with them.

Despite the antics of his father, whose existence RCA eventually began to hide from the general public, Elvis' popularity soared in the mid-fifties—in fact, the growth of Elvis' career in February 1956 was explosive. *Billboard* reported that "Heartbreak Hotel" was selling well on both the country and western and rock music charts. On February 5, 1956, when Elvis played at the Montecello Auditorium in Norfolk, Virginia, a number of local radio stations featured "I Was the One." The following night at the National Theater in Greensboro, North Carolina, there were loud screams from the audience requesting the song. Not surprisingly, it entered the *Billboard* Country and Western singles chart in the number 9 position. Things on the national level were beginning to happen instantaneously. Ironically, though, it was another two weeks before "I Was the One" was a top ten Memphis hit. For the very first time, Elvis Presley was more popular outside his hometown than he was inside it.

Elvis' record sales in both country and pop markets weren't the only aspect of his career in high profile during February. His songs were prompting the media to write about rock and roll music. Naturally, as before, not all of the articles were complimentary ones. In Birmingham, Alabama, the White Citizens Council circulated a brochure urging a ban on rock music. The Rev. William Shannon's article in the *Catholic Sun* charged that "Presley and his voodoo of frustration and defiance have become symbols in our country...." In Houston, Texas, local newspapers quoted John Orman, the Juvenile Delinquency and Crime Commission chairman,

on the need to ban rock music. This led to more than fifty songs being removed from local jukeboxes. Terry McGuire, a WCMC disc jockey in Wildwood, New Jersey, remarked on the air, "as a Christian I could not morally justify playing the music of Mr. Presley...." Bob Day, at WNIX in St. Johnsbury, Vermont, echoed this sentiment by labelling Presley's music "obviously in poor taste." In Seattle's Northgate shopping mall, a group of religious zealots handed out leaflets condemning Elvis.

The impact of all this criticism stung Gladys Presley. She loved Elvis' fame, but smarted from the "Yankee criticism." Gladys found that even her own personal life was being scrutinized. The cement that bound the Presley family together, the large, lumbering Gladys was becoming a media as well as a fan favorite. Uneasy in the spotlight, she more and more retired behind the walls of a series of new homes. The pressure on her grew, and her drinking increased accordingly. RCA didn't help. Heavy promotion concentrated upon the family and its importance to Elvis' music. There was a down-home character to it all that RCA's publicity attempted to reflect. The family was pictured as one that danced to Elvis' records in their living room. A wholesome image was deemed necessary to his continued success. It was all a tactic that helped to sell Presley's records. In the end, the media turned the Presley family into a hillbilly version of "The Honeymooners," complete with rock and roll music. Central casting could not have sent a better family to extol the blue-collar virtues of Elvis' music.

For his part, Colonel Parker continued to accumulate February bookings for Elvis, primarily in country music concert halls, even as the Dorsey show television appearances sold Presley's records in the pop market. Following each Dorsey telecast, there was a noticeable surge in Elvis' record sales in key Northern cities. At Seattle's "Music Museum," the February 1956 window display featured Presley's RCA press releases. In Los Angeles, a number of record stores catering to blacks prominently displayed advertisements for Presley's music. A Chicago record store in the Loop placed a huge sign in front of the store extolling the virtues of Presley's records. In Oakland and San Francisco, Elvis' records were displayed in a spot usually reserved for pop crooners. The merchandising of Elvis Presley was strong throughout the North and West, and it wasn't just in the larger cities—where one-stop distributors were constantly in touch with RCA for larger shipments of Presley's music—that Presley's sales surged. A store in Fargo, North Dakota, ordered a stack of Presley records, and a certain young man named Robert Thomas Velline purchased his first rock and roll record. The thirteen-year-old Velline would later change his name to Bobby

Vee, and would become a major record star in his own right. In February 1956, however, Velline was like many young fans just cutting their teeth on rock music with Presley's RCA singles.

Earthquake

In February 1956, RCA moved to capitalize on Presley's briskly-selling 45rpm record releases by issuing a long-playing album. What is notable about RCA's attitude is that they still weren't sure about Presley's long-term commercial appeal. Rock and roll was simply a phenomenon that RCA executives couldn't understand, clearly illuminating the fact that it was Steve Sholes who was responsible for much of Presley's early RCA success. After listening to the boxes of tapes that RCA received from Sun Records, Sholes would select a number of songs to include in Elvis' first RCA album. On Friday, January 20, 1956, Sholes had locked himself into an RCA studio and searched through the tapes for a song he could use immediately. There were two excellent takes of a lilting ballad, "I Love You Because." Sholes listened to the pops and hisses on the tape before he realized that the two cuts could be spliced into one exciting two-minute and thirty-nine-second record. Although "I Love You Because" was recorded in July 1954, it had a fresh, timeless quality to it. It was one of six singles RCA subsequently issued simultaneously to push Elvis' career.

Around mid-February, Elvis' Sun recording "I Forgot to Remember to Forget" reached the number 1 position on the *Billboard* Country and Western singles chart. Coupled with the notoriety Presley was already receiving as an RCA artist, many of the other major labels were spurred on to try to find their own rockabilly star. Elvis' music had broken in all markets, and this was enough to convince at least some record company executives to find their own rocker-in-the-Elvis-mold. (When things broke wide open, Elvis was selling up to $75,000 worth of records a day. His first album would sell 155,000 copies in two-and-a-half months, his singles were reportedly selling at a rate of up to fifty thousand copies a day, and EPs selling in excess of one thousand copies a day. Very soon, Elvis was generating fifty percent of RCA's popular record sales. A mini-industry in himself, Elvis truly changed the course of the entire record industry.)

When Capitol Records signed Gene Vincent, they were sure that he was the next Elvis. In the fall of 1955, Vincent had attended the Hank Snow All Star Jamboree at the Norfolk Municipal Auditorium. Like many other aspiring Virginia rockabilly artists, Vincent was determined to follow Presley in the music business. A Norfolk radio station, WCMS, often played Presley's

records, and Vincent used them to practice his act. Since Elvis was only a month older than Vincent, Sheriff Tex Davis, Vincent's manager, believed that they could follow in Presley's footsteps. In order to make sure that Vincent sounded as good as Elvis, his band, the Blue Caps, was augmented in the recording studio by some of Nashville's best session musicians. Grady Martin, Hank Garland, Buddy Harmon, and Bob Moore were brought into the Nashville recording studio to help record "Be-Bop-a-Lula," "Woman Love," and "Race with the Devil." Not only were the songs excellent, but this early 1956 recording session was to launch Vincent's career. Although he had his own highly developed talent, Gene Vincent's career was arguably an outgrowth of Elvis Presley's success.

Liberty Records groomed Eddie Cochran, who had issued Elvis-type records as early as 1955 on the Ekko label, to fill their Elvis slot. The Johnny Burnette Rock n Roll Trio, featuring the innovative guitarist Paul Burlison, was Coral's answer to Elvis. Ersel Hickey was signed by Epic Records almost two years after the initial Elvis surge, suggesting how lasting the Presley phenomenon was in the industry.

Smaller labels followed suit. Sun Records attempted to push Warren Smith's "Rock and Roll Ruby" as being in the Presley mold. The success that Sam Phillips experienced with Elvis Presley prompted small record

Elvis with Ace Records' would-be rockabilly star, Glen Glenn.

entrepreneurs to try to duplicate the Sun Records formula. Few labels missed the opportunity to record an Elvis-type singer. One of the most interesting was the Memphis-based Erwin Records. The belief that Memphis and the nearby Mississippi countryside was filled with talent much like Elvis Presley's prompted Marshall E. Ellis, a former musician, to organize the Erwin label. Ellis' label opened in a small office on Chelsea Avenue in Memphis, and he put out handbills advertising for singer-songwriters. Ellis, himself a big-band musician in the late forties, hoped to duplicate Sam Phillips' success in the hillbilly market. In 1954, Ellis' Erwin label issued two hillbilly songs by Carvis Turney. When these records failed to sell, Ellis noted Presley's success and began looking for rockabilly artists. It was not long before the area's finest rockabilly musicians streamed in to record.

In Memphis there were a number of excellent rockabilly artists who followed Elvis' lead. Eddie Bond waxed records with a Presley feel on the Ekko label in 1955. Bond, discussed earlier, was a well-known local act who appeared on both the prestigious "Big D Jamboree" in Dallas and Shreveport's "Louisiana Hayride." In 1953, it was Eddie Bond and the Stompers who had provided Elvis with his first local appearance; little wonder that they hoped to crack the national market with an their own rockabilly sound. Eddie Bond and the Stompers had played Elvis-type music long before Presley and Sam Phillips produced Elvis' famous Sun Records recordings.

Ray Smith, a rockabilly musician from Paducah, Kentucky, went on the road in the mid-1950s and eventually recorded for the Sun and Judd record labels. In 1960, Smith's "Rockin Little Angel" (Judd 1016) was a *Billboard* hit, and Smith remarked, "Without Elvis I wouldn't be here." The influence of Presley's music single-handedly brought rockabilly into the mainstream of American popular culture.

As a direct result of RCA's experience with Presley, the Decca label invited Buddy Holly to come to Nashville and cut four songs with his friend Sonny Curtis. Like Elvis, Holly was heavily influenced by rhythm and blues music. One of the songs Holly recorded, "Midnight Shift," was a takeoff on Hank Ballard and the Midnighters' "Annie" songs, and was another example of the fusion of r and b with country music. Eddie Crandall, a talent scout for Decca Records who also managed Marty Robbins, had "discovered" Holly performing as the opening act for a Hank Snow-Bill Haley concert in Lubbock, Texas. A shrewd judge of changing musical directions, Crandall attempted to interest every major Nashville record company in Holly as a "new style" country act. Crandall eventually convinced Decca to sign Holly, and he urged the Nashville establishment to pay close attention to Presley's music. Crandall defended the manner in which Steve Sholes recorded Elvis, and he also argued that Presley's new RCA material was commercially more attractive than his Sun recordings. As America's third largest label in the 1950s, Decca chased RCA and Columbia in the competitive record market. Crandall believed that he could come much closer to producing Presley's Sun sound, about which there was a great deal of industry gossip.

Despite Elvis' success, however, some executives at the larger record companies at first overruled in-house advocates of rock and roll, refusing to promote similar acts. Still, companies like Decca did at least bring in Holly and other rockabilly artists for brief recording sessions. At the time, however, producers and major executives on these labels preferred traditional country music artists, and simply failed to realize the potential financial significance of rock and roll records, despite the fact that they were many excellent rockabilly singers eager to sign record deals. A good example of this attitude prevailed at Columbia Records. The label was happy promoting Carl Smith and Lefty Frizzell as mainstream country artists; when Smith and Frizzell asked to record rockabilly numbers, they were turned down. Country music was still on the mind of many record industry people. Executives at Columbia wondered why RCA wasn't concentrating upon sure-fire hit artists like its own Lefty Frizzell and Carl Smith. This is surprising because in 1938 when William Paley purchased Columbia Records, they did a great deal of business in race records. Such blues luminaries as Bessie Smith and Ethel Waters made big money for the label. By 1956, however, RCA had passed Columbia as the major label. Consequently, they ridiculed Presley. "I tried to interest Columbia in Elvis early on," Arnold Shaw commented, "they told me they didn't want any hillbillies."

In spite of the naysayers at Columbia, one shrewd country performer, who recognized the importance of the rockabilly market, would not take no for an answer. Marty Robbins, realizing that there was an enormous market for rockabilly and rock and roll music, recorded an Elvis-inspired version of "That's All Right (Mama)" and a cover of Chuck Berry's "Maybellene." Steve Sholes had been furious with the Columbia executives who showed up at Elvis' first recording session; he was especially fearful of a country version of "Heartbreak Hotel." But, after watching Elvis in Nashville, the Columbia executives had concluded that Elvis was not a challenge to established artists, and that there was no sense wasting time and money on acts like him. The Columbia a & r people were convinced by Marty Robbins that any country singer could cover Elvis' rockabilly sound. In the end, even though there were a number of other significant rock and roll songs that Robbins recorded, notably, "Long Tall Sally." Ironically, in the long run, it was Robbins who didn't provide any serious competition to Elvis, just the reverse of Columbia's predictions.

One of the reasons that artists like Marty Robbins found it difficult to sell their own rock and rockabilly records in competition with Elvis was due to the impact that Elvis had in live performance, something others just couldn't match. By early 1956, rock and roll crowds were rushing to Presley's shows to see onstage moves they had never witnessed before. The market for Elvis' concert appearances was so strong that Colonel Tom Parker was forced to remodel and expand his Jamboree Attractions office in Madison, Tennessee. Parker's phone, Nashville 8-2858, rang incessantly. Carpenters and electricians barged through the offices making additions. The phones were handled by Tom Diskin, who bustled through the maze serving the Colonel's every whim and need. The Colonel, loving every minute of the carnival atmosphere, sat like a Wall Street banker in a big chair and barked out orders. To many observers, the Colonel was engaged in nonsensical pursuits. He ordered heart-shaped pillows, small decals, and labels with "Elvis" boldly emblazed on them—trinkets he loved to give away or, better still, charge money for. Despite all the Colonel's talk about accepting only big, high-guarantee concerts, Elvis continued to appear on the "Louisiana Hayride" and in other small-paying venues. To the Colonel, after all, wealth was only a wiggle away. The key was to keep Elvis wiggling.

The New Elvis

At the point at which RCA worked away at producing Elvis' first long-playing album, three significant changes had taken place in Elvis' career.

First, he was almost completely enveloped in a protective cocoon. A veil of secrecy and an aura of suspicion had grown up around him. He was no longer free to mix with the crowd. The first sign of this isolation occurred in February 1956 in Norfolk, Virginia, when a group of servicemen who were stationed nearby went to the Montecello Auditorium to chat with him. They remembered seeing him perform at Doc's bar in Frayser, a Memphis suburb. When they told the astonished security guard that they were from Doc's in Memphis and wanted to see Elvis, they were barred from the backstage area. Colonel Parker had made it very clear that most of Elvis' old Memphis cronies had to be kept away. In the end, the local sheriff had to be enlisted to escort the boisterous servicemen to their car. The ability to meet and talk with Elvis no longer existed. The Colonel had created a complex security system that he felt was essential to Elvis' image as a star.

The new Elvis—a star right down to the emblem on his cap.

Second, Elvis' music was changing. As a result of his compulsive perfectionism, he spent a great deal of time in the recording studio, soon discovering that he couldn't duplicate the familiar Sun sound. It was not just the technology that made Elvis' RCA recordings different from the Sun sessions. There was a feeling that he couldn't recapture. While critics have always assumed that Elvis didn't like the RCA sound—true enough in the sense that he had to readjust to a new place and couldn't dwell on past good times—there were some positive aspects to the new situation. In Elvis' mind, he was finally in a position to make perfect music. The technology and facilities in the RCA studios were infinitely superior to what Sam Phillips had offered at Sun. In addition, RCA ultimately granted Elvis *carte blanche* in terms of financial resources. He was able to select any song that he desired to record as long as there was a fair representation of Hill and Range material. "When you get an artist of Elvis' caliber, one who analyzes himself as closely as Elvis does," Steve Sholes remarked, "you know that all these things added together are what made him successful." Sholes had been the first to notice Presley's perfectionist nature, something that not only made his music stronger but took it in new directions. Now Elvis was able to perform or record a country, blues, or rhythm and blues tune in his own style

Steve Sholes: "Young Elvis appealed to everyone."

(rather than copying elements of style from other performers), and generally he seemed to improve upon the song. Elvis, as an artist, was now whole, someone for others to emulate.

Third, Elvis had developed an intuitive knack for recording the right pop songs, an ability which he had previously relied heavily on Sam Phillips to provide. He now had a show business instinct of his own for "commercial" songs. As Steve Sholes suggested, Elvis had "a feel for popular music much greater than other people...he was able to groove it in a direction that the kids liked...." Unwittingly, Sholes was describing Elvis Presley's greatest career asset—his ability to select and present a product that appealed to a wide variety of musical consumers. "No single group of people bought Elvis' records," Sholes concluded, "young Presley appealed to everyone."

The times were changing unalterably for both Elvis and RCA Records. The Sun Records era was behind him, and Presley was on his way to a national career. In the next two months, he would experience the final transformation into the King of Rock and Roll music. Security problems, the continual demand for a new product, constant badgering by the media, and the necessity to keep Elvis in the public eye would place an enormous strain on him. These pressures would eventually contribute to the decision to cast him in the movies and build his career outside of the traditional music industry. It is this successful attempt to make Elvis Presley a movie star, covered in the next chapter, that truly ends the Sun Records' era.

CHAPTER 15
"Cadillac Elvis": The Final Transformation, March-April 1956

Elvis Presley's final transformation into a musical superstar took place during March and April of 1956. By January 28, RCA had released six Elvis singles, and a month later plans were in the works for Elvis' first long-playing album. The commercial success of Presley's music astounded most RCA executives. By March, Elvis had charted six of RCA's twenty-five best-selling singles. His first album would sell 155,000 copies in two-and-a-half months. It was not just the records that made Elvis popular, however. As he appeared on black-and-white television sets across the nation, Elvis established not only his own remarkable public image but also the commercial possibilities of rock and roll music.

Movie moguls commented on Presley's potential impact upon the film business, and there was already talk about signing Elvis to a long-term movie contract. The movie industry had not been able to replace Frank Sinatra with a new bobbysox idol, and film producers envisioned Elvis as the next teenage heartthrob. In the mid-1950s, the easily produced exploitation movie was a profitable business venture, and many "b" movie producers believed that Presley's songs could and should be integrated into commercial films. There was an excitement attached to Presley's name that spelled big box-office dollars.

Good Fortune, Bad Vibes

Most fans and critics alike had been kind to Elvis throughout his Sun Records days. This would change abruptly in May 1956, when Elvis began his first tour north of the Mason-Dixon line, although, as noted, he had had his detractors all along, especially as his success carried him northward in January and February. March and April would be landmark months, but a May tour would be a mixed blessing. While it was successful, there was an aura of tension surrounding Presley's appearances. Rather than facing the laudatory Southern newspaper writers, Elvis was suddenly barraged with hostile questions from Yankee reporters. It was not a pleasant experience.

Elvis was surprised by the Northern critics. They attacked his music and made fun of his stage mannerisms. He hated confrontations, so he avoided reacting to the criticism. He just couldn't understand why the media was so hostile. "I know Elvis was concerned about his public image," Kenneth Herman remarked, "but he never complained about reporters. He knew that they

were necessary." Not only was Elvis badgered by the New York press, he faced serious ridicule as a result of contests held by local disc jockeys to judge his musical merits. Unwittingly, however, the disc jockeys' attacks upon Presley created even more demand for his records, prompting his youthful audience to rush to the defence of his music.

The press tried to elicit opinions from Elvis that could be used to create controversy. A good example of this tactic occurred on March 9, 1956, when Little Richard appeared on NBC's "National Radio Fan Club" performing "Slippin' and Slidin" and "Long Tall Sally." The NBC censors were concerned about lyrics that had Uncle John cheating on Aunt Mary with Sally. In order to create a confrontation, reporters asked Elvis if he thought Little Richard's lyrics were "dirty." With a bemused look, Elvis jokingly stated that he couldn't understand the words to the song, so he couldn't really say, one way or the other. Elvis then mentioned his respect for Little Richard's work and black music in general. Presley refused to be brought into a verbal battle over song content. He was a good interview and looked upon the press as a necessary evil, but Elvis wasn't stupid, so he handled the press with kid gloves. "I don't think those Yankee reporters ever listened to my music," Elvis remarked to Ronald Smith. Bands and singers were listening to Presley's music, though, and a revolution was taking place.

In an atmosphere much like that surrounding the mods and rockers in England in the mid-1960s, American rock enthusiasts demanded more, not less, of their favorite music. Many musicians used the Elvis model to make show business their goal. In Chicago, a thirteen-year-old, second generation American of German-Italian descent, Ralph Stuart Emanuel Donner, watched Elvis on television. By 1961, Ral Donner had recorded "You Don't Know What You Got" and "Girl of My Best Friend" for the Gone label. Donner, whose life was the basis for the Johnny Casino character in the hit musical "Grease," was typical of the fledgling singer encouraged by Elvis Presley's early career.

Record scouts inundated Memphis. "Those record people were everywhere looking for a new Elvis," Kenneth Herman recalled. They found one new Elvis' in Johnny Burnette's Rock 'n' Roll Trio. The group featured Johnny's brother, Dorsey, and the guitar genius of Paul Burlison. "We got our chance due to Elvis' break,"

Paul Burlison in the mid-1980s.

Burlison remarked in his Walls, Mississippi, home, "but we had the talent to become stars."

The Rock 'n' Roll Trio had been formed in 1953, and they came to New York to record for the Decca subsidiary Coral Records in May 1956, hot on Elvis' heels. After winning three times on the "Ted Mack Amateur Hour," the Rock 'n' Roll Trio was a well-known television act. While recording in New York, they were booked to appear on "American Bandstand," Steve Allen's "Tonight Show" and Perry Como's "Kraft Music Hall." When they returned home to Memphis they had established themselves as a rising rock act. (Unwittingly, Paul Burlison created a musical revolution during this tour. "One night I was carrying my amplifier on stage when I knocked it against a pole," Burlison remarked, "then I started playing it and it was distorted like a fuzz sound. I just pulled the blown tube out and played it that way.") Although mainstream commercial success evaded the Rock 'n' Roll Trio, Johnny and Dorsey Burnette later had hit records as solo artists and Paul Burlison went on to make his fortune in the construction business. Burlison has continued to play guitar over the years, and is regarded as one of the early innovators on the rock and roll guitar.

Of course, minor successes like those of the Rock 'n' Roll Trio would be more than overshadowed by events like Elvis' first gold record. Colonel Tom Parker, attempting to rope off a special place in the rock and roll music field for his protege, went so far as to discourage other major labels from promoting similar acts.

Profits and Puzzlement

The impact that Elvis Presley's music had upon the American music scene was immense. On March 3, 1956, *Billboard* reported that Elvis was RCA's most profitable recording artist. Since five of Elvis' singles were simply rereleases of Sun recordings, RCA indeed reaped enormous profits. There was no studio time or production expenses; the record masters were easily pressed and released. "Heartbreak Hotel" was the only major Presley hit record that RCA had to record from scratch, so it was easy to flood the market with Elvis songs. (As previously discussed, one real tragedy of the early RCA period is that no one paid more attention to the Sun tapes. They were passed from hand to hand, and even the otherwise astute Steve Sholes didn't even bother to have their contents catalogued. Apart from Sholes, no one searched them for new songs to release. Later RCA executives like Joan Deary were horrified by the casual disregard for the Sun tapes. The attitude within RCA's corporate headquarters was "why worry about this old music." They already had a mammoth hit record climbing the charts. It was time to promote the RCA product, not some old Sun recordings.)

In this initial period, as we have seen, RCA wavered back and forth in its perceptions of Elvis' potential. Many key executives were not convinced that Elvis' music and talent had a lasting quality, despite initial successes. They concluded that his record sales were a temporary phenomenon, and opted for momentary profits. RCA was placed in a position of promoting an act that many of its executives didn't believe could be successful over the long haul. This behavior is typical of the record industry. In the early 1970s, RCA management would repeat the same pattern with David Bowie. With Elvis, as with Bowie, RCA could not figure out what to do with his act.

What worried RCA was the possibility of being stuck with leftover Elvis records, which the Colonel had convinced reticent executives to press in large numbers. It didn't take RCA long to realize that the only way to guarantee a return on their investment was to organize an ingenious advertising campaign. The budget prepared for this venture exceeded $25,000, and it was designed to promote Elvis in markets where he was not yet well known. This had a blanketing effect and was instrumental in Elvis' growing national popularity.

In early March 1956, as "Heartbreak Hotel" crept into the number 68 spot on the *Billboard* Hot 100, RCA intensified its advertising campaign. On March 10, 1956, RCA placed a half-page ad in *Billboard* with a new slogan: Elvis "The Singing Rage." Although, within RCA, Elvis was identified as a country music artist, the label's executives were surprised by his appearance on the pop chart. They had reports that Elvis' radio play was also heavy on black radio stations. RCA was perplexed by letters from both country music and black rhythm and blues disc jockeys requesting promotional literature and interviews. Top 40 radio shows also featured his songs. Since Top 40 radio played the five to eight most popular songs continually, Elvis was always on the air. RCA marketing managers were used to categorizing acts, but Elvis seemed to defy strict labels. "I Was the One," which was the flip side of "Heartbreak Hotel," also entered the charts at the number 84 position. The strong mainstream reaction to "I Was the One" was yet another surprise to RCA management.

At the center of all this was the now-portly figure of none other than Steve Sholes. For the first time in his career, Sholes went out of his way to personally promote a performer. Over the years, Sholes had built up a great deal of good will in the music business, and he called in some of his markers for Elvis. Rhythm and blues and blues-oriented radio stations received calls from Sholes, and they responded by playing Presley's music. Steve Sholes was not surprised by the results. Not only was he the first RCA executive to recognize Elvis' crossover appeal, but it was Sholes who urged RCA's publicity department to increase its advertising. He pointed to Elvis' "atomic reaction" on the nation's jukeboxes. What Sholes was referring to was a record dealer, disc jockey, and jukebox operator survey that was used to compile the *Billboard* Hot 100. In great depth, this survey analyzed where Elvis' records were played and sold. The information it provided was reason enough for RCA to commit $25,000 to advertising, Sholes contended.

It was Steve Sholes' position that Elvis quite obviously had quick mobility on the charts, giving rise directly to the public relations term RCA next adopted for Elvis: the "Atomic Powered Singer." This was just the phrase RCA needed to focus its efforts, and the company publicity machine began turning out lengthy new press releases. Elvis' records enjoyed the benefits of innovative marketing when they began to be sold in Safeway, Woolworths, and other large department stores. As they headed into the check-out stands at Safeway, for example, shoppers were confronted with the picture sleeves of Presley's records. It was the early days of rack merchandising, and the sophisticated marketing scheme reached new consumers and reaped massive profits. After only three weeks in stores, "Heartbreak Hotel" had sold 300,000 copies.

"Elvis Presley," The Album

For his first album, Elvis covered a number of rhythm and blues and rock tunes. These included Ray Charles' "I Got a Woman," Little Richard's "Tutti Frutti," and Clyde McPhatter and the Drifters' "Money Honey." In addition to pioneer rock and roll songs, Elvis added a show tune, Richard Rodgers and Lorenz Hart's "Blue Moon." The latter is a good example of a show tune that appealed to RCA executives, although "Blue Moon"

was also one of Elvis' favorites, one which he recorded for Sam Phillips at Sun Records. (Phillips believed that "Blue Moon" was too pop for Presley's country and rock music fans, and might alienate his large and vocal Southern record-buying public, so it wasn't released initially by Sun.) When RCA executives heard Elvis' version of "Blue Moon," however, they were excited about its commercial possibilities. As a result, "Blue Moon" was one of a number of previously unreleased songs from the Sun recording sessions included on Elvis' first RCA album.

Sam Phillips, as we've seen, had a passion for perfection, and he appears to have had serious reservations about the recording quality of "Blue Moon." This was a common Phillips trait. He often refused to release a song because, as far as he was concerned, it was not quite right. There were other unreleased Presley songs—such tunes as "Just Because," "I'll Never Let You Go (Little Darlin')," and "I Love You Because"—that just did not meet Phillips' exacting standards. RCA, on the other hand, released versions of these tunes that contained, among other mistakes, flubbed vocal lines, rhythm guitar breakdowns, and flat bass notes. The reason that RCA executives ignored these weaknesses is that they were eager to fill Presley's first album without going back into the recording studio. It was corporate greed, not musical quality that motivated RCA. Nevertheless, these songs possessed commercial strength. They were raw, energetic tunes in which Elvis demonstrated his brilliance. The persistent rockabilly beat in Presley's music was what the fans wanted, and this was enough to convince RCA to include so many Sun recordings in the first album.

When **Elvis Presley** appeared on March 13, 1956, it sported a visually exciting green-and-blue cover, a dramatic change from RCA's conservative corporate image. The album was accentuated with Elvis' first name in large, bold pink letters; his last name, in large green letters, dominated the bottom of the album cover. A picture of Elvis gyrating to the music completed the effect. The graphic boldness of the cover intensified Presley's sullen qualities. The James Dean "Rebel-without-a-Cause" image was still popular, following hard upon the 1955 movie of the same name. The "misunderstood young man" was a highly marketable commodity, and RCA envisioned Elvis as the perfect embodiment of this mystique. The sensational album cover was not only a change in RCA's usual bland approach to marketing its product, but indicated a new direction for the rock music business.

Another departure from RCA's corporate tradition was the creation of a special fund to promote and advertise Presley's music. One of the best promotional gimmicks was a double-record extended play (EP) set of eight songs, also entitled **Elvis Presley**. The Presley EP sold very well, confirmed RCA's expectations for his commercial success, and was the first of ten EPs that RCA hurriedly released in 1956 to cash in on Presley's popularity. Such promotional tactics really worked, and Elvis' long-playing album entered the *Billboard* LP chart at the number 11 position.

Contagion

Elvis Presley, then, was a mixed bag of twelve songs blending old Sun recordings with newly-cut RCA material. Elvis confided to a close friend that "Blue Suede Shoes," a song that Presley picked up from Carl Perkins, was the tune closest to his old Sun sound. Although Elvis' version reached only number 24 on the *Billboard* Hot 100, it was a still a strong tune for him. It was also popular with other artists. During 1956, there were three versions of "Blue Suede Shoes" on the *Billboard* Hot 100. In addition to Elvis, Carl Perkins' original rendition reached number 4, while Boyd Bennett, a King recording artist, had a number 63 hit with it. The commercial appeal of "Blue Suede Shoes" was so strong that the tune was also recorded by Sid King, Pee Wee King, Jim Lowe, and Roy Hall.

Not only was "Blue Suede Shoes" a popular American song, but its solid rock and roll roots prompted cover versions by obscure local artists in Australia, Canada, and England. The initial phases of western-Canadian rock and roll, for example, were built upon Presley's Sun record sound. In Vancouver, British Columbia, Canadian rock and roll zealots reacted to "Blue Suede Shoes" by turning out in droves to see local artists perform it. The first Vancouver rock star, Jimmy Morrison, fronted a Presley-style band, the Stripes. "We listened to Elvis and were knocked out," Morrison re-

Elvis' 1957 visit to Vancouver.

called. Inasmuch as there was no record label to release their songs, Morrison founded the Arctic label and recorded a number of rockabilly, Elvis-influenced singles. His efforts brought other performers onto the Canadian rock scene.

In September 1956, Les Vogt introduced a Presley-inspired version of "I'm Gonna Sit Right Down and Cry (over You)" in Vancouver rock clubs. At the Penthouse Club, a motley assortment of hookers, players, and underage college students danced to Vogt's Presley-like renderings. Vogt became an immediate local star and eventually, in 1962, released the song on his own Jaguar label. "I realize now that back then we were all just nothing more than early Elvis impersonators," Vogt admitted.

As a result of the fact that Presley's music came to be featured on his show, the name of Jack Cullen's highly-rated radio program, "The Owl Prowl," was changed to "The Prowlers." The new program title was designed to appeal to late-night callers, who overwhelmingly requested rock and roll songs. Soon, a band, the Prowlers, featuring none other than Les Vogt, dominated the Vancouver concert scene. With such rockabilly records as "Rock Me Baby" and "Get a Move on Baby," Les Vogt's Prowlers became a rock and roll staple of Western Canada.

Down the road in Seattle, the Frantics emerged as a local band with enormous musical appeal. In 1956, the Frantics were an assemblage of four talented musicians who attended high school in Seattle's North End. Primarily an instrumental group, Ron Petersen, the Frantics' lead guitarist, played instrumental licks much like Scotty Moore's. Don Fulton's drums re-created D.J. Fontana's Presley sound. In time, Jim Manolides provided rhythm and blues-oriented vocals, and the band employed a predominantly black sound to win a large local following. As the Frantics' leader, Petersen recognized that the band had to move beyond the Elvis Presley sound, and they began playing Richard Berry's "Louie Louie" for local audiences. "We didn't play much of Elvis' music, but the beat of our music and the general rhythm and blues sound that Elvis had led us to copy other black r and b artists. Elvis got us started, whether we knew it or not," Petersen noted. "Without him, there would have been a different Seattle rock and roll scene."

A competing band, the Wailers, echoed the same sentiment. "We weren't like Elvis," Rockin' Robin Roberts remarked, "but he was the catalyst to the scene." Groups like the Frantics and Wailers combined rhythm and blues covers with original compositions. Not too far away, in a small garage in Tacoma, Washington, the Ventures practiced the guitar licks that made "Walk

Don't Run" a standard with rock and roll audiences. Again, it was Elvis who had opened the door for their act.

Much like the Vancouver music scene, Presley's influence was to heighten interest in rock and roll enough to give young bands in Seattle a chance to perform. Many, many vocal groups in Seattle owed Elvis a debt of gratitude even though they didn't specifically play his music. George Palmerton, the leader of Seattle's premier white doo-wop group, the Highlighters, remembered that Elvis' sound opened up the Spanish Castle and Dick Parker ballrooms to local bands. When "Elvis came to Seattle," Palmerton remarked, "his music helped us to land jobs in clubs and dance halls previously reserved for big bands." In addition to Presley's music, Palmerton recalled doing an early show with Paul Anka. "Rock and roll opened up for a lot of people after Elvis," Palmerton concluded.

There were also a number of fledgling black singers who looked up to Elvis. Ron Holden and Andy Duvall gained limited notoriety with Seattle's Playboys. Holden, who later went on to success with "Love You So," was not influenced directly by Elvis, but he remembers how much better the jobs were for rock bands after Elvis came to Seattle. At the Eagle's Ballroom, local bands began playing with the touring acts and soon the Spanish Castle and Parker ballrooms featured Pacific Northwest acts. This set the stage for the explosion of local talent. The result was such legendary Pacific Northwest acts as Paul Revere and the Raiders, Marilee Rush and the Turnabouts, the Sonics, the Ventures, Don and the Goodtimes, and the Kingsmen, all of whom earned recording contracts.

In San Francisco, the same scenario was repeated as a black entertainer, Bobby Freeman, appeared at local high school dances. While he didn't sing Presley-type songs, Freeman benefited from the demand for rock and roll music. Across the bay in El Cerrito, California, a town a few miles north of Oakland, two brothers named John and Tom Fogerty listened to Elvis' music. In 1959, they cut their first demo on the local Orchestra Record label and two years later the Blue Velvets were signed by Fantasy Records. In the late sixties, after changing their name to Creedence Clearwater Revival, they emerged as rock superstars.

All over the country this pattern continued as young, would-be rock and roll stars emerged. Small recording studios and labels sprung up to provide records for the growing rock market. It would be an exaggeration to credit Elvis alone with this musical explosion, but most artists pointed out that, as far as they are concerned, it was he who opened the doors to the world of rock and roll. Elvis' music was the trumpet call of a revolution.

In England there was a similar revolution. In 1956, Tony Sheridan, later to gain fame playing with the Beatles in Hamburg, Germany, was beginning his musical career in London's Soho district. While performing in the 2-Is bar in Soho, Sheridan introduced a new American song, 'Blue Suede Shoes,' to English audiences. "I'll never forget how I felt when I heard Elvis' version of "Blue Suede Shoes," Sheridan remarked, "it gave me goose bumps." It also provided Sheridan with an introduction to American rock and roll music. "We were all influenced by Elvis," Sheridan commented, and he emphasized that the small group of fledgling English rock and rollers all attempted to cover Elvis' songs.

Not only was Elvis' music a part of the English rock music scene, but the artists who imitated him won immediate, if not lasting, rock stardom. Tommy Steele had two British hits, "Rock with the Cavemen" and "Singing the Blues," in an Elvis vein. Steele's emergence as an English rock singer began almost by accident. While sailing to New York on a cruise ship—performing as Chick Hicks—Steele first heard Presley's music. He was smitten by the sound. A talented performer, Steele was careful to develop his own style, but it was Elvis that gave birth to his rock music successes.

There were a host of other English rock and roll stars who owed their success to Elvis Presley. When RCA released "Heartbreak Hotel" in England during the first week of March 1956, it reached a generation of eager European rock and rollers. In England, RCA's H.M.V. label included "I Was the One" as the b-side to "Heartbreak Hotel." The H.M.V. publicity releases called Elvis "the King of Western Bop," which was an odd phrase to the English. The *London Daily Mirror*'s critic wrote: "Will British girls fall for Elvis?" He then supplied the answer: "I think it's likely—in time." He was right, because it took some time for Elvis' first record to catch on in the English market.

Presley's importance is that young would-be performers like Harry Webb listened to him. It was not long before Webb changed his name to Cliff Richard and became one of England's early teen idols. Richard's success with Elvis-type songs was not immediate, but he had all the ingredients for eventual stardom. With his sullen snarl, dark greasy hair, and good looks, Cliff Richard was a natural to succeed as the English Elvis. From 1958 to 1963, Richard placed twenty hit singles on the British charts, and, before the Beatles revolutionized the rock music world, he had established an independent brand of British rock music. Richard wasn't a clone. He was a man with a unique style and a broad-based pop talent. His first hit single in August 1958, "Move It," had a Presley direction, but it also demonstrated his own unique talent. Although Richard's act was modeled on Elvis Presley's (with some Teddy Boy

Cliff Richard.

overtones), he soon changed his image. In early 1959, Richard's first English number 1 single, "Living Doll," prompted him to cut his sideburns and tone down his stage dress. Members of Richard's backup band, the Shadows (first known as the Drifters), also cut their hair and began sporting conventional dark suits with white shirts and discrete ties. Richard came on stage in a white suit and dazzled the girls with his dance steps. The act was clean, wholesome, and designed to offend no one. There was a mild reaction against Presley's music in England and Cliff Richard and the Shadows were taking no chances with their newfound commercial success. Unwittingly, the middle-of-the-road or adult-oriented rock was on its way to compromising the initial thrust of rock and roll music.

Cliff Richard became a superstar with the Presley sound. Others like Terry Dene and the Understudies, Vince Taylor and the Playboys, Wee Willie Harris, Marty Wilde, and Billy Fury hit the English pop charts from 1956 to the early 1960s with Presley soundalike records. The *New Musical Express*, *Melody Maker*, and *Disc* perennially selected Elvis as the top rock act, something that continued from 1956 until Presley's death in 1977. In England, Elvis Presley's records and career were synonymous with the rise of rock and roll, and the English fans were faithful to his music to the end.

We must not, of course, leave out a mention of perhaps the most important of the Elvis-influenced bands, the Beatles. As the number of English rock and roll musicians grew, German entrepreneurs realized that they could hire English bands for small sums. "We went to London," Horst Fascher remarked, "and found wonderful talent like Tony Sheridan." It was Fascher who convinced his boss, Bruno Koschmider, to bring Sheridan to the Kaiserkeller Club in Hamburg. When Sheridan moved from London to the German port town, he found, in the confines of Hamburg's Reeperbahn district, a place full of nightclubs, strip joints, and seedy bars. Sheridan was mesmerized by the energetic and wide open German society. To his amazement, he found the Reeperbahn populated by Indonesian bands with an Elvis Presley sound. They mouthed the words to American rock hits without understanding the subtle nuances of rock and roll music.

The stage was set for the burst of some of the most creative music in rock and roll history. "I'll never forget the first time I walked into the Blockhutte," Sheridan recalled. "It was a German bar where acts came in to sing like American cowboys. Soon it was full of rock and rollers." In 1960, it also became a hangout for John Lennon and Paul McCartney. "They went to the Blockhutte to hear Elvis Presley on the jukebox," Sheridan noted. In August 1960, when the Beatles arrived to play at Koschmider's Indra Club, they became good friends with Sheridan. Their common passion for Presley's music ignited the first sparks of friendship. The Beatles performed "That's All Right (Mama)" and, like Sheridan, preferred Elvis' Sun records to his RCA recordings.

Prior to the Hamburg years, of course, Elvis Presley had been a strong influence upon John Lennon. The founder and chief songwriter of the Beatles first heard Elvis on Radio Luxembourg in 1956. The strains of "Heartbreak Hotel" led John in full pursuit of Elvis' earlier Sun recordings. As Ray Coleman's monumental biography of Lennon suggests, "Elvis was an Americanized version of the teddy boy." Not only was Elvis Lennon's first hero, but he provided a role model for his personal behavior. The sneering lip that Presley proffered to the camera was also a staple in Lennon's early photos, one which played upon the image of the rough-hewn American. Leather jackets, swear words, and an ever-present cigarette was how Lennon envisioned the rock and roll personality. "To hell with conformity, and Hail, Hail, Rock and Roll," Lennon proclaimed to Cavern Club disc jockey Bob Wooler.

John Lennon and Tony Sheridan spent long hours talking about Elvis' English releases, and agreed that there was more musical education in these records than in any other source. Both Lennon and Sheridan recalled that the premier British music newspaper, *Melody Maker*, called Elvis' "Hound Dog," "a new low" in the recording industry. They loved these negative reviews, because they reinforced the notion that the critics didn't understand the new music. In fact, *Melody Maker*'s editorials continued to praise the smooth stylings of Ella Fitzgerald and Frank Sinatra.

One English writer did champion the new music, however. He was Ray Coleman, who wrote for such diverse newspapers as the *London Daily Mirror*, *Melody Maker*, and the *London Sunday Times*. As Coleman suggested, "John Lennon did not have to wait long for his Pied Piper. It was from...Elvis Presley's earth-shaking new anthem for rock 'n' roll, 'Heartbreak Hotel'..." that Lennon received his earliest inspiration. Coleman points out in his Lennon biography that the development of the English rock concert business could be traced to Presley's enormous popularity, much as it had been in America.

Smart English concert promoters like Larry Parnes took advantage of *Melody Maker*'s insensitivity to rock music. Many of Parnes' shows were billed as events that were meant to spite the music press, and the young British fans reacted positively to these events. Soon, another British publication, the *New Musical Express*, defended rock and roll music. It was not long before the *New Musical Express* record charts began to have a strong impact upon Elvis' record sales. Much of the debate over rock music in England during 1956 resulted from the songs that Elvis included on his first album.

The Colonel Keeps It Up

For his part, Colonel Tom Parker spent a good deal of time during this period organizing Elvis Presley Enterprises to license things like teddy bears, perfume, and lipstick. It was not until the late summer of 1956 that Elvis Presley Enterprises officially began licensing products, but the groundwork had been completed by April. Many of the ideas for Elvis products were actually quite good. An authentic Elvis Presley Victrola sold for $32.95, with an automatic 45rpm version merchandising for $44.95. The blue denim-covered record player included a free Presley recording. A coaster/ashtray with a porcelain base containing a photo of Elvis was available in Newberry's. Colonel Parker signed a contract with the Green Duck Company to manufacture small Elvis pins sold in penny gumball machines. A head scarf appeared in Woolworth's for $1.49, and a few months later a $1.29 turban scarf and $1.00 cotton scarf completed the headwear assortment. Elvis Presley Enterprises licensed pajamas, t-shirts, and a $1.00 pair of socks. Local dime stores were flooded with adjustable Elvis finger rings that sold for $.49 at Woolworth's and $1.00 in Nordstrom's department stores. In Oak Park, Illinois, Marshall Field featured Elvis Presley mittens in red, white, and blue for $1.50.

Many of these items were purchased by fan club

members, so the Colonel and Elvis spent as much time cooperating with the mushrooming fan clubs as they did in putting together merchandise lists. Fans were an integral part of the Presley phenomenon, and no effort was spared to keep them happy. In Shreveport, Louisiana, Jeanelle Alexander, president of the Shreveport-Bossier Elvis Presley Fan Club, organized Elvis' fans from the "Louisiana Hayride," and they marched around town with an "I told you so" air. Fans couldn't contain their emotions, and fan magazines had a field day. From the flashy pages of *Modern Screen* to the intellectual confines of *Harper's*, the curiosity over Elvis Presley's life and career erupted into a national phenomenon. Among those focussing on personal preferences, one of the more ridiculous articles appeared in *Movie Teen Illustrated*. In "What's Eating in Elvisville," Elvis purportedly listed such fine foods as pork chops, spaghetti, peanut-butter cups, and Hawaiian Punch among his favorites. Judging by the favorite-food lists furnished by others close to him since his death, Elvis was either telling the truth or someone at the magazine was making pretty accurate guesses.

When *Hit Parader* magazine announced a contest to meet Elvis, there were more than eighty thousand letters sent in describing—in a hundred words or less—"Why I Want to Meet Elvis." When the winner, dark-haired Andrea June Stephens, received the news about her winning letter at her home at 895 Eden Avenue, Atlanta 16, Georgia, she immediately began excitedly telephoning her friends. When she arrived in Jacksonville, Florida, where Elvis was performing, she was taken

Elvis dancing with Andrea June Stephens.

273

to his hotel room. It was not long before Elvis made her feel at home and soon she was sitting on Elvis' bed talking to him like an old friend. As they left the hotel to have dinner, a girl fainted in the lobby. As Elvis soothed the overcome youngster, Andrea stood by watching in amazement. For her well-publicized date with Elvis, Andrea wore a pink dress and, with her mother in tow, she and Elvis went to a nearby coffee shop to eat a ham sandwich.

Not to be outdone, *TV Radio Mirror* and *TV Star Parade* held reader polls to determine Presley's popularity. Elvis not only polled more than twice the votes of such challengers as Pat Boone, Paul Anka, Frankie Avalon, Bobby Darin, and Ricky Nelson, but he also sold more records than all of them combined.

The exploitation magazine *Confidential* published an article called "Beware of Elvis Presley's Ball Point Pen." The point of this pointless piece (pun intended) was that ladies should beware of Elvis if he had a pen in his hand, as he was notorious for attempting to sign his name on any female breast that presented itself to him. Publicity of this type—good, bad, and indifferent—helped Colonel Parker's Elvis Presley Enterprises sell more than twenty million dollars worth of souvenirs during Elvis' first year with RCA.

In March 1956, even as Elvis was promoted in the mainstream of the entertainment business, Colonel Tom Parker continued to book Presley into small-time, carnival-like venues. A good example of Parker's willingness to accept any booking occurred on March 14-15, 1956, at the Fox Theater in Atlanta, Georgia. In a brief thirty-minute show, Elvis appeared three different times—4:30, 7:18, and 10:06—followed by a Tony Curtis movie, "The Square Jungle." Mother Maybelle Carter and five other acts supported Elvis' show. The admission was eighty-five cents for the first show and a dollar for other remaining performances—not a booking strategy designed to make Elvis an instant millionaire. It did, however, guarantee a great deal of artist exposure. A parade of Atlanta radio personalities streamed backstage, making Presley's appearance an event that was discussed on the radio for weeks.

Colonel Parker believed that constant public performances would create a demand for Elvis' music. The Colonel conscientiously collected press clippings. When the *Atlanta Constitution* raved over Elvis' performances, the Colonel's assistant, Tom Diskin, carefully tucked away the reviews to use in future promotions. The scrapbook, as the Colonel fondly referred to his file, was used to garner even more Presley appearances. The press was treated like royalty, and Tom Parker never lost an opportunity to promote his fledgling star. "I think the Colonel lived and breathed Elvis in those days,"

Steve Sholes noted.

Oscar Davis, another of the Colonel's minions, defended the theater bookings as a means of convincing the movie people to sign Elvis. As one of Colonel Parker's advance men, Davis was instructed to book Elvis into a chain of theaters in Florida, as well as into various East Coast movie houses. It was a back-breaking schedule calling for Elvis to perform from two in the afternoon until eleven in the evening. "I exploited the dates, and we packed the theaters everywhere," Davis told biographer Jerry Hopkins. The Colonel was aware that Hollywood producer Hal Wallis had watched Elvis on the Dorsey shows. Not only that, but Wallis had called Parker and talked about what he saw as Presley's bright movie future. So the bookings, in the Paramount-controlled theater circuit, were designed to showcase Elvis' commercial potential. Wallis' minions, the Colonel supposed, were everywhere, and the bookings were undertaken to make it easy for Hollywood to keep a close eye on the Presley phenomenon.

Some months earlier, on August 15, 1955, Elvis and Colonel Parker had signed their first management agreement with a provision including Bob Neal as a partner (see Chapter 13). It was a strange agreement, because Neal continued to book and manage Elvis while Colonel Parker hovered in the background. What this contract demonstrates is that Parker had some doubts about Elvis' career. The Colonel was uncertain about Presley's long-term commercial future. By March 1956, however, Elvis and the Colonel finalized a new contract. Colonel Parker had the best of both worlds. He had a contract which made his commitment to Elvis a dubious one, but in the event of commercial success the agreement was strong enough to guarantee Parker's future financial success. Clearly designed to control Elvis' career, this contract had three sections that granted Parker enormous power, even as the Colonel continued to mesmerize the press with the story that he was working with Elvis on a simple handshake.

First, the Colonel worked out a contract with Elvis that shared in the songwriting royalties. He convinced fledgling songwriters to give Presley a portion of the writing credit in return for recording the song. The Colonel needed a publishing company that would quietly guarantee the extra profits from such an arrangement. Eventually, Hill and Range allowed Parker to offer new songwriters a deal they couldn't refuse. No one was forced to give songwriter's credit for a song, but the ethical questions about this practice were never resolved. "When I recorded in the 1950s, a man by the name of Bob Garlic took part of the writer's credit for 'The Walk,'" Jimmy McCracklin remembered. "You either accepted this practice or didn't record. Later I got full writer's credit back. But hell, I never even heard of any Bob Garlic. Leonard Chess cheated me." McCracklin's remarks suggest how widespread this practice was in the recording industry.

Certainly, it was all something new to Elvis. Suddenly, he was surrounded by people to whom business success mattered more than song quality. Colonel Parker saw few differences in Elvis' songs. To the Colonel, all of Elvis' records were potential hits. He didn't believe that it was necessary to find quality songs. The shortsightedness of Parker's views were what prompted him to sell the rights to Presley's music to RCA in 1973 for a paltry sum, an action buttressed by his belief that Elvis had a limited artistic future. It was time to cash in while the cashing in was good.

As discussed in previous chapters, there were many contradictions in Colonel Parker's personality. At times he was a brilliant businessman and promoter. In other periods of his life, he gave Elvis' business interests little attention. There was an unpredictable quality to Parker's management. When the Colonel was not the shrewd, manipulative promoter, he was a short-sighted businessman who chased small profits and ignored long-term interests, a schizoid heritage that ultimately hurt Presley's

Elvis and the Colonel—united in their deathly fear of being poor.

career. There is a contradiction between the Colonel's behavior in 1956 compared to that in 1973 which clearly points to a very erratic management over the long haul.

Second, the new contract between Colonel Parker and Elvis Presley was again virtually indentured servitude. There was a provision stipulating that Elvis would perform in forty-seven cities for Colonel Parker at fees ranging from $175 to $350 per concert. This was clearly a restraint upon Elvis' ability to negotiate higher concert fees. Even if larger concert gates emerged, Colonel Parker pocketed the excess profits. This agreement not only guaranteed Parker enormous profits, but it relegated Elvis to a servile economic status. Parker's experiences with Eddy Arnold had prompted him to bury Elvis in a contractual legalese from which Presley would never emerge. Another reason for Parker's actions was that he suspected Elvis might draw diminishing concert gates over time. This provision would allow the Colonel to keep his protege on the road at slave wages. None of the Colonel's investment would be lost, because he could make up any advanced money by invoking this clause. There is no doubt that Colonel Parker was astonished when Elvis' concert fees continued to increase out of sight. Again, Parker was the short-sighted pessimist who had little faith in his protege.

Third, the management contract specified that if Elvis was not a saleable commodity, he would have to pay the Colonel a $2,500 severance fee. There was an obsessive-compulsive quality to Parker's demands, and he was never able to separate his quest for money from a furtherance of Presley's career. Parker failed to realize that by publicizing and nurturing Elvis' music, the concert fees could only increase on the strength of Elvis' talent. The fact that Elvis did draw bigger crowds and earn more money was in spite of Parker's antiquated management techniques, not, as the Colonel believed, because of them.

Clearly, Colonel Tom Parker was not the legendary mastermind he made himself out to be. He played this role to the hilt, of course, and Southern and Yankee newsmen and disc jockeys rarely questioned his contentions. He was a "good ole boy" who knew the entertainment industry like the back of his hand, and nobody bothered to be anything but beguiled by his personality and deal-making ability. Red Robinson, a Vancouver, British Columbia, disc jockey, was a good example of the naive local dj who extolled Parker's virtues to his unsuspecting audience, referring to Parker as "a modern entertainment genius." The Colonel was a genius in using and manipulating local djs.

Marching On

On March 17, 1956, after the revised management

contract was signed, *Billboard* announced that "Heartbreak Hotel" was number 1 in Seattle, Washington. KJR, Seattle's premiere rock station, played the record twice an hour, and the drive-time disc jockey, Pat O'Day, enthralled his listeners with tales of Elvis' concert appearances. It was O'Day who first excited the Pacific Northwest about Presley (Elvis played in Seattle's Sick's Stadium the following year).

At Heiser's Shadow Lake, a country-western bar near Renton, a Seattle suburb, "Heartbreak Hotel" was the only non-country tune on the jukebox.

After playing a concert at Seattle's Eagles Auditorium, Little Richard took a taxi to Birdland, a black after-hours club on Capitol Hill, to sit in with the house band. During the break, Richard heard Elvis' version of "That's All Right (Mama)" blaring from the jukebox (Elvis was the only white artist with a song on the machine's playlist). When he came back on stage, he smiled to the audience and said, "our music is everywhere." Like many observers, Little Richard wasn't sure what to make of Presley's music. He sounded black. He sounded country. He sounded pop. And, whatever Little Richard thought, it was Elvis who was everywhere.

Like many black entertainers, of course, Little Richard Penniman acknowledged Presley's importance to the commercial success of rock and roll music. Both Pat Boone and Elvis Presley had covered Little Richard's "Tutti Frutti," and these versions helped rather than hurt the sales of Richard's original version. Elvis also covered "Rip It Up" and "Long Tall Sally." The result of such cover records was to bring Little Richard and other black artists into the white record-buying market as teenagers came to prefer the originals to the cover versions. "You know I was havin' so much fun in 1956, I didn't realize how much impact my music had," Little Richard has remarked. Indeed, black artists like Richard gave the music to white artists like Elvis, and white artists in turn gave back an atmosphere of acceptance and opportunities for black artists which they had never before enjoyed.

On March 22, 1956, Elvis appeared for two shows at the Mosque Theater in Richmond, Virginia. It was one of Colonel Parker's budget appearances, and Elvis was unhappy with it. This theater's bookings were controlled by Paramount studios, and Parker was using these performances to impress Paramount with Presley's movie star potential.

Despite commercial success, things were not running smoothly for Elvis and the Blue Moon Boys. Elvis stayed on the outskirts of Richmond, while Scotty and Bill had a hotel room near the Mosque Theater. The pair complained that they were not receiving their fair share of the personal appearance money. They also

resented the Colonel's manipulative personality, and continually voiced their dissatisfaction. The noticeable tension on stage during the two Richmond shows was evident to a Memphis air force officer who attended the concert. "I didn't know what was wrong, but they didn't act like they were having fun." Elvis hurriedly sang three or four numbers and exited the stage quickly following each show. There was a television commitment to fulfill, so Elvis left immediately for New York.

After a leisurely drive back to New York, Elvis checked into the Warwick Hotel. The sixth appearance on the Dorsey show was scheduled for March 24, 1956. Colonel Parker had scheduled a series of interviews prior to the show. The media frenzy over Elvis' last appearance on the Dorsey show reflected how strong interest in him had become since the first show a scant two months before. The Nielsen rating for this show was 20.9 percent of the audience, which was only a two percent increase over past shows, but Elvis' performances were widely credited with creating new interest in the show. Not only did Elvis' success on the sixth Dorsey stage show boost his chance for a movie career, but surging record sales further convinced Hollywood of his commercial prowess.

The Dorsey shows led to extensive press coverage of Presley's early career. Typical of the positive reaction to Elvis was the conclusion to an article in *Record Whirl*: "Elvis Presley is now a national craze." There was not unanimous agreement among critics that Presley was a future star, however. In the next few months, Elvis was severely chastised by New York television, magazine, and newspaper critics. One critic, John Crosby, a television commentator, remarked that Elvis is "a shouter...who yells a song...and seems to have some sort of St. Vitus dance." Jack Gould, the *New York Times* television critic, wrote: "Mr. Presley has no discernible singing ability." Jack O'Brien, a New York *Journal-American* critic, retorted, "He [Elvis] can't sing a lick...." As for Elvis' dancing, O'Brien commented, it was like "an aborigine's mating dance." The positive side of all this criticism was that it caught the attention of Hollywood producers by creating controversy over Elvis' talent—the important thing for moviemakers was that it fostered public demand to view Elvis' spectacular and often-criticized act.

The reaction of the New York media did bother Elvis, though. He confided to a number of friends, notably Jim Denson, Ronald Smith, and Kenneth Herman, that he was nervous about the unwarranted criticism. As Elvis' old Memphis friend Kenneth Herman remarked, "Only New Yorkers and Yankees wrote about Elvis; funny—they didn't seem to understand us Southern boys." These sentiments were echoed by another long-time friend, Ronald Smith, who pointed out that many people who were not close to Elvis in high school suddenly became his best friends. "I remember one politician-type who would have nothing to do with Elvis," Smith smiled "Then he [Elvis] became famous and they were best friends." What Smith and Herman were referring to were the hangers-on, or the so-called Memphis Mafia members that began to isolate Elvis from the outside world.

Because Elvis was always out to please, was very sensitive and vulnerable to criticism, it was hard for him to trust people. As a result, he tended to surround himself with individuals who were uncritical—or at least openly so—supportive, and accepting. This tendency opened the door to anyone who was either genuine or dissembling enough in their reactions to him to make Elvis believe in their undying loyalty.

The staunchest Presley defender, George Klein, was formerly the president of the L.C. Humes High School student body. He achieved a peer group popularity and success at Humes that Elvis found impossible to attain. As a result, Elvis identified with Klein for the rest of his life, and it was easy for him to become part of Presley's inner circle. For his part, the lithe, smooth-talking Klein has built a career around his friendship with Elvis. On Memphis radio and on national television shows, Klein has perpetuated the myths and stereotypes that Elvis' fans have always loved; to do otherwise would nullify his ability to continue to exploit his

Memphis disc jockey George Klein.

self-appointed position as "Elvis' best friend."

The Movies

One of the most significant things to occur during this period was the sudden interest of movie producers in Elvis. Hollywood was intrigued by the publicity surrounding his singing. As names like "Elvis the Pelvis" made front-page headlines, movie talent scouts and promotion-minded agents speculated that Presley could be a promising source of instant profits. The Colonel quickly realized that he had a potentially hot property, but, uncertain about how to negotiate a profitable movie deal, he resorted to one of his time-tested management techniques. The Colonel let it be known that he would deal only with "familiar movie people." When he had managed Eddy Arnold and Hank Snow, Colonel Parker had dealt with Paramount Studios, so it was unsurprising when Parker contacted Paramount to arrange a screen test for Elvis with producer Hal Wallis.

The Colonel feared that Elvis' diction, poor skin tone, bad teeth, and protruding nose would be detrimental to his prospects, so he hired a voice and elocution coach for Elvis. "When Elvis came back to Memphis, he was a new man," Kenneth Herman recalled. From 1953 to 1955, as a member of Eddie Bond's Stompers, Herman had often talked music and the movies with Elvis. "He had not only changed the way he spoke, but there was a new confidence to Elvis," continued Herman. "When Elvis went to Hollywood for his screen test, he had done his homework. He knew what the movie people wanted and gave it to them."

Kenneth Herman remembers that when Elvis returned from his April 1956 Hollywood screen test, he also had a different look. His skin had cleared up. His speech and manners were polished. Herman believes that Elvis had minor plastic surgery in addition to speech and elocution lessons. "It was a different Elvis," Herman recalled. "I was amazed by his good looks and slick-talking way. Yet, I knew it was the old Elvis when he looked at me and said, 'Kenneth, you'll never believe it, I passed my screen test. I can't believe it. If I pinch myself the dream will end'." Herman laughed along with Elvis, because Presley believed he had put something over on the Hollywood magnates.

Ronald Smith was another old friend who remembered the "new" Elvis. His nose was different, his chin line was modified, and his pockmarked face had a new vitality. "Elvis winked at me and asked if I liked the 'Cadillac Elvis'," Smith remembered.

After the last Dorsey brother's stage show, Elvis caught a plane for Los Angeles to complete his screen test for Hal Wallis, set for April 1. Before that, how-

Along the road to film stardom—Elvis seated between
actors Robert Wagner and Alan Hale, Jr.

ever, he was scheduled to meet with Wallis. Unfortunately, Elvis' plane was caught in a snowstorm shortly after taking off from LaGuardia. The engines iced over, causing an emergency landing. Elvis was so severely shaken by the ordeal that he took the time to drive to Los Angeles. The drive to Hollywood was a relaxing one, and Elvis came into town ready for his screen test.

When Elvis arrived in the movie capital he was a strange sight. Presley's long hair, outlandish clothes, and tendency to draw large crowds was unique even by Hollywood standards. Many of filmland's rich and powerful producers were put off by the Presley persona. Hal Wallis, who had worked with such Hollywood luminaries as Dean Martin and Jerry Lewis, puzzled many industry insiders by his interest in Elvis.

Wallis had watched Elvis on the Dorsey show, and believed that Presley offered a new commercial direction for the movie industry. Frank Sinatra's early movie success was a parallel that Wallis considered. In a memo to management, Wallis pointed out that Frank Sinatra's 1940 movie "Las Vegas Nights" offered some valuable insights into Presley's possible potential. Sinatra had appeared in "Las Vegas Nights" as an anonymous band singer performing "I'll Never Smile Again." The young girls in the audience still screamed when Sinatra came on screen, but few Sinatra fans attended the movie because his appearance was not well publicized. The Tommy Dorsey Orchestra was featured in ads for the film, and this proved to be a box-office mistake. Wallis' memo made it clear that Elvis had to be the centerpiece of any movie, and that a combination of singing

and drama was needed to draw the fans. Wallis' memo didn't excite Paramount executives, however, because they, like RCA management, initially had no idea how to merchandise Presley.

Like many Americans who tuned in Elvis' performances, Wallis recalled many things about his first view of this young performer. In retrospect, Wallis remembered that he was motivated by curiosity rather than an interest in rock music. As a seasoned observer of popular culture, Wallis was struck by the audience reaction to Presley's show. During his last appearance on the Dorsey show, Elvis' singing and visual stage manner electrified Wallis. After the June Taylor Dancers finished the opening number, Elvis came out and performed "Money Honey," then closed with "Heartbreak Hotel." The audience's heady applause sprinkled with some laughter intrigued Hal Wallis. He saw Elvis as a talent who could transfer his excitement to the movie screen. After each Dorsey stage show, CBS had been bombarded with telegrams, phone calls, and letters, something which Wallis learned after having quietly called CBS executives to inquire about Presley's stage manner. "Was Elvis a problem backstage?" Wallis asked. "Did he have an excessive ego?" Jack Philbin response was unequivocal: "Elvis is a nice kid, he is very professional, and easy to direct."

Elvis and Hal Wallis.

Wallis described his reaction to seeing Presley on the Dorsey show as follows: "I was sitting at home spinning the dial of my television set...when I first saw this remarkable performer." The sport coat Elvis wore on the show was too large for him and the black pants were too tight, an odd combination which fascinated Wallis. "At first, he looked like any other teen-age bopper, but when he started to sing, twisting his legs, bumping and grinding, shaking his shoulders, he was electrifying."

It was a tough job for Wallis to convince Paramount big-wigs that Elvis had talent, but very soon a number of Paramount executives realized that Presley was the forerunner of a new musical sound. The change in attitude occurred after a series of concerts Elvis performed in San Diego a few days after his screen test. Even as Colonel Parker and Paramount were negotiating a contract, the San Diego performances, witnessed by Paramount executives, produced a crowd reaction that convinced many of them that Elvis was indeed a hot commercial property. Elvis performed two shows in the San Diego Arena. The April 4-5, 1956, live performances were well received, and Elvis also appeared in local record stores to promote his first album. The line of record buyers waiting to see him at one record store was over five thousand strong. The magic between Elvis and his fans was clearly evident to even the most casual observer.

On April 3, 1956, before the San Diego concerts, Elvis had appeared on "The Milton Berle Show," which was broadcast from 8:00 to 9:00 on ABC-TV. This Tuesday-night live show from the deck of the aircraft carrier USS Hancock was also an impressive one, with Elvis performing "Blue Suede Shoes," "Shake Rattle and Roll," and "Heartbreak Hotel." Elvis demonstrated

Elvis became fast friends with actor Nick Adams.

some acting talent in a comedy sketch with Berle, and appeared at ease in front of the TV cameras.

As a result of these appearances, Paramount signed Presley to a seven-year contract, although they then confirmed that they didn't yet have a suitable picture in which to showcase Presley's talent. Elvis was unable to convince Paramount to make music the centerpiece of his first movie. Instead, the studio called a press conference on Friday, April 6, at which it was announced that, although general plans for Elvis' first three pictures had been discussed, he would be loaned to 20th Century Fox in the short term for a western drama, "The Reno Brothers," a title later changed to "Love Me Tender." Fox signed Richard Egan and Debra Paget to add depth to the cast.

After Paramount signed Elvis, Hal Wallis remarked that young Presley had certainly done his homework, and was obviously familiar with the type of character actors and leading men that Hollywood preferred. Elvis came off convincingly as a cross between James Dean, Marlon Brando, and Paul Newman. During his screen test, he displayed a natural acting talent in his scene with veteran character actor Frank Faylen.

Once "Love Me Tender" triumphed at the box office, Paramount accelerated plans to produce a music-oriented picture. The artistic failure of "Love Me Tender" was all but ignored due to the immense box office, and, in 1957, "Loving You" became the first of nine Wallis-produced Presley movies to extend the tradition of extraordinary profitability associated with Elvis on the big screen.

By the end of April 1956, Elvis Presley was firmly established as a major musical, television, and movie act. The old Sun Records days were over, and he was a national star. The innocence and good times, intertwined with frustration and heartbreak, of 1954-1955 gave way to a new feeling. Elvis was not only a star, but had an entourage befitting a major entertainment figure. The long, hard climb was over.

While he didn't give birth to rock and roll music, Elvis did become its first million-dollar superstar. When "Heartbreak Hotel" became a top five record on all three *Billboard* charts—the pop, country, and rhythm and blues lists—it was the first record to achieve such a status. On the country and pop charts it rose to number 1, and peaked at number 5 on the rhythm and blues chart. From May 5 to June 16, 1956, "Heartbreak Hotel" would hold the number 1 spot on the *Billboard* Hot 100. This feat helped to establish rock and roll music as a highly profitable entertainment form, a success which forced RCA and other major labels into grudgingly acceptance of rock music.

CHAPTER 16
The Price of Fame and Fortune,
Late April-July 1956

By the summer of 1956, Elvis Presley was at the height of his success. What price did Elvis Presley really pay for his rise to fame and fortune? Put simply, the pressures of recording, touring, making movies, and public celebrity were even now beginning the process of creating a prison from which Elvis would never escape—until his tragic and untimely death twenty years later.

Las Vegas

On April 11, 1956, even as *Variety* reported that the single "Heartbreak Hotel" had sold more than a million copies, Colonel Parker signed Elvis to appear at the New Frontier Hotel's Venus Room in Las Vegas, Nevada. Parker held a press conference and bragged to the press that Presley's contract at the New Frontier was the beginning of a new phase in Elvis' career. The media was at first surprised by the Vegas booking, because Elvis didn't fit the mold for headliners in the resort town. The hotel received an unprecedented sixty-five requests for complimentary press passes, and major media outlets were all set to continue their coverage of Presley. The denigration of Presley's act began to intensify following Colonel Parker's announcement of the late-April Las Vegas booking, however, and the triumphs that Elvis was to experience in May and June 1956 were bittersweet ones because of persistent press criticism.

Presley's two weeks at the New Frontier began on April 23. *Variety* was the first to question Presley's talent in its May 2, 1956, issue. Little more than mid-way through his stay at the New Frontier, the entertainment tabloid noted that Elvis "doesn't hit the mark." Presley had been signed by Samy Lewis to appear in a show entitled "Musical Fantasy," in which Elvis was one of three headline acts. The others were bandleader Freddy Martin and comedian Shecky Greene. The two-dollar admission price drew a strange group of middle-aged tourists and their children, but it soon became apparent that it was not yet time to bring Elvis' brand of rock and roll music into the desert oasis. The predominantly adult audiences preferred Freddy Martin and His Orchestra to young Presley. Whether or not Elvis' initial Las Vegas engagement was successful is difficult to analyze, however. Rock music was an entertainment form that the Las Vegas critics couldn't understand, and they reacted to it with a torrid spate of faultfinding. "From an audience appeal point of view," one critic wrote, "the young man appeared to score with his 'geetar' playing, but as the numbers progressed they seemed to be similarly repetitious."

Colonel Parker quickly recognized the fact that Elvis just wasn't going over in the big way he had expected him to and, in an attempt to dampen any negative publicity, the Colonel subsequently perpetuated the myth that Elvis had left the show after only a couple of performances, something that was patently untrue—Elvis finished his two-week engagement...quietly. As D.J. Fontana recalled, "We not only had big crowds, but every celebrity in town turned out to see Elvis."

To Vegas locals and visitors alike, Presley cut an odd figure. He was polite off stage and raucous on stage. A cult of personality developed around him. You liked him or you didn't—there was no middle ground. He had a different, yet deferential, air about him, a contradiction that ultimately frustrated the press. Largely as a result of his non-Vegas persona, the newspaper reviews of Presley's New Frontier appearances were hostile ones. Another of the reasons for negative reviews was the fact that Elvis had failed to show up for an interview with United Press' Hollywood columnist, Aline Mosby. When it was discovered that Elvis had gone to see a Randolph Scott western instead, some

Las Vegas was chorus girl heaven for Elvis.

rather unkind comments appeared in print. The press ravaged Elvis' act, while at the same time praising Shecky Greene's comedy and Freddy Martin's musical numbers. The juvenility reached a new low when one local columnist went so far as to wander around town making crude public jokes about Presley's singing.

Elvis was hurt by the press backbiting, but tried not to let it bother him. Unlike his future visits to Vegas, Elvis was usually up by noon, tooling around town. A string of movies, a bevy of chorus girls, and attendance at all the shows filled his off-stage time. Elvis spent four nights watching Billy Ward and the Dominoes perform in one of the downtown clubs. Jackie Wilson, the Dominoes' featured vocalist, performed Elvis' "Don't Be Cruel," and Elvis remarked that "his version was much better than mine." "He was on the floor after the song and I was on the table cheering him," Elvis later recalled. The diction and enunciation in Wilson's voice intrigued Elvis, who chuckled at the manner in which Wilson pronounced the word "telephone." Presley's re-

Elvis met Liberace and brother George in Vegas.

marks were praiseworthy, and he marvelled at Wilson's talent. Jackie Wilson's artistry later prompted Elvis to record a demo version of "Paralyzed" in the black singer's style.

The stint in Las Vegas did have a temporary impact upon his career, however. Hoping to capitalize on Presley's popularity, RCA had taped his last appearance, but the controversy over Presley's show discouraged release of the album.

Nevertheless, the May 1956 performance did reveal a mature performer who paced his show admirably and excited the crowd. Elvis opened with "Heartbreak Hotel," changing the song title to "Heartburn Motel" to vent his feelings over the rude Las Vegas reception. Once Elvis began singing "Long Tall Sally," he quietly added the opening bars of "The Ballad of Davy Crockett." This was Elvis-the-unrequited-rebel at his best. The media criticism, as well as the attitude of some of the professional Las Vegas entertainers, had stung him, and Presley struck back in his own way.

During Elvis' introduction to "Blue Suede Shoes," he let the audience know that "Heartbreak Hotel" was a million-seller. After some verbal clowning around with the Freddy Martin Orchestra, Presley recognized two celebrities in the audience—Ray Bolger and Phil Silvers. When Elvis closed the show with "Money Honey," the applause was long and loud.

During Elvis' two-week stint at the New Frontier, he played a special show for teenagers. This Saturday, April 28 show demonstrated that Presley was indeed a strong act with the right audience. The largely female crowd showed up to have their bras and panties autographed, and Elvis met many of his fans at a special autograph table.

In the end, Elvis left Las Vegas unhappy with the booking, however. The crowds were too sedate and the special teenager's show was contrived. Colonel Tom Parker realized that the New Frontier Hotel booking had been a mistake. It was time to go back to Memphis for a short rest before resuming his tour schedule. When he returned home, Elvis met Marion Keisker on the street in front of Sun studio. "I asked Elvis about Las Vegas," she remarked. "He passed it off as people who didn't understand his music; he had no bitterness," Keisker concluded.

Bodyguards

When Elvis arrived back in Memphis, he purchased a house at 1034 Audubon Drive for $40,000. It was a green-and-white, one-story house built in the popular ranch style of the 1950s. Located near Memphis State

Snapshots from Audubon Drive

1034 Audubon Drive (the carport is on the left).

Vernon and Gladys in the carport
—with two Cadillacs and Elvis' motorcycle.

Elvis and his cycle at Audubon Drive.

University, the Audubon Drive home was in an upper middle-class neighborhood, and possessed an understated elegance. The small fence in front of Presley's new home failed to discourage the fans, however, who wandered onto the property at will. For months there were people walking around the front and backyard. Whenever Elvis went outside, he was mobbed by adoring fans. Gladys Presley worried that something would happen to her son, and was nervous about all the young girls hanging around the house. When Kenneth Herman and Ronald Smith visited, they were taken aback by the few opportunities Elvis had for solitude, something they knew he enjoyed. "I don't think that Elvis was comfortable with the situation in that house," Ronald Smith remarked about Elvis' lack of privacy. "He was a country boy thrust into the spotlight."

Elvis didn't have an entourage of bodyguards when he returned from Las Vegas, so he had taken a cab home from the train depot. After he purchased the Audubon Drive home, though, the problems involving unwanted visitors prompted Elvis' friends Red West and George Klein to urge Presley to hire some bodyguards. Reluctantly, Elvis hired West, an old high school friend, Bitsy Mott, Colonel Parker's brother-in-law, and Junior Smith, Elvis' cousin, to act as security, the vanguard of an ever-expanding group that ultimately became known to the media as the "Memphis Mafia."

Red West, an excellent bodyguard, had the knowledge and innate intelligence to avoid confrontations. A huge, muscular man, West was also thoughtful and gentle. In contrast, Bitsy Mott dressed and acted like a television gangster. A former semi-pro baseball player who grew up in Chicago, Mott was a small man with an inferiority complex who enjoyed pushing around people who wanted to see Elvis. On more than one occasion, Red West bailed Mott out of serious trouble. Junior Smith, whose personality was basically psychotic, made it impossible for Elvis to relax. Mott and Smith lured girls backstage with promises of meeting Elvis, thereby creating many of Elvis' problems. Not content to merely guard Presley, the pair baited and taunted young men whose dates they brought backstage, creating an hysterical atmosphere which bred violence. Mott had no deep feelings for Elvis, and his actions were typical of the sycophantic hangers-on—like Junior Smith, who lived off of Elvis, but who was "family"—who would plague Elvis throughout ensuing his career.

Red West was vital to Elvis' stability. It was West who quietly carried out security procedures. Not only had they been friends since their Humes High days, but Elvis genuinely admired Red's quick wit, intelligence, and physical prowess. West was also a jack-of-all-trades. Between concerts he drove the band's equipment from one town to another, acted as a roadie, se-

In a taxi surrounded by fans, Elvis lights Junior Smith's cigarette.

curity guard, and general counselor. Much of what Red West learned in these years contributed to his later success as a character actor on television and in the movies. All of this made Red West doubly valuable to Elvis, because he could control both Smith and Mott. There is no doubt that at this point West was Elvis' closest friend. (Sadly, as it appears, over time West's loyalty seems to have given way to the same tendency to capitalize on his friendship with Elvis that has afflicted so many other of Elvis' so-called friends. For his part, West and the other co-authors of *Elvis—What Happened?* would insist that they acted solely out of love for Elvis, hoping to shock Elvis back to reality by revealing what they claimed were the lurid details of his private life.)

But the truly saddest part of the change in this aspect of Elvis' life is that other old and trusted friends like Kenneth Herman and Ronald Smith were estranged from Elvis, refusing to become part of the show business farce that, with the Colonel's blessing, steadily grew up around Elvis.

Crest of the Wave

Even as show business security was becoming an integral part of Presley's life, he was again honored by *Billboard* magazine. The day after Elvis bought the Audubon Drive house, he was voted *Billboard*'s top new country and western artist. RCA announced that

Presley's record, "I Want You, I Need You, I Love You," had the largest pre-release order of any RCA-Victor record. The 300,000 advance copies indicated that Presley would soon have two instant, million-selling records. ("Heartbreak Hotel" continued to sell seventy thousand copies a week, and Presley's LP was destined to become the biggest selling album in RCA history.)

The degree of Presley's success had been demonstrated earlier, when the April 18 issue of *Billboard* reported that "Heartbreak Hotel" was number 1 in Baltimore, Buffalo, Chicago, Cincinnati, Denver, Detroit, Kansas City, Milwaukee, Minneapolis-St. Paul, New Orleans, St. Louis, Seattle, and Toronto. The *Billboard* publicity increased the demand for Presley concerts, and Colonel Parker continued to plan extensive tour schedules. In addition, the April 30 issue of *Life* magazine had featured Elvis in an article entitled "A Howling Hillbilly Success." The first truly national article on Elvis, it reflected upon his financial successes. There was no new information on his family or his career, and the piece reeked of Colonel Parker's publicity handouts, but it nevertheless added to Elvis' notoriety.

On May 4, RCA released "I Want You, I Need You, I Love You" backed with "My Baby Left Me." With five days remaining in his Las Vegas engagement, Elvis was elated with the news that "Heartbreak Hotel" was number 1 on the *Billboard* singles chart and his album was number 1 on the album chart. As industry endorsements, awards, and staggering record sales continued to accumulate, radio airplay went through the roof. At WSLM in Salem, Indiana, for example, it was announced that the station was going to begin broadcasting a weekly program called "Rockin' with Presley."

In early May 1956, news about Elvis dominated *Billboard*. A review of "My Baby Left Me" backed with "I Want You, I Need You, I Love You" was featured in all three of its "Review Spotlight" sections. *Billboard*'s pop, country and western, and rhythm and blues review sections also stimulated Presley's record sales. He was listed as the number one artist in sales, jukebox play, and disc jockey favorites.

About a week after Elvis left Las Vegas, on May 13, he performed two shows in a St. Paul, Minnesota, auditorium. The publicity over Presley's record sales had prompted the promoter to hire ten extra policemen. Surprisingly, though, Elvis played to an only partially filled house. The age of mass marketing and large rock concerts was still a decade away, and Colonel Parker's greed had prompted him to overbook—he had selected a venue so large that neither Elvis nor any other rock act of the time could have filled it.

Another reason for empty seats was the excessive hype and negative publicity surrounding Presley's ca-

able to the press, Jones stomped off in disgust. He vowed to make Presley look silly. What Jones didn't realize was that Colonel Parker had arranged for Elvis to meet with major media representatives, resulting in a great deal of positive national publicity that more than offset diatribes of the type he generated on a local level.

Despite the empty seats in the Twin Cities, *Time* and *Newsweek* magazines both covered Elvis' rise to stardom. The May 14, 1956, *Newsweek* featured a story, "Hillbilly on a Pedestal," which unfortunately continued the myths about Elvis' "poor, white trash background." That night Elvis performed two shows in La Crosse, Wisconsin, before more than five thousand fans. At both shows, fans carried copies of the *Newsweek* issue and proudly held up pictures of Presley. They experienced a rare treat as Elvis sang the Platters' "Only You," and extended his show by almost a half hour. Whenever Elvis was in high spirits he would stay on stage for a longer period of time. The positive national publicity had obviously made him buoyant, and he treated his fans to a hard-driving show.

Because of the length of this show, however, Elvis missed his plane home to Memphis, where he was to scheduled to appear as a headliner at the Memphis Cotton Carnival. When he arrived in town late on the afternoon of May 15, he went straight to Ellis Auditorium, where he shared the bill with Hank Snow. After-

reer. Colonel Parker's whirlwind promotional techniques had indeed created a ground swell for Presley's concerts, but many of the public at large were still baffled by Elvis' persona. To many people, he was an interesting oddity. When the concert gates were large, it was because the Colonel had gotten the word out to the fan clubs. When the venues went unfilled in places that were not hotbeds of Presleymania, Parker increased the hoopla and hype surrounding the dates, sometimes having the effect of dispelling the latent interest of the merely curious rather than reinforcing it.

For its part, the press continued to hammer away at Elvis' performances. Will Jones, a local Minneapolis reporter, wrote that Elvis was in the Twin Cities because "he flopped at a Las Vegas, Nev., nightclub." Jones, a middle-aged critic, was used to covering Frank Sinatra, Tony Bennett, and jazz acts. Presley made him nervous, and he confessed that he didn't understand rock and roll music. Not only did Jones not understand the music, but he had no knowledge of the blues, country, or rhythm and blues music. His review of Presley's performance made it clear that serious rock music criticism was still a decade away.

After Presley's concert, Jones went backstage to interview Elvis. He began talking to Red West and grew very uncomfortable around the bodyguards. When it became apparent that Presley wasn't going to be avail-

ward, he again left Memphis, spending five days on the road appearing in Little Rock, Arkansas, Springfield, Missouri, and Lincoln and Omaha, Nebraska.

After four days off, Elvis appeared in Kansas City, Missouri, before a small crowd of 2,500 in a 12,500-seat coliseum. Playing large, partially-filled auditoriums and baseball stadiums depressed Elvis. The smaller auditoriums filled to capacity allowed both Elvis and his fans to go away with a positive feeling. Elvis told Ronald Smith that he was sure that the latter approach would inevitably create a greater demand for his product.

The mixture of half-full houses and sold-out concert sites was typical of the 1956 shows. At one concert Elvis would fill the place and the next night the concert hall might be half full. Although the Presley hysteria was universal, it didn't always translate to packed houses. It is known that Colonel Tom Parker and Elvis fought over the booking policy the Colonel had adopted. In fact, Elvis was outraged with many of the Colonel's promotional schemes. The pillows, teddy bears, buttons, and gadgets that the Colonel contracted for drove Presley crazy. Privately, he confided to half a dozen friends that Parker was a crude pitchman. Why play to the small crowds that turned out in the larger concert venues? Elvis was adamant that the Colonel bring him into smaller theaters where he could be intimate with his audience. He wanted to play movie theaters and smaller concert halls—his type of venue, one that he sparkled in on stage. A good example of the type of concerts that Elvis enjoyed occurred on Friday, May 25, 1956, when he appeared for three shows at Detroit's Fox Theater. Elvis drew a near-capacity crowd and earned a net take-home wage of $10,000. The comments of fourteen-year-old Ernestine Waynick were typical of Presley's audience. "I saved $4.50 worth of pop-bottles to see all three Elvis shows."

The local press, however, still wasn't convinced. Charles Manos, reporting for the *Detroit Free-Press*, treated Presley's act as a curiosity, and wrote that rock music was not a commercial phenomenon. The death knell for Presley's brand of rock and roll was of course premature, and critics like Manos may have unwittingly increased rock music's popularity by their constant barrage of negativism.

Elvis sensitivity to criticism was further illustrated when, on May 26, he was awarded the "Jimmie Rodgers Achievement Award" for 1956. When the honor was bestowed, however, Elvis was not present to receive it. He received a telephone call about his selection while at his hotel in Columbus, Ohio, as he was waiting to perform two evening shows. He didn't mention the award to anyone, however, and refused to return the Rodgers committee's phone call.

During his stay in Las Vegas, reporters had continually asked Elvis about the negative side of his career and, in a heated private exchange with one newsman, Elvis was accused of not being truthful with the press. As a result, Presley spent an entire afternoon recalling his problems in Meridian, Mississippi, at the Jimmie Rodgers Memorial celebration he had attended in 1955. For a year, Elvis had unburdened himself to anyone who would listen that he felt he had been sabotaged by his own people—Elvis was booed by the crowd. Young toughs had made fun of his clothes, and it was difficult to sing over the catcalls. The idea that the good people of Meridian, Mississippi, had ridiculed one of their own during a parade had totally enraged him. Because he had been so poorly treated by the celebrants, Elvis had publicly vowed never to return to the sleepy Mississippi town, something which may have influenced the committee, by way of apology, to present him with the award. True to his word, Elvis stayed away.

Onward and Upward

The day after his Detroit concert, Elvis discovered that his picture was on the front cover of *Cashbox*. The shot showed Elvis in front of the New Frontier Hotel with Colonel Parker and Freddy Martin, Elvis holding a gold record for "Heartbreak Hotel." And it was one

tired-looking Elvis, to be sure. He had played hard in Las Vegas, and the girls in the local chorus lines had kept him busy. One of Elvis' favorite memories was being able to use the New Frontier Hotel pool. He felt like a star for the first time. It was this stay at the New Frontier, in fact, that convinced Elvis to add a swimming pool to his new Audubon Drive home.

As "I Want You, I Need You, I Love You" reached the top three on the *Billboard* Hot 100, Elvis continued to tour and draw large crowds. A concert in Columbus, Ohio, drew almost two thousand people and, for the first time, Colonel Parker asked $2.50 a ticket. There was astonishment over the ticket price, because a $1.50 ticket was usual. The publicity in national magazines continued to generate interest in Presley's career, however, and with a mini publicity industry growing up around Elvis, the Colonel had decided to test the limits of his celebrity.

The May 1956 issue of *Country and Western Jamboree* featured an article "Overnight Stardom Comes to Elvis Presley." The article, which read like a publicity handout from Colonel Parker, traced Elvis' short-term popularity, ignoring the years he had worked at his craft in favor of a false view emphasizing a quick and effortless rise to fame. The inconsistency of the media bothered Elvis tremendously, and he didn't like reading the early accounts of his life. Sometimes it seemed to Elvis that if he wasn't being vilified by the press, he was being damned by faint praise.

In June 1956, Elvis signed a contract to appear at the Mississippi-Alabama State Fair in Tupelo. The prospect of this appearance, scheduled for September, pleased Elvis immensely, and his concerts were more energetic as a result. After flying into San Francisco on June 3, 1956, Elvis appeared at the Oakland Auditorium. This northern California town was located across the bay from San Francisco. The Oakland Auditorium was a large hall with a basement bar, and it was the bastion of big band and dance enthusiasts. Periodically, a drunken sailor from the nearby Alameda Naval Station wandered into the hall. Oakland city officials were nervous due to the publicity surrounding Presley's meteoric rise to stardom. After posting a $10,000 bond, Colonel Parker began taking charge. The result was the best rock concert ever to appear in Oakland. In the front row, a twenty-three-year-old sailor, W. Reed Severson, sat transfixed, staring at the Presley phenomenon. "It was an event that was like nothing I had ever seen," Severson remarked. "The girls were screaming, the police looked perplexed....It was something new and we didn't know how to react to it," Severson concluded.

After finishing his two sellout concerts in Oakland, Elvis flew to Los Angeles, where he slept for a few hours at the Knickerbocker Hotel before he began re-

hearsals at ABC-TV for the "Milton Berle Show," which was broadcast on June 6 from 8:00 to 9:00 p.m. Elvis sang "I Want You, I Need You, I Love You" and "Hound Dog." This was the first time that "Hound Dog" was performed on national television. The show also included a short sketch in which Elvis was mobbed by girls. Elvis demonstrated an easy-going acting style, and he joked with Berle about his career. The live show also included Debra Paget, Elvis' co-star in "Love Me Tender."

In its June 13 issue, *Variety* was again hostile in its review of Elvis' Berle show appearance, suggesting that he added nothing to the program. The same day, NBC-TV announced that Elvis would not be allowed to bump or grind when he appeared on the "Steve Allen Show" on July 1. The negative publicity created an unprecedented demand for Presley's concerts, and his appearances drew even larger crowds. *Billboard* was on the money when it suggested in an article—"Presley on Pan but Cash Keeps Rolling"—that whether or not you liked Elvis, there was no denying his popularity.

Back to Recording

Even as his successes accumulated, Elvis was faced with the problem of selecting new material to record for RCA. If he was to continue to sell records, he had to find the right songs. During the spring of 1956, Elvis picked a song from his own 45rpm collection, "Hound Dog," as a potential cover record. The Willie Mae Thornton song had been issued on the Peacock label in 1953, and Elvis recorded his own version on July 2.

Ostensibly penned by Johnny Otis, rights to "Hound Dog" were acquired in 1956 by songwriters Jerry Leiber and Mike Stoller as a result of a nasty lawsuit. They claimed that they had written the song, and that Otis had stolen it. Johnny Otis insisted he wrote the song, but the underage Leiber and Stoller nevertheless won a court judgement against him. Leiber and Stoller, who at the time were not yet twenty-one years old, alleged that Otis had taken advantage of them. Otis tells a quite different story. He points out that Leiber and Stoller "cut me out by some legal maneuver called 'disaffirm the contract'...." Mike Stoller tells the story in another manner. He alleges that he and Jerry Leiber presented Otis with the song, and that Otis allowed the recording of Big Mama Thornton's version of "Hound Dog," claiming authorship for himself.

After losing the case, Johnny Otis went back to the clubs in East Los Angeles and on Western Avenue near Hollywood. As far as he was concerned, the trend of ripping off black artists had continued, and much of the best of mid-1950s rock and roll was the product of black singers and songwriters who received neither royalties nor artistic recognition.

When Elvis decided to record "Hound Dog," Hill and Range, at the behest of Elvis Presley Music, set out to acquire half the musical rights. Elvis did not record it until July, but it was released less than two weeks after it was cut. By the time the legal problems over "Hound Dog" were resolved in the courts, the song had sold more than two million copies, and the controversy had so elevated the importance of Leiber and Stoller as songwriters that Colonel Tom Parker signed them to write Elvis' next big hit, "Jailhouse Rock."

After a series of West Coast concerts in San Diego, Long Beach, and Los Angeles, Elvis flew to Ocean Springs, Mississippi, to spend some time with June Juanico. At the Gulf Hills Dude Ranch, Elvis was joined by his parents, and the week was a pleasant one. The time in Mississippi was important for Elvis, because he was finally able to reflect on his success. Juanico was an old friend, and Elvis could confess his hopes, fears, and thoughts about the future to her.

There was still time for hometown fun, so Elvis went back to Memphis to appear on Channel 13 with an old friend, Wink Martindale. Elvis appeared on Martindale's "Dance Party" program on KLAC-TV. In a brief interview, Presley showed signs that the criticism was hurting him. Nevertheless, the days he spent vacationing and at home helped Elvis to cleanse his mind and store up energy for future tours. There was enormous pressure upon Presley, and the brief respite prepared him to answer the media's renewed assaults. Indeed, it would not be long before Elvis had the chance to defend himself. To make matters worse, Vernon Presley harped at his son to mind his manners, then took off for the beer bars and began to use his celebrity status to chase after as many young girls as possible. Elvis was angered by his father's actions, but he had more serious concerns—despite his penchant for cooperation, the media continued to crucify him for reasons he couldn't understand.

The press couldn't seem to get enough of Elvis. They followed him everywhere, constantly seeking out anti-Elvis spokespersons. In a 1956 issue of *Life* magazine, a Florida preacher is pictured with a strongly-worded statement that Elvis had sold his soul to the devil. Elvis responded to these irresponsible attacks in an interview with Hollywood gossip columnist, Louella Parsons. "I belong to the First Assembly of God Church and have gone to church since I could walk," Elvis protested. "My mother was very mad about this article because it hit at my religion...." To Ronald Smith, Elvis once remarked that he would never let these comments destroy him, although he also admitted that they hurt his feelings enormously.

Mother and Son

When *New York Herald-Tribune* columnist Hy Gardner called Elvis on July 1, 1956, to inquire about his career, Presley was ready to answer Gardner's questions. Displaying a disarming honesty, Elvis informed Gardner that things were happening so rapidly that, yes, he was a bit "confused" by it all. When Gardner tried to embarrass Elvis by asking him if he had smoked marijuana, Presley laughed and denied the rumor. This was the first of many attempts to tie Elvis to drug use or other forms of depraved behavior, none of which were successful. Elvis knew that facing questions and dealing with rumors like these was simply one of the hazards of stardom. The intense pressure that Elvis faced during his first year with RCA took its toll, however. Presley became more and more wary of the press, and increasingly concerned about his image. He seemed to be faced with pressures that would never cease. Being the focus of attention was a tough situation for any average twenty-one-year-old, let alone one who had been thrust into the national spotlight. Constantly on the road, forever unable to rest, Elvis' mother became, now more than ever, the source of stability and love that he needed to survive the swirling cauldron of controversy.

There was never any real conflict between Gladys and Elvis—they had a special relationship. She was

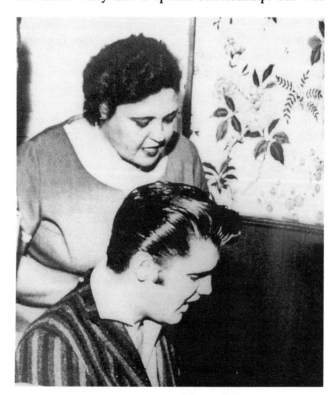

Elvis and Gladys—a special relationship.

the only person Elvis trusted without reservation. As soon as Elvis signed with RCA, signs that the demands of his career were becoming a strain were apparent to Gladys. He was gone from home so much that she complained to Elvis' that his health would suffer. The Protestant ethic of hard work that was an integral part of Elvis' personality prompted him to ignore his mother's warnings. Everyone laughed about Gladys' natural concern for her son's well-being, and urged her to look on the positive side—the family finally had enough money to enjoy themselves. The problem was that Elvis found it increasingly impossible to be alone with his family.

Gladys herself was constantly hounded by the fans. With Vernon out every night drinking beer and basking in the limelight of being the father of the King of Rock and Roll, Gladys was forced to spend a great deal of time alone. Worried that the impression she made was not the right one for her son's image, she began taking diet pills and often went on crash weight-loss programs. Her behavior became increasingly erratic. The dieting was mixed with occasional drinking sprees, and the weight would quickly return, bizarre behavior similar to that which Elvis would engage in later years, behavior in which he would see-saw back and forth between dieting and binging. Much like Elvis in the last weeks of his life, Gladys Presley's moods were sour. Her inability to handle the pressures that resulted from fame and fortune was indeed a harbinger of things to come for her son.

Few people saw the real Gladys Presley in the last two years of her life. She hid behind the fresh-cut flowers, the new furniture, and the shiny cars. The transition to a life of luxury was actually a death sentence for her. She was unable to enjoy the small pleasures of life that were important to her. Gladys' sister Lillian complained that Colonel Tom Parker was the source of the family problems. As Lillian shrewdly observed about the Colonel, "He didn't look like our kind of people." Even Vernon was beginning to get nervous, because the Colonel didn't seem to be interested in anything but business. Initially, Parker had won Vernon's friendship with gifts of hundred-dollar bills, money which Vernon took to local bars and waved under the noses of the awe-struck clientele. It was a time for Vernon to gloat and finally feel like a real man. A few years later, however, Vernon had become as wary as anyone else about the Colonel's obsessive promotions. When the Colonel recognized that Vernon was becoming disenchanted, he slipped him more money and appealed to Vernon's considerable ego, tactics which worked time and time again.

Isolated in this way, then, it was Gladys Presley, who faced most of the family pressures growing from Elvis' stardom. In 1956, a number of Mississippi-Ten-nessee preachers used Presley's rock music stardom to preach against the evils of the new music, prompting Gladys' guilt to increase and leading to a feeling that she had abandoned her religious beliefs. She began having severe headaches each time a preacher denounced her son and rock music in general. Preacher Jimmy Rodgers Snow, Hank's son, was the most conspicuous anti-Presley exponent. Snow had seen fit to tour as a country singer with Elvis in 1954-1955, yet, ironically, a year later, he was splashed all over television and movie screens denouncing the evils of rock and roll. When Snow told his audience that he had been there and watched the devil's music corrupt youth, Gladys became physically ill. As Snow pounded on his Bible and moved his wiry little body around the television screen, Gladys fidgeted uncomfortably and wished her son had taken another path. It hurt Gladys especially deeply to see Southerners vilify Elvis.

Throughout the summer of 1956, the flurry of activity surrounding Elvis' music and blossoming movie career relegated these incidents to the background, however. His appearances on the "Ed Sullivan Show," and the completion of the movie "Love Me Tender," kept him busy. The resulting publicity from his record and movie endeavors made him a superstar but, unfortunately, drove frenzied fans in ever-increasing numbers to the Audubon Drive house. There never seemed to be a private moment. Gladys was a prisoner in a glass menagerie. When out of town, Elvis was on the phone every day to his mother, but this was never enough to reassure and satisfy her.

Although Elvis kept Gladys informed of his triumphs, she was unable to reach any form of inner contentment. While Elvis' telephone voice temporarily soothed her, she soon complained to those around her that stardom had taken her son from her. She could never fully confide her fears, talk about her dreams, or explain her future plans to Elvis. He was simply too busy and excited about his show business success.

When Elvis called to inform his mother that he would return to Tupelo to perform during Elvis Presley Day at the Mississippi-Alabama Fair, she was overjoyed. The concert was located just a mile from where Elvis grew up, and it would be fun to return triumphantly to Tupelo. The celebration, scheduled for September 26, again caused Gladys to worry about her physical appearance. The old snubs from Tupelo's better citizens were still a bitter memory, and Gladys wanted to look her best for the show. After all, she was scheduled to ride in a special parade down Main Street with her famous son. Although the Presleys had all the money anyone could want, Gladys herself made Elvis a garish blue velvet shirt with bright rhinestone buttons to wear in the parade. It was her way of showing the locals that she was still a down-home woman. After shopping for dresses in downtown Memphis, she finally sewed herself a shiny brocade dress with an exaggerated print. Musing that the fabric was her favorite, she decided that the locals would simply have to accept the old Gladys. The dress shows up repeatedly in Gladys' pictures during the last two years of her life. It was her form of rebellion—a homemade dress. A trait that her son possessed in abundance—rebelliousness—was an inherent part of Gladys Presley's personality.

On the day of the parade, Vernon Presley, true to form, reacted just like the "good ole boy" he was, openly flashing the three one-hundred-dollar bills that the Colonel had handed to him just before the parade. It was as if the highest thing that Vernon could aspire to was to be Orville Bean—a big man in a small town who played a special role. "I think that Mr. Presley had a lot of bad feelings about Tupelo," Oleta Grimes recalled. Another local remembers Elvis' dad as "the old tightwad, Vernon." "Vernon never spent his money, he was just showing it off," was a common observation. Mrs. Grimes, one of Presley's grade school teachers and Orville Bean's daughter, was in awe of Elvis as she sat in her Tupelo home talking about the King. A small, frail woman, Mrs. Grimes seemed to say "I'm sorry" to the Presley's for the Tupelo indignities.

The 1956 Tupelo benefit performance was followed by another one the next year, and the proceeds were earmarked to build an Elvis Presley Youth Center. The City of Tupelo announced that it would purchase the land adjacent to the Presleys' former East Tupelo home from none other than Orville Bean. Elaborate plans were announced to install a guitar-shaped swimming pool as part of the complex. In the end, these grandiose schemes never materialized. To this day, Tupelo residents talk about the money that was "embezzled" from Elvis' early concerts. No one has ever substantiated these charges, but it is clear that the failure to carry through on the plans were just the final insult to Elvis Presley. He had donated his time, energy, and considerable reputation to a charity project that was destroyed by local greed and petty politics. "Tupelo was a place where people were concerned about social class," Professor W. Kenneth Holdwitch remarked. A high school classmate of Presley's, Holdwitch was not surprised by the "petty" local attitudes.

When Elvis returned to Memphis, he was plagued by incidents growing out of his celebrity. While having dinner one night in a local restaurant, Elvis playfully put his head on a young girl's shoulder. She threatened to sue, and he settled out of court for $5,550. A few weeks later, Elvis was involved in a fight with Ed Hop-

Signing off.

per, a local gas station attendant, and was forced to appear in a Memphis court. Not only was Elvis cleared of the assault charge, but the court indicated that the incident was Hopper's fault. As Elvis was filling his car up with gas, he had been besieged by fans. Presley ignored Hopper's initial request to move on, and they became involved in a heated argument. When Hopper struck Elvis in the back of his head, Presley responded with a punch to the attendant's mouth. The police arrived, and the minor incident made national headlines. There was a farcical note to the entire court proceeding, and Elvis learned a bitter lesson about the price of fame. He quietly vowed never to become involved in another personal confrontation in public.

The gas station incident also frightened Gladys, who now began to imagine that Elvis' life might be in danger. The problems that she associated with his success prompted her to decide to have a long talk with her son. A face-to-face discussion was impossible because of Elvis' schedule, but every time Elvis called home, Gladys implored him to get out of show business and open an automobile dealership. She made a strong case that he could become a respected local businessman. Elvis laughed at the idea, but Gladys continued to lecture him about the pressures and perils of stardom. She warned him time and time again that the business would kill him. She was right.

The neverending road of movie production, Las Vegas openings, and countless concerts occupied Elvis for the next twenty-one years. By the time of his death, the Sun Records and early RCA days were a dim memory. The image of a "Mythical Elvis" had taken over, and Presley's career reached truly epic proportions. Greil Marcus summarized Elvis' plight: "We see him singing to himself in limousines, backstage...as he waits for his cue." The controlled, mechanical aspects of Presley's later years were an enormous tragedy. He was caught in a career vise that eventually killed him, one which stifled and subverted, rather than enhanced, the com-plete development of his immense talent.

Since his death, the Presley myths have fed incessantly upon themselves. Exploitation books, movies, memoirs, and hidden personal treasures continue to surface at breakneck speed. RCA, having acquired the next best thing to the Midas touch from Colonel Parker, is acutely aware of the necessity to put out "new" Presley products—they simply dust off old relics, repackage the material, continue the hype, and rake in the profits. Somewhere, in the best Elvis tradition, the King of Rock and Roll is cracking a joke about the hideous displays of corporate greed and fan mania which continue in his name. The reason he's grinning is because he doesn't have to be part of it any longer. Indeed, perhaps in his early death it was Elvis who truly had the last laugh.

Early Elvis Presley Concerts & Reviews, 1952-1955

May 1952 Elvis played with Ronald Smith's group at a party.

May 1952 Hi-Hat Supper Club. Elvis was a special guest vocalist with Ronald Smith's group, members of which were essentially the same people as those in Eddie Bond's Stompers.

November 15, 1952 Amateur Show, South Side High School. The concert at 8:00 p.m. was sponsored by the South Side High School band. Elvis and Ronald Smith played acoustic guitars and sang. The Shelby Falen Band, featuring Paul Burlison, played during the contest, but didn't compete for a prize as they had local bookings.

April 9, 1953 Humes High Band Presents Its Annual Minstrel Show, 8:00 p.m. Elvis was listed on the program as the sixteenth performer, a guitarist, and his name was misspelled Elvis Prestley.

Spring 1953 Two appearances with the East Trigg Baptist Church choir, 1189 Trigg Avenue, Memphis. Pastor W. Herbert Brewster.

May 1953 Silver Stallion Nite Club, 1447 Union Avenue, Memphis (amateur night).

May 1953 Coral Club. Elvis sat in with Ronald Smith.

May 1953 Palms Club, Summer Avenue, Memphis (amateur night).

May 1953 Columbia Mutual Towers, Memphis, with a group formed by Ronald Smith.

May 1953 Home for the Incurables, Memphis, with Eddie Bond and the Stompers.

May 1953 Hi-Hat Supper Club, Memphis (amateur night).

June 1953 Goodwin Institute, Memphis.

June 1953 Teen Canteen, Memphis.

June 1953 Doc's Bar, Frayser, Tennessee (Friday night).

June 1953 Creole Club, Memphis, intermission song. B.B. King performed.

June 1953 J. and S. Motors. Elvis sang "Your Birthday Cake" with the Johnny Burnette Trio.

June 1953 VFW hall, Hernando, Mississippi.

August 1953 Airways Used Car Lot. Elvis sang "Take Your Fingers Out of It" and "It Didn't Belong to You" with the Johnny Burnette Trio.

August-September 1953 Audition for the Ouachita Valley Jamboree, Monroe, Louisiana.

September 1953 Red Coach Club, Monroe, Louisiana.

October 1953 Red's Place, Memphis (amateur contest).

November 1953 Eagle's Nest Night Club, Memphis. Elvis sang "That's Amore."

November 1953 Palms Club (amateur night).

January 1954 Cotton Club, West Memphis, Arkansas.

February 1954 Red's Place, Memphis (amateur contest).

March 1954 Memphis (amateur contest).

June 1954 The Earl's Club parking lot, performing on the hood of a car.

June 1954 Doc's Bar, Frayser, Tennessee.

June 1954 VFW hall, Hernando, Mississippi.

June 1954 Home for the Incurables, with Eddie Bond and the Stompers.

Late June 1954 Firestone Workers' Union Hall with Doug Poindexter.

July 1954 Bon Air Club, with Doug Poindexter and the Starlite Wranglers.

July 27, 1954 In an interview with Edwin Howard, Elvis was featured in the *Memphis Press Scimitar*.

July 29, 1954 Bon Air Club, with Doug Poindexter and the Starlite Wranglers.

July 30, 1954 Overton Park Shell, with Slim Whitman, Billy Walker, Sugarfoot Collins, Curly Harris, and Sonny Harvelle. Tickets were $1.00 in advance, $1.25 reserved, general admission $1.00, and kids $.75.

Early August 1954 Corinth, Mississippi. Radio interview on Buddy Bain's radio show (WMCA).

August 7, 1954 Eagle's Nest, with the Tiny Dixon Band. *Billboard*, the nation's top trade music weekly, reviewed Elvis' first single in the "Review Spotlight" section.

August 9, 1954 "Grand Ole Opry" audition.

August 10, 1954 Overton Park Shell with Webb Pierce, Carl Smith, Slim Whitman, Billy Walker, the Louvin Brothers, and Minnie Pearl. Two shows.

August 14, 1954 Bel Air Night Club, with the Jack Clement Band.

August 16, 1954 Eagle's Nest Night Club, with the Jack Clement Band.

August 18, 1954 Benefit performance at Bellevue Park, Memphis.

August 19, 1954 "Louisiana Hayride" Audition (probable).

August 21, 1954 "Louisiana Hayride" Audition (probable).

August 21, 1954 Gladewater, Texas.

August 22, 1954 Magnolia Gardens, Houston, Texas.

August 27, 1954 Eagle's Nest Night Club, with Tiny Dixon Band.

August 28, 1954 Kennedy Hospital, benefit appearance. *Billboard* listed "Blue Moon of Kentucky" on its "Country and Western Territorial Best Sellers," a number 3 hit in Memphis.

August 28, 1954 Late night guest appearance at the Bel Air Club with Jack Clement.

August 31, 1954 Afternoon radio show on KSIJ, Gladewater, Texas, with DJ Tom Perryman.

August 31, 1954 Eagle's Nest Night Club, intermission spot during the S.E.J. Fan Club Dance with host Bob Neal.

September 2, 1954 High school auditorium, Bethel Springs, Mississippi. Carl, Jay, and Clayton Perkins were in the audience. They had a club date in a small bar twenty-five miles out of town.

September 3, 1954 Art's Barbecue, Memphis.

September 4, 1954 Cherry Valley High School, Cherry Valley, Arkansas. Ronald Smith and Kenneth Herman went along and played with Scotty Moore and Bill Black. Bob Neal booked the date.

September 8, 1954 *Memphis Press Scimitar* special supplement on the opening of the Lamar-Airways Shopping Center at 2256 Lamar Avenue featured a picture of Elvis.

September 9, 1954 Lamar-Airways Shopping Center opening.

September 9, 1954 Eagle's Nest Night Club, Memphis (late night solo spot).

September 11, 1954 School auditorium, Poukeepsie, Arkansas. Ronald Smith and Kenneth Herman went along on this date booked by Bob Neal.

September 16, 1954 High school auditorium, Helena, Arkansas, with Maxine and Jim Ed Brown and the Louvin Brothers.

September 18, 1954 Eagle's Nest Night Club, with Sleepy-Eyed John Lepley and the Tiny Dixon Band.

September 24-25, 1954 Eagle's Nest Night Club, with the Tiny Dixon Band.

September 1954 Elvis was signed to appear at the American Legion Hall in Greenwich, Mississippi, by Roundman Knowland. The concert was cancelled because of complaints about Presley's music.

September 1954 KWEM interview with Doug Poindexter, West Memphis, Arkansas.

October 1, 1954 Eagle's Nest Night Club, with the Tiny Dixon Band.

October 2, 1954 "Grand Ole Opry," Nashville. Elvis appeared on the Hank Snow section with Eddie Hill and the Davis Sisters.

October 2, 1954 Ernest Tubb's "Midnight Jamboree" (radio broadcast)

October 6, 1954 Eagle's Nest Night Club (ladies night).

October 9, 1954 Eagle's Nest Night Club.

October 13, 1954 Eagle's Nest Night Club (ladies night).

October 15, 1954 Eagle's Nest Night Club.

October 16, 1954 "Louisiana Hayride," Shreveport. Elvis' first appearance on the show from the Municipal Auditorium broadcast over KWKH. Admission to the "Hayride" was $1.50. *Billboard*, in its "Folk Talent and Tunes" section, reported on Elvis' planned tour with the Louvin Brothers and Jim Ed and Maxine Brown.

October 17, 1954 Lake Cliff Club, Shreveport.

October 20, 1954 Eagle's Nest Night Club (ladies night).

October 22, 1954 "The Old Barn Dance," New Orleans, Louisiana. A New Orleans radio personality, Keith Rush, booked the show and helped Elvis to garner local airplay. "Blue Moon of Kentucky" rose to number 3 on New Orleans radio shortly after this concert.

October 23, 1954 "Louisiana Hayride." During Elvis' second appearance on the "Louisiana Hayride" "Blue Moon of Kentucky" charted at number 6 in Nashville.

October 24, 1954 Lake Cliff Club, Shreveport. Hoot and Curly were also on the bill.

October 29-30, 1954 Eagle's Nest Night Club, with Chuck Reed, Herb Jeffries, and the Tiny Dixon Band.

Late October 1954 The Old Corral, Houston, Texas.

November 4, 1954 The first ad in a Shreveport, Louisiana, newspaper advertised Elvis' appearance on the "Louisiana Hayride."

November 6, 1954 "Louisiana Hayride." Elvis read a commercial for Southern Doughnuts. *Billboard* called "I Don't Care if the Sun Don't Shine"/"Good Rockin' Tonight" a "solid record" in its "Review Spotlight." Elvis signed a one-year contract with the "Louisiana Hayride."

November 13, 1954 "Louisiana Hayride." Tommy Collins, Justin Tubb, Jimmy and Johnny, Maxine and Jim Ed Brown, Rita Robbins, Skeeter Bonn, Jimmy Newman, Willie Jackson, and Faron Young were guests on the "Hayride." *Billboard*'s annual disc jockey poll placed Elvis number 8 in the "Most Promising Country and Western vocalist" category.

November 17, 1954 Eagle's Nest Night Club. "Louisiana Hayride" artists Jimmy and Johnny appeared with Elvis. A $1.00 admission was charged at the door.

November 20, 1954 "Louisiana Hayride." *Billboard* recognized Elvis' recent appearances on the "Louisiana Hayride."

November 27, 1954 "Louisiana Hayride."

December 4, 1954 "Louisiana Hayride."

December 11, 1954 "Louisiana Hayride." Elvis also

guested on the "Red River Roundup" on KWKH at 11:00 p.m. following the "Hayride" show. *Billboard*'s "Folk Talent and Tunes" section mentioned Presley's "hillbilly blues beat" on the "Louisiana Hayride."

December 18, 1954 "Louisiana Hayride."

December 22, 1954 Eagle's Nest, Memphis. (Impromptu show to gauge audience reaction to "Milkcow Blues Boogie."

December 28, 1954 Cook's Hoedown, Houston (Galena suburb). Floyd Tillman and others appeared. Admission was $1.25.

December 31, 1954 Eagle's Nest, Memphis

Late December 1954 Helena, Arkansas, High School with Jim Ed and Maxine Brown and the Louvin Brothers.

Late December 1954 Texarkana, Texas. Interview with Uncle Dudley (Ernest Hackworth) on KTWN.

Late December 1954 Texarkana, Arkansas, High School with Jim Ed and Maxine Brown and the Louvin Brothers.

January 1, 1955 Grand Prize Saturday Night Jamboree, Houston, Texas. The guests included Tommy Sands, George Jones, and Jerry Jerico. Gabe Tucker was the master of ceremonies and he played guitar on stage with the bands.

January 8, 1955 "Louisiana Hayride." *Billboard*'s "Folk Talent and Tunes" column mentioned Bob Neal's management of Presley and his continued popularity.

January 12, 1955 Clarksdale, Mississippi, with Jim Ed and Maxine Brown, Texas Bill Strength, and other members of the "Louisiana Hayride."

January 13, 1955 Helena, Arkansas. A performance from the back of a truck with a $12 guarantee.

January 15, 1955 "Louisiana Hayride."

January 16, 1955 Booneville, Mississippi. Jim Ed and Maxine Brown were on the bill. Before the show, Elvis did an interview with Lynn McDowell on WBIP.

January 17, 1955 Sheffield, Alabama.

January 18, 1955 Leachville, Arkansas.

January 19, 1955 Sikeston, Missouri.

January 22, 1955 "Louisiana Hayride."

January 23, 1955 Gladewater, Texas, area (high school gyms; promoted by Tom Perryman).

January 24, 1955 Midland, Texas, with Billy Walker. The audience was a hefty 1,600 people.

January 25, 1955 Boston, Texas (Colonel Parker in audience).

January 26, 1955 Gladewater, Texas.

January 27, 1955 Cotton Club, Lubbock, Texas, with the Jimmy Rodgers Snow show.

January 28, 1955 Creole Club, Mobile, Alabama.

January 29, 1955 Eagle's Hall, Houston, Texas. *Billboard* reviewed "Milkcow Blues Boogie," rating it an 80, and "You're a Heartbreaker," rated 76.

Late January 1955 Creole Club, Mobile, Alabama.

February 3, 1955 Town and Country Club, Donaldsonville, Louisiana. This show was booked by Ralph Falsetta, who later became Donaldsonville's mayor.

February 4, 1955 Golden Cadillac Lounge, St. Claude Avenue, New Orleans. This show was booked by Keith Rush. The club catered to a white audience but often featured a black band.

February 5, 1955 Louisiana Hayride. "Uncle Pen" was performed.

February 6, 1955 The Five Star Jamboree at the North Hall Auditorium, Memphis, with Faron Young, Martha Carson, Ferlin Huskey, the Wilburn Brothers, Jim Ed and Maxine Brown, George McCormick, Bill Strength, and The Taters. The admission was $1.00 to $1.75. There were shows at 3:00 and 8:00 p.m.

February 7, 1955 Ripley, Mississippi.

February 10, 1955 Alpin, Texas.

February 11, 1955 Sports Arena, Carlsbad, New Mexico.

February 12, 1955 Legion Hut Dance, Carlsbad, New Mexico.

February 12, 1955 "Louisiana Hayride."

February 13, 1955 Colonel Parker and Bob Neal announced that Elvis was booked for a five-day tour with Hank Snow through the Southwest. No locations and dates were announced but the tour included New Mexico, possibly Arizona, and Texas.

February 15, 1955 Albuquerque, New Mexico, with Faron Young.

February 16, 1955 Odessa, Texas. Elvis joined the Hank Snow jamboree featuring Jimmy Rodgers Snow, Charlene Arthur, and the Duke of Paducah. A crowd of 4,000 turned up at the Odessa show.

February 18, 1955 Monroe, Louisiana, with Hank Snow jamboree.

February 19, 1955 "Louisiana Hayride."

February 22, 1955 Hope, Arkansas, with Mother Maybelle and the Carter Sisters, Jimmy Rodgers Snow, Charley Steward, Uncle Dudley, and the Duke of Paducah.

February 24, 1955 Bastrop, Louisiana (tour ends).

February 26, 1955 Circle Theater, Cleveland, Ohio. The 7:30 p.m. country show was broadcast on WERE. There was a second show at 10:30. Faron Young, the Wilburn Brothers, the York Brothers, and Justin Tubb were on the program.

March 5, 1955 "Louisiana Hayride" (TV). Elvis performed "Uncle Pen" in his first "Hayride" TV show. Later in the year a bootleg 45 of the song appeared in the South.

March 7-11, 1955 Elvis completed a five-day tour of small towns in Tennessee, Mississippi, and Texas, with Jimmy Work, Betty Amos and the Duke of Paducah.

March 12, 1955 "Louisiana Hayride."

March 14, 1955 TV interview on WMAL-TV, Washington, DC. The "Town and Country Jubilee Show" was broadcast over WMAL-TV, an ABC-TV affiliate.

March 15, 1955 "Arthur Godfrey Talent Scouts" and Ted Mack "Amateur Hour" auditions.

March 19, 1955 G. Rolle White Coliseum, Texas A & M University, with Flatt and Scruggs, Little Jimmy Dickens, Archie Campbell, Wilma Burgess, and Debbie Day. (Late afternoon-early evening slot for Elvis.)

March 19, 1955 Eagle's Hall, Houston, Texas. This concert was with Hoot Gibson, a disc jockey on KGRY in Gary, Indiana, Sonny Burns, the Brown Brothers, Tommy Sands, James O'Gwynn, Coye Wilcox, the Dixie Drifters, Ernie Hunter, and Herb Remington.

March 21-25, 1955 Elvis completed a five-day tour of Tennessee, Arkansas, Mississippi, Louisiana, and Missouri, with the Duke of Paducah, Jimmy Work, and Betty Amos. He then flew to Cleveland, Ohio, for a series of concerts.

March 26, 1955 "Louisiana Hayride."

March 28-31, 1955 Circle Theater, Cleveland, Ohio, with Faron Young, the Wilburn and York Brothers, and Justin Tubb.

March 28, 1955 After the Circle Theater jamboree show in Cleveland, Ohio, Bill Randle interviewed Elvis over WERE.

April 1, 1955 Odessa, Texas, at Ector County Auditorium with Onie Wheeler and Floyd Cramer. Admission was $1.25 and the show began at 8:15 p.m.

April 2, 1955 "Louisiana Hayride."

April 3-8, 1955 Arkansas tour with Onie Wheeler (El Dorado, Helena, Pine Bluff, Swifton, Pochahantas, and Texarkana).

April 9, 1955 "Louisiana Hayride."

April 16, 1955 "Big D Jamboree," Sportatorium, Dallas, Texas, with Sonny James, Hank Locklin, Charlene Arthur, and the Belew Brothers, among others. J.F. Dolan promoted this show.

April 23, 1955 "Louisiana Hayride," from Waco, Texas.

April 24-29, 1955 Arkansas tour (Little Rock, El Dorado, Texarkana, and Helena).

April 30, 1955 "Louisiana Hayride," from Gladewater, Texas.

April 1955 Odessa, Texas (late).

April 1955 El Dorado High School (late).

April 1955 Memphis, Tennessee. Catholic girls' high school with Barbara Pittman.

April 1955 Helena, Arkansas (late).

April 1955 Little Rock, Arkansas (late).

April 1955 Hot Springs, Arkansas (late).

April 1955 Texarkana, Arkansas.

May 1, 1955 New Orleans, Louisiana. Elvis joined the Hank Snow jamboree for a twenty-one day, twenty-town tour booked by Colonel Tom Parker. There were thirty-one performers on the show at various times. Among them were Faron Young, Martha Carson, Onie Wheeler, Slim Whitman, Jimmy Rodgers Snow, the Wilburn Brothers, the Davis Sisters, Mother Maybelle and the Carter Sisters, and, of course, Hank Snow.

May 4-5, 1955 Mobile, Alabama, with Hank Snow.

May 6, 1955 Birmingham, Alabama, with Hank Snow.

May 7, 1955 Daytona Beach, Florida, with Hank Snow.

May 8, 1955 Tampa, Florida, with Hank Snow.

May 9, 1955 Macon, Georgia, with Hank Snow.

May 10, 1955 Ocala, Florida, with Hank Snow. A crowd of almost 3,000 showed up. Nervous Ned Needham, a country and western disc jockey on WMOP, Ocala, interviewed Elvis.

May 11-12, 1955 Florida tour (possibly Sarasota and Tampa).

May 13, 1955 Gator Bowl, Jacksonville, Florida, with Hank Snow. A crowd of 14,000 showed up and Elvis' Lincoln Continental was smeared with lipstick. Singer Johnny Tillotson was in attendance at this show.

May 14, 1955 *Billboard* reviewed "Baby Let's Play House" and gave it a 77. The flip side, "I'm Left, You're Right, She's Gone," was rated at 71 and *Billboard* called it a song with "an unusual, rhythmic country chant."

May 15, 1955 Norfolk, Virginia, Arena with Hank Snow (see May 17 for performers).

May 16, 1955 Richmond, Virginia. Elvis closed the show at the Mosque Theater with Martha Carson and Slim Whitman.

May 17, 1955 Norfolk, Virginia; two shows with Hank Snow, Slim Whitman, the Davis Sisters, Onie Wheeler, and Jimmy Rodgers Snow.

May 18, 1955 Roanoke, Virginia, two shows with Hank Snow, Slim Whitman, the Davis Sisters, Onie Wheeler, and Jimmy Rodgers Snow.

May 19, 1955 New Bern, North Carolina, with the Davis Sisters and Martha Carson.

May 20, 1955 Chattanooga, Tennessee. This was the last show of the Hank Snow jamboree tour.

May 21, 1955 "Louisiana Hayride" (special guest: Onie Wheeler). *Billboard*'s annual review of country and western music labelled Presley "the freshest, newest voice" in country music.

May 22, 1955 Magnolia Gardens, Houston, Texas. Onie Wheeler shared the bill with Elvis.

May 23, 1955 Breckenridge, Texas, American Legion Hall.

May 24, 1955 Snyder, Texas, with Dub Dickerson, Chuck Lee, and Gene Kay.

May 25, 1955 Third Annual Jimmie Rodgers Day, Meridian, Mississippi. There was a parade in the morning at which Elvis was booed loudly by local roughnecks. An afternoon barbecue was held at Highland Park. That night at five different locations there was music by various country and western artists.

May 26, 1955 Baseball stadium, Gainesville, Texas, with Onie Wheeler and Frank Starr and the Rock-a-Way Boys.

May 27, 1955 Kilgore, Texas, with Jim Ed and Maxine Brown. An interview with Rex Lawrence was broadcast over radio station KOCA.

May 28, 1955 "Big D Jamboree," Dallas, Texas, with Arlie Duff and Texas Bill Strength.

May 29, 1955 Northside Coliseum, Forth Worth, Texas (afternoon). Martha Carson, Ferlin Huskey, the Carlisles, and Jim Ed and Maxine Brown appeared in a 4:00 p.m. show with a $1.25 admission price ($1.00 advance).

May 29, 1955 Sportatorium, Dallas, Texas (evening). Martha Carson, Ferlin Huskey, the Carlisles, and Jim Ed and Maxine Brown appeared in a show at 8:30 p.m. with a $1.25 admission ($1.00 advance).

May 30, 1955 Fair Park Auditorium, Abilene, Texas.

May 31, 1955 Midland, Texas (7:30 p.m.). Billy Walker appeared with Elvis.

May 31, 1955 Odessa, Texas (8:30 p.m.). Billy Walker appeared with Elvis.

June 1, 1955 Guymon, Oklahoma.

June 2, 1955 City Auditorium, Amarillo, Texas.

June 3, 1955 The Johnson-Connelley Pontiac show room featured Elvis in a 7:00 p.m. concert. He left after an hour for the show at the Fair Park Coliseum later that night.

June 3, 1955 Lubbock, Texas. Ferlin Huskey, Bill Carlisle, Martha Carson, Jim Ed and Maxine Brown, Onie Wheeler, George and Earl, and Simon Crum were on a bill at the Fair Park Coliseum. An ad for the 8:00 p.m. show in the Lubbock *Morning Avalanche* featured Presley's picture next to Ferlin Huskey's.

June 3, 1955 Cotton Club, Lubbock, Texas (midnight session for $100).

June 4, 1955 "Louisiana Hayride."

June 7, 1955 Marianna, Arkansas, with Johnny Cash and Carl Perkins.

June 9-10, 1955 National Guard Armory, Lawton, Oklahoma. Elvis joined the Hank Snow jamboree.

June 11, 1955 "Louisiana Hayride."

June 13, 1955 Bruce, Mississippi.

June 14, 1955 Tupelo, Mississippi. An interview with Bobby Ritter of WTUP was conducted with Elvis to announce that the First Annual WTUP Country and Western Popularity poll placed Elvis first among male singers. Kitty Wells was the top female artist and the Simmons Brothers were voted the most popular band. Cards and letters from sixteen states determined the winner.

June 15, 1955 Gobler, Missouri (B & B Club).

June 16, 1955 El Dorado, Arkansas, High School auditorium with Onie Wheeler, Betty Amos and T. Tommy and Band.

June 17, 1955 Stamford, Texas.

June 18, 1955 "Big D Jamboree," Dallas.

June 19, 1955 Magnolia Gardens, Houston, Texas.

June 20-21, 1955 Beaumont, Texas, with Marty Robbins, the Maddox Brothers, Sonny James, the Belew Twins, the Texas Stompers, and Retta Maddox. This unit continued through June 24, 1955 (two shows).

June 22, 1955 Vernon, Texas.

June 23, 1955 Big Springs, Texas (afternoon barbecue).

June 23, 1955 Lawton, Oklahoma (McMahon Auditorium). Elvis appeared with Leon Payne, Joe Carson, Chuck Lee, and KSWO DJ Cecil Lee.

June 23, 1955 Southern Club, Lawton, Oklahoma (midnight session).

June 24, 1955 Altus, Oklahoma.

June 25, 1955 "Louisiana Hayride."

June 26, 1955 Slovonian Lodge, Biloxi, Mississippi (afternoon show).

June 26, 1955 Municipal Auditorium, Biloxi, Mississippi, with Marty Robbins and Sonny James.

June 27-28, 1955 NCO Club, Keesler Air Force Base, Mississippi.

June 29-30, 1955 Curtis Gordon's Club, Mobile, Alabama, with Marty Robbins and Sonny James.

July 1, 1955 Baton Rouge, Louisiana, Lou Millett booking.

July 2, 1955 Waco, Texas. Elvis appeared on local radio station KEYS to promote his show the following night. *Cashbox* voted Elvis the "Up and Coming Male Vocalist."

July 3, 1955 Shows in Corpus Christi with the Blackwood Brothers and the Statesmen, and in Waco, Texas (exact order not determined).

July 3, 1955 Waco, Texas, with the Statesmen Quartet and the Blackwood Brothers. Lou Millett booking.

July 4, 1955 *Billboard* reported that Elvis had toured the West with stops in Los Angeles and San Francisco. Local newspapers fail to support this, however.

July 4, 1955 City Recreational Building (afternoon), Stephenville, Texas, with the Statesmen Quartet and the Blackwood Brothers. Lou Millett booking.

July 4, 1955 Evening show, DeLeon, Texas, with Slim Willet and the Farren Twins.

July 7, 1955 Sportscenter on Barton Springs Road, Memphis.

July 22, 1955 Pioneer Jamboree, Odessa, Texas, with Ferlin Huskey, the Browns, Tibby Edwards, and Sonny James.

July 23, 1955 "Big D Jamboree," Dallas.

July 24, 1955 The Round-Up Club, 2005 S. Ervay, Dallas, Texas.

July 25, 1955 Tampa, Florida, with Andy Griffith, Ferlin Huskey, Jimmy Rodgers Snow, Marty Robbins, Tommy Collins, Frank Evans, and Glenn Reeves. The show was held at the 116th Field Artillery Armory.

July 26-27, 1955 Orlando, Florida, with Andy Griffith show.

July 28-29, 1955 Baseball stadium, Jacksonville, Florida.

July 30, 1955 Daytona Beach, Florida.

July 31, 1955 Community Center, Sheffield, Alabama, with Webb Pierce, Johnny Cash, Bud Deckelman, and Wanda Jackson.

July 1955 Shelbyville, Tennessee.

August 1-2, 1955 Municipal Auditorium, Little Rock, Arkansas.

August 3, 1955 Tupelo, Mississippi.

August 4, 1955 Camden, Arkansas.

August 5, 1955 Bob Neal's 8th Anniversary Jamboree, Overton Park Shell, Memphis, Tennessee, with Webb Pierce, Red Sovine, Sonny James, Jim Wilson, Johnny Cash, Wanda Jackson, Texas Bill Strength, Bud Deckelman, Charlie Feathers, and The Neal Boys. A reported 4,000 fans showed up.

August 6, 1955 "Louisiana Hayride."

August 8-10, 1955 Gladewater, Texas area, with Jim Ed and Maxine Brown. KSIJ in Gladewater interviewed Elvis.

August 11, 1955 State fair, Dallas, Texas.

August 12, 1955 San Antonio, Texas.

August 13, 1955 Houston, Texas.

Mid-August 1955 Skyline Club, Austin, Texas.

August 15-20, 1955 Elvis made a five-day tour of small clubs and high schools in West Texas. On August 20, 1955, *Billboard*'s "Review Spotlight" lauded "I Forgot to Remember to Forget" and called it a song "certain to get strong initial exposure."

August 22, 1955 Wichita Falls, Texas. This five-day

tour featured Johnny Horton, Betty Amos, David Houston, Tillman Franks, Sonny Trammell, Ray Gorman, and Woody Birdbrain.

August 23, 1955 Saddle Club, Bryan, Texas.

August 24, 1955 Conroe, Texas, with Johnny Horton et al.

August 25, 1955 Sports Arena, Austin, Texas, with Johnny Horton et al.

August 26, 1955 Gonzales, Texas.

August 27, 1955 "Louisiana Hayride."

August 31, 1955 Interview on WMPS in Texarkana, Arkansas.

September 1, 1955 Golden Cadillac Lounge, New Orleans, Louisiana. This date was again booked by Keith Rush.

September 2, 1955 Municipal Coliseum, Texarkana, Arkansas, with Johnny Cash, Charlene Arthur, Floyd Cramer, and Jimmy Day.

September 3, 1955 "Big D Jamboree," Dallas

September 4, 1955 The Round-Up Club, Dallas, Texas, with Dub Dickerson.

September 5, 1955 Forrest City, Arkansas, with Eddie Bond, Bud Deckelman, and Johnny Cash.

September 6, 1955 Bono City, Arkansas. Although Bono had a population of only 311, the paid attendance was 1,152.

September 7, 1955 Sikeston, Missouri.

September 8, 1955 Clarksdale, Mississippi.

September 9, 1955 McComb, Mississippi.

September 10, 1955 "Louisiana Hayride." (Scotty Moore, Bill Black, and D.J. Fontana were driving to Virginia.)

September 11-12, 1955 Norfolk, Virginia, with the Hank Snow All Star Jamboree featuring Cowboy Copas, the Louvin Brothers, and Jimmy Rodgers Snow. Broadcast over WCMS and promoted by Sheriff Tex Davis, the co-writer of "Be-Bop-a-Lula."

September 14, 1955 Asheville, North Carolina.

September 15, 1955 American Legion auditorium, Roanoke, Virginia.

September 16, 1955 New Bern, North Carolina, with the Louvin Brothers and Cowboy Copas.

September 17, 1955 Wilson, North Carolina. *Billboard*'s listing of the "Country and Western Territorial Best Sellers" showed "I Forgot to Remember to Forget" in the Top Ten in Dallas-Fort Worth, New Orleans, Houston, St. Louis, and Richmond.

September 18, 1955 Raleigh, North Carolina.

September 19, 1955 Thomasville, North Carolina.

September 20, 1955 "Old Dominion Barn Dance," Richmond, Virginia. The shows were broadcast over WRVA at 2:30 and 8:30 p.m.

September 21, 1955 Danville, Virginia, with the Louvin Brothers and Cowboy Copas.

September 22, 1955 Kingsport, Tennessee. Elvis followed the Louvin Brothers and sang Bill Haley's "Rock around the Clock." Cowboy Copas closed the show.

September 24, 1955 "Louisiana Hayride."

October 1, 1955 "Louisiana Hayride."

October 3-6, 1955 Tour of small Texas towns.

October 7, 1955 Longview, Texas.

October 8, 1955 "Louisiana Hayride."

October 9, 1955 Lufkin, Texas.

October 10, 1955 Memorial Hall, Brownwood, Texas.

October 11, 1955 Abilene, Texas. The Elvis Presley Jamboree featured Jimmy Newman, Jean Shepard, Bobby Lord, Johnny Cash, Floyd Cramer, Porter Wagoner, Jimmy Day, and Wanda Jackson. There were two evening shows at 7:00 and 9:15 p.m. Admission was $1.00.

October 12, 1955 Elvis Presley Jamboree, Midland, Texas, High School auditorium.

October 13, 1955 Elvis Presley Jamboree, Amarillo, Texas.

October 14, 1955 Elvis Presley Jamboree, Odessa, Texas.

October 15, 1955 Fair Park auditorium, Lubbock, Texas, with Buddy Holly and Bob Montgomery, Jimmy Newman, Floyd Cramer, Jimmy Day, Johnny Cash, and Bobby Lord.

October 15, 1955 Cotton Club, Lubbock (midnight show).

October 16, 1955 Hub Motors, Lubbock, Texas, with Buddy Holly and Bob Montgomery.

October 17, 1955 El Dorado, Arkansas (Jaycee sponsored show).

October 19, 1955 Elvis appeared at mid-day assemblies at Brooklyn High School and St. Michaels High School, Cleveland, Ohio. A short film entitled "A Day in the Life of a Disc Jockey" was shot with Pat Boone, Bill Haley and the Comets, and the Four Lads. The film was never released, according to *Billboard*, due to a technicians' strike. The film was designed to promote disc jockey Bill Randle's career. There was talk that Randle was being groomed to take over Alan Freed's role in the New York radio industry.

October 19-20, 1955 Circle Theater, Cleveland, Ohio, with the Roy Acuff show.

October 21-23, 1955 St. Louis, Missouri, with the Roy Acuff show.

October 24, 1955 Silver Moon Club, Pine Bluff, Arkansas, with the Moonlighters featuring Sonny Burgess.

October 26-28, 1955 County fairgrounds, Prichard, Alabama.

October 29, 1955 "Louisiana Hayride."

October 31-November 5, 1955 Elvis was booked for $85 for the week as a solo act at the NCO club at Keesler AFB. Scotty Moore and Bill Black were back in Memphis. On opening night, New Orleans disc jockey Bill Bennett of WTIX shared the bill with Elvis. Jim Russell, a promotion man who recently migrated to New Orleans from Ohio, introduced Elvis the first night.

November 6, 1955 Sie's Place, Biloxi, Mississippi.

November 7, 1955 NCO club, Keesler AFB. A one-night return after the strong showing late in the previous week.

November 8, 1955 Amory, Mississippi.

November 12, 1955 Carthage, Texas (afternoon).

November 12, 1955 "Louisiana Hayride" (evening).

November 13, 1955 Ellis Auditorium, Memphis, with Hank Thompson, Charlene Arthur, and Carl Perkins. A farewell concert for Texas Bill Strength, who was moving to Minneapolis.

November 14, 1955 Forrest City, Arkansas, with Hank Thompson, Charlene Arthur, and Carl Perkins.

November 15, 1955 Sheffield, Alabama.

November 16, 1955 Camden, Arkansas.

November 17, 1955 Texarkana, Arkansas.

November 18, 1955 Longview, Texas.

November 19, 1955 "Louisiana Hayride." Elvis sang LaVern Baker's "Tweedle Dee." The show was broadcast from Gladewater, Texas.

November 25, 1955 Woodrow Wilson Junior High School auditorium, Port Arthur, Texas.

November 26, 1955 "Louisiana Hayride."

December 2, 1955 Sports Arena, Atlanta, Georgia.

December 3, 1955 State Coliseum, Montgomery, Alabama. "The Talent Search of the Deep South" featured Roy Acuff, Kitty Wells, Johnnie and Jack, Jack Turner, Fred Wamble, and Buddy Hawk. A crowd estimated at 15,000 attended the show.

December 10, 1955 "Louisiana Hayride."

December 16, 1955 L.C. Humes High School benefit, Memphis.

December 17, 1955 "Louisiana Hayride." This show was broadcast from the Hirsch Memorial Coliseum in Shreveport and was a benefit for the YMCA.

December 19, 1955 Swifton, Arkansas, with Johnny Cash and the Moonlighters featuring Sonny Burgess.

December 20, 1955 Little Rock, Arkansas, with Jim Ed and Maxine Brown and the Louvin Brothers.

December 31, 1955 "Louisiana Hayride."

Elvis' Top Ten Memphis Nightclubs:
The Influence of Local Venues

The following list of ten Memphis clubs and dance venues provides an interesting look at the type of music and night life that shaped Elvis Presley's career in the 1953 to 1955 period.

1. **Goodwin Institute:** This was a hall that Marcus Van Story played in, bringing his brand of rockabilly and blues music to Memphis' young people. Elvis played at the Institute in 1953 and 1954 and this venue was instrumental in allowing Presley's talent to develop.

2. **The Teen Canteen:** This was a small room in a building adjacent to Lauderdale Court where fledgling musicians like the Burnette Brothers and Elvis Presley played for free to curious kids.

3. **Doc's Bar:** Located in Frayser, a suburb of Memphis, near Millington AFB, this club allowed Elvis to come in on Friday from 5:00 to 8:00 p.m. and sing for the locals. The club attracted servicemen and Elvis got along very well with the clientele.

4. **VFW Hall, Hernando, Mississippi:** This large, rustic white building was the scene of a number of Presley performances with Eddie Bond and the Stompers. Elvis generally sang pop tunes.

5. **The Home for the Incurables:** This was a state agency for the handicapped. Eddie Bond and the Stompers featuring Ronald Smith and Kenneth Herman played this venue, and Elvis showed up to sit in with the band.

6. **The Eagle's Nest:** This Memphis club had Sleepy-Eyed John Lepley as the booking agent; he allowed Elvis to perform in the club at intermissions. After Presley's first record, the Eagle's Nest was one of many venues that helped to develop Elvis' talent. It was a large, cavernous building that locals frequented in the mid-1950s for the swimming pool as well as the music and liquor.

7. **Silver Stallion Nite Club:** This club featured strange entertainment. A group of performing horses were brought in one night, and Elvis showed up to perform on the amateur nights while he was still in high school.

8. **Bon Air Club:** This club is important because Elvis learned a great deal about the guitar from Doug Poindexter and the Starlite Wranglers. Not only did Poindexter play an innovative guitar, but he allowed Scotty Moore to solo. All this influenced Presley's approach to the music.

9. **The Bel Air Club:** Another important venue that allowed Presley to perfect his act. The Bel Air had a wide variety of music and it allowed more freedom than many of the other clubs.

10. **Palms Club:** This Summer Avenue night spot was a favorite hangout for the locals because of its willingness to allow anyone on stage. It was a crazy place where fights were commonplace and the musicians learned to please the boisterous audience.

Appendix 3
Elvis' Sun Sessions
And Other Early Recordings

THE SUN RECORDS SESSIONS

The Sun Records sessions were ones about which Sam Phillips didn't keep careful written records. In November 1955, when RCA purchased Elvis Presley's contract, fifteen boxes of tapes were forwarded to RCA's Steve Sholes. In Nashville, Sholes listened to the songs on the tapes and made his own notes. Sholes' assistant, Joan Deary, has made the notes available to researchers and, although very cryptic, they cast a great deal of light on the Presley-Sun recordings mystery. (As an example, Sholes frequently wrote the word "Satisfied" in his notes. No one knows if this was a reference to the song of that name, or a reference to the quality of a particular recording session. A source inside RCA, who requested anonymity, recalled hearing fragments of the song "Satisfied" on the Sun tapes when Steve Sholes listened to them in Nashville.)

It is impossible to accurately verify all of the songs that Elvis recorded for Sun, but the following list builds on the pioneering work in Lee Cotten's *All Shook Up: Elvis Day-By-Day, 1954-1977* (Ann Arbor, 1985; available only from Popular Culture, Ink.). Stan Kesler, Ronald Smith, Doug Poindexter, Malcolm Yelvington, Marcus Van Story, Kenneth Herman, Paul Burlison, and Eddie Bond also contributed their recollections of the days at Sun Records. The recordings marked with an asterisk (*) are included because of interviews with the above listed Sun session musicians. Due to the intervening years, these recordings may or may not exist today. (Note: This discography omits the Ed Leek disc "My Happiness"/"That's When Your Heartaches Begin," recorded July 18, 1953, which was not commercially recorded, although it was released by RCA in 1990.)

JULY 5, 1954

1. "Harbor Lights"—Alternate takes 1 through 4.
2. "Harbor Lights"—Master take. This song was first released on the album **Elvis—A Legendary Performer, Volume 2**. (Source: Harry Owens And His Royal Hawaiians)
3. "I Love You Because"—Takes 1 through 5.
4. "I Love You Because"—Two master takes exist for this song: one is a composite of takes 3 and 5, and the other is a composite of takes 2 and 4. In 1974, RCA released take 1 on the album **Elvis—A Legendary Performer, Vol-**

ume 1. (Source: Leon Payne, 1949, and Eddie Fisher, 1950)
5. "That's All Right (Mama)"—Alternate take.
6. "That's All Right (Mama)"—Master take. (Source: Arthur "Big Boy" Crudup, 1947)
7. "I'll Never Let You Go (Little Darlin')"—Probable alternate take; incomplete version.
*8. "Satisfied"—Fragmented; probable uncompleted rehearsal version. (Source: Martha Carson, 1954)
*9. "I'll Never Let You Go (Little Darlin')"—Probable uncompleted rehearsal version. (Source: Jimmy Wakely, 1943)

Musicians: Scotty Moore, guitar; Bill Black, bass; Elvis Presley, guitar.

JULY 6, 1954

1. "Blue Moon Of Kentucky"—Four takes. (Source: Bill Monroe and His Bluegrass Boys, 1947)
2. "I'll Never Let You Go (Little Darlin')"—Fragment or alternate take.
*3. "Blue Moon"—Probable. (Source: Billy Eckstine, 1948, and Ivory Joe Hunter, 1952)
*4. "Just Because"—Probable uncompleted rehearsal version. (Source: The Shelton Brothers, 1942)
*5. "Tomorrow Night"—Probable. (Note: A new backup track was recorded on March 18, 1965, with Chet Atkins as producer. The overdubbing session featured: Grady Martin, guitar; Henry Strzelecki, bass; Buddy Harman, drums; Charlie McCoy, harmonica; and the Anita Kerr Singers, vocals (Source: Lonnie Johnson, 1948)

Musicians: Scotty Moore, guitar; Bill Black, bass; Elvis Presley, guitar.

AUGUST 19, 1954

1. "Blue Moon" (Note: This is an extraordinary session, as Sam Phillips devoted it entirely to one song. There is (or was) a full tape of "Blue Moon" cuts somewhere in the RCA-Victor archives.)

SEPTEMBER 10, 1954

*1. "Tomorrow Night"—Probable long version. (Source: Lonnie Johnson, 1947)

2. "Blue Moon Of Kentucky"—Probable. (Source: Bill Monroe)
*3. "I'll Never Let You Go (Little Darlin')"—Master tape (probable two takes). (Source: Jimmy Wakely, 1943)
*4. "Just Because"—Probable. (Source: Frankie Yankovic, 1948)
*5. "Satisfied" —Small fragment. (Source: Martha Carson, 1954)
6. "Good Rockin' Tonight" (Source: Roy Brown, 1947, and Wynonie Harris, 1948)
7. "I Don't Care If The Sun Don't Shine"—Two incomplete takes and one final take. (Source: Patti Page, 1950) (Note: According to RCA, "I Don't Care If The Sun Don't Shine" was at first not considered for release because the guitar solo was never completed. When finally released in 1965, Chet Atkins had been enlisted to overdub the guitar solo. A version of the undubbed master was later released on **The Complete Sun Sessions**.)

Musicians: Scotty Moore, guitar; Bill Black, bass; Doug Poindexter, guitar; Buddy Cunningham, drum sound; Elvis Presley, guitar.

NOVEMBER 16, 1954
1. "I'm Left, You're Right, She's Gone"—Takes 7 through 12 (two reels of this song existed at one time). (Source: Stan Kesler and Bill Taylor; original song written for Elvis)
*2. "My Baby's Gone"—Probable fragment. (Note: This is a slow, bluesy version of "I'm Left, You're Right, She's Gone.")

Musicians: Scotty Moore, guitar; Bill Black, bass; Johnny Bernero, drums; Elvis Presley, guitar.

DECEMBER 8, 1954
*1. "Uncle Pen"—Probable. (Source: Bill Monroe)
2. "Tomorrow Night" (Source: Lonnie Johnson, 1948)
*3. "Juanita" (Source: Rufus Thomas)
*4. "Blues Stay Away From Me"—A Scotty Moore rehearsal recording session with Elvis' voice off mike.
*5. "How Do You Think I Feel"—A Scotty Moore rehearsal recording session with Elvis' voice off mike.

DECEMBER 20, 1954
1. "Milkcow Blues Boogie" (Source: Kokomo Arnold, 1935; Johnnie Lee Wills, 1941; Moon

Mullican, 1946; and Bob Wills and the Texas Playboys)
2. "You're A Heartbreaker" (Source: Jack Sallee; original song written for Elvis)
*3. "How Do You Think I Feel"

Musicians: Scotty Moore, guitar; Bill Black, bass; Jimmy Lott, drums; and Doug Poindexter, guitar.

JANUARY 1955 (Taped practice session)
1. "I'll Never Let You Go (Little Darlin')"—Alternate version.
*2. "Tomorrow Night"—Probable.
*3. "Satisfied"—Unreleased version. (Source: Martha Carson)

FEBRUARY 5, 1955
1. "Baby Let's Play House" (Source: Arthur Gunter, 1954)
2. "Tryin' To Get To You" (Source: The Eagles, 1954)
3. "I Got A Woman" (Source: Ray Charles, 1955)

Musicians: Scotty Moore, guitar; Bill Black, bass; Doug Poindexter, guitar; Elvis Presley, guitar; and perhaps Johnny Bernero (drums) on "Tryin' To Get To You."

MARCH 5, 1955
1. "I'm Left, You're Right, She's Gone"
2. "I'm Left, You're Right, She's Gone" (Note: The outtakes of "I'm Left, You're Right, She's Gone" (slow version) have been released on **The Complete Sun Sessions**.
*3. "How Do You Think I Feel"—Rehearsal version or fragment with Scotty Moore's guitar.
*4. "You're A Heartbreaker"—Rehearsal version.

Musicians: Scotty Moore, guitar; Bill Black, bass; Doug Poindexter, guitar; Jimmy Lott, drums; Elvis Presley, guitar.

JULY 11, 1955
1. "Mystery Train" (Source: Little Junior's Blues Flames (Little Junior Parker), 1953, and the Turtles.) (Issued by RCA in November 1955.)
2. "I Forgot To Remember To Forget" (Source: Charlie Feathers and Stan Kesler; original song written for Elvis)
3. "Tryin' To Get To You" (Source: The Eagles, 1954)
*4. "When It Rains It Really Pours"—Three takes; one is incomplete, one is a rehearsal cut, and

there is one complete take. (Source: Billy "The Kid" Emerson, 1955.)

*5. "Tennessee Saturday Night"—Probable.
*6. "Tweedle Dee"—Probable. (Source: LaVern Baker)

Musicians: Scotty Moore, guitar; Bill Black, bass; Doug Poindexter, guitar; Johnny Bernero, drums; Smokey Joe Baugh, piano; Elvis Presley, guitar.

LIVE BROADCAST RECORDINGS FOR KWKH's "LOUISIANA HAYRIDE," SHREVEPORT, LOUISIANA, 1954-1956

MUNICIPAL AUDITORIUM, SHREVEPORT, LOUISIANA, OCTOBER 16, 1954

1. "That's All Right (Mama)"
2. "Blue Moon Of Kentucky"

Musicians: Scotty Moore, guitar; Bill Black, bass; Elvis Presley, guitar.

KWKH STUDIO: OCTOBER 25-28, 1954—POSSIBLE RECORDINGS

1. "Give Me More, More, More (Of Your Kisses)"
2. "Blue Guitar"
3. "That's What You Gotta Watch"
4. "Always Late (With Your Kisses)"
5. "Uncle Pen"

ON LOCATION: GLADEWATER, TEXAS, DECEMBER 18, 1954

1. "Tweedle Dee"

Musicians: Scotty Moore, guitar; Elvis Presley, guitar; Bill Black, bass; Jimmy Day, steel guitar; Floyd Cramer, piano.

ON LOCATION: LUBBOCK, TEXAS, JANUARY 27, 1955 (COTTON CLUB)

1. "Shake, Rattle And Roll"—Acetate demo.

Musicians: Scotty Moore, guitar; Bill Black, bass; Unidentified, piano; Elvis Presley, guitar.

MUNICIPAL AUDITORIUM, SHREVEPORT, LOUISIANA, AUGUST 1955

1. "Baby Let's Play House"
2. "Maybellene"
3. "That's All Right"

Musicians: Scotty Moore, guitar; Bill Black, bass; Elvis Presley, guitar.

OTHER LIVE RECORDINGS

EAGLE'S HALL, HOUSTON, TEXAS, MARCH 1955

1. "Good Rockin' Tonight"
2. "Baby Let's Play House"
3. "Blue Moon Of Kentucky"
4. "I Got A Woman"
5. "That's All Right (Mama)"

Musicians: Scotty Moore, guitar; Bill Black, bass; Elvis Presley, guitar.

"LOUISIANA HAYRIDE," SHREVEPORT, LOUISIANA, DECEMBER 16, 1956

1. "Love Me Tender"
2. "I Was The One"
3. "Hound Dog"
4. "Pink Cadillac"

SUN RECORD RELEASES
(FIVE PRESLEY SINGLES)

1. Sun 209 "That's All Right (Mama)" b/w "Blue Moon Of Kentucky" (Release date: July 19, 1954)
2. Sun 210 "Good Rockin' Tonight" b/w "I Don't Care If The Sun Don't Shine" (Release date: September 22, 1954)
3. Sun 215 "Milkcow Blues Boogie" b/w "You're A Heartbreaker" (Release date: January 8, 1955)
4. Sun 217 "I'm Left, You're Right, She's Gone" b/w "Baby Let's Play House" (Release date: April 25, 1955)
5. Sun 223 "Mystery Train" b/w "I Forgot To Remember To Forget" (Release date: August 1, 1955)

Appendix 4
Other Presley Recordings
From the Sun Records Era

ALLEGED/UNRELEASED
PRESLEY SUN RECORDINGS

The following songs were reportedly recorded by Elvis Presley while under contract to Sam Phillips at Sun Records or during the early years of his RCA contract. These songs may or may not exist, but they have been widely reported by collectors, fellow musicians, and record company executives.

"Won't You Play That Simple Melody"
"I Don't Hurt Anymore"
"Tennessee Saturday Night"
"Oakie Boogie"
"That's The Stuff You Gotta Watch"
"Night Train To Memphis"
"Gone"
"You Are My Sunshine"
"Who's Sorry Now"
"You'll Never Walk Alone"
"Without You"
"Love Bug Itch"
"Tiger Man"
"Blue Guitar"
"I Really Don't Want To Know"
"Uncle Pen"
"Casual Love Affair"
"I'll Never Stand In Your Way"
"Rags To Riches"
"I Got A Woman" (RCA lists as on tape)
"Keep Them Cold, Cold Icy Fingers Off Of Me"
"Go Go Go (Down The Line)"
"Always Late With Your Kisses"
"Satisfied" (RCA lists as on tape)
"Tennessee Partner"
"Mona Lisa"
"I'm Beginning To Forget You"
"Earth Angel"
"Rag Mop"
"Cryin' Heart Blues"
"Maybellene"
"Little Cabin On The Hill"
"Juanita"
"Tweedle Dee"
"Noah"
"Give Me More, More, More Of Your Kisses"
"How Do You Think I Feel" (1955; released by
    Bear Family Records)—Scotty Moore instru-

mental rehearsal
"16 Tons"
"The Big Hurt"

(Note: Some of the songs listed above have been released over the years. The released songs are included to suggest that other tunes included in this listing may surface in time.)

SELECTED SONGS PERFORMED BY
ELVIS PRESLEY
ON RADIO & TV SHOWS, AND IN MOVIES:
THE SUN RECORDS PERIOD

The following list is live performance material that appeared on radio, television, and in unreleased movies. This list of songs performed is restricted to the Sun Records era.

**LOUISIANA HAYRIDE SONGS BROADCAST ON
RADIO AND TV 1954-1956**
"That's All Right (Mama)"
"Baby Let's Play House"
"Blue Moon"
"I Forgot To Remember To Forget"
"Blue Moon Of Kentucky"
"I Love You Because"
"Just Because"
"Uncle Pen"
"Tweedle Dee"
"Maybellene"
"Always Late (With Your Kisses)"
"Oakie Boogie"
"Hound Dog"
"Gone"
"I Was The One"
"Love Me Tender"
"That's The Stuff (You Gotta Watch)"
"Cryin' Heart Blues"
"Little Cabin On The Hill"
"Juanita"
"Noah"
"Give Me More, More, More Of Your Kisses"
"Pink Cadillac"

"GRAND OLE OPRY" APPEARANCE

"That's All Right (Mama)" (May have been cut from the program)
"Blue Moon Of Kentucky"

HOUSTON, TEXAS, JANUARY—MARCH 1955

"I Got A Woman"
"Blue Moon Of Kentucky"
"Baby Let's Play House"
"Good Rockin' Tonight"

CLEVELAND'S CIRCLE THEATER, 1955

"I Forgot To Remember To Forget"
"That's All Right (Mama)"
"Blue Moon Of Kentucky"
"Good Rockin' Tonight"

UNIVERSAL STUDIOS MOVIE, CLEVELAND, 1955

In 1955, Elvis Presley appeared at the Circle Theater in Cleveland, Ohio. This was a country music concert hall, and Universal Studios contracted Elvis to appear in a short movie about Cleveland dj Bill Randle. For some time Randle had been an admirer of Elvis Presley's music, and he urged Universal Studios to include Elvis in a movie about Randle's disc jockey experiences. The songs Elvis performed in this movie, which was never released due to a movie technicians' strike, are as follows:

"Blue Moon Of Kentucky"
"That's All Right (Mama)"
"I Forgot To Remember To Forget"
"Good Rockin' Tonight"

The Sun Label' Influence on Elvis Presley

The following list of Sun recordings was compiled through interviews with friends, close associates, and people in the record business. The songs listed below are ones that Elvis listened to before and during his years with Sam Phillips' Sun label. The purpose of this list is to demonstrate the musical diversity and in-depth knowledge of various types of music in Elvis Presley's early life. How much these songs influenced Presley's own performances is unknown, but the list provides a look into Elvis' musical personality.

SUN SESSIONS INFLUENCING ELVIS: BLUES SESSIONS

Jackie Brenston, "Rocket 88." Recorded: March 1951. Released by Chess Records (Chess 1458).

James Cotton, "My Baby" and "Straighten Up Baby." Recorded: December 7, 1953. Released by Sun Records (Sun 199).

Billy "The Kid" Emerson, "When It Rains It Really Pours." Recorded: September 18, 1954. Released by Sun Records (Sun 214).

Rosco Gordon, "Booted." Recorded: August 1951. Released by Chess Records (Chess 1487).

Howlin' Wolf, "Moanin' at Midnight." Recorded: Late 1950. Released by Chess Records (Chess 1479).

Howlin' Wolf, "Saddle My Pony." Recorded: April 17, 1952. Released by Chess Records (Chess 1515).

Herman "Little Junior" Parker, "Love My Baby" and "Mystery Train." Recorded: 1953. Released by Sun Records (Sun 192).

Rufus Thomas, "Juanita." Recorded: April 21, 1952. Released by Chess Records (Chess 1517).

SUN SESSIONS INFLUENCING ELVIS: BLUES-GOSPEL VOCAL GROUPS

The Prisonaires, "Baby Please" and "Just Walkin' in the Rain." Recorded: June 1, 1953. Released by Sun Records (Sun 186).

SUN SESSIONS INFLUENCING ELVIS: COUNTRY MUSICIANS

Carvel Lee Ausborn (Mississippi Slim), "Try Doin' Right." No recording date. Unissued (Bear Family Release-1980s); "Nicotine Fit (Coffin Nails)." Originally unreleased, issued by Redita Records.

Charlie Feathers, "Peepin' Eyes." Recorded: February 17, 1955. Released by Flip Records (Flip 503); "I Forgot to Remember to Forget." Recorded: June-July 1955. Originally unissued.

Harmonica Frank Floyd, "Rockin' Chair Daddy." Recorded: July 1, 1954. Released by Sun Records (Sun 205).

Sidney "Hardrock" Gunter, "Gonna Dance All Night." Recorded: April 1954. Released by Sun Records (Sun 201). (Not recorded in the Sun studio.)

Clyde Leoppard, "Lonely Sweetheart" and "Split Personality." Recorded: February 1955. Released by Flip Records (Flip 502).

Carl Perkins, "Movie Magg" and "Turn Around." Recorded: January 22, 1955. Released by Flip Records (Flip 501).

Carl Perkins, "Gone, Gone, Gone" and "Let the Jukebox Keep on Playing." Recorded: July 11, 1955. Released by Sun Records (Sun 234).

Earl Peterson, "Boogie Blues." Recorded: March 1954. Released by Sun Records (Sun 197).

Doug Poindexter and the Starlite Wranglers, "Now She Cares for Me" and "My Kind of Carrying On." Recorded: May 25, 1954. Released by Sun Records (Sun 202).

Ripley Cotton Choppers, "Silver Bells." Recorded: July 11, 1953. Released by Sun Records (Sun 190).

Howard Seratt, "Troublesome Waters." Recorded: Unknown. Released by Sun Records (Sun 198).

Maggie Sue Wimberly, "How Long." Recorded: September 1955. Released by Sun Records (Sun 229).

Malcolm Yelvington, "Drinkin' Wine Spodee-O-Dee." Recorded: September 1954. Released by Sun Records (Sun 211).

Appendix 6
Musicians Influencing
Elvis' Sun Years

The following list includes musicians who played at Elvis' Memphis recording sessions, influenced his music, or had records that aided in the development of his act. The list also includes singers with an Elvis style who may not have influenced Presley but were important to the developing rockabilly scene.

Many of these artists recorded for Sun Records and played in the same local clubs where Elvis performed. Those listed who didn't record for Sam Phillips' Sun label were important because they drew local musicians to the Memphis clubs. In the late 1940s and early to mid-1950s, the "Golden Age of Rhythm and Blues" brought many black performers to Beale Street and white artists to other local clubs. (Elvis Presley, like many young aspiring white musicians, regularly snuck into these clubs to watch the black, country, and hillbilly acts from the audience.) A number of seminal black blues artists who played in Memphis are listed here, along with other black artists who came into town. The large number of white, country, rockabilly artists who influenced Elvis is important because many of these people recorded after Elvis did. Yet, they had often performed their music in front of Elvis before they themselves went into the studio. A classic case in point is Eddie Bond, who had a Presley rockabilly style before Elvis developed it.

Still others listed below were established recording artists whose 78s influenced Elvis and other Memphis musicians. Some of the artists performed with Presley in 1954-1955 or sought him out for advice. Many of those listed have suggested how pervasive Elvis' influence was during the formative years of rock and roll music, and how he affected them. It is an eclectic list that is designed to show how wide and varied Presley's musical interests and experiences were in the mid-1950s.

Ronald Smith spent more than a hundred hours with me going over the performers and influences shaping Presley's career. Extensive interviews with Stan Kesler, Eddie Bond, Kenneth Herman, Marcus Van Story, Leroy Green, and Paul Burlison were helpful in filling in the blanks.

The choice of recommended albums is one of personal preference and should be viewed in this light. The anthology selections, which also reflect this author's tastes, have one or more cuts by the artist being discussed. This list was compiled after identifying performers who Elvis definitely listened to (according to

friends of his) during the formative years of his career, including artists that Elvis himself never mentioned.

JOHNNY ACE: This legendary blues singer was born John Marshall Alexander on June 9, 1929, in Memphis. After attending LaRose Grammar School and Booker T. Washington University, Ace served in the navy and then joined the Beale Streeters. Working with a young B.B. King, Ace became a major rhythm and blues star. He died backstage during a concert in Houston, Texas, in 1954. A blues singer with a pop vocal style, Ace was one of Presley's favorite singers. His stylish rhythm and blues vocals crossed over into the white-dominated pop market much the way that Presley's songs did a few years later.

Recommended Album(s):
Johnny Ace, Duke Records (EP)-80
Johnny Ace Memorial Album, Duke Records DLP-71

KOKOMO ARNOLD: Born in Lovejoy, just South of Atlanta, Georgia, on February 15, 1901, Arnold was an unlikely musical influence upon Elvis Presley. Arnold moved from Georgia to Buffalo, New York, where he learned his music in the streets. In 1929 Arnold moved to Chicago where he made and sold bootleg whiskey much of his life. He was also a musician who had a race hit in 1934, "Old Original Kokomo Blues." The flip side to this record was "Milk Cow Blues," which Elvis later recorded as "Milkcow Blues Boogie." By 1941 Arnold had given up music and returned to work in local steel mills.

Recommended Album(s):
Kokomo Arnold, Masters of the Blues, volume 4, Collector's Classics CC25
Blues Classics by Kokomo Arnold and Peetie Wheatstraw, Arhoolie Records, edited by Chris Strachwitz

SMOKEY JOE BAUGH: The original piano player with the Snearly Ranch Boys, Baugh was a multi-talented musician. He recorded for Sun Records and hung around Phillips' recording studio in 1954-1955. Like most musicians, Elvis admired the extraordinary talent that Baugh brought to the piano. Stan Kesler and Bill Taylor wrote a blues-based song for Baugh, "The Signifying Monkey," which became a regional hit. Later Chuck Berry took this tune and rewrote it into "Jo Jo Gunne." "The Signifying Monkey" was popular on New

York radio stations, but when the Apollo Theater called Sam Phillips to book Baugh, the Southern musician declined. Alan Freed loved Baugh's piano and was shocked to find out he was a white, country musician. Baugh continues to play with various bands throughout Texas. As a frustrated piano player, Elvis watched Smokey Joe Baugh intently and learned a great deal about the piano.

Recommended Album(s):

Sun Sounds—Special Raunchy Rockabilly, Charly Records CR 30147

Rock Bop Boogie...to the Hula Hop, Sun Records, Charly, LP1021

DEAN BEARD: A Texas-born rockabilly musician, Beard was on the scene in Memphis in the 1950s. He was one of the fledgling acts in Memphis in the mid-1950s, and eventually became the piano player for the Champs. Sam Phillips had Beard record two songs, "Rock Around the Town" and "Rakin' and Scrapin," both of which were not released.

Recommended Album(s):

The Roots of Rock, Volume 5, Rebel Rockabilly, Charly Records CR 30105

Rock Around the Town, Bopcat-700

JOHNNY BERNERO: A studio drummer who played on some of Elvis' Sun cuts, Bernero set a high standard for drummers. He recorded with Thurman Enlow for Sun and such tunes as "Bernero's Boogie," "Rockin' at the Woodchoppers Ball," and "Cotton Pickin' Boogie" were evidence of Bernero's talent. He was the session drummer that Sam Phillips used when he wanted to change his musical direction.

Recommended Album(s):

Sun Box 106, Released by Bear Family Records (5 Bernero tunes are included in this box set)

BILL BLACK: As the original bass player with Elvis, Bill Black has received a great deal of attention. He played with the Starlite Wranglers and was a well-known musician around Memphis before he teamed up with Elvis. A hard-drinking man with a penchant for onstage clowning, Black was instrumental in teaching Elvis how to perform in front of large crowds. In the later part of 1954, Black was important to Presley's success because he was able to neutralize the often hostile country music audiences. In 1958, after a salary dispute with Colonel Tom Parker, he formed the Bill Black Combo. In December 1959, "Smokie, Part 2" hit the *Billboard* pop charts, and the Bill Black Combo had seven more hits over the next two years. On October 22, 1965, Bill Black died while in surgery, and the Bill Black Combo continued under the leadership of

Ace Cannon. Vernon Presley attended the funeral but Elvis was unable to attend and pay tribute to his old friend.

Recommended Album(s):

Bill Black's Greatest Hits, Hi Records SHL 32012

BLACKWOOD BROTHERS: A gospel quartet from Ackerman, Mississippi, that was originally formed in 1939, they once considered Elvis as a replacement member in the group. The Blackwood Brothers also had a younger group, the Songfellows, and both of these quartets influenced Elvis. Because they were Gladys Presley's favorite group, he requested the Blackwood Brothers to sing at her funeral.

EDDIE BOND AND THE STOMPERS: Bond was born on July 1, 1933, in Memphis. He attended Pine Hill Junior High School and South Side High School and then worked for Campbell and Son as a salesman after being discharged from the navy. In the early 1950s Bond played with the Snearly Ranch Boys, and he developed a strong interest in country music. By 1953 Eddie Bond and the Stompers were a fledgling country and western band with rockabilly overtones. Bond, who graduated from Memphis' South Side High School two years before Elvis, was a well-known musician who signed a recording contract with Ekko in 1955 and Mercury in 1956. His band, the Stompers, included two fine musicians, one of whom—guitarist Ronald Smith—was an important influence upon young Elvis. Historians have overlooked the influence of Eddie Bond and the Stompers upon Elvis, because Bond recorded after Elvis was already a regional star. In 1953-1954, however, Bond hired Elvis to sing "pop songs" at the Stompers' engagements. As a result, Elvis was influenced by Bond's rockabilly and country singing style and intrigued by Smith's guitar work. When Elvis' Sun Records sound emerged, it depended heavily upon Bond's style. Bond went on to score the 1973 movie "Walking Tall" and ran for sheriff in Hernando, Mississippi, in 1974. He continues to be an outstanding performer with a strong European following. A successful businessman in Hernando, Bond's records are released to large European sales.

Recommended Album(s):

Eddie Bond: Original Early Recordings, White Label Records, WLP 8876

JOHNNY BRAGG: Johnny Bragg was the lead singer in the Prisonaires. The group was made up of inmates from the Tennessee State Penitentiary. They wrote and recorded for Sun Records. The Prisonaires' best-known song was an r and b hit, "Walking in the Rain." Johnny Ray recorded the song and it became a number 1 pop hit. Johnny Bragg was an important influence upon Elvis' style, and the Prisonaires allegedly appeared with Elvis. It is impossible to confirm when, but they were paroled in 1955. Johnny Bragg was one of the vocalists that Elvis used to develop his style.

Recommended Album(s):
The Prisonaires: Five Beats Behind Bars, Charly Records, CR30176, liner notes by Martin Hawkins

CHARLES BROWN: As a young Texas bluesman, Brown established his fame as a singer and piano player with Johnny Moore's Three Blazers. Born in Texas City, Texas, in 1920, Brown made his fame in Los Angeles blues clubs. After leaving Johnny Moore, Brown had seven Top Ten *Billboard* rhythm and blues hits. There was a cool, relaxed cocktail bar sound to Brown's vocals. When he moved to Memphis, Elvis bought a copy of Brown's "Merry Christmas Baby," which had been on the charts from 1946 to 1948 and continued to sell every year in the Christmas market.

Recommended Album(s):
Charles Brown, Ballads My Way, Mainstream Records S/6035
Charles Brown and Johnny Moore's Three Blazers, Race Track Blues, Route 66 Records, KIX-17
Charles Brown and Johnny Moore's Three Blazers, Sunny Road, Route 66 Records, KIX-5

ROY BROWN: When Roy Brown wrote and recorded "Good Rockin' Tonight," he provided Elvis Presley with his first rock and roll song. Born in New Orleans on September 10, 1925, Brown recorded "Good Rockin' Tonight" in 1948 for de Luxe. In 1950, "Hard Luck Blues" further established Brown's rhythm and blues credentials. He appeared in Tupelo and Memphis in the late 1940s and early 1950s, and Elvis watched him in concert. Edgar Blanchard, Brown's bandleader and guitar player, had Elvis bring him liquor when the group was in Tupelo and Memphis, and this suggests the degree of Brown's influence. The hard-rocking vocal style of Roy Brown had a direct impact upon Presley's own stage show.

Recommended Album(s):
Roy Brown, Boogie at Midnight, Charly R and B Records, CRB 1093

JACKIE BRENSTON: In the debate over what is the first rock and roll song, Jackie Brenston's "Rocket 88" is invariably mentioned. There is no doubt that this song was one of the first, if not the first, rock-oriented tune to influence Elvis Presley. Brenston was born on August 15, 1930, in Clarksdale, Mississippi, a delta town where Highway 49 meets Highway 61. Son House, Charley Patton, and Robert Johnson worked

in the juke joints in the area, and Brenston's music reflected the local blues roots. John Lee Hooker and Eddie Boyd were born in the same area. When Elvis listened to Memphis radio in 1951-52, "Rocket 88" was a major hit. The road to success for Brenston began in February 1951 when he drove north on Highway 51 to Memphis with Ike Turner's band. Sam Phillips was then a twenty-eight-year-old recording neophyte who was interested in finding new acts. On March 3, 1955, at Phillips' Memphis recording studio, Ike Turner's band—featuring the new singer, Jackie Brenston—recorded "Rocket 88." The drive and intensity of Brenston's vocals was impressive to young Sam Phillips, and he never forgot the song. In April 1951, Leonard Chess purchased the "Rocket 88" master and it became one of Chess Records' earliest hits. Not only did "Rocket 88" reach number 1 on the *Billboard* Rhythm and Blues charts, but it prompted Sam Phillips to begin recording local artists. The driving piano accompaniment and the smooth, energetic vocal style in "Rocket 88" appealed to young Elvis. By 1954 Brenston had left Ike Turner and was playing saxophone in Lowell Fulson's band. There is a good possibility that Elvis saw Brenston, because Lowell Fulson was an artist that Elvis went to see at the Club Handy in 1954-1955. While Fulson's band was in Memphis, Brenston was the lead singer. It was ironic that Brenston died at the Kennedy VA Hospital in Memphis on December 15, 1979. He outlived Elvis by more than two years and died in the hospital where Elvis gave his first benefit performance. In his later years, a severe alcohol problem limited Brenston's musical dates. He never recovered from Ike Turner's unwillingness to let Brenston perform "Rocket 88" with the Kings of Rhythm.

Recommended Album(s):
Jackie Brenston and His Delta Kings: Rocket 88, Chess PLP-6027

SONNY BURGESS: Born on May 28, 1931, in Newport, Arkansas, Burgess' formative years were influenced by country music. By the early 1950s, Hank Williams and Lefty Frizzell were Burgess's models In 1953 he formed a band, the Moonlighters. On December 19, 1955, the Moonlighters played in Swifton, Arkansas, with Elvis Presley and Johnny Cash. It was at this concert that Elvis sang the Platters' recently released "Only You."

Recommended Album(s):
Sun—The Roots of Rock, Volume 8, Sun Rocks, Charly Records CR 30115

PAUL BURLISON: The lead guitarist with Johnny and Dorsey Burnette's Rock 'n' Roll Trio, Burlison was an extraordinary guitar player who taught Elvis a great deal about music. Not only did Elvis play with the Rock 'n' Roll Trio at an Airways auto dealership, but they were close friends prior to Elvis' fame. A quiet unassuming man, Burlison became a well-to-do figure in the construction industry while continuing to pursue his musical interests. After Johnny and Dorsey Burnette's deaths, Burlison and more than a dozen Memphis music figures put out a tasteful tribute to the Rock 'n' Roll Trio. At the present time he is the lead guitarist in the Sun Rhythm Section. An extraordinarily gifted musician who has never gotten full recognition for his innovative talents, Burlison remains a gifted guitarist.

Recommended Album(s):

Johnny Burnette's Rock 'n' Roll Trio and Their Rockin' Friends from Memphis: A Tribute to Johnny and Dorsey Burnette, Rock-A-Billy Records-1001

Johnny Burnette, the Rock 'n' Roll Trio: Tear It Up, 17 Rockabilly Classics, Solid Smoke Records-8001, liner notes by Tom Henneberry

DORSEY BURNETTE: The older brother of rockabilly-pop artist Johnny Burnette. Born in Memphis on December 28, 1932, Dorsey began his musical career as a bass player with the Rock 'n' Roll Trio. Like his brother, he worked at Crown Electric with Elvis and was a Golden Gloves boxer. His solo career included the hits "Tall Oak Tree" and "Big Rock Candy Mountain." He also wrote hit songs for Ricky Nelson and Jerry Lee Lewis.

Recommended Album(s):

Dorsey Burnette's Greatest Hits, ERA Records HTE-800

Dorsey Burnette, Things I Treasure, Calliope Records CAL 7006

Dorsey Burnette, Capitol ST-11219

JOHNNY BURNETTE: Born on March 25, 1934, Burnette was musically active in Memphis in 1953, and he was a distinct influence upon Presley. While working at Crown Electric, Burnette put together the Rock 'n' Roll Trio with his brother, Dorsey, and guitar whiz Paul Burlison. During his Memphis years Burnette was musically close to Elvis and they shared a common interest in rockabilly records. As Elvis' music matured it was heavily influenced by Burnette's trio. He wrote hit songs for Ricky Nelson and had solo hits before his untimely death on August 14, 1964.

Recommended Album(s):

Johnny Burnette, the Rock 'n' Roll Trio Tear It Up, 17 Rockabilly Classics, Solid Smoke Records, 8001

JACK CLEMENT: Born in 1932 in Memphis, Clement began his career in a bluegrass duo, Buzz and Jack. In this group, Clement demonstrated that he was a master mandolinist, skilled bassist, innovative steel guitarist, lead guitarist, and part-time drummer. It was as a result of this experience that he became a valued session musician for Sam Phillips at Sun Records. His influence upon Presley was subtle but very direct. He was a session musician when Elvis recorded, and his freewheeling, gregarious personality prompted Clement to give Presley a lot of advice. Elvis used it to his own advantage. In 1955, as a member of Slim Wallace's Dixie Ramblers, Clement played a type of rockabilly music that Elvis loved.

Recommended Album(s):

Sun—The Roots of Rockabilly, Volume 4, Cotton City Country, Charly Records CR 30104

JACKIE LEE COCHRAN: He was born on February 5, 1941, while his parents were visiting relatives in Dalton, Georgia. Growing up in the Louisiana and Mississippi Delta area, Cochran was infused with a love for blues, country, and what became rockabilly music. Jimmy Reed, John Lee Hooker, Muddy Waters, Hank Williams, and Hank Snow's music formed the basis of his unique sound. Cochran was a regular performer in the Dallas area. His appearances on the Cowtown Jamboree in Fort Worth were excellent ones. The "Louisiana Hayride" and the Dallas "Big D Jamboree" were other venues that Cochran successfully performed on in the mid-1950s. Unfortunately, he was labelled a Presley copycat. This caused his unique and well-developed talent to go unnoticed. Although there is no direct evidence that he influenced Elvis, Tommy Sands and others remember Elvis watching Cochran with great interest. His style was much like Presley's but they were friendly and talked together about the new music.

Recommended Album(s):

Swamp Fox, Rollin Rock (M) LP005

ARTHUR "BIG BOY" CRUDUP: A Delta blues musician, Crudup recorded for RCA's Bluebird label. In 1944, "Rock Me Mama" set the standard for postwar blues tunes. "That's All Right (Mama)," "My Baby Left Me," and "So Glad You're Mine" were Crudup tunes that Presley covered. In fact, each of those songs is so similar to Elvis' recorded version that there is no doubt he mimicked Crudup's style. In Crudup's music there is a blues direction that is infused with a hillbilly tone. The songs that Crudup recorded for RCA from 1941 until he left the label in 1954 are significant influences upon Presley.

Recommended Album(s):

Crudup's Rockin Blues, RCA-NL8938, liner notes by Rony Rounce

JACK EARLS: Born on August 23, 1932, in Woodbury, Tennessee, Earls played with Johnny Black in a Memphis band in 1954. Since Black was friendly with Elvis, Earls became a minor influence upon Presley. In 1956 Earls recorded at Sun with Bill Black and Luther Perkins. Earls' band, the Jimbos, cut tunes for Sam Phillips. The Jimbos' 1955 recording, "If You Don't Mind," is an excellent example of Earls' talent.

Recommended Album(s):

The Best of Sun Rockabilly, Volume 2, Charly Records, CR 30124

Rock Around the Town, Bopcat-700

Cotton Chopper Country, Redita-126

BILLY "THE KID" EMERSON: Born William R. Emerson on December 21, 1929, in Tarpon Springs, Florida, he learned to play the piano and joined the Billy Battle Band in 1946. While in the army, Emerson came to Memphis and joined up with Sam Phillips' Sun label. He was an early musical influence and a personal friend of Elvis', and his seminal tune, "When It Rains It Really Pours" was a key blues influence upon Presley.

Recommended Album(s):

Sun Sound Special, Shoobie Oobie, Charly Records, CR 30148

CHARLIE FEATHERS: Born in Holly Springs, Mississippi, on June 12, 1932, Feathers was a studio musician, recording artist, and full-time club performer. His earliest musical training was with friends and family members. Feathers' brother-in-law, Dick Stewart, got him a job working at radio station KWEM, and it was not long before he started playing with a group. A musical genius with a rockabilly tinge to his country voice, Feathers is an innovative guitarist and a gifted singer. He cut some of the most important dubs, "I Forgot to Remember to Forget" and "Good Rockin' Tonight" for Elvis during the Sun years. In an interview in a 1980 issue of the British magazine *Not Fade Away*, Feathers recalled going over to Elvis' house and teaching him to sing some of his early Sun songs. During extensive interviewing in Memphis, I found many people who corroborated Feathers' story. Marcus Van Story and Stan Kesler recorded with Feathers and they give him a great deal of credit for Presley's evolution as a serious musician.

Recommended Album(s):

Charlie Feathers, That Rock-a-Billy Cat, Barrelhouse Records BH 014

Rockabilly's Main Man—Charlie Feathers, Charly Records, CR 30161

Charlie Feathers: The Legendary 1956 Demo Session, Zu Zazz Records ZZ 1001-A

Charlie Feathers: Good Rockin' Tonight, Barrel-

house Records BH-03

The Living Legend—Charlie Feathers, Redita LP-107

HARMONICA FRANK FLOYD: Frank Floyd was born on October 11, 1908, in Tacapola, Mississippi. His early musical influences resulted from medicine shows that traveled through the South. Harmonica Frank, as he called himself, learned a talking blues style that he mixed with hillbilly and pop music. For a time he lived in Memphis as a pig farmer. Harmonica Frank appeared on local radio stations and in concert with the Eddie Hill Band. His eclectic musical style, including the ability to play a harmonica while it was inside his mouth, was a strong influence upon Presley.

Recommended Album(s):

Harmonica Frank Floyd, Adelphi Records, AD 1023

LOWELL FULSON: A Los Angeles-based blues guitarist, Fulson was born in Tulsa, Oklahoma, in 1921. Fulson's "Reconsider Baby" had a strong early influence upon Elvis' blues direction. A powerful guitarist with a smokey blues voice, Fulson played in Memphis and Elvis saw him in concert in 1954 and 1955.

Recommended Album(s):

Lowell Fulson, Chess Blues Masters Series, 2A CMB-205

ROSCO GORDON: Another Sun Records performer, Rosco Gordon was a dynamic blues piano man. Born in Memphis in 1933, Gordon recorded for Sun Records. Gordon had a big hit with "Booted," a tune that Sam Phillips sold to Leonard Chess' Chess label. It was while performing at the Palace Theater on Beale Street in Memphis that Elvis watched Gordon perform. In 1955, "The Chicken" was a Top Ten *Billboard* Rhythm and Blues hit. There is a picture of Elvis and Rosco in the Sun studio control room, which suggests that they were fast friends. Another blues voice who influenced Elvis.

Recommended Album(s):

Rosco Gordon, Keep on Doggin', Mr. R & B, R&B 103, notes by Hank Davis

Rosco Gordon, No More Doggin, Charly CRB 1044, notes by Cliff White

Rosco Gordon, volume 1, Ace Records, CH 26, notes by Ray Topping

Rosco Gordon, volume 2, Ace Records, CH 51, notes by Ray Topping

The Legendary Sun Performers: Rosco Gordon, CR 30133, notes by Martin Hawkins

ARTHUR GUNTER: Born in Nashville on May 23, 1926, Gunter was one of a very few black blues artists attempting to make it in music in the country music capital. The Nashboro Record label in Nashville brought in Arthur Gunter to record "Baby Let's Play House." It was a minor r and b hit for Gunter, but a king size record for Elvis. Ernie Young, the owner of Nashboro, bought the song for $500 from Gunter and it made Young a fortune. It was Gunter's ability to combine blues and country music that helped Elvis break through with his own unique blend of music.

Recommended Album(s):
Arthur Gunter, Blues After Hours, Blue Horizon Records, 2431 012

HARDROCK GUNTER: In 1950, Hardrock Gunter's first record, "Birmingham Bounce" on the Bama label, established Sidney Louis Gunter as an innovative musical figure. Red Foley, a major country music star, covered "Birmingham Bounce," and it rose to number 1 on the country charts. Gunter's songwriting future appeared bright. During the next decade Gunter's mainstream commercial success was minimal, he was an important influence upon the development of rockabilly music. His best-known song, "Jukebox Help Me Find My Baby" on the Cross Country label, was released by Sam Phillips' Sun Records label. This tune was an important influence upon young Elvis Presley. Gunter, who was born on February 27, 1925, eventually became a well-known radio and TV personality in Birmingham, Alabama. In 1951, Hunter's song "Boogie Woogie on a Saturday Night" was released by Decca, and it appeared that Hardrock Gunter was destined for musical stardom. But Uncle Sam intervened, and he was called up from reserve duty for a two-year stint in the armed forces.

Gunter's significance to Elvis Presley's music was in his ability to incorporate a black boogie woogie piano style into his music. It was the feeling and direction of Gunter's music that prompted Elvis to unwittingly incorporate a rock sound in his country tunes. In sum, it was the ability to switch from country to rhythm and blues music that distinguished Gunter's style. It provided the bridge that Elvis needed to infuse traditional country songs with an r and b feeling.

Recommended Album(s):
Hardrock Gunter, Boogie Woogie on a Saturday Night, Charly Records, London, liner notes by Adam Komorowski

WYNONIE HARRIS: Born in Omaha, Nebraska, in 1915, Harris was a jump blues performer who recorded "Good Rockin' Tonight" on December 28, 1947. He beat Roy Brown out with this song and Elvis listened intently to Harris' blues sounds.

Recommended Album(s):

Wynonie Harris, Rock Mr. Blues, Charly R and B Records, CRB 1097

KENNETH HERMAN: A steel guitar player who toured with Jerry Lee Lewis, Johnny Cash, and Roy Orbison, Herman is an inordinately talented musician who fused country and rockabilly music. Herman could also play the bass, and there was talk for a time that he would replace Bill Black and tour with Elvis. Like Ronald Smith, Herman played with Elvis prior to the Sun days and was a close friend of Presley's. An intelligent maverick, Herman carved out a reputation in Memphis as a private investigator while continuing to pursue country music as an avocation. He currently lives in Florida and pursues country music.

Recommended Album(s):
Eddie Bond Sings Carl Smith, Balser Records EB-8983. Herman plays steel guitar on this record.

STAN KESLER: Perhaps the single, most under-rated person at Sun Records—Kesler, a quiet, professorial-type musician, is an arranger and producer of great skill. As an assistant to Sam Phillips at Sun, Kesler was a behind-the-scenes genius who helped to mold the Sun sound. He was also a songwriter and composed "I Forgot to Remember to Forget," "I'm Left, You're Right, She's Gone," and "Playing for Keeps." In the 1960s, Kesler produced two albums for Jerry Lee Lewis and singlehandedly produced the material that made Sam the Sham and the Pharaohs a national act. As a steel and bass guitarist, Kesler remains an outstanding musician. Presently, he is in charge of Sam Phillips' record affairs.

Recommended Album(s):
The Sun Rhythm Section, Old Time Rock N Roll, Flying Fish Records FF445

B.B. KING: Born Riley King on September 16, 1925, in Indianola, Mississippi, King moved to Memphis in 1946 to live with his cousin, Bukka White. He became a well-known dj on WDIA and organized a band, which played on KWEM with Sonny Boy Williamson. He recorded one of Sam Phillips' most acclaimed records, "Three O'Clock Blues," and was the master of ceremonies at clubs that had amateur nights. Elvis frequented these spots and King's music was an important early influence.

Recommended Album(s):
B.B. King on Stage—Live, United Records, US 7736

SID KING AND HIS FIVE STRINGS: In 1953, Sid King appeared as a solo act on the "Big D Jamboree" in Dallas, Texas. Hailing from Denton, Texas, King put together the original Five Strings by recruiting high school friends. A radio show on KDT in Denton made the band a popular local act. Soon they played the Cotton Club in Lubbock, the Cobra Club in Amarillo, a high school gym in Tyler, and were signed by Columbia Records. As one of the groups attempting to make it while Elvis was a Sun recording artist, Sid King and the Five Strings were a strong influence upon Elvis. They played many shows with him and rumor has it that Sid King has a tape with Elvis. Sid King's style was a mixture of country, rockabilly, and early rock and roll, and he had a blues feeling in many of his songs. Elvis loved the group and stayed around to listen to them on the many shows in which they appeared together. Sid King recalled that the shows at the Sportatorium were among his favorites, but he also appeared with Elvis in Austin, Texas.

Recommended Album(s):

Sid King and the Five Strings, Gonna Shake This Shack Tonight, Bear Family Records, BFX 15048

LITTLE JUNIOR PARKER: It was as a harmonica player that Little Junior Parker became recognized as a consummate bluesman. Born on March 27, 1932, in West Memphis, Arkansas, Parker played in Howlin' Wolf's band from 1948 to 1950. Parker had learned much of his technique from Rice Miller in West Memphis. He soon formed his own band, Little Junior's Flames, and Matt Murphy's guitar work distinguished this tight unit. It was after Pat Hare and John Bowers were added on guitar and drums that Parker's music caught Sam Phillips' attention at Sun Records. Parker's first record for the fledgling Sun label, "Feelin' Good," was a rhythm and blues hit. The song that influenced Elvis Presley was Parker's "Love My Baby," because it contained the exact guitar licks and musical tone of Elvis' recording of Little Junior Parker's classic song "Mystery Train." Little Junior Parker's early recordings often featured a saxophone, but they remained in the Delta blues tradition. Pat Hare's lead guitar was the model for Scotty Moore, and Parker's country sounding harmonica was instrumental in shaping Elvis' music. In the early 1950s Little Junior Parker often played on Beale Street, and he was close to B.B. King throughout his professional life. There was a tone to Little Junior Parker's vocals that Elvis imitated. Presley also spent a great deal of time listening to "Mystery Train," and "Feelin' Good."

Recommended album(s):

The Legendary Sun Performers: Junior Parker and Billy Love, Charly Records CR 30135, liner notes by Martin Hawkins

Bluesway Records Presents Junior Parker, Bluesway, ABC Records, BLS-6066

CLYDE LEOPPARD: Born in Arkansas, Leoppard moved to Memphis in 1949 and played with the Snearly Ranch Boys. He was initially a guitarist but took up the bass in 1952 and later switched to the drums. Leoppard's importance is in putting together groups. At the Cotton Club, Leoppard and the Snearly Ranch Boys established a reputation as a top western swing or hillbilly dance band. When the Cotton Club opened in West Memphis in 1949 it was largely due to Leoppard's promise to provide danceable music. The Snearly Ranch Boys and Clyde Leoppard's subsequent bands set a standard for excellence that made other bands strive for a professional sound.

Recommended Album(s):

Sun—The Roots of Rock, Volume 10, Sun Country, Charly Records CR 30117

JIMMY MCCRACKLIN: In the 1953-1955 period, Jimmy McCracklin was a talented blues performer who had not yet had a major hit. Working in Texas, McCracklin toured Mississippi and worked Memphis clubs. His music was played on blues and rhythm and blues radio stations. A prolific songwriter and a dynamic showman, McCracklin played Beale Street and toured the South in 1954-1955 when Elvis was beginning his career. Although they never performed together, Presley had an affinity for McCracklin's hard-driving blues. When "The Walk" became a major hit for McCracklin in the late 1950s, Presley added the record to his collection. Kenneth Herman remembers McCracklin's records playing at Graceland.

Recommended Album(s):

Jimmy McCracklin, Every Night, Every Day, Imperial 12285

Jimmy McCracklin, Think, Imperial, LP 12297

MISSISSIPPI SLIM: A shadowy figure in Elvis' life, Mississippi Slim was Presley's first musical influence. While living in Tupelo, young Elvis listened to Slim on WELO and crafted his early country music sounds to his music. Born Carvel Lee Ausborn just after the turn of the century, Mississippi Slim was an original, and his 1954 Redita song "Nicotine Fit" is a testimony to his country-rockabilly roots.

Recommended Album(s):

Cotton Chopper Country, Redita-126

BILL MONROE: Born in 1911 on a farm in western Kentucky, Bill Monroe and the Blue Grass Boys bridged the gap between the country music style of the 1930s and the modern country sound. Although Monroe is credited with popularizing "bluegrass" music, he was equally adept at hillbilly and rockabilly music. Elvis listened to Monroe's version of "Uncle Pen" and "Blue

Moon of Kentucky." Like Elvis, Monroe was influenced by black music. Arnold Schultz, a black guitarist and fiddler, worked with Monroe at country dances and helped to develop his infused blues style. During interviews Monroe frequently mentioned that he loved "Negro music." The song "Uncle Pen" was written for his mother's brother, Uncle Pen Vanderver, a fiddler, who inspired Monroe musically.

Recommended Album(s):
Monroe Brothers, Early Bluegrass Music, Camden 774

SCOTTY MOORE: One of the finest rockabilly guitarists in Memphis, Moore was born on December 27, 1931, in Gadsden, Tennessee. After serving an apprentice period as a dj on a country radio show on WBRO in Washington, Moore moved on to Nashville session work. He began recording in the early 1950s, appearing on Eddie Hills' "Hot Guitar" record for Mercury. Soon Moore was a regular with a number of Memphis bands. In 1954, he became Elvis' guitarist and first manager. He is considered one of the finest guitarists in music history and continues to be active in Nashville music circles.

Recommended Album(s):
Guitar That Changed the World (Plays Elvis Hits), EPIC LN 24103

EARL PETERSON: Peterson was born on February 24, 1927, in Paxton, Illinois. He began studying law but drifted into country music. As a teen-age dj on WOAP in Owosso, Michigan, Peterson developed a following and moved on to WOEN in Mt. Pleasant, Michigan. After forming "Earl's Melody Trails Show," Peterson came to Memphis in 1954 and recorded for Sun. It was Peterson's musical direction and singing style that was important in influencing young Elvis Presley.

Recommended Album(s):
Sun Sounds Special Tennessee Country, Sun Records, Charly Records CR 30150

BARBARA PITTMAN: In 1954, Barbara Pittman's mother brought her to the Eagle's Nest where she sang at intermissions. She also sang with the Snearly Ranch Boys at the Cotton Club in West Memphis, Arkansas. Legend has it that Elvis recommended Barbara to Sleepy-Eyed John Lepley at the Eagle's Nest and he signed her after an audition. She also dated Elvis for a time, and went on to record for Sun. Stan Kesler's tune "Playing for Keeps" was the demo song she used when auditioning for Sam Phillips at Sun. The song had been written for Elvis, and Barbara performed it in a Presley vein. She was one of the most talented female country-rockabilly singers in Memphis.

Recommended Album(s):
Barbara Pittman, the Original Sun Sides, Rockhouse Records-LPM 8307

DOUG POINDEXTER: This talented musician was the leader of the Starlite Wranglers. The band included Scotty Moore and Bill Black and was a country band with rockabilly overtones. An innovative guitarist, Poindexter played on Sun sessions for Elvis and Johnny Cash. He never received the proper credit, because Sam Phillips didn't register Poindexter with the musicians' union. The major thrust of Poindexter's talent was as a guitarist, but he was also a carefully organized businessman. His band was one of the three most professional bands in Memphis. The others were the Snearly Ranch Boys and Malcolm Yelvington's group. In the Sun studio, Poindexter was a creative musical force who freely shared his ideas on musical production.

Recommended single and album(s):
Sun 202, "Now She Cares No More for Me" b/w "My Kind of Carrying On," and **Sun—The Roots of Rock, Volume 4, Cotton City Country**
Cotton Chopper Country, Redita-126

BILLY LEE RILEY: Born on October 5, 1933, in Pocohontas, Arkansas, Riley moved to Memphis in 1955 to become a record star. By the summer of 1956 he quit his job to play music full time. In late 1955, Riley worked around Memphis with the Dixie Ramblers and he played in local clubs that Elvis frequented. A fine blues harmonica player, Billy Lee Riley had a sound that Elvis liked. While not an influence upon Elvis, Billy Lee Riley is important as an artist who reflected the mid-1950s Memphis music scene.

Recommended Album(s):
Sun—The Roots of Rock, Volume 8, Sun Rocks, Charly Records CR 30115

RIPLEY COTTON CHOPPERS: The high point of Elvis Presley's early career may have occurred when the Ripley Cotton Choppers refused to let him sing with them. They were a country music band that recorded the single "Blues Waltz" backed with "Silver Bells" (Sun 190). This 1953 record was the first country release on Sun, and it was played extensively on Memphis radio. One of the Ripley Cotton Choppers, Ernest Underwood, was a country music devotee who was openly hostile to the emerging rockabilly music. As a result of the popularity of rockabilly music, Underwood persuaded the group to record only once with Sam Phillips at Sun. Some historians feel that Raymond Kerby, a house painter, was the group's leader. It was Kerby's uncle, Jesse Frost, who sang lead on many of their songs. This may be the reason that Kerby rejected Sam Phillips' suggestion that they use Elvis Presley as the lead singer. The Ripley Cotton Choppers took their name from a group of Tennessee musicians who were popular during the Great Depression. They played live over WREC in Memphis and were a popular local band. One of their earliest recordings, "Paint Slinger Blues," cut in 1952, is a collector's item. Frost's vocal on "Paint Slinger Blues" demonstrates a blues direction despite their country roots.

Recommended Album(s):
Cotton Chopper Country, Redita-126

TOMMY SANDS: Born in Chicago on August 27, 1939, Sands grew up in Texas and Louisiana. He was a regular on Cliffie Stone's Hometown Jamboree in Dallas and appeared as a regular on the "Louisiana Hayride." A rockabilly singer managed by Colonel Tom Parker, Sands toured extensively with Elvis in 1954-1955. Scotty Moore and Bill Black approached Sands to become the lead singer in the Blue Moon Boys after they fought with Elvis. Sands was uncomfortable with this idea, but he played one concert date with Scotty and Bill. His early rockabilly and country recordings were all but forgotten in 1956 when he appeared in the TV show "The Singing Idol." This program catapulted Sands to stardom as a teen idol. During the time he was a rockabilly singer, Sands was close to and very friendly with Elvis. He lives in Hawaii and is presently active on the Oldies but Goodies circuit.

Recommended Album(s):
Sands Storm, Capitol T1081

RONALD SMITH: A South Side High School student who later graduated from Mann Private, Smith dated Barbara Hearn, who eventually went out with Elvis. During his high school years, Smith was a professional musician playing nightly in Memphis clubs. He had to leave South Side High and enroll at Mann Private because of the rigorous demands of his music career. Most Memphis observers rate Smith's guitar work as superior to Scotty Moore's. Because of his musical skill, Ronald became a close friend of Elvis' during his last year at Humes and often went out with him. It was Smith who organized Elvis' first band. In May 1952, they played their first gig at the Hi-Hat and Ronald Smith remembers they didn't get paid. At the Hi-Hat, Mark Waters played drums, Dino Dainesworth played saxophone and clarinet, Smith guitar, and Aubrey Meadows played piano. This band played pop music and hired Elvis as the lead singer. This was essentially Eddie Bond's band, but they were musicians who played rhythm and blues and dance music. This band, with some change in members, played the Columbia Tow-

ers, the Home for the Incurables, and the Kennedy Hospital with Elvis as the lead singer. In September 1954, Smith played at Cherry Valley High School in Arkansas and at the Poughkeepsie, Arkansas, high school. Bob Neal booked these concerts, Elvis got paid, but Ronald Smith, Curtis Alderson, Kenneth Herman, Scotty Moore, and Bill Black didn't get paid for these gigs. "I wasn't hostile, we were young and it was fun playing with Elvis," Smith remarked in 1986. Smith was also the guitarist with Eddie Bond and the Stompers, and his rockabilly guitar riffs were an important influence upon Elvis. Smith also helped Elvis select 45 records and generally talked music with the future King of Rock and Roll. A dedicated historian, Smith has preserved records, badges, memorabilia, and artifacts that trace Presley's musical roots. He is still active as a performer in the Memphis area.

Recommended Album(s):
Smith is the guitarist on Charlie Feathers' song "One Black Rat." At Sun, Smith is the guitarist on Ernie Barton's "Stairway to Nowhere." Sam Phillips listed Roland Janes as the guitarist on this song because Ronald Smith was not in the musicians' union.

WARREN SMITH: Born on February 7, 1933, in Louise, Mississippi, Smith joined Clyde Leoppard's Snearly Ranch Boys and bought a song from George Jones for forty dollars. He took this tune, "Rock and Roll Ruby," to Sam Phillips and it became a Sun Records hit in 1956. The slapping bass of Jan Ledbetter, the drums of Johnny Bernero, and Smith's energetic vocals made this a classic rockabilly record. For years Warren Smith played with Marcus Van Story, Stan Kesler, and a host of talented Memphis musicians. His recording of "Ubangi Stomp" was another successful tune, but it was not long before Smith faded into oblivion. He was not a major influence upon Elvis, but his style and energetic rockabilly records were a subtle reminder to Presley that he would have to continue his rockabilly direction with a high degree of professionalism.

Recommended Album(s):
Warren Smith, Real Rock and Roll, Sun Records, 2 LPs issued by Charly Records, 1988, CDX 23

Sun—The Roots of Rock, Volume 8, Sun Rocks, Charly Records CR 30115

SNEARLY RANCH BOYS: This group was named for Ma Snearly's boarding house, a place some of the local musicians called home. Stan Kesler, Marcus Van Story, Paul Burlison, Warren Smith, Clyde Leoppard, and a host of other musicians played in this impromptu group. The music was hillbilly, western swing, and old-time country. There was often a blues direction, because the musicians were heavily influenced by local black artists.

JAMES VAN EATON: Born on December 23, 1937, in Memphis, Van Eaton was a session drummer for Sun and other labels. His work with Billy Lee Riley on a 1978 session demonstrated that his talent lasted for a long time.

MARCUS VAN STORY: Another relatively obscure, yet seminally important figure in the Sun Records story. As a young man in Mississippi, Van Story was heavily influenced by black blues musicians. When he heard Deford Bailey's harmonica on the "Grand Ole Opry," Van Story was surprised to find that Bailey was black, and he began to eagerly learn from local black artists. As a result Van Story became a multi-talented artist who could play any instrument. In the early 1950s, Van Story played with the Snearly Ranch Boys, and he toured with Warren Smith. Van Story's singing style was one that used a blues harmonica, and he often sang "Milkcow Blues" and Arthur Crudup's "My Baby Left Me." In 1954-1955, Elvis performed with Marcus Van Story on a number of occasions and they were friends from 1953 to 1955. Although he raised a family and worked a day job, Van Story's vocal performances and musical skill had an enormous impact upon young Presley. The significance of Marcus Van Story is that he helped Elvis to pace his early shows. At the Goodwin Institute, where Van Story had a regular show, he taught Elvis to calm down and work the audience. Another important aspect of Van Story's influence is that he taught Elvis to wait for the instrumental break in a song and then give the musicians a chance to finish their licks. "I think Elvis learned a lot from the shows in Memphis," Van Story remarked in 1986.
Recommended Album(s):
Johnny Burnette's Rock 'n' Roll Trio and Their Rockin' Friends from Memphis: A Tribute to Johnny and Dorsey Burnette, Rock-A-Billy Records-1001

ONIE WHEELER: Born on November 10, 1921, in Sikeston, Missouri, Wheeler was a talented musician who formed the Ozark Cowboys in 1950. He was Roy Acuff's harmonica player for a time (mid-1960s) and in the mid-1950s was a fledgling solo artist. A country musician heavily influenced by the blues, Wheeler toured with Elvis in 1954-1955 and was a keen observer of the Presley phenomenon. The intense harmonica solos and rough rockabilly vocals that Wheeler displayed in 1954-1955 were not lost on Presley. As he watched Wheeler work his audience, Elvis learned a great deal about keeping the country crowd entertained.
Recommended Album(s):
Sun—The Roots of Rock, Volume 10, Sun Country Sun Records, Charly CR30117

MALCOLM YELVINGTON: One of the key figures in the Memphis music scene in 1953 through 1955. Yelvington's Star Rhythm Boys employed a growling, rockabilly sound. With a honky-tonk piano, acoustic bass guitar, electric guitar, steel guitar, and piano, the Star Rhythm Boys were Memphis' most innovative sound. Yelvington's musical direction on "Gonna Have Myself a Ball," "Drinkin Wine Spodee-O-Dee," "Rockin with My Baby," "Trumpet," "Mr. Blues," "First and Last Love," "Goodbye Marie," "It's Me Baby," and "Yakety Yak" provided some of the most interesting moments in Memphis rockabilly history. Yelvington's sides on Sun and Meteor are some of the finest cuts in rockabilly history. Yelvington was one of a very few musicians to encourage Elvis Presley to continue his quest for a musical career. Many times Yelvington urged the roughs and the less-talented musicians to leave Elvis to his music. This was partially due to Yelvington's respect for Presley, but the lanky rockabilly artist also performed a similar type of music.
Recommended Album(s):
The Best of Sun Rockabilly, Volume 2
Sun—The Roots of Rock, Volume 10, Sun Country Sun Records, Charly CR30117
Sun Sounds—Special Tennessee Country, Charly Records CR 30150
Rollin' Rockin' Country Style, Sun Records, issued by Charly LOP 1030
Rock Bop Boogie...to the Hula Hop, Sun Records, Charly LP 1021

Sun-Era Elvis Presley
Bootleg 45s, EPs and Albums

This section is a listing of Elvis Presley bootleg 45s from the Sun Record era. The records are divided into two sections: 45s and EPs, and Albums. This is only a partial listing of bootlegs, counterfeits, and other nefarious products. For a complete list of Elvis bootlegs see Lee Cotten and Howard DeWitt's *Jailhouse Rock: The Bootleg Records of Elvis Presley, 1970-1983* (Ann Arbor, 1983; available only from Popular Culture, Ink.).

45 AND EP RECORDS

"Baby Let's Play House"/"Let Yourself Go"
(Marquis Records M 101, 1979, America)

This is a rare release of "Baby Let's Play House." There is no electronic echo and as a result the sound is extremely pure. Speculation is that this is an original Sun recording that was either taken from Sun Records or quietly lifted from the RCA archives. The flip side, "Let Yourself Go," is a primarily instrumental song from a bootleg album **The 68 Comeback**.

"Baby Let's Play House"/"I'm Left, You're Right, She's Gone"
(RCA Victor 47-6383 (counterfeit), 1973, America)

This record was issued to fill the demand for a good counterfeit copy of Elvis' Sun single after it was released by RCA in November 1955. Later black-and-white picture sleeves were added by devoted collectors. This record was printed in large quantities and fifteen years after its release it is still being sold in collector stores. There is also a counterfeit 78 of this record pressed on vinyl of various colors, including black.

"Baby Let's Play House"/"I'm Left, You're Right, She's Gone"
(Sun Records 217 (counterfeit), 1973, America)

This reproduction of Elvis' Sun recording is a triumph for the bootlegger. It deserves a Grammy Award. Not only is the Sun logo perfectly reproduced, but the original 45rpm records were mastered with a 78rpm stylus to produce a sound identical to the original. This is one of five singles on which bootleggers seem to have spent an inordinate amount of time and money in order to recreate the early Sun Records sound. Some of these records were issued with picture sleeves and others were not. (The best known Elvis bootleggers were involved in the simultaneously released five Sun Elvis records.) Taking a chapter from Colonel Tom Parker and RCA, a cadre of bootleggers quietly announced that the five original Sun Elvis Presley records were again available. It is odd that it never occurred to RCA to take the same time and trouble with Elvis' early music. These records flooded vinyl swaps in the 1970s.

"Baby Let's Play House"/"I'm Left, You're Right, She's Gone"
(Sun Records 217 (second counterfeit), 1974, America)

The quality of the second counterfeit pressing is poor.

"Baby Let's Play House"/"I'm Left, You're Right, She's Gone"
(Sun 217, 1977, America)

This release has a light brown cover highlighted with dark brown ink and a picture of Elvis performing at the 1956 Mississippi-Alabama State Fair.

"Baby Let's Play House"/"You're A Heartbreaker"/ "Mystery Train"/"I Forgot To Remember To Forget"
(Sun Records EP 102, 1978, America)

This is a nicely packaged EP. The cover photo is from Elvis' 1956 appearance at the Mississippi-Alabama State Fair in Tupelo. The front cover has a yellow border, which highlights Elvis' picture.

"Blue Moon"/"Just Because"
(RCA Victor 47-6640; picture sleeve only)

A 45 picture sleeve released in 1973. RCA never released a picture sleeve to package these songs. This was counterfeited and produced by an ardent Presley collector.

The Early Days
(Rockin' Records 45-001 (EP), 1976, America)
"I Don't Care If The Sun Don't Shine"/"I'll Never Let You Go (Little Darlin')"/"My Baby Is Gone"/ "Blue Moon Of Kentucky"
(Rockin' Records 45-001 (EP))

The four cuts on this EP were studio outtakes recorded in the Sun studio from July 1954 through February 1955. The songs on this EP were featured on the 1970 bootleg album **Good Rocking Tonight**. An excellent historical document. This EP was reissued two more times with the title **Elvis Presley** (Rockin' Records 001).

Elvis Presley
(Rockin' Records 45-001 (EP—two issues of this
    record), 1977)
    This is a reissue of the double EP "The Early Days."

**"Good Rockin' Tonight"/"I Don't Care If The Sun Don't
    Shine"**
(RCA (counterfeit 45), 1973, America)
    This is one of many counterfeits of this particular
record.

Good Rockin' Tonight
(Sun Records EP 101, 1978, America)
    This EP has four cuts: "Milkcow Blues Boogie,"
"My Baby's Gone," "I'm Left, You're Right, She's
Gone," and the title cut.
    There are at least five different bootlegs or counter-
feits of this Sun record.

The Hillbilly Cat
(Rockin' Records 002 (EP), 1976, America)
    1. "Jailhouse Rock"
    2. "The Truth About Me"
    3. "The Lady Loves Me"
    4. "Tryin' To Get To You"
Only part of the material on this EP is related to
the Sun years. However, the inclusion of the duet with
Ann-Margret, "The Lady Loves Me" from the movie
"Viva Las Vegas," is reason enough to search for this
EP.

"I Got A Woman"/"I Love You Because"
(Sun Records 524 (45), 1978, America)
    There was no Sun record 524, so this is a unique
bootleg version of two of his Sun recordings. Definitely for the hard-core collector.

Live On The "Louisiana Hayride"
(Rockin' Records 45 006 (EP), 1979, America)
    This EP includes three cuts from the "Louisiana
Hayride," along with "I Got a Woman" from a live
Eagle's Hall show in Houston, Texas, in early 1955.
An interesting cover and fine live performances high-
light this EP.

"Milkcow Blues Boogie"/"You're A Heartbreaker"
(Sun Records 215—Various bootlegs and counterfeits
    dating from 1973 through 1977)
    There are at least five different versions of this
Sun record.

"My Baby's Gone"/"Baby Let's Play House"
Sun Records 45—Various bootlegs and counterfeits
    dating from 1970 through 1978)
    There are at least four bootleg or counterfeit ver-
sions.

"Mystery Train"/"I Forgot To Remember To Forget"
Sun Records 223 AND RCA Victor 47-6357— Vari-
    ous bootlegs and counterfeits dating from 1973
    through 1977)
    There are at least five versions of this record.

"That's All Right (Mama)"/"Blue Moon Of Kentucky"
(Chicken Records 101 (counterfeit 45), 1979, America)
    This is my favorite counterfeit Elvis record. The
record label has a chicken looking into a Victrola. The
label is from Catahoula, Louisiana, and is remixed by
Wild Dog Lewis. An inspired piece of counterfeiting
that sold at record swaps for one dollar in the 1970s. A
rare collector's item. There are at least nine counterfeit bootleg versions of this record. Enjoy.

"Tweedle Dee"/"Lawdy Miss Clawdy"
(Sun Records 526 (45), 1979, America)
    There wasn't a Sun record 526. This single is one
of the best early Elvis items for the collector. LaVern
Baker even bought one.

**ELVIS PRESLEY BOOTLEG ALBUMS
FEATURING SUN RECORDS SONGS**

Elvis (LP)
(King Kong Records, 1974)
    1. "Good Rockin' Tonight"
    2. "My Baby Is Gone"
    3. "I Don't Care If The Sun Don't Shine"
    4. "Blue Moon Of Kentucky"
    5. "I'll Never Let You Go (Little Darlin')"
    6. "Mystery Train"
    7. "I Forgot To Remember To Forget"
    8. "Teen Parade"
    9. "Teddy Bear"
    10. "Got A Lot O' Livin' To Do"
    11. "Treat Me Nice"
    12. "Jailhouse Rock"
    13. 1958 Interview
    Cuts one through seven were recorded in the Sun
studio circa 1954-1955. With the exception of "Good
Rockin' Tonight," the remainder of the Sun tunes are
outtakes. This is a poorly packaged bootleg, which had
neither a graphic album cover or liner notes. This is
designed merely to separate you from your money. Avoid
this LP at all costs.

Elvis Special, Volume 2
(Unknown, (10-inch LP))
1. "Peace In The Valley"
2. Uncle Tom's Cabin Interview
3. "Little Darlin'"
4. "Uncle Pen" (Not an Elvis recording)
5. "Separate Ways"
6. "Burning Love"
7. "Ready Teddy"
8. "Twelfth Of Never"

This is a strange mixture of tunes highlighted by the Sun-era's "Uncle Pen," which is not Presley's long-suspected recording. A difficult album to find, it is worthy of the collector.

Elvis You Ain't Nothing But The King
(King Record Company, LPS 2722 (LP), 1979 America)
1. "Ready Teddy"
2. "I Need Your Love Tonight"
3. "Shake, Rattle And Roll"/"Flip Flop And Fly"
4. "I Got A Woman"
5. "Good Rockin' Tonight"
6. "That's All Right (Mama)"
7. "I Don't Care If The Sun Don't Shine"
8. "Rip It Up"
9. "Blue Moon Of Kentucky"
10. "I'll Never Let You Go (Little Darlin')"
11. "Loving You"
12. "Jailhouse Rock"
13. "King Creole"
14. Elvis Tells
15. "I Want You, I Need You, I Love You"
16. "My Baby's Gone"

This album contains material from the Dorsey stage shows, the Eagle's Hall, the 1961 Honolulu benefit show, cuts from the soundtracks of "Loving You," "Jailhouse Rock," and "King Creole." "The Steve Allen Show" and a radio show from 1978 featuring Sam Phillips are sources for other cuts on this LP, which should be entitled **Sun Elvis Meets Movie Elvis**. This is a beautifully packaged bootleg and the sound quality is better than most RCA records. A first class LP that belongs in any collection. The high points include the "electronic duets" with Bill Haley and Elvis Presley singing "Rip It Up," and another spliced version of Buddy Holly and the Crickets performing "Ready Teddy" with Elvis.

The Entertainer, 1954-1976
(Rooster Record Company R LP 501 (LP), 1978, America)
1. "That's All Right (Mama)"
2. "Blue Moon Of Kentucky"
3. "Tweedle Dee"

4. "Flip Flop And Fly"
5. "Good Rockin' Tonight"
6. "Baby Let's Play House"
7. "I Got A Woman"
8. "Blue Moon Of Kentucky"
9. "That's All Right (Mama)"
10. "Polk Salad Annie"
11. "Kentucky Rain"
12. "I Got A Woman"
13. "Don't Cry Daddy"
14. "It's Your Baby, You Rock It"
15. "Don't Think Twice, It's All Right"
16. "Wooden Heart"/"Young And Beautiful"
17. "What Now My Love"
18. "Folsom Prison Blues"/"I Walk The Line"
19. "Return To Sender"

The first eight cuts on this record are live from the "Louisiana Hayride," the Dorsey stage show, and the Eagle's Hall in Houston, Texas. The photos on the cover show Elvis in the 1950s and 1970s. The liner notes are informative and the production is excellent. The sound quality on this LP is superb. A must for the serious Elvis collector.

The First Year—Recorded Live December 1954-February 1955
(Black Belt Records 2 LPS (LP), 1979, America)
1. "Good Rockin' Tonight"
2. "Baby Let's Play House"
3. "Blue Moon Of Kentucky"
4. "I Got A Woman"
5. "That's All Right (Mama)"
6. Interview with Elvis following his last appearance on the "Louisiana Hayride"
7. "Tweedle Dee"
8. "That's All Right (Mama)"
9. "Blue Moon Of Kentucky"
10. The Texarkana Interview

This album contains cuts from the Eagle's Hall, Houston, the Jay Thompson interview from Wichita Falls, Texas, in 1956, "Louisiana Hayride" selections, and an interview by Bob Neal on WMPS radio in Memphis in 1955 to promote a Texarkana, Arkansas, show. This has a newspaper-type cover with an early black-and-white photo of Elvis. The album is on colored vinyl and is an excellent package for the Presley collector. The sound quality is good, considering that some of these recordings were made with early tape recorders.

The First Years
(HALW, Inc. HALW 00001 (LP), 1979, America)
1. First Meeting
2. Discovery of Elvis by Sam Phillips

3. The First Recording Session
4. The Second Recording Session
5. Shows With the Starlite Wranglers
6. On Their Own
7. Stranded in Shreveport, Louisiana
8. "Grand Ole Opry" Appearance
9. "There's Good Rockin' Tonight"
10. "Baby Let's Play House"
11. "Blue Moon Of Kentucky"
12. "I Got A Woman"
13. "That's All Right (Mama)"

This is an historically significant album. It contains key interviews, live performances, and "Scotty Moore Tells His Story" in a revealing interview. The packaging is fair, but the sound quality is excellent. Scotty Moore's interview bits are very important in piecing together the early Elvis Presley story. A "must" for the collector.

Good Rockin' Tonight
(RCA 130.252 (10-inch counterfeit LP), 1978, France)

This is the counterfeit of an album originally released by RCA in France in 1956, and the eight cuts are original Sun recordings. The original 10-inch LP quickly went out of print and is now valued at over $2,000 per copy. It has been counterfeited for years, and bootleg copies regularly turn up in used record stores. Pick this version up, it's a bargain.

Good Rocking Tonight
Bopcat Records (LP), 1974, Holland
1. "Good Rockin' Tonight"
2. "My Baby Is Gone"
3. "I Don't Care If The Sun Don't Shine"
4. "Blue Moon Of Kentucky"
5. "I'll Never Let You Go (Little Darlin')"
6. "Mystery Train"
7. "I Forgot To Remember To Forget"
8. "The Return Of Jerry Lee"
9. "Savin' It All For You"
10. "Milkshake Madamoiselle"
11. Studio discussion
12. "Great Balls Of Fire"
13. "Rock With Me Baby"
14. "Trouble Bound"

This excellent LP from Holland is the Cadillac of Elvis bootleg musical vehicles. If Elvis Presley met Jerry Lee Lewis on vinyl this record would be the instrument. Not only is the album admirably conceived but the packaging and sound quality is superior to many RCA products. But what isn't? The liner notes provide an excellent history of Sun Records. This album was limited to 500 copies and it is the best bootleg LP from the Sun years.

The Nashville Outtakes and Early Interviews
Wizardo Records 312 (LP), 1974, America
1. "Good Rockin' Tonight"
2. "My Baby Is Gone"
3. "I Don't Care If The Sun Don't Shine"
4. "Blue Moon Of Kentucky"
5. "I'll Never Let You Go (Little Darlin')"
6. "Mystery Train"
7. "I Forgot To Remember To Forget"
8. Early interviews

Wizardo Records specializes in bootlegging from other bootleggers. They are the K-Mart of bootleggers. The quality is poor and the product is inferior. Avoid this album as the material is available on other LPs.

Radio Thrills
(Moon Records 101 (LP), 1979, America)
1. Interview with Scotty Moore
2. "That's All Right (Mama)"
3. "Blue Moon Of Kentucky"
4. Texarkana interview
5. "Good Rocking Tonight"
6. "Baby Let's Play House"
7. "Blue Moon Of Kentucky"
8. "I Got A Woman"
9. "That's All Right (Mama)"

This album has a nice cover but the material is available on other bootlegs. The LP contains many early interviews and a number of excellent songs. The sound quality is fair to poor on this bootleg, which should be avoided.

The Rockin' Rebel, Vol. II
(Golden Archives Records GA 300 (LP), 1979, America)
1. "Good Rockin' Tonight"
2. "Baby Let's Play House"
3. "Blue Moon Of Kentucky"
4. "I Got A Woman"
5. "That's All Right (Mama)"
6. "That's All Right (Mama)"
7. "Blue Moon Of Kentucky"
8. "Tweedle Dee"
9. "I Was The One"
10. "Love Me Tender"

The highly professional cover features black-and-white photos of Elvis in 1955, as well as some excellent backstage shots at the "Louisiana Hayride" in 1956. Inside the LP there is a booklet of photos of Elvis live in 1955. This is one of the best bootlegs available, and the sound and packaging is superb. It is an historically significant document and a wonderful bootleg.

The Sun Years

(Sun International Corporation SUN 1001 (LP), 1977,
America)

1. "I Love You Because"
2. "That's All Right (Mama)"
3. "That's All Right (Mama)"
4. "Blue Moon Of Kentucky"
5. "Blue Moon Of Kentucky"
6. "Blue Moon Of Kentucky"
7. "I Don't Care If The Sun Don't Shine"
8. "Good Rockin' Tonight"
9. "I Don't Care If The Sun Don't Shine"
10. "Milkcow Blues Boogie"
11. "You're A Heartbreaker"
12. "My Baby's Gone"
13. "I'm Left, You're Right, She's Gone"
14. "Baby Let's Play House"
15. "Mystery Train"
16. "I Forgot To Remember To Forget"
17. "Mystery Train"
18. "Heartbreak Hotel"
19. Interview
20. "Shake, Rattle And Roll"
21. "Don't Be Cruel"
22. "Love Me Tender"
23. "Hound Dog"
24. Interview
25. "Blue Suede Shoes"
26. Radio announcements

The cover of this LP is not very professionally done. Shelby Singleton's Sun Records company issued this album. It is a travesty and has little to offer the serious collector.

Jerry Osborne's
Elvis Presley Recording

Jerry Osborne, former publisher of *DISCoveries,* one of the premier magazines for rock and roll record collectors, is also a well known author and something of a record detective. After a great deal of investigation, Osborne discovered some important new Presley recordings from the "Louisiana Hayride." He also coordinated the release of the picture disc **To Elvis: Love Still Burning.** This LP was one of the world's first commercially-issued picture disc album. At that point in record collecting history only promotional records were released as picture discs. Released in May 1978, the eleven-song album contained tribute tunes by a wide variety of artists. A portion of the proceeds from the album was donated to the Elvis Presley Memorial Foundation. The album was something of a media sensation and was featured on the front page of *Billboard.* It was coveted by collectors and created a demand for new Presley material. The word on the street was that there were no new Presley recordings to be found, but Osborne didn't believe it.

The most important discovery in Jerry Osborne's research journey came when Dave Kent, the owner of the "Louisiana Hayride," wrote to Osborne and asked if he could help him with some Presley tapes. It was at this point that Osborne found out that there were Presley recordings from the "Louisiana Hayride." Kent wanted to put out an Elvis record with RCA's blessing.

This was Osborne's cue to negotiate a record deal with RCA. "I never had a single problem with RCA. I went to them and went over everything with them," Osborne remarked. These negotiations took place shortly after Presley's death. In 1979, the first edition of Osborne's book *Presleyana,* published by O'Sullivan and Woodside, was dedicated to Dave Kent and the "Louisiana Hayride" for "the extreme confidence he placed in us." I asked Osborne what he meant by this remark. "For trusting me with a copy of the master tape for every single Presley track that he had in his vault," was his reply. This was the first time that Kent had let anything out of his sight because he feared bootleggers. (At that point in time, bootlegging resulted in about ten Elvis LPs a year, as well as six or seven 45s issued during a given twelve month period. There were often as many as six releases of the same album or 45 in various forms. The demand for new Presley records was overwhelming after his death, and for certain collectors the bootlegger filled the void.)

Osborne dealt with RCA in 1979, and they were initially very interested in the material. But only Joan Deary, who was based in Hollywood, realized the historical importance of these cuts. Deary, the head of all Presley record releases at this time, was enthusiastic about the new songs. She recognized the historical value of the "Louisiana Hayride" cuts and did her best to convince RCA's corporate moguls of their importance. Equally impressed was RCA's Canadian President. In Montreal, J. Edward Preston envisioned a worldwide market for any new Presley items, and he urged New York's RCA executive board to consider the new cuts. But the project was doomed to failure. The legal department at RCA, also based in New York, believed that the project lacked commercial appeal. They argued that there was a certain "hillbilly sound" to the "Louisiana Hayride" recordings that made Elvis come across like an amateur. It was the age of disco and the RCA corporate brain trust was listening to the Village People, not to Presley fans. They hadn't yet heard Elvis' version of "Maybellene," but believed the rest of the "Louisiana Hayride" cuts were trite.

The one track on tape that RCA was ultimately interested in releasing was destined to remain outside its grasp. This cut was Elvis' version of Chuck Berry's "Maybellene" and it appealed to the RCA executive who finally heard it. "We didn't want to sell them one track," Osborne recalled, "they made a complete album if you did them all." As RCA didn't want the other tracks, Osborne broke off negotiations. He was determined to release a full Presley record with all the new tracks.

Because of RCA's reluctance to release these songs, a separate agreement was made with Marshall Sehorn and he put out two LPs on his label, Music Works. The two albums on the Music Works label were titled **Elvis: The First Live Recordings** and **Elvis: The Hillbilly Cat.** They were marketed by JEM, and presented the full range of the "Louisiana Hayride" material. The songs included "That's All Right (Mama)," "Blue Moon of Kentucky," "Good Rockin' Tonight," "I Got A Woman," "I Wanna Play House With You," "Maybellene," "Tweedle Dee" and "Hound Dog."

The new songs that Osborne had uncovered excited him. He also felt especially privileged because the "Louisiana Hayride" had selected him to bring the project to fruition. "Dave Kent had never before released the tracks. He sent me a tape with these songs in a box entitled 'Elvis at the Hayride.' The tape was dated Dec 21, 1979 and the record came out in 1981."

Jerry Osborne reminisced: "I went to the 'Louisiana Hayride' and I went through every tape in their vault. It was a marvelous chance to listen to the history of the Hayride. I pulled out songs by a number of artists that I released on an EP: Marty Robbins, Ray Price, etc. I didn't turn up any other new Elvis material. My belief was that there are other songs. I took the tape on his behalf and negotiated with Joan Deary and J. Edward Preston, who represented Canada, and the head of Canadian RCA wanted these songs badly. They really liked 'Maybellene.' It is obvious that RCA didn't realize the full importance of the material. But eventually RCA made an offer of $25,000 for 'Maybellene,' but they didn't want the other cuts. They only wanted 'Maybellene'."

Dave Kent and Osborne reached an agreement two years later in 1982 whereby RCA agreed to manufacture fifty thousand copies of the album at their India-napolis plant and press it on the "Louisiana Hayride" label. RCA would also do all the art work and graphics. The deal also specified that RCA would treat the project as though Kent and Osborne were a regular production customer. The Hayride was given the right to market the material in any way they chose in the U.S. In exchange, RCA received the material and the rights to market and distribute the exact same LP in the rest of the world. When RCA finally released this album, it used the same liner notes, graphics and production package for world market release. The RCA record was essentially the Kent-Osborne release.

"So **Elvis: The Beginning Years** was pressed in Indianapolis and they were shipped to the 'Louisiana Hayride'." As Jerry Osborne came to the end of this story, he made a point that I agreed with, one which I have stressed in this book: RCA just didn't know how to produce and merchandise Presley's records.

The Sun Records Era:
A History of Authenticity

The five Sun Records 45s and 78s that Sam Phillips recorded and released for Elvis Presley are among the most bootlegged and counterfeited records in the industry. The easiest way to identify the originals pressed in Memphis is by the "Push Marks" left by the machine that pushed the final copy of each record off the spindle during the manufacturing process. The push marks are three small circular indentations in a triangular configuration on the label around the spindle hole. Those copies pressed in Los Angeles can be identified by the triangle and handwritten number (known as a Delta number) in the "dead" wax next to the label. Another good clue is that the color of the yellow label and the brown print differs slightly on the original Sun Records from later bootlegs.

There have been a number of attempts to judge the value of the Sun Records that Elvis Presley recorded in 1954 and 1955. Jerry Osborne's book, *Official Guide To Memorabilia of Elvis Presley and The Beatles,* published in 1988, listed the value of the Sun singles. It is currently the best and most accurate book on Presley records. By analyzing the value he places on the records with current market conditions it is possible to gain an insight into the purchase of rare records.

"That's All Right (Mama)" backed with **"Blue Moon of Kentucky"** (Sun Record 209) is listed in the Osborne guide as a $375 to $400 value for a 45 and $200 to $300 for a 78. Neal Umphred's *Elvis Presley Price Guide 1985-1986,* published in 1985, lists this record at $400. This is the Sun Record that has proven easy for collectors to obtain and it's usually purchased below the listed collectors price. However, "Mystery Train" remains the singular easiest record to find for the searching collector.

Recent Record Store Prices: $500.00

"Good Rockin' Tonight" backed with **"I Don't Care If The Sun Don't Shine"** (Sun Record 210) is listed in the Osborne guide as $375 to $400 for a 45 and $200

to $275 for a 78. Neal Umphred's *Elvis Presley Price Guide*, lists the record at $400 for a 45 and $200 for a 78. The obvious conclusion is that the 78 record is one with limited demand for the collector and the 45 is no longer increasing in value.

Recent Record Store Prices: $500.00

"Milkcow Blues Boogie" backed with **"You're A Heartbreaker"** (Sun Record 215) is listed in the Osborne guide as $375 to $425 for a 45 and $200 to $300 for a 78. Neal Umphred's *Elvis Presley Price Guide* lists the record at $500 for a 45 and $250 for a 78. This is the most difficult Presley single to find on the Sun label as it sold poorly, prompting Sam Phillips to press a smaller quantity.

Recent Record Store Prices: $750.00

"Baby Let's Play House" backed with **"I'm Left, You're Right, She's Gone"** (Sun Record 217) is listed in the Osborne guide as $350 to $400 for a 45 and $200 to $250 for a 78 record. Lee Cotten's *The Elvis Catalog,* published by Doubleday in 1987, lists this record for $250. Neal Umphred's *Elvis Presley Price Guide,* 1985-1986, published in 1985, lists the price of Sun Record 217 at $360. This indicates that in three years there was no increase in the value of this Sun single, the first Elvis record to sell well enough to make the national charts.

Recent Record Store Prices: $400.00

"Mystery Train" backed with **"I Forgot To Remember To Forget"** (Sun Record 223) is listed in the Osborne guide as $250 to $300 for a 45 and $200 to $275 for a 78. Neal Umphred's *Elvis Presley Price Guide* lists this record at $360 for a 45 and $180 for a 78. This record sold well at the time, reaching number 1 on the national country charts. In the 1990s it is the easiest Sun single to find. Frequently, it is advertised in collector periodicals at a price below its market value.

Recent Record Store Prices: $300.00

Bibliographic Essay

BIOGRAPHIES

Albert Goldman's *Elvis* (New York, 1981) remains the most interesting general study of Presley's career. Unfortunately, the usefulness of this biography is limited by the author's bias against rock and roll. The research and factual base of Goldman's study is excellent in spots, but his use of psychology and pseudo pop cultural analysis hurts the final product. Jerry Hopkins' two books, *Elvis: A Biography* (New York, 1971) and *Elvis: The Final Years* (New York, 1980), remain the standard interpretive works on Presley's life. An equally important volume is Lee Cotten's *The Elvis Catalog* (New York, 1987), which combines a fine biographical analysis with a collection of memorabilia, icons, and collectibles concerning Presley's career. Cotten's book is a valuable, interpretive work that places Elvis in proper perspective. It is very useful in challenging old stereotypes and questioning many of the common assumptions about Presley's career.

The large number of Presley biographies and recollections by associates has led to some interesting responses from critics. The most thoughtful comments on Presley's career are: Dave Marsh's "A Bad Year For Elvis," *Rolling Stone* (December 24, 1981): 27; Greil Marcus's "He May Be Dead But He's Still Elvis," *Rolling Stone* (October 2, 1980): 87-91; and, finally, Nick Tosches' "The Rise Of Rockabilly," *Country Music* (January-February 1980): 32-35. The Tosches article is particularly useful in defining Presley's early greatness.

Chet Flippo's essays, "Jerry Lee Lewis And The Elvis Demon" and "Saint Elvis," reprinted in *Everybody Was Kung-Fu Dancing* (New York, 1991) are excellent journalistic pieces on Presley's influence upon other performers and on popular culture. These artcles, along with Lester Bangs' "Where Were You When Elvis Died," in editor Greil Marcus' *Psychotic Reactions And Carburetor Dung* (New York, 1987), are important biographical pieces.

On Elvis' early life, the best book is Elaine Dundy's *Elvis And Gladys* (New York, 1985). Dundy lived in Tupelo and gathered a great deal of new information about Elvis and his mother. While the book is marred by a general lack of knowledge concerning rock and roll, nevertheless, it is a sensitive and well-written portrayal of Elvis' life. Priscilla Beaulieu Presley's *Elvis And Me* (New York, 1985) is a sugar-coated look at Priscilla's life with Elvis. The book is basically an apol-ogy for her behavior, with no analysis of Elvis' music. (Priscilla comments that in the late 1960s she knew Elvis was recording good songs, but she wasn't sure which ones were the best. She was too busy doing her hair to notice.)

Marty Lacker, Patsy Lacker, and Leslie S. Smith's *Elvis: Portrait Of A Friend* (New York, 1980) is one of the few books written by an Elvis insider with accurate material and a clear presentation of Elvis' significance to rock music. There is neither hatred nor vengeance in Lacker and Smith's book; Smith has constructed an inside view of Presley's life with emphasis upon the Humes High years. The book is useful in analyzing Elvis' relatives and the role they played in his life.

One of the best academic biographies of Elvis is Patsy Hammontree's *Elvis Presley, A Bio-Bibliography* (Greenwood, CT, 1985). This biography by an English professor and popular culture specialist at the University of Tennessee combines biographical and bibliographical information. In 1972, after watching the documentary film "Elvis: That's the Way It Is," Hammontree began her work about Presley's influence on popular culture. Although she describes herself as a simple fan, her book is the work of a serious scholar. Professor Hammontree has taken all the extant knowledge about Elvis and distilled it into a carefully researched and well-written book. The main value of this volume is its research and careful categorization of periods in Presley's life.

Robert Matthew Walker's *Elvis Presley: A Study In Music* (London, 1980) is the most sophisticated analysis of Presley's musical output. Walker, an English record executive, is thoroughly grounded in Presley's music, and he is able to delineate the best and worst of Presley's songs.

The best example of a fan club book is Valerie Harms' *Trying To Get To You* (New York, 1979). This volume, by the founder of one of Elvis' earliest West Texas fan clubs, is a thoughtful and honest look at Presley's career. As a contemporary of Elvis Presley, Harms analyzed the forces and influences that shaped his character. She is particularly adroit in pointing out how he reacted to the taunts and catcalls of his high school peers and many of those in attendance at his early concerts.

Another charming book by a fan is Arlene Cogan and Charles Goodman's *Elvis, This One's For You* (Castle Books, 1985). As one of four teenage girls that Elvis

331

talked to at Graceland's gate, Cogan was able to create a memoir of Presley's kind and thoughtful manner. This book suggests that there was a wholesome side to Elvis when it came to his fans. It also demonstrates the intense feeling between Presley and his legion of devotees.

Pete Nelson's *When Elvis Rocked The World* (London, 1985) is a highly speculative look at Presley's career, with some excellent pictures from the early years. Nelson adopts a novelist's license to offer some of Presley's thoughts on his high school years. No one in Memphis remembers Nelson coming around to interview the Humes High graduates, but the book is highly entertaining.

The worst books by those close to Elvis include Red West, Sonny West, and Dave Hebler's *Elvis: What Happened?* (New York, 1977). This book, ghost-written by a sensational-minded journalist, Steve Dunleavy, is the first kiss-and-tell book. It presents a great deal of valuable information about the tragic side of Elvis' life, but the volume spends too much time on Red and Sonny West's missionary attempts to save Elvis from "sex, drugs and rock and roll." This is the worst form of exploitative journalism, and it is difficult to verify the accuracy of the material. Almost the very worst book on Elvis is Ed Parker's *Inside Elvis* (Orange, CA, 1978). A Mormon with a strong feeling for Elvis, Parker naively writes that Elvis' fans killed him. A karate instructor, Parker's prose reads like a second-grade storybook and his analysis combines the intellectual qualities of the Three Stooges with the subtle nuances of Don Rickles. The West and Parker volumes fail to analyze Elvis' Sun roots, and are simply examples of exploitation. Becky Yancey and Cliff Lindecker's *My Life With Elvis* (New York, 1977) is a personal glimpse of Elvis' life by a fan who became his private secretary. Yancey was a wide-eyed, fourteen-year-old Memphis teenager when she met Elvis in 1954; by the early 1960s, she was one of Graceland's marginal employees. Her book adds little to Elvis' story.

An important British work is Richard Peters' *Elvis: The Golden Anniversary Tribute* (London, 1984). The Peters volume is a collection of key dates, testimonials by close friends and colleagues, and a listing of songs. As a research tool it is an important asset. Roy Carr and Mick Farren's *Elvis Presley: An Illustrated Record* (New York, 1982) is beautifully illustrated and offers a solid look at Presley's music.

Vince Staten's *The Real Elvis: Good Old Boy* (Dayton, OH, 1978) is an excellent, if somewhat ignored, study of Presley's early years. Although incomplete in research, nonetheless, Staten's work is the first to cover the early Sun years. Interviews with people close to Elvis aided the book's objectivity. It is weak in analyz-

ing the music and there are gaps in the story, but Staten has provided an important link to the early years.

Dee Presley and Martin Torgoff's *Elvis: We Love You Tender* (New York, 1979) is an attempt by Vernon Presley's second wife to cash in on Elvis' death. Thanks to Martin Torgoff's writing skills, the book offers some important windows into Elvis' life. The Sun years are the weakest, but the recounting of Dee Presley's early life offers some interesting insights about growing up during and after World War II.

The worst gossip books on Elvis include May Mann's *Elvis And The Colonel* (New York, 1975). Mann's volume is the "Hollywood gossip columnist" type. She failed to listen to Presley's music, and often misunderstood what he suggested in the interview that made this book possible. To compound this book's problems, it was revised by Mann in 1977 and reappeared under the titles *The Private Elvis* and *Elvis, Why Won't They Leave You Alone*. Mann, who was once Miss Utah, claims that Elvis insisted she tell his story. The only problem was that Mann knew nothing about rock and roll and very little about Elvis Presley.

A very good short biography on Elvis is Todd Slaughter's *Elvis Presley* (London, 1977). As president of the *London Daily Mirror* pop club, Slaughter has clout in English rock politics. He is also an active Elvis collector and a serious mail-order dealer. For years Slaughter has brought planeloads of English fans to Las Vegas, Memphis, and Hollywood. Consequently, Colonel Tom Parker granted Slaughter special privileges in Las Vegas. Slaughter's book has a nice, chatty tone to it.

One of the strangest books on Elvis is Samuel Roy's *Elvis: Prophet Of Power* (Brookline, MA, 1985). Roy's study employs loaded language, stilted prose, and imprecise facts. It is in the same league as Robert Graham and Keith Baty's *Elvis: The Novel* (London, 1984).

In the menagerie of bad books about Elvis, the absolute worst is Jess Stearn's *Elvis: His Spiritual Journey* (Norfolk, VA, 1982). This is an examination of the spiritual side of Elvis' life from someone close to him. The material for Stearn's book comes from Larry Geller, Elvis' personal hairstylist and part-time spiritual adviser. According to the book's publicist, Mr. Geller's specialties are meditation, yoga, healing, and nutrition. English grammar, factual knowledge of Presley's life and music, and editorial humility are apparently *not* his specialties, as they are definitely *not* a part of this book. Even more ludicrous is the fact that Jess Stearn and Larry Geller had the same book published two years earlier as *The Truth About Elvis* (New York, 1980). In the first edition, the publisher, Jove Books, proclaimed on the back cover: "For the first time, here is the long-hidden truth about Elvis--in the remarkable book he yearned to write...Elvis's powers of psychic healing...his vision in the desert...."

Although not the poorest study of Elvis, Paul Lichter's *The Boy Who Dared To Rock: The Definitive Elvis* (New York, 1978) is flawed by the tendency to discuss the author more than Elvis. Lichter's book is unreliable and spends an inordinate amount of time examining the author's alleged relationship with Presley.

John Tobler and Richard Wootton's *Elvis: The Legend And The Music* (New York, 1983) is a beautifully produced Elvis book with a minimum of text.

Marian J. Cocke's *I Called Him Babe* (Memphis, 1980), although low on the overall list of "insider" tomes, is still an interesting book by Presley's nurse. It highlights his compassionate nature and suggests many of Presley's positive human qualities. For the real story on Presley's last years and death, see Charles C. Thompson II and James P. Cole, *The Death Of Elvis: What Really Happened?* (New York, 1991).

Dave Marsh's *Elvis* (New York, 1982) is a large coffee table book with excellent photos and a critical analysis of Elvis' career. Marsh's is a fine popular biography of Elvis in print.

Neal and Janice Gregory's *When Elvis Died* (Washington, DC, 1980) is an important source for Elvis' place in American history. In Chapter 10, "Interpreting the Myth," the Gregorys analyze Elvis' impact upon American popular culture.

Earl Greenwood and Kathleen Tracy's *The Boy Who Would Be King: An Intimate Portrait Of Elvis Presley By His Cousin* (New York, 1990) purports to be an insider book by a close relative. The book is riddled with factual errors, and contains no new information on Elvis. During all my interviews, no one recalled a cousin named Earl Greenwood, presently a real estate agent in Los Angeles. Greenwood's book fails to take account of the material contained in Chapter 2 of the present work, material which was available from the Lee County Archives and the Tupelo Public Library.

PERIODICAL ARTICLES ON ELVIS: THE ROCK PRESS

The rock music press is filled with Elvis material. For blues influences upon Elvis, see Clive Anderson, "How Elvis Bleached the Blues: Black Roots," *Let It Rock* (December 1975). A series of articles in England's *Melody Maker* were helpful. While these articles often ranged beyond the Sun years, nonetheless, they provided important insights into Elvis' musical character and personality. For the most useful articles see, for example, T. Brown, "Elvis Presley," *Melody Maker* (21 July 1956): 3; B. Case, "The Night the Music Died," *Melody Maker* (6 October 1979): 11; Ray Coleman, "El-

vis: A Social Phenomena," *Melody Maker* (4 May 1963): 4; C. King, "Elvis: The Living Legend," *Melody Maker* (13 September 1959): 2; H. Lucraft, "Elvis Says, I've Never Written a Song, I Can't Play the Guitar," *Melody Maker* (2 November 1957): 1; C. O' Curran, "At Last the Truth about Elvis," *Melody Maker* (27 July 1959): 3; D. Shout, "Historic Beatles-Elvis Meeting," *Melody Maker* (4 September 1965): 5; H. Whiston, "Elvis Forgot the Hole in His Sock," *Melody Maker* (27 April 1957): 7; and R. Williams, "From Elvis Came Rock," *Melody Maker* (27 August 1977): 5.

Wayne Russell's "Elvis Presley--Itinerary for 1954 and 1955," *Goldmine*, no. 64 (September 1981): 171, is an inaccurate and incomplete list of Presley's early tours. A good article on Elvis' growth since the Sun years is F. Segers, "Presley: From Backwoods Phenom in 1956 to Polished Superstar in 1972," *Variety,* 267 (14 June 1972): 52.

On Scotty Moore and Bill Black's influence see "Albums: Elvis, Scotty and Bill: The First Years," *Melody Maker* (1 December 1979).

The moral controversy surrounding Elvis' music is reflected in "Baptist Minister's Sermon vs. Elvis: He'll Hit the Skids," *Variety* (17 October 1956): 1. An interesting view of Presley's death is "ABC Seeks Elvis' Autopsy Report," *Rolling Stone* (29 November 1979): 11. For Colonel Parker's manipulation of Presley's career see, for example, Matty Brescia's "Judge Pulls In Tom Parker's Reins Over Elvis' Estate," *Variety* (17 February 1982): 2ff; Matty Brescia's "Presley Estate Guardian Avers 'Cheat Scam' By Colonel Parker And RCA: Report To Court," *Variety* (5 August 1981): 2ff; Rose Clayton's "Colonel Parker Accused Of Ripping Off Elvis," *Rolling Stone* (17 September 1981): 8-9; and Rose Clayton's "Elvis Estate Sues Parker Over License," *Billboard* (20 February 1982): 4.

Chris Woodford's "The Songs of Leiber and Stoller," *Now Dig This,* 53 (August 1987): 12-13, is an excellent brief look at two important songwriters. For an interesting comparison with an early British rock star, see Ray Coleman's "Cliff v. Elvis," *Melody Maker* (24 March 1962): 9.

POPULAR PERIODICAL ARTICLES ON ELVIS

C. Brown's article, "Craze Called Elvis," *Coronet* (September 1956): 153, is an early attempt to explain Presley's appeal. From the British view, A. Bryant's "Elvis Presley and the Universal Worship He Engenders," *Illustrated London News* (9 February 1957) is a similar attempt to analyze Presleymania. Dave Marsh's "Elvis: The New Deal Origins of Rock 'n' Roll," *Musician,* no. 50 (December 1982): 18-24, 110-12, is valuable in placing Elvis' music in the context of American history. Marsh argues that "Presleymania has a political dimension." He brilliantly demonstrates how Elvis' Tupelo roots shaped his sound, a sound that Northerners couldn't understand. For Presley's role in the early rock music revolution, see Richard Welch's "Rock 'N' Roll And Social Change," *History Today*, vol. 40 (February 1990): 32-39. Also see Richard Moody's "Elvis Speaks," *Harper's* (August 1988): 32; Richard Corliss' "The King Is Dead, Or Is He?" *Time* (10 October 1988): 90; "Can 50 Million Americans Be Wrong?" *Downbeat* (September 1989): 40; Neil Asher's "Elvis: The Myth Lives On," *Archaeology*, vol. 43 (July-August 1990): 80; Bob Greene's "The Nixon-Elvis Papers," *Esquire*, vol. 110 (October 1988): 63; Greil Marcus's "Still Dead: Elvis Without Music," *Artforum*, vol. 27 (February 1989): 14; J. Hoberman's "On American Myths," *Artforum*, vol. 27 (February 1989): 14; J.D. Reed's "The Mansion Music Made; There's Still Good Rockin' At Elvis Presley's Graceland," *Time* (19 December 1988) 10. The above articles define Presley's continued importance to pop culture.

Jay Cocks' "Last Stop on the Mystery Train," *Time* (29 August 1977): 56-59, is the best analysis of Elvis' career at the time of his death. Stanley Booth's "A Hound Dog to the Manor Born," *Esquire* (February 1968): 106-8, is a perceptive analysis of Elvis' influence upon rock music.

When Elvis died there were a spate of obituaries that brilliantly summarized his place in rock history, see, for example, Chet Flippo, "Funeral in Memphis," *Rolling Stone* (22 September 1977): 38; Ben Fong-Torres, "Broken Heart for Sale," *Rolling Stone* (22 September 1977): 42; Greil Marcus, "Elvis: Spirit and Flesh," *Rolling Stone* (22 September 1977): 56ff; Dave Marsh, "Elvis in the Promised Land," *Rolling Stone* (22 September 1977): 58; Robert Ward, "Down at the End of a Lonely Street," *Crawdaddy* (November 1977): 29-34; Michael Watts, "The Phenomenon," *Melody Maker* (27 August 1977): 6; and Jean Williams, "Boy from Tupelo Did Much to Bridge Black-White Gap," *Billboard* (27 August 1977): 82. Dave Marsh's "Elvis: His Impact on American Music," *TV Guide*, no. 31 (9 April 1983): 34-38, is an excellent survey of Presley's cultural importance.

For the early reaction to Presley's music during the RCA era see, for example, "Howling Hillbilly Success," *Life* (April 1956): 64; "Hillbilly on a Pedestal," *Newsweek* (14 May 1956): 82; "Presley Spells Profit," *Newsweek* (14 May 1956); Colin Brown, "Craze Called Elvis," *Coronet* (September 1956): 153-57; Evelyn Condon, "What Is an Elvis Presley," *Cosmopolitan* (December 1956): 54-61; "Elvis Presley: Dig the Greatest," *Hep Cat's Review* (February 1956): 13-45; "Elvis

Presley, He Can't Be, but He Is," *Look* (August 1956): 82-85; and Jerry Baxter, et al., "Man in the Blues Suede Shoes," *Harper's* (January 1958): 45-47. Tom Ayres' "Elvis," *Country Music* (December 1977): 24-28, is excellent for a post-mortem on Presley's career.

When Presley left the army and returned to appear on the Frank Sinatra special, there were numerous articles. The best piece is "Idols Team Up on TV," *Life* (16 May 1960): 103-4. Some of the changes in Presley's career are covered in J. Archer's "Presley Swooners Now Gone Sedate," *Variety* (5 January 1972): 24ff.

Sun Records And Sam Phillips: Specialized Books And Articles

The major books on Sun Records are Colin Escott and Martin Hawkins's *Sun Records: The Brief History Of The Legendary Record Label* (New York, 1980), and Colin Escott and Martin Hawkins' *Good Rockin' Tonight: Sun Records And The Birth Of Rock 'N' Roll* (New York, 1991). This is the starting point for anyone researching Elvis' Sun career, and it is a groundbreaking book. Charlie Gillett's *Making Tracks: Atlantic Records And The Growth Of A Multi-Billion-Dollar Industry* (New York, 1974) is a model study of Ahmet Ertegun's label, and Gillett covers a great deal of ground concerning Presley's early career.

John Jackson's "A Tour of Sun Records Studios: It's Even on Union Avenue," *Goldmine*, no. 80 (January 1983): 14-15, is essential in understanding the Sun atmosphere. Also see Randy Haspel's "Tell 'Em Phillips Sent'cha," *Memphis* (June 1978).

Kevin Ford's "Elvis--The Sun Years," *Time Barrier Express*, no. 25 (July-August 1979): 18-22, is a brief but interesting analysis. Also see, Gareth L. Pawlowski, "Elvis: 1955's 'Folk Music Fireball'," in *Our Best To You: From Record Digest*, ed. by Jerry Osborne (Prescott, AZ, 1979): 6-10; Nick Tosches, "Elvis--Getting the Ink, 1954-1955," *Goldmine* (January 1982): 14; Nick Tosches, "Elvis: The Shocking Hillbilly," *Country Style* (August 1981): 14-21; and Nick Tosches, "The Provenance of Elvis Presley's Sun Songs," *Goldmine* (January 1983): 15.

Stan Kesler's importance to Sun Records and Elvis Presley is demonstrated in an excellent interview. See Jim Newcombe, "An Interview with Stan Kesler," *Now Dig This*, 62 (May 1988): 4-6. Also see Newcombe's "An Interview with Jack Clement," *Now Dig This*, 62 (May 1988): 24-27.

Barbara Barnes' "Sun Records: An Insider's View," *New Kommotion*, 2 (Spring 1977): 30-31, is informative. For another view of Sun Records, see the short history of Phillips International in Robert J. Becker's

"Phillips Findings," *Record Exchanger* (February 1973): 12-13, and Paul Vernon's *The Sun Legend* (London, 1969).

For an inside look at Sam Phillips' recording techniques see, for example, Rose Clayton, "Rock's Roots Recalled in Sam Phillips Studio Sessions," *Billboard,* 93 (4 April 1981): 42; Bill Daniels, "Before Sunrise: The Early Recordings of Sam Phillips," *Record Exchanger,* 5 (1977): 16-17; Robert Dermann, "Sunrise to Sunset," *Country Style,* no. 69 (August 1981): 33-34.

"Charly Shelves Presley Sun Set (Recording: Sun Years)," *Billboard* (29 October 1977): 76, is an interesting look at the controversy over unreleased Sun materials. Peter Guralnick's essay, "Boppin' the Blues: Sam Phillips and the Sun Sound," in his *Feel Like Going Home: Portraits In Blues And Rock N Roll* (New York, 1971), 171-75, is the best piece on Phillips' production genius. Also see Guralnick, "Million Dollar Quartet," *New York Times Magazine* (25 March 1979): 28-30; Greil Marcus' provocative tome on popular culture, *Mystery Train: Images Of America In Rock 'N' Roll Music* (New York, 1975), 11-13, 18-20, 163-65, 185-86, 199-201, provides an excellent assessment of Sam Phillips' contribution to Presley's music. Nick Tosches' *Country: The Biggest Music In America* (New York, 1977), 36-43, is a valuable look at Phillips' career and ties many old country hits into Elvis' career.

The "Louisiana Hayride" offered Elvis a chance to experiment with his music. An excellent article on the Hayride is Walter Bronson's "Flashback: Louisiana Hayride Revisited," *Song Hits* Magazine Tribute to Elvis (Winter 1984): 62-63. Almost Slim's "The Louisiana Hayride," *Wavelength,* Issue 30 (April 1980): 14-17, is a brief look at Elvis on the Hayride.

Walter Dawson's brief article, "Sunset," in *Country Music: Elvis,* 8 (January-February 1980): 76, provides some interesting quotes from Sam Phillips on Elvis' Sun years. Nick Tosches' "The Rise of Rockabilly," *Country Music: Elvis,* 8 (January-February 1980): 33-35 analyzes the reason that rockabilly was such an important new musical force in the mid-1950s.

The question of what is left of the early Sun recordings is addressed in Jack Helinski's "What's in the Can," *Music World,* no. 88 (August 1981): 8-12, and Helinski, "Elvis: What's in the Can, an Update," *Goldmine* (23 October 1987): 36-37. Also see Jack Helinski, "The Sun Controversy," *Music World,* 89 (September 1981): 27. In December 1956, Elvis, Johnny Cash, Carl Perkins, and Jerry Lee Lewis engaged in a famous session. For the best review of this, see Peter Guralnick, "Million Dollar Memories," *New Kommotion,* no. 25: 7-12.

A very strange article on Elvis' Sun days is Ed Gorman's "I Forgot to Remember to Forget," *The Record Spinner* (1 August 1983): 7. Gorman's article focuses upon one song during the Sun days.

Robert Hilburn's "Sam Phillips: The Man Who Found Elvis and Jerry Lee," *Los Angeles Times Calendar* (19 April 1981): 1, 56-58, is the best recent look at Sam Phillips' contribution to Presley's music. Another view of Sam Phillips is Walter Dawson's "Presley and Phillips Had Nothing to Lose by Being Different," *Memphis Commercial Appeal* (13 August 1978): B-3. The importance of disc jockey Dewey Phillips is examined in Randy Haspel's "Tell 'Em Phillips Sent'cha: Dewey Phillips--the First Rock and Roll Deejay," *Memphis* (June 1978): 52ff.

Peter Guralnick's "Faded Love: A Personal Memoir," *Country Music* (December 1977): 36, is a touching commentary on Elvis' death and importance by one of rock's more academic writers. Equally important as a memoir is Greil Marcus' "Elvis: Spirit and Flesh," *Rolling Stone* (22 September 1977): 58. Dave Marsh's "Elvis in the Promised Land," *Rolling Stone* (22 September 1977): 58, adds a great deal to Guralnick and Marcus' commentary on Elvis' importance to American culture.

There are many articles on Sam Phillips. The best are Walter Dawson, "Sunset: An Interview with Sam Phillips," *Country Music* (December 1977), 58-59, also reprinted in *Creem,* 7 (December 1977): 58-59; Peter Guralnick, "Sam Phillips Talking," *Lost Highway: Journeys And Arrivals Of American Musicians* (Boston, 1979), 324-39.

Big Al's "The Hardrock Gunter Story, Parts I and II," *New Kommotion* nos. 24-25 is an excellent analysis of an obscure country-rockabilly artist who unwittingly influenced Elvis.

PERSONAL REMINISCENCES ABOUT ELVIS

The most sensational personal reminiscence about Elvis is Lucy de Barbin and Dary Matera's *Are You Lonesome Tonight: The Untold Story Of Elvis Presley's One True Love And The Child He Never Knew* (New York, 1987). It is an undocumented story that Elvis fathered a love child. When Presley left Ms. de Barbin's life, John Wayne walked into it. What is amazing about this book is that a major New York publisher, Villard Books, bought a story with so little documentation. The facts, dates, and general knowledge of Presley's career are not consistent with this book's assertions.

Dave Oksanen's "D.J. Fontana Interviewed," *Music World,* no. 88 (August 1981): 40-45, is an interview providing a clear picture of the drummer's relationship with Elvis. Also see J.D. Sumner's *J.D. Sumner: Gospel Music Is My Life* (1971) for a distorted view of Presley. An interesting view of Presley during the late July 1955 Florida tour is provided by singer Jimmy

Velvet's "Interview for the Record," *Elvis: The Record,* 2, no. 3 (October-November 1980): 7-8. Jean-Charles Marion's "Requiem for the Hillbilly Cat," *Record Exchanger,* no. 25: 6-7, is an interesting personal overview of Presley's impact upon American culture. Vester Presley's *A Presley Speaks* (Memphis, 1978) is a brief ghost-written look at the Presley family by Uncle Vester, and is a rich source for the early years.

Billy Smith's "The Audubon House," *Elvis: The Record* (June 1979): 8-10, is an eyewitness account regarding Elvis' first big house.

Nancy Anderson's "Elvis by His Father, Vernon Presley," *Good Housekeeping* (January 1978) is an interesting post-mortem look at Presley's life. Harold Loyd and George Bough's *The Graceland Gates* (Memphis, 1978) is a work along the same lines (mourning Elvis' death).

"Marty Lacker Interview," *Elvis: The Record* (May 1979): 17-19, is an interesting reminiscence by one of the Memphis Mafia. A similar interview is George Klein's "Interview for the Record," *Elvis: The Record* (June 1979). Lorraine Smith's "Some Hard Times," *Elvis: The Record* (May 1979): 21, is a brief recollection by Travis Smith's wife. She recounts some hard times in Tupelo in 1948.

Marge Crumbaker with Gabe Tucker, *Up And Down With Elvis Presley* (New York, 1981) is an excellent look at Colonel Tom Parker's influence upon Elvis by a musician and publicity man who worked for Parker. Alternately praising and condemning Colonel Parker, Tucker's book reveals the intricate interrelationship of the Parker-Presley partnership. Also see Jim Van Hollebeke's "The Colonel Parker Story," *Goldmine,* no. 66 (November 1981): 179.

"Kathy Westmoreland Interview," *Record Exchanger,* 5, no. 3: 10-14, is a useful look at Presley's life by a back-up singer who was close to him. Also see Kathy Westmoreland with William G. Quinn's *Kathy And Elvis* (Glendale, CA, 1978) for Westmoreland's memoirs of her years with Presley. This book is a dim-witted recounting of her life, and it suggests that only someone who really knew Elvis should write a book. Equally insipid is David Stanley with David Wimpish's *Life With Elvis* (Old Tappan, NJ, 1986). It is an apology for the Stanley family that blames Elvis for most of their problems. The good Reverend David Stanley has found Jesus and apologizes for his past. The long-haired young man who sat in the Hilton bars attempting to pick up girls is gone, and in his place is a mature young man who sees all of Presley's faults. A nice piece of fiction.

Bob Battle's "Flashback: The Early Years," *Song Hits* Magazine's Tribute to Elvis (Winter 1984): 34-35, is a brief personal reminiscence of an encounter with Presley.

Peter Haining's *Elvis In Private* (New York, 1987) is a valuable collection of personal reminiscences and anecdotes concentrating upon Presley's early years. Vester Presley, Bill Leaptrott, Johnny Burnette, Judd Phillips, Scotty Moore, Rufus Thomas, Anita Wood, Steve Sholes, D.J. Fontana, Chet Atkins, and Gordon Stoker provide excellent material on the early Sun Records years. Todd Slaughter, the president of the British Elvis Presley Fan Club, contributes a sensitive introduction to this material. For a brief view of Anita Wood, see Wayne Russell, "Anita's the Name of His Latest Flame," *Now Dig This,* no. 32 (November 1985): 6.

REFERENCE SOURCES ON ELVIS PRESLEY, ROCK AND ROLL, AND BLUES

Colin Escott and Martin Hawkins' *The Complete Sun Label Session Files* (Swift Record Distributors, East Sussex, England, revised edition 1978) is an indispensable source for analyzing Sam Phillips' record label and its impact upon Elvis' music. An update of the Escott-Hawkins book is *Sun Records: The Discography* (Bear Family Records, Germany, 1987). Ernst Jorgensen, Erik Rasmussen, and Johnny Mikkelsen's *Elvis: Recording Sessions* (Denmark, 1984) is a complete and incisive catalog of Presley recordings.

The best overall book on blues discography is Mike Leadbitter and Neil Slaven's *Blues Records, 1943-1966* (New York, 1968). Also see Fred L. Worth and Steve D. Tamerius' *All About Elvis* (New York, 1981) for an excellent encyclopedic view of Presley's life. Lee Cotten's *All Shook Up: Elvis Day By Day, 1954-1977* (Ann Arbor, 1985; available only from Popular Culture, Ink.) is the best factual treatment of Presley. Cotten's work is accurate and well written, and examines all aspects of Elvis' life. Peter Jones' "Elvis Presley's U.K. Singles," *Record Collector* (June 1980): 4-10, is an important tool for analyzing the impact of Presley's Sun singles and career upon the English record market. A dated work is Roy Barlow, *The Elvis Presley Encyclopedia* (England, 1964). For Elvis bootleg records, see Lee Cotten and Howard A. DeWitt, *Jailhouse Rock: The Bootleg Records Of Elvis Presley, 1970-1983* (Ann Arbor, 1983; available only from Popular Culture, Ink.).

The best book on Elvis' recordings is Ernst Jorgensen, et al., *Reconsider Baby: The Definitive Elvis Sessionography* (Ann Arbor, 1986). This volume is a Popular Culture, Ink. revised reprint of *Elvis: The Recording Sessions* originally printed by Jee Productions in Denmark. Ron Barry's *The Elvis Presley American Discography* (Phillipsburg, NJ, 1980) is a useful brief reference for Presley records. A more complete guide is Neal Umphred, *Elvis Presley: Record Price Guide*

(Phoenix, 1986). John A. Whisler's *Elvis Presley: Reference Guide And Discography* (Metuchen, NJ, 1981) is also useful.

The best price guide to Presleyana is Jerry Osborne's *Presleyana 3: The Elvis Presley Record Price Guide* (Osborne Enterprises, PO Box 255, Port Townsend, WA 98368). Not only is the Osborne guide the most recent, there is simply none better for gauging price and demand.

MUSICIANS AND ELVIS PRESLEY

Dan Forte's "Pioneers of Rock and Roll Guitar," *Guitar Player,* no. 174 (June 1984): 60-61, offers some interesting commentary on the rock guitar. Without mentioning Scotty Moore, Forte points up the key changes in guitar styles. Although he did not play with Elvis until the late 1960s, James Burton's guitar styling was an important influence upon the development of rock and roll. For information on Burton see, for example, Steve Fishell, "James Burton," *Guitar Player,* no. 174 (June 1984): 88-101. An important source in analyzing Carl Perkins' impact upon Elvis and rock music is Dennis Hensley, "Carl Perkins," *Guitar Player,* no. 99 (March 1975): 18, 39-40.

Adam Komorowski's "Ray Smith," *New Kommotion,* 3, no. 2: 20-24 is an excellent piece on a talented musician who developed during Elvis' Sun years. The Komorowski article, while not directly related to Elvis' rise to prominence, is, nonetheless, important in piecing together the early history of rockabilly music.

For information on a rival music label, see Roger Weeden and George A. Moonoogian's "Duke Records: The Early Years," *Whiskey Women And...,* Issue 14.

Peter Guralnick's "Charlie Feathers," *New Kommotion,* 3, no. 2: 30-33 is the best article on Feathers and is reprinted in Guralnick's seminal study, *Lost Highway.* Another interesting look at Feathers' music is Roger Ford's "Charlie Feathers," *Not Fade Away,* no. 16 (1980): 24-25.

Dick Grant's "The Eddie Bond Story," *Now Dig This,* no. 30 (September 1985): 9-12, filled in many holes about Bond's contribution to the Memphis rockabilly scene. Trevor Cajiao edited the work.

Barry John's "The Era of Glen Glenn: A Hollywood Rockabilly," *New Kommotion,* no. 27 (1983): 10-12, suggests some post-Presley Sun rockabilly influences. Dick Grant's "Blues Blues Blues with Hayden Thompson," *New Kommotion,* no. 27 (1983): 24-27, adds another dimension to the mid-1950s rockabilly story. Adam Komorowski and Clive Anderson's "Presleyana," *New Kommotion,* no. 27 (1983): 29, reviews some early key Elvis records.

Jim Newcombe's "A Tribute to Dorsey Burnette," *Not Fade Away,* no. 16 (1980): 44-46, provides some anecdotes about one of the Burnette brothers.

Trevor Cajiao's "Jackie Lee Cochran," *Now Dig This,* no. 24 (March 1985): 17-20, adds to an obscure local rockabilly singer's place at Sun Records.

Martin Hawkins' "Malcolm Yelvington," *New Kommotion,* 3, no. 2: 39-40, is important in analyzing Yelvington and his band's influence upon Elvis. Bill Millar's article, "Johnny Bragg," places the Prisonaires influence and gospel music in general in Presley's musical development.

Adam Komorowski's "Jack Clement," *New Kommotion,* 30, no. 2: 46-47, contains important material on a musician close to Elvis. Also see Adam Komorowski's "Warren Smith," *New Kommotion,* 3, no. 2: 48-51, for another superb article on a Memphis rockabilly legend.

"Jerry Capehart Remembers," *Now Dig This,* no. 25 (April 1985): 3-5, details some of the highlights of Eddie Cochran's career by a co-producer, manager, and personal friend.

Rick Whitesell's "The Jordanaires: Standing Out in the Background," *Goldmine,* no. 58 (March 1981): 184-86, provides some background into Presley's early music.

Adam Komorowski's "Echoes: Start Rockin', Son-- That's an Order," *Melody Maker,* no. 54 (29 December 1979): 22, and "Ray Smith," *New Kommotion,* no. 22 (1979) are important articles in understanding the influence of a key Sun Records artist.

GENERAL HISTORIES OF ROCK MUSIC

An important starting point in understanding the birth of early rock and roll is Charlie Gillett's *The Sound Of The City: The Rise Of Rock And Roll* (New York, 1970). Gillett's monumental work is significant in demonstrating the force of rhythm and blues music in Elvis' early career. Carl Belz's *The Story Of Rock* (New York, 1969) is a good overview of the 1950s and 1960s. Mike Jahn's *The Story Of Rock: From Elvis Presley To The Rolling Stones* (New York, 1973) offers a segmented view of rock trends that is important in analyzing the different types of music emerging as rock and roll.

Herbert I. London's *Closing The Circle: A Cultural History Of The Rock Revolution* (Chicago, 1984) is a much ignored but important interpretation of rock and roll by a knowledgeable academician. Professor London himself cut two records between 1959 and 1961, and his book offers the insights of someone who was in the midst of the rock revolution. Simon Frith's *Sound Effects: Youth, Leisure And The Politics Of Rock 'N' Roll* (New York, 1981) is the work of a British sociologist, and it is very useful in examining the negative reaction to rock and roll music.

Henry Pleasant's *The Great American Popular Singers* (New York, 1974) is a scholarly attempt to place Elvis within the framework of modern music. This volume suggests that Elvis' singing talent had a great deal in common with Frank Sinatra, Judy Garland, and Bing Crosby.

Don J. Hibbard and Carol Kaleialoha's *The Role Of Rock: A Guide To The Social And Political Consequences Of Rock Music* (Englewood Cliffs, 1983) is a well-researched tome on the significance of rock and roll music. Also see Charles T. Brown's *The Art Of Rock And Roll* (Englewood Cliffs, 1983) for a textbook look at rock music. For the role of radio disc jockeys, see Arnold Passman's *The Dee Jays* (New York, 1971).

In exploring the political and commercial side of the music industry, the following books are important resources: Simon Garfield, *Money For Nothing: Greed And Exploitation In The Music Industry* (Boston, 1986); Reebee Garofalo and Steve Chapple, *Rock And Roll Is Here To Pay* (Chicago, 1977); and John Street, *Rebel Rock: The Politics Of Popular Music* (London, 1986).

Arnold Shaw's *Honkers And Shouters: The Golden Years Of Rhythm and Blues* (New York, 1978) offers an insider's view of rhythm and blues music. Shaw was one of the first entertainment industry figures to champion Elvis' music, and this makes the book especially appealing. The best source for early rhythm and blues/ rock and roll record releases and concert appearances is Lee Cotten's *Shake Rattle And Roll: The Golden Age Of American Rock And Roll, Volume 1* (Ann Arbor, MI: Popular Culture, Ink.)

The best general history of rock and roll is Ed Ward, Geoffrey Stokes, and Ken Tucker's *Rock Of Ages: The Rolling Stone History Of Rock and Roll* (New York, 1986). Also see, Jann S. Wenner, *20 Years Of Rolling Stone: What A Long, Strange Trip It's Been* (New York, 1987), an excellent anthology tracing key changes in rock music.

R. Serge Denisoff's *Solid Gold: The Popular Record Industry* (New Brunswick, 1975) is an interesting look at the music industry. Also see his *Tarnished Gold* (New Brunswick, 1987) for the sequel to *Solid Gold*.

A pioneering work in popular culture is B. Lee Cooper's *Images Of American Society In Popular Music: A Guide To Reflective Teaching* (Chicago, 1982). Professor Cooper is the foremost practitioner of pop culture and rock and roll writing from an academic perspective. An extension of this approach is Cooper's *Popular Music Perspectives: Ideas, Themes And Patterns In Contemporary Lyrics* (Bowling Green, 1991).

ACADEMIC STUDIES: BLUES, COUNTRY, AND ROCK MUSIC INFLUENCES

B. Lee Cooper's "Contemporary Singers as Subjects for Biographical Study," *Library College Experimenter,* 5 (May 1979): 13-28, is a model for implementing rock biography within a larger framework. Robert Palmer's *A Tale Of Two Cities: Memphis Rock And New Orleans Roll* (New York, 1979) is a brief sketch of both cities and their impact upon rock music. Palmer, the rock music critic for the *New York Times*, completed this study for the Institute for Studies in American Music, Brooklyn College, and it is an excellent monograph on Memphis' musical heritage. Also see Jack V. Buerkle and Danny Barker's *Bourbon Street Black* (New York, 1973); Samuel B. Charters' *The Country Blues* (New York, 1975); Charles W. Crawford's *Yesterday's Memphis* (Miami, 1976); Margaret McKee and Fred Chisenhall's *Beale Black And Blue: Life And Music On Black America's Main Street* (Baton Rouge, 1981); and Paul Oliver's *The Story Of The Blues* (London, 1969) for detailed information on Memphis and Beale Street. Oliver's book is the best single study of the blues. Giles Oakley's *The Devil's Music: A History Of The Blues* (London, 1977) is the best source on early blues music. Paul Oliver, et al.'s *Recording The Blues* (New York, 1970) is an important source for the early days of the blues recording industry. Editor Paul Oliver's *Stewart-Baxter, Derrick, Ma Rainey, And The Classic Blues Singers* (New York, 1970) helped to recreate the influences of some minor blues figures.

Robert Palmer's *Deep Blues* (New York, 1981) is the best single book on the blues. It contains a great deal of material about Memphis and the influences that permeated Presley's music. Other books important to blues influences are David Evans, *Tommy Johnson* (London, 1971); John Fahey, *Charley Patton* (London, 1970); William Ferris, *Blues From The Delta* (New York, 1978); Paul Garon, *Blues And The Poetic Spirit* (New York, 1978); Paul Garon, *The Devil's Son-in-Law: The Story Of Peetie Wheatstraw And His Songs* (London, 1978); and Simon A. Napier, *Back Woods Blues* (London, 1968).

Jac L. Tharpe's *Elvis: Images And Fancies* (Jackson, MS, 1980) is a collection of academic essays on Presley's life and music. Most are specialized examinations of Presley's career concentrating on his impact upon American popular culture. Editor Ger Rijff's *Long Lonely Highway: A 1950s Elvis Scrapbook* (Ann Arbor, 1987; available only from Popular Culture, Ink.) is an excellent source- book of Presley newspaper clippings and other scrapbook material from the 1950s. This volume is thoughtfully put together and contains a great deal of important material.

In a more specialized vein, see Fred Hutchins' *What Happened In Memphis* (Kingport, 1965) and Fred Hutchins, "Beale Street as It Was," *West Tennessee Historical Society Papers,* XXVI (1972): 56-63, for an excellent analysis of the changing nature of Beale Street. George W. Lee's *Beale Street: Where The Blues Began* (College Park, 1934) is a useful look at the musical changes that helped shape Elvis' career.

Mike Rowe's *Chicago Breakdown* (Chicago, 1973) is a model study of Chicago blues, and Rowe has a great deal to say about Memphis blues. For the Memphis blues, see Bengt Olsson's *Memphis Blues* (London, 1970). This is a narrow, limited study, but it helps to place Memphis blues influences in perspective. See Charles S. Murray, "The Blues Had a Baby and They Called It Rock and Roll," *New Musical Express* (30 April 1977) for a brief connection between the blues and rock and roll music.

Helen Doob Lazar's "Living Blues Interview: James Cotton," *Living Blues,* no. 76 (1987): 22-33, is an excellent overview of Cotton's career and a fine interview. It helps put some perspective on Cotton's influence upon Presley's music. Howery Pack's "The Blues Had a Baby," *Living Blues,* no. 76 (1987): 34-37, is an excellent list of songs by blues artists that have been recorded by mainstream rock and roll acts.

Among the numerous blues artists who influenced Elvis, Roy Brown is one of the most important. See John Broven, "Roy Brown: Hard Luck Blues, Part 2," *Blues Unlimited,* no. 124 (March-June 1977): 14-21, for an in-depth look at Brown's relationship with Elvis. See "Valerie Wilmer Talks to Roy Brown," *New Kommotion,* 2, no. 10 (Summer 1978): 53-54, for more information on Brown's relationship with Presley. Paul Harris' interview "Roy Brown Reminisces," *Not Fade Away,* no. 17 (1981): 40-47, is an important interview with Brown.

Stuart Colman's *They Kept On Rockin: The Giants Of Rock 'N' Roll* (London, 1982) is a brilliant interpretive work on early American and British rock and roll artists. The sketch on Elvis, entitled "Elvis Presley--Once a King" on pages 122-127, is one of the finest brief articles on Presley's influence upon rock and roll. Howard Elson's *Early Rockers* (New York, 1982) contains an excellent sketch of Presley's career on pages 116-127.

Although not particularly strong on Elvis, the following books are important to understanding the blues. See, for example, Bruce Cook, *Listen To The Blues* (New York, 1973); LeRoi Jones, *Blues People* (New York, 1963); Charles Keil, *Urban Blues* (Chicago, 1966); and Tony Russell, *Blacks, Whites And Blues* (New York, 1970).

The history of the phonograph industry is impor-

tant and Oliver Read and Walter Welch's, *From Tin Foil To Stereo: Evolution Of The Phonograph* (Indianapolis, 1959, rev. ed., 1976) is an indispensable look at it. Ian Whitcomb's *After The Ball: From Rag To Rock* (New York, 1972) is an essential book for understanding how ragtime and jazz influenced early blues and rock and roll music. Bill C. Malone's *Country Music USA--A Fifty-Year History* (Austin, 1968) is the work of a serious student of American culture and music. Charles R. Townsend's *San Antonio Rose: The Life And Music Of Bob Wills* (Urbana, 1976) is the official biography of one of America's great musicians, and is a monumental work. Nolan Porterfield's *Jimmie Rodgers: The Life And Times Of America's Blue Yodeler* (Urbana, 1979) is another important work on country music. Eddy Arnold's *It's A Long Way From Chester County* (Old Tappan, NJ, 1969) offers some insights into Colonel Parker's relationship with his performers. James Rooney's *Bossmen: Bill Monroe And Muddy Waters* (New York, 1971) is an excellent study of Monroe's influences upon Elvis. Also see Neil Rosenberg's *Bill Monroe And His Bluegrass Boys: An Illustrated Discography* (Nashville, 1975).

Trevor Cajiao's article, "Jackie Lee Cochran," *Now Dig This* (March 1985): 17-20 provides excellent background material on the rockabilly revolution. While Cochran's success was limited and historically later than Elvis', nonetheless, this article suggests the conditions that contributed to rockabilly's musical success. Hank Taylor's "From One Cut to Another: The Sid King Story," *Not Fade Away,* no. 17 (1981): 28-38, provides some interesting comments by King on the mid-1950s.

H.F. Mooney's "Popular Music Since the 1920s: The Significance of Shifting Taste," *The American Quarterly* (1968) reprinted in *The Age Of Rock: Sounds Of The American Cultural Revolution*, edited by Jonathan Eisen (New York, 1969) is a pioneering attempt to place popular music in a cultural perspective. In the same volume, Stanley Booth's "A Hound Dog to the Manor Born" is a highly interpretive look at Presley's life. Booth's article was written in 1968 and brilliantly analyzes Elvis' impact upon American music.

Howard Junker's "The Fifties," in *The Age Of Rock: Sights And Sounds Of The American Cultural Revolution*, edited by Jonathan Eisen (New York, 1970) is an excellent analysis of the values of the 1950s. Also see David Dalton's "Elvis Presley: Wagging His Tail in Las Vegas" in Ben Fong-Torres' *The Rolling Stone Rock N Roll Reader*.

Fan Clubs, Tour Magazines, and Fanzines

In 1955, Hank Snow's show featured a souvenir

photo book with a useful sketch on Elvis Presley. In 1956, an Elvis Presley souvenir photo album sold during the summer months, and a magazine tour book was released in November containing with pictures from the movie *Love Me Tender*. Each provided some insight into Presley's performing skills.

Once Elvis became a major star, he was featured in mass market magazines aimed at his fans. Despite the commercial aspect of these magazines and the juvenile mentality of the articles, they provide an interesting look at Presley. The best of these are *Teenage Rock and Roll Review* (October 1956) and *Dig* (November 1956/January 1957). Both articles in *Dig* featured Elvis as a cover story.

The *Hillbilly And Western Scrapbook* for 1957 features Elvis along with many of the country stars. This interesting book suggests how much country music helped Presley's early career. The first book on Elvis was editor James Gregory's *The Elvis Presley Story* (New York, 1957). This little volume was simply a reprinting of an article in the magazines *Movieland* and *TV Times*. With an introduction by Dick Clark, this book has become a valued collector's item.

Pioneer Figures In The History Of Blues And Rock And Roll Music

A number of important books suggest the role of early rock and roll pioneers. Charles White's *The Life And Times Of Little Richard: The Quasar Of Rock* (New York, 1984); John Swenson's *Bill Haley* (London, 1982); Nick Tosches' *Hellfire: The Jerry Lee Lewis Story* (New York, 1982); Myra Lewis with Murray Silver's *Great Balls Of Fire: The Uncensored Story Of Jerry Lee Lewis* (New York, 1982); Britt Hagarty's *The Day The World Turned Blues* (Vancouver, 1983): Howard A. DeWitt's *Chuck Berry: Rock N Roll Music* (Ann Arbor, 1985; available only from Popular Culture, Ink.); John Goldrosen's *The Buddy Holly Story* (New York, 1975); James Brown's (with Bruce Tucker) *James Brown: The Godfather Of Soul* (London, 1986); Charles Sawyer's *The Arrival Of B.B. King* (New York, 1980); and Jeff Hannusch's *I Hear You Knockin': The Sound Of New Orleans Rhythm And Blues* (New Orleans, 1985) offer valuable comments on rock and roll in the 1950s. All of these books were significant in tracing Presley's career.

Useful in a limited way was Jason Berry, Jonathan Foose, and Tad Jones' *Up From The Craddle Of Jazz: New Orleans Music Since World War II* (Athens, 1986); Ben Fong-Torres' The Rolling Stone Interviews, 1967-1980: *Talking With The Legends Of Rock And Roll* (New York, 1981); and Bill Flanagan's *Written In My Soul: Conversations With Rock's Great Songwriters* (Chicago, 1987).

John A. Jackson's *Big Beat Heat: Alan Freed And The Early Years Of Rock And Roll* (New York, 1991) is an important source on Freed and early rock music. Also, see Jackson's *Big Beat Legends: Television's Golden Age* (Point Pleasant, NJ, 1987).

Greil Marcus' *Dead Elvis: A Chronicle Of Cultural Obsession* (New York, 1991) is an attempt to place the years after Presley's death into a broader historical perspective. There are numerous telling insights into Presley's Sun years in this rather obtusely argued work.

Sources

The following list of sources consists primarily of interviews. A few of the key books necessary to each chapter are also listed; however, the bibliographic essay contains a complete survey of the secondary sources that were most important to this study. The following list of interviews is an attempt to suggest from where the conversations, names of recordings which influenced Elvis, and other important historical facts were derived during the writing of this book. All sources within RCA Records, with one exception, requested anonymity.

CHAPTER 1
ELVIS PRESLEY:
AN INTRODUCTION TO SUN ELVIS

Jerry Hopkins' *Elvis: The Final Years* (New York, 1980) is the best source on Elvis in the 1970s. The best single book on Elvis' life, his records, and memorabilia is Lee Cotten's *The Elvis Catalog* (New York, 1987). The Cotten volume is also the best interpretive biography. For a compendium of reliable and well-researched materials on Presley, see Fred L. Worth and Steve Tamerius' *Elvis: His Life From A To Z* (Chicago, 1988). The Worth volume is interpretive and replete with encyclopedic information on Presley. The most sensational Elvis biography is Albert Goldman's *Elvis* (New York, 1981). This book provides not only a negative view of the last few years of Elvis' life, but it distorts Presley's influence upon the history of rock and roll music. Despite his conclusions, Goldman's research uncovered new material about Presley's life. Neal and Janice Gregory's *When Elvis Died* (Washington, DC, 1980) is a well-documented study of Elvis' death and its impact upon American popular culture. The Gregory volume is useful for its collection of newspaper articles and editorials on Presley's death. An inside view of Elvis' last years is Kathy Westmoreland's (with William G. Quinn) *Elvis And Kathy* (Glendale, CA, 1987). A back-up vocalist for Elvis, Westmoreland had a brief affair with him. As a result, Westmoreland's book reads like a soap opera; she insists that she alone could have saved Elvis. The Westmoreland book is a classic example of why insiders should not write books.

Many of the conclusions in this chapter were derived from the reminiscences of more than fifty fans. Their observations of Elvis in the 1970s helped to form much of the introductory chapter. While working at RCA, Joan Deary attended fan conventions, and she patiently answered my questions about these gatherings. She also provided some important thoughts on Steve Sholes and RCA's packaging of Presley's records. Although Deary was never critical of RCA, she did provide important insights into company policy.

Robin Rosaaen, a dedicated Presley fan, provided pictures, memorabilia, bootleg recordings of Elvis' concert appearances, key historical sources, and a well-balanced picture of those who protected the King of Rock and Roll. As one of many fans who frequented Elvis' inner circle, Ms. Rosaaen provided a different view of Presley than that presented in the media. Ms. Rosaaen's voluminous collection of bootleg tapes of Presley's shows recreated conversation and music that allowed me to analyze the Elvis of the 1970s. For almost a decade, Robin set up her tape recorder on stages in Las Vegas and Lake Tahoe. Her tapes document Elvis' performing and personal decline while demonstrating that his voice continued to be strong.

Ron Freitas, a California automobile magnate, talked about his business dealings with Presley and offered important observations on Elvis' security and daily life. Marie Fletcher of the "Elvis Memories Collectors Club" contributed important bits of information on Elvis since the 1960s. Renee Kearns, a young German girl who first met Elvis in Las Vegas in 1969, provided pictures and clear memories of Elvis from 1969 until 1977. Kearns was in the unique position of being a fan who got inside. She maintained a quiet presence and was allowed into gatherings held after concerts. Naomi Frisbee, a long-time Elvis fan, provided a great deal of support and inside information covering more than a decade. Not only is Ms. Frisbee a collector, but she was one of the most important fans in maintaining an historical archive, material she graciously shared with me. W. Reed Severson, a dedicated fan since 1956, offered his insights into Presley's early California appearances.

The best of the insider or inner circle books is Marty Lacker, Patsy Lacker and Les Smith's *Elvis: Portrait Of A Friend* (Memphis, 1979). The worst are Marian Cocke's *I Called Him Babe: Elvis Presley's Nurse Remembers* (Memphis, 1979); Larry Geller, et al., *If I Could Dream: Elvis' Own Story* (New York, 1989); Charlie Hodge with Charles Goodman, *Me 'N Elvis* (Memphis, 1984); Billy Stanley with George Erikson, *Elvis, My Brother* (New York, 1989); and David Stanley with David Wimpish, *Life With Elvis* (Tappan, NJ, 1986).

In 1983, Clive Epstein spent more time talking about Elvis Presley's influence upon his famous brother, Brian, than he did reminiscing about the Beatles. It was through Epstein's gracious conversations that I came to realize Presley's seminal importance to the emergence of British rock and roll.

Kenneth Herman, who had played with Elvis in 1953 as a member of Eddie Bond's band, was instrumental in recreating the Memphis atmosphere. Of all the sources used in this book, the most important one was Ronald Smith. Not only was Smith a fine guitar player, but he was one of Elvis' closest friends. His recollections help to recreate conversations, buildings, the musical atmosphere, and the economic struggles of the 1950s. Smith also led me to a number of Presley's other friends. Many of the photos, research materials, and corroboration of facts could not have been obtained without Smith.

An interview with Rock And Roll Hall Of Fame member LaVern Baker in early 1993, even as this book was in its final editing stage, added new material to this chapter.

Eddie Fadal in Waco, Texas, offered his considerable insights into Presley's development as an entertainer. Fadal also shared his personal experiences with the King of Rock and Roll.

The comments of blues giant Willie Dixon, expressed during a visit to Oakland, California, a year prior to his death, were an important contribution. Dixon read Chapter 1 and added important insights.

In Hawaii, Rodney Masuoka provided detailed information about Presley's visit to Honolulu and a wealth of research material on Presley's career.

On Presley's death, see State of Tennessee v. George C. Nichopoulus, M.D., Criminal Court, 16th Judicial Circuit, indictment, proceedings, and investigative interviews; Copyright Office of the United States of America, Library of Congress, Number TXu 18-490: Grob, Richard as told to Dan Mingori, *The Elvis Conspiracy*, book synopsis, 1979; Cyril H. Wecht, "Post Mortem On Elvis Presley Won't Die," *Legal Aspects Of Medical Practice* (December 1979); Robert Hilburn, "Eternal Revenue—Why Elvis Is Worth More Now Than The Day He Died," *Los Angeles Times Magazine* (June 11, 1989).

CHAPTER 2
ELVIS' ROOTS TO 1941

Elaine Dundy's *Gladys And Elvis* (New York, 1985) is an important study of the family, with an emphasis upon Gladys Presley. Albert Goldman's *Elvis* (New York, 1981) is also strong on the Presley family. Much of the material for this chapter is the result of research in the National Archives, Washington, DC; the Public Record Office, London, England; the Tupelo Public Library; and Memphis State University, Memphis. Adam Eterovich of the Ragusan Press provided research assistance concerning the Presley, Smith, and Love families. The Tupelo Public School District office provided local history material and a great deal of information on schools and students. This material helped to fill in parts of the Presley and Smith family backgrounds.

CHAPTER 3
COURTSHIP, MARRIAGE, AND FAMILY:
GLADYS AND VERNON,
1932-1941

Leroy Green, a lifetime Tupelo resident, was significant in pointing out the key influences in Elvis' early Tupelo years. Rocky Ausborn provided excellent material on the changes in Tupelo and the early career of Mississippi Slim. Clyde Thomas, a black resident of Tupelo, analyzed the changes in Shakerag during the Great Depression. Mrs. Johnny Crabb talked about the times that she did Gladys Presley's hair in her beauty parlor. Located in her home, Mrs. Crabb's parlor was the scene of many of Gladys' most private confessions. Donald L. Dunavent, Pastor of the East Heights Assembly of God church provided extensive interviews about the Presleys, and he searched back into church records to validate many points. Blues musician Roy Brown recalled the atmosphere when he played in Tupelo, and provided fond memories of the various sheriffs. Jim Denson, a Memphis resident, went to Tupelo with Elvis, and his recollections are important ones. Denson remembers that the Presleys often came to Memphis prior to 1948, and he remembers them living for a time in Memphis in 1947. Not only are Denson's observations excellent, but he helped to reconstruct some of the tales that Vernon Presley told about the Tupelo days.

Marcus Van Story, a Memphis musician raised in Mississippi, helped to fill in a great many facts about growing up in the state. A talented musician, Van Story told a number of key tales about how black musicians influenced the growing rockabilly movement of which both Van Story and Elvis were a part.

R.L. Burnside, a blues musician from Holly Springs, Mississippi, talked about Southern Blues and Elvis Presley at J.J.'s Blues Lounge in San Jose, and he provided some interesting anecdotes about the influence of black musicians upon their white counterparts.

The Tupelo Public Library has a special collection of Presley material and this was very useful in developing a feel for the times. The Tupelo Public School

District provided materials on Milam Junior High and a general history of the growth of its school system.

CHAPTER 4
TUPELO:
THE ADOLESCENT YEARS, 1941-1948

Leroy Green provided information on Elvis' school years. W. Kenneth Holdwitch of the University of New Orleans recreated the social atmosphere in Tupelo, and he provided detailed information about teachers and the school system. The Reverend Donald Dunavent and Rocky Ausborn shared their recollections of the WWII and postwar years. Orville Bean's daughter, Mrs. J.C. Grimes, offered detailed reminiscences of the Presley family. Joyce Miller of the Tupelo school district allowed me to copy documents pertaining to the history of local schools. Nell Robins' "History of Milam Junior High School" (unpublished manuscript, 1962) and "History of the Tupelo Public Schools" (n.p., n.d.) were important in assessing Elvis' educational background. A taped interview with F.L. Bobo recalled how he sold Elvis a guitar, and also documents the Presley's time in Tupelo.

Jimmy McCracklin, an Arkansas native, recalled the musical forces of the 1940s as they influenced the artistry of Elvis Presley. Other musicians, notably Charles Brown and Bob Geddins, provided a number of tales about white artists showing up to hear their music. What is remarkable about their story is the manner in which black rhythm and blues and blues music were integrated into early rock and roll.

CHAPTER 5
MEMPHIS:
THE OBSCURE YEARS, 1948-1952

The early Memphis years were recreated through interviews with many people close to the Presleys. Jim Denson, who lived in the Lauderdale Court, was instrumental in reshaping the period from 1949 to 1952 and provided a great deal of material. His brother, Jesse Lee Denson, recalled his days playing and singing with Elvis. Evan "Buzzy" Forbess was another Lauderdale Court resident who recreated these early days. Ronald Smith, who attended South Side High School, was one of Elvis' early musical friends, and Smith's lengthy interviews recreated the musical influences dominating Presley's early life. Kenneth Herman was another friend who observed Elvis' musical growth. Paul Burlison, a local musician, was one of the first to recognize Elvis' talent. Other Memphis musicians who cooperatively discussed this period with me were Paul Burlison, Doug

Poindexter, Charlie Feathers, Stan Kesler, Eddie Bond, and Marcus Van Story.

CHAPTER 6
THE MAKING OF A PERFORMER, 1953

Stan Kesler, Paul Burlison, Marcus Van Story, Charlie Feathers, and Malcolm Yelvington were important Memphis musicians who recalled their experiences with young Elvis Presley. They all provided detailed information on the clubs and musical influences of the day. Jimmy McCracklin and Charles Brown provided significant insights into blues artists who influenced Presley in this period. Rufus Thomas suggested some of the problems of the day on Beale Street, and reflected on his early memories of Elvis Presley.

Doug Poindexter was extremely helpful in recreating the atmosphere at Sun Records and in the local clubs. With a nearly photographic memory, Poindexter suggested the degree of jealousy that some musicians felt towards Elvis, and he sketched the music scene in detail. Much of the information about the clubs comes from Poindexter.

Ronald Smith and Kenneth Herman, who played in Eddie Bond's Stompers, were remarkably clear about where and when they played with Elvis. They also provided the substance of conversations, influential recordings, and the atmosphere of the Eisenhower years as they influenced Elvis.

Eddie Bond provided detailed information about the times he hired Elvis to play in his band. Bond also assembled Ronald Smith, Kenneth Herman, Stan Kesler, Marcus Van Story, and Paul Burlison, who all graciously showed up at Bond's Hernando Club and played for a weary, traveling author. It was not only a thrill, but the evening began the gathering of material that led to this book. Edyth Peeler, of Hernando, Mississippi, recalled the night she saw Elvis at the local VFW hall with clarity and wit.

Johnny Tillotson, Tommy Sands, and Bob Luman provided important insights into the relationship of rockabilly music to rock and roll in this period.

At the office of the Jimmie Rodgers Day Celebration in Meridian, Mississippi, the staff provided important information.

CHAPTER 7
THE KEY INFLUENCES:
COLONEL TOM PARKER AND SAM PHILLIPS

The material on Colonel Tom Parker depends very heavily upon the Elvis biographies of Albert Goldman and Jerry Hopkins. Tommy Sands also shared his intimate knowledge of Colonel Tom Parker, and he related a number of tales about travelling with the Colonel in 1954. On the country influences upon Colonel Tom Parker, Onie Wheeler and Ernest Tubb talked about the 1940s and early 1950s. Research into Hank Williams' influence upon Parker is discussed in this author's "Hank Williams: The Road To Stardom Runs Through The 'Louisiana Hayride'," *Blue Suede News*, no. 22 (Spring 1993): 6-8. Bob Luman and Johnny Tillotson spent time recalling their amazement at Presley's early talent, and also provided a number of anecdotes about Colonel Parker.

Stan Kesler, Marcus Van Story, Ronald Smith, Eddie Bond, Marion Keisker, Kenneth Herman, and Joan Deary provided additional information in key interviews on Sam Phillips and the early Sun Records days. Doug Poindexter spent two evenings describing how Phillips recorded, and discussed why union rules prevented many non-union musicians from being listed as having played at various Sun sessions. The Charly Records box set, **Sun Records: The Blues Years, 1950-1956,** contains an excellent booklet on this period. Martin Hawkins, Colin Escott, and Hank Davis provided the material for this excellent booklet, and it was useful in reconstructing the Sun years.

Further on Sam Phillips, the following sources were useful: Robert Palmer's *Deep Blues* (New York, 1981); Randy Haspel's "Tell 'Em Phillips Sent'cha," *Memphis* (June 1978); Charles Raiteri's "Interviews With Sam Phillips," *Red, Hot And Blue* (Zu-Zazz Z2012 recording); and, Colin Escott and Martin Hawkins' *Good Rockin' Tonight* (New York, 1991).

A number of blues musicians—Lowell Fulson, Johnny Otis, Jimmy McCracklin, Rufus Thomas, Charles Brown, and Guitar Mac—provided important interviews on the relationship of the blues to Sun Records. A brief conversation with Chuck Berry in 1981 helped to clarify his relationship with Elvis Presley. My book, *Chuck Berry: Rock N Roll Music* (Ann Arbor, 1985; available only from Popular Culture, Ink.) was used to place Sam Phillips and Colonel Tom Parker in the proper historical perspective. My European collaborator, Morten Reff, sent hundreds of items on Presley's career culled from European newspapers, magazines, and obscure fanzines. Reff's knowledge and devotion to rock music was a major source in the compilation of this book.

Ike Turner, now living with his daughter in Vallejo, California, recalled the importance of Sam Phillips to black music in the 1950s. For research on Howlin' Wolf in Memphis, see this author's "Howlin' Wolf: Sam Phillips And The Memphis Years," *Blue Suede News*, no. 18 (Spring 1992): 10-12.

For early Sun Records information, see Ger Rijff's

Long Lonely Highway (Ann Arbor, 1987; available only from Popular Culture, Ink.); Peter Guralnick's liner notes to **The Complete Sun Sessions** (RCA 6414); Escott and Hawkins' *Good Rockin' Tonight* (Chapter 4), and Stanley Booth's "A Hound Dog To The Manor Born," *The Age Of Rock* (New York, 1969).

CHAPTER 8
EARLY SUN ELVIS, JANUARY—JULY 1954

The early days of the Memphis music scene were recalled in an interview with Ronald Smith, Kenneth Herman, Doug Poindexter, Malcolm Yelvington, Marcus Van Story, and Eddie Bond. Stan Kesler provided not only information on the early Sun days, but he reconstructed the Snearly Ranch Boys influence upon artists like Elvis. The interviews with early Memphis musicians provided much of the material on Elvis' pre-Sun Records days. Charlie Feathers was cooperative in recalling the early 1954 era, while Jim and Jesse Lee Denson recreated Elvis' old Lauderdale Court neighborhood. The Johnny and Dorsey Burnette influences were mentioned by a number of people, but it was Paul Burlison's recollections of those days that were most significant. Jerry Hopkins' biography contained a wealth of information in a few pages on the early Sun Records days.

Marion Keisker graciously recreated how Elvis approached her at the time he cut his first vanity and demo records. She laughingly suggested that Elvis "haunted" Sun Records in those days.

In a short interview in April 1993, B.B. King provided anecdotes for this chapter.

Mark Naftalin, formerly of the Paul Butterfield Blues Band and now a respected solo blues performer, helped me understand the blues influence upon rock and roll music. Ron Thompson, another blues artist, helped me relate key blues tunes to Presley's career.

The influence of Leonard Chess, the Bihari brothers, and Don Robey upon Sam Phillips' early records was clarified by the recollections of blues giant Jimmy McCracklin. McCracklin appeared in Memphis and he recorded for Chess, the Biharis, and Robey. My book, *Chuck Berry: Rock N Roll Music* (1985), provided many anecdotes from this period. Bo Diddley helped to reconstruct the early Chess Record days, and in his reminiscences he added a great deal about the link between Sam Phillips and Leonard Chess. In Los Angeles, Lowell Fulson provided some important tips on the blues and its relationship to early rock and roll music.

CHAPTER 9
THE SUN BEGINNINGS,
AUGUST—DECEMBER 1954

The early days of the "Louisiana Hayride" were vividly recalled by Tommy Sands. There were also a number of other musicians from the Hayride days who recalled them for me. The most helpful source was Charles Tyson, who played with a number of artists as a Hayride musician. An interview with Roy Brown when he played in San Francisco a few years prior to his death contained a great deal of information about Presley's impact on black musicians. Jimmy McCracklin and Charles Brown provided detailed interviews about the blues music scene in 1954, and they both offered valuable perspectives on Presley's early career. Guitar Mac, a San Jose, California, blues musician, helped to reconstruct the blues scene in Tennessee-Arkansas-Mississippi during the early 1950s. Bob Geddins, an Oakland, California, blues pioneer who migrated from Texas in the 1930s, provided extensive comments on the relationship between the blues and rock music. In the late 1980s, Stevie Ray Vaughan (now deceased) and Johnny Winter have recorded tunes that Geddins wrote in the 1950s. Geddins believed that Elvis, like Vaughan and Winter, was influenced by the blues.

Malcolm Yelvington, Doug Poindexter, and Eddie Bond talked about leading bands during this period, while Stan Kesler, Ronald Smith, Kenneth Herman, and Marcus Van Story recalled the trials and travails of those days as country-rockabilly musicians.

During an interview in San Francisco, Roy Brown talked about the old days in Memphis and the condition of the blues in the South. At Mooney's Irish Pub, Brown went on at great length about the changes that Presley brought to the music business.

Tommy Sands added his intimate knowledge of the changes in rockabilly music and his first-hand observations of Presley's success.

CHAPTER 10
BUILDING A REPUTATION,
JANUARY—APRIL 1955

Ronald Smith worked closely with Elvis and Bob Neal during this period, and Smith was also a session guitarist with Sun. Tommy Sands toured and played in the same circuit with Elvis and recalled his impact. Bo Diddley became aware of Elvis in this period, and provided his initial reaction to Presley's music. Tommy Roe added his impressions of Presley's early career.

Stan Kesler, Marcus Van Story, Eddie Bond, Kenneth Herman, Paul Burlison, and Rufus Thomas added

to the story by recalling Elvis' musical impact. In 1965, Bob Luman, during a 1965 appearance in Seaside, California, reminisced about Elvis in the 1960s. This interview was important because Elvis' Texas appearances were still fresh in Luman's mind. Jimmy McCracklin recalls the times he crossed paths with Elvis. "I played the black clubs and Elvis played the white clubs, but we was in town in Texas at the same time." Charles Brown also recalls Elvis' early impact and its significance for blues musicians.

CHAPTER 11
SUN MANIA, MAY—AUGUST 1955

Once Elvis Presley became a commercial property for Sun Records, there was a "mania" attached to his public appearances. Tommy Sands, Bob Luman, and Onie Wheeler provided interviews regarding Presley's early concerts. The most revealing was Onie Wheeler's interview at San Francisco's Great American Music Hall where he described Presley as the man who "changed the music." Ronald Smith often played with Elvis in these early days, and he was able to recount the changes in the crowds' reaction to Elvis' music.

Charles Gillett's book, *The Sound Of The City*, is important in placing Presley's music into the rhythm and blues mold. Nick Tosches' *The Unsung Heroes Of Rock and Roll* contains an essay on Jesse Stone which reveals a great deal about black music and Elvis Presley. Jimmy McCracklin provided many insights about blues and rhythm and blues artists who were instrumental in Presley's success.

CHAPTER 12
SUN RISE,
SEPTEMBER—OCTOBER 1955

Tommy Sands and Eddie Bond recalled how Presley's popularity helped their music. Ronald Smith and Kenneth Herman reflected on the changes in Presley's life due to his popularity. Paul Burlison, Marcus Van Story, and Stan Kesler suggested how important Elvis was to the success of other musicians in this period. A brief five-minute interview with Bill Haley in 1967 in Redwood City, California, elicited strong praise about Presley's music and a few anecdotes about their meetings. Gene Vincent's daughter, Melody Jean Vincent, provided some useful commentary on her father's love of Elvis Presley's music. At the Wee Drop Inn in Sumas, Washington, in 1961, I worked as a waiter and had the chance to spend the afternoon with Jim Reeves, who was performing at the club. Reeves talked a long time about Elvis' country music ability and suggested that he was much smarter than the "Yankee press" recognized.

An interview with Roy Brown in San Francisco brought forth a great deal of information on Presley. The significance of the blues upon Elvis was stressed time and again in conversations with Sacramento blues artist and disc jockey, Guitar Mac.

Lowell Fulson, Jimmy McCracklin, Johnny Otis, and Bo Diddley offered a blues perspective on the material in this chapter and a number of significant anecdotes. My book, *Chuck Berry: Rock N Roll Music* (1985), contained a great deal of material used in this chapter.

CHAPTER 13
SUN BURST,
NOVEMBER—DECEMBER 1955

As Elvis Presley signed with Colonel Tom Parker and RCA Records, a number of people witnessed changes in his career. Bo Diddley provided a number of insights into the early musical explosion surrounding Presley's career. Bo recalled the night that Elvis showed up to see him in New York. Jimmy McCracklin, Jimmy Beasley, and Buddy Ace suggested some important points about Don Robey and Duke/Peacock Records. Big Mama Thornton was interviewed on her Oakland, California, porch in the 1970s and was nervous as she talked about Johnny Ace. Johnny Tillotson, Tommy Roe, and Donnie Brooks offered comments from the standpoint of young men interested in rock and roll who watched Elvis come of age. All three went on to become major recording stars, and they each provided some exceptional material on Presley's impact upon their own lives and careers. Billy Vera's comments on his early career helped my understanding of rock and roll music.

Lowell Fulson, who recorded for Stan Lewis' Jewel label and for Don Robey's Duke/Peacock label, spent hours reminiscing about Presley's impact on black music. Fulson's version of his song "Reconsider Baby" influenced Elvis to record it.

In New Orleans, Professor W. Kenneth Holdwitch reminisced about going to Milam Junior High School with Elvis, and he provided a wealth of information about Tupelo. Professor Holdwitch graciously lent me interviews with F.L. Bobo and other people in Tupelo who touched Presley's early life. Cosimo Matassa supported many of Holdwitch's conclusions from another vantage point.

Marion Keisker recalled how Sam Phillips hoped to make Carl Perkins into a Presley-type singer. Ronald Smith, Kenneth Herman, Eddie Bond, and Paul Burlison added material on Perkins.

Jim Russell, a New Orleans record store pro-

prietor, offered a healthy amount of material on Elvis in 1954-1955. As a former promoter, dj, and wheeler-dealer, Russell had a great deal to say about the music business. Jeff Hannusch, a.k.a. Almost Slim, provided some information about the New Orleans music scene, and his wife graciously recalled Donaldsonville, Louisiana.

A lengthy conversation with Solomon Burke helped me to understand the importance of Presley's RCA contract. Burke suggested that it "opened up Atlantic Records to my music when they missed out on Presley."

CHAPTER 14
THE NEW ELVIS:
JANUARY—FEBRUARY 1956

The shift in Elvis' musical career in January and February 1956 is important. Jimmy McCracklin and Charles Brown, two veteran blues artists now residing in Oakland, California, provided extensive interviews on the relationship of black and white music. Johnny Tillotson, who watched Elvis in Florida, offered his insights into changes in the record business due to rock and roll music. Bob Luman and Eddie Bond recalled the rise of country music, rockabilly, and rock and roll in the mid-1950s. Stan Kesler, who had written and helped record many of Elvis' early songs, was able to suggest what the RCA transition meant to Elvis' career. Marcus Van Story, Kenneth Herman, and Ronald Smith remembered the changes in Elvis as a result of his fame and fortune. Jim Denson, a close friend of the Presley family since the late 1940s, was present for many of the early show business triumphs and in his candid manner pointed out key changes in Elvis' life. Jesse Lee Denson suggested the problems that fame may have brought to Elvis Presley. Paul Burlison, Tommy Sands, and Doug Poindexter recalled the general impact that Elvis had upon the television and record industries.

The comments made by Marion Keisker concerning Presley's reaction to the RCA recording sessions were important in reconstructing his attitudes. She recalled conversations, but I didn't use them because of the inability to interview those with whom she talked.

Melody Jean Vincent, Gene's daughter, provided extensive interviews on her father and Eddie Cochran. She recalled how influential Elvis was upon both artists. She pointed out that they were instructed by their record labels to downplay Elvis' influence, and, as a result, never were able to fully acknowledge Presley's importance.

Donald L. Dunavent, pastor of the East Heights First Assembly of God church, candidly pointed out Vernon Presley's relationship to the church. He also recalled, from interviews and research that he has conducted, a vivid picture of Elvis and Gladys Presley.

CHAPTER 15
"CADILLAC ELVIS":
THE FINAL TRANSFORMATION, MARCH—APRIL 1956

The rise of Presleymania is extensively documented in the press. Johnny Otis provided some important insights into how rock and roll changed as a result of Elvis Presley. Bo Diddley was also important in recalling the phenomenal success that Presley experienced and what it meant to black artists. Kenneth Herman was often at Elvis' house during this period, and he suggested many of the key ideas that make up this chapter. Ron Peterson, Don Fulton, Chuck Schoning, and Joel Goodman, original members of the Frantics, helped to recall the rise of rock and roll. George Palmerton, lead singer in the Highlighters, helped to retrace Elvis' impact upon Seattle groups. The late Rockin' Robin Roberts offered his insights into Presleymania. Little Bill Engelhardt of Seattle, former front man for Little Bill and the Bluenotes, was also helpful in reconstructing Presley's influence upon struggling young rock singers. Ron Holden and Andy Duvall of the Playboys, a 1950s Seattle group, provided important comments about the influence of Presley upon blues and r and b musicians. Tony Sheridan, now residing in Hamburg, Germany, spent hours recalling the impact of Elvis upon rock and roll music in England and Europe. Horst Fascher, the Beatles' bodyguard in Hamburg, analyzed the German reaction to early Presleymania. In Liverpool, Charlie Lennon, John's uncle, recounted John Lennon's fascination with Elvis. Joe Flannery, a professional entertainer in England in the 1950s, spent some time suggesting Presley's importance to future rock musicians. Bob Wooler, the compere at the Cavern Club, dug into his extensive British record collection and suggested some of the key songs that influenced the Beatles and other English rock groups.

In Las Vegas, Freddie Bell offered an extensive interview in 1991 on Presley's 1956 Las Vegas escapades. Bell gave Elvis a copy of his "Hound Dog,," and they played it over and over at Bell's place. "When Elvis recorded 'Hound Dog,'" Bell related, "he copied my version. He left out one chorus, but otherwise it's the same song."

In Memphis, Jim Denson and his brother Jesse Lee were an extraordinary research aid as they recounted the changes that came over Elvis during 1956. The most important source for this book, Ronald Smith, corroborated some of Denson's tales and added new insights into Elvis' stardom. Not only was Smith the single-most important source, but he led me to a number of

new areas of research.

There were many professional entertainers who shared their feelings about Elvis. The most significant were Tommy Roe, Billy Vera, Donnie Brooks, Bo Diddley, and Jim Reeves. Mark Naftalin, a San Francisco blues artist who began his professional career with the Paul Butterfield Blues Band, had given me a number of insights into the blues and rock and roll in general. Johnny Otis graciously answered questions about his career and the role of Elvis Presley in the early rock music revolution.

Rip Lay, owner of Star Fire Records, answered numerous questions about 1950s rock and roll and provided the material about Elvis Presley's relationship to Ral Donner.

In New Orleans, sitting with me in his grocery store in the 1980s, Cosimo Matassa recalled how Elvis Presley burst upon the New Orleans record scene and the impact that this had upon the sale of local black artists. Jim Russell, a figure in the New Orleans music business, supplied anecdotes about Elvis and some tales from firsthand contact with young Presley.

Arnold Shaw talked with me at length about Presley's success.

CHAPTER 16
THE PRICE OF FAME AND FORTUNE,
LATE APRIL TO JULY 1956

The material for this chapter is drawn from a mixture of interviews. Professor W. Kenneth Holdwitch of the University of New Orleans helped to recreate the atmosphere, rumors, and facts surrounding Presley's return to Tupelo. As a guest at a wedding Presley attended, Holdwitch was able to swap stories with him about Tupelo.

The reminiscences of Kenneth Herman and Ronald Smith were important in reconstructing the rise of Presley to fame and fortune. Eddie Bond recounted stories of conversations with Presley after he reached fame. From his Alameda, Califronia, home, Jumpin' George Oxford, a San Francisco disc jockey, talked about Elvis. In 1956, Oxford's KSAN radio program featured Presley's music. Arnold Shaw provided an in-depth interview about the musical styles and entertainment structure of Las Vegas. A long interview with Oleta Grimes, Orville Bean's daughter, shed a great deal of light on the conflicts that Presley experienced with rock music stardom.

Before she retired from RCA, Joan Deary provided a number of important insights into Presley's early career. Jerry Osborne, the publisher of *DISCoveries*, provided a great deal of information about the "Louisiana Hayride" and the Presley phenomenon.

Barbara Lynn, whose hit "If You Lose Me, You Lose A Good Thing" established her as a blues artist, discussed her admiration for Elvis. Ms. Lynn was a young girl living in Texas at the time, and was well aware of the impact of Elvis' music upon black listeners and performers. Lowell Fulson echoed Barbara Lynn's comments.

Index

About the Author

Howard A. DeWitt is a Professor of History at Ohlone College, Fremont, California. DeWitt taught previously at the University of California-Davis, Cochise College, and Chabot College. He has taught the History of Rock and Roll in the classroom for more than twenty years.

After receiving his Ph.D. from the University of Arizona, DeWitt began a prolific writing career. He is the author of fourteen other books, seven of which also deal with rock and roll music. These include: **Chuck Berry: Rock And Roll Music** (1985; available from Popular Culture, Ink.); **Jailhouse Rock: The Bootleg Records of Elvis Presley** (1983; co-authored with Lee Cotten and also available from Popular Culture, Ink.); **Van Morrison: The Mystic's Music** (1983); **The Beatles: Untold Tales** (1985); **Beatle Poems** (1987); and **Paul McCartney: From Liverpool to 'Let It Be'** (1992). The latter four titles are available from Horizon Books.

DeWitt is a regular contributor to a wide variety of rock music magazines, including DISCoveries, Blue Suede News, Juke Box Digest, and Record Profile Magazine.

In addition to his writing, DeWitt is one of California's most noted record, CD, and rock music memorabilia collectors. He is featured in a commercial video entitled "Elvis and The Beatles," produced by Front Row Videos of New Jersey.

The author is currently working on a new project, **Stranger in Town: The Mysterious Life of Del Shannon.** Anyone who would like to add corrections, new information, or offer research materials for this project

Professor Howard A. DeWitt

or revisions of any previous title may write directly to the author: Howard DeWitt, P.O. Box 3083, Fremont, CA 94539.

ML 420 .P73 D48 1993
DeWitt, Howard A.
Elvis, the Sun years
77590

DEC 1 2 1998

MAR 0 6 2002

NOV 2 9 2003

DEC 2 2 2003

VILLA JULIE COLLEGE LIBRARY
STEVENSON, MD 21153

DEMCO